SOCIAL ACCELERATION

NEW DIRECTIONS IN CRITICAL THEORY

NEW DIRECTIONS IN CRITICAL THEORY

Amy Allen, General Editor

New Directions in Critical Theory presents outstanding classic and contemporary texts in the tradition of critical social theory, broadly construed. The series aims to renew and advance the program of critical social theory, with a particular focus on theorizing contemporary struggles around gender, race, sexuality, class, and globalization and their complex interconnections.

SOCIAL ACCELERATION

A NEW THEORY OF MODERNITY

Hartmut Rosa

Translated by Jonathan Trejo-Mathys

COLUMBIA UNIVERSITY PRESS   NEW YORK

COLUMBIA UNIVERSITY PRESS
Publishers Since 1893
New York Chichester, West Sussex

cup.columbia.edu

Beschleunigung: Die Veränderung de Zeitstrukturen in der Moderne copyright © 2005 Suhrkamp
 Verlag Frankfurt am Main
English translation copyright © 2013 Columbia University Press
All rights reserved
Library of Congress Cataloging-in-Publication Data
Rosa, Hartmut, 1965–
 [Beschleunigung. English]
 Social acceleration: a new theory of modernity / Hartmut Rosa; translated by Jonathan
Trejo-Mathys.
  p. cm. —(New directions for critical theory)
 Includes bibliographical references and index.
 ISBN 978-0-231-14834-4 (cloth: alk. paper)—ISBN 978-0-231-51988-5 (e-book)
 1. Time perception. 2. Time pressure. 3. Time—Sociological aspects. 4. Social
change. 5. Civilization, Modern—21st century. I. Trejo-Mathys, Jonathan. II. Title.
 HM656.R6713 2013
 303.4—dc23

2012029515

Columbia University Press books are printed on permanent and durable acid-free paper.
 This book is printed on paper with recycled content.

Printed in the United States of America
c 10 9 8 7 6 5 4 3 2 1

COVER ART: Joseph Mallord Turner, Rain, Steam, and Speed–The Great Western Railway, 1844.
 © National Gallery, London/Art Resource, NY
COVER DESIGN: Catherine Casalino

CONTENTS

ILLUSTRATIONS

TRANSLATOR'S INTRODUCTION: MODERNITY AND TIME

The most insignificant man can be complete if he works within the limits of his capacities, innate or acquired; but even fine talents can be obscured, neutralised, and destroyed by lack of this indispensable requirement of symmetry. This is a mischief which will often occur in modern times; for who will be able to come up to the claims of an age so full and intense as this, and one too that moves so rapidly?

—JOHANN WOLFGANG VON GOETHE, *Maxims and Reflections*

THE DRASTIC SOCIAL TRANSFORMATIONS THAT accompanied the industrial revolution forced themselves on the attention of any half-awake observer of nineteenth-century society, but it took the rise of the sociological imagination with thinkers like Karl Marx and Alexis de Tocqueville to discern the hidden connections between various surface phenomena of the new dispensation. Events like the sudden economic collapse of the centuries-old craft of the Silesian weavers, for no reason apparent to local German observers, prodded acute and probing intellects like Marx's to uncover the far-flung, transnational causal nexus of the newly expanding modern capitalist economy and its revolutionary power to reorganize human social and political relationships.[1] That things in general—history, the social and political order, fashion, etc.—seemed to be changing faster and faster was also a common observation of the times. However, the idea that the diverse perceptions of increasing speed in disparate social domains might themselves be systematically linked by some subterranean bond was not formulated until Henry Adams's speculative and unmethodical postulation of a universal-historical "law of acceleration" that leads inexorably to the "whirl" of the modern world (oo).[2] Though various social thinkers after Adams recognized and analyzed the central role of speed in particular areas of modern social existence,[3] it would be a long time before someone systematically worked up these scattered insights of the sociological tradition into the provocative and challenging thesis that social acceleration is the key to understanding modernity and the modernization process. The substantiation of this claim is the burden of Hartmut Rosa's *Social Acceleration*. In addition, it aims to be a methodological demonstration that an acceleration-theoretical starting point possesses a unique capacity to simultaneously illuminate other more conventional or familiar dimensions of modernity.

Such a thesis will inevitably have something of the paradoxical air that surrounds many characteristically sociological insights.[4] It will seem intuitive to the extent that the experience of things moving too fast, of there simply not being enough time to do everything one is called upon to do, and of the almost vertiginous technological change in everyday life is almost universal in modern societies. But it will seem counterintuitive in that the notion that these widely strewn experiences in diverse domains of social life might be connected by one single hidden thread is hardly something suggested by common sense. To help in this regard, in the next section I survey some recent examples of social acceleration that illustrate the way its consequences are anything but a trivial matter. In addition, I will show how the concerns at the heart of the book, though quintessentially modern, have deep roots in Western social and political thought before moving on to a summary of the striking and counterintuitive connections embodied in the basic claims of Rosa's theory of acceleration. Then I turn to discuss the distinctive contribution Rosa's work can make to a broader moral-philosophical debate concerning the key normative concepts of the right and the good and the relative weight they ought to bear in critical social theorizing. Last, in the final section I briefly indicate two lines along which the critical theory outlined in *Social Acceleration* has been and continues to be further developed.

SOCIAL ACCELERATION: SOME EXAMPLES

In the wake of the worldwide financial crisis of 2008 and the global economic recession that followed it, obscure, complicated financial instruments like credit default swaps, collateralized debt obligations, and the now notorious species of derivative, the mortgage-backed security, became household words.

Much was made of the anonymity and lack of transparency in the derivatives markets that lay at the heart of the crisis. But little was made of a related and equally troubling aspect of contemporary stock exchanges: the destabilizing and unpredictable effects of the acceleration of transaction speeds. With the emergence of so-called high frequency trading since the authorization of electronic exchanges in 1998, the ability to gain a slight edge in the number of transactions per second or the speed at which the algorithms in one's computer program can process information and switch trading strategies can mean tens of billions of dollars in annual profits.[5]

Although such acceleration does not per se lead to inevitable catastrophe, portents of the potential damage that might result were witnessed on the afternoon of May 6, 2010, when the Dow Jones Industrial Average plunged 700 points in seven minutes. There had not been such a great loss in such a short period of time since the great crash of October 1987. This time, however, after billions in share values had been lost almost in an instant, the market just as rapidly regained its preplunge levels. After "a report traced the main trigger of May's big crash to a poorly timed trade by a mutual fund in Kansas," the response of regulators was "to put in place circuit breakers to halt trading and reset prices in case stocks plunge."[6] Yet since that time there have been scores of "mini flash crashes" of individual stocks. To give just one example, four months later the value of Progress Energy, a 107-year-old utility company with 3.1 million customers and 11,000 employees, dropped 90 percent and was almost wiped out in a matter of seconds. Neither its executives nor active traders in the utility markets had any idea why. It later became clear that "a wayward keystroke by a trader somewhere had unleashed a powerful computer algorithm that had devoured Progress Energy's stock in moments." The resulting trades were canceled out and the damage was undone. But many are worried that these phenomena are signs that larger-scale crashes could occur and wreak damaging havoc in electronic markets that are paradoxically both highly integrated and very fractured.

In a brilliant analysis of what the May 6 flash crash revealed about the current structure and dynamics of electronically mediated markets, Paul A. David highlights the fact that the acceleration enabled by electronic exchanges and computer trading algorithms is very unevenly distributed among market actors and different stock exchanges. This led to a dramatic form of what Rosa, from a sociological point of view, describes as dysfunctional desynchronization. The circuit breakers built into the major electronic exchanges like the New York Stock Exchange (NYSE) worked as they should.[7] But the NYSE, which as recently as 2005 was home to three-fourths of the volume of stock trades on U.S. exchanges, is now only the location of around 30 percent of such trades. The rest mainly occur in a network of relatively unregulated private and unregistered equity trading venues that are, on the one hand, relatively invisible to actors not involved in them (most importantly to the public regulatory agencies like the Securities and Exchange Commission) and, on the other hand, also interconnected with the large, established exchanges that are now equipped with safety catch mechanisms.[8] So when the "circuit breakers" were triggered in the major exchanges like the NYSE, the speculative trading of the relevant stocks simply shifted over to the scores of smaller unregulated, satellite-based electronic exchanges that are connected to the larger exchanges and to each other by dense but nontransparent networks. This had perverse effects on the system as a whole. Many observers wondered why these smaller private exchanges did not voluntarily install safety mechanisms similar to those that government regulators have required the major exchanges to put in place. That they did not is no doubt due in part to the fact that the resulting volatility is very good for the profit-making activities of high-frequency traders. But one could also argue quite plausibly that another factor is the sheer speed with which the speed-inducing networked electronic exchanges have sprung into existence. In a matter of several years they have transformed the trading landscape. The slowness of governmental regulation, and of democratic law more generally, in comparison with the increasingly rapid pace of social change is just another theme of Rosa's comprehensive sociological analysis of the constitutive role of social acceleration in the past, present, and future of modern society.[9]

Equally striking examples from other domains can be found. During the twentieth century the nuclear military standoff between the USA and the USSR sharpened as both the amount of time nuclear weapons required to reach their targets and the warning time before impact lessened to a matter of minutes and seconds. The result was the establishment of a direct line (the "hot line") between the offices of the chief executives of the two powers and the negotiation by Richard Nixon and Leonid Brezhnev of the first strategic arms limitation agreement. As Paul Virilio observes, these measures are in large part about "the preservation of a properly 'human' political power, since the constant progress of rapidity threatens to reduce the warning time for nuclear war to *less than one fatal minute*—thus finally abolishing the head of state's power of reflection and decision in favor of a pure and simple *automation* of defense systems."[10] In a more geographical vein, the remarkable growth of an ever denser cross-border network of interconnections between so-called "global cities" such as New York, London, Paris, Tokyo, Hong Kong, Singapore, Frankfurt, Washington DC, and Beijing is intimately bound up with the technological acceleration of transportation, communication, production, and exchange and the corresponding intensification of the need for various kinds of services by transnational firms.[11] Turning to politics and going further back, Marx had already noted how the accelerating effects of mass communication and rail transport could actually empower regressive social forces as in Louis-Napoléon Bonaparte's blitzkrieg-style political campaign across mid-nineteenth-century France to consolidate his hold on power (he eventually crowned himself emperor): "Bonaparte used not only the accelerating effect of mass publication and the telegraph but, above all, the speed of the railways to establish in France a style of electioneering that was highly innovative, thoroughly organized in terms of its propaganda, entirely state-wide—indeed, campaign-like, in the military sense. With such means he was able to establish his presence in the entire country and to organize plebiscites whose acclamation was achieved through manipulation."[12]

This now ever present possibility of, as Theodor Adorno put it, "enlightenment as mass deception" seems to have been most recently illustrated by the rushed march to war in Iraq orchestrated by the Bush administration beginning in September 2002. If these examples aren't enough to establish the significance of the relative and absolute speed of material and social processes for social thought, perhaps a complementary look back at the history of Western political thinking and the rise of sociology will suffice.

SPEED AND RHYTHM AT THE HEART OF POLITICAL PHILOSOPHY AND SOCIOLOGY

At the very beginning of Western social and political thought, in the philosopher Plato and the historian Polybius, one can already observe the importance of time and temporal concepts such as rhythm and tempo. They play a central role in images of order and change in the polity, both in terms of the actual dynamics of human communities and the ideals with which they should be brought into conformity. The ancient Greek polis was seen as requiring not simply certain fixed structures and static patterns of order but also the forms of movement necessary for genuine collective agency. The question was how to ensure that this social motion was "controlled motion."[13] Plato famously presented the issue in the context of a myth: if the "golden age" in which a god had his hand on the wheel of the cosmos, guiding it with divine wisdom, has irrevocably passed, how can human beings maintain appropriate order, pursue desirable change, and prevent a descent into chaos in their affairs?[14] Such existential questions became burning ones again during the Renaissance revival of ancient republican thought as political thinkers and political communities strove to gain intellectual purchase on a tumultuous world of mundane events whose origins and interconnections seemed inscrutable to human understanding and therefore threateningly beyond the control even of political communities composed of citizens of comparatively great civic virtue (*virtù*). The importance of decisively performing the right action at the right moment, of recognizing and seizing what J. G. A. Pocock has styled as the "Machiavellian moment," whether as an individual political actor (the prince) or as a collective one (the republican citizenry), was paramount.[15]

With the rise of modernity this constellation seemed to be so dramatically transformed that the major changes which led to it all came to be described as revolutions—successive scientific, political, and industrial ones—in a wholly new and modern sense of the term. Indeed, one could say half-facetiously that this was a revolutionary use of the term "revolution." Whereas before the term referred to a return to a prior state of affairs after a disturbance or deviation, it has ever since implied a relatively rapid and very extensive change in regnant ideas, institutions, practices, or social relationships that results in something historically new.[16] Modernity also gave rise to the promise that human beings would finally be able to collectively shape their common life together and achieve that controlled motion of social affairs to which classical and renaissance thinkers had only aspired. The result would be a rational social and political order, one in which freedom, prosperity, and happiness could be at least possible for all.

But as the effects of early modern capital accumulation, the dislocation of rural populations, political upheaval, urbanization, and industrialization became ever more strikingly visible and pathological, the classical philosophical problems of combining order and change in controlled rhythms of social motion returned in a sharpened fashion. To meet this challenge, a new form of thought emerged that would eventually become the discipline of sociology.[17] Hartmut Rosa's *Social Acceleration* is a remarkable contribution to both these streams of thought.

Combining the engaged philosopher's concern for the personal and collective pursuit of freedom and the good life and the sociologist's interest in the integration, structure, and dynamics of society as a whole, he arrives at a striking synthesis of these two irreducible points of view. For almost two centuries modern society has appeared to be in principle capable of autonomously giving itself the shape it desires and allowing individuals to do the same with their lives—but for the last two or three decades this appearance has faded and given way to a widespread sense that "utopian energies" are exhausted, that we have reached the "end of history" or *posthistoire*, and that the modern promise of personal and collective autonomy cannot be redeemed. According to Rosa, both these phenomena can be explained by the multidimensional acceleration of social processes and events that has been bound up with the modernization process from the very beginning. During the period of "classical" modernity, the temporal structures that resulted from the interaction of this principle with the initial conditions of early modern societies gave rise to a window of opportunity for that quintessentially modern promise of self-determination on both the individual and collective levels. Yet the further operation of the complex self-reinforcing syndrome of factors driving social acceleration now seems to have closed that window. The increases in speed that made classical modernity possible, with prospects at once both liberating and frightening, now both render it obsolete and threaten to break it apart at the seams and leave us in a paradoxical, characteristically late modern condition of frenetic standstill. Such is the claim that Rosa seeks to make plausible and convincing in the ambitious and wide-ranging theory developed in this book.

MODERN SOCIETIES AS ACCELERATION SOCIETIES

Rosa's theory belongs to the broader tradition of critical social theory, and, like much work in this family, it has four features that are often separated in other social-scientific research traditions: it is diagnostic, normative, integrative, and empirical. It is *diagnostic* in at least two senses. First, it proceeds in a differential and comparative way analogous to aspects of the technique of differential diagnosis in the clinical practice of medicine and psychology, in particular in the collection and ordering of information as an aid to diagnosis in a second, normative sense.[18] The differentiation and comparison are focused on understanding the respective features of premodern and modern societies, and also the developmental process leading from the former to the latter, with a view to evaluating claims concerning the presence of a contemporary transition or break between the modern period and a post- or late modern one. Since diagnosis here eventually moves into a second dimension involving the use of a standard that distinguishes between broadly good or desirable states and broadly bad or undesirable ones (e.g., health/sickness, functional/dysfunctional, normal/pathological, intact/damaged, and so on), the question of the source and validation of such a standard becomes immediately relevant.[19]

For Rosa, following the venerable precedents of Hegel, Marx, and the various "generations" of the Frankfurt School tradition, this *normative* dimension is rooted in the experiences and avowals of members of society, certain central social practices, and general elements of the wider culture.[20] Writers in this tradition thus practice an "internal" or "immanent" form of critique that seeks to find its critical standards *in* the objects upon which it reflects or which it subjects to judgment.[21] Indeed, instead of the political or juridical metaphor of subjection to judgment, one could also say that immanent critique seeks to express, articulate, or set free the critical "voice" or "claim" of the object itself, whether the object is a social-political order, a modernist artwork, a social group, or an individual.[22] In chapter 13 Rosa makes clear that a critical theory of social acceleration is rooted in the actual experiences of suffering and alienated human beings and ultimately in ideas of autonomy that are deeply rooted in the social institutions and culture of modern society, in what Rosa, following Jürgen Habermas, calls "the project of modernity."

The third feature of Rosa's theory is its *integrative* construction. At its core is an attempt to assimilate what Rosa deems to be the central insights of four classical sociological thinkers regarding the process of modernization: Marx, Émile Durkheim, Georg Simmel, and Max Weber. Since each of the these thinkers initiated entire traditions of research, such a methodology can claim, at least in principle, to integrate important insights of these various streams of sociological theory. Such a process is inevitably a critical one, something that was already clear in the stance of Plato and Aristotle toward the thought of their philosophical predecessors, let alone in more recent feats of integration in the major works of sociological theorists like Talcott Parsons and Habermas.[23] It requires that one carefully distinguish between the lasting contributions and the dispensable elements of each integrated theory and incorporate only the former. Finally, there is the *empirical* grounding of the theory in a diverse and interdisciplinary evidential base that draws on, among others, cultural history, comparative sociology, political economy, recent Marxian scholarship on the interrelationships of culture (Fredric Jameson), geography

(David Harvey), and modern capitalist society, clinical and personality psychology, quantitative studies of time use and empirical-psychological studies of the effects of media, entertainment, and communications technologies on memory and the experience of time.

This wide-ranging array of evidential material is worked up into, first, the aforementioned integrative account of modernization and, second, a model of the self-reinforcing spiral of acceleration that constitutes modern societies as acceleration societies. Rosa sees modernization as having been analyzed by the classical sociological thinkers in the four key dimensions of *culture, personality structures, social structures,* and society's relation to *nature.*[24] This generated accounts of modernity as, respectively, rationalization (Weber), individualization (Simmel), functional differentiation (Durkheim), and the domestication of nature (Marx). For each of these, so to speak, "positive" dimensions of modernization, there is also a paradoxical "negative" flip side. The rationalization of cultural and social life leads to an erosion of meaning resources. The same processes that lead to the greater prominence of individuality in modern life also seem bound up with the emergence of an industrially produced and stereotyped "mass culture," the social and political salience of "the masses" and other forms of "massification" that plague modern societies and seem to make nonsense of their promise to liberate individuals to realize their own "unique" possibilities.[25] Increasing functional differentiation, and the related phenomena of a division of labor and increasing specialization, lead to impressive gains in productivity and the general ability to process complexity, but also a tendency toward societal disintegration. Finally, the advancing technological domestication of nature that promised to liberate humankind from material want and thus usher in a transition from the realm of necessity into the realm of freedom increasingly seems to threaten human society with ecological catastrophe.[26]

According to Rosa, however, time cannot simply be seen as another dimension alongside culture, personality, social structure, and the relation to nature, since it cuts across all four of them. In addition, it is a theoretically strategic focal point because it marks a privileged site for the coupling of social structure with the self-understanding and identity of agents. Further, the dynamic interrelationship between this coupling of structure and agency and the wider cultural realm is a powerful influence on the symbolic possibilities of expression that are available to agents.[27] As Rosa notes, the time structures of a given society are inevitably encountered by its members as normative expectations. The development of standardized clock and calendar times and ever more regularized schedules for trains, school days, stock markets, factory work, and so on, compels individuals to conform their behavior and plan their lives around the socially dominant time schemes. Hence any social theory that maintains a constitutive linkage to normative principles must take into account the impact of social time structures on the moral identities and aspirations of individuals. One necessary tool for doing so is a typology of the main dimensions of change in social time structures.

In Rosa's view the three main types of acceleration in modern society are *technical* acceleration (this category includes both acceleration achieved through improvements of the techniques used by agents in carrying out a given activity as well as that which results from the introduction of new technologies), the acceleration of *social change*, and the acceleration of *the pace of life*.[28] These types are internally related to each other in the sense that their respective modes of functioning result in mutual causal reinforcement. This is what Rosa calls "the circle of acceleration." Simply put, technical acceleration tends to increase the pace of social change, which in turn unavoidably increases the experienced pace of life, which then induces an ongoing demand for technical acceleration in the hopes of saving time, and so on back around the circle.[29] However, each of these forms of acceleration also has an external driver or "motor" that injects further energy into the circle of acceleration.[30] When the effects of these external motors are combined with the internal interaction of the forms of acceleration, the result is a self-propelling "spiral" of acceleration that takes on a life of its own and does the lion's share in generating the experience of a "runaway world."[31] The result is an *acceleration society*, defined as a society that simultaneously exhibits technical acceleration and the acceleration of the pace of life (i.e., an increasing scarcity of time): in other words, where rates of *growth* (in the quantity of goods/services produced, messages communicated, actions performed, experiential episodes, etc.) outpace rates of *acceleration* of those activities.[32]

Technical (and technological) acceleration is driven by the *economic motor* symbolized in the proverbial expression "time is money," whose grammatically indicative form hides, so to speak, the categorical capitalist imperatives of maximizing the amount of salable goods or services produced per unit of time and of being the first to introduce innovations. Especially when operating at large scales and volumes, small temporal advantages over competitors can mean immense profits for those in the lead—and ruin for those behind. The acceleration of social change, on the other hand, is propelled by the *social-structural motor* of functional differentiation, which is more colloquially known to us in our everyday lives in the form of professional specialization and the division of labor. This extraordinarily consequential aspect of modernization typically allows immense gains in processing speed and productivity. But these gains themselves tend to induce faster social change because they multiply social arenas of action; as a result there arises a very serious need for coordination and synchronization across domains that can only be met in the first instance by strict temporal regimentation and time discipline. Last, the acceleration of the pace of life is externally driven by the *cultural promise of acceleration* in the form of a secularization of the religious promise of eternal life. In premodern society the social and natural world were viewed as fundamentally unchanging or as at most rotating among stages of an already known "cycle." One missed nothing by living only several decades, since in that span one could see most of the central things existence could offer. In addition, even as the processes leading to modernity began to take hold, the culturally dominant religious conception of an eternal life after death automatically brought the time of life into congruence with all that the world and its time could offer. Then the crossing of the threshold to modernity, the rise of the idea of progress, and the related sense that society itself is in motion, in conjunction with the shattering of the cultural hegemony of religious ideas, opened up a terrifying gap between the seemingly infinite experiential possibilities that will develop in an ever more perfect future and the starkly limited span of one human life in a still unperfected society here and now. Therefore the prospect of accelerating our ability to have different experiences, and thus to exhaust the available possibilities, becomes extremely seductive. The more we can accelerate our ability to go to different places, see new things, try new foods, embrace various forms of spirituality, learn new activities, share sensual pleasures with others whether it be in dancing or sex, experience different forms of art, and so on, the less incongruence there is between the possibilities of experience we can realize in our own lifetimes and the total array of possibilities available to human beings now and in the future—that is, the closer we come to having a truly "fulfilled" life, in the literal sense of one that is as *filled full* of experiences as it can possibly be. This utopian and ultimately chimerical idea depends on our ability to approach an infinite acceleration of our capacity to experience and act. It is self-contradictory to the extent that the very means by which the acceleration is to be achieved, typically technological ones, generate new possibilities of experience. Hence it will often even be the case that a new technology will yield a net *decrease* in the ratio of actual to possible experiences. Yet this ersatz form of redemption or salvation through a "fulfilled" life is deeply entrenched in modern culture. Consider as evidence the following statement made by Angelina Jolie in a recent interview in which she unintentionally demonstrates the power of the cultural promise of acceleration: "I was actually quite a cool kid. I was not tough. I was certainly independent and bold. I was never teased. I never had any trouble from anybody. But I was never satisfied. I had trouble sleeping. I didn't really fit. I always feel that I'm searching for something deeper, something more, more. . . . You want to meet other people that challenge you with ideas or with power or with passion. I wanted to live very fully. I wanted to live many lives and explore many things."[33]

Because their status and livelihood depend on it, mega-celebrities like Jolie are necessarily sensitive seismographs registering the subterranean movements of culture. They are thus interesting sources of evidence for hypotheses linking cultural phenomena with social and personality structures. So it is noteworthy that Rosa's theory of acceleration provides a plausible explanation for another otherwise paradoxical phenomenon that appears in Jolie's statement: the fact that she claims she "didn't really fit" and at the same time that she was "cool" (for modern culture perhaps *the* prototypical way of "fitting in"). The key to understanding this lies somewhat surprisingly in the way the development from premodern to classical modern to late modern forms of social structure and identity lines up with a progression from multigenerational to generational to intragenerational rates of social change.[34] When structurally relevant social change generally requires more than the length of the three to four generations that coexist at any given time, there is little perception of a change of society as such. Beneath this multigenerational threshold, however, a sense that society itself is undergoing changes within the living memory of coexisting generations becomes endemic. The approach toward a generational pace of change is experienced as an acceleration *of* society with an accompanying shrinkage of the amount of time during which expectations formed on the basis of past experience are reliable guides for action (a phenomenon Rosa calls, following Hermann Lübbe, "the contraction of the present").[35] The shift in the tempo of cultural and social change corresponds on the level of personality to a shift from what Rosa calls "a priori substantial identities," the content or substance of which is determined by one's place in long-enduring social structures, to a posteriori chosen identities, the content of which is determined by selection from a set of structurally available options. Yet choice-based *identities* (or enduring personality structures) definitely depend upon the maintenance of the structural prerequisites of a certain time horizon, roughly the span of a lifetime or at least of its adult portion, since decisions to be this or do that for two weeks don't rise to the level of identity-constituting factors, while a time horizon longer than an average human lifetime can hardly be the object of a rational choice of identity (one can only decide how to spend the time one actually has). This is why Rosa refers to this form of identity as an "a posteriori stable identity." A definite set of classical modern institutions helped to secure and protect these time-structural preconditions, including bourgeois marriage and the nuclear family, the industrial work(time) regime with its strict separation of factory or office from home and work time from free time, and the legal-political framework of the welfare or "social security" state. If social changes are now occurring faster than the time horizons of these arrangements permit, it is no coincidence that these patterns of identity are eroding before our eyes and giving way to highly improvisational and reactive forms of "situational" identity and politics.

Therefore, when rates of social change reach an intragenerational pace, our relationships to things and material structures, to people and to ourselves become pressured to take on a similar mutability. There are less and less ready-made social slots into which one might, like finding the right spot for a puzzle piece, "fit." One could say: when all the solutions to the puzzle of social identity are taken away, all one is left with are puzzling pieces. But the idea of voluntarily determining the shape of our own identities and lives over the long haul through a free and reflective choice is remarkably persistent. This is evident in another example from the interview with Jolie: "Brad [Pitt] and I are raising our children to respect everyone. We have a bookshelf in the house that has the Bible, the Torah, the Koran, everything. We will take our children to church, temple, Buddhist ceremonies, Mosques, teaching them about all faiths. Whatever religion they choose, the choice will be theirs."

Against the background of the just discussed theorems of the theory of acceleration, it can hardly be a surprising feature of Jolie's earlier testimony that she says she "was never satisfied." But now we are in a position to see that the forces of social acceleration have also long since placed in question the possibility that the conscious, deliberative exercise of individual choice could fill in that socially induced gap in subjective experience and remedy the sense of perpetual dissatisfaction felt even by the coolest of cool celebrities. Jolie's optimistic view of the benefit she is providing her children clearly presupposes the background conditions of a posteriori stable identities of choice. But the shift toward the more fluid "situational" forms of association and identity, even in the traditionally rigid domain of religious identity, makes this optimism seem ill-founded. Rates of conversion are increasing both in the developed world (from one religious identity to another or out of organized religion altogether) and in the developing world (typically to Evangelical and Pentecostal forms of Christianity). In the latter case, one may conjecture that this is a response to rates of social change that are rapidly increasing as Asia, Africa, and Latin America ("emerging markets") are integrated into the high-speed exchange networks of contemporary global markets in securities, capital, goods, and services. The theory of acceleration makes clear why such an environment favors the relatively loose and fluid associational and doctrinal structures of, e.g., Pentecostalism. However, in the developed world at least, the flip side of this is a declining number of people who identify with any "organized" religion (including people identifying with doctrinally rigid structures of atheism like those of the increasingly organized network of the so-called New Atheists). There are parallels in the decline of the number of those who identify with organized political parties and ideologies.[36]

A further weighty obstacle to the realization of any ethical life project lies in the way individuals are increasingly caught in an ever denser web of deadlines required by the various social spheres ("subsystems") in which they participate: work, family (school and sports activities of children), church, credit systems (i.e., loan payment due dates), energy systems (utility bills), communications systems (Internet and cell phone bills), etc. The requirement of synchronizing and managing this complicated mesh of imperatives places one under the imperious control of a systemically induced "urgency of the fixed-term" (Luhmann).[37] In practice, the surprising—and ethically disastrous—result is that individuals' reflective value and preference orderings are not (and tendentially cannot) be reflected in their actions. As Luhmann explains, "the division of time and value judgments can no longer be separated. The priority of deadlines flips over into a primacy of deadlines, into an evaluative choiceworthiness that is not in line with the rest of the values that one otherwise professes. . . . Tasks that are always at a disadvantage must in the end be devalued and ranked as less important in order to reconcile fate and meaning. Thus a restructuring of the order of values can result simply from time problems."[38]

People compelled to continually defer the activities they value most in order to meet an endless and multiplying stream of pressing deadlines inevitably become haunted by the feeling expressed in the trenchant bon mot of Ödön von Horváth cited by Rosa: "I'm actually a quite different person, I just never get around to being him."[39] In view of these challenges, we might safely presume that the odds are stacked against the possibility that, even if they in some sense wanted to, Jolie's children will actually be able to carry through an existential choice in favor of one the presented ethicoreligious options.

Therefore, while on the "surface" contemporary acceleration societies present us with a kaleidoscopic juxtaposition of cultural fragments and identity options, their underlying processes militate against the realization of any "deep" identity-constituting projects that are not in conformity with the structurally advantaged form of flexible, situational selves. With these conclusions of his social theory in mind, it is not surprising to find Rosa concerned to highlight the central importance for any adequate contemporary critical project of eudaimonist turns of thought (that is, use of concepts like the good life, happiness, well-being, or human flourishing).

TOWARD A EUDAIMONISTIC TURN IN CRITICAL THEORY

Critical theory has been concerned from its inception to preserve the heritage of the classical ethical-political questions of the Western philosophical tradition, even if this requires transforming it to an extent commensurate with the epochal changes leading to modern societies.[40] In the classical view, as expressed by figures such as Plato and Aristotle, philosophical understanding is inevitably bound up with the idea and practical pursuit of the good life in a just and free society. Critical theorists similarly maintain that social theory is radically incomplete without a connection to emancipatory interests in human flourishing, freedom, justice, and relief from suffering.[41] Against modern competitors for whom "sociological enlightenment" involves the abandonment of these concerns as merely "Old European" cultural leftovers from premodern and early modern social formations, critical theory seeks to reformulate them in plausible ways in light of contemporary circumstances and current epistemic standards of inquiry.[42] Accordingly, Rosa's work vigorously asserts the legitimacy and even necessity of evaluative and normative engagement on the part of any adequate sociology. Yet it also occupies a particular place within the tradition.

For within critical theory, as in the broader stream of contemporary social thought that maintains the classical normative orientation, there is an ongoing debate concerning the nature and relationship of the concepts of the right and the good. This debate concerns both the particular domains of morality, law, and politics and the basic conceptual framework of social theory more generally. There are various ways in which the issue has been framed. John Rawls provides one when he writes that "the two main concepts of ethics are those of the right and the good; the concept of a morally worthy person is, I believe, derived from them. The structure of an ethical theory is, then, largely determined by how it defines and connects these two basic notions."[43] Next he defines *teleological* theories as ones that define the good independently of the right, e.g., in terms of pleasure, preference satisfaction, happiness, or cultural excellence (and often subsequently define the right as the maximization of the good as specified), while *deontological* theories are characterized negatively as theories that do not define the good independently of the right. This way of putting it is somewhat unfortunate, though, for it would arguably count Plato and Aristotle as "deontological" since for them justice (the right) is a constituent of the good life, both in the individual and the polity (not to mention the fact that the notion of maximization that Rawls strongly associates with teleological theories has no clear place in their ethics). However, in another place Rawls provides a slightly different way of framing the issue that has, I think, proven to be more influential or at any rate more prominent in the literature. He presents his own theory of justice as asserting that the right has *normative priority* over and/or *conceptual independence* from the good.

Among critical theorists the tone was set by Habermas, who has defended a strong conceptual separation between "moral" issues of justice or rightness that are universal (or universalizable) in nature and "ethical" issues concerning the good that inevitably involve the particular conceptions of the good held by individuals or social groups.[44] For him this is also bound up with the related theses, first, that from a normative point of view the right *always* trumps the good if they come into conflict and, second, the view that in the pluralistic milieus of modern societies philosophy has no role to play in offering substantive guidance concerning which lives are the good ones. At most it can clarify the nature of the question as it confronts individuals and communities and elucidate the process of reflective self-understanding and self-interpretation required for them to answer it for themselves. Beyond this, the good has little role to play in moral, social, or political theory, or at most a subordinate one.

Those who have dissented from Habermas (and Rawls) on these points have done so in diverse ways. Some have questioned whether the conceptual separation can be as sharp as the thesis requires and also whether it needs to be.[45] Others have taken a different tactic and argued for the centrality of the idea of the good (life) in practical reasoning. This tends to lead to the rejection of the normative priority of the right.[46] Yet others have offered a somewhat more ambivalent, and perhaps therefore potentially more interesting, response that does not clearly reject the priority of the right in cases of conflict in the domain of practical reasoning per se, but instead vigorously asserts the central and unavoidable role of the notion of the good in social theory. The most important recent contribution in this vein has been the work of Axel Honneth, whose social theory of recognition culminates in a "formal conception of the good life" that, following Hegel, conceptually intertwines the good of individuals and the institutional arrangements of "rational" or legitimate sociopolitical orders in a way that is reminiscent of the classical theories of Plato and Aristotle.[47]

Rosa's work has been in this latter camp from the very beginning: his dissertation was in fact a comprehensive critical exploration of the methodological and normative implications of Charles Taylor's work for political philosophy.[48] Taylor's central contention is that the identity of human beings is necessarily constituted by what he calls "strong evaluation," namely, the interrelation of 1. a distinction between some good or set of goods (alternatively, some value or set of values) that are seen as incomparably higher in worth than other goods (or values) and 2. the corresponding motivational or attitudinal commitments on the part of the agent with those evaluative views.[49] The necessity involved here is transcendental. It does not imply that one must strongly evaluate any particular good or set of goods, only that there must be *some* such good(s) strongly evaluated on pain of failing to be a human agent at all. For Rosa, this fact proves to be of crucial importance for social criticism and a critical social science in two ways, one normative and the other social-theoretical.

First, from a *normative point of view* it allows one to approach the question of the relevance of the idea of the good life for social and political theory from a different standpoint than the state-centered one that has dominated the liberal-communitarian debate in political philosophy during the last two decades of the twentieth century. The result of this latter standpoint is that the central question becomes whether the *state* or polity should be "neutral" with respect to the diverse comprehensive doctrines, religions, cultures, and worldviews of its citizens or whether it should promote some particular one, perhaps the one that is true or most justified or that best promotes liberty or autonomy or solidarity or some other value.[50] In light of the tremendous cultural diversity of almost all modern constitutional-democratic states, it is quite plausible from this point of view that the state must, in order to treat all of its citizens with equal respect, avoid directly *establishing* legal privileges for any particular way of life or conception of the good through the means of coercively enforced laws. However, laws whose provisions do not themselves establish such "non-neutral" outcomes may, given the circumstances, happen to *engender* the decrease or even disappearance of certain ways of life or conceptions of the good as a result of morally unobjectionable processes. In itself this is a morally neutral fact. Basic moral norms entail respect for persons, not forms of life or traditions or worldviews as such. But the case is slightly different when background conditions *foreseeably and reliably* engender disadvantages for some ways of life or, more important, foreseeably provide powerful, perhaps even overwhelming, incentives to pursue a specific and possibly highly restricted range of goods (or conceptions of the good).[51] In Rosa's view this is precisely the case in modern liberal polities, not as a positive result of state action, but because they are embedded in capitalist socioeconomic orders. For this reason, the apparently extensive and endlessly celebrated individual liberty that is supposedly ensured by the neutral or impartial norms of liberal constitutions leads to a surprisingly homogeneous and limited set of realized possibilities with regard to conceptions of the good, possible careers, educational options, personality structures, consumption choices, leisure activities, and family structure, among others. "Liberal freedom" ironically turns out to go hand in hand with "capitalist necessity."[52] This reality is occluded by the usual state-centric focus of the "right versus good" debate in mainstream political philosophy.

That fact seems to be related to neglect of an insight that was poignantly expressed by Walter Benjamin: one can imagine a society in which basic needs of order and security are met and human relationships and social structures are ordered in perfectly just ways, but in which individuals are dreadfully unhappy, in which there seems to be grave difficulty in finding "meaning" in individual and collective life, in which human beings do not seem to find it possible to genuinely flourish, but instead live lives of quiet, though unresentful and even dignified, desperation. As Habermas puts Benjamin's point: "wouldn't it be as possible to have emancipation without happiness and fulfillment as it is to have a relatively high standard of living without the abolition of repression?"[53] Hence along with the cramped fixation on the state, which given the extraordinarily concentrated police and military powers of modern states naturally has an unimpeachable motive, there is a parallel hardening of the gaze on the figure of justice, which perhaps itself results from the justified fear of what might happen if particular religious or moral conceptions of the good were to be directly enforced by the coercive arms of the state. Yet this can distract us from structural conditions that both transcend (though they naturally also involve) the state and constitute something approaching a functional equivalent for the coercive enforcement of a particular (capitalist-consumerist) mode of life. The real and observable impact of these factors on the freedom, autonomy, and modes of well-being, flourishing, or happiness available to human beings surely also demands the attention of theorists pursuing the emancipatory aims that critical theory has claimed as its own from the beginning. But while the inherently accelerating dynamics of capitalist competition for profitability are certainly a powerful influence on the types and extent of good realized in human lives in modern society,[54] cultural factors like the aforementioned secularization of the promise of eternal life under the guise of an accelerated exhaustion of experiential options and social-structural factors like the intensifying need for synchronization and coordination that results from the differentiation of social subsystems must also be taken into account.[55] To understand their cumulative interplay, one must shift from a directly normative to a sociological standpoint.

Thus, second, from a *social-theoretical point of view* the insight into the identity- and agency-constituting nature of a relationship to the good, when conjoined with a sociological perspective on the similarly constitutive nature of time horizons and time structures, promises to shed new light on an age-old question in critical social thought, one that has astonished and vexed it since the days of Jean-Jacques Rousseau and Marx, namely, the way the systemic or functional requirements of a social formation often seem to almost effortlessly find their complementary reflections in the beliefs, desires, moral sentiments, dispostions, and practices of social subjects. Since time horizons and time structures, alongside their centrality to agency and self-understanding, are also deeply shaped by social structures and cultural ideas that are not at the disposal of any given individual or group but instead confront them as social facts, "temporal structures form the central site for the coordination and integration of individual life-plans and 'systemic' requirements, and, further, insofar as ethical and political questions basically concern *how we want to spend our time*, they are also the place where social-scientific structural analyses and ethical-philosophical inquiries can and must be tied together."[56] Considerations like these have led Rosa more recently to make the even stronger claim that "the ultimate, though mostly unspoken, and also often unconscious object of sociology is *the question of the good life*, or more precisely: the analysis of the social conditions under which a successful life is possible."[57]

One might say that where someone like Martin Heidegger engages in a philosophical exploration of the relationship between being and time, Rosa's work can be seen as a critical social theory of the relationship between social criticism and time.[58] Beginning with the broadly Heidegger-inspired insight that the question how we want to live is equivalent to the question how we want to spend our time, the temporal-structural approach to critical social science reveals that "the manner of our *being-in-the-world* depends to a great degree on the temporal structures of the society in which we live." The acceleration-theoretical account of modernization then reveals that

> instead of the dreamed-of utempian affluence of time a grave and sharpening scarcity of time has arisen in the social reality of Western societies — the *crisis of time* that places in question the traditional forms and possibilities of both individual and political self-determination [*Gestaltungsfähigkeit*] and has led to the widespread perception of a social *time of crisis*, where, paradoxically, the feeling spreads that a deep-seated structural and cultural stasis is hidden behind the permanent, dynamic transformation of social, material, and cultural structures in the "acceleration society," a fundamental historical rigidity in which *nothing essential* changes anymore, however rapidly things alter on the surface.[59]

The promise of modernity, the conviction that scientific, technological, and social progress would make a life of material, social, and political freedom available to all, has not only remained unfulfilled: it is itself among the mechanisms that generated a paradoxical inversion into its opposite. According to Rosa, this process is incomprehensible without grasping the aspirational ideals that were among its driving forces. While it is clear that struggles for justice and political freedom were and are an inextricable aspect of the modernization process, the interlocking dynamic of the economic, social, and cultural motors that unleash the spiral of modern acceleration also bears an ineliminable reference to a historically contingent but fateful "utempian" vision of the good. If this is right, then a critical social theory of the acceleration societies of modernity requires not just the analytical and deontological sword of discourses of justice but also the light shed by the eudaimonistic critique of distorted and self-undermining conceptions of the good.

FURTHER DIRECTIONS FOR THE THEORY OF ACCELERATION: THE CRITIQUE OF CAPITALISM, THE DIAGNOSIS OF ALIENATION, AND A CRITICAL THEORY OF WORLD RELATIONS

The theory presented in this work is not something that is complete in itself and closed off from further development. It ends not with deterministic predictions but rather open-ended reflection concerning four possible scenarios for the future evolution of the acceleration society. In addition, it has proven to be fruitful groundwork for further theoretical projects. Since the publication of the German original of *Social Acceleration*, Rosa has deepened the thematic focus and widened the conceptual framework of the theory of acceleration. Thematically, he has continued to develop the critique of capitalism set out in earlier work that was briefly discussed earlier. Perhaps the most significant expression of this line of research to date is a collaborative work produced with some of his colleagues from the University of Jena, the primary purpose of which is to resuscitate the critical engagement with capitalism that has been central to the sociological tradition from the start.[60] A second but not unrelated project involves an attempt to retrieve and reformulate the Hegelian and Marxian concept of alienation (*Entfremdung*) for contemporary critical theory.[61] Rosa contrasts experiences of alienation with experiences of what he calls, drawing again on Charles Taylor, "resonance," in particular resonant experiences in the domains of art, religion, and nature.[62] Both of these are embedded in a wider, third project that consists in the elaboration of a critical theory of our relationships to the world (*Weltbeziehungen*).[63] This is meant to be a kind of pendant or counterpart to the theory of acceleration in that it attempts to specify the normative and evaluative basis of the critical or negative diagnosis of the pathologies of acceleration societies by articulating the experiences and utterances of individuals themselves and making explicit the standards implicit therein. The aim is also to disclose a more positive perspective on the possibilities of a good or successful life in such societies. This kind of theory could provide orientation for individual or collective projects of emancipation and fulfillment or, if there are no viable ways of escaping the dominance of the forces of acceleration over the forces of progress and collective political self-determination, the weaker strategy of melioration.

IN PLACE OF A PREFACE

BEFORE THE INVENTION OF TECHNOLOGY, if Longheart of Kairos wanted to send some news to his friend Shortwhile in Chronos, which also lay in the Kingdom of Utempus (this was a time when people didn't take the distinction between Greek and Latin morphemes so seriously), he'd have to cover the distance on foot, which took six hours, or on a donkey, which still took about three and a half hours. Both options would leave him short on time since either he couldn't get back before lunch, or, if he left after lunch, he needed to stay in Chronos overnight, which not only led to fights with his wife but also made him lose a day of work. Nowadays, though, Longheart picks up the phone with a smile on his face, conveys the news to Shortwhile and chats with him a bit about the weather before he leisurely smokes a pipe, feeds his cat, works for half an hour and then makes lunch with his wife—and for that they mostly use the microwave.

Ah yes, even at the office things are different than before. Before the introduction of technology he had worked the entire day on the books he needed to replicate as the city copyist. If the book was thick, sometimes he hadn't even copied out one by nightfall. Nowadays though he just calmly turns on the copier in the morning, drinks a cup of coffee until the machine warms up, and copies the manuscript ten or twenty times, depending on how great the need for copies in Kairos is that day, none of which takes more than twenty minutes. Afterward he goes swimming at the beach. In the evenings, meanwhile, Longheart doesn't work at all.

At last he has time to sit in the garden, talk with his wife, play some music or philosophize, or read the books he's copied if they are interesting. It is magnificent to be able to enjoy his life without being pressed for time or pressured by deadlines. If he wants to have a picture of his wife, his cat, or the sunset over the sea so that his great-grandkids may remember them, he leisurely fetches his digital camera from the living room and presses the button. The finished image, glorious and true to life, appears after a few moments in the printer tray. He no longer needs to commission his friend, the painter Aeternus, who had always been busy before and, even when available, had to guide the brush for hours on end while Longheart kept the cat still with either caresses or force. On the other hand, Longheart only notices every once in a while the desire to preserve something in an image in order to enjoy it later or pass it on to posterity.

If he wants to stay comfortably warm inside when it gets cold in the evenings, he doesn't have to go into the forest and gather wood just to struggle to light it later and even then only enjoy the warmth for a limited time. He simply turns on the heater that is connected to windmills on the coast and, literally with a turn of the hand, it grows as warm in the living room as a balmy summer afternoon. Longheart is happy and feels he is rich. He has won time, almost inexhaustible amounts of time, and the strangest thing is that he is also no longer visited by the uncomfortable feeling of boredom that he used to feel before. He has at last found leisure. This surplus, this immeasurable wealth of time, has made him a new man, and Utempus a new society.

This, or something like it, is how we could picture a world in which a certain dream of technological promise had become reality, one that captivated people's imaginations well into the twentieth century: namely, the dream of an emancipated world in which there was no such thing as a scarcity of time, where time had even been transformed from a scarce good into an overabundant one.

The belief that modern technological and economic efficiency would produce such a "utempian" society was hardly ever doubted by the advocates of economic and technological progress. One still finds it in, for instance, Ludwig Erhard.[1] As the Swedish economist Staffan B. Linder strikingly remarked, "we had always expected one of the beneficent results of economic affluence [brought about by technological progress — H. R.] to be a tranquil and harmonious manner of life, a life in Arcadia."[2] The English philosopher Bertrand Russell, in his essay "In Praise of Idleness," written in 1932, defended the view that this arcadian-utempian society had in principle already been achieved. Only an unreasonable ("Protestant") work ethic as well as a misallocation of labor prevented its full realization.[3] As late as 1964, the American magazine *Life*, warned of an imminent massive overflow of free time in modern society that would cause serious psychological problems: "Americans Now Face a Glut of Leisure—The Task Ahead: How to Take Life Easy," ran the headline of the February 21 issue of that year.[4]

Our society seems like the utempian city of Kairos in many ways, and yet it is also radically different. But why? The "tempo of life" has increased, and with it stress, hecticness, and lack of time. One hears such complaints from all sides, even though, just like in Kairos, in almost every sphere of social life there are enormous gains in time by means of technology. *We don't have any time although we've gained far more than we needed before.* The aim of my book is to elucidate this monstrous paradox of the modern world.

My thesis is that this requires the deciphering of the logic of acceleration. In the context of the story it seems natural to start with the suggestion that the time Longheart gains simply gets lost again because the copier, the photo apparatus, and the heating system that help him save so much time have themselves to be manufactured or earned in the first place. If we assume that even in Kairos things are produced by a division of a labor, then after the "invention" of technology Longheart has to copy proportionately *more* books than before (which itself presupposes that the *demand* for books in Utempus correspondingly increases as well). In this way the relationship between one's available budget of time and the promises of technology may have become a zero-sum game (or even a negative-sum game): the inhabitants of Utempus would need just as much or even more time to produce and earn the time-saving devices as they save by using them. This reminds one of the story, told in many places and in different versions, of the poor fisherman and the successful entrepreneur.[5]

In an isolated part of rustic southern Europe, a fisherman is sitting on a flat seaside beach fishing with an old traditional fishing rod. A rich businessman, enjoying a vacation alone by the sea, passes by during a walk, watches the fisherman a while, shakes his head, and starts to speak to him. He asks him why he's fishing here and says that out there on the rocky cliff he could surely double his catch. The fisherman looks at him, bewildered, and asks uncomprehendingly, "What for?" Well, the entrepreneur goes on, he could sell the additional fish at the market in the next town and with the earnings acquire a new fiberglass rod and highly effective special bait. That way he could easily double his average daily catch yet again. "And then what?" asks the fisherman, still puzzled. The entrepreneur becomes impatient but continues, saying that he could soon purchase a boat, head out into deep water, and haul in ten times as many fish, so that in a short time he would be rich enough to get a modern ocean trawler! The businessman is beaming now, inspired by his vision. "All right," says the fisherman, "and what do I do then?" Then, the businessman enthused, he would soon dominate the fishing industry along the entire coast and he could have an entire fleet of fishing boats working for him. "Aha," replied the fisherman, "and what do I do when they all work for me?" Well, then he could sit by the beach all day, enjoy the sun, and fish. "Uh huh," says the fisherman, "I'm already doing that now."

Naturally the story seems a bit naive. It suggests that the highly improbable ending of the arduous narrative of progress that the businessman wants to make palatable is identical with its beginning, so that in the end, even when the fisherman supposedly succeeds, he actually gains nothing. So the businessman appears to be an unambiguous victim of the "protestant work ethic" decried by Russell: work is for him a pure end in itself, and the path from the starting point to the final result is like a zero-sum game—in the best-case scenario. Of course, the story is in fact *not* circular. The beginning and the end are only apparently identical. In truth, they are very different. The fisherman *has to* fish because that is how he makes his living and he has no alternative. The rich entrepreneur, on the other hand, *can* fish, although he can also do a thousand other things. *The expansion of our horizon of possibility* is thus an essential element of the promise of technology. But this phenomenon also changes the nature of fishing on the beach in a rather underhanded way. The businessman is aware that he could do many other things with the time he spends fishing: there's the boat tour, the opening of the golf course, the drive to the next tourist highlight, etc. If his fishing pastime gets disturbed by this train of thought, then he appears to us in a very familiar contemporary guise, though one no less foolish: the fear of missing something prevents him from "being-in-the-world" in the way the (idealized) fisherman is.

But his anxiety about missing something does not have purely hedonistic roots. There are also good business reasons: While he fishes on the beach, the competition is developing newer, better ships, acquiring expanded fishing rights, placing his monopoly on the coast in question, and thus always on the point of ruining his seaside vacation. Meanwhile the rates are changing for the health insurance, telephone and electricity bills of both his company and his household, and the investment conditions under which he manages his wealth are likewise in flux. Maybe he'd be better off looking after these matters instead of absent-mindedly fishing. Otherwise tomorrow he might not even be able to fish anymore. Also, he urgently needs some new clothes since what he's wearing went out of fashion two years ago, and his sunglasses don't meet the latest UV-protection standards, so they're rather unhealthy. His friends are constantly moving too. Maybe he should head home and give them a call before he's completely lost track of them. After all, now that he's on vacation he finally has time for that. And his wife has been coming home later and later recently. Maybe she's planning on leaving him. No, he should definitely not sit on the beach and fish while the world changes around him at a scorching pace. (Damn! His computer has gotten so old in the meantime that it can't even load the newest software that would help him manage all the addresses. It's too hard to always write down postal addresses, telephone numbers, cell phone numbers, fax numbers, and e-mail addresses by hand. The address book has become unreadable and tattered after writing over so many old entries.)

So while the entrepreneur would like to sit on the beach and leisurely fish, he has the feeling that he is sitting on a or, more precisely, several slippery slopes or standing on a descending escalator: he had better start running so he can stay in place, so he can stay *current*. Therefore, it is not only the promise of technology that drives him to increase the tempo of his life but also the highly dynamic nature of his technological, social, and cultural environment, which has become more and more complex and contingent and thus compels him to do this. Yet this shows that the second answer to the parable of the fishermen is still naive. It's not the case that the entrepreneur simply *can* fish while the poor fishman *must* do it. He can of course consciously take some "time off" and "give" himself a couple of days (more rarely weeks) on the beach (without his cell phone or an Internet connection or a TV), but he pays a price for his stay in this "oasis of deceleration," where what the fisherman does out of poverty appears to be an unheard-of luxury. The world will have changed when he comes back, and he will have to catch up or put up with a backlog. This consciousness makes clear that between the beginning and the end of the story there is not just a change in the social world but also in the very personality of the fisherman-entrepreneur. He has a different conception of the relation between future, present, and past. The future world of the entrepreneur is radically distinct from his past, while the fisherman (similar to Longheart in the first story) knows what to expect of the future on the basis of his experience of the past. The horizon of expectation (*Erwartungshorizont*) and the space of experience (*Erfahrungsraum*) are broadly congruent for the fisherman, but maximally distinct for the entrepreneur.[6] The latter has a different feeling for the lapse of time and a different conception of the value of time.

If our protagonist is an entrepreneur of the usual variety, then he will find himself very stressed for time. He will try to maintain control over his life and his company (and the social changes relevant to him) and also plan scrupulously for future developments. However, the more dynamic his environment becomes, the more complexly and contingently its chains of events and horizons of possibility take shape, the more unfulfillable this intention will become. For this reason, our fisherman-entrepreneur will, if possible, transform himself once again. He will give up his pretensions to control and management and become a "player" who allows himself to be driven by events: "If the competition leaves my ships worthless the day after tomorrow, then I'll just open a casino or write a book, emigrate to India to seek my guru, or go back to school to study something new. Who knows? I don't have to decide today. I'll let it depend on how I feel the day after tomorrow and what opportunities present themselves to me then. The world is full of unexpected opportunities and possibilities." With this move he becomes in many respects like the fisherman again, who also did not try to alter the future in accordance with long-term plans. Perhaps he will even win back a moment of leisure. But the environment of a player remains highly dynamic: the respective horizons of expectation and experience remain separated. That is why the (late modern) player is *in the world* and *in time* differently than both the (premodern) fisherman and the (classical modern) entrepreneur.

In this book I will show that the manner of our being-in-the-world depends to a great degree on the *temporal structures* (*Zeitstrukturen*) of the society in which we live.[7] The question how we want to live is equivalent to the question how we want to spend our time, but the qualities of "our" time, its horizons and structures, its tempo and its rhythm, are not (or only to a very limited degree) at our disposal. Temporal structures have a collective nature and a social character. They continuously confront acting individuals as a solid fact. The time structures of modernity, as we will see, stand above all under the sign of acceleration. The acceleration of processes and events is a fundamental principle of modern society. However, as the two stories make clear, the causes and modes of action of this principle are extraordinarily diverse, complex, and at times paradoxical. The protagonists see themselves up against not one but three different kinds of acceleration. In the first place, they have to deal with *technological acceleration*, which, as the story of Kairos illustrates, should have a decelerating effect on the tempo of life when seen from an abstract or purely logical perspective. In fact, however, the *acceleration of the tempo of life* presents us with a second form of social acceleration that is, in view of technological acceleration, paradoxical and in addition, as the previous consideration of the fisherman-entrepreneur's dilemma shows, may be connected with a third, analytically independent manifestation of social acceleration: *the acceleration of the social and cultural rate of change.*

I will explain how the complex interaction of these forms of acceleration is responsible for the fact that, instead of the dreamed-of utempian affluence of time, a grave and sharpening scarcity of time has arisen in the social reality of Western societies, a *crisis of time* that places in question the traditional ways in which individuals and polities could secure the possibility of shaping their own existence. This has in turn led to the widespread perception of a social *time of crisis*, where, paradoxically, the feeling spreads that a deep-seated structural and cultural stasis is hidden behind the permanent, dynamic transformation of social, material, and cultural structures in the "acceleration society," a fundamental historical rigidity in which nothing essential changes anymore, however rapidly things may alter on the surface. It is easy to conceive of new patterns of identity and sociopolitical arrangements that are appropriate for the altered structures of time, but they require that we give up the deepest ethical and political convictions of modernity, that we give up on the (failed) project of modernity.

The composition of a habilitation thesis and then a book manuscript is in many ways itself a battle with time and a race against the clock. That I have been able to finish this work in what I hope is an acceptable way is something for which I thank a large number of friends, advisers, interlocutors, and companions who have supported me in various ways over the years and thereby significantly strengthened the book: naturally, I bear sole responsibility for the remaining weaknesses. In the first place, I would like to mention Hans-Joachim Giegel, Klaus Dicke, and Axel Honneth, who, not only as committee members but beyond this as discussion partners and critics from three different disciplines, played a large role in sharpening my argument, giving me encouragement in the course of my work, and saving me from errors. The same goes for Herfried Münkler, who in particular provided inestimable support during the early phases of the formulation of my project and offered his research colloquium as a valuable forum for discussion. For that I give him special thanks.

I have received helpful references and stimulation from too many colleagues to name them all. However, I am particularly indebted to the Graduate Faculty of the New School University in New York, where I stayed from September 2001 to August 2002 with the help of a Feodor-Lynen Research Grant that was generously awarded me by the Alexander von Humboldt Foundation and where (aside from certain events in world politics) I was able to work undisturbed. In particular, my thanks are owed Andrew Arato, Richard Bernstein, and Nancy Fraser. Due to the closeness of the themes of our work, William Scheuerman was an extraordinarily important conversation partner—and a good friend. The same is true for Manfred Garhammer. I received important professional help from Hanns-Georg Brose, Barbara Adam, and Martin Kohli. I would also like to thank my Jena colleagues Michael Beetz, Michael Behr, Robin Celikates, Klaus-M. Kodalle, Jörn Lamla, Lutz Niethammer, Mike Sandbothe, Rainer Treptow, and especially Ralph Schrader and Andrea Kottmann. André Kaiser was an indispensable adviser on every professional decision. Along with the Humboldt Foundation I would like to thank the Körber Foundation for its support of my work and for its outstanding cooperation.

Friendly conversations with Elisabeth Herrmann, Carola Lasch, James Ingram, Christian Kraus, Paulus Liening, Jörn Arnecke, Stephan Zimmermann, Stefan Amann, and Freider Weis have all inspired decisive intellectual breakthroughs—many insights came to me during endless Sundays with the youth of TC Grafenhausen at Gegners tennis courts and intense discussion with the engaged participants of the Deutschen SchülerAkademien in Braunschweig from 1998–2003. Heiko Steiniger made himself invaluable through his tireless dedication to tracking down needed literature. Ursula May edited the entire manuscript with impressive precision and good judgment, as did Bernd Stiegler of Suhrkamp: to them both I owe my thanks.

I dedicate this book to my siblings, Armin and Christine.

SOCIAL ACCELERATION

INTRODUCTION

As to what social theory can accomplish in and of itself—it resembles the focusing power of a magnifying glass. Only when the social sciences no longer sparked a single thought would the time for social theory be past.

—JÜRGEN HABERMAS, The Theory of Communicative Action

1. TEMPORAL STRUCTURES IN SOCIETY

The belief that all events, objects, and states of affairs in the social world are dynamic processes and that time is therefore a key category for any appropriate analysis of society has become a commonplace in the social sciences. But it looks as if even disciplines that realize this have not known how to make much of it. Over and over one finds the astonished realization that almost all social phenomena can be "temporally reconstructed," that is, redescribed in terms of their temporal aspects, whether it be techniques of domination, class distinctions, intercultural problems, socioeconomic underdevelopment, gender relations, welfare regimes, or the experience of hospitals, prisons, and drugs.[1] As a general rule, however, this observation fails to have any lasting effect. The redescription of the phenomena of the respective problem area in terms of time results in little cumulative gain for either sociological theory or practice and the findings of disparate investigations of this sort hardly seem capable of being brought together in a systematic sociology of time.

So it is hardly surprising that even into the late 1980s treatises on the sociology of time consistently began with the almost stereotypical observation that time is a fundamental category of social reality and that until the appearance of the respective work there was no sociology of time worth mentioning, which the author of course intended to change.[2] Yet, in important and detailed literature reviews at the beginning of that decade, Robert Lauer and Werner Bergmann had already shown that, contrary to this stubbornly persistent conviction, there was in fact a large amount of research on the sociology of time.[3] Nevertheless their verdict was that a social-scientific analysis of time that carefully linked theory formation and empirical research was still lacking.

In view of this, Bergmann claims that the principal obstacle for the sociology of time consists in the lack of a well-founded, systematic connection to general sociological theory formation. As a rule, existing social-scientific studies of time are based on pretheoretical and arbitrarily selected models of time that for the most part rest loosely on philosophical, anthropological, or even everyday concepts. As a consequence, the sociological literature on time is made up of a variety of unconnected, noncumulative studies that are virtually "solipsistic" since they lack a sufficient connection to general approaches in social theory.[4] So far not much has changed in this respect. Of course today books hardly ever begin with the assertion that until they appeared there was practically no sociology of time. Instead they usually start off with an overview of the most important philosophical or sociological studies, organized either chronologically or by subdiscipline, and these inquiries are then said to be unconnected and unsatisfactory. What follows, though, is all too often yet another "solipsistic" treatise, typically one that makes selective use of authors or theses that support its argument.[5]

As a result, existing social-scientific work on the theme of time can be grouped in general into three categories. In the first falls a surprisingly large number of survey works that take up and systematize previous reflections on the sociology of time from extremely diverse points of view. These treatises almost always culminate in the claim that the surveyed material is sufficient to show how important and diverse temporal structures are in the social world and why it is urgently necessary to devote more attention to them.[6] The second category includes an increasingly salient group of very detailed studies of time and temporal structures that belong to particular subdisciplines of the social sciences. In the overwhelming majority of these cases one can add that the analyses remain too immediately focused on the particular phenomena being investigated. Rather theoretically impoverished and methodologically eclectic, they tend to treat time as a self-evident quantity.[7]

Finally, by way of contrast, the third category encompasses a series of theoretically oriented analyses of time that aim at the systematic clarification of a
social-scientific or social-philosophical concept of time. They rise to such a
high level of abstraction, though, that the investigation of empirically relevant
phenomena not only completely drops out of view but also threatens to become unworkable[8] —not to mention the fact that so far these attempts at conceptualization also operate in a predominantly "solipsistic" fashion. Because
of this they do not open up the prospect of a unified, social-scientific concept
of time. As Barbara Adam remarks: "None of the writers has the same focus.
Everyone asks different questions. No two theorists have the same view on
what it means to make time central to social theory. . . . There are no signposts
for orientation in this maze of conceptual chaos."[9] So, despite promises by
Giddens and Luhmann to make time an essential concept in the formation of
their own theories,[10] a systematic linkage of the sociology of time to the development of empirical research programs is still an unfulfilled desideratum.

The suggestion, made by Adam and others, that in such a difficulty we
should fall back on a *philosophical* approach to time as a unified foundation
for our efforts, quickly proves to be just as unpromising when we take a closer
look: philosophical concepts of time, formulated by the likes of Augustine, Immanuel Kant, Henri-Louis Bergson, John Ellis McTaggart, Martin Heidegger,
or Margaret Mead and debated in their wake, are no less heterogeneous, incommensurable, and incompatible. These thinkers disagree on even the most
elementary questions concerning the reality of time, whether it is a natural
category, or one belonging to intuition or the understanding, or rather instead
a social construct.[11] Approaches based on the philosophy of time are thus just
as much inclined to let time appear to be an unfathomable puzzle as the
more theoretical investigations of the sociology of time are, while the empirical analyses that remain closer to the phenomena are equally disappointing
since as a rule they simply take time to be a self-evident quantity. Thus, at first
glance, the problem noted by Tabboni, that analyses of time fall with great
regularity into either the "self-evidence trap" or the "enigma trap," seems to be
irresolvable.[12] So it is hardly surprising that in the debate on the nature of time
the favorite citation continues to be that pregnant passage from Augustine's
Confessions, where he states his own back-and-forth oscillation between these
two poles: "What is time? When no one asks me, I know. But if I seek to explain it to someone who asks me about it, then I do not."[13]

The consequences of the sociology of time's rather weak condition are serious not only in view of the difficulties of establishing it as a subfield within

the canonical disciplines of the social sciences but above all with respect to the contemporary formulation of theories of society, analyses of modernity, and diagnoses of the times. Because research in the sociology of time has so far been relatively unfruitful and difficult to connect to theoretical projects in the social sciences and social philosophy, these have been practically forced to continue operating in a way that excludes a temporal perspective. So Pierre Bourdieu's dictum that the practice of social theory is so "detemporalized" that it even rules out the very idea of what it excludes still seems correct, despite all the metatheoretical protestations and pronouncements to the contrary.[14]

Against this background the present work is *not* envisaged as a contribution to the sociology of time as such, i.e., it does not ask what time is, nor in what way it enters into and affects social practices and structures. Instead it seeks to contribute an adequate social-theoretical grasp of current social developments and problems in the context of the process of modernization and also the debate concerning a fracture in this process between a "classical" age of modernity and a "second" age of *late* or *post*modernity. Further, it aims to systematically work out their ethical and political implications. My guiding hypothesis is that modernization is not only a multileveled process *in* time but also signifies first and foremost a structural (and culturally highly significant) transformation *of* time structures and horizons themselves. Accordingly, the direction of alteration is best captured by the concept of *social acceleration*. The thesis is that without treating the temporal dimension as a categorial and central consideration in social theory one cannot account for present-day changes in social practices, institutions, and self-relations in Western societies. The point is neither to establish a further subfield ("the sociology of acceleration") nor to justify an existing one ("the sociology of time"), but rather to reconceptualize contemporary social theory. Thus in what follows I will generally draw on ideas from the philosophy and sociology of time only where this seems appropriate for systematic reasons.

One decisive advantage of temporal-analytic points of entry to social-theoretical questions consists in the fact that temporal structures and horizons represent one, if not *the*, systematic link between actor and system perspectives. As is well known, social changes can be either analyzed "macrosociologically" as alterations in "objective" social or systemic structures or investigated "microsociologically" from the viewpoint of a subject-centered social science as a transformation of logics of action and self-relations. While almost all varieties of social theory since Talcott Parsons have striven to overcome this structure/agency division, the question concerning the mechanisms by which systemic-structural logics and imperatives and actor orientations become mutually adjusted to one another or mediated with each other still remains perhaps one of the most puzzling and least well-understood problems of the social world.

Thus it is more or less obvious that social-structural processes of modernization cannot occur without some correspondence in the construction of subjective senses of self, in other words that social-structural transformation through modernization must necessarily go hand in hand with a transformation of identity.[15] It is very unclear, however, how in fact actors in liberal societies, who not only respect but also actively cultivate the principle of individual ethical autonomy, develop the action orientations that are required from a systemic point of view.[16] In this context, analyzing the almost miraculous mutual adjustment of systemic logics and those of action from the perspective of time appears to be a promising method. On the one hand, time horizons and time structures are constitutive for action orientations and self-relations. On the other, they are not at the disposal of individuals insofar as time, regardless of its social construction and systemic production, confronts actors as a "natural fact" or a "given." Because the solid facticity of time and its nonetheless social nature are therefore indissolubly intertwined, temporal structures form the central site for the coordination and integration of individual life plans and "systemic" requirements. And, furthermore, insofar as ethical and political questions basically concern *how we want to spend our time*,[17] they are also the place where social-scientific structural analyses and ethical-philosophical inquiries can and must be tied together.

Research in the sociology and ethnology of time present us here with one unanimous finding containing two essential points: first, measurements of time, perceptions of time, and time horizons are highly culturally dependent and change with the social structure of societies. Otthein Rammstedt worked this out systematically in an influential essay that postulates four forms of experienced time and time consciousness that unfold in accordance with the evolutionary development of social structures and are accompanied by very different time horizons and thus produce radically different action orientations and self-relations.[18] According to this scheme, simple, undifferentiated societies tend to have an "occasional" time consciousness whose experience of time only differentiates in general between a "now" and a "not now," so that past and future are fused together as the (mythically constituted) Other of the present. The claim that human beings "always already" had at their disposal quite concrete and similar representations of past and future is thus rendered permanently suspect.[19]

This conception portrays segmental and archaic caste-differentiated societies as dominated by a cyclical time consciousness in which time is experienced as a circulation of continuously recurring processes and states of affairs. Therefore the primary form of experienced time differentiates between *before* and *after*. Nevertheless, past and future are structurally identical here: the memory of the past is equivalent to the prediction of the future; the space of experience and the horizon of expectation are congruent.[20] This experience of time appears in an extreme form as the "eternal return of the same" (Friedrich Nietzsche), in which memory extends across the future. In contrast to this, in the more starkly differentiated societies of early modernity a linear time consciousness gradually prevails that replaces the circle of time with an irreversible line running from the past through the present into the future. Here, for the first time, the dominant experience of time is one oriented by the difference between past, present, and future, with the future in particular appearing as fixed or closed in the sense of a *telos of history* (for instance, in Christianity or Marxism).[21]

In the functionally differentiated society of high modernity, finally, a linear time consciousness with an open future predominates: historical development is no longer understood as running toward a determinate goal, and its ending remains uncertain. According to Otthein Rammstedt, the corresponding experience of time is that of continuous movement or acceleration. Naturally this typology is schematic and simplified and hence empirically questionable. Rammstedt himself emphasizes that the four forms of time consciousness are superimposed on each other and do not form a historically unambiguous series. Empirical research has verified this supposition: for instance, coexistent cyclical and linear conceptions of time are found in almost all cultures, albeit with different emphases and characteristics.[22] The central claim that the experience of time and the consciousness of time vary depending on social structures and cultural models is thus not placed in doubt by such objections.[23]

Second, the temporal structures of a given society are both cognitively and normatively binding as well as anchored deep within the personality structure that determines the habitus of individuals. Thus Norbert Elias emphasizes, on the one hand, the functional character of concepts of time, which for him serve primarily to coordinate and synchronize social processes and therefore develop and become further refined to the extent that the growing social complexity and length of chains of interdependence require more precise planning, regulation, and ordering of time. On the other hand, he stresses that the individual's socially produced consciousness of time is, as a social habitus and as it were second nature, an inextricable component of one's personality: "The experience of time of an individual belonging to a society that strictly regulates time is one example out of many for personality structures that are no less compulsory than biological characteristics and yet are socially acquired."[24]

Interestingly, Elias already sees in this interlacing of systemic and individual-psychological structures an explanation for the (rapid) tempo of life in modern societies.

> One of the characteristics which make this connection between the size of and pressure within the network of interdependence on the one hand, and the psychological make-up of the individual on the other particularly clear, is what we call the "tempo" of our time. *This "tempo" is in fact nothing other than a manifestation of the multitude of intertwining chains of interdependence which run through every single social function that people have to perform* . . . [it] is an expression of the multitude of interdependent actions, of the length and density of the chains composed by the individual actions, and of the intensity of the competitive chains composed by the individual actions. . . . A function situated at the junction of so many chains of action demands an exact allocation of time; it makes people become accustomed to subordinating momentary inclinations to the overriding necessities of interdependence; it trains them to eliminate all irregularities from behavior and to achieve permanent self-control.[25]

In the following chapters I will explore in detail the connection between social structure and pace of life postulated by Elias. For the moment, let me just emphasize that the normalizing character embodied in the temporal structures of society unfolds, as it were, behind the backs of actors in such a way that a higher degree of social normalization, on the one hand and a lower degree of morally authoritative codes or a maximum degree of individual ethical self-determination, on the other become compatible.[26] The works of Elias and Michel Foucault thus suggest that the modern "disciplinary society" essentially achieves its disciplining and planning power by means of the establishment and internalization of time structures. And indeed, as countless studies have shown in the meantime, the key institutions of the disciplinary process, prisons, schools, barracks, hospitals, and workhouses, are characterized above all by their strict regulation of time.[27]

Nevertheless the process by which systemic temporal perspectives and patterns are aligned with those of individuals, and thereby social-structural requirements with individual dispositions, is not limited to specific institutional contexts but occurs continuously in all realms of life and society. Following Peter Ahlheit and Anthony Giddens, from the actor perspective one can situate the process of temporal mediation at three levels.[28] Actors always simultaneously develop three distinct temporal perspectives whose relations with each other they must repeatedly reconsider and work out in their temporal practices. In the first place, they must deal with the time structures of their everyday lives, for instance, the recurring routines and rhythms of work and leisure time, waking up and going to sleep, etc., and the connected problems of synchronization, speed, duration, and the sequencing of actions. (How will I manage to get my work done at the office and pick up my daughter from kindergarten on time? Should I go shopping before or after swimming?) The extent to which time becomes a problem on this plane also depends upon the degree of routinization and habitualization, which in late modernity seems to be decreasing again. Nevertheless, everyday time has had to this day a mostly repetitive and cyclical character, since it is, as Giddens emphasizes, constitutive for the reproduction of social structures.[29]

In the second place, however, actors also constantly develop a temporal perspective on life as a whole in which they reflect upon their "lifetime." The question how we wish to spend our time is not only posed to us with respect to our everyday life but also with respect to our life as a whole, which is why Giddens reverts to Heidegger's concept of *Dasein* for this temporal dimension. Here as well the questions of synchronization, speed, duration, and the sequencing of actions are posed. *How long do I want to (may I) go to school? Do I want to (can I) have kids, before I'm done with my degree? Do I really want to be a judge all my life? When will I retire?*

In the third place, actors experience their everyday time and their lifetime as embedded in the encompassing time of their epoch, their generation, and their age (*longue durée* in the terminology Giddens uses following Fernand Braudel). "Our time" is therefore always simultaneously the time of our days, our lives, and our epoch, something that becomes clear when older people say "in my time things were different," "in our time these traditions are obsolete," or when people speak of "Goethe and his time."

Only the interplay of all three of these levels of time and their respective time horizons determines the being-in-time of an actor,[30] and they must be brought into accord with each other in a continuously renewed fashion. For example, when the daily routine of a student consists in waking up at noon, then going to the café, and finally to the revolutionary student club, sooner or later the pressing question will arise whether this is compatible with his plan to become a bona fide university professor and spend his retirement comfortably in Tuscany and whether this kind of routine can be seriously maintained if he doesn't want to be economically excluded in the middle to long run. Similarly, the question will arise whether his life plan is in general still in step with the times—and whether it is still in step with the times to make long-term life plans.

Formulated more generally, this means that the allocation of temporal resources always depends on considerations pertaining to all three levels: how much time someone spends on professional work, family, leisure activities, and physical well-being depends on her daily routines, her life perspective, and her estimation of what is "in step with the times" (or of the demands of time and the future). Enduring divergences in perspectives force one to adopt strategies of adaptation: either the daily routine gets changed or the long-term life goal is redefined. (The possibility of a strategic alteration of the temporal patterns and perspectives of a given epoch only enters the consciousness of actors in exceptional situations.) All three levels have, first, their own temporal patterns (rhythms, sequences, speeds, synchronization requirements) and perspectives (i.e., their own conceptions or horizons of past, present, and future and of their relevance for the given action).[31] Second, they are to a great extent determined by social structures. The rhythm, speed, duration, and sequence of our activities and practices are almost never determined by us as individuals but rather almost always prescribed by the collective temporal patterns and synchronization requirements of society (by hours of operation, transportation schedules, institutional rhythms, time-regulating contracts, deadlines, etc.).[32]

The social-structural constitution of temporal practices is illustrated particularly well by the time patterns of modern society. Again and again one finds the fact that individuals in Western societies rigidly plan and sequence their time, in other words, that the duration of events and the order of activities follows an abstractly fixed time plan external to the actions themselves, bemoaned by cultural critics and celebrated as an achievement by handbooks of time management. Yet this temporal practice is not the consequence of individual decisions or life plans, but results almost inevitably from the structural principle of functional differentiation according to which particular social spheres each follow their own respective temporal logic and individuals are only partially embedded in the respective areas of work, family, union, church, party, committee, department of government, etc. For this reason, as Georg Simmel and Talcott Parsons had already noticed, and as Eviatar

Zerubavel worked out in great detail,[33] they are compelled on pain of exclusion to precisely sequence their involvement in the respective social spheres with the help of hourly, daily, weekly, monthly, and yearly planners and, correspondingly, to synchronize the respective area-specific time patterns. So the oft-remarked dominance of abstract time over "event time" in modern societies—something revealed, for instance, by the fact that events like a talk, a seminar, or a workday do not end when the relevant tasks are finished, but rather when a certain period of time has elapsed—is not some cultural peculiarity, but rather a social-structural necessity. The apparent possibility of reversing it in favor of a "(re-) temporalization of time" in present-day society therefore requires a meticulous cultural and structural analysis, as will be shown in part 4 of this book.

The collective nature of each respective concrete time pattern results in particular from the need for synchronization. We constantly have to orient our action toward the complementary activities and time patterns of our interaction partners and secure at least temporary synchronization. In functionally differentiated societies, this unavoidably leads to a large amount of shorter or longer waiting times, on the one hand, and to correlative phenomena of time pressure, on the other. Something similar holds true for our life perspectives. As will be shown more clearly in the course of the argument, both the idea of a *life* plan and its ideal-typical division into the three phases of education, gainful employment, and retirement, or childhood (in the family of origin), adulthood (with one's own nuclear family), and old age (after the kids have moved out), are sociocultural constructions that cannot in anyway claim universal validity and definitely show signs of eroding in contemporary society. Whether, how, and to what extent the future is planned depends to a great degree on the stability and predictability of the social and cultural environment. Finally, the third plane of time, historical time or the epoch, almost entirely eludes the possibility of being shaped by individuals. Here individual actors only retain the possibility of behaving affirmatively or negatively to the respective demands of "their time." Therefore the meaning of past, present, and future (i.e., temporal perspective) and the temporal pattern of action, which together determine the manner of our being-in-time, are always the complex product of structural and cultural relations and their refraction through the perspective of particular acting subjects.

The interconnection of the three levels of time in the perspective of actors always follows narrative patterns. Everyday time, biographical time, and historical time are related to each other, and mutually criticized and justified, in cultural and individual narratives. The meaning and relative weight of the past, present, and future and thus also the relevance and relative weight of tradition and change are determined simultaneously in narrative schemata (*Entwürfe*). In them every present appears grounded upon a past and related to a future. Cultural and institutional forms of change and persistence are legitimated, and sometimes criticized, through the narrative interrelation of everyday time, life history, and world history, though of course the balance between dynamic and stabilizing forces, between *movement* and *inertia*, varies historically.

As philosophers like Charles Taylor and Alasdair MacIntyre have recently emphasized, the linkage of past, present, and future in one's own life history is always performed against the background of the historical framework of a cultural community or a narrated world history.[34] Knowledge of the finitude of individual existence allows the discrepancy between a limited lifetime and the perspectivally unlimited time of the world to become a narrative and practical life problem.[35] In almost all developed cultures the problem of reconciling this discrepancy is solved by the introduction of a fourth level of time through the notion of a sacred time.[36] This "holy time" over arches the linear time of life and history, establishes its beginning and its end, and sublates life history and world history in a common, higher, and, so to speak, timeless time.

In Christian life, for instance, the time of life and the time of the world are brought together in such a way that both aim toward a future end of the world in the final judgment. In contrast to the linear, quantitative profane time that belongs to the immanent world and everyday ("work day") life, sacred time has a timeless, cyclical, qualitative character and belongs to another or higher world.[37] It is bound together with profane time in extraordinary or more-than-everyday "nodal" points, i.e., in specific moments, rituals, and festivals (e.g., in Christian cultural milieus Sundays, Christmas, or Easter) when it clearly interrupts everyday time, as it were, in a "time-out," and thereby also gives the sequential flow of the latter a structure.[38]

With the help of sacred time, everyday time, the time of life and the time of the world are bound together in a meaningful whole that orients culture and action, one in which cultural patterns and structural necessities, systemic requirements and actor perspectives are made congruent. This temporal concordance is by no means always already secured. Instead it has to be produced in political and social processes of contestation. This makes clear how much the establishment and harmonization of the three social levels of time is always connected to questions of social and political power. The question *who* determines the rhythm, duration, sequencing, and synchronization of activities and events forms a central arena for conflicts of interest and power struggles. *Chronopolitics* is thus a central component of any form of domination, and in the historical process, as, above all, Paul Virilio never tires of postulating and elucidating, domination is as a rule the domination of *the faster*.[39]

So, in the context of everyday practices, temporal strategies like letting others wait, holding back, beating them to the punch, hesitating, changing the rhythm, varying the duration, etc., often lie at the center of social contestation,[40] while on the middle level of time the struggle for time in life, that is, concerning time for education and retirement, vacations and holidays, weekend and night work, or periods of compensation for sickness or unemployment, often shapes economic and political debates in capitalistic societies even more than demands for a certain wage level.[41] This type of controversy encroaches on the third level of culturally and politically determined epochal time in a fluid manner, as is easily seen in the conflict over Sundays and holidays, which was historically played out as a power struggle between church and capital and thus one between sacred and profane time.

It is not a coincidence that political upheavals have again and again played out as struggles over the determination of the calendar (something easily demonstrated by the history of the establishment of the Gregorian calendar) and that new holders of power often seek to cement their position by introducing a new one: for instance, at the beginning of modernity in the new time of the revolutionary calendar of 1793 or in Stalin's efforts at calendar reform.[42] The fact that both attempts at reform ultimately failed makes strikingly clear again just how much inherited time structures and perspectives become, so to speak, second nature to actors. The reformed calendars appeared "unnatural" or "contrary to nature," even though—at least in the case of the revolutionary calendar—they explicitly strove to be closer to nature.[43] The high degree of internalization of time patterns is therefore also responsible for the fact that the temporal dispositions of actors can often be adjusted to new structural conditions only through a long and generally violent process of reeducation, as E. P. Thompson made clear in his celebrated work on the "new dispensation" of time in the lives of workers during early industrialization.[44]

Consequently, if temporal patterns and perspectives represent the paradigmatic site for the mediation of structure and culture, of systemic and actor perspectives, and therefore also of systemic necessities and normative expectations, this immediately suggests that they disclose a privileged point of entry for the social-scientific analysis of the entire cultural and structural formation of an age. Whoever wants to investigate an entire sociocultural arrangement of systemic necessities and cultural orientations—in other words, whoever attempts to get to the bottom of, say, the nature of that meaningful and structural whole that we call modernity with regard to its statics and its dynamics, its inherent tensions and developmental tendencies—would do well to be guided in their work by the specificity, logic, and development of just those structures of time we are exploring here, because the principles and tendencies that underlie modernity are revealed in them as in a magnifying glass. The present work is therefore based on the conviction that adequate social-scientific diagnoses of *the times* (*Zeitdiagnose*) should in fact literally be diagnoses of *its time*, i.e., its temporal structures (*Zeit-diagnosen*). If it has become the conspicuous problem of the diagnostic disciplines that they can no longer find a common focus and therefore take up, in a seemingly arbitrary fashion, particular structural and cultural phenomena and make them each respectively into an anchor of diagnoses of society as a whole—something that has led to the bewildering proliferation of definitions of contemporary society, e.g., as a work, leisure, experience, risk, information, and multi-option society as well as all the *post* societies (postconventional, postindustrial, posthistoire, postmodern, postcapitalist, posttraditional)—then the proposed, as it were, "double" diagnosis of the times indicates a promising way out of this dilemma.[45] The justification of this postulate is the aim and task of the present study.

2. TWO CONTEMPORARY DIAGNOSES OF THE TIMES

The feeling that one's own age is "out of joint" is certainly nothing new. The critical observer's gaze discerns symptoms of a "time of crisis" almost without fail and in cultural history this appears to be virtually constitutive for all attempts at characterizing one's own position or epoch. However, as Reinhart Koselleck has meticulously shown in various works, within the horizon of modernity a new experience is added to this: the feeling, even the explicit conviction, that it is the time itself that is out of joint,[46] that the ongoing time of crisis is the result of a crisis of time.[47]

Observers of modernity are at one in their diagnosis of the kind of transformation of time at issue, even if they disagree about how to evaluate it: reports of the perception of an immense acceleration of time and history, often expressing a state of bewilderment, appear in rapidly increasing number since roughly 1750, which is identified by the editors of the *Geschichtliche Grundbegriffe* series as marking an epochal threshold (literally a "saddle period": *Sattelzeit*).[48] Note that this is long before the beginning of the industrial revolution and even before the French Revolution.[49] With the introduction of the railroad this feeling intensified, and in the wake of the industrial revolution the practice of everyday life became, as it were, experientially saturated by it. As I show in the next chapter, in the subsequent historical process of modernity there followed wave after wave of diagnoses of an acceleration of tempo (of life, of the world, of society, of history—or even of time itself), so that Peter Conrad, in his mammoth cultural history, *Modern Times, Modern Places*, can make the brief and trenchant declaration: "Modernity is about the acceleration of time."[50]

The experience of acceleration remains crucial today and has left its trace in almost every popular and academic diagnosis of the times. In fact, in the wake of the political revolution of 1989, the roughly contemporaneous "digital revolution" in communications technology, and the strengthened processes of global interconnectedness they both made possible, a new discourse about acceleration arises. In 2000 Gundolf S. Freyermuth, here representative of legions of essayists, op-ed writers, politicians, and economists, and with full awareness of the historical career of diagnoses of acceleration, summarizes this discourse as follows: "We are contemporaries of a phase of acceleration that is unique in the history of humankind—and makes industrialization look cozy in hindsight."[51] From the ivory tower, philosophers like Stefan Breuer ("Speed is doubtless the god of our era")[52] and sociologists like Frederic Jameson ("Time is today a function of speed, and evidently perceptible only in terms of its rate or velocity as such")[53] confirm this culturally predominant perception.

"Everything's getting faster and faster." Everything is constantly in flux, and the future is therefore completely open and uncertain and no longer simply derivable from the past and the present. This basic experience of modernity, characteristic of all its phases, only defines one side of the currently prevalent critical diagnoses of the times. Alongside it there is, paradoxically, a second, diametrically opposed observation society makes of itself. Even though it was already formulated by, for instance, Max Weber and Alexandre Kojève and was present as, so to speak, a subtext from the very beginning of modern times, toward the end of the twentieth century it occupies increasing amounts of space in the public mind and appears to affect the experience of reality of the majority of our contemporaries. People speak here of a "crystallization" of the cultural and structural formations of their own age, of its appearing to be an "iron cage" in which nothing essential changes anymore and nothing new occurs. In this view of contemporary society, the current epoch is characterized precisely by the way all motion seems to come to an end: utopian energies are exhausted because all the intellectual and spiritual possibilities appear to have been tried, and this threatens to expand into an uneventful (*ereignislose*) boredom. One finds the most striking formulations of this thesis, of course, in the discourse of *posthistoire* and Fukuyama's claim about the "end of history,"[54] but it is also reflected in the *ex negativo* definitions of one's own age as a "post" and "end" period, a post-age at the end of reason, the subject, values, education, narratives, politics, history, etc. These last diagnoses of an epochal shift are naturally historically new insofar as they appear asymmetrical or "halved": they are observations of an epochal break without a corresponding vision of a cultural new beginning, thus without a new meaningful linkage of past, present, and future.[55]

The two diagnoses of the time that appear so contradictory, social acceleration and societal rigidity, are only at first glance contrary to one another. In the memorable metaphor of a "frenetic standstill" (*rasender Stillstand*), which we owe to an inspired translation of Paul Virilio's *inertie polaire*, they are synthesized into a *posthistoire* diagnosis in which the *rush* of historical events only provides scant cover for (and ultimately, in effect, produces) a *standstill* in the development of ideas and deep social structures.[56] In the next chapter I will attempt to show that the complementarity of these critical experiences of time is not just an academic construct estranged from reality but is emphatically reflected in the cultural self-expression of society.[57]

Under this description the paradoxical basic structure of time in modernity (and, a fortiori, in late modernity), namely, that experiences of acceleration can repeatedly flip over into their diametrical opposites, can be observed not only on the level of historical time but also on the levels of lifetime and everyday time. Analogous to the paradoxical "double diagnosis" of the simultaneous acceleration of social change and halting of social development, one finds in the history of modernity periodic complaints about an increase in the pace of life and an ever more hectic lifestyle, which is said to have all manner of pathological characteristics, especially in the form of overstimulation and task overload (*Überforderung*). This grievance is interestingly accompanied by an opposing subtext in which the uneventful boredom of modern life is bemoaned. *L'ennui* becomes a catchword precisely at the time the industrial revolution is multiplying "velocity in all realms of human experience," as Peter Conrad remarks.[58] These are accompanied by the feeling that life "flies by" faster and faster, although the average lifespan in Western societies has continuously lengthened. The experience of *time standing still* becomes pathological here in the form of clinical depression. More than a few psychologists suspect that this represents a reaction to unfulfillable expectations of acceleration. According to many studies, depressive ailments appear to be on the rise in contemporary society.[59]

The accelerated transformation of social circumstances, institutions, and relationships, that is, the acceleration of social change, poses the following problem to individuals: they have to plan their lives over the long term in order to lend them an element of time-resistant stability, although in view of the growing contingency of social relations they cannot do this rationally. As I will show in part 4, this difficulty, one that sharpens in late modernity, is not just posed to individual actors but also to society as a whole, and to its subsystems, as the problem of steering (*Steuerung*) or coping with contingency. It proves to be a fundamental problem of "our time."

Finally, from the perspective of everyday life in modern societies, as everyone knows from their own experience, time appears as fundamentally paradoxical insofar as it is saved in ever greater quantities through the ever more refined deployment of modern technology and organizational planning in almost all everyday practices, while it does not lose its scarce character at all. On the contrary: "the more time we save, the less we have," runs a well-known piece of folk wisdom impressively illustrated in Michael Ende's *Momo*.[60] Despite a quantitatively large amount of "free time" in the sense of free time resources that do not have to be spent on the performance of necessary productive or reproductive activities, social scientists since Staffan B. Linder's influential study, *The Harried Leisure Class*, have diagnosed an acute "time starvation" that afflicts contemporary society and is manifest at all three levels of time.[61] "At present, American Society is starving—not the starvation of the Somalis or other traditional cultures, who die for lack of food, but for the ultimate scarcity of the postmodern world, time," write the time-budget researchers John P. Robinson and Geoffrey Godbey (who are, incidentally, strictly empirically oriented). They add that "starving for time does not result in death, but rather, as ancient Athenian philosophers observed, in never beginning to live."[62]

Whether acceleration per se is judged to be a malign or benign temporal change depends of course on the consequences taken into consideration. In view of the essential limitation of a human lifetime one may assume that the acceleration of goal-directed processes (the production of goods or states of affairs, the traversal of transport routes, the transmission of information) is, in principal, viewed as desirable. Nevertheless, an evident danger here consists in the potential desynchronization of processes, systems, and perspectives as a result of one-sided acceleration. Acceleration in one subregion of society only remains compatible with the rest of society if corresponding increases in tempo at structural and cultural points of intersection allow for frictionless "translation."[63] In a growing number of diagnoses of the time, however, one finds the implicit or explicit claim that just this "translation" or "resynchronization" is becoming increasingly problematic in many areas of society. If one tries to systematize these desynchronization diagnoses, it becomes apparent that they involve three analytically distinct developments. In the first place, as I have already made clear, it is always possible that systemically institutionalized or structurally induced temporal patterns and perspectives, on the one hand, and the temporal patterns and perspectives of actors, on the other, increasingly diverge, i.e., that these two structures of time fall apart (and thus desynchronize) as a consequence of migration or a rapid system change. As Simmel already lucidly observed, the institutionally and structurally induced tempo can be too high for acting subjects or, conversely, appear to the latter as having an excessive amount of rigidity and inertia.[64] So both structural developments and cultural changes can be the (endogenous) cause of such a temporal bifurcation (*Entzweiung*).[65] The resynchronization process can then run in favor of the one side or the other: either actors take on and internalize new temporal orientations, as in the process described by E. P. Thompson, or a systemic change occurs in whose course the overly inflexible and sluggish structures are replaced by faster and more mobile arrangements (or vice versa), as happened, for example, in the case of the former socialist states of eastern Europe.

A diagnosis of the times that fits this pattern is presented by many social scientists when they argue that systemic processes of modern society have become too fast for the individuals that live in them.[66] The converse reproach — that actors are too inflexible, sluggish, and comfortable, in other words too slow for the "challenges of the time" — is not infrequently made by employers, economists, and politicians when they need to explain systemic deficiencies or misallocations (e.g., unemployment).

In contrast, a second form of desynchronization is represented by Peter Ahlheit's postulation of a growing incongruence of the three actor-guiding horizons of time (that is, a disintegration of the perspectives of everyday time, biographical time, and historical time) in modern capitalist societies. In his view their irreconcilability causes individuals to perceive "their" time (in all three frames of reference) as "alienated." This leads to a loss of the ability to narratively embed one's own life in a past giving one a point of reference and a future lending meaning to one's endeavors such that, at least in the middle term, a time-resistant action orientation is achieved.[67] Naturally this actor-related form of desynchronization can be a consequence of desynchronization processes of the first kind. This is made clear, for instance, in the work of Richard Sennett.[68]

In the third place, social subsystems or functional systems can also be desynchronized with respect to each other. This is the gist of a widespread diagnosis of the times found in the social sciences and even in the op-ed pages and everyday politics according to which, roughly, the economy, science, technology, and the developments to which they give rise, have become too fast for a political steering and legal regulation of social transformation; the economy, science, and technology, on the one hand, and law and politics, on the other, have fallen "out of step," that is, become desynchronized.[69] Later on I will come back to all these forms of desynchronization and attempt to elucidate their internal connection to the tendencies of acceleration inherent in modernity. Here it is enough to observe that the (ongoing) acceleration of even one social subsystem can raise problematic temporal side effects for the other systems, and the individuals acting within them, in virtue of the temporal aspects of the "structural coupling" of social systems and the need for synchronization that results from it.[70]

If one tries to survey the current diagnoses of the times (and diagnoses of time) as a whole, it is striking that on one critical point they appear to converge. Common to a great variety of otherwise rather different contemporary interpretations of society is the belief that one can discern a more or less accentuated *break* in the development of modernity that forces one to redefine the present age as a second modernity,[71] a reflexive modernity,[72] an extended liberal modernity,[73] a late modernity,[74] or even a postmodernity.[75] However, the basis on which this postulated break rests (is it structural or cultural?), where and when it sets in historically (is it a matter of a new age? if so, when does it begin?), and how far-reaching it is are all highly contested topics in the social sciences. Is it a question of a break *in* modernity or of a break *with* modernity? The concepts just mentioned already make clear that most of the interpreters incline to the first diagnosis and claim to observe a *radicalization* of modern principles. But then it becomes questionable what is genuinely new about the identified historical period.[76]

The path to an adequate answer to this question opens up only when one takes a look at the diagnoses of time already discussed: phenomena of acceleration and desynchronization lie at the heart of almost all definitions of the "new age." This is particularly true of those diagnoses of the time that closely connect the postulated new social formations to the phenomena gathered together under the catchword *globalization*. As I argue in the chapter 9, the genuinely new thing about present-day globalization consists not in the appearance of the processes discussed under this heading, but rather in the *speed* with which they transpire.

This particular process of acceleration undoubtedly brings with it a series of structural and cultural consequences that lead to noticeable differences from the social formation of "classical modernity."[77] At first glance, of course, it proves to be an unprecedented process of global *synchronization*: the "age of globalization" is emblematically condensed in the placeless, "u-topian" Internet, where all events occur simultaneously worldwide. Nevertheless, complementary to this, as it were, intersocietal, intercontinental synchronization, almost all the intrasocietal phenomena of desynchronization discussed appear to sharpen. The information and financial markets in which transactions span the world in fractions of a second now hardly allow for a resynchronization of actor and system perspectives and, above all, no longer admit of political, and in part not even of legal, steering. Individuals and nation-states have grown too slow for the rate of transaction in globalized modernity. Education, politics, and law cannot keep pace with the developments of the era. At the same time, quantitatively large but marginalized groups in the so-called Third World, and certainly in the industrialized societies as well, are becoming "desynchronized" in that they are excluded from the decisive structural and cultural developments. All the diagnoses of globalization agree that the simultaneity of the nonsimultaneous is rapidly increasing: the Stone Age and the Cyber Era exist next to each other in an unmediated fashion.

Indeed, it appears that an acceptance of these processes of desynchronization is the common core of what apologists of the "postmodern" celebrate and their opponents are battling against. The surrender of a political steering of economic, technological, and social processes of development (the "end of politics") or even of the attempt to understand these developments at all (the "end of Science/Reason"); the renunciation of the demand for a meaningful, narrative integration of the past, present, and future, both biographical and collective ("the end of metanarratives"), and thus for an integration of everyday time, biographical time, and historical time in the project of a personal identity ("the end of the subject/the terror of identity"); the acceptance of desynchronized and disintegrated processing on the part of social subsystems ("the end of Society") and finally acquiescence in the desynchronized and disintegrated development of different social groups—all these characterize the essence of both the postmodern philosophical ideology and the postmodern sociological diagnosis of the times. Therefore in what follows I argue that the assumption of a temporal perspective makes it possible to bring together the manifold observations of a "break" in the development of Western societies in such a way as to allow for an account of this break that is theoretical in substance, empirically verifiable, and capable of giving a selective, and hence normatively useful, diagnosis of the times. My guiding heuristic hypothesis here is that *the acceleration that is a constitutive part of modernity crosses a critical threshold in "late modernity" beyond which the demand for societal synchronization and social integration can no longer be met.*[78]

The consequence of this, as will be shown, is a fundamental, qualitative transformation in the forms of societal steering and individual identity that entails the abandonment of the claim to individual and collective autonomy and thus of the normative project of modernity. At this point of inflection, the quality of biographical and historical time changes as well: individual and collective time patterns and perspectives become situational and are continually redefined with the flow of time in a context-dependent manner in historically novel forms of "situational identity" and "situational politics." Finally, in light of these considerations, one can theoretically locate and analytically specify the paradoxical simultaneity of diagnoses of a "total" dynamization of all social relations and a contemporaneous complete rigidification of historical and life-historical development of any kind, both of which show up precisely in diagnoses of "postmodernity."[79]

3. A THEORY OF SOCIAL ACCELERATION: PRELIMINARY CONSIDERATIONS

As I have tried to show, the requirement that we make temporal structures themselves the focus of social-scientific diagnoses of the times and definitions of modernity arises as it were naturally from the self-observation of modernity and in effect imposes itself on the sensitive social researcher. It grounds the hope that the cogent aspects of the various diagnoses and postulates concerning contemporary developments (globalization, disintegration, individualization, the information society, etc.) will reveal themselves to be diverse manifestations of a unified developmental logic. Therefore in the next chapter I interrogate the systematic content of the available self-observations of modernity regarding time more rigorously in order to lay down the foundations of my own theory of acceleration. In the first place, though, the methodological and theoretical presuppositions of such an enterprise should be made clear.

The initial hypothesis of this work runs as follows: *the experience of modernization is an experience of acceleration.* However, the question of which analytical categories lead to the most revealing interpretation and explanation of the structural and cultural developmental dynamics of modernity can only be answered by social-scientific analysis itself. So the cogency and explanatory potential of the conjecture that acceleration is the central feature of the transformation of time structures, and as such a fundamental force that shapes the culture and social structure of modernity, has to prove itself in what follows. In contrast, several authors have recently objected that the defining experience of time in late modernity is no longer that of acceleration, but rather that of the simultaneity of highly heterogeneous events and processes, which leads to the temporal perspective of a prolonged (Hanns-Georg Brose) or stretched (Helga Nowotny) present.[80] I agree with this diagnosis to a great extent, but I will argue that this observed alteration in the consciousness of time and the time horizon represents a consequence and manifestation, or a new level, of the process of acceleration and cannot be interpreted as its replacement by a new temporal principle. Thus we are dealing with something that *results from* processes of acceleration.

According to another objection to the acceleration diagnosis, processes of acceleration are almost always accompanied by complementary tendencies of hesitation, delay, and slowing down such that changes in time structures invariably have to be interpreted as complex manifestations of this reciprocal relationship. Acceleration and deceleration have, in this view, an equal claim to being universal basic temporal tendencies. While I accept this objection to the extent that any theory of acceleration with a systematic intent has to take into consideration corresponding processes of slowdown, I am convinced I can show that in the modernization process forces of acceleration and deceleration do *not* balance out, but are instead very unequal in distribution: discernible tendencies of deceleration can be interpreted either as residual or as reactions to acceleration processes (and occasionally as functional for the latter). They are therefore in all cases secondary to the forces of acceleration. This holds true irrespective of the observation that lies at the heart of this book, namely, that the forces of acceleration bear within themselves a time-altering quality that leads to epiphenomenal appearances of inertia.

A social-theoretical definition of modernity that takes as its starting point the category of acceleration confronts in the first place the question, as obvious as it is difficult to answer, of what social acceleration is and what exactly is actually being accelerated in the modernization process. In fact, just as much confusion and disagreement reigns regarding the correct answer to this question as there is agreement about the fact of social acceleration as such. There is today no cleanly defined social-scientific concept of acceleration, let alone a theory of it.[81] Very often, with a culpable neglect of logic and the categories of physics, the concepts of speed and acceleration are used synonymously, i.e., perceptions of acceleration and processes occurring at great speed are taken to be the same thing. Nevertheless, things are no better with regard to the concept of speed, which has also been given no precise meaning over and above its physical one, as Stefan Breuer remarks in his study of Paul Virilio's "dromology" (which unfortunately rejects exact definitions of concepts as a matter of principle): "How little we know about speed! Sociology deals with meaning, economics with wealth (or poverty), political science with domination—in other words, phenomena that have little or nothing to do with speed. . . . Should the equation $v = s/t$ be all there is to say over a phenomenon on which nothing less than the continued existence of this planet depends?"[82]

What is unclear here is not just what one conceives of as pertaining to social acceleration but also that to which it actually refers, that is, what its object domain comprises. Up to now the diagnoses of the times that are available in the social sciences, high culture, and everyday life offer a series of candidates, usually without further justification. History,[83] culture,[84] society, the pace of life,[85] or even time itself is accelerating.[86] Similarly in the course of the modernization process, from its very beginning to the present day, such things are claimed again and again, but here the diagnoses can be combined at will and as a rule their concepts can be used to describe the same phenomena, i.e., used as synonyms and hence without the power to discriminate analytically between different things. So it can hardly be surprising that in countless works of social science (and not only second-rate ones) one finds the crude and unqualified assertion that in modern or contemporary society absolutely *everything* is accelerating.[87]

That this is false hardly bears mentioning. Even a cursory glance at daily life shows that a wide array of processes are slowing down (most unhappily, for example, in traffic and legislative deadlock), while others stubbornly resist any attempts at acceleration (the most palpable here are those relating to one's own body, e.g., colds and pregnancies). For this reason, a systematic theory of acceleration cannot avoid undertaking an analytically precise categorial definition of acceleration phenomena (chapter 2.1–2 and chapters 3–5), and it is particularly important to determine to what extent the identified phenomena of acceleration, taken together, can be described as an acceleration *of* society (as a whole). This is a claim that is categorically distinct from the thesis of an acceleration of central developments *within* society. One can only decide between these when one places alongside the definition of processes of acceleration an analogous but contrasting categorial identification of the socially relevant phenomena of slowdown and inertia (chapter 2.3). On this basis, then, the crucial task will be to understand more precisely the interrelationship of the forces of acceleration and deceleration (or of movement and stasis) (chapter 2.4).

For this reason, in part 2 I undertake a "phenomenological" analysis, that is, an analysis of the manifestations and modes of functioning of the three domains of social acceleration whose categories have been distinguished earlier—technological acceleration (chapter 3), the acceleration of social change (chapter 4), and the acceleration of the pace of life (chapter 5)—before I turn in part 3 to an identification of the context in which these processes of acceleration occur and the forces that drive them. Only if it can be shown that these phenomena of acceleration cannot be reduced without remainder to side effects of other basic tendencies of the modernization process (e.g., functional differentiation or individualization) can my hypothesis, namely, that acceleration constitutes an independent basic principle of modernity, claim a certain amount of plausibility in the first place. As I will demonstrate, the modern dynamic of acceleration can indeed be identified as a self-propelling circular process (the circle of acceleration) that is set in motion and driven forth by three analytically distinguishable "external" motors, of an economic, cultural, and social-structural nature, with which it stands in a dynamic reciprocal relationship (chapters 6 and 7). Compared to this, the tremendously historically influential accelerators represented by the state and the military recede into the background in late modernity and today appear to exert a decelerating force on social processes of development rather than an energizing one (chapter 8).

In the fourth and final part of the book, then, I will turn to the consequences of the process of social acceleration worked out in the previous parts. As has been shown, an analysis of the time structures of society offers the possibility of grasping, on the one hand, structural and systemic developments and, on the other, changes related to actors or subjects at the same time and also in relation to each other. As I have already indicated, the forces of acceleration in contemporary society at the transition from the twentieth to the twenty-first century are in fact causing just as much of an alteration and redefinition of individual and collective self-understandings (*Selbstverhältnisse*), i.e., dominant forms of identity, as they are of the shape taken by the political self-intervention or steering of society (chapters 10 and 11).

My argument assumes that the acceleration process of modernity does not take a simple linear form. Due to the complex multidimensionality that has already been discussed, the acceleration of social processes and developments is not simply a process of quantitative increase that would leave the nature of those processes and developments unchanged. Just as, for instance, the acceleration of a series of pictures beyond a certain speed can suddenly bring it to life, in that a movie emerges from individual photos, or again as the accelerated motion of molecules alters at critical points the aggregate condition of matter (frozen, liquid, gaseous), so too the acceleration of social processes beyond certain speeds causes a transmutation of these processes themselves. The thesis developed in chapters 9 through 12 states that the dynamics of the time structures of early modernity produced fundamentally different consequences than those of the transition into the twenty-first century. The latter generate a transformative break in the social structure, culture, and forms of identity of modern society that in fact results in a different society.

Having set myself the objective of defining and locating the dynamic of acceleration in the structural and cultural web of modernity, I conceive of this work as a contribution to a systematic theory of society anchored in empirical research and a social-theoretical redefinition of modernity. Although, like any theory of society that wants to be taken seriously, it orders and attempts to interpret empirical phenomena by postulating structural and cultural interconnections that of course can and must be subject to empirical testing, it does not claim to be itself an empirical investigation. Insofar as it diagnoses and postulates social developments, it obviously lays itself open to the possibility of empirical confirmation or critique. However, the cogency of the fundamental reflections underlying this work cannot be tested by means of a unified, closed methodology, because there is no method of empirical social research that can *simultaneously* grasp the interrelated theoretical observations concerning structures, actions, and subjects and the complexity of the differently scaled temporal structures and perspectives.

As I hope to make clear in the next chapter, the demand for such a controlled and unified method shackles the gaze to sharply restricted surface phenomena and does not allow one to grasp deep structures and distant connections. In particular, the temporal linkage of structural necessities and cultural perspectives is quite systematically lost from view in empirically oriented studies (as in analyses of time budgets or investigations of the time patterns and time requirements of organizations). The connection of my work to empirical research is therefore twofold: first, wherever the argument rests on empirically testable assumptions, I will make use of available data drawn from a multitude of a very different studies in the sociology and psychology of time in a necessarily eclectic fashion. In this respect, it belongs to the "intellectual honesty" already demanded by Max Weber not to proceed in accordance with a logic of subsumption, only accounting for those inquiries that confirm the hypothesis of acceleration, but rather to examine all findings in an impartial spirit.[88]

Here, for instance, the copiously available analyses of time usage are very informative.[89] They are indispensable when it comes to the confirmation of an increase in the pace of life, even though, as will be shown, they are more appropriate for the analysis of the highly temporally differentiated arrangements of classical modernity than they are for the investigation of the dedifferentiated time structures of late modernity. In the latter context they display grave conceptual and methodological inadequacies for an inquiry into the compression of episodes of action and experience and fail to register the relevant key indicators. So just as indispensable are qualitative investigations that try to probe the experience and perception of time by individuals and the reasons for changes in their temporal practices and perspectives.[90] Without consideration of such qualitative findings, the logic of the translation of systemic imperatives into individual motives for action cannot be deciphered.

Thus, in order to discern the temporally specific alterations in patterns of identity, I will draw on sociological and psychological identity research. Where it is rather a matter of deciphering systemic time patterns, I will make use of investigations of structures and horizons of time in politics, law, and the economy. Information on temporal-structural changes in contemporary society can also be gleaned from analyses of so-called globalization and investigations of the geography of time.[91]

There is another particular difficulty involved in empirically testing the postulated acceleration of social change. The problem here is not simply the general lack of comparative historical data. The situation is further complicated by the fact that there is no consensus in the social sciences about what constitute valid indicators of social change—and thus still less clarity concerning how one might ascertain an acceleration of this change. One hypothesis that suggests itself, namely, that acceleration can be defined in terms of an increase in the rate of innovation, fails empirically from the very start since it is unclear what counts as an innovation baseline in the respective realms of society (e.g., in science, in the economy, in art, etc.). I will thus first develop a definition of the acceleration of social change oriented by the philosopher Hermann Lübbe's concept of a "contraction of the present" and only then search for evidence and counterevidence for a corresponding change in the rate of change. Analyses of change in the structure of education, occupational life, and the family, for instance, might yield decisive indications on this point.

This already makes clear the second way in which this work is tied back to empirical research. As a social-theoretical investigation, it claims to open new horizons of inquiry for future empirical research and to offer new guidance here through its capacity to translate a thesis, as diffuse as it is pervasive, of "general acceleration" in social life into a field of empirically specifiable research questions.[92] In accordance with the definition of the relation between social theory and the social sciences from Jürgen Habermas cited at the beginning of this introduction, this work aims to have the "focusing power of a magnifying glass" and establish a new research paradigm at whose center stands an acceleration in the temporal structures of modern society.

Before I begin the actual investigation, I would like to respond to three predictable methodological objections. The first touches on the question of the systematic significance of empirical findings. A foundational problem of investigations aimed at diagnosing the times consists in the fact that for every observable trend there are countertrends that can be found and for all the evidence there is counterevidence. This difficulty is essentially responsible for the uncertainty that predominates regarding, for instance, the significance of diagnoses of globalization and individualization. Problems are posed in a similar way for a theory of acceleration that, in the first place, must be able to determine empirically the systematic importance of phenomena of deceleration in such a way that they appear as residual, as reactions to or side effects of primary processes of acceleration. In the second place, it has to answer the question of the systematic significance of quantities. If the main hypothesis of this work is that acceleration phenomena are fundamental to the cultural and structural development of modern society, it is not refuted by a demonstration that large groups within the population are excluded by the identified phenomena of acceleration because they are, say, unemployed, sick, without rights, or marginalized in some other way. Insofar as they are excluded from precisely those social spheres that are decisive for social development, their importance for the structural and cultural transformation of society remains limited regardless of their quantity.[93] So an increasing number of forcefully decelerated "victims of modernization" does not falsify the thesis that acceleration is a defining characteristic of modernization.

In view of group-specific differences in the experience and shaping of time, there is a further continuing debate in the social sciences concerning the question of the "genderedness" of time, i.e., the differences in the temporal behavior and experience of men and women and their cultural and structural causes. That this question is not given much attention in the present work does not mean that I think it is irrelevant. However, it appears to me to be of rather secondary importance with respect to a systematic acceleration-theoretical analysis of modernity. The compulsions to accelerate affect men and women alike, although it can probably be shown that working women with children are subject to it in greater measure than men, since they are still burdened with the brunt of the tasks of family life.[94]

Doesn't someone who demands a temporal-analytical redefinition of the modernization process culpably neglect the complementary transformation of the qualities of space? *Whoever speaks of time must also speak of space* runs the second methodological objection to be discussed here. This idea rests on a considerations going back to Kant and Émile Durkheim according to which space and time have to be taken as equally fundamental forms of intuition or understanding. As a consequence of this, many of the developments in contemporary social science that are central for this work are described in terms of the inclusion of the spatial dimension as "Time-Space-Distanciation,"[95] "Time-Space-Compression"[96] or as the annihilation of space by time,[97] or even under a prioritization of the spatial perspective as a liquefying of space into *flows* and *scapes*.[98]

That perception and the mastery of space and time are tightly linked to one another is incontestable. Yet if these categories count for Kant as given a priori, for Durkheim they appear as a historically and culturally variable social construct, although one individuals in any given society cannot avoid.[99]

In what follows I hold that, with respect to the modernization process, space and time do not have the same status. It is incontestable that the experience of space has both phylogenetic and ontogenetic priority over the experience of time.[100] If the former more strongly suggests a Kantian a priori, the latter displays in far greater measure the characteristics of sociohistorical variability. Ontogenetically there can hardly be any doubt that the sense of space and the spatial orientation of the child develop much earlier than the sense of time. In virtue of the force of gravity and the physical order of the sense organs and limbs, the distinctions between *above* and *below* and between *in front of* and *behind* are directly embodied (due to the symmetrical construction of the body, the difference between *right* and *left* is, in contrast, an artificial synthetic achievement that children learn much later and sometimes master only incompletely). Over against the primary spatial distinctions, temporal orientations, i.e., the capacity to estimate temporal distances or the duration of events, are essentially more complicated and abstract and are first learned much later. The sense of time is only fully developed in the period of adolescence.[101] Phylogenetically the priority of space lies in the fact that perceptions and concepts of time develop in accordance with changes in spatial qualities: the locally observable differences between day and night and between the seasons, along with the natural and social rhythms connected to these, are the starting points for the determination of time and the development of a temporal vocabulary.[102] Thus in cultural development time is always in the first place local time, determined by the position of the sun and the seasonal development of nature at a specific location.

The reason why temporal structures and perspectives are more sociohistorically variable quantities, however, lies precisely in their weaker anthropological anchoring in comparison to the perception of space. Temporal structures can alter to an extent that spatial ones never can. Therefore changes in the "space-time regime" of a society always arise from altered temporal structures and not from spatial changes. The birth hour of modernity, one might say with some plausibility, was the emancipation of time from space that stands at the beginning of the acceleration process. Through the introduction of the mechanical clock and, later, standardization, time is liberated from place and can be indicated independently of the qualities of the latter. Philosophically, the emancipation of time is achieved with Hobbes (and modern physics), in that the principle of *movement* (as freedom) finally gains priority over (Aristotelian) rest, and in the thought of Kant, who allows time to have a greater weight than space insofar as it constitutes the inner sense.[103] Similarly it is not controversial in recent discussions of the change in how space is perceived to hold that here one is dealing with consequences of transformations in temporal structures.[104] The often observed progressive contraction of space since the introduction of railroads and steamships is a consequence of the faster crossing of distances. The compression of space postulated by the geographer David Harvey is explicitly introduced by him as an "annihilation of space *through time*" caused by temporal processes of acceleration.[105] And the "flows" and "scapes" of globalized modernity that loose themselves from a stable fixation in geographical space can hardly be grasped otherwise than as consequences of a rate of circulation of streams of information that has been sped up to the point of global simultaneity. Therefore my claim runs as follows: *there is no independent spatial moment of change in modernity analogous to acceleration; the transformation of spatiotemporal structures is primarily driven by its temporal dynamic of change.*

The postulation of a sociological priority of time (in contrast to an anthropological priority of space) will certainly provoke opposition and at this point is only intended to help kick off a debate. The theoretical fruitfulness of the guiding hypothesis and overall approach of the present work do not depend on the correctness of this postulate. Change in temporal structures and its causes, effects, and consequences can be analyzed independently of the question how, parallel to this, spatial structures change. That does not at all mean that there are no highly relevant empirical connections between the two, for instance, regarding the organization of political domination. For this reason, space will play a significant role in the following investigation. Yet, in contrast to time, it appears primarily as a dependent variable.

Finally, the third and last objection to be discussed here concerns the question of the concept of time underlying a theory of acceleration. Doesn't the focus on the acceleration of processes and changes imply a certain Eurocentric conception of time, i.e., a linear, abstract, commodified one? Isn't it the case that anyone who tries to develop a "theory of acceleration" must extensively study the time patterns and perspectives of non-European peoples and cultures? My reply to this criticism is that the present investigation does not aim at being a universal history of time or at the development of an ahistorical concept of social time, but rather represents an attempt to understand the essence and the developmental dynamic of modernity following Western patterns. It is an engagement with the temporal structures and perspectives of modernized Western societies. One may conjecture, with sufficient empirical plausibility, that wherever processes of modernization occur they will bring in train a corresponding transformation of concepts of time.[106] A systematic analysis of premodern or non-European cultures in which modernization processes have not yet transpired is not required for this enterprise. I will therefore only make use of related ethnological and historical studies of time to the extent that they help illuminate, by way of contrast, the change in the temporal structures and perspectives of modernity.

The same holds true for the "new" concepts of time that are forming in the natural sciences. In the social-scientific literature it has almost become an obsession to make reference to the relativization and revision of the linear, abstract Newtonian concept of an "absolute mathematical time" and the importance of the insights of, in particular, Albert Einstein's general relativity theory, quantum physics, and Ilya Prigogine's theory of dissipative structures as well as the discovery of a number of forms of intrinsic biological temporalities (*biologischer Eigenzeiten*). Repeated stereotypically here is the assertion that these insights revolutionize our understanding of time and have powerful consequences for society and hence also for any social-scientific conception of time.[107]

On the basis of an often astonishing mixture of esoteric and holistic ideas whose respectability in the natural sciences is certainly a matter of dispute, interesting though they may be, the emergence of a completely new understanding of time is announced, one which, so we are assured, will not only revolutionize the social sciences but also life in modern society as a whole: "A different picture emerges . . . once we put the Newtonian and Cartesian understanding aside and concentrate on the infinite connections and relations. With such a shift of focus and emphasis, existing assumptions and classifications begin to become meaningless."[108] As if in confirmation of this claim, the popular time researcher Karlheinz Geißler announces that as a result of Einstein's relativity theory the end of clock time, punctuality, and the distinction between past, present, and future is in sight, even with regard to our everyday life: "Einstein proved in his relativity theory that clocks in moving systems run at different speeds when the systems themselves have different speeds. . . . With this pathbreaking insight clock time was relativized. . . . In 1955, Einstein remarked in a letter that time is 'only an illusion, even if a stubborn one.' This illusion no longer appears to be so stubborn after all. The once solid belief in the all-powerful time of the clock is disappearing."[109]

Now I do not mean in any way to contest the extraordinary interest that the discoveries of physics have for our theoretical and philosophical understanding of time, nor even the idea that in the long run they will probably have effects on our social practices.[110] At present, however, they help at most to strengthen the enigmatic character of time. Therefore I hold both of these assertions to be mistaken: the relativization of time in the natural sciences does *not* lead to the collapse of temporal structures in our social institutions and our temporal orientations and horizons. It leaves time structures and perspectives at all three levels (everyday time, the time of life, and historical time) untouched. At best, "relativized time," especially when combined with esoteric bodies of thought, may take on the functions of a new sacred time for some actors. Even then they cannot bring about any immediate practical consequences for human action, since in particular the relevant phenomena of physics remain entirely inaccessible to direct experience.

So if there is any empirical evidence for the change in temporal experience and practice postulated by Adam and Geißler, its explanation must be sought in the context of social and cultural practices. A half-baked esoteric-holistic, pseudo-scientific concept of time cannot contribute very much to social science research and work in social philosophy on this point.

The popularity of non-European, esoteric-mystical, and alternative quantum- or astrophysical concepts of time is due to the hope that they might provide a foothold for the development of a normative critique of late modern, late capitalist society on the basis of its treatment of time. As I have argued, this move has an initial plausibility because temporal structures carry fundamental normative implications. Insofar as the basic ethical question of the good life is the question how human beings desire to or should spend "their" time, time structures and horizons, which are always social in nature, lie at the center of ethics.[111] So it is hardly surprising that even empirical studies of time tend to discuss questions of the good life and alternative ways of living.

This work certainly shares the basic intention of social criticism. Nevertheless it seeks to obtain its criteria for the diagnosis of "pathological" developments, as it were, from *within* society by on the one hand drawing our attention to the phenomena of desynchronization and disintegration resulting from social acceleration and on the other holding the temporal perspectives relevant to action and culture up against the structurally imposed patterns of time. Where the three (or, if one includes sacred time, four) levels of the individual's experience of time can no longer be brought into accord with one another and with the systemic patterns of time, severe consequences unavoidably result for actors, both individual and collective. A resynchronization is then only possible at the cost of a (temporal-) cultural or (temporal-) structural "revolution." In this respect, I also understand the following reflections as a contribution to an as-yet-unwritten *sociology of the good life*. Unlike a philosophy of the good life, which would have to develop abstract ethical criteria for the conduct of life, this form of critical sociology wields the socially predominant ideas of a successful life, whether explicitly formulated or implicitly held, against the structural conditions under which those conceptions are pursued.[112]

PART ONE

THE CATEGORIAL FRAMEWORK
OF A SYSTEMATIC THEORY OF
SOCIAL ACCELERATION

1

FROM THE LOVE OF MOVEMENT TO THE LAW OF ACCELERATION: OBSERVATIONS OF MODERNITY

1. ACCELERATION AND THE CULTURE OF MODERNITY

Since the Renaissance, which began a historically reconstructible debate concerning the "newtime" (*neue Zeit*), the defenders and the despisers of modernity have agreed on one point: its constitutive experience is that of a monstrous acceleration of the world, of life, and of each individual's stream of experience. A series of recent historical works has made clear just how much the entire cultural history of modernity to the present day can be interpreted in light of this basic experience. Their common focus lies in the construal of the cultural self-understanding of modernity as a reaction to a changed experience of time and space.[1]

Like Peter Conrad, for whom modernity is quite simply a matter of the acceleration of time (and linked to this the dissolution of fixed spaces),[2] the political scientist and urbanist Marshall Berman defends the thesis that the term *modernity* describes a condition of ceaseless dynamism that finds its most vivid expression in the oft-cited formulation from The Communist Manifesto: *all that is solid melts into air*.

In his book of that title (with the subtitle *The Experience of Modernity*) Berman writes:

> There is a mode of vital experience—experience of space and time, of the self and others, of life's possibilities and perils—that is shared by men and women all over the world today. I will call this body of experience, "modernity." ... Modern environments and experiences cut across all boundaries of geography and ethnicity, of class and nationality, of religion and ideology: it pours us all into a maelstrom of perpetual disintegration and renewal, of

struggle and contradiction, of ambiguity and anguish. To be modern is to be part of a universe in which, as Marx said, "all that is solid melts into air."[3]

Berman then traces the way this experience of dynamization, transformation, and the continual unsettling of certainties accompanies all processes of modernization. The culture of modernity thus consists in working out, interpreting, and more or less bringing this experience under control. (Berman consistently speaks of modernism as a reaction to modernization.)

He lets modernity in this sense begin with Rousseau's observation of the *tourbillon social* or "social whirlwind" in Émile and achieve its first complete artistic expression in Goethe's *Faust*.[4] In the fate of Philemon and Baucis, who in the last act of *Faust* are literally victims of the setting in motion of the Earth and hence symbolically represent the passing away of the old world of inertia or persistence, Goethe makes visible just how much the social whirlwind links together internal and external changes. As Friedrich Ancillon had already remarked in 1823, this culturally shifts the burden of proof, as it were, from movement to inertia: "Everything has begun to move or will be set in motion. And with the intention or under the pretense of perfecting everything, everything is called into question, everything is doubted and we approach a universal metamorphosis. The love of movement for its own sake, even without a purpose and without a definite goal, is what has resulted from the movement of the times. In it, and in it alone, the true life is sought."[5] The burden of proof was borne from then on not by those who wished to change things, but by those who held fast, whether in everyday life, politics, or culture, to what currently existed, something Berman makes clear with a quotation from the New York developer Robert Moses: his bulldozers demolished large parts of New York, and especially the Bronx, with Faustian violence in the middle of the twentieth century (similar to the machines of Haussmann in Paris a hundred years earlier), and, according to him, people who "love things the way they are" have "no hope" in modernity.[6] The love of movement for its own sake, as Ancillon formulated it, appears to be the fundamental modern principle.

Of course, this principle is experienced as ambivalent from the very beginning, both as a path to the true life and a promise of progress and as a limitless abyss and an all-devouring whirlpool. This ambivalence is constitutive for the entire culture of modernity. It can be seen in Goethe, who vacillated between enthusiasm and admiration for the social and technological achievements of the new world, on the one hand, and concern regarding the deeply destructive qualities of its "velociferian," Mephistophelian tempo,[7] and also in Nietzsche, whose dynamic, energetic Overman is overshadowed by the fear of a new barbarism: "With the tremendous acceleration of life mind and eye have become accustomed to seeing and judging partially or inaccurately. . . . From lack of repose our civilization is turning into a new barbarism. At no time have the active, that is to say the restless, counted for more. That is why one of the most necessary corrections to the character of mankind that have to be taken in hand is a considerable strengthening of the contemplative element in it."[8] In the *Untimely Meditations* Nietzsche leaves no doubt that the acceleration, liquefaction, and dissolution of existing relationships and convictions, "the madly thoughtless shattering and dismantling of all foundations, their dissolution into a continual evolving that flows ceaselessly away, the tireless unspinning and historicizing of all there has ever been by modern man, the great cross-spider at the node of the cosmic web," is the basic principle of modern culture.[9]

Nietzsche believed that this development was the seed of decline and decadence. When he "thinks of the haste and hurry now universal, of the increasing velocity of life, of the cessation of all contemplativeness and simplicity," it almost seems to him that "what he is seeing are the symptoms of a total extermination and uprooting of culture."[10] This ambivalence may also explain the effect of Charles Baudelaire's influential characterizations of modernity. In his essay, "The Painter of Modern Life," Baudelaire defines (and celebrates) modernity as the passing and always already disappearing, as "the transient, the fugitive, the contingent, one half of art, whose other half is the eternal and the unchangeable."[11] The fleetingness of the modern moment thus actualizes in a new way the longing for the eternal and permanent, the *other half* of art, on whose behalf Baudelaire greets the constitutively modern idea of (technological) progress with nothing but hatred and contempt, as when he observes that the will to self-annihilation that inhabits the thought of progress is suicidal and leads to eternal despair.[12]

Nevertheless the question here is not that of appraising the experience of an expanding dynamism, but rather of demonstrating its effect on the character of modern culture. From architecture, painting, and sculpture to literature and music, it was definitive in all fields of cultural production.[13]

In the works of the cubists and futurists, like those of Fernand Léger, Jean Metzinger, Giacomo Balla, or Umberto Boccioni, but also of course in the works of William Turner[14] or Marcel Duchamp, who attempted in his picture of 1912, *Nude Descending a Staircase*, to artistically put into practice Einstein's idea of expressing space and time through the abstract representation of movement, one sees clearly the effort to translate the dynamization and fragmentation of the experience of space and the world into a new formal language (*Formensprache*).[15] Drawing on the work of Stephen Kern, David Harvey shows how much, say, Robert Delaunay's cubist painting of the Eiffel Tower (1911) expresses precisely the same idea of representing time through the fragmentation of space that underlies Henry Ford's acceleration of industrial production through the assembly line.[16]

It has often been observed how much the tempo of the performance of classical works in music has sped up since the nineteenth century. If one compares the average duration of recordings of a given work over the decades, one can in fact detect unambiguous "tendencies of compression," leaving aside a few countermovements that aim at "deceleration."[17] It has, moreover, been claimed that, in view of the faster pace of contemporary life, works like Beethoven's symphonies *must* be played faster in order to bring about comparable effects.[18] However, even in the compositional techniques themselves, contrasts of tempo and hence dynamic effects become more and more important from at least the Baroque period onward. A piano sonata of Schumann rather astonishingly begins with the prescribed tempo "as fast as possible" only to immediately follow this with an indication of "even faster."[19] The most pronounced experimentation with dynamic effects is perhaps that of Maurice Ravel, whose *Boléro*, for example, achieves an illusory effect of acceleration through changes in instrumentation. Finally, Darius Milhaud heightens the idea of musical acceleration to the point of absurdity in his three *operas minutes* (1927) by running through the material of three Greek tragedies in a few minutes.

The musical forms of jazz and many styles of pop and rock music have also repeatedly been interpreted as reflections of the breathless pace of modern urban life. The word jazz itself appears to be a slang expression for speed.[20] It doesn't seem implausible to conjecture that new stylistic movements in pop music display a tendency to become ever faster for a time until a critical limit is reached (that of playability or intelligibility). After this, new forms of expression have to be found or one faces the threat of a loss of popularity. The same holds true for the punk music of the 1970s and '80s, for heavy metal, which achieved and passed its zenith of popularity in the second half of the 1980s in its breathtakingly fast variety of "speed metal," and for the techno music of the '90s, in which there was a genuine competition over the highest number of "beats per minute."[21] The effect of such music on the hearer can be thoroughly ambivalent: for example, in her book, *Teenage Wasteland*, Donna

Gaines writes that "thrash [a closely related variety of speed metal —H. R.] is so fast it actually calms you down; it's relaxing, like Ritalin," and, regarding the perception of time in the techno scene, Barbara Volkswein reports the effect of a "flipping over" (*Umschlagen*) of the experience of racing time into a feeling that time is congealing and even standing still that will be central to my general theory of social acceleration.[22] Things are different with another phenomenon: the attraction of disco music, as well as a large part of techno music, is clearly in some way essentially related to the fact that its basic tempo lies just above the normal human heartbeat and thus has a snappy stimulative and accelerating effect. Nevertheless, it is in this case much less about artistically working through a transformed experience of time and space than it is about industrially reproducing it. Its traces can also be seen in other developments in popular culture and the media landscape: for instance, in the way image sequences and editing have grown faster and faster in the course of the twentieth century, reaching the point at which the principle of linear narrative connection is technologically replaced by fragmentary, associative, and kaleidoscopic transitions, as, e.g., MTV made popular worldwide through its ads and music videos.[23]

Last, in the literature of modernity encounters with that "social whirlwind," the ongoing, accelerated metamorphosis of existing social forms and the traumatic, shocklike experience of technologically altered lifeworlds are ubiquitous. We find them not only in Goethe and in the novels of Rousseau but also in, for instance, the poetry of the Romantics: in Adelbert Chamisso's "The Steam Horse," in the "model of all that is fast," that "the course of time" leaves behind it,[24] in Heinrich Heine's only half-ironic observation about the annihilation of our basic concepts of space and time by the railroad,[25] or in the testimonies of expressionism, for instance, in Georg Heym or Georg Trakl, for whom the "demonic" quality of cities lay in their violent pace of change and dynamic movement.

The great novels of the twentieth century can also be understood as reactions to modernity's expectations of acceleration. James Joyce's *Ulysses* transforms and represents them in a stream of consciousness that appears to only allow for the present, while Marcel Proust sets off in search of a past that seems to be, in the "age of speed," always already converted into a museum piece and irretrievably lost.[26] Thomas Mann sets up his *Magic Mountain* as a "novel of time" that not only reflects on the paradoxes of the experience of time but even makes acceleration the principle of its narrative structure: time flows faster and faster as the novel progresses, so that the same number of pages recount a few hours of narrated time at the beginning of the book that later portray days and then weeks, until by the end of the work months and years are compressed into a few pages.[27]

From these observations, David Harvey concludes that the culture of modernity as a whole can only be understood as a reaction to the transformed, crisis-ridden experiences of space and time that result from successive waves of "time-space-compression" and thus must be conceived as consequences of the acceleration of the pace of life and the annihilation of space through time.[28]

This leads me to conjecture that waves of acceleration, as the core of the modernization process, are produced in particular by technical innovations and their industrial implementation. The introduction of the steam engine into factories and, soon after, the construction of railroads; the mass diffusion of bicycles and then automobiles and later planes; the acceleration of communication through telegraphs and then through telephones and finally through the Internet; the social entrenchment of transistor radios and "moving pictures": all these forms of the technological acceleration of transport, communication, and production altered the lifeworld and everyday culture in occasionally shocking and traumatic ways and led to a shifting sense (*Empfindung*) of being-in-time and being-in-the-world. Since the industrial revolution, as Stefan Breuer remarks drawing on Virilio, this world appears to *befall* subjects "unceasingly, with the violence of an accident,"[29] so that medical concepts of *shock* and *trauma* appear to be completely appropriate categories to use. In short, these changes led to what Harvey calls time-space compression.[30]

Ambivalent evaluations of these transformations are characteristic of modernity and show up over and over again in cultural conflicts about each of these innovations: in contemporary testimonials of various associations one often recognizes the experience of the "alluring and at the same time frightening" remarked by Heine. For instance, in 1877 W. G. Greg already formulates it like this: "doubtless the outstanding mark of life in the second half of the nineteenth century is *speed*—the hurry that fills it, the speed with which we move, the great pressure under which we work—and it behooves us, first, to consider the question whether this great speed is something intrinsically good, and second, the question whether it is worth the price we pay for it—a price that we can only estimate and reliably determine with difficulty."[31]

The introduction of each speed-enhancing innovation led to a form of culture war in which the defenders of the new technology who praised the new possibilities it promised faced off against just as determined opponents who warned of both a loss of human scale and control of the lifeworld as well as the physically and psychologically damaging consequences. The warnings ran the gamut: from "bicycle face" caused by high wind resistance to brain damage and digestive problems caused by the high velocity of railroad and later automobile travel[32]—all the way to apocalyptic visions of the complete disappearance of culture as a result of massive television consumption or incurable depressive isolation caused by the expansion of e-mail communication and excessive use of the Internet.[33] Seen in this light, the widespread warnings of harmful effects on the brain from cell phone use give one a sense of déjà vu.

Three systematic conclusions can be drawn from the history of cultural war over technologies of acceleration: first, the technological acceleration process does not run in a uniformly linear fashion, but comes in surges, continually encountering obstacles, resistances, and countermovements that can slow it down, interrupt it, or even temporarily reverse it.[34]

Second, almost every surge of acceleration is followed by a discourse of acceleration and deceleration in which, as a rule, the call for deceleration and the nostalgic desire for the lost "slow world," whose slowness first becomes a distinct quality in retrospect, outweighs the excitement about gains in speed.[35] Cultural movements like Marinetti's futurism (in particular his manifesto of 1909) that euphorically celebrate the intoxication and triumph of the newly created and from then on "eternal, ever-present speed," glimpsing in it at first a new aesthetic and later even a new religion and morality, remained the exception.[36] In this vein the oppositional adherents of a deliberative deceleration were also never at loss for original ways to express their protest against speed, whether it be in the manner of the Parisian fad of taking turtles for walks on the boulevards in 1840, noted by Walter Benjamin in his essay on the flaneur, or in the manner of Peter Heintel's present-day *Union for the Slowing Down of Time* (*Verein zur Verzögerung der Zeit*).[37]

Third, even in the face of the discursive hegemony enjoyed by decelerators in high culture, every single one of these "culture wars" has so far ended with the victory of the accelerators, i.e., with the introduction and entrenchment of the new technology. The triumphal march of the accelerating technologies is flanked here by a popular culture enthused by promised time gains in advertisement, sports, and everyday life, some of whose paradigmatic expressions are, for instance, the fascination with, and success of, "fast food," *Blitzkrieg*,

Formula One racing, luge, or radio stations that broadcast the news two minutes before the hour and advertise themselves with slogans like "on Radio Such-and-Such, always informed two minutes earlier."

Although it is rather pointless to argue about when exactly the strongest phase of acceleration occurred since, on the one hand, technological and organizational innovations are always appearing and the cultural debate about the dynamization of life never quiets down and, on the other, the phases of innovation in the various fields of transportation, production, and communication do not always occur simultaneously, there is nevertheless a broad consensus in the scholarly literature about two significant waves of acceleration. First, it is undisputed that a revolution in speed occurred in the decades before and after 1900 as a result of the industrial revolution and the wide impact its technological innovations had on almost all spheres of life.[38] It is certainly not a coincidence that right about this time (1886 and 1904, respectively) Werner Siemens and Henry Adams each independently postulate a "law of acceleration" in the development of culture. The "clear and evident law of our current cultural development is that of continuous acceleration," explains Siemens,[39] and in his autobiographical work *The Education of Henry Adams* Adams delivers us an impressive and palpable example of the experience of modern culture as steered by explosive, violent, inescapable, and impersonal powers. (Adams continuously speaks, somewhat mysteriously, of "the force" and "the forces" that drive the acceleration process forward.) It is instructive to consider a longer excerpt from a chapter entitled "A Law of Acceleration" that deals with the transformations observed by Adams after the 1890s:

> Nothing so revolutionary had happened since the year 300. Thought had more than once been upset, but never caught and whirled about in the vortex of infinite forces. Power leaped from every atom, and enough of it to supply the stellar universe showed itself running to waste at every pore of matter. Man could no longer hold it off. Forces grasped his wrists and flung him about as though he had hold of a live wire or a runaway automobile; which was very nearly the exact truth. . . . Impossibilities no longer stood in the way. One's life had fattened on impossibilities. Before the boy was six years old, he had seen four impossibilities made actual—the ocean steamer, the railway, the electric telegraph, and the Daguerrotype; nor could he ever learn which of the four had most hurried others to come. . . . Every day Nature violently revolted, causing so-called accidents with enormous

destruction of property and life, while plainly laughing at man, who helplessly groaned and shrieked and shuddered, but never for a single instant could stop. The railways alone approached the carnage of war; automobiles and fire-arms ravaged society, until an earthquake became almost a nervous relaxation.[40]

If we view the emergence of a new medical-pathological discourse of acceleration or the widespread diagnosis of a new speed-induced kind of sickness as the most unambiguous symptom of a phase of comprehensive acceleration, as Joachim Radkau suggests, then the flood of talk about "neurasthenia" that followed the introduction of this diagnostic category by George M. Beard in 1881 (and is echoed in Adams's text) also bears witness to the significance of the changes occurring around 1900.[41] It is this that leads Radkau to name the first decade of the twentieth century the "age of nervousness" (Nervosität).[42] If one uses this kind of indicator, then it turns out that there are strong signs of a new, recent phase of acceleration in the transition from the twentieth to the twenty-first century: from "hurry sickness" and "yuppie flu" to the recently ubiquitous *attention deficit disorder* in children and youth and on to clinical depression as a reaction to the speed demands of a globalized society, the diagnoses of speed-induced sicknesses are proliferating at present.[43]

In agreement with this, from 1989 to the turn of the century the discourse of acceleration and deceleration has swelled as a reaction to the increase in speed through the digital and political revolutions of this period. Lack of time and acceleration are continuous themes in the popular science media and in the op-ed and essay sections of the major newspapers, works offering guidance and counseling about improved time management sell rapidly,[44] and the admonitory voices of oppositional decelerators launch into a mighty crescendo. Books and movements that have committed themselves to a conscious slowing down, for example, Fritz Reheis's best seller *The Creativity of Slowness* or Sten Nadolny's *Discovery of Slowness* or even the aforementioned *Union for the Slowing Down of Time*, have such a wide appeal that Peter Glotz sees in them the emergence of a new, dominant oppositional ideology.[45]

At the same time, both the apologists and the critics of a new culture of "postmodernity" agree that one has to include the recent increase in the speed of social processes among its distinctive characteristics and driving forces.[46]

Here the question whether the digital revolution and the increased speed of transactions discussed under the heading of globalization are actually without historical precedent or whether they instead pale by comparison with the transformations of experience wrought by the industrial revolution (even if only because, as Reinhart Koselleck conjectures, we can become accustomed even to experiences of acceleration) is both hardly capable of being answered and also not particularly relevant.[47] Insofar as the phenomena in question concern the heightening of speed in transportation, communication, and production, the individual mechanisms of acceleration have a cumulative effect: the corresponding processes become ever more accelerated.

In contrast, a different, far-reaching question is whether the process of acceleration itself accelerates insofar as the waves of acceleration in the various spheres of life appear in ever thicker sequences, such that the rate of change itself increases until we arrive at a permanent transformation, an idea suggested by the "laws of acceleration" postulated by Siemens and Adams.[48] An acceleration process of this kind cannot be understood as a form of technological acceleration, but must instead be conceived as a symptom of the acceleration of social change.

Two further phenomena to be explained also speak in favor of the necessity for a social-scientific analysis of the modern dynamics of acceleration that is systematic in intent. The first concerns the fact that the experience of acceleration and shortage of time that stands in the center of the modernization process is in no way a simple *consequence* of technological acceleration. Quite to the contrary, the former appears to be a presupposition of the latter. As authors like Hans Blumenberg, Reinhart Koselleck, Helga Nowotny, or Marianne Gronemeyer have shown, the Enlightenment developed a characteristic form of impatience as a result of the separation of the historical space of experience from the horizon of expectation. This impatience, and associated ideas of Progress, a belated Reason, and an acceleratable History, are constitutive presuppositions for the triumphs of the natural sciences and the industrial revolution that follow.[49]

Koselleck impressively retraces the way the perception of a (secular) social and historical acceleration (partly rooted, of course, in older eschatological expectations) emerges sometime around 1750. It follows the development of a new, "temporalized" understanding of history on the basis of which the space of experience of history and the horizon of expectation of the future can gradually come apart. Wholly independent of but in agreement with these considerations, Marshall Berman and David Harvey also date the beginning of the modern dynamization or time-space-compression from the Renaissance.[50]

The principle of dynamization and acceleration thus appears to be inherent in the culture of modernity from the very beginning, even before becoming observable in its material structures.

Interestingly, the same historical connection is also revealed with respect to the already emphasized "flip side" of acceleration, which characterizes the second of the phenomena that require explanation here, namely, the expanding experience of *processes of rigidification*. These are not only discernible in theoretically oriented sketches and diagnoses of the times. One also reads them attested in cultural self-observations like a subtext that becomes stronger as modernity moves forward. Experiences of standing still go along with the feeling of a heightening rate of change and action and even seem to be its complement or flip side. Thus long before the industrial revolution, but unmistakably within the horizon of modernity, we find in the culture and discourse of sensitivity (*Empfindsamkeit*) various countersymptoms to the symptoms of acceleration. For instance, counterposed to Simmel's qualitative and quantitative "escalation of nervous life" (*Steigerung des Nervenlebens*) there is "black" melancholia, which leads its victims (who are typically identified as "high-strung over-sensitive types" [*überspannte Empfindler*]) into a condition of paralysis and stasis, of a pastless and futureless temporal void.[51] This experience returns during the second half of the nineteenth century and the fin de siècle in a stronger and discursively different form as the existential feelings of *l'ennui*, *Langeweile*, and *boredom*, which were particularly widespread in literary circles. This was a time when the circumstances of life were indeed undergoing breathtaking change as a result of the industrial revolution: "As if in reaction to the force so freakishly expended in manufacturing and engineering . . . the busiest century in the world's history was also the one afflicted by enervation, attracted by sleeping sickness."[52]

While Baudelaire saw *l'ennui* as an unavoidable consequence of the bourgeois culture that gave itself over to the worship of the fleeting moment, Nietzsche also thought he perceived the eternal return of the same behind the furious change of modern society and interpreted its cultural tendencies toward acceleration as a flight from a steadily expanding sense of tedium.[53] Then in the early twentieth century the very same symptoms were held to be the expression of the acceleration sickness *neurasthenia*. Thus, if one follows Radkau, the *mal du siècle* already identified by Alfred de Musset in 1836 becomes, under a new name, the sickness (or guiding discourse) of the early twentieth century.[54] And, as we have already seen, the experience of time tamely flowing or standing still, of the collapse of a meaningful past or future horizon, is the reverse side of the perception of "racing time" and pervades the culture of Western societies in the transition to the twenty-first century: pathologically as a symptom of clinical depression, discursively in the "posthistory" (*posthistoire*) debates, and literarily perhaps most clearly in the stories of Douglas Coupland, whose book, *Generation X*—it was stylized as the "catechism of a late modernity" and a "book of truths at the end of the century" by the *Frankfurter Allgemeine Zeitung,* one of Germany's most important newspapers and at the same time furnished sociology with a keyword for a whole generation[55]—seems to confirm Frederic Jameson's thesis of an imminent collapse of the antinomies of change and stasis when he offers us the following definitions of the symptoms of late modern "history poisoning": "*Historical Underdosing*: To live in a period of time when nothing seems to happen. Major symptoms include addiction to newspapers, magazines, and TV news broadcasts. *Historical Overdosing*: To live in a period when too much seems to happen. Major symptoms include addiction to newspapers, magazines, and TV news broadcasts."[56]

All this makes sufficiently clear that the connection between acceleration and modernity is just as deep as it is complex and that the causal effects of the increases in tempo are manifold and contradictory. Therefore in the next two sections I will turn to the sociological and social-scientific tradition to see what conceptual and methodological resources it offers us for the purpose of comprehending and locating the process of dynamization within the context of modernity from a systematic point of view.

2. MODERNIZATION, ACCELERATION, AND SOCIAL THEORY

A) ACCELERATION IN CLASSICAL AND CONTEMPORARY SOCIAL THEORIES

There can be no doubt that the rise of sociology and its establishment as an academic discipline was in large part a reaction to the basic experience of the liquefaction and dynamization of social relations and the revolutionization of their temporal structure. Nor can there be any doubt that the sociological analyses of the so-called founding fathers of the discipline—Weber, Durkheim, Simmel, and also Ferdinand Tönnies, which emerge during precisely the time frame shown in the previous section to be perhaps the sharpest period of acceleration ever, represent, in this sense, analyses of modernity.[57] The question that interests us here is what contribution the conceptual schemes of the sociological "classics" can make to the systematic and categorial analysis of the modern process of acceleration, its causes, manifestations, and consequences. Their reflections are attempts to locate the basic cultural experience of modernity within the structural transformation processes of *modernization*. It is of interest, in this vein, to first go back one step behind that generation of disciplinary founders and return to the other ancestor of modern social theory: Karl Marx.

The formulation from *The Communist Manifesto* taken up by Marshall Berman, according to which all that is solid is always already dissolving and being transformed or melting into air, already makes clear how much Marx's reflections are shaped by the nineteenth-century experience of a shocking mobilization and dynamization of all material and social relations . In Marx's view the reason for this is the capitalist mode of production, which makes the continual revolutionizing of the means of production a necessity and hence also the transformation of social relations as well as the constant annihilation of what already exists and has been produced. According to Marx, it is the core principle of all modernization processes. It is also a historically new form of social acceleration because all older socioeconomic formations tend to lay down and naturalize relations of production once they are established, statically preserving them from change for as long as possible, in contrast to capitalism, for which the primacy of change over inertia is constitutive.

> The bourgeoisie cannot exist without constantly revolutionizing the instruments of production, and thereby the relations of production, and with them the relations of society as a whole. Conservation of the old modes of production in unaltered form, was, on the contrary, the first condition of existence for all earlier industrial classes. Constant revolutionizing of production, uninterrupted disturbance of all social conditions, everlasting uncertainty and movement distinguish the bourgeois epoch from all earlier ones. All fixed, fast-frozen relations, with their train of ancient and venerable prejudices and opinions, are swept away, all new-formed ones become antiquated before they can ossify. All that is solid melts into air, all that is holy is profaned.[58]

So in Marx's analysis of history and capitalism the modernization process does indeed appear to be an acceleration process, one in which two distinct principles of acceleration can be analytically distinguished. In the first place, as is well known, Marx defends a dynamic understanding of history according to which historical development transpires on the basis of a dialectical interplay between the forces of production that continually further unfold and the relations of production that alter in a corresponding fashion (i.e., at one moment favoring the development of the forces of production, in the next moment hindering it and then being revolutionized). Insofar as factors that are endogenous to capitalism drive this process forward, it accelerates the development of the unfolding productive forces, and hence ultimately the progress of history, in a historically unprecedented way: "The bourgeoisie, during its rule of scarce one hundred years, has created more massive and more colossal productive forces than have all preceding generations together. Subjection of Nature's forces to man, machinery, application of chemistry to industry and agriculture, steam-navigation, railways, electric telegraphs, clearing of whole continents for cultivation, canalization of rivers, whole populations conjured out of the ground—what earlier century had even a presentiment that such productive forces slumbered in the lap of social labour?"[59]

Marx's approach is therefore a truly paradigmatic example of the development of Koselleck's "temporalized" conceptions of history, in which history itself has a direction and becomes as it were a collective subject, which is itself a presupposition of the idea that history can accelerate (and be accelerated). Historical materialism's image of history, then, is based on the notion of a linear historical time that approaches a more or less "closed," that is, predictable future. However, Marx's observation of the transformative dynamics of capitalist societies is independent of the assumption of such a telos of history.

In the second place, and quite independent of this historical dimension, time is a factor of production and therefore a scarce good when considered as a resource within the capitalist process of production. Since gains in time can immediately be converted into the (surplus) profits necessary for survival, time comes to stand out as a factor of competition in the modern economic system, one related in multiple ways to money and acceleration (of processes of development, production, and circulation).[60] This explains in great measure why the acceleration imperatives of modernity aim at the instrumental enhancement of velocities (in transportation, communication, production, and organization) and an increase in the speed of capital circulation and also clarifies the resulting alterations in ways of dealing with time. I will return to this point in chapter 7, where the driving forces of the acceleration process are discussed. Here it is sufficient to note that even though acceleration is only a subordinate, underdeveloped, and rather marginal aspect of a theoretical edifice centered on the basic social contradiction of class conflict, Marx's approach actually does offer a foundation for the explanation of all three forms of acceleration—technological acceleration, the acceleration of social change, and the acceleration of the pace of life (resulting for Marx and Engels only derivatively from permanent existential insecurity, economic competition, and the subjection of workers to the temporal dictates of machines). A systematic theory of acceleration undoubtedly does well, then, to take seriously the results of the Marxian analysis of capitalist economic processes and to integrate them within itself. As I will show in chapter 7, it is the escalatory principles (*Steigerungsprinzipien*) of growth and acceleration anchored in the capitalistic economic system that shape the culture and produce the structures of modern society and the modern form of life.[61]

Max Weber also had these in mind when he identified capitalism as "the most fateful force in our modern life" in the preliminary remarks to his collected essays on the sociology of religion and thus in the context of his investigations concerning the internal connection between the Protestant ethic and the capitalist form of economic life.[62] In so doing he makes clear that the analysis of modern time structures should guard itself against an overhasty economistic reductionism. As is well-known, Weber was above all interested in the motivation of action in capitalism. His study of the capitalist ethos, the attitude and conduct of life corresponding to its economic form, reveals a transformation of time horizons that is both analogous to the structural logic identified by Marx and impossible to reduce to it in an economistic fashion. He thereby provides an impressive confirmation of the thesis formulated in the introduction, namely, that the systemic-structural requirements and the orientations of actors are joined together in the temporal structures of society.

For Weber too a defining characteristic of this ethos consists in the treatment of time as a scarce good of the highest rank. This is clear right at the beginning of his essay on the spirit of capitalism in the famous quotation from Benjamin Franklin that starts with the admonition "remember that time is money." The categorical imperative of the Protestant ethic and the capitalist ethos consists in the obligation *to use time as efficiently as possible*, to systematically eliminate waste of time or idleness and to give an exact accounting of how time has been spent. According to Weber, then, the restlessness and agitation, the acceleration of the pace of life through the systematic elimination of pauses and absences and the categorical economization of time in the conduct of life that shape the cardinal experience of modernity are the consequence of an originally (Calvinist, Puritan) Protestant spiritual mindset that is later secularized. In this view a second lost once is a second lost forever and the loss of time is the first and "deadliest of all sins." Through it the, as it were, temporaly ascetic systematization and disciplining of the conduct of life becomes a core element of the modern attitude to life.[63] From this perspective, time discipline appears to be much more a cultural presupposition of capitalism, rather than a structural consequence. I will come back to this cultural dimension of the causation of the modern acceleration process in more detail later.

In the context of a search for the starting points of a theory of social acceleration, however, it is above all interesting that for Weber too the Protestant-capitalist evaluation of time is part of an encompassing (and accelerating) historical movement, namely, the underlying Western processes of *rationalization*.[64] Insofar as this process is rooted in shortening and enhancing the efficiency of means-ends relations in the sense of instrumental rationality, it can be described as an acceleration process that aims at the accelerated realization of ends through the minimization of the necessary steps or an increase in the effectiveness of the means employed. Rationalization in this sense means to be able to achieve *more in less time* (and with less input). But the increase of quantities per unit of time, as I will argue, is the most abstract and generalized definition of acceleration. It is this enhancement of speed that, according to Weber, characterizes the main Western forms of rational organization and domination—bureaucracy,[65] a state under the rule of law (*Rechtsstaat*), and a capitalistic economic order—and also grounds their historical superiority over all other social formations. For Weber too, then, at the center of the modernization process stand principles of acceleration (although, of course, he was even further away than Marx from developing a theory of social acceleration).

The rationalization of social processes that is central for Weber's analysis of modernity is inherently linked to the development of the social division of labor or, in other words, the *social differentiation* of functional and value spheres that stands at the heart of Durkheim's understanding of modernity. At first glance, Durkheim's works hardly offer points of approach for a theory of social acceleration and a corresponding redefinition of the modernization process. However, after a closer look it turns out that his intensive search for new forms of social integration and social solidarity is motivated, just like the social theories of the other classical thinkers, by the cardinal experience of a dynamized, fragmented, and accelerated society that results from the conden-sation of social intercourse.[66] In his analysis of anomic forms of the division of labor, which he viewed as one of the greatest dangers of the modern differen-tiation process, he identified social anomie as *a consequence of overly fast so-cial change*. As a result of the high rate of change, the awareness and the rules of social interdependence erode before new modes of social integration have enough time to form. Therefore social change and increasing differentiation per se are not the problem for society, but rather their (too) fast tempo.[67]

Durkheim was interested in how social order and stability is possible in the face of the ongoing acceleration and fragmentation of social relations. Never-theless his reflections offer neither a systematic cultural grounding for the ex-perience of acceleration nor an analysis of its social-structural consequences. For this reason it was left to Niklas Luhmann and representatives of the sys-tems theory he developed to analyze the temporal consequences of functional differentiation and to indicate the systematic internal connection of processes of differentiation and acceleration. According to Luhmann, system structures and temporal structures are tightly correlated, such that the differentiation of modern functional systems also involves the differentiation of their time structures as well as the past and future time horizons they involve.[68] Here Luhmann shares Koselleck's view that there has been a "temporalization" or dynamization of time in modernity that is not just an *effect* of structural differentiation but also just as much underlies it: "with the rise of bourgeois society the structure of time drastically shifted in the direction of higher com-plexity . . . [therefore] *we must assume that this restructuring has an impact on each social structure and every concept*. Nothing will retain its earlier meaning. Even if there is a formal continuity in institutions or terminologies, this only hides the fact that each individual form has achieved higher contingency and higher selectivity."[69]

Through the "temporalization of complexity" characteristic of function-ally differentiated societies—which, as I will try to show in chapter 7.3, can be understood as a third structural "motor" of the modern acceleration pro-cess—we arrive not only at a progressive shortening of time horizons, and thus possibly an "acceleration of the evolutionary process which is unparalleled in history,"[70] but also at the *desynchronization* of the respective systemic time structures discussed in the introduction. Luhmann emphasizes how impor-tant a systematic analysis of these developments is for the understanding of modern societies and at the same time makes clear that the conceptual ap-paratus for this task is dramatically underdeveloped.

We would need to be in a position to estimate the degree of heterogeneity in temporal structures which we can tolerate in the various subsystems of our society; it would be important to know how the shrinking time horizons of families affect the economy and how we could counter the well-known negative influence that the time perspectives of a growing economy have on the political system. . . . It is hard to see how one might go about working on these questions or even trying to answer them. Systems theory appears to be the only conceptual frame of reference equipped with sufficient complexity. Up to now, however, systems theory has only applied very simple chronological concepts of time and futurity and conceived the future simply as the state of a system at a later moment of time.[71]

Regrettably, Luhmann did not further work out a theory of time despite his repeated affirmations of the indispensable importance of temporality for the understanding of social systems. Instead it was Armin Nassehi who wrote *The Time of Society*, where, however, acceleration does not even appear as a keyword.[72] Contrary to Luhmann's hope, the systems-theoretical conception of time appears to be rather poorly suited for the development of a theory of acceleration since the distinctions employed by it make an analysis of the diachronic change of temporal structures harder rather than easier. This is because it first constitutes time as the difference of past and future in the operations of a given system and only then grasps it chronologically through observation of that system.[73] Yet in its reflections on the temporalization of complexity and the influence on social decisions of the "urgency of the short-term" (*Vordringlichkeit des Befristeten*) that accompanies the scarcity of time in differentiated systems,[74] systems theory does make an important contribution to a theory of acceleration. I will return to this in the course of the argument.

Meanwhile, the social division of labor and functional differentiation have a necessary correlate in the process of *individualization* that is a further unmistakable characteristic of modernization and stands at the center of the sociological and social-psychological analyses of George Simmel and work influenced by him. It is not a coincidence that for Simmel the metropolis, as the paradigmatic site of modernity, represents at the same time the site of the most extreme individualization and the most advanced division of labor.[75] Simmel ties these processes back to the cultural experience of modernity in a much stronger way than Weber, Marx, or Durkheim. For him too this experience is dominated by the overwhelming feeling of an intensification and acceleration of social processes of exchange and a ceaseless dynamization of all social relations. "The metropolitan type of individuality," writes Simmel at the very beginning of what is perhaps his most influential essay, "The Metropolis and Mental Life," rests on the

> *intensification of nervous stimulation*, which results from the swift and uninterrupted change of outer and inner stimuli. Man is a differentiating creature. His mind is stimulated by the difference between a momentary impression and the one which preceded it. Lasting impressions, impressions which differ only slightly from one another, impressions which take a regular and habitual course and show regular and habitual contrasts—all these use up, so to speak, less consciousness than does the rapid crowding of changing images, the sharp discontinuity in the grasp of a single glance, and the unexpectedness of onrushing impressions. These are the psychological conditions which the metropolis creates. With each crossing of the street, with the tempo and multiplicity of economic, occupational and social life, the city sets up a deep contrast with small town and rural life with reference to the sensory foundations of psychic life. The metropolis exacts from man as a discriminating creature a different amount of consciousness than does rural life. Here the rhythm of life and sensory mental imagery flows more slowly, more habitually, and more evenly.[76]

In harmony with this characterization, in "On the Influence of Money on the Pace of Life," a work that appeared in 1897, and whose fundamental arguments return almost word for word in the central closing chapter of *The Philosophy of Money* ("On the Style of Life"), Simmel defines the tempo of life as the "product of the sum and depth" of the changes in the ideational contents of consciousness per unit of time .[77] In addition, he emphasizes that in modern society this tempo increases violently and without cease.

In fact all the elements invoked and presented by Simmel as "elective affinities" that distinguish modern life from that of previous eras stand out for their intensified dynamics and movement. According to Simmel, what is characteristic of modernity are the fast city as against the slow countryside, the dominance of the mobile intellect over the more static, slowly changing emotional life, dynamic individualism in the sense of a liberation of individuals from fixed, stable traditions and bonds as against the collective social fabrics of the past that change only incrementally and with difficulty, and thus a specific "disloyalty" (*Treulosigkeit*) regarding associations, values, and activities as well as a related preference for the rapidly alternating tempo of fashion, etc.[78] Simmel then brings all these tendencies into close connection with the expanding monetarization of the modern economy, something that appears to him to be both a cause of social acceleration and an expression of it (pictured in the "rolls of coins" sweeping through social life without resistance).[79] Modern monetary exchange enables, increases, and accelerates social and commercial transactions and economic circulation and thereby mobilizes almost all social relations. As Simmel summarizes his reflections on the connection between the modern (capitalist) monetary economy and the pace of life: "All this illustrates to what great extent money symbolizes acceleration in the pace of life and how it measures itself against the number and diversity of inflowing and alternating impressions and stimuli," and he continues, "the tendency of money to converge and accumulate . . . to bring together the interests of and thus the individuals themselves . . . and thus, as determined by the form of value money represents, to concentrate the most diverse elements in the smallest possible space — in short, this tendency and capacity of money has the psychological effect of enhancing the variety and richness of life, that is of increasing its pace."[80]

Simmel thus follows Baudelaire in defining modernity as an experience of the transitory and the fleeting and he explains it in terms of functional differentiation and especially the effects of money.[81] Yet for him modernization also primarily means a transformation of individual personality structures. These react to the social demands of an accelerated modernity with a change in their inventory of feelings (*Gefühlshaushaltes*), their attitudes (*Gemütsstruktur*), their patterns of stimulation (*Nervenlebens*), and the relationship between feeling and intellect. This is the basis of Simmel's rather idiosyncratic-sounding definition of the essence of modernity in his essay on the art of Auguste Rodin, where he writes: "The essence of modernity in general is psychologism, experiencing and interpreting the world in accordance with our interior reactions and, in fact, as an interior world, dissolving fixed contents in the fluid element of the soul, which is purified of everything substantial and whose forms are only forms of movement."[82] Simmel thus conceives of the modernization process as a shifting of the balance between the universal principles of movement and inertia in favor of the former,[83] and thus also as the dissolution of fixed rhythms in favor of permanent change. In this respect money is for him the symbolic manifestation of the "absolutely dynamic character of the world."[84] Individuals react to this shift with, on the one hand, a blasé attitude and indifference toward the contents of the world, and, on the other, in a kind of dialectical inversion, with an addiction to ever newer and more extreme experiences and arousing stimuli:[85] in short, with all the symptoms of the "neurasthenia" that very much characterized Simmel's own personality, according to his contemporaries Ernst Troeltsch and S. P. Altmann.[86] Of all the classical figures of sociology, Simmel thus places the facet of acceleration closest to the center of his definition of modernity, without, however, giving it a self-standing theoretical formulation. Yet those paradoxical processes of individualization (or transformation in personality structures) are what really form the systematic center of his rather fragmentary, sometimes frankly impressionistic works, whose methodology is, as it were, an adaptation to their object domain.

The result of this review of the interpretations proposed by the "classics" is as follows: their still influential definitions of modernity as a process of individualization, rationalization, differentiation, and increasing domination of nature as a result of the development of the forces of production possess a common core that lies in the experience of an immense acceleration, mobilization, and dynamization of social life. They represent at the same time responses to and systematic explanations of that basic experience of modernity. But the transformation of temporal structures itself does not stand in the systematic epicenter of the modernization theory of any of these authors, although it is thematized and serves as a motif in all of them. And thus it was possible for the acceleration process to lose more and more importance relative to other processes in the overwhelmingly "detemporalized" development of sociological and social-scientific definitions of modernity and to play almost no role in later theories of modernization.

This could explain the almost total absence of a theory of acceleration in contemporary social theory. While overflowing debates have been and are conducted about the other basic tendencies of modernization—about the definition and interpretation of processes of rationalization, differentiation, individualization, and domestication (i.e., the development and institutionalization of instrumental reason)—with respect to acceleration one only finds a cluster of individual studies oriented to the manifestations and effects of dynamization regarding particular phenomena in the media,[87] in the labor market,[88] in new information technologies,[89] in the economy,[90] etc., as well as treatments in the genres of popular science and cultural history[91] that do not allow a systematic location and definition of this tendency within the context of a cultural *and* structural analysis of the modernization process.[92]

Some of the few exceptions are the works of Paul Virilio, Fritz Reheis, and Kay Kirchmann, who all set themselves the task of a theoretical definition of social acceleration. While I will draw selectively on their work in what follows, in the end they appear to me to offer, for various reasons, an inappropriate basis for a systematic theory of social acceleration. Virilio's call for and attempt at the founding of a "dromology" as the science of (increasing) speed certainly represents the most prominent approach in the literature. For Virilio, not only modernity but world history in its entirety can be reinterpreted as a history of acceleration in which speed becomes as it were a historical agent (*Geschichts-subjekt*). His historical reconstruction is moreover an eminently political one because he believes he can discern the driving force of the acceleration process in the *domination of the fastest*.[93] Since historically power has been above all the power of movement, the military and weapons-technological struggle for control proves to be a continuous struggle to achieve greater speed. This battle lies at the root of the "dromocratic revolution" (which is how Virilio interprets the industrial revolution),[94] in the course of which "metabolic" speed (of human and animal bodies) is replaced by a new, ever increasable "technological" speed.

By means of successive waves of acceleration through revolutions in transportation, transmission, and, most recently, transplantation (i.e., increases in speed through the organic fusion of body and machine, of genetic engineering and computer technology) we arrive at the victory of time over space.[95] The space-time *dispositif* is replaced by a speed-space, the coordination of action increasingly takes place in and through time and less and less through space, and chronopolitics gains in importance relative to geopolitics. Virilio's reflections are particularly stimulating where it is a matter of interpreting the consequences of technological acceleration and its military-political driving forces or the complementarity of accelerating and inertial tendencies. Nevertheless his diagnosis is that the logical endpoint of acceleration lies in a completely rigid state, a frenetic standstill (*inertie polaire, rasender Stillstand*).[96] I will come back to both these aspects of Virilio's thought. But one cannot get a systematic foundation for a theory of acceleration from his work, because, first, he rejects systematic theory building out of principle and instead structures his works with associative leaps, amassing countless neologisms, obscure analogies, and seemingly esoteric allusions, and second, with the self-confidence of an autodidact he foregoes any links to existing social theories. Yet it seems to me that the weightiest objection lies in the fact that Virilio's approach remains conceptually truncated since he only conceives acceleration as technological acceleration and leaves no categorial place for the other two analytically independent aspects of acceleration, those of social change and the pace of life.

Fritz Reheis's best seller, *The Creativity of Slowness* (*Die Kreativität der Langsamkeit*), presents us with a critique of the social demands of acceleration in modern society from a psychological and ecological perspective. Reheis builds his analysis of the temporal structures of late capitalist society, which are, in his view, dysfunctional, on the systems-theoretical model of three nested basic systems. The *environment* or nature forms the comprehensive system for all social processes and is fundamental for the second level, the system *culture/society*, which in turn is prior to the physical and psychological system of the *individual*. Alterations at one level always affect both the other systems, though naturally the rates of change and the characteristic tempos (*Eigenzeiten*) of the respective systems differ: individuals can transform themselves or adapt faster than societies, and nature requires still longer periods of time to reproduce its resources or regenerate itself. The explicitly Marx-inspired "ecological-materialist" central thesis is then that unfettered capitalism (as the core element of the modern culture/society) disrespects the natural rhythms and tempos of all three systems because of an inherent compulsion to accelerate rooted in the law of profit.[97] This desynchronizes and overtaxes the other systems' capacities to adapt and learn both separately and in their mutual relationships, and that in turn leads to dysfunctional phenomena within and between all three systems.[98] But Reheis's analysis of the dynamic of acceleration itself does not go beyond Marx if he sees it as rooted in the evolutionary logic of capital. And furthermore he proceeds very selectively and one-sidedly in his interpretation of the consequences and limits of acceleration by reducing them all to the common denominator of "diseased people, declining society and desiccated nature."[99]

Last, Kirchmann draws on Norbert Elias in his systematic investigation of the connection between the acceleration of social processes and the development of the media in modernity in that he interprets both as complementary elements of the modern civilizing process.[100] His work also provides a series of interesting insights. However, it is too fixated on the analysis of acceleration in the mass media to serve as a starting point for a systematic account of the causes, characteristic phenomena, and consequences of social acceleration. In

particular it remains unclear in the final analysis what drives forth the mechanism of escalation (*Steigerung*) in the interplay between the media, speed, and
the civilizing process as a procedure of condensation or slowdown.

Thus in view of the current state of theory on this subject, and in accordance with the goal of the present work—namely, to provide a theoretically substantial, empirically grounded account of the functioning, scope,
and influence of the acceleration process and also of its limits and effects in
the context of modernization—the most promising course in the search for a
systematic approach is to build upon the foundation of the classical sociological theories of modernization discussed in this chapter.

B) ACCELERATION AND MODERNIZATION: ATTEMPT AT A SYSTEMATIZATION

Dealing with the heterogeneous and partially contradictory multiplicity of
both processes of change and analytical perspectives is a fundamental problem for every systematic theory of modernization. Drawing on a suggestion
of Hans van der Loo and Willem van Reijen,[101] who themselves unmistakably build upon the (notoriously detemporalized) general action schema of
Talcott Parsons,[102] it seems sensible to me to distinguish between perspectives focused on *social structure*, on *culture*, on *personality structure* (or on
the subject), and finally on society's relationship to *nature*. Social formations
and social developments can then be investigated under each of these four
aspects in a principled way. If one places these perspectives in relation to the
approaches that were reviewed in the previous section, it becomes apparent
that the modernization process can be and has been culturally interpreted as
rationalization, social-structurally as *differentiation*, with respect to the development of the predominant subjective self-understanding or personality type
as *individualization* and in terms of the relation to nature as instrumentaliza-
tion or *domestication* (see figure 1.1).[103]

In the works of the sociological classics and contemporary research that
follows them one mostly finds that a single aspect serves as a central, guiding perspective. Thus, for instance, Max Weber understands modernization
above all as a process of rationalization. This also constitutes the core of the
project of modernity as it has been defined by, for instance, Jürgen Habermas
and his followers.[104] In contrast to this, processes of the division of labor and
functional differentiation stand, as we have seen, at the center not only of
Durkheim's investigations but also of contemporary systems theory. In turn,

after having been thematized in a multifaceted way by Simmel, individualization is a social tendency that takes on central importance in, for instance, the
diagnoses of the times of Ulrich Beck or Gerhard Schulze. Finally, the way in
which nature, and consequently the character of an individual and a society,
is processed and transformed constitutes the starting point for the analyses of
modernity of Karl Marx and the social scientists inspired by him. From this
point of view, modernization appears to be in the first instance the immensely
successful tendency to instrumentalize and thereby domesticate both inner
and outer nature, i.e., to make it controllable and useful for human ends.
The ambivalence of this tendency was perhaps most strikingly worked out by
Horkheimer and Adorno in *Dialectic of Enlightenment*.[105]

Of course in all four dimensions one finds that modernization processes
not only display a profound ambivalence but also invariably seem to carry
their own contradiction with them as a paradoxical flip side.[106] Thus as a result
of its unintended consequences mastery *over* nature threatens to turn into the
annihilation or destruction *of* nature or into an annihilation of the basis of
human life *by* nature in the form of an ecological catastrophe. Similarly, according to its cultural critics modernity is not just characterized by a tendency
for individual particularities to develop but just as much by one toward "massification" (*Vermassung*) in a homogenized *mass culture*. This is why Simmel
believed he could observe not only the increase of "quantitative" individuality but also, at the same time, the disappearance of original, "qualitative"
individuality as a result of the subordination of subjective culture to objective
culture.[107] Again, Weber already saw the flip side of the Western process of
rationalization as an ongoing *erosion of meaning resources* resulting from inherent necessities (*Sachzwänge*) that arise from the ruthless autonomization
of structural dynamics and that in the end take the form of a spiritless iron
cage whose logic (e.g., escalation and acceleration) cannot be stopped even
when its continued existence proves to be highly irrational.[108]

It is somewhat more difficult to identify a paradoxical flip side of the process of differentiation. Here, in fact, two paradoxical developmental tendencies immediately come into view: on the one hand, processes of ever finer
differentiation are accompanied by a parallel growth of (today global) chains
of interdependence and, on the other hand, the unity and coherence of the
whole of society seems to disappear in the wake of (stability- and efficiency-
increasing) differentiation: as Luhmann never tires of emphasizing, modern
society must get along without a peak, a center, or a "central perspective."[109]
In this sense the flip side of differentiation is social *disintegration*.

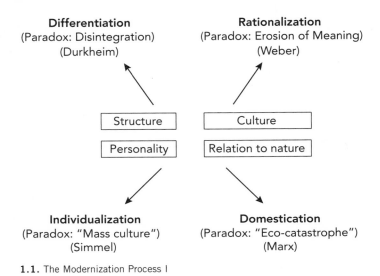

1.1. The Modernization Process I

In light of this grid (see figure 1.1), whose respective elements have so far dominated sociological analyses of modernity, it is difficult to indicate a systematic location or starting point for a reinterpretation from the perspective of social acceleration. The first thought that occurs is simply to solve the problem by introducing an additional perspective: just as modernization from a cultural point of view can be understood as rationalization and from the standpoint of personality psychology as individualization, so it can be understood with respect to the dimension of time or temporal structures as acceleration. And just as, for instance, processes of individualization or rationalization do not transpire evenly or continuously, but rather come in waves, so too with processes of acceleration (as we have seen). Just as surges of individualization are accompanied by "communitarian" fears and corresponding countermovements and as "traditionalist" warnings and efforts grow loud in the face of each wave of rationalization,[110] rejection and resistance are mobilized against each new round of acceleration. And in each case, even if there are hesitations and modifications in the end, the modernization process inexorably advances. Further, exactly as in the case of the other four basic processes of modernization, social acceleration always carries its own paradoxical countertendency within itself: social rigidity. Therefore the central question for an understanding of the statics and dynamics of modernity is *how to conceive social acceleration and societal crystallization together* on both cultural and structural levels.

Only an analysis that is capable of giving an account of this can claim to do theoretical justice to the historical formation of modernity.

Nevertheless it seems to me that this solution to the conceptual problem is extremely unsuitable.[111] From a conceptual point of view, time cannot simply be placed next to culture, structure, nature, and personality, since it is rather a central and constitutive dimension of them. Furthermore, acceleration proves to be an aspect and element of each of the four types of development linked to it. Indeed it actually seems to represent the principle that connects and drives them, in which respect it appears now as a cause and then as an effect of the other tendencies of modernity.[112] In part 4 I will pursue various indications that acceleration is more fundamental than the other categories insofar as processes of differentiation, rationalization, or individualization come to a standstill or even turn into their opposite just in case they become dysfunctional for further social acceleration. It does not in fact seem implausible, as we will see, to interpret those four modernization processes as (unintended) consequences of social acceleration: social disintegration would accordingly be a consequence of growing societal desynchronization, environmental devastation an effect of overtaxed natural regeneration times, the loss of "qualitative" individuality a side effect of the increased pace of life, and the surrender of rational autonomy the result of the "temporalization of time." From this perspective, the other modernization tendencies thus appear to be, as it were, modes of functioning or manifestations of acceleration.

If one accepts that social acceleration irreducibly cuts across the cornerstones of the "classical" analytical grid, then it seems that Luhmann's suggested distinction between material, temporal, and social (Sach-, Zeit-, Sozial-) dimensions of meaning offers a second strategy for locating acceleration in the categorial framework of modernization theory. Acceleration would then be simply a central developmental principle of the temporal dimension of modernity. Yet even this method of reducing complexity necessarily fails: the characteristic transformation of temporal structures occurs precisely in the material and social dimensions of modern society. Indeed I hold that development in the material and social dimensions follows precisely the specific transformational logic of acceleration. Therefore the reinterpretation of modernization in terms of social acceleration makes a more comprehensive claim than the distinction between the three dimensions would suggest.

For this reason, my strategy cannot be satisfied with analyzing acceleration as an isolatable, partial aspect of modernization. It cannot avoid defining and analyzing the process of acceleration along all four dimensions (structure, culture, nature, and personality) and with respect to all three dimensions of meaning. The categorial framework that has been worked out is meant to serve as a heuristic tool for the analytical differentiation of theoretical perspectives that can also sharpen our view of the complexity of the modernization process and of the diverse interactions between identified developmental tendencies. It is their dynamic that now has to be deciphered. However, the layout of the book's argument does not follow the, as it were, "external" specifications of the categorial system, but rather the "internal" conceptual and material logic of social acceleration itself. Nevertheless, at the end of the book I will attempt to reintegrate the results of the inquiry into this schema so that I can, in accordance with the aim of the work, render more precise the account of the function and status of acceleration in the context of modernization.

2

WHAT IS SOCIAL ACCELERATION?

1. PRELIMINARY CONSIDERATIONS: ACCELERATION AND ESCALATION

In view of the notorious lack of clarity regarding the concept of acceleration in the contemporary social science literature, the introduction of an analytically adequate and empirically useful definition of acceleration stands first and foremost as a desideratum for any social theory.[1] Of course, one problem that immediately arises is that there are quite heterogeneous acceleration phenomena in different areas of society that are both difficult to bring together under a single concept and at first glance not clearly connected to one another. For instance, what do the following facts have to do with each other: that speed records in sports are broken with increasing regularity (which can partly be traced to improved technology, partly to more precise measurement of minuscule time intervals); that new computer models increase their processing speed every couple of months; that in modern Western societies the average time spent sleeping and eating seems to steadily decrease while, on average (statistically), change of intimate partners, place of residence, and membership in civil society associations as well as fashion and product cycles occur faster and faster?[2]

If one searches for a definition of acceleration that can encompass all these phenomena, one thing that quickly proves unhelpful is a recourse to conventional definitions from high school physics that measure acceleration in terms of the amount of distance traveled, e.g., $a = v/t$ or $a = 2s/t^2$. In fact, this would only cover the first kind of phenomenon mentioned. The inappropriateness of such a narrow physical definition can be seen clearly, for instance, in Helga Nowotny's definition of acceleration. She first claims that "acceleration does not just mean . . . increased speed of all [!] social processes," yet then surprisingly in the next sentence she appears to reduce it to the faster traversal of distances when she continues, "it conditions a temporal norm of generally increased mobility which is the result of both technologically and economically mediated processes for the transportation of goods, human beings, energy and information *that have to overcome spatio-temporal distances*."[3] Just after this, however, she indicates that acceleration or mobility has become a general social norm: "goods, human beings, energy, money and information should change their locations *with increasing frequency* in order to circulate in a comprehensive sense, both economically and culturally."[4] Contrary to the misleading association with distance traveled, an accelerated changeover in place of residence cannot be captured by that physical formula. In this case there is no question of distances that are covered *faster*. Rather, they are covered *more frequently*, a distinction that makes a decisive difference.

Nowotny's reflections make clear that the articulation of a workable definition of social acceleration should involve a strict analytical distinction between two basic forms of acceleration. Numerous phenomena can be described as forms of 1. an *intentional* and *goal-directed* and therefore in the widest sense "technical" acceleration of particular processes (e.g., enhancements of performance in sports, transportation, or computer technology). To be distinguished from this form of technological-teleological acceleration are 2. increased social *rates of change*, that is, for instance, the acceleration of changeover in jobs, political party preferences, intimate partners, and membership in voluntary associations or of change per unit of time in occupational and family structures, artistic styles, etc., i.e., the acceleration of social changes that are not inherently goal directed.[5]

If you consider the list of acceleration phenomena you will very quickly discover that these two specifications of the concept of acceleration still do not cover all the relevant phenomena: the attempt to save time through fast food, speed dating, power naps, or multitasking, i.e., by shortening or condensing episodes of action, represents a reaction to a *scarcity of time* that can be classified under the heading neither of accelerated social change nor of technical acceleration. In view of the manifold types of technological acceleration, the fact that time becomes scarce is actually in itself a paradox that requires explanation. For this reason, there can be no doubt that 3. the *heightening of the pace of life through an increase of episodes of action and/or experience per unit of time* that is linked with a scarcity of temporal resources and the resulting "lack of time" constitutes an independent third category of social acceleration in modern society.

In almost all the studies done on the theme of acceleration, *one* of these three forms or spheres of social acceleration is, for the most part unreflectively, placed front and center while phenomena in the other domains are falsely subsumed under the chosen category. Thus the work of Paul Virilio, for instance, circles around the phenomena of technological acceleration, while Hermann Lübbe or Matthias Eberling concentrate on the acceleration of social change, and Georg Simmel or Robert Levine occupy themselves with the acceleration of the pace of life. Doubtless the most interesting question, however, concerns the *internal connection* between these categories of acceleration. Before we can pursue this matter further, we should first take up the question whether the concept of acceleration can be defined in such a way that it can simultaneously capture the relevant phenomena in these three analytically independent domains and thereby allow us to determine their *logical* relation to one another and thus help guide research on their *empirical* interconnection.

The recourse to Newtonian physics is more helpful if one replaces the distances contained in the given equations with an abstract quantitative variable. Acceleration can then be defined as *an increase in quantity per unit of time* (or, logically equivalent, as a reduction of the amount of time per fixed quantity). Various things may serve as the quantity measured: distance traveled, total number of communicated messages, amount of goods produced (category 1) or the number of jobs per working lifetime or change in intimate partners per year (category 2) or action episodes per unit of time (category 3; see figure 2.1).

Now to understand the relationship between technical acceleration and acceleration of the pace of life it is of decisive importance to get the exact connection between quantitative growth and acceleration into view. If it is a matter of processes of continuous (i.e., uninterruptedly advancing) "production," then acceleration results in exponential growth (cf. figure 2.2). A paradigm example of this kind of growth curve is, for instance, the increase in world population during the last three hundred years.[6] Similar acceleration curves are found in, say, the rampant growth of cancer cells and also in the increase in the diffusion of commodities or technological innovations: for example in the amount of scientific publications or the number of Internet connections or e-mails sent per year.[7]

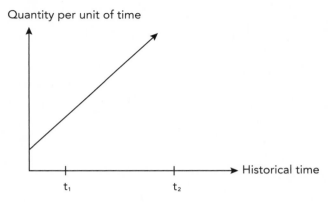

2.1. Acceleration as Increase in Quantity Per Unit of Time

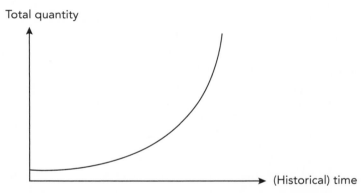

2.2. Exponential Growth as a Result of Acceleration of Continuous Processes

However, it is of crucial significance that processes of transportation, production, and communication, which constitute the focal points of technological acceleration, are all *noncontinuous* and therefore display no intrinsic tendencies of growth. The fact that today it is possible to cover the distance from A to B in a shorter time neither logically nor causally implies that we do (or should) cover these distances more frequently or control larger expanses, and, likewise, the possibility of communicating a certain quantity of signs in less time (across a certain distance) neither logically nor causally brings with it the duty or even the tendency to communicate larger quantities or more often. In itself the capability of producing a given quantity of goods faster is independent of any *escalation of production*. Yet if the quantity transported,

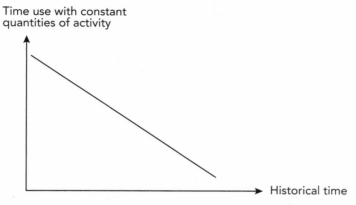

2.3. Time Use with Constant Quantity of Activities in an Age of Technological Acceleration

communicated, or produced remains constant, the "pace of life" decreases rather than increases as a logical consequence of technological acceleration, since the time needed for the fulfillment of a given task shrinks: "free time" arises in the sense of a freeing up of formerly tied-down time resources (cf. figure 2.3). Under these conditions the problem of time scarcity progressively slackens.

So if the subjective phenomena of stress, hecticness, and lack of time are traced back over and over again in pop science literature to the immense *technical acceleration* of numerous processes, which at first glance appear to be the most powerful drivers of a ubiquitous social and cultural acceleration, then this is a result of the unreflective assertion that in modernity more or less "everything" becomes faster. This fallacy is as blatant as it is widespread. The dynamics and the temporal compulsions of social and psychic life in industrial and postindustrial society cannot be derived from achievements in technologically supported acceleration, since in fact the latter stand in direct logical contradiction to the former. The heightening of the "pace of life," the temporal scarcity of modernity, arise not *because* but rather *even though* enormous gains in time through acceleration have been registered in almost all areas of social life.

On the basis of this insight it is clear the acceleration of the pace of life or the growing scarcity of time is a consequence of a quantitative increase that has to be logically independent from the processes of technical acceleration: we produce, communicate, and transport not just faster but also *more* than earlier social epochs. For a progressive shortfall in time resources can in principle only arise if either more time is needed to tackle a given task, i.e., in cases of technical deceleration, or if the *growth rate* (of production of goods and services, of the number of transmitted communications, of distances covered, of activities to be completed) outpaces the *rate of acceleration* of the corresponding processes. Only in the latter case do technical acceleration and the acceleration of the pace of life appear simultaneously. This case occurs where, for instance, the quantity of distance to be covered (of goods to be produced, of communications) at an initial point in time t_1 triples at a later point in time t_2 while the speed of movement (of production, of communication) has only doubled. The more strongly the rates of acceleration lag behind the rates of growth, the greater the shortage of time will be; on the other hand, the more the former exceed the latter, the more time resources will be set free, i.e., the less scarce time will become. If the two rates of increase are identical, then the pace of life or the shortage (or excess) of time will not change, regardless of how high or low the rates of technical acceleration may be (figure 2.4).[8]

Thus the guiding hypothesis of this work runs as follows: *modern society can be understood as an "acceleration society" in the sense that it displays a highly conditioned* (voraussetzungsreiche) *structural and cultural linkage of both forms of acceleration*—technical acceleration and an increase in the pace of life due to chronic shortage of time resources—and therefore also a strong linkage of acceleration and growth. This implies that the average rate

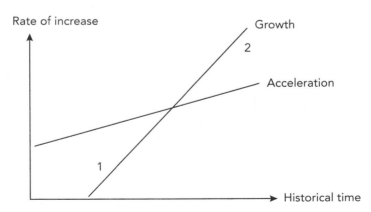

2.4. "Free Time" and "Time Scarcity" as Consequences of the Relation of the Rates of Growth and Acceleration. (1)=Decreasing, (2)=Increasing pace of life. When the rates are identical the pace of life does not change.

of growth (defined as increase of the total quantity of things produced, communicated, distances covered, etc.) *exceeds* the average rate of acceleration.[9]

And in fact there is now sufficient empirical evidence for the claim that the temporal resources "gained" or set free by technological acceleration, for instance, in the household by means of washing machines, microwaves, vacuum cleaners, etc., are simply tied up once again through corresponding quantitative increases in activity. Thus investigations from the 1960s and '70s indicate that the time spent at home surprisingly tends to increase rather than fall with the number of household appliances. According to an extensive countrywide American study of time use from 1975 involving 2,406 respondents, owners of dishwashing machines spent on average one minute and owners of laundry machines four minutes *more* at home each day than adults without these appliances, and the vacuum cleaner saved only one minute.[10] From this, John Robinson and Geoffrey Godbey conclude, in agreement with the hypothesis developed here, that "what likely occurred with other technology is happening with the microwave oven: potential time savings are turned into increased output or improved quality."[11]

This pattern is also confirmed by the effects of the automobile on time resources: the possession of a passenger car did change the amount of time spent underway, but not in the direction of less. Instead, the acceleration-induced gain in time is invested in more frequent or longer travels so that in time budgets the time allotted for transportation seems to be invariant relative to the speed of movement.[12]

From the observation that the usage of time in particular fields of activity like the household and transportation remains relatively stable, i.e., behaves largely neutral with respect to technological innovations, Robinson and Godbey conclude that growth and acceleration rates develop in parallel, hence that gains in time from technology and losses in time from qualitative and quantitative intensification stay in balance. According to the definition we have developed, congruent rates of growth and acceleration are neutral with respect to the pace of life, although Robinson and Godbey as well as those questioned by them assert an *acceleration* of the pace of life (one the authors find inexplicable). If one assumes that it is not *merely* a question of an objectively unjustified phenomenon resulting from distorted subjective perception,[13] then two mutually supplementary possible explanations present themselves, both of which are difficult to operationalize in time use studies: first, relative constancy in the time resources devoted to a particular kind of activity does not in any way confirm an agreement in rates of growth and acceleration since higher growth rates can be balanced out by a condensation (or thickening) of episodes of action or by "multitasking."[14] For instance if the speed of movement doubles through technological innovation, but the distance to be covered triples, then one way of keeping the transport time constant is to reduce time spent resting. Similarly, if the increase in the quantity of tasks outpaces technological acceleration, then the time spent at home can be held constant by, say, cooking and vacuuming *at the same time* where these activities were previously done *in succession*.[15] In such cases the growth rate exceeds the rate of acceleration and, as a consequence, the pace of life quickens, since formerly free microtemporal resources *within* the time dedicated to a given field of activity now become tied up.

A second explanation for the quickening of the pace of life can be found in a specific "side effect" of new technologies: the opening up of new fields and new possibilities of action. Making use of these often requires additional time resources (one thinks for instance of the time use effects of the video recorder), and this may even lead to a net loss of *free* time resources. I will come back to this later. However, we can already conjecture at this point that the multiplication of options and contingencies is among the main causes of the acceleration of the pace of life.[16] The former is nevertheless in no way a simple consequence of technological innovations. Indeed it is not even in general derivable from them without further assumptions (e.g., regarding why the complete exhaustion of new options or the opening up of new fields of action appears attractive in the first place). As will be shown later, it can only be more precisely understood in the context of the phenomena that have been classified here under the category of the acceleration of social change.

Taken as a whole, then, these preliminary considerations make clear that the various acceleration phenomena can in fact be grasped with a unified concept, although they show at the same time that there is no direct logical or causal connection between the three designated domains of acceleration. So what results is a new desideratum for research, namely, to answer the question regarding the more complex *empirical* links between the partial dimensions of social acceleration: what drives forward the process or, better, the processes of acceleration, and what structural and/or cultural linkages can be found between the quantitative logic of escalation (*Steigerung*) and the acceleration dynamic of modernity? Before I try to give this question a systematic answer in part 3, we must first make more precise both the definitions of the three dimensions of acceleration and also their delimitation from one another (chapter 2.2). This will facilitate the investigation of their empirical manifestations and their structural and cultural consequences in part 2. In the meantime, however, what follows is a categorial specification of the phenomena and social domains that withdraw from or oppose the identified accelerative tendencies of modernity, that is, a categorial definition of forms of social deceleration (chapter 2.3), and then an empirically supported analysis of the relation between the accelerating and decelerating tendencies of modern society (2.4). The verdict that modern society is an acceleration society can only be justified if it can be shown that in modernity the forces of movement systematically outweigh the forces of inertia.

2. THREE DIMENSIONS OF SOCIAL ACCELERATION

The conceptual proposal I have made suggests that for the purposes of a systematic study of social acceleration and its constitutive role in modernity, we must distinguish between three types of phenomena that are analytically distinct but interconnected, logically irreducible to each other, and empirically related in complex and partly paradoxical ways. These three forms of acceleration, which will now be precisely defined and delimited from each other, are technical acceleration, the acceleration of social change, and the acceleration of the pace of life.

A) TECHNICAL ACCELERATION

The most evident and consequential shape that modern acceleration takes is the *intentional, technical, and above all technological (i.e., machine-based) acceleration of goal-directed processes*. Paradigmatic examples are processes of transportation, communication, and production (of goods and services). This is the form of acceleration that can be most easily measured and demonstrated (despite all the problems confronting an exact establishment of average velocities).

The history of the acceleration of movement from premodern and preindustrial society to the present, and hence from travel on foot, horse riding, and the steamship to the railway, the automobile, and finally to the airplane and the spaceship is familiar to everyone and well documented, so it requires no repetition. In its course top speeds multiplied from roughly 15 to well over 1,000 kilometers per hour, or, if one takes into account space travel, to several thousand kilometers per hour, therefore at least by a factor of 102.[17] Leaving aside the absolute top speed, the speed limits of the particular modes of transport also climbed at the same time: cars, ships, locomotives, airplanes, space shuttles, and even bicycles today achieve much higher speeds than when they were introduced, although we are approaching the limits of the possible (and reasonable).

For the thesis of a general mobilization and dynamization of society, however, the increase in *average* speeds is far more important than top speeds. Even though there can be no doubt that here too there have been tremendous increases since the industrial revolution, it is much more difficult to establish precise values. The most exact measure for the form of social acceleration connected to the acceleration of transport would be the quantity of goods and persons that can be transported per unit of time and their average velocity.[18] As we will see in the next section, these two values sometimes stand in a negative relationship to each other: the more persons that simultaneously wish to move, the lower their average speed if congestion effects occur as a result of overloaded infrastructures. This explains why the average speed of several forms of transport (for instance, urban traffic) seems to sink rather than climb.

Increases in the speed of transportation lie at the root of the pervasive modern experience of a "shrinkage" or "compression" of space. The experience of space is to a great extent a function of the length of time it takes to traverse it. ("How far is it from Berlin to Paris?" — "10 hours by car or one hour by plane.") While in the eighteenth century it took several weeks to get from Europe to America, today the journey only requires around six hours by plane. As a consequence the world seems to have shrunk to something like a sixtieth of its original size. Accelerating innovations in transportation are therefore mostly responsible for what can be described, following David Harvey and others, as "the annihilation of space by time."[19]

While the inversion of the priority of space into a priority of time has been caused by the acceleration of movement, the acceleration of information transmission has been just as influential. The narrative of acceleration in this case is also well-documented and familiar: from "marathon runners" through horse-riding messengers, smoke signals, and mail pigeons to telegraphs and telephones and finally to the, in the truest sense of the word, u-topian, spaceless Internet, where pieces of information lose their location and can be transmitted at the speed of light. In the course of this development it was not just the speed of message transmission but also the quantity transmittable per unit of time (in a particular medium) that continuously grew. This "transmission revolution" comes a bit later chronologically than the "transport revolution" and appears to be in various respects a reaction to the latter.[20] According to Karlheinz Geißler's estimate, in the twentieth century alone the speed of communication increased by a factor of 107; Francis Heylighen even calculates the increase during the last two hundred years to be a factor of 1010.[21] Presumably, however, what is decisive for the character of interpersonal communication is less the quantity of data that machines can make available worldwide at the speed of light than the fact that both asynchronous (i.e., through e-mail or answering machine) and synchronous communicative interactions are possible at any time independent of the respective location of the conversation partners.

Technical acceleration designates not only the faster movement of humans, goods, messages, and (as Virilio emphatically points out) military projectiles across the earth but also the more rapid production of goods, the speedier conversion of matter and energy, and, though in lesser measure, the acceleration of services.[22] As James Beniger thus correctly remarks, "by far the greatest effect of industrialization . . . was to speed up a society's entire material processing system."[23] The story of acceleration to be told here describes the path from the steam engine to the utilization of hydraulic power and the combustion engine, on down to electricity and the technologies of industrial mass production and the assembly line, arriving finally at the microtechnologies of the computer age.[24]

The industrial revolution, interpreted by Virilio as a "dromological" revolution, is therefore in the first instance also a revolution of production speeds, one that continues in the "digital revolution" during the transition to the twenty-first century. As Gundolf Freyermuth writes, "the replacement of physical processes by virtual ones promises the desired acceleration of reaction times and cycle times in the direction of real time. While under analogous circumstances it often required weeks to recognize and satisfy a change in demand, this can occur many times faster through a complete networking of all members of the chain of supply and distribution, from the suppliers and the participants in the actual production and distribution process down to the final customers."[25]

So acceleration is achieved either by the immediate virtualization and digitization of once material processes (for example, in the development of a model), which indeed allows an acceleration to the speed of light in some areas, or rather by building digital information transmission into analog ones, i.e., material processes and chains of action, which thereby fall under further pressure to accelerate. In fact, in the new possibilities of virtualization and digitization the three predominant forms of technological acceleration overlap: the conventional transport of goods like recording media or books is replaced through digitization by a form of pure information transmission, and similarly material processes of production (for instance, the development of designs or architectural models) can be transformed into information processing procedures through virtualization. The speed of data processing also rose by a factor of around 106 in the twentieth century.[26] Yet this does not mean, as Geißler supposes, that the end of the acceleration process has been reached because the speed of light represents a final limit. Data can be *transferred*, but not *generated*, at the speed of light, and the pressure to accelerate at material interfaces has grown immensely as a direct result of the possibilities of digitization.[27]

In the capitalist economic system, however, the continually rising speed of production necessarily goes hand in hand with the escalation of speeds in distribution and consumption, which are in turn driven by technological innovations and thus share responsibility for the fact that the material structures of modern society are reproduced and altered in ever shorter periods of time. Yet a precondition of this was and is that modernization, beyond these basic forms of *technological* acceleration, is simultaneously characterized by an acceleration of processes of organization, decision, administration, and control—for example, in modern bureaucracies and ministries—that falls into the category of *technical* acceleration in the wider sense (i.e., intentional acceleration of goal-directed processes through innovative techniques).[28]

B) THE ACCELERATION OF SOCIAL CHANGE

If one takes a closer look at the way technical innovations affect social institutions and practices it becomes clear that social change and technological innovation can be analytically distinguished even though they naturally often go hand in hand empirically and historically. I have defined technological acceleration as the *intentional acceleration of goal-directed processes*, whereas the acceleration of social change relates to the tempo of change in, on the one hand, practices and action orientations and, on the other, associational structures and patterns of relationship. An accompanying postulate is that the *rates of change themselves change*, i.e., they accelerate. So, for instance, the replacement of an early capitalist organization of labor by a Taylorist labor regime represents at once a form of social change and a phenomenon of technical acceleration, but taken by itself it is not at all an example of the *acceleration* of social change. Only a reorganization of the labor process that appears at ever shorter intervals could be so understood. Conversely the replacement of party platforms with a four-year term by a two-year term represents an example of accelerated social change that contains no element of technical acceleration. The difference can also be illustrated with an example from the history of innovation diffusion: the period from the invention of the radio at the end of the nineteenth century to its distribution to 50 million listeners lasted 38 years; the television, introduced a quarter of a century later, needed only 13 years to achieve this, while the Internet went from the first to the 50-millionth connection in barely 4. In view of this finding, Thomas H. Eriksen asks rhetorically, "is anybody still in doubt as to whether [social —H. R.] change accelerated during the twentieth century?"[29] F. Heylighen presents a similar numbers game when he lays out how the period from the invention of the typewriter in 1714 to successful diffusion through marketization lasted 174 years, for inventions like the freezer and the vacuum cleaner at the beginning of the twentieth century around 30–40 years, for new technologies like the CD player or video recorder, in contrast, only a decade until their mass diffusion.[30]

What is decisive here is the fact that the tempo of the social implementation of new technologies, i.e., the spatial extension of alterations in practices and action orientations, is neither logically nor causally reducible to technological acceleration itself (leaving aside, naturally, infrastructural preconditions). Insofar as, for example, the sheer increase of processor speeds in computers is accompanied by neither a significant alteration of action orientations nor a shift in social patterns of association, it has an entirely neutral relationship to social change (not to deny that, empirically speaking, technical innovations often have changes in practices and/or patterns of relationship as consequences).

Contrary to the widespread assertion that society today is being transformed at historically unprecedented speeds,[31] Eriksen's rhetorically intended question cannot be as easily brushed aside as he believes because there is no agreement in the sociological literature about how *social change* as such can be precisely defined, what its indicators are, and which innovations are to count as fundamental ones—consequently the assertion of its acceleration is also not on solid ground.[32] Thus Marie Jahoda remarks, "while there is much talk about . . . the increasing rate of change in complex societies, how to define *rate of change* is an as yet unsolved problem in the social sciences,"[33] while the historian Peter Laslett distinguishes between nineteen (!) types of social change divided into four categories of speed, in an elaborate and overcomplex system of classification (political change and the tempo of life are said to be the fastest, while changes in the relations of production and social structure occur most slowly; in between these are technical and economic change and the alteration of attitudes and mentalities), yet then observes in regard to the question of acceleration that despite numerous evidences of it research is still compelled to rely on intuitions and impressions.[34]

In view of this situation, I would like to propose that we define the acceleration of social change using the concept of the *contraction of the present* introduced by Lübbe and also suggested by Luhmann's systems theory. With Lübbe we can define the *present* as a time period (*Zeitraum*) of stability in which, in Reinhart Koselleck's terms, the space of experience and the horizon of expectations are unchanged and thus congruent. Only within such time periods can conclusions about the present and the future be drawn from previous experiences, and only in them do experiences and learning processes have an action-orienting power, because expectations find a certain measure of security.[35] From this perspective, then, the past characterizes everything that *is no longer valid*, whereas, in contrast, the future encompasses that which *is not yet valid*.[36]

This definition allows a differentiation or pluralization of the past into various realms of value, function, and action and thereby the introduction of the idea of the *noncontemporaneity of the contemporaneous*[37]: what is still valid within one geographical or social realm has already lost its validity in another; what is already realized here, still lies in the horizon of the future there. In the context of this definition, Lübbe's conjecture is that modern societies experience an ongoing contraction of the present as the result of an increasing social and cultural "rate of obsolescence" or a growing sociocultural "compression of innovation."[38] This conjecture is strengthened by Koselleck's observation that the perception of such a compression in the form of a historical experience of acceleration has really defined modernity from the very beginning.[39]

The acceleration of social change can thus be defined as an increase of the rate of decay of action-orienting experiences and expectations and as a contraction of the time periods that determine the present of respective functional, value, and action spheres. Such a standard of stability and change can be applied to social and cultural institutions and practices of any kind: the thesis of a general acceleration of social change states that the "present" contracts as much in politics as in the economy, science, and art, in work relations as much as in family arrangements, and just as much in moral as in practical everyday orientations. Hence the present contracts from both a cultural as well as a structural perspective. Armin Nassehi, drawing on Luhmann, finds the same: "the present, the concrete, evental now of social situations, is exposed to a new situation in comparison with earlier social forms: it is becoming ever smaller and more limited and falls under the pressure of earlier events and above all of those expected in the future."[40] Where that is the case, one can rightly speak of an acceleration *of* society, whereas the phenomena of technical enhancements of speed falling under the first category of acceleration are to be understood rather as accelerations of this or that phenomenon *within* society. Of course it is also conceivable that this process of contraction occurs at differing speeds in the various spheres and that in particular realms of society a standstill or, conversely, even an "expansion of the present" may arise, which might lead to phenomena of increased social desynchronization. Therefore an acceleration-theoretical diagnosis of the times cannot avoid scrupulously examining the society being investigated for evidence of the developments just described. In the next section I will attempt to develop the categorial apparatus necessary for this.

While the acceleration of social change is defined in the first place by Lübbe in an action-theoretical way, it finds a surprising correspondence and confirmation in the systems-theoretical reflections of Niklas Luhmann. For Luhmann "the present" is, in the first instance, constitutive for each system operation insofar as it continually redifferentiates past and future; where the past appears as determined, the future, on the other hand, as (still) undetermined. In a further sense, however, he understands it also as a time period within which (from the perspective of a system) the time horizons of the past and future, and consequently the basis for expectations and decisions (or selections), remain stable, and he leaves no doubt that modernity is characterized by a progressive shortening of these time periods.[41]

From this point of view, "contraction of the present" or social acceleration means that past and future must be rewritten in the various areas of society at ever shorter intervals.[42] For Luhmann it is not so much actual social change that becomes a problem in modern society as it is the growing instability of time horizons and bases of selection produced by the ongoing revision of expectations and reconstructed experiences.[43] I will come back to the difference between instability and change in chapter 4, where the manifestations and side effects of, as well as the empirical evidence for, this second form of social acceleration, which is on the whole far less evident than in the case of technical acceleration, will be discussed. However, at this point let me already suggest that altering time horizons and expectations are themselves to be grasped as manifestations of social change.[44] Their stability can then be made into a measure of the acceleration or slowdown of social change.

C) THE ACCELERATION OF THE PACE OF LIFE

As I already tried to show in chapter 2.1, the heightening of the tempo of life, understood as an increase in episodes of action or experience per unit of time, cannot simply be derived from the acceleration of social change, even if, of course, it represents an obvious (although not necessary) reaction to the latter development.[45] On the contrary, the shortage of time resources and the consequent "lack of time" (*Zeitnot*) stand in a directly paradoxical relation to the category of technical acceleration. Therefore, the escalation of the pace of life that is particularly central to popular science diagnoses of acceleration and gives the strongest impulse to the call for deceleration constitutes an analytically independent third category of social acceleration.

This third kind of acceleration can be defined by means of an objective and/or a subjective component. *Objectively*, the acceleration of the tempo of life involves a shortening or condensation of episodes of action that can be identified in principle by, for instance, time budget studies, as presented by, among others, Manfred Garhammer, Jonathan Gershuny, and Robinson and Godbey. What is meant by this are, for example, the shortening of mealtimes or amounts of sleep or of the average time spent communicating in the family, but also attempts to reduce the total duration—i.e., the stretch of time between the ending of a previous activity and the beginning of the next one—of a trip to the cinema, a feast, a burial, etc. This can be achieved, on the one hand, by a direct increase in the speed of action (*eat or pray faster*) or, on the other hand, by a decrease in rests and empty times between activities, which may also be described as a "condensation" of action episodes.[46] As we have already seen, however, this condensation and thus increase of action episodes per unit of time may be reached not only by a direct acceleration but also by stacking them up, i.e., by simultaneously performing several activities (*multitasking*), which may lead to a de facto diminishment of the speed of individual activities but nevertheless make possible a faster completion of a set of actions taken as a whole.[47] If such temporal transformations form a consistent pattern, they lead cumulatively to an increase in the number of episodes of action or experience per unit of time that can be objectively verified by the methods of empirical social research.[48]

Since the heightening of the pace of life should be understood as a result of the scarcity of time resources, which means that the increase of the quantity of actions exceeds the technical enhancement of the speed of performance (cf. figure 2.5), *subjectively* it is expressed in the growing sense that one lacks time or is pressed for time and in a stressful compulsion to accelerate as well as in anxiety about "not keeping up." The acceleration and condensation of action episodes then represents an obvious reaction to these perceptions. Moreover, the scarcity of time resources presumably constitutes here (alongside the experience of a contraction of the present) the main cause for the *feeling* that time itself is going by faster. In fact, such experiences of time have in the meantime been quite well confirmed in highly industrialized societies. The inhabitants of rich industrial states do indeed feel themselves increasingly pressed for time (which speaks in favor of an exponential acceleration or at least for the encroachment of a new wave of acceleration), and they complain on a massive scale about the scarcity of time.[49] Yet the fact that this experience of time has accompanied modern society in continually repeated waves since at least the eighteenth century does not prove that the pace of life in modernity has always been high, but rather strongly indicates that it *constantly accelerates*: it is a result of ever more scarce time resources. Strictly speaking, it says nothing at all about the "absolute" tempo of life.

This is not the place, however, to argue about the causes, manifestations, and consequences of the acceleration of the tempo of life, since I will come back to these in chapter 5. In the context of this categorial explication of the basic framework of my theory of social acceleration, I would simply like to point out a problem of demarcation regarding the first and the third of the suggested dimensions of social acceleration. In many cases the shortening of episodes of action is directly connected to the introduction of new techniques, that is, with technical acceleration. When, for instance, a long-distance runner covers a ten-thousand-meter distance in a shorter time because of the development of new breathing and running techniques, then according to the definitions so far developed it seems to be a form of technical acceleration (i.e., the intentional acceleration of a goal-directed process through the utilization of a new technique) as well as a phenomenon of accelerated life tempo (i.e., the acceleration of an episode of action). The latter definition, however, appears to be counterintuitive in the context of this example, if not absolutely absurd: to interpret the improvement of running time as a heightening of the pace of life is more a light-hearted jest than an enlightening academic (non-)achievement. This indicates that, first, one must proceed with caution when defining action episodes: not the run itself but rather participation in the entire corresponding event should be understood as a completed episode of action. Episodes are not just determined through one's own activity but also through the given context. The shortening of track and field competitions from six to four hours, for example, by running the hammer throw and the long-distance run at the same time, would in fact constitute an example of the heightening of the tempo of life. Second, however, this example makes clear that the shortening of particular episodes of experience or action taken by itself does not suffice to verify an acceleration of the pace of life: the freeing up of time resources (through technological acceleration or by foregoing activities) per se, i.e., without new commitments, is in fact an indicator of an abatement of the tempo of life, as I have shown. Only the increase of action episodes per unit of time (e.g., day, week, or year) satisfies the definition given. That requires, to stick with our example, that our runner uses the gain in time to, say, get to the cinema earlier, which could then indeed be interpreted as a heightening of the pace of life.

Beyond the measurable and objective definition proposed here, the prevailing sense of the scarcity of time and the quickness of social life in modern societies is an extraordinarily complex social-psychological phenomenon that cannot be adequately understood and explained without a systematic incorporation of *cultural* factors. One result of their analysis in chapter 5 will be that the experience of an acceleration of the pace of life in modernity encompasses both an increase of the *speed of action* and a structurally induced alteration of the *experience of time* in everyday life.

3. FIVE CATEGORIES OF INERTIA

In view of the danger of following a simple logic of subsumption and interpreting *all* regions and phenomena of social life as determined by the acceleration dynamic along the three analytically distinguished dimensions, it is essential to undertake an exact characterization of the forms, function, and status of those processes and phenomena that evade a dynamization or even actively resist it by either not being acceleratable or by having tendencies to slow down. In both cases they serve as a "brake" or "decelerator" in accelerating social environments. Only when we can determine their relation to the forces of acceleration will we be in a position to say in exactly what sense one can speak of an acceleration *of* society. Analytically, one can distinguish here five categories of deceleration or inertia that, as it were, cut across the three identified dimensions of acceleration.[50]

A) NATURAL LIMITS TO SPEED

First, there are quite evident (geo-)physical, biological, and anthropological limits to speed, i.e., processes whose duration and velocity absolutely cannot be manipulated or can be only at the price of a massive qualitative transformation of the process accelerated. To this class belong, for instance, the speed limits of the brain (e.g., perception, stimulus processing, and reaction as well as regeneration times) and the body (one thinks of processes of growth or the overcoming of sicknesses),[51] but also of the tempo of reproduction for natural raw materials, for example, the conversion of ocean deposits into oil. Beyond this, perhaps one of the most momentous limits to speed is represented by the capacity of the ecosystems of the earth to process toxic substances and waste materials.[52] The seasons and days also cannot be accelerated, although their effects can now be manipulated and simulated: for instance, by altering the temperature with heating systems and turning night into day with artificial light. In agriculture there have been several cases in which the natural speed limits of biological processes, for example, the egg laying of hens, were successfully augmented by shortening the daily alternation of light and dark to twenty-three hours using artificial lights. The same is true of growth processes through the use of breeding: trees planted using the so-called tall spindle system, for instance, bear fruit after only four to five years while conventional tree varieties need fifteen or more years for this. However, they also become fruitless in a shorter period of time. They are, in a certain way, disposable trees.

Wherever the acceleration of social processes is hindered by natural speed limits attempts are made to push these back, and these efforts are often astonishingly successful. Therefore caution is warranted when postulating absolute limits to speed. In particular one has to be on guard against rashly viewing the insecurities and psychic or even physical irritations that result from a massive surge of acceleration as insurmountable or even anthropologically grounded barriers. This can be impressively illustrated with the history of railroad travel. In his brilliant reconstruction of the transformation of our consciousness of space and time in the wake of the institutionalization of the railroad, Wolfgang Schivelbusch demonstrates that the "annihilation of space and time" (or the annihilation of space by time), which is even today stylized as the central characteristic of late modernity, already dominated the early discourse about the railroad in the first half of the nineteenth century.[53] However, the first railroad travelers did not just feel that space and time were apparently being annihilated. They also imagined themselves to be at the limits of what the human body can cope with and the senses process: the "panoramic gaze," which is directed into the distance and not fixed on things and is thus capable of perceiving and enjoying the passing landscape even while moving at high speeds, had to be at first gradually developed and practiced. Early passengers often became physically ill as a result of their exposure to the rapid change of impressions, persons and landscapes while looking out of the railcar window.[54] As Schivelbusch shows, the technological innovations of the railroad gradually brought about a new relationship to space and time that incorporated mobility as a constitutive factor, and little by little new modes of perception and behavior developed that were adapted to the accelerated tempo and transformed something that at first appeared to be frankly pathological into a new form of normality that even became an unavoidable social demand.[55]

The displacement of the limits to speed and the related changes in the perception of quickness and slowness are revealed in the fact that the railroad counts today as a slow and peaceful mode of transportation, one that is, compared to the highways and airplane travel, even a paradigmatic medium of "Slow Time" (Eriksen), while it appeared to the eighteenth century to be inconceivably fast and damaging to human health (and meanwhile has reached much higher velocities).[56] Quite similarly, today certain forms of jazz music that, at the time of their emergence in the first half of the twentieth century, were experienced as breathless, hectic, exceedingly fast, maschine-like, and stupefyingly chaotic—and thus as fitting reflections of their era—are touted as "music for tranquil hours" or "jazz for a peaceful afternoon."[57]

In view of such phenomena and drawing on Sigmund Freud, Norbert Elias, and Walter Benjamin in a train of thought reminiscent of Simmel's reflections on the metropolis, Schivelbusch conjectures that the civilizing acceleration of social life exposes moderns to an ever denser sequence of new and aggressive stimuli that have disturbing and irritating effects so long as the psyche of the affected does not respond with a (consciousness- and perception-altering) reinforcement of the "stimulus defense mechanism."[58] Therefore it is an empirically open question whether the rise in anxieties observed in the discourse of late modernity in the face of a further round of acceleration actually represents a reflexlike repetition of a well-known cultural reaction to a new surge of acceleration before the formation of appropriate new modes of perception and behavior or in fact signals the arrival at more massive social, ecological, and perhaps anthropological limits, the exceeding of which could cause the structural and cultural arrangements of modernity to collapse. In the fourth part of this inquiry I will consider and attempt to systematically link together several signs that point in the latter direction. With respect to the surmountability of physiological-anthropological limits to speed, one has to take into account the new possibilities that loom in genetic technology and its fusion with computer technology, something Virilio sees as the beginning of a "transplant revolution" that may bring with it yet another revolutionary overcoming of previously immutable barriers.[59] The requirements of cultural and structural reproduction may therefore constitute weightier limits to speed than biophysical processes.

B) ISLANDS OF DECELERATION

Further, one naturally finds both territorial and social niches or oases of deceleration that have until now been partly or entirely left out of the accelerating processes of modernization. In these places, in these groups (e.g., in certain sects like the Amish communities in Ohio or in socially excluded groups) or these contexts of practice,[60] it literally appears that "time stood still": this customary figure of speech indicates a social form that is resistant to such processes, one that becomes increasingly anachronistic in comparison with the surrounding temporally dynamic social systems. Sticking with the metaphor, the clocks run there "as they did a hundred years ago." Such oases of deceleration fall under strong territorial, cultural, and economic pressures of erosion. The temporal distance to their readily and willingly accelerating environments becomes ever greater and thus more costly, while at the same the braking effect they have at the interfaces to the accelerated social world increases. Of course, places and forms of practice that have been consciously created or preserved as islands of deceleration (for instance, "wellness oases") are excluded from this erosion and fall under the fourth category of deceleration identified here. As Helga Nowotny and Hermann Lübbe remark, these acceleration-immune phenomena gain "nostalgic" value and make more enticing promises the rarer they become.[61]

C) SLOWDOWN AS DYSFUNCTIONAL SIDE EFFECT

Slowdown and stoppage are appearing in modern society ever more frequently and in increasingly severer forms as *unintended consequences* of acceleration processes. Dysfunctional deceleration phenomena and pathological forms of slowdown belong here. Without a doubt, the most well-known example of dysfunctional deceleration is the traffic jam: for instance, for several years the average speed of traffic in American urban centers has been sinking as a result of the continuous rise in traffic levels. With respect to pathological slowdowns, recent research yields increasing support for the notion that depression and related disorders may appear as a pathological reaction to and withdrawal from the social pressure to accelerate. In phases of depression it often seems to the sick person that time stands still or turns into a toughened mass.[62] One can also include in this category the exclusion of employees from the labor force insofar as its structural ground lies in escalations of tempo (and hence productivity) in the production process, something that often results in the inability of those affected to keep up with the high speed of work and innovation demanded, leading to extreme deceleration in the form of undesired unemployment.[63] Economic recessions, characterized in English-speaking regions precisely as "slowdowns," can themselves also presumably be interpreted as dysfunctional side effects of the successful acceleration of the production process.[64]

However, slowdown does not only emerge as an immediate side effect of processes of acceleration. It is also, to a far greater extent, a sideeffect of (acceleration-induced) desynchronization phenomena, e.g., in the form of waiting times. In functionally differentiated societies, wherever goings-on must be synchronized with one another or temporally geared to each other, a temporal change like the acceleration of processes leads to potential friction problems at the synchronization points. This is especially problematic and immediately detectable where highly accelerated processes impact upon "backward" systems: that which can go faster is, over and over again, slowed down or stopped by that which goes slower.[65] In some situations this desynchronization leads (temporarily) to massive real slowdowns, as when complicated chains of work fall so far out of step that blockages occur. The *impression* of delay, however, can also generally arise where different speeds encounter each other, even if no actual braking effect is observed. For instance, the unbearable impatience that sets in when the Internet search engine becomes torturously slow in delivering results seems to represent an interesting example of this.

Even here one is dealing in the end with a synchronization problem. The computer "simulates" a dialogue and answers questions, but with continual delays that lie well beyond the frame of the conversationally tolerable three-second window of attention. Thus the feeling emerges that one is being "held up" by the computer, although it is precisely the computer that achieves immense time savings in comparison to previous methods of obtaining information.[66]

Finally, beyond this slowdown and delay can also set in as dysfunctional side effects of (as a rule temporally concentrated) events like accidents, natural catastrophes, or wars (these last are also sometimes used to delay developments in hostile countries, in which case they fall under the next category).

D) TWO FORMS OF INTENTIONAL DECELERATION

Intentional efforts and often ideologically justified movements toward conscious deceleration and social slowdown must be strictly distinguished from phenomena of unintended and dysfunctional deceleration. They can be further subdivided into genuine (ideological) decelerating movements, which often appear as a basically oppositional force with decidedly antimodern features, and slowdown efforts that aim at maintaining or even promoting functional and accelerative capabilities (whether individual or social) and thus actually represent, in the end, strategies of acceleration.

DECELERATION AS IDEOLOGY As is clearly shown in the examples of resistance to new technologies like the mechanical loom, the railroad, or the telegraph, the call for decisive or radical deceleration has constantly accompanied surges of acceleration in the history of the modern era up to the present day, and it often blends together with a fundamental critique of modernity and principled protest against (further) modernization.[67] This is not at all strange if the thesis of this work is valid, namely, that the modernization process is best understood as, in the first instance, a process of acceleration. The longing for a lost world of calm, stability, and leisure that is almost constitutive of modernity is borne by fantasy images of premodernity that become connected in social protest movements to the ideas of a decelerated post- or countermodernity. So it can hardly be surprising that the fundamentalist demand for radical slowdown, which is becoming louder in industrial societies as a result of the previously diagnosed waves of acceleration caused by the digital and political revolutions at the end of the twentieth century, often appears in the garb of a radical criticism of modern culture and society.[68] In fact, political radicalism in the twenty-first century is increasingly directed against continual change and aims at preservation of and stasis for the status quo. This leads Peter Glotz to surmise that at the moment deceleration is becoming "the aggressive ideology of a currently emerging and rapidly growing class (or social stratum) of victims of modernization" and is, moreover, on the verge of replacing socialist conceptions as an ideological model (*Leitbild*).[69] The goal of this ideology is to bring the acceleration process of modernity to a halt in the name of a better society and form of life. It is nourished from very different sources, including religious, ultraconservative, or anarchistic ones as well as the deep ecology movement.[70]

The slowdown movement promises "a new well-being through deceleration"[71] and is organized partly in intellectual, partly in grassroots associations like the "Union for the Slowing Down of Time" or the "Happy Unemployed" who celebrate themselves as "leisure gangsters"[72] and thus place themselves in a tradition that includes Paul Lafargue and Bertrand Russell.[73] Although the widespread representations and fantasies of radical slowdown in this milieu have strong currency on the plane of ideas, that is, in lectures, conferences, and publications, they only seldom reach the structure-relevant plane of action.[74] This can be accounted for in part by the fact that the price of individual slowdown in postindustrial societies is very high: whoever withdraws herself from the pressure of an accelerated tempo (for instance by joining a sect, taking over an ecofarm, or plunging into a time-forgetful drug culture) risks missing the boat and finding no chance for readmission. When after several years she is ready to return to mainstream society, her resources are hopelessly obsolete. It remains to be seen whether initiatives like the slow food or the voluntary simplicity movements can spread to such an extent that they actually achieve relevance for society as a whole.[75] Furthermore, in the end many, if not in fact most, of the desires for deceleration are not directed against modern society as such, but rather against particular consequences of it, e.g., the hurried workplace, the speed of traffic in the neighborhood. However, precisely on account of their particular nature, they are often incongruent. Many of our everyday needs for deceleration are so selective that they contain their own negation: we wish, for instance, that we would finally have time for ourselves, for family, for hobbies, etc., and precisely in order to achieve this we simultaneously desire and demand that *everyone else* hurry up: the cashier in the supermarket, the official in the tax ministry, etc. Even the traffic light should turn green and the tramcar go faster. Therefore selective deceleration in complex and networked societies is only possible to a very limited degree.

Nevertheless that does not provide an absolute objection to the effort to establish, as it were, protected spaces in the sense of the aforementioned islands of deceleration that enable other, i.e., slower experiences of time. To be counted among this form of intentional deceleration are also, for instance, forms of "aesthetic-artistic" slowdown through scene setting in the arts, which can not only enable the enduring presence (*Präsenthalten*) of other experiences of time but also help bring about a transformed perception of the temporal structures of late modernity.[76] Interestingly, such experiences of deceleration also occur sometimes precisely as a consequence of higher speeds: for instance, when people can relax during high-speed rides on the highway (or the rollercoaster) through the externalization of unrest.[77] They thereby attain deceleration through acceleration. With this we have already arrived at those forms of intentional deceleration that are not directed *against* the time structures of the "acceleration society," but may rather be entirely *functional* for it.

SLOWDOWN AS A STRATEGY OF ACCELERATION Of exceptional significance for the functional capacity of modern societies are processes and institutions of purposeful partial and temporary deceleration that must not be confused with the efforts of the ideological countermovement against the acceleration dynamic. These strategies of slowdown may be indispensable presuppositions for the further acceleration of *other* processes. They are implemented by both individual actors and social organizations.

On the level of the individual, one can count retreats at monasteries or courses in meditation, yoga techniques, and so on as belonging in this category insofar as they are meant in the end to serve the goal of coping with the swift-paced life of the workplace, relationships, or everyday routine even more successfully, i.e., faster, afterward.[78] They represent oases of deceleration where one goes to "refuel" and "get going again." In addition, attempts to, for instance, assimilate more learning material in a shorter time through the conscious slowing down of particular learning processes or to heighten innovativeness and creativity through deliberate breaks for rest unmistakably constitute strategies of acceleration-through-slowdown.[79]

On the collective level, various forms of moratoria are developed and implemented in a similar way, above all in politics, in order to make time for the solution of fundamental technical, social, legal, or even environmental problems that appear to be an obstacle to further endeavors to accelerate or modernize.[80] From this standpoint, an important insight into the interconnection of stability and dynamization in modern societies presents itself. Namely, given the fact that the call for deceleration can be nourished by both these very distinct motives—an antimodern and, so to speak, a "functionalist" one—it is clear that Glotz makes it too simple for himself when he simply brands deceleration as an ideology of the victims of modernization. In so doing he overlooks the fact that *acceleration by means of institutional pausing and the guaranteed maintenance of background conditions* is a basic principle of the modern history of acceleration and an essential reason for its success as well. In central areas acceleration is made possible precisely by the fact that authoritative institutions like law, political steering mechanisms, and the stable industrial work(time) regime, together with leading abstract cultural orientations such as values and ideas of progress, rationalization, individualism, universalism, and activism,[81] were themselves exempted from change and therefore helped create reliable expectations, stable planning, and predictability. This in turn must be viewed as the foundation of economic, technical, and scientific acceleration and perhaps also of an accelerated individual conduct of life.[82] Only against the background of such stable horizons of expectation does it become rational to make the long-term plans and investments that were indispensable for numerous modernization processes. The erosion of those institutions and orientations as a result of further, as it were, "unbounded" acceleration, propagated by the followers of postmodern or neoliberal philosophies and diagnosed in postmodernity by various social scientists, might undermine their own presuppositions and the stability of late modern society as a whole and thereby place the (accelerative) project of modernity in greater danger than the antimodern deceleration movement.

Joseph Schumpeter had already indicated the possibility that the attempt to clear away all barriers to speed in the service of a maximal acceleration, that is, the unleashing of the "total market," could achieve the opposite of what was intended: the collapse of the developmental dynamic and hence economic slowdown through recession and depression. Even from an economic point of view, then, "shackles and brakes"[83] might prove to be functional for further acceleration.[84]

Lübbe presents this argument from a culture-theoretical perspective when he places the stability and preservation (*Bestandsgarantie*) of some cultural fixed points among the presuppositions of successful cultural reproduction, in particular under the conditions of flexible and accelerated social change: "Highly dynamic cultural development presupposes a high constancy in the validity of some cultural elements. Dynamic cultures put themselves at risk from the rapid obsolescence of tradition that complements their dynamism, and in order to cope with this, declining traditional resources, whose validity demonstrates constancy, become all the more important. In other words, there seem to be limits, from both an individual and an institutional perspective, to the capacity to process innovation."[85]

In this sense, to say it once more, selective social deceleration for the purpose of hindering an erosion of institutions necessary for the continued existence of society may be, from both a cultural and structural perspective, a functional requirement of the contemporary acceleration society. The investigation of such tendencies of erosion under the pressure to accelerate of late modern societies will therefore be a central object of part 4.

E) STRUCTURAL AND CULTURAL RIGIDITY

Perhaps the most interesting form of an (at least superficially) opposing deceleration in the context of a theory of social acceleration are the phenomena of cultural and structural rigidification or crystallization, already encountered multiple times, that constitute the fifth and last category of slowdown or inertia. As has been shown, they are paradoxically closely connected to social manifestations of acceleration and have led to theories, such as those of the "end of history," the "exhaustion of utopian energies," "cultural crystallization" and the "utopia of the zero-option,"[86] that postulate a paralyzing standstill in the inner development of modern societies complementary to the diagnosis of an acceleration of social change. Underlying them is the suspicion that the apparently limitless contingency and openness of modern societies and their rapid, continuous change are merely appearances at the "user interface,"[87] while the solidification and hardening of their deep structures goes unnoticed. In chapter 1.3, I formulated the fundamental hypothesis of this work, namely, that these complementary processes of social hyperacceleration and societal rigidity, which find their most eloquent expression in the metaphor of "frenetic standstill," are systematically and not contingently connected to each other. The forms of slowdown included in this category are thus not opposed to the modern dynamic of acceleration but instead represent an *internal* element and an *inherent* complementary principle of the acceleration process itself. Since an entire chapter in the last part of this book is dedicated to their analysis, and since what are here loose ends of the developing theory of acceleration will systematically converge there, further discussion of this category right now is unnecessary.

4. ON THE RELATION BETWEEN MOVEMENT AND INERTIA IN MODERNITY

The categories of *inertia* introduced in the last chapter have made clear the untenability of the notion that "everything" became faster with the advent of modernity. Much remains as fast (or slow) as it ever was, and some things are even slower. Reflected in that quite stubbornly repeated formula, though, is the almost constitutively modern conviction of a ceaselessly advancing shift in the balance between the elements of inertia and movement in favor of the latter.[88] Now that we have defined the forms of social acceleration and deceleration, we are in a position to make their relations to each other more precise and thus test the cogency of that view.

In principle, two possibilities are conceivable here. The first consists in a basic equilibrium of the forces of inertia and movement, i.e., we find processes of both acceleration and deceleration in the temporal structures of society without being able to identify a dominant long-term trend. The second, in contrast, rests in the possibility that the balance actually shifts in the direction of movement and acceleration, i.e., in favor of progressive dynamization. Such a diagnosis would be justified if (and only if) discernible (and nonfunctional) elements of slowdown and inertia were proved to be either *residual* or *reactive* with respect to the forces of acceleration.

My thesis is that the latter condition is in fact fulfilled in modern society. It rests on the two assumptions that, first, the listed categories of inertia exhaust all the relevant phenomena and, second, none of them embody a structural and/or cultural countertrend that could equal the acceleration dynamic of modernity. The justification for this claim runs as follows: The phenomena listed under categories (a) and (b) describe the (retreating) *limits* of social acceleration; they do not at all represent a contrary force. The slowdowns of the third category are *side* effects of acceleration, and as such they derive from it and hence are secondary in status. The processes classified under category (d2), on the other hand, are of more fundamental importance for the acceleration process itself in that they either appear as elements of it or at least must be counted among its conditions of possibility and/or preservation. In either case, they also fail to represent any countertendency. Furthermore, the efforts of intentional resistance to social acceleration and the deceleration ideology listed under (d1) are without a doubt *reactions* to the pressure to accelerate and its side effects. They appear anew with each wave of acceleration in modernity, and even though there is no guarantee that it will also be this way in future, so far they have always been rather short-lived and in the end very unsuccessful. There may even be a change looming in the way the acceleration dynamic is dealt with, one whose cause could be precisely the repeated experience of the futility of resistance. It is expressed in the way the Techno Generation distinguishes itself from its predecessors, especially among the youth movements. Previous movements like the '68ers, hippies, greens, new age groups, etc., were shaped by, among other things, resistance to the compulsions to accelerate (of society and machines). At least in this respect they have on the whole failed. Today's Techno Generation has perhaps drawn from this the lesson that resistance should be given up: similar to the (disappearingly small group of) futurists in their own day, its representatives set themselves up at the forefront of the acceleration process, using all time-saving devices and the fastest media and technologies to regain their temporal and technical sovereignty and impose their will on the machines instead of pulverizing themselves in a senseless revolt against them. However, as I will argue in chapters 10 and 11, the price for this seems to be the abandonment of the project of modernity. In both cases, nevertheless, it remains true that these deceleratory forces are neither structurally nor culturally on a par with the acceleration dynamic. Instead they seem to behave in an almost parasitical fashion toward it.[89]

Only the processes of cultural and structural rigidification included in the fifth category cannot be explained in this way as secondary, reactive, or residual phenomena. They seem to be rather an inherent and constitutive element of the acceleration process itself and to belong to modernity just as indissolubly as it does. With them one is dealing with the (acceleration-specific) reverse side of the modernization process that is characteristic of all its basic tendencies—differentiation, rationalization, domestification, individualization, and acceleration—and it stands to reason that they wax or wane with the forces of acceleration themselves.

Even if there can be no doubt that no equivalent force stands against the tendency of acceleration, it is nevertheless of great significance to understand the contribution that the institutional immobilization (*Stillstellung*) of central social background conditions has made to the accelerative success of modernity. For its part, this fixation of background conditions, which consisted in particular in the laying down of stable *developmental tracks*—of legislation, of political steering, of economic growth, of educational and professional paths, etc.—followed a prior phase in which these social realms were liquefied and dynamized in early modernity and the industrial revolution. From the very beginning of modernity, the placing in question of traditions and traditional principles of validity, the establishment of new practices in the sphere of production, and the processes of urbanization allowed the contingency of social institutions to become visible, and this very fact dynamized or "liquefied" society as a whole. The institutional reconsolidation (or, in Peter Wagner's terms, organization) of the social framework through the unfolding of the modern rule of law and the welfare state (*Rechts- und Sozialstaates*) did not supersede that inherent contingency and mutability (since modern law and democratic politics are essentially dynamic), but rather guaranteed that alterations ran along stable paths or transpired in accordance with predictable rules.[90]

For individuals, there emerged reliable lifelong career paths that guided them from birth through education and on to retirement, and, for economic development, stable, long-term foundations were created for calculation and secure expectations. As I have tried to show, it was precisely this "slowness of the rules of the game" that made possible the immense acceleration of material reproduction and scientific-technological progress as well as the liquefaction of many, if not all, social relationships.[91] Modernity thereby created in its leading institutions its own moment of *inertia*, as it were, one that was in peculiar tension with its dominant core tendency of setting "all that is solid" in motion and transforming it. This contradiction between the idea of *institutions*, whose etymological roots in Latin already indicate something standing, *inert*, and subject to at most incremental change, and the "spirit of modernity" was already seen by Nietzsche in the following formulation of his critique of modernity: "The West as a whole has lost the instincts that give rise to institutions, that give rise to a *future*: it might well be that nothing rubs its 'modern spirit' the wrong way more than this. People live for today, people live very fast,—people live very irresponsibly: and this is precisely what one calls 'freedom.' The things that make an institution into an institution are despised, hated, rejected."[92]

According to the thesis I will justify in what follows, the institutions of that spirit can no longer provide resistance because the forces of acceleration have developed so far that even the institutional structures that brought about and supported their unfolding can no longer keep up with them. Thus they become hindrances to acceleration and braking forces at the threshold of *another* modernity. Social acceleration has outgrown them and is now beginning to erode them and thereby introduce the end of the phase of institutionally immobilized social background conditions in which the space of experience and the horizon of expectation were congruent with respect to the rules of the game. As I will show in chapter 8, this holds true, for instance, for the nation-state and its bureaucracies (celebrated by Weber as accelerators, they have become too slow and inflexible in the age of hyperacceleration), but possibly also for the institutions of representative democracy, for the work (time) regime of "classical modernity" and its institutional separation of production and reproduction or work and free time, for the life course regime, for the "institution" of stable personal identities, and even for law.[93] The consequences of this development are still hardly foreseeable. They could paradoxically immobilize the acceleration dynamic in two different ways: on the one hand (in a limited sense), through the appearance of a "frenetic standstill," a situation brought about by the abandonment of a perspective and "path" of progress and characterized by the absence of any direction of development and, on the other, through the unsettling of the very foundations of the previously "ultrastable" cultural and structural societal framework of modernity by "postmodern" processes of erosion.[94]

Thus it becomes apparent that the relationship between inertia and movement in the history of modernity is not to be understood as a linear advance from the former to the latter and hence as a linear acceleration of social change. Rather, in a peculiar way, it follows more closely the dialectical developmental logic of forces of production and relations of production worked out by Marx and Engels. It seems that the dynamic forces of acceleration themselves produce the institutions and forms of practice they need in accordance with the respective requirements of their further unfolding and then annihilate them again upon reaching the speed limits those forms have made possible. From this perspective, surprisingly, it appears that it is the *increase of speed* rather than the unfolding of forces of production (though these are naturally closely connected to the acceleration dynamic) that is the real driving force of (modern) history. However, such a way of looking at the modern process of acceleration naturally harbors the danger of unreflectively making acceleration into a macrosubject of history. In order to meet this threat head on, I will investigate the historical causes and social mechanisms of the modern circle of acceleration in part 3.

PART TWO

MECHANISMS AND MANIFESTATIONS:
A PHENOMENOLOGY OF
SOCIAL ACCELERATION

3

TECHNICAL ACCELERATION AND THE REVOLUTIONIZING OF THE SPACE-TIME REGIME

IT WOULD NEVER OCCUR TO anyone to doubt the everyday experience of and the well-documented empirical evidence for a massive acceleration of processes of transportation, communication, and production in the history of modernity, so there is no need to discuss this in a detailed fashion. However, the way human beings are "in the world," that is, in space and time and in relation to each other, was fundamentally changed as a result of technical acceleration, which furthermore revolutionized the dominant ways that self and world were interpreted and thus heavily influenced the forms of subjectivity and society.[1] One does not at all need to defend a technological determinism in order to maintain this thesis: technical acceleration, as will be shown later, is itself a consequence of cultural, economic, and social-structural presuppositions, and the fact that it heavily influences social forms and modes of subjectivity does not mean that it determines them. There is a mutual influence and a mutual conditioning between alterations in the perception and conceptualization of space and time and technological innovations with respect to the ways we move within and deal with them. As a matter of fact, a palpable acceleration of transport and communication had already set in prior to and independent of the great technological innovations like the steam engine and the telegraph that led to the industrial revolution:

> The premechanical increase in speed had been apparent in many ways since the seventeenth century. The construction of networks of roads and canals increased the volume of freight and the distance it could be carried.[2] . . . The average speed of private carriages on French roads more than doubled from 1814 to 1848, from 4.5 to 9.5 kilometers per hour. In Prussia during the same period the time of the mail coach journey from Berlin

to Cologne shrank from 130 to 78 hours. . . . We find another precursor of increasing speed in the seas. In the first decade of the nineteenth century, North Americans developed the clipper ship, a narrow sailing ship with tall masts, which cut the time to travel from New York around Cape Horn to San Francisco (19,000 km) from 150–190 to 90 days[,] . . . an average speed of around 15 nautical miles per hour, which steam would only beat much later.

Something similar can be observed in communications. Before the electrical telegraph prevailed . . . optical telegraph networks, whose tradition stretched back to antiquity, were developed to their final perfection. The speed of signaling was increased enormously, whether through the necessary shortening of baroque administrative texts or the construction of a system of signals, which were transmitted from tower to tower.[3]

Such *technical*, but, as it were, pre*technological* accelerations of transport and communication already signal a transformation of the consciousness of space and time that is primarily expressed in the advancing disentanglement of spatial perception from location and temporal perception from space. The diffusion of the technical, scientific innovations of the map and the mechanical clock were very significant in this context. The increasing use of maps transformed the "natural," place-bound idea of space, the center of which was constituted by "the village," as the main standpoint of the observer whose lifeworld horizon was arranged in concentric circles of decreasing familiarity, into a somewhat "placeless" form of abstract spatial perception with a variable center. It is easy to see that this perspective opens up new possibilities of conceptualizing space as controllable and conquerable because it places the observer into a transformed relationship to space.[4]

Closely linked to this is the disentanglement of time from space, which was chiefly made possible by the invention and diffusion of the mechanical clock. As we have already seen, the perception of time is, in the first place, a function of the perception of space: a feeling for time develops because spatial qualities in our vicinity change; it becomes light as day and dark as night, warm as summer and cold as winter. Therefore it is not surprising that deep into the nineteenth century the time of day differed from place to place or at least from region to region: daytime was when the sun was at its zenith (and autumn began when certain fruits ripened in the fields, etc.). In the end this remained the case up to the establishment of the railroad, which forced, at the very least, a national standardization of time in order to consolidate the railway schedule (here the dialectical interplay between technology and consciousness appears again).[5] In contrast, the mechanical clock allowed the separation of time from place.[6] It made it possible in principle to determine time not only independently of spatial *qualities* but also entirely independently of a concrete place of residence. Then in 1912, at an international conference on time in Paris, a unified and globally valid *world time* was introduced, something that had already been conceived in 1884. Analogous to the placeless definition of space using a globe, this made possible an, as it were, placeless definition of time.[7]

If through these developments time established itself as an independent dimension of the world on an equal footing with space, then it was the accelerative revolution in the transportation sector in particular that further revolutionized the socially dominant space-time regime by "shrinking" the perception and relevance of space for many social and cultural processes and in the end even making it into a *function of time*. As an illustrative example of this kind of reconceptualization of space and time, Koselleck cites an entry in *Brockhaus der Gegenwart* on the essence of the railroads from 1838: "They annul spatial separation by getting closer in time. . . . For all spaces are only distances for us through the time we need to traverse them; if we accelerate this, then the influence of space itself on life and social intercourse is curtailed. . . . Railroads reduced Europe to roughly the size of Germany."[8]

In the twentieth century, this process of spatial shrinkage or *time-space compression* is driven further by the invention and diffusion of the automobile and the airplane and, finally, the space shuttle, even if it has not yet become an immediate component of the everyday (*lebensweltlichen*) consciousness of space. Even leaving the latter aside, from this perspective space has shrunk to around a sixtieth of its former size since the eighteenth century (see figure 3.1).

The effect this process of spatial shrinkage had on the experience of space and time can be intuitively reconstructed from a phenomenological point of view. As Virilio and also for instance Marianne Gronemeyer have shown, the consciousness of space is tightly linked to the type of movement in space at issue:[9] as long as we move forward on foot, we perceive space in all its immediate qualities, we feel, smell, hear, and see it. With the construction of roads begins the leveling of the terrain, the overcoming of hindrances, the manipulation of the quality of space. We no longer roam through it; we single-mindedly cut across it. With the invention of highways, then, space is already shortened, jammed together, faded out. Taking one's eye off the monotonously unchanging road and glancing into space would be life threatening. The driver locates himself not by using the passing landscape, but rather the

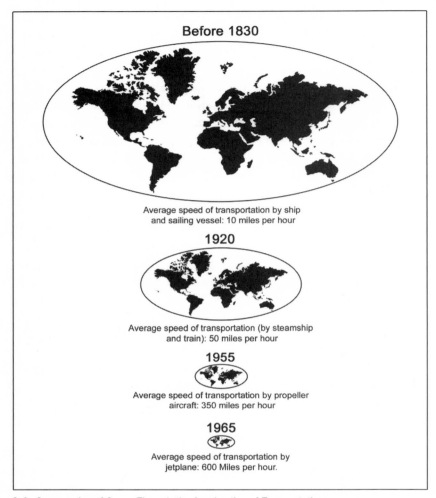

3.1. Compression of Space Through the Acceleration of Transportation

abstract symbols on the side of the road or even on the display of his GPS device. In this sense, the fundamental modern experience of the "annihilation of space" has a real basis. Finally, whoever flies completely breaks loose from the topographical space of life and the surface of the earth. For him, space is only an abstract, empty distance measured by the duration of the flight. Instead of struggling to overcome the difficulties of space, the modern traveler fights against the clock because he has to make connecting flights and keep appointments. Here too we see the priority of space as an orienting dimension turned into a priority of time, at least as concerns the planning of action and the appearance of hindrances. Quite often space becomes in a literal sense a function of time: where someone is depends on what time it is, whereas the converse no longer holds.[10]

Last, space completely loses its orienting function where material transportation processes are replaced by the electronic transmission of information: indeed, on the Internet the time at which information is sent or requested is registered, but not the place. The latter has become meaningless for many processes, while indications of time are gaining more relevance for the coordination and synchronization of global chains of action. In this way more and more social events in the age of globalization become, as it were, placeless.

Space's loss of meaning through this process produces a merely apparent paradox when, contrary to the trend just analyzed, geographical and geopolitical space and sometimes even the local specifics of place suddenly attain new significance for a series of decisions and developments. Precisely because space has become contingent and interchangeable for, say, economic investment and siting decisions, *local and regional differences* (e.g., climatic, infrastructural, or political ones) suddenly become very important, which can even lead (temporarily) to an upward revaluation of regional identities and particularities and above all to a repoliticization of space.[11] This gain in relevance, however, is only apparent or secondary: it rests on the fact that, in many respects, space has lost its property of *immutable givenness*, of being an *unchangeable background condition*, and stepped into the characteristically modern realm of the contingent, optional, and transitory.

In this way the "transmission revolution" of the (late) twentieth century interestingly inverts the direction of movement of the "transportation revolution" that reached its highpoint at the end of nineteenth and in the twentieth century: the latter's dynamizing achievement consisted in moving humans and goods in growing number and increasing tempo across the surface of the earth. In contrast, the former's dynamizing achievement rests on, as it were, reduplicating places and goods through virtualization and digitalization and making them accessible from anywhere in a stationary fashion. The transport revolution brought human beings to the world, whereas the transmission revolution (virtually) brings the world to human beings. Hence, for Virilio, this process of dynamization dialectically flips over into a process of rigidification in which humans and even goods themselves practically no longer move. This culminates in a scenario where everything dynamic is a result of flowing streams of data. By means of data gloves and cybersensory suits, or even newfangled connections between computers and bodies, in the wake of the current "transplant revolution" these (could) transmit all the spatial qualities of the earth and even other planets to any place in the world with such verisimilitude that an attempt to determine where one "really" is would be pointless: this is Virilio's vision of a terminal "polar inertia," of what I call frenetic standstill.[12]

Even though educators, psychologists, and pediatricians today are increasingly drawing our attention to the fact that in developed countries children and adolescents spend too much time passive and motionless in front of computers and TV screens, which threatens to stunt their faculties of spatial orientation and their capacity for movement,[13] there can be no doubt that this diagnosis describes at most a logical tendency: human beings and goods are moving through space not only virtually but also really in historically unprecedented numbers and with great speeds. However, the worldwide simultaneous access to information of all kinds and the "shrinkage of space" as a consequence of the acceleration of transport have lent an immediate and intuitive quality to metaphors like McLuhan's global village or—one made plausible by satellite images—spaceship earth or even the slogan from a telecommunications firm's advertisement, "There will be no more 'There,' we will all be 'Here.'" This is strengthened by the fact that as a consequence of these combined accelerations new fashion waves, social movements, and lifestyles as well as sicknesses, forms of terror, etc., also now appear worldwide almost simultaneously.

Moreover, as sociologists like Manuell Castells, Anthony Giddens, or John Urry have shown, the processes described by the catchwords of *globalization* and the *information* and *communication revolutions* do not only lead to an altered meaning and experience of space but also change the form and perception of social time. As a result of the nearly unlimited recording capacity of the new media and the already discussed increase in occurences of a *simultaneity of the nonsimultaneous*, time is beginning to lose its unilinear, orientation-giving character because the connection of sequences and chronologies appears to be progressively dissolving.

This can be illustrated with five examples. 1. For instance, in the Internet there are pieces of information and data, entered at different moments in time and pertaining to various historical epochs, that stand seamlessly and without hierarchy next to one another and thereby systematically undermine the possibility of a temporal orientation by allowing a kaleidoscopic, fragmentary pattern to emerge in place of ordered and stable chronologies. This phenomenon of temporal-sequential disorientation finds its cultural reflection in numerous products of the video, film, and television industries in which the chronological-sequential and linear narrative order of the images and messages are replaced by associative, kaleidoscopic transitions between spatiotemporal fragments.[14] 2. In the same way, contemporary forms of asynchronous communication (e-mail, answering machines) have made it possible to, as it were, "detemporalize" communicative connections and reactivate them at will again at points in time and in sequences of our own choosing. 3. Likewise, the dominant principle of style in cultural postmodernity, in art and architecture, fashion and lifestyle, and at times even in politics and science, is that elements from the most diverse epochs are placed on an equal footing and eclectically juxtaposed and connected in various ways. 4. On the stage of world politics as well as at the level of everyday life, events and episodes that seem to belong to different eras of world history show up in apparently random order, either one after the other or at the same time[15]: after September 11, 2001, in Afghanistan the warfare and world politics of the twenty-first century struck a medieval religious state (and its slow form of war), one that had moreover allied itself in a novel way with a highly modern form of terror, only to soon fall back again into an age of premodern tribal war. Similarly, on the streets of a "global city" it is possible to wander from a part of the city with medieval-looking scenes of market life and religion into a twenty-first-century center of finance and communication and immediately thereafter into a manufacturing district reminiscent of the industrial revolution. It is just as possible, of course, that elements of these three eras will collide in one and the same quarter of the city. 5. Finally, biological age is losing its sequencing, ordering function with respect to the course of life: phases of education and training can take over from periods of professional work, parenthood is possible at a relatively advanced age, and, even in retirement, single life can follow a phase of married life, etc.

Anthony Giddens identifies in such processes a transformation and broadening of "time-space distantiation" that is characterized above all by the disembedding of social events from traditional time-space patterns,[16] and Manuel Castells coins the concept "timeless time," reminiscent of "placeless space," for the dominant temporal form of the information age: "I propose the idea that timeless time, as I label the dominant temporality of our society, occurs when the characteristics of a given context, namely, the informational paradigm and the network society, induce systemic perturbation in the sequential order of phenomena performed in that context. This perturbation may take the form of compressing the occurrence of phenomena, aiming at instantaneity, or else by introducing random discontinuity in the sequence. Elimination of sequencing creates undifferentiated time, which is tantamount to eternity."[17]

It is obvious, then, that not just space but also time, in some contexts at least, loses its orienting function. This seems to make the formation of new modes of sensory orientation indispensable in late modern circumstances of action. I will come back to this in the discussion of the consequences of social acceleration.

However, the transformation of our relationship to time and space, or the *social space-time regime,* is not the only way in which the mode of subjects' "placement-in-the-world" is revolutionized by technical acceleration. Rather, one can assert in a simplified and schematizing formula that just as our *relationship to space* was above all transformed by the acceleration of transportation, our *relationship to human beings* was revolutionized by the acceleration of communication and our *relationship to things* by the acceleration of (re)production. All three types of acceleration have therefore contributed to the transformation of our *relationship to time* itself (cf. figure 3.2).

The transformation of our relationships to space, to other humans, and to the material structures of the world of things follows the shared logic that is characteristic of the modernization process as a whole: it becomes, as it were, "liquefied," i.e., transitory, quickly changeable, and contingent.[18] Thus the mobilization of society through transportation technology dissolves the

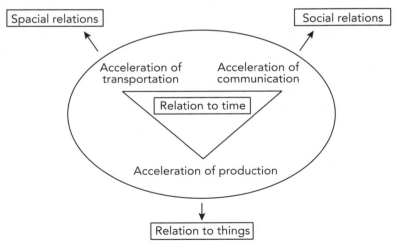

3.2. Technical Acceleration and the Transformation of Relations to the World

archaic bond between subjects and territorially delimited spaces, while the development of communications technology in modernity, which tends to bring *each person into communicative connection with every other person around the world at all times,*[19] represents an essential presupposition for the transformation of social relationships in the modernization process. This transformation consists, in the first place, in the fact that patterns of association and relationship are no longer or to a lesser extent bound to one common geographical space (and thus, on the one hand, easier to dissolve and to change while, on the other, also capable of being maintained over large distances); in the second place, in the increase and rapid turnover of communication partners; and, in the third place, in the alteration of communications *media*, which undeniably influences the quality of social interaction and hence social relationships themselves. The manifold differences between face-to-face contact and mediated interaction are the most well-known example of this.[20]

Finally, the acceleration of *production* constitutes a central precondition for the permanent (ex)change of the material structures that surround us: our clothes and shoes, our homes or at least our furniture, kitchens, and bathrooms, our home appliances and work tools and instruments, our cars and luxury goods. The massive speeding up of their production has made possible what the economic imperative of the capitalist order demands: the acceleration of the entire social system's conversion of matter into useful commodities and thereby the turnover speed of capital.[21] In this way both the everyday objects that surround us and the material structures of our lifeworld as a whole become contingent and transitory. It is reasonable to suppose that this greatly changes the relationship between persons and things. Due to the way objects ceaselessly become obsolete and out of date (the computer that promised acceleration yesterday is today already a brake in view of faster programs) and the economic rationality of *discarding* and *replacing* things instead of repairing them,[22] identity-constituting processes of adapting to and growing accustomed to things become increasingly improbable.[23] From this point of view, modernity is characterized by the continuous displacement of *physical wear* by *moral wear* (Marx) as the main cause for the material replacement of objects and arrangements: in the course of the last few centuries, the latter have become unusable less and less often because their material substance is used up or worn out (i.e., irreparable); rather they become "out of date" or obsolescent relative to technology or fashion. As a result, and in contrast to premodern societies, they are almost never reproduced identically, but rather nearly always in an *altered form*.

Even when people *do not* change where they live, their social partners, and important material objects like their house or their car, or even their purse, within the horizon of (late) modernity these relationships have become contingent to such an extent that their alternation is at every moment a real possibility, and "inertia" in the face of movement is, as it were, something that demands a justification. Here one can see just how far the acceleration of transportation, communication, and production has influenced the socially relevant patterns of identity: identification with spaces, with fixed communication partners and reference groups, and with things takes on a temporally delimited and contingent character. The person is compelled to distance or emancipate herself from them to the extent that she can withstand a change (whether voluntary or forced) without a loss of self. Human existence thus tends to become *placeless*, just as places become *devoid of identity and history*.[24] At first this claim must remain a mere postulate. I will return to the question of the alteration of patterns of identity and relationships to self in the wake of social acceleration in greater detail in chapters 5.3 and 10.

In any case, we have already gone quite far beyond the realm of technical acceleration as such. The diagnosed alterations of the space-time regime, of our social relationships, and of our relation to the material structures of our environment are not simply a result of technological inventions. The former are not logically implied by the latter; rather their empirical manifestations are indissolubly linked with the acceleration of social change and the pace of life. This can be seen especially in regard to the alteration of our relationship to other people or our social circumstances: rapidly changing and qualitatively transformed interaction patterns are, as will soon be shown, at least as much a form and result of accelerated social change as they are a consequence of the development of communications technology or, put otherwise, the specific effects of the latter first unfold in the context of the former. In a similar way, the ever faster revolutionizing of the structures of our material environment is not goal directed as such, so it is actually a manifestation of the acceleration of social change. Technical acceleration is therefore just the *material basis* of and a *condition of possibility* for the various social processes of acceleration that underlie those transformations and are discussed today primarily under the catchphrase *globalization*. It thereby forms at the same time the material basis for both the other forms of social acceleration, which then in turn serve as a "motivator" (*Motivgeber*) that drives technological acceleration. This makes clear once again that the distinction between the three dimensions of social acceleration is an *analytical* one: in order to understand the empirical manifestations and mechanisms of social acceleration, one absolutely has to take account of all three dimensions at the same time and to study their *interactions* in particular. So before I further interrogate the causes and the broader consequences of social acceleration, I would like to turn now to a phenomenological stocktaking of the other two dimensions of acceleration. Then in chapter 6 it will be systematically shown how technical acceleration, the acceleration of social change, and the acceleration of the pace of life propel each other in a reflexive circle.

4

SLIPPING SLOPES: THE ACCELERATION OF SOCIAL CHANGE AND THE INCREASE OF CONTINGENCY

IN *ELECTIVE AFFINITIES* GOETHE HAS Eduard complain, "it is terrible that one can't learn anything for life anymore. . . . Our ancestors held firm to what they had learned in their youth; but we have to learn everything over again every five years if we are not to be totally behind the times." Reinhart Koselleck sees in this *shortening of the temporal rhythms of relearning* (or the half-life of knowledge), which is a correlate of the contraction of the present, the core of a perception of accelerated social change.[1] The parts of knowledge given up to accelerated obsolescence pertain to practices and action orientations as well as associational structures and patterns of relation; they concern knowledge of the world and social knowledge as well as the cognitive elements of the relationships subjects have to themselves and they embrace the structural as well as the cultural side of social reality. Modern society is characterized by a historically unprecedented amount of "kinetic energy" or transformative unrest, which lends plausibility to the metaphors of a continual melting, evaporating, and liquefying of social structures that have been used from Karl Marx to Marshall Berman and Zygmunt Bauman.[2]

At the end of the twentieth century, an erosion of the economic, legal, political, and welfare-providing institutional framework connected to the national state set in, a framework that developed during "classical modernity" and up until that point proved to be surprisingly stable. In view of this metaphors of "flows" and "fluids" have gained a new currency in contemporary diagnoses of the time: authors like Manuel Castells, Bauman, John Urry, or Arjun Appadurai attribute the property of liquidity to the streams of persons, information, financing, and commodities that circulate rapidly and almost without resistance across the globe. They can be quickly disseminated anywhere, but they can also be made to flow in other directions or through other channels or even be taken back again at the slightest territorial or political change. In other words, they never achieve any stable or long-term aggregate state or any fixed connections to each other. In this diagnosed triumph of modern dynamization over the institutional forces of inertia (which are, of course, also to be attributed to modernity), *no* new principle becomes visible. Instead one simply reaches a further stage of the process of acceleration and liquefaction that is a primordial aspect of modernity.

Appadurai's image of the dissolution of firmly established, historically and geographically stable social aggregates in favor of more fluid, permanently mobile, and shifting *ethno-, techno- , financial- , media- ,* and *ideoscapes* offers a striking expression of, and a potential benchmark for, this development. As *cultural flows*, these separate from one other and displace each other disjunctively, such that they are, as it were, no longer representable by conventional maps, but rather only in the dynamic visualization of continually changing screens.[3] Such flows always appear in plural: what is decisive for the understanding of contemporary societies is the fact that territories, ethnic groups, financial and ideological streams as well as forms of cultural, religious, and political practice are tending to become independent from one another, such that these streams can flow in various directions—i.e., in almost arbitrary (re)combinations—but also appear to be largely beyond intentional control (*Steuerung*).

Even with respect to the tempo of social change, one should assume that a progressive quantitative escalation can lead to qualitative shifts in the constitution of social reality when critical threshold values are reached. As authors like Jan Assmann or Reinhart Koselleck have shown,[4] the temporal extension of the communicative social memory is limited to around eighty to one hundred years, which means that the divergence of the space of experience and the horizon of expectation that is characteristic of modernity, and hence the experience of a "contraction of the present," can only appear once significant transformative processes have transpired *within three to four generations.* If, on the other hand, social change, i.e., the transformation of structural and cultural certainties, reaches a higher tempo than the basic sequence of generations, one may conjecture not only that serious consequences follow for intergenerational relations, as Karl Mannheim already assumed, but also that the erosion of lifeworld certainties achieves a new quality, which cannot help but affect cultural reproduction as well as the form of subjective relationships to self.[5] Finally, beyond a still higher, though hardly unambiguously determinable threshold value, change is no longer perceived as a transformation of fixed structures, but instead as a fundamental and potentially chaotic *indeterminacy*.[6] The attractiveness of postmodern ideas in the present age may therefore be a signal that just such a threshold value has been reached, beyond which the forms of narrative, cumulative and linear world disclosure can no longer be maintained.

The thesis of a progressive acceleration of social change in the course of the modernization process can thus be formulated in a sharper way as follows: the tempo of this transformation has been heightened from an *intergenerational* speed of change in early modernity through a phase of approximate synchronization with the sequence of generations in "classical modernity" to a tendency toward an *intragenerational* tempo in late modernity.[7] As I have already shown, it is difficult to strengthen this conjecture empirically, above all because in the social-scientific debate it is unclear which innovations are to be counted as foundational (*Basisinnovationen*) and which indicators evince genuine social transformation. Nevertheless, according to a broad-reigning consensus, the foundational institutions of a society are those that organize the fundamental processes of production and reproduction.[8] For Western societies since early modernity, these have remained the institutions of the family and the (capitalistic) employment system, which is why analyses of social change very often concentrate on just these realms.

Despite all the discrepancies in the empirical findings regarding these two dimensions of society, it is not implausible to postulate for both realms just such an acceleration of change from an intergenerational through a generational to a potentially intragenerational tempo if one only considers the societally endogenous, i.e., self-produced causes of change, which are all that matter in this context (and not exogenous events like enemy raids, natural catastrophes, etc.). Thus in what concerns, for example, the life cycle of families as economic units or as "households," the ideal-typical family structures in agarian societies tended to be stable across a long chain of generations: the turnover of generations left the basic structures untouched and simply replaced, as it were, the individual role bearers. Thus Arthur Imhof describes the maintenance of stable family structures across many generations using the example of a north Hessian household in the following way (in this case it is a farmstead, although lines of succession in households and royal dynasties were structurally similar)[9]: "The individual Johannes Hoos, who was born and died in this or that year, was not of crucial significance. What was significant was rather that there was always a descendent by the name of Johannes Hoos who stood ready to bear the role of steering the destiny of the household through his physically best and socially most strongly integrated years. In this way, the household was not merely in the possession of Johannes Hoos for ten or twenty or thirty years, but continually over the course of four and a half centuries. Truly an astonishing stability despite uncertain lifespans!"[10] That many members of society were forbidden to start their own families does not at all contradict this finding: their societal position was defined by their relationship to the supporting family structures; they were in part simply a component of the familial household. The structurally (and culturally) authoritative (*maßgebend*) family structures were therefore intended and disposed to endure for the long run. Then, in classical modernity, the extended family, and hence the transgenerational family bond and the corresponding structure directed toward long-run stability, is replaced by the ideal-typical nuclear family tailored to *one generation* and centered around a married couple whose structure collapses with the death of that couple. *Starting a family of one's own* that as an economic unit (at least in theory) only ceases to exist after the death of both spouses becomes nothing less than the identity-constituting and autonomy-securing task of the modern bourgeois individual (and increasingly also the "proletarian" one). In late modernity, finally, family cycles display an unmistakable tendency to take on an infragenerational lifespan, for which increasing divorce and remarriage rates as well as the rearrangement or disintegration of households are the clearest evidence.[11] Today the life *period* partner is tending to replace the *life* partner. This argument does not by any means suppose the decline of the ideal of the bourgeois family per se, on the contrary: it is entirely consistent with the empirical finding that this form of life is in fact a social model to an increasing degree and that individuals today are still inclined to enter into (new) familial ties.[12] However, lifelong monogamy is being replaced ever more frequently by a new form of "serial monogamy" or "romantic partners for a time."[13] As Thomas H. Eriksen remarks, one is dealing here with a remarkable manifestation of that "frenetic standstill" that characterizes late modernity as a whole.[14]

Despite all the obvious empirical reservations concerning such a schematic presentation of the transformation of family structures, it can in any case hardly be denied that the *consciousness of contingency* in family ties is being heightened even among those who decide to remain together for their entire lives: the awareness that things could also be otherwise, not only through the choices of another but also through one's own, and the resulting uncertainties and compulsions to justify inertia are undeniably increasing. Sighard Neckel has given this an apt formulation: "The simple fact that everyone knows that things are done otherwise by other people places one's own course of life under an obligation to justify itself and gives birth to the necessary action of inventing oneself as a person. . . . This establishes a symbolic reality behind which the individual cannot get. This already alters society independently of whether everything is actually different than in times when it was composed of a few great groups."[15] And in contrast to exogenous contingencies and vicissitudes like diseases, natural catastrophes, the repercussions of violent relations of domination, etc., that often threatened premodern family structures with disintegration, the contingencies of late modern family structures are of a self-produced nature endogenous to the family.

This finding of dynamization also holds good (and in even greater measure) for the development of employment relations. Here too one can argue in an ideal-typical and sharpened way that occupations in pre- and early modernity tended to be passed down from fathers to sons such that occupational and employment structures displayed a cross-generational stability. The free, but as a rule one-shot choice of one's own, lifelong, and identity-constituting occupation would then become a constitutive feature of "classical" modernity in which occupational structures exhibited a "generational" stability.[16] *Find your calling!* became, alongside *start your own family!* the second identity-constituting task, first for young men and then increasingly for young women in modernizing societies. In late modernity, in contrast, occupation and employment relations seem ever more seldom to last an entire career: multiple changes of occupation and/or place of employment *within* one professional life (often accompanied by longer or shorter periods of unemployment) seem to have gone from being the exception to being the rule according to the overwhelming majority of the empirical findings. For instance Richard Sennett finds that "today a young American with two years of college education must reckon on changing positions eleven times and retraining three times within forty years of work."[17]

Meanwhile even in Germany, whose model of high occupational stability has previously displayed particular resistance to efforts at making them more flexible,[18] one can discern an unmistakable tendency of acceleration in the structural transformation of employment and in the turnover rate in positions for the employed. In the context of their analysis of the structural transformation of the labor market by means of an evaluation of the microcensus and the BIBB/IAB survey of the employed between 1975 and 1997, the research group of Christoph Köhler and Olaf Struck observe a "steady erosion of stable and secure employment,"[19] and while their findings are not always very pronounced, they point in an unambiguous direction. They find a clear shortening of the average length of employment at an enterprise, an increase in job changes between firms, a rising mobility of labor, an increase in short- and mid-term employment contracts, and, on the whole, a growing instability of employment relations. The (subjective) risk of layoff also markedly increased.[20] Thus "it is shown that in the 1990s relations in the labor market changed in the direction of shorter duration and higher mobility."[21]

Such findings strengthen the thesis that late modern society is also characterized by a transition from a generational to an intragenerational structural transformation of employment and labor force replacement.[22] In addition, more than in the forms of family life (which in limited measure have been likewise pluralized in late modernity),[23] in the employment sector it is not only the *relations* of employment but also the range of the *forms* of employment and the professions that have rapidly altered. The deregulation of labor relations produced new forms of employment, for instance, temporary work and various forms of part-time work, while it was above all information technology that created entirely new professions that accompanied the disappearance of numerous traditional occupations. Moreover, it also holds true here that the dynamic of transformation is of a socially endogenous nature, that changes can be brought about by one's own decision or that of others, and that the consciousness of contingency, i.e., uncertainty about the short-, mid- and long-term employment situation, even increases where there are *not* changes in occupation or employment opportunities.[24]

I argue, then, that the acceleration of social change as a whole is most clearly legible in the state of intergenerational relations: from a premodern situation in which structural and cultural stock was simply passed down through many generations, it led to a modernity in which, as Ansgar Weyman observes, "generations [functioned] as innovative and structure-building collective actors," which thus allowed one to read off transformations from the change of generations,[25] and then finally to a late modernity in which social relations are subject to fundamental change within the timespan alloted to a single generation.

If one defines the contraction of the present as the *general decrease of the length of time for which there prevail secure expectations regarding the stability of the circumstances of action*, then it is immediately evident just how much forms of professional and familial instability can be interpreted as symptoms of the acceleration of social change. However, the rapid transformation, revisability, recombinability, and hence increasing contingency of practices, scenarios

(*Konstellationen*), and structures also affects other realms of society, both those that are central to the social structure of everyday life and those that are peripheral. In today's highly accelerated "global" society, the same uncertainty tends to prevail about the central dimensions of modern mobility,[26] such as future life partners and employers, place of residence, political affiliation,[27] and religious orientation,[28] as about the stability of action contexts in peripheral dimensions of social life: that is, which telephone companies, insurance providers, or energy suppliers, which recreational associations, investors, and pension funds will still exist "tomorrow" (which in Lübbe's sense is inching ever closer to "today") and offer favorable conditions is something just as uncertain as the question of which newspapers, journals, television networks, Internet providers, search machines, etc., with acceptable offerings will be available—not to mention the uncertainty about which new fields of action and forms of practice will emerge. (Consider that the question concerning the Internet provider and the Web search engine, or the right telephone company, would have been absolutely meaningless just a few generations ago.)

As a rule, we hold the (accelerated) change of fashions, product ranges, and styles of art to be less problematic since these areas are constituted by an orientation toward transformation, although a feeling of insecurity in everyday life can certainly arise when familiar products and brands of clothing, food, cosmetics, etc., are no longer available. The shortening of product life cycles becomes especially problematic for retailers and buyers where the speed of innovation has gotten so high that distinguishing between old and new models requires a serious effort.[29] Naturally, as we have already seen in chapter 2.2b, the "present," i.e., the temporal space of stability, is of different lengths in the various realms of society: for instance, it is as a rule longer with respect to life (period) partners than it is regarding fashion. The thesis of a general acceleration of social change, however, states that it is contracting either in *all* realms or at least in its aggregated value across all (weighted) fields.

Significant desynchronization phenomena caused by differing speeds of transformation and adaptation appear not only in the relationships of functional systems to one another (for example, the speeds of change and innovation in education and politics are longer than those in the economy and technology) but also in the relations of different social groups and particularly between the generations living within a society. If social change rises to an *intragenerational* tempo, then one should expect that this will have far-ranging consequences for the possibilities and forms of social integration and cultural reproduction. Thus Lübbe conjectures: "The intergenerational transfer of cultural information is potentially threatened if the cultural orientations of the two generations living together in the small modern family unit drift too far apart. Processes of growing up, just like processes of growing old, become precarious if the quantity of cultural resources that have consistent validity over the short duration of an average life dissolves with disorienting consequences."[30]

Even if one can question the extent of the consequences of disorientation on the grounds of a lack of empirical proof, the observable symptoms of a growing intergenerational "rift," especially with regard to contemporary popular culture and media, remain unmistakable: young and old people increasingly live isolated from each other in subworlds in the sense that they not only use different communications media but also play different games, frequent different locales, follow different TV and news programs, read distinct newspapers and magazines, prefer different styles of music in divergent milieus, wear distinct kinds of clothing that they buy in respective age-specific stores, and even eat distinct kinds of food and speak different languages.

In this context the notion of a *progressive* contraction of the present implies that not only one but rather two or more such generational faultlines have developed. Intergenerational relations thus become, as it were, a manifestation of the *noncontemporaneity of the contemporaneous* and hence of the problem of social desynchronization: the experiences, practices, and stock of knowledge of the parental generation increasingly become for the youth anachronistic and meaningless, indeed, insofar as knowledge is bound to participation in a practice, actually *incomprehensible* (and vice versa). The world of Gameboys, the Internet, and SMS messages is already for many parents, and even more so for many grandparents, as unintelligible and foreign as the mores and practices of a geographically distant culture. An empirical indication of the fact that the "older" forms of praxis are also at the same time the *slower* ones is provided by studies that attribute entirely new abilities and skills to youths in contrast to older persons, such as "polychronicity" or multitasking, i.e., the capacity to simultaneously process several sources of information and types of activity.[31] In an accelerating world, therefore, the abilities and stock of knowledge of the young and the old are not only different but appear to give a systematic advantage to the former. Gerhard De Hann concludes from this that the education of the younger generation by the older has come to an end, and he calls for a "special right of adults as a past generation" as a "final pedagogical maxim" or, as it were, a preserve for the lifeworld of older persons in the sense of an intentionally conserved oasis of deceleration.[32] In any case, this indicates a differentiation of generational lifeworlds or worlds of experience that is alarming with respect to the chances of intergenerational integration and solidarity.[33]

The consequences of this "generational break" are manifold. With respect to cultural reproduction, it is generally uncontroversial that children and adolescents today acquire more and more orienting knowledge from their peers and less and less from those who are older because the experiences and the stock of knowledge of the old become devalued faster and faster as an unavoidable side effect of the contraction of the present.[34]

This means that the status of age in society inevitably changes. An institution that was self-evident for traditional societies, namely, that of "wise elders," to whom an outstanding status was attributed because they had "seen everything" and hence could no longer be surprised by any of the troubles of life, has practically disappeared in late modern society: instead the old are stigmatized by the fact that they *no longer know their way around* and can *no longer keep up*. The threatened loss of openness and flexibility in old age is a stigmatizing handicap in a society with high rates of change, as is shown for instance in those professions in which even forty year olds are no longer employed because they do not appear flexible and venturesome enough, which leads moreover to the acceleration of professional careers today, such that, for instance, they have to be sucessfully launched between the ages of twenty-five and forty-five.[35] The "obsession with youthfulness" of (late) modern society so often mocked in cultural criticism has its acceleration-induced roots here: the ideal image of older human beings is no longer that of a "wise elder," but rather that of the still flexible, versatile, *not really old* person who does not shy away from actively adapting to the new. The compulsion to be youthful, or indeed to "eternal puberty," is irrevocably inscribed in the time structures of late modern society and does not stem from a mere cultural mood.[36]

The constitutive instability of the material and social conditions of situations, choices, and actions due to the acceleration of social change forces individuals as well as organizations and institutions to permanently revise their expectations, reinterpret experiences, redefine what counts as relevant, and repeatedly carry out coordinating and synchronizing operations. Without a doubt the flexibilization and deregulation of numerous social practices under the sign of neoliberal "globalization" has driven this process further in the wake of the digital and political acceleration revolution at the end of the twentieth century.

From a phenomenological perspective, just as technical acceleration has altered our relations to space, time, things, and society, so too the acceleration of social change and the "liquefying" of social and material relationships has grave repercussions on the (late) modern way of "being-in-the-world." Elsewhere I have tried to describe the feeling of existence produced in modernity and generalized and heightened in postmodernity as being characterized by the perception of standing, in all areas of life, on a slippery slope or on a down escalator.[37] I have meanwhile come to think that the metaphor of *slipping* slopes is better suited for the interpretation of the late modern condition (*Befindlichkeit*): actors operate under conditions of permanent multidimensional change that make standing still by *not acting* or *not deciding* impossible. Whoever does not continually readapt to the steadily shifting conditions of action (updating or actualizing, in a literal and figurative sense, both "hardware" and "software") loses the connections that enable future options. From a more practical standpoint, this means that if you do not constantly strive to stay up to date, your language, your clothing, your address book, your knowledge of the world and of society, your skills, your recreational gear, your retirement fund and investments, etc., will become anachronistic.[38] In this context it is definitely not only one's own movements that bring about change (as the image of *slipp*ery slopes suggests), and it is not only a matter of the danger of a unilinear anachronization, as the image of the escalator implies; rather, it has to do with the situation of action and decision in a highly dynamized social world that the metaphor of *slipping* slopes tries to capture. The circumstances of action and choice themselves alter continuously and along multiple dimensions such that there is no longer a resting place from which one might "calmly" explore options and connections. As in an earthquake, not all layers (of the ground) shift at the same pace: as I have already tried to show, desynchronization phenomena arise through which the various realms of society move at different speeds, and individual oases of deceleration repeatedly form that, like stable rock ledges in an earthquake, promise a limited stability in rapidly changing surroundings. The result is nevertheless a permanent reformation of the "decision landscape" that not only continually devalues experiences and stored knowledge but also makes it almost impossible to predict *which* connections and opportunities for action will be relevant and important in the future. However, where it becomes difficult to foresee relevancies a natural reaction is to attempt to keep open as many options as possible, or even all of them, for later realization: this is precisely what Luhmann describes as the *temporalization of complexity*, which in turn induces further acceleration.[39]

Perhaps the most revealing symptom of social dynamization is the introduction of the newspaper at the end of the eighteenth century. It was a reaction to the growing need of people to be informed about the rapid changes in various spheres of society and so in a certain way it reproduced each day a new "map" of politics, the economy, cultural life, sports, etc.[40] Its "use by date" amounted to exactly one day: nothing is so obviously anachronistic as yesterday's newspaper. In the meantime, however, the daily reassessment of the terrain is no longer sufficient: Internet editions of journals are increasingly transitioning to updating their news several times per day, per hour, or even "online."[41] Similarly, the weekly newsreels in the cinema have long been replaced by daily news shows, and modern news broadcasters like CNN keep their viewers up to date with up to three scrolling lines of news (the news ticker or crawler) in addition to image-based reporting. These mobile lines of text (not only on computer and TV screens but also on display panels on municipal buildings and public transportation centers) that promise news in "real time" thus become the symbol of a society of "nonstop" change.

Naturally, one can raise against this argument the justified objection that the possibility of an accelerated transmission of news reports cannot simply be equated with a real acceleration of the social processes to which they refer. Yet here we find a further example for the interaction of technological acceleration and the acceleration of social change: the faster dissemination of news reports makes possible a quicker reaction to changes (as the development of the stock and financial markets have strikingly shown) and thereby leads to a real acceleration of social change. Moreover, the accelerated updating of news reports represents a paradigm case of the contraction of the present: the knowledge of the world one has at 10 A.M. is already obsolete at 4 P.M.,[42] its "use by date" shrinks in the face of the news ticker to nearly zero. Once again it is instability rather than actual change that is responsible for the loss of certainty in many realms; most of the reported states of affairs remain the same six hours later, but they *could* have changed, at least with respect to their *relevancies*.

There are obvious consequences for the feeling, triggered by the acceleration of social change, that one is standing on slipping slopes in all realms of life. The logic of culture corresponds exactly to that of physiology here: actors feel placed under stress and time pressure to keep up with changes and not lose options or connectivity (*Anschlusschancen*) because of the obsolescence of their knowledge and skills. The *cultural processing* of new pieces of information, i.e., their embedding in systematic knowledge of the world and narrative structures of interpretation, is unavoidably *costly in time*. This is an essential reason for the experience of "time pressure, under which one experimentally attempts, individually as well as institutionally, to culturally process the temporally compressed assault of innovations."[43] Therefore it is entirely conceivable, as I have already tried to show drawing on Lübbe's work, that the temporal limits of our processing capacity have been surpassed by social change and consequently there has been a recent *qualitative* ("postmodern") transformation of culture and subjective relationships to self due to a *quantitative* escalation of speed. Peter Conrad, standing in here for many observers of our culture, describes on the first page of his cultural history of modernity the everyday life experience of people at the end of the twentieth century by saying, "we run as fast as we can in order to stay in the same place." The time use researchers Robinson and Godbey confirm this experience on the basis of their empirical findings with almost the same words: "we dance faster and faster just to stay in place."[44] With this we already find ourselves in the realm of phenomena that, according to the definitions developed in chapter 2.2, fall under the category of an acceleration of the pace of life whose phenomenological stocktaking is the aim of the next chapter. I will return in greater detail to the problem of the crossing of critical threshold values in the individual and collective processing of social change in part 4.

5

THE ACCELERATION OF THE "PACE OF LIFE" AND PARADOXES IN THE EXPERIENCE OF TIME

AS GEORG SIMMEL HAD ALREADY remarked in 1897, "one often hears about the 'pace of life,' that it varies in different historical epochs, in the regions of the contemporary world, even in the same country and among individuals of the same social circle."[1] Just as little has changed in this respect, as in the related fact that this pace continually *escalates* in modern society, so that each of its periods can successively claim to live at a historically unprecedented record pace.[2] As we have seen in part 1 of this study, this realization has almost always been accompanied by the fear that the pace of life has gotten *too fast*. Unfortunately, however, despite all the time use studies we have, the question how to *measure* it and thus how to empirically test the acceleration thesis is just as unclear today as in Simmel's time.

Simmel himself suggested that the pace of life be defined as the "product of the number and intensity" of the changes in the ideational contents of consciousness per unit of time,[3] a definition that is, although intuitively plausible, as curious as it is empirically unoperationalizable. He conjectured that this tempo correlated with the available quantity of money and its speed of circulation.[4]

In an award-winning social-psychological study in which the pace of life of large cities in thirty-one different countries from four regions of the earth was measured, the Californian sociologist Robert Levine and his team proposed another definition of the speed of life, one relatively easy to operationalize empirically. According to their definition, the respective culturally determined tempo of life can be established using three indicators: "First, we measured the average walking speed of randomly selected pedestrians over a distance of 60 feet. . . . The second . . . focused on an example of speed in the workplace: the time it took postal clerks to fulfill a standard request for stamps. . . . Third, as an estimate of a city's interest in clock time, we observed the accuracy of 15 randomly selected bank clocks in main downtown areas in each city."[5] This definition has the advantage of allowing accurate intercultural comparisons that actually do generate several interesting results.[6] Nevertheless its methodology appears rather dubious and its empirical relevance quite limited. In particular, the question *what* is actually being measured thrusts itself on us: the pace of social life? The selectivity of the indicators already speaks against this. Post offices in New York are, as the author knows from painful experience, unusually and, in comparison with European standards, even scandalously slow, something presumably connected with the low estimation and chronic underfinancing of the public sector in the United States.[7] Yet to take this as an indicator of an overall slow pace of life in that metropolis appears rather questionable. Conversely, the surprising fact that the *Irish* show the highest foot speed could possibly be explained not by their generally fast pace of life but by the frequent rainy weather in Ireland.[8] Therefore, in order to adequately take into account the temporal peculiarities of particular cultural practices while determining the pace of life, the action tempo of an entire series of very diverse processes from different fields of action must be considered and aggregated.

The question concerning what exactly is being measured is also emphatically raised, however, with respect to Levine's third indicator. Karlheinz Geißler has observed that clocks in the public realm, and in particular at the nodal points of metropolitan life like modern airports, are increasingly losing significance and disappearing from the streetscape (or falling into neglect). If that is correct,[9] then the suspicion arises that the precision of public clocks might rather be a sign of *backwardness*, of being stuck inertially in "classical" modernity, rather than one of arrival in the quick-paced "postmodernity."[10] Finally, Levine's indicators in and of themselves say nothing about the "condensation" of action episodes and subjectively felt *time pressure*, which play a constitutive role for at least the subjective *perception* of a high tempo of life and are not at all connected in a linear way with the performance tempo of individual actions. Whoever is in a position to perform an action faster than others may thereby precisely decelerate her life: but only provided that she uses the freed-up time resources for breaks or recuperation.

Due to these kinds of difficulties, I proposed in chapter 2.2c that the acceleration of the pace of life be defined as the *increase of episodes of action and/or experience per unit of time as a result of a scarcity of time resources.* I then separated it into an objective and a subjective component. *Objectively,* at least in principle, the condensation of episodes of action and/or experience can be measured by means of time use studies, while *subjectively* the experience of stress, time pressure, and "racing" time are empirically ascertainable indicators for the perception of a scarcity of time resources and an accelerated elapse of time.[11] The acceleration of the pace of life contains, then, an *increase in the aggregated speed of action* as well as the *transformation of the experience of time* in everyday life.

In what follows I will first investigate the manifestations of and evidence for an objective condensation of episodes of action and experience in order to then return in greater detail to the question of the subjective feeling of time pressure, the perception of time resources, and the tempo at which time transpires. In the last section of the chapter I work out a further dimension of the acceleration of the pace of life, which remains hidden at first, one that goes beyond modes of action and experience and relates to "modes of being," i.e., socially constitutive forms of identity. Their transformation turns out to be a cultural consequence of the acceleration of social change and the pace of life. It therefore represents a necessary effect of the "circle of acceleration" that will be presented in chapter 6 as a kind of summation of the previous considerations.

1. OBJECTIVE PARAMETERS: THE ESCALATION OF THE SPEED OF ACTION

In the dimension testable by the methods of quantitative empirical social research, the thesis of an acceleration of the pace of life postulates a heightening of the number of episodes of action and/or experience per unit of time. To this end, there are in principle three different but combinable strategies available: first, action itself can be accelerated (walk, eat, read faster); second, breaks and idle times can be reduced or eliminated; and, third, several actions can be performed simultaneously (multitasking). In their time use study Robinson and Godbey describe such strategies as "time-deepening" and add to them a fourth, namely, the replacement of slow activities by faster ones, for instance, cooking by calling for takeout pizza.[12]

In its general form, the thesis defended here states that *since the beginning of modernity the average pace of life has accelerated, though not in linear fashion but in phases interrupted by pauses and small trend reversals.*[13] By themselves, the length of the work day and the quantity of time free outside work tell us nothing about the pace of life. If people worked up to fourteen hours a day in early modernity, this does not mean that the speed of action and experience was particularly high. Presumably it was quite low, although long work hours may compel a thickening of action in the scarce hours of free time. On the other hand, the *intensification* of work and the closure of the "pores of the workday" observed by Karl Marx in the first volume of *Capital* form a splendid example of the first and second aforementioned strategies of acceleration; they are a direct consequence of the *shortening of the workday*.[14] Here, at the very least, the work-related tempo of life heightens as a direct result of the shortening of labor time in the capitalist economy, whereas the pace of life in leisure time is not correlated with the latter's length: it can sink or rise while leisure time increases; however, it displays a tendency to rise when material well-being does.[15] Insofar as feelings of time pressure and stress are indicators of an acceleration of the pace of life, their measurable increase alongside a shortening of work time in Western societies should not be surprising. The contradiction between these two quantities (growing stress despite rising free time), overemphasized by Robinson and Godbey, proves to be merely apparent after a closer analysis.

Numerous and diverse examples of all three (or four) strategies of temporal condensation can be found in everyday life, essays and op-eds, and works of cultural criticism. They run from guides to "power naps" and shortened and condensed "quality time" with the kids in the evening to speed reading and speed dating (a form of coupling in which potential "dates" are encountered, as it were, on an assembly line) on down to the drive-through funeral. English names are usually used for such innovations, perhaps because Americans are pioneers in this area too. Furthermore, one finds reports about the widespread tendency of, e.g., the length of performances of classical symphonies and plays as well as news reports on television and the radio to become shorter and shorter.[16] Even the speed of our talking has supposedly accelerated significantly: while this intuitively makes sense for radio and television and is surely easy to verify,[17] the result of a study by the political scientist Ulf Torgersen showed that the number of phonemes articulated per minute in the yearly budget debates of the Norwegian parliament continually rose between 1945 to 1995 from 584 to 863, an increase of almost 50 percent.[18]

As suggested above all by the works of Gerhard Schulze,[19] the pace of life, in particular in late modern society, is determined not only by the number of (active, objectively measurable) episodes of action but also by the quantity of (even passive, subjective) episodes of experience. For while not all experiences can be qualified as actions,[20] it is precisely the former whose quality and quantity make up the center of social life in the "experience society," according to Schulze, and provide it with, as it were, a focus for the definition of the good life: the cultural maxim of this society runs, if we follow Schulze, *the more episodes of experience that can be savored for the enrichment of one's inner life in less time, the better.*[21] However, independent of the question concerning this foundational cultural project (to which I will return in chapter 7.2), the thesis of the acceleration of the pace of life states that the number of episodes of experience per unit of time also increases, hence a kind of "compression of experience" occurs.

It is obvious that just such an idea already lay behind Simmel's definition of the tempo of life when he connects it to the heightening of the number and contrast of changing contents of consciousness. We can find a form of this compression of experience in, for instance, the shortening of the duration of ads on CNN in 1971 to 30 seconds, a brevity that was relatively avant-garde at the time, although today they only last 5 seconds. Thus the viewer is exposed every 5 seconds to completely different "contents of consciousness," each with their own fragments of narrative structure.[22] The switching is still faster in the case of contemporary TV "grazers," who change the channel on average every 2.7 seconds.[23] Someone who watches an ad-free channel for a while finds herself exposed to image editing that is essentially faster than it was even in the 1970s, for instance. If we assume Simmel's definition and an average length of time watching television of two hours per day, this finding can already be interpreted as a significant indication of an acceleration of the pace of life: from this perspective, the phenomenon observed with astonishment by Robinson and Godbey, namely, that the more time people spend in front of the television, the more they seem to complain about stress and lack of time, hardly seems paradoxical.[24]

Naturally one difficulty here is that it is unclear what can count as a self-contained episode of experience. Insofar as experiences are always also defined by their context and need narrative closure from subjects,[25] it may appear implausible to define every new ad or every narrative sequence as an episode of experience. But, even if one uses a broad definition of experiences, the assumption of a steady escalation of their episodic density remains plausible. The temporal structures of late modernity seem to be characterized in large measure by fragmentation, i.e., by the breaking down of series of actions and experiences into ever smaller sequences with shrinking windows of attention. Eriksen sees here an outstanding marker of the late modern "tyranny of the moment" that is caused by permanent availability for communication (and hence vulnerability to a variety of external interruptions), the flexibilization and deinstitutionalization of practices, and also excess information and material abundance. This creates a situation, "where both working time and leisure time are cut into pieces, where the intervals become smaller and smaller, where a growing number of events are squeezed into decreasing time slots."[26] Also of interest in this connection are multitasking phenomena: they force an alternation of consciousness among multiple action contexts per second such that they lead, as it were, to an overlapping of experiences as well as actions. Moreover, as we will see in the next section, there are empirical indications that the shortening and condensation of episodes of experience can lead to a significant transformation of the experience of time and to the perception that it is flowing faster.

In any case, it can hardly be doubted that a growing number of available and potentially interesting goods and pieces of information shortens the span of time that can be devoted to each particular object: if we dedicate a constant proportion of our time budget to reading books, listening to CDs, and answering e-mails, then the average length of time we can devote to each book, CD, or e-mail drops in line with the number of books and CDs we acquire (or borrow) per unit of time or the number of e-mails we receive and send.[27] Similarly, the amount of time we can allot to the dutiful perusal of an academic journal decreases in lockstep with the increase in the number of relevant journals: examples of these kinds of compulsions to accelerate can be multiplied at will, and they simply reveal, once again, how much the logics of escalation and acceleration are intertwined in modern society. Because the rates of escalation are higher than the rates of acceleration, a scarcity of time resources and a heightening of the tempo of life occur.

This is driven, moreover, by the fact that the required time for making rational and informed choices and for coordinating and synchronizing actions steadily increases. An escalating quantity of ever more complex goods and services, on the one hand, and the deregulation, flexibilization, and deroutinization of types of action (*Handlungspraktiken*), on the other, are equally responsible for this. The joint result is that decision-making processes themselves become ever more complex in view of the various options that arise ever more frequently within the course of life and everyday practice and therefore take more time because the consequences of decisions (and their interdependencies) become unforeseeable and force one to expend more and more on the acquisition and processing of information.[28] What results for our temporal practice is almost always a feeling of dissatisfaction: in the end, one makes either 1. an at least partially contingent decision on the basis of unsatisfactory information (e.g., "of course it's possible that another computer model at some other dealer's would be a better deal, but who wants to invest even more time in finding that out"—Linder views the capability of making *suggestion* into the functional equivalent of *information* as the secret mechanism of advertising)[29]—or 2. one meticulously gathers information and then later has the feeling that one spent way too much time on this one decision or 3. one avoids making a decision and sticks with one's present computer model, one's existing health insurance, one's old-fashioned savings account, etc.[30] According to Linder's analysis, this situation has as an inevitable consequence a diminished quality of individual decisions, i.e., their objective appropriateness; the requirements of temporal rationality force one into an increasing substantive irrationality.[31] As I would like to show in chapter 11, collective political decision-making processes find themselves in just the same kind of dilemma, which exerts an immense influence on the ability of society to steer itself and thus on its political self-understanding.

Meanwhile, the temporal deregulation and deinstitutionalization of numerous fields of activity in late modern society has massively heightened the cost of planning and thus the time required to coordinate and synchronize everyday sequences of action. The consequence of the surrender of collective rhythms and time structures is that daily, weekly, and yearly processes are no longer self-evidently prestructured,[32] but instead have to be repeatedly planned, negotiated, and agreed upon with cooperation partners all over again.[33] If neither sunrise and sunset (as was customary for centuries) nor the factory sirens and no longer even the television sign-off and sign-on can serve as routine initiators of getting up and going to bed, then every individual must plan and reflect and make such decisions for himself. "Today whoever gets out of bed with a good conscience, or is inclined to do so, needs a motive," remarks the time researcher Karlheinz Geißler.[34] The additional burden caused by such (temporally costly) decision and planning processes clarifies one of Arnold Gehlen's central arguments, namely, that social institutions perform an important burden-easing function in view of the essential openness of action and choice in human existence.[35] The contemporary social deinstitutionalization of numerous practices thus leads consistently to an *additional* (temporal and cognitive) burden, which significantly contributes to the scarcity of time resources and thereby to the heightening of the pace of life.

What is highly interesting with respect to the question of temporal rationality here are the interactions between the new possibilities of technological acceleration and flexible availability and social expectations. In fact, appointments today are themselves becoming increasingly "temporalized" in the sense that they no longer have to be fixed for certain ahead of time, but can be negotiated *on the move* by e-mail and cell phone ("let's meet around noon" versus "when I'm ready I'll call you to see if you've arrived"). In his comparative study of European, Japanese, and American patterns of time use, Manfred Garhammer has even derived the general tendency to replace activities with higher levels of time (and social) commitment by those with lower levels of commitment.[36] This raises planning costs and the time required for coordination enormously because the number of variables and contingencies proliferates, but it shortens waiting times and avoids temporal rigidities (e.g., the premature breaking off of the previous activity). In view of the ambivalent consequences for one's time budget, it would be, on the one hand, *rational in a higher-order sense* to save time and energy by doing without a "mobile" and flexible planning of appointments, but, on the other hand, with respect to concrete individual decisions it can be highly *irrational* to do so ("what do you mean you can't call me when you're ready?!"). In a similar way, it is highly irrational *not* to keep channel surfing when faced with a boring made-for-TV film; *not* to check one's messages all day long (and thus run the risk of missing something important), since e-mail connections take mere seconds; or even to routinely plan entire work days during which colleagues will be unavailable (and thereby create in a certain way a temporary, artifical oasis of deceleration in the sense defined above), something Luhmann proposes as a solution to the problem of the "tyranny of the moment."[37] If the most important conference of the year or the visit of a colleague from another country fell on just such a day, however, even the most convinced defender of this sort of rule would allow for an exception. Yet it is precisely the more undramatic everyday coordination problems that make such a strategy irrational and/or antisocial: "if you don't send me the attachment tomorrow, I'll miss my application deadline"; "if you don't come to our meeting down the corridor tomorrow, I'll have to make an additional trip to the city again two days from now." The costs of such macro time-saving strategies are, as a rule, too high for oneself and for others (contrary to most how-to guides on time management)[38]—unless, that is, one reinstitutionalized them as collectively binding.[39]

Finally, the technical acceleration of processes simultaneously changes the socially established standards of temporal rationality: to wait seven days for the answer to a letter taking eight days to arrive appears just as appropriate as the same length of time appears inappropriate when answering an e-mail that turns up in its recipient's mailbox after a few seconds. Technical acceleration does not force a heightening of the pace of life, but it changes the *temporal standards* that underlie our actions and plans.[40]

Unfortunately, in the usual time use studies all of these developments are basically not registered (which is why acceleration practically never shows up in the data records that have by now been systematically collected in all the large industrial countries). So whoever hopes to find systematic empirical evidence for such processes of compression and acceleration in the now over-flowing research on time use becomes bitterly disappointed. Time budgeting research in its present form concentrates on the *allocation of time* among actors and different fields of activity—i.e., on the question who performs what kind of activity for how long—and thereby ascertains the differences between various groups of the population, diachronic developmental trends in the rededication of time resources (where it finds, for instance, that the average time at theater visits has dropped slightly, while, in contrast, time spent in front of the computer has risen; although a bitter dispute regarding the development of the relation between work time and free time prevails),[41] and connections between work time behavior and free time behavior,[42] etc. However, the acceleration phenomena postulated here cannot be captured by the survey instruments designed for these questions. The total time available always amounts to twenty-four hours a day, so time saved on one activity (e.g., household chores) is spent on another (e.g., watching TV); as a result, one is always dealing with speed-indifferent zero-sum games.[43] Whether during work hours one works more and hence faster, during hours spent reading more is read, or in time spent communicating more contacts are made remains uninvestigated. Even the shortening of breaks and idle times, which can be easily ascertained with the help of time diaries, is made invisible partly by the researchers and partly by the respondents in that it is attributed to the sub-stantial fields of activity (e.g., transportation, sleep, or communication). Thus the question whether and to what extent there is an escalation of the episodic density of action and experience per unit of time cannot be answered using the time budget studies published so far.

Consequently, an urgent desideratum for scholarship is the development of innovative research designs that can systematically register the three (or four) diagnosed forms of acceleration: the speeding up of individual actions, the elimination of breaks, the temporal overlapping of activities (multitasking), and the replacement of temporally costly with time-saving activities. A fundamental problem here is the fact that statements about acceleration are relational and therefore can really be tested only by diachronic, iterated surveys (panel studies in particular).

In the absence of such studies, the only possibility that remains is to disclose acceleration processes *indirectly* by identifying shifts in time budgeting that can be interpreted as the shortening of action episodes. Time spent on personal regeneration (eating, sleeping, body care) offers a particularly good means for this: a shortening here suggests an inference of acceleration in the corresponding processes.

And, in fact, the existing studies are revealing in this respect: the previously justified supposition that the years of the digital and political revolutions around and after 1989 were characterized by a clear surge of acceleration seems to be reflected in the data from the large, countrywide U.S. time use study (the "Americans' Use of Time Project") from 1985 (n = 5, 300) and 1995 (n = 1, 200). During this period, in particular with respect to men, the time spent weekly on body care decreased by 2.2 hours, eating by 1.8 hours, and sleeping by a half hour, which suggests that the respondents ate, slept, and washed themselves faster (the data for women are -1.9 for body care, −1.5 for eating, but +1.3 for sleeping).[44] This result is confirmed by the European time use data analyzed by Garhammer, from which he likewise derives a clear trend toward a "compression of personal needs" and consequently an acceleration of corresponding activities.[45] Especially striking in this context is the finding that the average duration of sleep has fallen around 30 minutes since the 1970s and 2 hours (!) from the previous century.[46] Yet just this number makes clear the caution that is necessary when interpreting such results. For, in the first place, the number is contested by other researchers,[47] and, in the second place, it would be premature to interpret it as a symptom of a restless, nonstop society: it *could* also be simply an effect of the fact that heavy physical labor becomes rarer and people become older in postindustrial society and hence the "objective" need for sleep lessens.[48]

Moreover, the available data strengthen the postulated development in a further respect: the trends toward an increase in *multitasking* and a growing *fragmentation* of activities are by now quite uncontroversial.[49] Yet precisely this undermines the validity of time use studies: if several activities are performed in parallel within a given time frame (possibly without a clear hierarchization into primary, secondary, and tertiary activities), this poses notorious problems for the attribution of units of time. Even more serious are the consequences of the fragmentation of time and the dedifferentiating dissolution of boundaries between the types, sites, and times of activity: where professional work and household activities or child care as well as free time activities are all done at home, where leisure time activities are coordinated from the workplace, where, say, e-mails regarding matters of private and professional life as well as honorary offices or volunteer work are handled, and corresponding phone calls made, in no particular order, temporal accounting is significantly more difficult. It becomes near impossible where activities no longer permit any unambiguous classification because the spheres of work, family, and leisure time blur together to the point of indistinguishability. A person who listens to Beethoven at work but for this reason discovers the solution to her weightiest professional problem while at the concert hall and arranges her friendships and her free time in such a way that they constantly serve the advancement of her career by fulfilling the ever more important functions of networking just falls through the nets of time budget research.[50] It might very well turn out that the survey instruments of time use research are a manifestation of highly temporally differentiated "classical" modernity but are only of rather limited value for analysis of the time structures of late modernity.

In view of the current state of the evidence, then, it is all the more surprising that both the most comprehensive current time budget studies, Robinson and Godbey's *Time for Life: The Surprising Ways Americans Use Their Time* and Manfred Garhammer's *How Europeans Use Their Time* (*Wie Europäer ihre Zeit nutzen*), agree that acceleration and temporal compression are the main trends in the development of time use patterns and dedicate great attention to them—without, however, being able to be justify this using their data. Garhammer puts acceleration at the top of his summary list of the ten most important trends in the contemporary development of temporal structures, but, significantly, he refers in support of his diagnosis to, among others, Levine's study.[51] He designates compression, i.e., the shortening and simultaneous performance of activities, as a further main trend, which, according to the definition used here, can likewise serve as an indicator of an acceleration of the pace of life. Conversely, Robinson and Godbey dedicate a chapter to the diagnosis of an unprecedented acceleration of the tempo of life before laying out and discussing their empirical data and spend thirty full pages on the phenomena of temporal compression and time scarcity; nevertheless, they too fail to make any real connection to the time use data that follows.[52] On the contrary, their analysis of this data leads them to imply to the reader, against their own diagnosis, that the acceleration of the pace of life is (purely) a fact about subjective perceptions.[53] While I have argued that there is a massive and observable "objective" or material basis for the diagnosis of an acceleration of the tempo of life (though it remains to a great extent hidden in time use data), still there can be no doubt about Robinson and Godbey's conclusion that it is above all the experience of time that has changed as a result of altered practices in everyday life: *the quantitative heightening of the objective pace of life seems to lead to a qualitative transformation of the subjective experience of time.* This phenomenon, which cannot be explained solely with time budget research and the analysis of empirical evidence for acceleration, now needs to be subjected to a systematic investigation in the following section.

2. SUBJECTIVE PARAMETERS: TIME PRESSURE AND THE EXPERIENCE OF RACING TIME

As the conceptual discussion of social acceleration in chapter 2.1 has shown, the heightening of the pace of life is a paradoxical phenomenon in view of the continual technical acceleration of transportation, communication, and production. Technical acceleration shortens the time bound up in such processes and partially frees considerable time resources such that for a constant quantity of actions and experiences *more time* is available: thus one would expect a *slower pace of action, longer breaks,* and *less overlapping of actions.* For just this reason, the "problem of free time" was understood well into the 1960s not as that of, for instance, free time stress, but rather the "problem" that people (particularly the "uneducated masses," of course) do not have a clue what to do (rationally) with the "immense reserve capital of freed-up time" (as the *Bayerische Gewerbefreund* said in an article from 1848 entitled "Excess Steam and Excess Time")[54] that was always imagined as lying in the immediate future. Even in 1964 the cover of *Time* magazine read, "Americans Now Face a Glut of Leisure—the Task Ahead: How to Take Life Easy."[55]

In contrast, a heightening of the pace of life represents a reaction to a scarcity of time resources: for particular actions (or experiences) there is *less time* available than before. The simultaneous appearance of both forms of acceleration is conceivable only if there are *growth processes* in which an increase in the quantity of actions exceeds the increase in speeds of performance. Subjectively, i.e., in the way acting subjects experience time, such a scarcity of time resources is expressed in a feeling that *time passes more rapidly*,[56] but above all in the experience of a *lack of time* and stress and in the feeling that one does not "have" any time (unless the actors had been previously bored).

Now there can be little doubt that just this perception of time has almost continually increased in all Western industrial states since the beginning of corresponding surveys in the 1960s.[57] For instance, one gathers from the data reproduced in Robinson and Godbey's study of the U.S. national time budget surveys that the number of eighteen to sixty-four year olds who indicate they *always* feel in a hurry or under time pressure rose in stages between 1965 and 1992 from 24 percent to 38 percent, while the number of those who *almost never* felt under time pressure in the same period fell from 27 percent to 18 percent. In contrast, the number of respondents that indicated they *quite often* had free time resources ("time on your hands that you don't know what to do with") fell by more than half between 1965 and 1994 from 15 percent to 7 percent, while the percentage of those that answered the same question with *almost never* rose from 48 percent to 61 percent.[58] It seems beyond question that the increasing scarcity of time resources is documented in such numbers.

Nevertheless, Robinson and Godbey think they find increasing signs that the feeling of stress and time pressure as symptoms of increasingly scarce time resources has slightly but unmistakably diminished since the mid-1990s and that the numbers signal a trend reversal (the number of those that are *always in a hurry* dropped from 1992 to 1995 by 6 percent and the percentage of respondents who indicated they have *less free time than five years ago* dropped by nine points to 45 percent).[59] But, contrary to the interpretation of the authors, what is reflected therein is not a slowing down of the pace of life ("The Great American Slowdown"), but rather a subsiding of acceleration: time resources are just becoming scarce less rapidly. The sensation of stress expresses nothing about the *absolute* tempo of life, but only about its *change*. Therefore it is not at all surprising, though Robinson and Godbey suppose otherwise,[60] that the inhabitants of *Russia* give relatively high responses concerning the experience of stress and time pressure since 1990 (26 percent of Russian adults indicate, for instance, that they no longer have any time for amusements, compared with "only" 23 percent of Americans), although the pace of life in Russia is presumably still clearly slower than in the U.S.: the rate of acceleration in Russia may be significantly higher in the wake of the transformation after the end of the Soviet Union.

Robinson and Godbey's data still await confirmation by other studies, particularly from other industrial nations.[61] If they prove valid, they could be interpreted as an impressive confirmation of the thesis that around 1990 what is for the time being the last wave of acceleration reached its high point and has been ebbing since.

However, there is another surprising variant of the paradox introduced at the beginning of this section that is reflected in the data of the time use researchers: the dramatic rise in feelings of stress and lack of time between 1965 and 1995 is accompanied by an equally significant *increase in free time*, which already suggests a growth in free time resources. In time budget research, free time is normally not simply defined as time outside remunerated labor, but rather as the time resources that are not bound up in obligatory activities, and over which one may therefore dispose more or less at will, i.e., as time that remains left over after subtracting work time, family and household time (child raising, grocery shopping, housework), and personal care time (eating, sleeping, body care). This "free time" climbed continually between 1965 and 1995 for practically every population group, even for working women (by 5.6 hours per week in comparison to 10.3 hours for housewives; working men gained almost 6 hours of free time per week). Responsible for those figures are sinking work times and, above all, diminishing housework times that were more than able to offset the growth in paid labor time that has occurred in particular since the 1990s.[62] Here is the reason for Robinson and Godbey's assumption that the heightening of the pace of life might be overwhelmingly a problem of perception.

Even if the reflections of the last section have shown that the heightening of the tempo of life in the sense of a rise in the episodes of action and experience per unit of time can certainly be accompanied without contradiction by a lengthening of free time, it remains to be explained why respondents complain of growing *time pressure* and of being *compelled* to accelerate. In view of the data, the pace heightening per se is not astonishing, but the feeling of being rushed is. This is reflected in the finding that the respondents have the impression, in a certain way inversely proportional to the evidence, that their free time is constantly dwindling. Perplexingly, subjectively estimated free time decreases in parallel with the increase of "actual" free time. It not only often amounts to less than half the free time calculated using time journals, but even falls on average under the de facto time spent in front of the television![63] At first glance, the only thing that can be inferred from this with any certainty is that the observed free time is not experienced by actors as a reservoir of free time resources, but rather as a quickly passing quantity of time tied up in actions (and experiences).[64]

Starting with this paradox, and on the basis of reflections from social psychology and the philosophy of culture, I will try to find an explanation for the transformation of the modern (and a fortiori late modern) experience of time that is reflected in such findings and in doing so to ferret out its internal connection with the escalating density of action and experience.

In the first place, two natural causes for the feeling of time pressure are the *fear of missing out* and the *compulsion to adapt*, which have thoroughly distinct roots. The fear of missing (valuable) things and therefore the desire to heighten the pace of life are, as I will show in chapter 7.2, the result of a cultural program that began developing in early modernity and consists in making one's own life more fulfilled and richer in experience through an accelerated "savoring of worldly options"—i.e., by escalating the rate of experience—and thereby realizing a "good life." The cultural *promise of acceleration* lies in this idea. As a result subjects *want* to live faster.

In contrast, the *compulsion to adapt* is a consequence of the structural dynamic of late modern societies, more specifically of the acceleration of social change. As I have tried to demonstrate, the more rapid alteration of not just the material structures of the environment but also the patterns of relationship and structures of association, forms of practice and action orientations, unavoidably leads to an existential feeling of standing on slipping slopes, the "slipping slope syndrome." As a result of the "contraction of the present," in a dynamic society almost all one's stock of knowledge and property is constantly threatened with obsolescence. Even in those intervals of time during which a subject has free time resources at her disposal, her surroundings continue to change at a rapid pace. After they have passed, she will have fallen behind the times in many respects and consequently be compelled to catch up: for example, after eight days of vacation a scholar finds an overflowing e-mail account with queries of all kinds, a series of exams to be graded, an impressive number of new publications relevant to his research, new software and hardware offers, etc. It is easy to understand how the feeling of rapidly elapsing time emerges in a highly dynamic society, generating pressure even in periods free of work. The "objective flow of events" transpires more rapidly than the speed at which it can be reactively processed in one's own action and experience.[65] Herein lies modernity's structural compulsion to accelerate. As a result, subjects *must* live faster.

To decide whether the fear of missing out or the compulsion to adapt (which, naturally, cannot always be cleanly separated empirically) makes a stronger causal contribution to the acceleration of the pace of life, quantitative or standardized investigations of time allocation are insufficient, as even time use research has recognized by now.[66] Instead what can first shed light on this point is an analysis of the *motives* for respective (free time) activities and shifts in allocation.

Of course one must keep in mind here that time pressure has a positive connotation in the patterns of modern social recognition: not to have any time signals desirability and productivity. Time scarcity is therefore without doubt a communicatively strengthened, if not produced, phenomenon. However, it is entirely conceivable that the tempo-related pattern of distinction in the concept should be flipped around: if faster previously meant better because it signaled higher competencies and resources and thus an evolutionary and social advantage, then in late modern society slowness may definitely become a marker of distinction: whoever manages to leave oneself time, controls one's own availability, and enjoys free time resources has the advantage.

In any case, in the absence of systematic surveys on the matter, when it comes to explaining or justifying its allocation, the degree to which a vocabulary of *must* and *obligation* dominates the social semantics of free time is remarkable. In glaring contradiction to the prevailing ideology of individual freedom and the minimally restrictive ethical code of modern society, and in a way that cannot be explained simply by the social attractiveness of time scarcity, social actors surprisingly speak continually of their activities as obligatory: "I really have to read the newspaper again"; "I ought to finally do something for my fitness, buy new clothes, learn a foreign language, pay attention to my hobbies, meet up with my friends again, yes, go to the theater, take a vacation, etc."[67] It would hardly be surprising if this "must" semantics dominated nonproductive activities more strongly in Western societies than in any highly normatively regulated traditional society. It seems to be a natural reaction to the situation of living on slipping slopes: "we dance faster and faster just to stay in place"; it is becoming more and more difficult to stay *up to date*. "Daily life has become a sea of drowning demands, and there is no shore in sight," finds Kenneth Gergen, while Robinson and Godbey and the leisure time researcher Opaschowski agree in noting that there seems to be an exponential multiplication of the *necessary* and *indispensable* even in free time.[68] Moreover, insofar as the slopes become steeper, i.e., the rates of change increase, an inherent tendency toward a gradual shift in motives seems to develop: the rhetoric of the promise of acceleration is increasingly replaced on the individual and political level by that of the compulsion to adapt. In place of an orientation toward long-term goals there appears an effort to remain open to options and opportunities in a world characterized by change, contingency, and uncertainty.[69]

This suggests a speculative conjecture for which there are in any case several sources of empirical support: behind the striving to keep pace with change, and its resulting demands, and the attempt if not to increase the number of available options, which Heinz von Foerster calls the ethical categorical imperative of modernity,[70] then at least to maintain them in the face of the growing imponderability of both the world and one's own needs, activities that are held to be valuable or choiceworthy for their own sake disappear from view. No time is left over for "genuinely" valuable activities. This is at least as true of work as it is of free time. Everywhere it seems like there is no time available for long-term goals—in the example of the scholar, for instance, writing her new book—because of the constant pressure of little demands in the meantime, things which are very often directly related to keeping open opportunities. In support of this claim, which may at first glance appear unfounded, one can, first, identify a consequential principle of social functioning and, second, present some striking survey data.

Sequencing represents an almost natural means of weighting and ordering activities in accordance with their value.[71] Do the most important or valuable thing first, then the second most important, etc., and the less important things will get done if afterward there are still time resources available. In a functionally differentiated society with widely linked interaction chains, however, this ordering principle is replaced more and more by deadlines and appointments for coordinating and synchronizing action. In view of this prevailing *orientational primacy* of time, Luhmann states that "it seems as though the division of time has confounded the order of values."[72] "The power of the deadline" now determines the serial order of activities and, under conditions of scarce time resources, brings it about that goals that are not bound to deadlines or appointments are lost from view because the burden of what "has to get done (before)" smothers them, as it were—they leave behind only a vague feeling that one doesn't have time to do "anything" anymore. We are constantly "putting out the fires" that flare up again and again in the wake of the many-layered coordination imperatives of our activities and no longer get around to making, let alone pursuing, long-term objectives.[73] As Luhmann further observes, "the division of time and value judgments can no longer be separated [in the traditional way — H. R.]. The priority of deadlines flips over into a primacy of deadlines, into an evaluative choiceworthiness that is not in line with the rest of the values that one otherwise professes."[74] He thereby makes clear that a kind of duplication of the order of values occurs in light of these temporal structures. We "profess" the higher worth of certain activities or even ways of life (e.g., walking on the beach, going to the theater, civic engagement, playing the violin, writing a novel), although this "discursive" order of values is hardly reflected in the order of preferences expressed in our actual activities.

And just this has been confirmed by empirical surveys that connect time use data with questions of the quality of life. According to them, actors spend their time by and large on activities that they not only hold to be of little value, but that, according to their own reports (among others those recorded in time journals), also give them little satisfaction. This holds true in particular for watching TV: respondents not only value it least among all free time activities but also draw even less satisfaction from it than from work.[75] In a countrywide American survey, on a scale of satisfaction running from 1 to 10, TV received an average score of 4.8, in contrast to work at 7.0 (in 1975 even 8.0) or shopping (6.4 in the 1985 survey); in 1995 the female respondents at least actually drew more satisfaction from cleaning work around the house (5.6!) than from time spent in front of the TV, while men said they got more enjoyment from cooking (5.5) than from TV.[76] Yet inhabitants of Western industrial states devote on average almost 40 percent of their free time to just this activity: more than two hours a day and much more than any other free time activity. In contrast, only minimal (and in the years since 1965 tendentially decreasing) time resources are allocated to many activities that actors hold to be integral components of a "good life" and that in fact produce feelings of great satisfaction in them.[77] "In other words, the allocation of free time to such 'worthwhile' leisure activities as reading serious literature, engaging in community activities, or attending cultural events is a blip on the free-time radar screen," as Robinson and Godbey summarize their results and state an unmistakable *disparity* between what the actors say they like to do and what they actually do in spite of this.[78]

At first glance, though, this finding is, in *one* respect, strikingly opposed to the line of argument developed so far: the fact that the respondents can spend so much time on watching television, an activity that they themselves see as of little worth, seems incompatible with the thought that it is the *urgency of the fixed* term and time scarcity that hinder them in the pursuit of more satisfying activities. Yet a closer look reveals that this finding does not absolutely contradict that thesis, but may rather even lend it support. For, first, it is incontestable that TV is one of the few activities that can always be used to fill up short fragments of time and bridge gaps (i.e., breaks): it requires neither buildup nor follow-up. Quite logically, the studies also demonstrate that TV consumption during holidays, when free time resources are less fragmented, markedly declines (while the activities held to be more valuable come into their own), although free time resources increase.[79] Second, however, TV also requires only a minimal expenditure of psychological and physical energy. Leaving aside sleeping and dozing, no other activity calls for such comparatively low operative "input," which is why TV consumption is also generally seen as an especially "passive activity."[80] For this reason it seems (misleadingly) particularly well-suited to serve as an "activity" that can compensate for stressful everyday experiences under intense time pressure.[81] This corresponds to the observation of a "polarization" of everyday time into phases that are characterized as stressful, burdensome, and very demanding and complementary compensating times that are characterized by passivity.[82] Nietzsche already diagnosed this tendency of modern life to place subjects under stress and time pressure in such a way that when they at last have time for themselves what they want is "not only to let themselves go, but to *stretch out* at length as ungainly as they happen to be" (or even what Nietzsche couldn't yet do: watch TV).[83]

But, third, TV consumption thus represents one of those activities, so characteristic of late modern entertainment culture, in which the "input-output" relation is especially positive regarding immediate satisfaction: the TV promises "instant gratification" without previous expenditure of time and energy, an inestimable advantage in a society marked by high rates of change and oriented to short-run time horizons. Now one further factor is important for understanding the psychological attractions of TV (and other entertainment media designed for passive consumption): research subjects generally report distinctly higher satisfaction values *during* the activity of watching TV than after, and as a rule they *experience* viewing more positively than they judge it to be from a more distanced perspective with respect to a scale of activities held to be satisfying or worthwhile. The short-term experiential gain of TV is thus relatively high, though the "enduring" value is not: this is shown not merely "subjectively" in the low valuation of TV consumption in questionnaires but also in psychophysical investigations of mood, degree of contentment, and capacities of concentration and attention after the end of the activity; TV apparently tends to leave behind tired, hardly recuperated spectators who are in a bad mood.[84] In fact, the creeping "restructuring of the order of values by time problems" indicated by Luhmann might take place in cultural life in the following way: since the social structure rewards short-run orientations because of high rates of instability and change, and the entertainment industry opens up any number of literally "attractive" experiential possibilities that offer "instant gratification" with a favorable input-output relation, less and less time resources are expended for those activities held to be more valuable and satisfying on a cognitive, abstract level that require large or long-run investments of time and energy.[85] One may consider opera to be more valuable than a musical, but nevertheless go to the latter; judge a good restaurant to be more satisfying than McDonald's and still stop at the fast food chain; ascribe much value to playing the violin, but instead of that try out the latest CD releases at the cultural entertainment store; have experienced engagement with poetry as extraordinarily satisfying and still turn on the TV in its place; hold the writing of a novel to be the most worthwhile activity of all, but wind up playing a computer game while looking for the corresponding file; indeed, we might even be absolutely certain that we would get more from a demanding film classic than from a Hollywood action comedy and nevertheless buy tickets for the latter.

Thus in the long run the activities originally held to be worthwhile get forgotten and devalued: "tasks that are always at a disadvantage must in the end be devalued and ranked as less important in order to reconcile fate and meaning. Thus a restructuring of the order of values can result simply from time problems."[86]

Reflections of this kind naturally have an undertone of cultural criticism, but they are in accord with the finding that what actors hold to be valuable and experience as satisfying and what they *do* significantly diverge in Western industrial states. And anyone who wants to defend a diagnosis of cultural decline would do well, in my opinion, to give central place to an analysis of the dimension of time.

However, the indicated revision of the social order of values would be an unreflective and *unintended consequence* of temporal-structural social developments. A democratically constituted political community that wanted to hold fast to the idea of collective autonomy in the face of social processes that are taking on a life of their own (*sich verselbständigende*) could definitely come to the conclusion that it must counteract this politically. But it would have to resort to thoroughly ambivalent methods of binding itself in a deliberative democratic but, as it were, "auto-paternalistic" fashion in order to hinder the erosion of cultural practices that it views as valuable (and that need long-run investments of time) by an uncontrolled "market paternalism" that favors short-run realities.[87] Younger generations will involve themselves with (and hence experience the value of) practices that unfold over the long run and require large prior investments only if they are encouraged to do so by stable trust relationships and reliable role models. Moreover, trust relationships of this sort only develop in the long run. Therefore, what would be culturally required is, as it were, the establishment of "oases of deceleration" protected by the state, within which the corresponding experiences could be had.[88] However, the chances of such an intervention depend decisively on the structural presuppositions of a political steering of societal development. Yet these are noticeably worsening in contemporary society as a result of the acceleration-induced *desynchronization of functional spheres*, as I would like to demonstrate in part 4.

In any event, one can derive from these considerations an illuminating explanation for the widespread feeling of urgent time scarcity despite greater time resources: on account of the offerings (which function literally as psychophysical "attractors") of ample experiences with better input-output ratios and an immediate satisfaction of needs, there remains in late modern society no time for things that are held to be "really important"; *we literally never get to (do) them anymore*, even though we may console ourselves with the thought that we will at last take the time to do them *some other time*. For the time being we orient ourselves to the urgency of the fixed term—regardless of how great our free time resources may be. Thus, in a countrywide American study of participation in the arts from 1993, the majority of respondents indicated that their reason for staying away from cultural events and museums was that they "had no time" (this answer was four times more common than *lack of money*), even though, in agreement with the "more-more pattern," it was (even after controlling for education and income) precisely the people with the *fewest* uncommitted time resources (or the greatest number of work hours) who participated most frequently.[89] Nevertheless, that answer need not simply be a cheap excuse. Astonishingly, the feeling of time scarcity sets in whenever we take into consideration only the activities named first in each of the examples in the list given four paragraphs earlier but not the second, with which we spend far more time.

Moreover, Kubey and Csikszentmihalyi explain the differences in the long-run satisfaction values using the concept of *flow*. According to this idea, the most intensive (and enduring) feelings of happiness occur in the performance of activities that are done for their own sake, unencumbered by difficult circumstances, in which abilities and challenges are balanced at a high level: if we are not challenged, i.e., abilities clearly exceed the challenges, then boredom threatens; if, in contrast, we are overly challenged, we react with stress and anxiety. The higher the balanced level, the greater the chances of an experience of flow. Tennis or playing the violin, writing a novel, running a boarding school, or even learning to understand a complicated piece of twelve-tone music are good candidates for this. They all presuppose long-term investments and the readiness to delay gratification.[90]

One can certainly suppose that an elitist, culture-critical bias lies behind these reflections even if they are supported by empirical evidence. Nevertheless they have a highly interesting and until now unnoticed correlate in the paradoxes of temporal experience that may prove to be fruitful for the explanation of the sense of "racing time."

As Hans Castorp remarks in Thomas Mann's *Magic Mountain* and William James tries to justify psychologically, experienced time has the peculiar property of in a certain way "inverting" itself in memory when compared with lived experience: "In general, a time filled with varied and interesting experiences, seems short in passing, but long as we look back. On the other hand, a tract of time empty of experiences seems long in passing, but in retrospect short."[91] The experience of time thus yields either a *short-long* pattern (short experiential time, long remembered time) or a *long-short* pattern (long experiential, short remembered time). As a so-called *subjective paradox of time*, this phenomenon is well-documented and also entirely explicable: episodes of lived experience that are felt to be interesting leave behind more pronounced traces in memory than the boring ones, and their larger memory content operates as an *extension* of the remembered time and vice versa.[92]

On the other hand, a second phenomenon that runs contrary to this pattern has hardly been studied. I will call it, following Ariane Barth, the *television paradox*.[93] Time spent in front of the TV (for instance, watching a crime drama) displays all of the features of short experiential time (high stimulus density, emotional involvement—when the killer arrives or the shooter begins his penalty kick approach, one's heartbeat, blood pressure, and galvanic skin response change—and the feeling that time is "flying"),[94] but as soon as the TV is turned off, and especially later in memory, it behaves like long experiential time: it "leaves nothing behind." The remembered time rapidly shrinks, which is why test subjects often report a "great void" after the end of TV consumption that is surprising in light of the high density of experience. This may be in large measure responsible for the bad "mood values" after this activity. Kubey and Csikszentmihalyi quote for instance an English teacher who summarizes his experience as follows: "I find television almost irresistible. When the set is on, I cannot ignore it. I cannot turn it off. I feel sapped, willless, enervated. . . . So I sit there for hours and hours. . . . I remember when we first got the set I'd watch it for hours and hours, whenever I could, and I remember that feeling of tiredness and anxiety that always followed those orgies, *a sense of time terribly wasted*. It was like eating cotton candy; television promised so much richness, I couldn't wait for it, *and then it just evaporated into air. I remember feeling terribly drained after watching for a long time.*"[95]

Thus TV watching apparently tends to produce a *short-short* pattern that is novel and paradoxical relative to the "traditional" experiences of time, which is not to say that it always does: under certain conditions, to which I will return shortly, it can doubtless produce "normal" patterns of temporal experience. Unfortunately, methodologically rigorous empirical investigation of this TV effect remains for the time being an unfulfilled desideratum.[96]

However, presumably television is not the only activity that generates a short-short pattern. Computer games, for instance, seem even more relevant to the production of these patterns: they seduce players into occasionally hours-long feverish activity, with high stimulus density and a high degree of involvement, but at the point of departure (in particular, when one stops before reaching the goal of the game) an overpowering feeling of the "shrinkage" of time sets in. Interestingly, the "shut-down second," i.e., the short time the computer needs to end the program, is often felt to be unbearably long and extraordinarily torturous; perhaps because in it the "shrivelling up of time" is quite clearly experienced. So this short period may even behave in accordance with a long-long pattern where the flow of time seems to slow down, one that is otherwise well-documented as a mode of temporal experience in extreme situations or in decisive moments in sports.[97] Successful athletes supposedly possess the ability to perceive fast athletic happenings, as it were, in "slow motion" and therefore dispose over sufficient time to react. Presumably this experience of time is also unaltered in memory (table 5.1).

The question what time pattern a visit to the cinema leaves behind is instructive here. It seems that contextual conditions and the subjective *meaning* the film has for the moviegoer exert a decisive influence. This might actually also give us a crucial clue to an explanation of the television paradox: my conjecture is that in the case of television (and computer games) memory

TABLE 5.1 Paradoxes in the Experience of Time

	TIME IN LIVED EXPERIENCE	TIME IN MEMORY	EXAMPLE
Subjective time paradox	short	long	Vacation
	long	short	Waiting room
Television paradox	short	short	TV drama, computer game, experience of crises, sports, shutdown moment (?)
	long	long	

traces are erased so quickly because the experience is, first, desensualized and, second, as a rule decontextualized. *Desensualization* means here that it is exclusively sight and hearing that are addressed, while tactile sensations, smells (which are, as is well-known, of great significance for long-term memories), and tastes are absent. In addition, all stimuli come from a narrow, spatially limited "window." Relevant studies have shown that the degree of neural activation and brain functioning is, when compared to other activities, altered or limited.[98] Nevertheless it seems to me that the phenomenon of *decontextualization* is of even greater importance here: what happens on the screen does not stand in any relation to the rest of our experiences, moods, needs, desires, etc., and does not react to them; it is, in the narrative context of our life, almost completely "contextless" or unsituated and therefore cannot be transformed into the experiential constituents of our own identity and life history. They are stories of strangers without any internal connection to what we are doing before or afterward or what we believe ourselves to be, so "nothing remains behind." Things are different when, in contrast, such connections can be made: for instance, to *Star Wars* fans who live with and through their heroes, collect the memorabilia, read magazines, etc., watching the newest episode is *not* contextless. It can be narratively assimilated into the horizon of their life and identity with ease. So it stands to reason that in such cases the television or cinema experience follows the short-long pattern.

Moreover, the short-short pattern could prove to be very instructive regarding the (late) modern experience of "racing time." It is conceivable that everyday experience in contemporary society increasingly produces this temporal pattern because the episodes of experience that densely follow one another display a tendency toward decontextualization: lived experiences that are short, stimulation-rich, but remain isolated from each other, i.e., without any internal connection, and replace each other in rapid transitions such that time begins to race in a certain way "at both ends," that is, it elapses very fast *during* the activities, which are felt to be brief (and often stressful), but at the same time it seems in hindsight to "shrink" so that days and years hurry by as if in flight. In the end we have the feeling that we have hardly lived, although we may be old in years. Thus we lived, so to speak longer (objectively), and shorter (subjectively) at the same time.[99] Objective evidence that in contemporary society time in fact seems in retrospect to have gone by faster than expected is provided by an empirical study of Michael Flaherty with 366 experimental subjects from three age groups that were supposed to indicate how fast last year had gone for them on a five-point scale from 1 (very slow) to 5 (very fast).[100] The average answer turned out to have a value of 4.216, thus between *fast* and *very fast*![101]

One cause for the assumed decontextualization of episodes of action and experience might lie in the already discussed progressive destructuring of everyday life and the related permanent availability of other possibilities of action and experience. When ginger bread cakes, strawberries, and the possibility of going swimming are available 365 days of the year, they become detached from specific spatial, temporal, and social contexts and make a linkage of the experience bound up with them to further experiences and memories impossible or improbable.[102] In any case, this destructuring and decontextualization is making the centuries old (Judeo-Christian) proverb that there is "a (specific) time for everything" (and, one could add, a fixed *place*) increasingly obsolete: many things are becoming permanently available and almost arbitrarily combinable with other things.

In this context the cultural and historical-philosophical reflections of Walter Benjamin seem to be extraordinarily clear-eyed and far-seeing. He lays out the reasons why the incongruence of the space of experience and the horizon of expectations, on the one hand, and the accelerating succession and stringing together of noncumulative, isolated episodes of experience, on the other, lastingly alter the structure of subjective (temporal) experience.[103]

Benjamin diagnoses an advancing *loss of experience* (*Erfahrungsverlust*) in modern society that results from the inability of subjects to transform the variety of abrupt lived events (*Erlebnisse*) in everyday life (which was paradigmatically embodied for him as for Simmel in metropolitan life) into genuine experience (*Erfahrung*).[104] *Experience* is for Benjamin ineradicably linked to the embedding of what has been lived in an experienced history and a lived tradition. It emerges in an "appropriation" of what has been lived with the help of stable, narrative patterns anchored in memory and in the light of historically established, antecedent horizons of experience. So lived events can become experiences only if they can be placed in a meaningful relationship to an individual and collective past and future. As one can derive from this, genuine experiences enter into the identity of a person, his or her life history; memory traces of them are largely resistant to erosion. However, they become impossible in a world of permanently changing horizons of expectation and continuously reconstructed spaces of experience.[105] Therefore, the shorter the period of time in which the space of experience and the horizon of expectation are congruent (the present), and the greater the number of lived events per unit of time, the more improbable the transformation of lived events into experiences becomes.[106] Modern time is thus for Benjamin the time of *players*, devoid of experience and strung together as a chain of noncumulative, disconnected, and abrupt lived events from which no experiences result, but which subjects later try to recall with the help of "souvenirs" (also in the form of photos).[107] The activities of watching TV and playing computer games could be taken as paradigmatic for such a succession of isolated lived events: their nontranslatability into experience makes them remain mere episodes and thereby accelerates the erosion of the memory traces connected to them.

As these considerations show, the society characterized by the short-short pattern is a society *rich in lived events* but *devoid of experience*. Time slips through its hands like water at both ends—in living it and in remembering it. Thus one may conclude from the television paradox that, from the perspective of the subjective experience of time, the flow of time itself indeed accelerates for social-structural reasons.

3. TEMPORAL STRUCTURES AND SELF-RELATIONS

As part 2 has already shown, the processes of technical acceleration equally affect the relationships of subjects to space and time and to people and things, while the acceleration of the pace of life alters their action and experience by heightening the number of actions and lived events per unit of time. From this it necessarily follows that the modern acceleration dynamic not only transforms the way subjects *do* things but also the way they *are*, i.e., their identities or the way they relate to themselves, because these are constituted by those relationships and actions. Our sense of *who we are* is really a function of our relationship to space, to time, to our fellow human beings and the objects of our environment, and to our action and experience, and vice versa our identity is reflected in our actions and relationships: the two sides are thus interdependent.[108] In sociology the claim that social structure and the structures of the self are correlated with one another, so that, for instance, there must necessarily be some correspondence between societal modernization processes and the construction of subjective relations to self, is practically a truism.[109] As I stated in the introduction, my thesis is that temporal structures (of society and of subjects) are the precise link between the two sides and, as it were, guarantee their "structural coupling." So in this section it is now time to pursue the question concerning the ways in which transformed time structures find expression in modern and late modern forms of identity. Is there such a thing as a dynamization or acceleration of identity, of the relationship we have to ourselves, of our *way of being (Seinsweise)*?

To answer this question one should keep in mind that self-relations have an indissolubly temporal structure in which the past, present, and future of a subject are connected.[110] Who one is is always also defined by how one became it, what one was and could have been, and what one will be and wants to be. In every identity-constituting, narratively constructed life history it is not only the case that the past is reconstructed; at one and the same time the present is interpreted and a possible future is projected. Therefore, self-relations are always also relations to time, and they can exhibit large, culture-dependent variations. In some cultural milieus identity seems to be primarily developed through an orientation to the past and to traditions (and the obligations and status definitions derived from one's ancestry), while in other cultures meaning is shaped for the self by expectations and plans for the future (as a time to be consciously created or one that will be fulfilled like a destiny). By contrast, in a society where the past has lost its obligating power, while the future is conceived as unforeseeable and uncontrollable, "situational" or present-oriented patterns of identity dominate.[111] At the same time, in subjects' "daily identity work", several time horizons of differing scopes are constantly interwoven: the patterns of time and identity of the respective situation, of the given form of everyday practice, of the overarching perspective on one's own life as a whole, and, finally, of the historical epoch must continually be brought into accord with each other.[112] Transformations in society's temporal structures and horizons therefore exert an inescapable influence on the temporal structures of identity formation and maintenance. Furthermore, according to the thesis I develop in chapter 10, it is here more than anywhere else that one can discern a break between classical modernity and what one may label *late* or (depending on one's viewpoint) *post* modernity.

The diagnosed quickening of social change to an *intra*generational tempo and the accompanying escalation of contingency and instability are of fundamental importance for the transformation of the temporal structure of identities as a result of social acceleration. This is responsible for the fact noted by Lyotard, namely, that in "postmodernity" all identity-constituting relationships and statuses require a temporal marker: if families, occupations, residences, political and religious convictions and practices can *in principle* be changed or switched at any time, then one no longer *is* a baker, husband of X, New Yorker, conservative, and Catholic per se. Rather one is so for periods of an only vaguely foreseeable duration; one is all these things "for the moment," i.e., in a present that tends to shrink; one *was* something else and (possibly) *will be* someone else.[113] Social change is thereby shifted, as it were, into the identity of subjects. Of interest here are the questions whether those relationships can still in general define our identity and whether we disregard identity predicates in our self-description because they suggest a stability that cannot be made good: it is not that one *is* a baker, rather one *works* as one (for two years now); not that one *is* the husband of X, rather one lives with X; not that one *is* a New Yorker and conservative, rather one *lives* in New York (for the next few years) and *votes* for conservatives.[114]

In the end such a perspective leads to the thesis of a shrinkage of identity. The self collapses into an, as it were, predicateless "punctual self" that no longer identifies (without remainder) with its roles and relationships but instead takes on a more or less instrumental attitude toward them.[115]

More commonly, in identity research the observed change (whose magnitude and scope are, of course, heavily contested, though the developmental tendency cannot be doubted)[116] is interpreted as a *dynamization* of identity or the self: subjects are still defined by their roles, relationships, and convictions and acquire their self-understanding in and through them—they *are* still bakers, husbands, and Catholics—but the (substantial) identities that rest on these (including preferences and evaluative beliefs) are becoming temporally unstable. They tend to change from situation to situation and from context to context.[117] In chapter 10 I will show that these two diagnoses are not necessarily incompatible. They simply concern, as it were, the two distinct sides of the process of self-determination that can be expressed by "I determine myself." The subject side in this process (the *who* of identity) shrinks to a predicateless point, while the object side (the *what*) appears situationally fluid.[118]

The concept of a stable personal identity may thus prove to be a natural correlate of a type of social change whose pace is synchronized with the change of generations and hence a constitutive sign of classical modernity. In traditional societies with *lower* rates of change, individuals find themselves defined by antecedent, enduring structures and thus, in a certain way, by intergenerational identities, whereas stable, long-term individual identities cannot withstand the fast pace of change in late modern society and become, so to speak, broken up, such that intragenerational (or even intrapersonal) identity sequences arise. A highly dynamic society like that of late modernity therefore compels a corresponding dynamic in individuals' self-relations and patterns of identity by awarding flexibility and a willingness to change in contrast to inertia and continuity: subjects must either conceive themselves from the very beginning as open, flexible and eager to change or run the danger of suffering permanent frustration when their projected identities are threatened with failure by a quickly changing environment.

I will attempt to give a more detailed account of the kind of "situational" identity that results from this in part 4, which deals with the consequences of social acceleration. However, as a provisional finding one can state that the acceleration of the pace of life does in fact seem to imply something like a sequencing and dynamization of forms of existence: there is an acceleration not only of what individuals do and experience but also of what they *are*.

PART THREE

CAUSES

6

THE SPEEDING UP OF SOCIETY AS A SELF-PROPELLING PROCESS: THE CIRCLE OF ACCELERATION

WHY DOES PRACTICALLY "EVERYTHING" IN modern society seem to go faster and faster? As the discussion in chapter 2 revealed, this question is, at the very least, misleading as the starting point for an analysis of the modern acceleration dynamic. In the first place, not *everything* is accelerating: many things simply cannot be accelerated, and a whole series of processes are even slowing down. In the second place, not all observable acceleration processes are of the same kind: rather the three forms of social acceleration worked out here—the *technical acceleration* of goal-directed processes, the *acceleration of social change*, and the *acceleration of the pace of life*—must be logically and analytically distinguished from one another in a strict way. Not only can they not be reduced to each other, but they stand in frankly paradoxical relationships to each other, at least in the case of technical acceleration and the acceleration of the pace of life: by definition technical acceleration generates free time resources and therefore works against the scarcity of these resources and hence also the acceleration of the tempo of life. However, the analysis of the manifestations of social acceleration in the previous part of this work has brought to light a variety of *empirical* interactions and causal interdependencies among the three domains of phenomena defined by those forms. These empirical relationships need to be brought together and systematized in this chapter. This will yield our first answer to the question about the root or driving force of the seemingly ubiquitous dynamic of acceleration in modern society.

The thesis I would like to justify here is that *in the modern world social acceleration has become a self-propelling process* that places the three realms of acceleration into reciprocal relationships of mutual escalation. Therefore, within this circle acceleration always and inevitably produces *more* acceleration: it becomes a self-reinforcing "feedback system."

Since the causal chain we are investigating is circular in nature, analysis can begin at any given place. On heuristic grounds, however, it is most fruitful to look at the interactions in an order opposite to that in part 2 and start off with the problematized relationship between the pace of life and technical acceleration.

The social aim and the immediate effect of technical acceleration is *to save time*, i.e., to decrease the time required by certain processes and thereby create free time resources. This is the societal function of the acceleration of, for instance, transportation, communication, or production: the corresponding processes are shortened, and more time is available for other activities. Just for this reason it is an obvious social answer to the problem of time scarcity, though one which, as we have seen, causes a heightening of the pace of life. Actors react to the scarcity of time resources with a *compression of episodes of action*: they can achieve this by either implementing techniques of acceleration *or* by shortening breaks and by overlapping activities (multitasking).[1] Because the latter possibilities of acceleration are by nature limited, however, it is apparent that the *more scarce time resources become, the greater is the need for techniques and technologies of acceleration and hence the faster the pace of life becomes too.*

Therefore, the widespread sensation of stress and lack of time discussed in the last chapter (regardless of what their causes might be) and the scarcity of time resources of individual and collective actors *form a powerful mainspring for the process of technical and technological innovation aimed at the acceleration of goal-directed processes.* The greater the lack of time is, the stronger will be the call for faster transportation connections, faster computers, and shorter waiting times, and the more outrageous any imposed slowdowns will seem to be. Wherever it is *possible* to save time through improved techniques—even in administrative processes, in legislation, in education, indeed in recreation or entertainment—there is great social pressure to develop and implement them in order to have newly available freed-up time resources. In addition to this, the holding open of *future opportunities to accelerate*, e.g., by acquiring more powerful hardware, wider streets, greater energy storage, and so on, than one currently needs, likewise becomes an imperative of social action. A failure in this regard generally becomes costly (temporally and financially) for actors to bear in the long run. The expectation of technical acceleration (and the corresponding *quantitative growth* of transportation, information processing, energy demand, etc.) is thus, as it were, always already "built in" to the social and material infrastructure. *Technical acceleration is therefore a direct conse-*

quence of the scarcity of time resources and hence of the heightening of the pace of life (arrow 1 of the circle of acceleration in figure 6.1).

Moreover, the technical acceleration of goal-directed processes, and above all the introduction of new accelerating technologies, does not simply cause a quantitative change in the time resources necessary for their performance but also leads us to certain inflection points at which a fundamental *qualitative* transformation occurs in our relationship to space and time, to the world of objects, and to the social world, and hence to a change in our form of life, as the analysis of the corresponding acceleration processes in chapter 3 showed (cf. figure 3.2).

A mere passing glance at the historical impact that basic technological innovations in transportation, communication, and production had on forms of life in modernity makes the connection clear: as we already saw in the case of the railroad, adaptation to the possibilities of accelerated movement even demanded the development of new modes of perception and new psychophysical patterns of behavior in order the make the "high" speeds psychologically and physically tolerable as well as capable of being mentally processed.[2] Quite similar to this, psychologists and educators today claim that the rapid tempo of late modern information streams in the media lead to the formation of new capacities of simultaneous information processing in children and youth.[3]

The social effects of the mass diffusion of automobiles and hence individual transport several decades later have been by now well documented in the literature on the "automobile" society. Using them, one can demonstrate the acceleration-induced change in structures of association and patterns of relationship in particular: the introduction of the automobile transformed the spatiality of social relationships and geography of industrial society by allowing greater distances, for example, between residence and workplace and in this way massively influencing the layout of housing developments in cities, suburbs, and even rural areas.[4]

The transformation of work (and, as a result, social) relationships as a consequence of the acceleration of society's processes of production and hence its material "metabolism" during the *industrial revolution* requires no further discussion. Sociologists and historians have covered all the details many times over.[5]

The most recent and yet ongoing "wave of acceleration," the *digital revolution*, which began in the late twentieth century, is concentrated on the acceleration of streams of communication and information following the introduction of new computer and media technologies. Its repercussions on the social world are also serious in that they bring with them new occupational structures, new modes of production, altered patterns of communication, and a further round of time-space compression. The switchover from a quantitative escalation of speed to a qualitatively new social form can be given a particularly striking illustration in the transformation of the financial markets. The possibility of almost unhindered, worldwide financial transactions in mere seconds has drastically changed investment patterns, trading practices, opportunities for speculation, the relationship between monetary and fixed capital,[6] and, as a result, the political risks of economic action (as the crises in Mexico, Asia, and Argentina have made abundantly clear), and hence, finally, the maneuvering room for political action.[7] In light of such processes of change, social scientists like Castells or Eriksen have even diagnosed the completion of a new social revolution that is in no way less significant than the industrial revolution and, consequently, the emergence of a new form of society (*The Information Age*).[8]

Finally, as I tried to show in chapter 5.3, the change in our relationships to space, time, things, and other actors as a result of the technical acceleration of goal-directed processes is also accompanied by a transformation of the forms of subjectivity. Practices of socialization and subjectivation, and hence patterns of identity and personality structures, are a function of those relationships; if the latter change as a result of technical acceleration, then the former are influenced as well.[9]

At this point in the argument, however, it is undeniably clear that *technical and, above all, technological acceleration serves as a powerful driver of social change.* Its empirical-historical mechanisms lead to a constant alteration of practices and action orientations, of associational structures and patterns of relationship, and even of self-relations and psychophysical dispositions. However, in chapter 2 I defined the acceleration of social change as the escalation of the *tempo* at which just those structures and orientations—and hence social forms of life—change. Because the development and mass diffusion of technological innovations contributes immensely to the escalation of the corresponding rates of change, *the acceleration of social change is a direct (and, in the end, unavoidable) consequence of technical acceleration* (arrow 2 of the circle of acceleration in figure 6.1).[10]

Furthermore, the third and last of the constitutive interdependence relationships of the circle of acceleration involves the way in which the acceleration of social change implies a growing separation of the space of experience and the horizon of expectation and thus the shortening of the stability of time horizons in the sense of a "contraction of the present": the circumstances of action lose their constancy and situation definitions remain valid for ever shorter intervals of time. However, as we saw in the analysis of chapter 4, this leads to an existential situation characterized by the "slipping slope syndrome" not only for individual actors but also for organizations and institutions: horizons of expectation and experience must be continuously revised; actors see themselves compelled to keep pace with the rapid tempo of multidimensional change in their environment and successfully make corresponding adaptations. As we have seen, this brings about an erosion of all conceivable resting places: *standing still* inevitably becomes a form of *falling behind* not only in the economy but in all dimensions of social life. Consequently, there is an expansion of the scope of what is absolutely necessary, of the (adaptative) behaviors to be performed, as well as of the list of what is possible: for social actors (and systems) time becomes scarce.

The way time resources become scarce, as Luhmann already observed, is a consequence of the fact that there seems to be no time scarcity for changes in the environment, whereas the resources of each respective individual for processing these changes are inevitably limited: the time horizon (of each respective individual) and the ("objective") structure of expectations increasingly come apart,[11] or, in Blumenberg's categories, the *time of life* and the *time of the world* become more and more incongruent. For this reason, the always temporally costly attempt to culturally process accelerating social changes, i.e., to appropriate them in their historical meaning using narrative patterns of interpretation (a presupposition for the transformation of lived events into experiences), becomes ever more problematic.[12] Even where reactive action in the face of higher rates of change is still possible, where we, in Luhmann's words, "still function in cooperative contexts" and "transfer pieces of information from one work context into another," it becomes difficult to integrate developments into cultural world pictures, narratives, educational institutions, and patterns of interpretation. This dimension of time pressure is at the root of the culturally widespread idea that the world "no longer has time for words" or that philosophy is too slow for late modern society.[13] It is the meaning-processing property of the human being that makes it "antiquated," as Günther Anders already conjectured. He also expressed the structural ineliminability of the scarcity of time resources when he observed that in the modern world everything that requires a long time lasts too long, and everything that asks for time asks for too much time.[14]

However, the increasing scarcity of time resources necessarily and by definition leads to a heightening of the pace of life, i.e., to the compression of episodes of action and experience in the face of time pressure[15]: —*accelerated social change is therefore a potent driver of the acceleration of the pace of life.* The generalizable cause of the ubiquitous feeling of being, as it were, "always already too late" with respect to a "runaway world"[16] is not an individual or collective waste of time or "dawdling," but rather the growing structural incongruence of the time of the world and the time of life in the advance of modernization. *The heightening of the pace of life in view of newly scarce time resources is thus a direct (and in the end unavoidable) consequence of the acceleration of social change* (arrow 3 of the circle of acceleration in figure 6.1).

In light of this basic existential situation of scarce time resources, however, the demand for relief by the time-saving technical acceleration of all goal-directed processes seems like a strategy to which there are no cultural or structural alternatives—and the circle of acceleration thereby closes. Here lies a first and fundamental answer to the question why "everything" in modern society seems to get "faster and faster" or why speed, in Eriksen's formulation,[17] is "infectious": *in modernity social acceleration becomes a self-propelling process.*

The circle of acceleration is thus a good example of the divergence of individual and collective rationality: what appears to be a solution to the problem of time scarcity from a microsocial perspective—the technical acceleration of goal-directed processes—proves to be an essential element of its causation at the macrosocial level. In everyday practical contexts this state of affairs is reflected in our desire for the maximal acceleration of all routine processes, which implies that *everyone else* with whom we come into contact should

Driving Forces of Acceleration I: The Circle of Acceleration

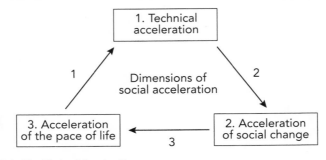

6.1. The Circle of Acceleration

hurry up as much as possible so that *we* can have some time—an obviously self-undermining strategy. As we have already seen, though, the paradoxical time-reducing effect of technical acceleration shows up in still another way in our everyday behaviors, namely, in the alteration of the implicit temporal standards and rationalities of action: we send an e-mail message instead of a letter because this saves time resources (and of course also mental energy) and thereby risk already getting an answer a few hours (instead of several days) later and hence once again being under pressure to act. As the line of argument developed here has shown, this is also a form of the "contraction of the present," one that harbors an inherent impulse toward the accelerated continuation of chains of communication and action.

However, this immediately raises the question at what point the self-propelling circle of acceleration can potentially be stopped or interrupted.[18] If we take a closer look, we see very quickly that the processes marked by arrows 2 and 3 are to a great extent immune from intentional control or steering: the effects of technical acceleration on our social practices and relationships are, as a rule, side effects of technical innovations that are just as unintended as they are inevitable. An interruption of the feedback systems at this point seems basically excluded from the start. This holds a fortiori for the ramifications that accelerated social change and the resulting contraction of the present have for our time resources: according to the logic of "slipping slopes," the increasing scarcity of time resources is unavoidable if actor orientations are to remain synchronized with structural developments.

Therefore, the process indicated by arrow 1 seems to be, as it were, the "natural" or predestined site for a (political) intervention into the now autonomous acceleration dynamic of modernity: the technical answer to the problem of increasingly scarce time resources is not logically compelling and seems accessible to intentional intervention. Nevertheless, the circle of acceleration turns out to be largely immune to *individual* attempts to interrupt it, *pace* the recommendations of self-help manuals. Whoever individually refrains from using time-saving techniques pays the price of a partial desynchronization: she cannot stay "up to date" and loses opportunities (which potentially become relevant to her later) because, for reasons of time, she must drop out of at least some contexts of interaction.

The alteration of temporal rationalities of action can thus make what was a sign of poverty and backwardness in the temporal daily life of early modernity and in "classical modernity," namely, *slowness* and temporary *unavailability*, appear to be an expensive time luxury in the late modern world. Imagine, for example, a remote farm in the Black Forest just a century ago: the next village was two hours away on foot, there was no car, no telephone, no television, no Internet connection, and perhaps not yet even any electricity. In contrast, someone who takes a trip to the Black Forest for a weekend today will be confronted with, say, the following "To-Do List": "When you arrive send me the file we're working on as an attachment. Call me sometime over the weekend. When you're in the Black Forest, you absolutely have to visit Freiburg, I mean it's at most an hour away. This weekend you'll finally have time to take a look at our Web site. On Sunday, by the way, there's an interesting show on channel such and such that's right in line with your topic, etc." In view of all this, a late modern weekend in the Black Forest *without* car, phone, or Internet connection represents a prime example of an "oasis of deceleration": it promises time for going on a walk, chopping wood, looking at the stars, etc.[19] The only ones who can manage this (especially on a repeated basis) are those who are not dependent on holding all options open and who can, possibly by letting others work for them, ensure that in the following week they can catch up on the accumulated "time arrears": one's e-mail account will be full, the call will be made as well as the visit; if the TV program is really important, one can get the DVD, etc. All this leads to a sharpened scarcity of time resources *outside* the oasis of deceleration and thus several opportunities will be irrevocably lost. And, even aside from this, someone who stops being available in this way has to reckon with social obligations of justification since the technological possibilities have been incorporated into social expectations: "how come you didn't visit me, call me, e-mail me?"

In view of the considerable costs of individual deceleration, a rational actor will presumably choose the option of spending a weekend on the farm that keeps open all the technically possible opportunities, though with a strong resolve not to use them. Yet the fact that it would be easy to "just quickly send off the attachment" or "watch just this one TV program" or "drive to Freiburg for just this one concert" significantly changes the cost-benefit calculation regarding the use of technology and thus also shifts the burden of justification *against* the intended deceleration. If the possibilities of acceleration are even available on site, the "oasis" can hardly be preserved.

As we have already seen with Luhmann, the only way to avoid the exhaustion of technically possible gains from acceleration is through "institutionalized excuses," i.e., collectively binding decisions. Thus it seems that the acceleration of goal-directed processes to the limits of what is technically (or financially) possible can only be prevented via the path of purposeful political intervention. This is why the establishment of new "oases of deceleration" and the protection of existing ones, as well as the creation of "political moratoria," i.e., artificial time delays or periods of recess, are central demands of the defenders of (at least a partial) social deceleration like Fritz Reheis, Matthias Eberling, Jeremy Rifkin, or Thomas H. Eriksen.[20] These can be interpreted as attempts to interrupt the structurally and culturally routinized circle of acceleration at the interface between the increasing scarcity of time resources and the effort to reclaim them through technical acceleration (designated by arrow 1 in figure 6.1).

Yet for two reasons that will be explored in the following chapters this enterprise proves to be much more difficult than many followers of the ideology of deceleration imagine. In the first place, social acceleration in modernity is not *only* driven by its own internal dynamic but also by, as it were, "external" cultural and structural causal factors that set the circle in motion and maintain and heat up the complex reciprocal dynamic of growth and acceleration even where it does not result from the feedback circle itself. The next chapter is dedicated to the identification of such external driving "motors" of social acceleration. Thus an intentional political interruption of the circle of acceleration must be capable of opposing the independent cultural and structural forces of acceleration and not just its internal dynamic.

In the second place, however, the idea of an intentional political interruption (or modification) of the circle of acceleration rests on the notion of a (preferably democratic) political steering of societal development. However, this very possibility is not without temporal presuppositions. On the contrary, a democratic self-steering and self-binding of society, as I will show in chapter 11, is dependent on cultural, structural, and institutional presuppositions that seem to be rapidly eroding in late modernity precisely as a consequence of social acceleration.[21] Therefore it is highly unlikely there can be an effective interruption of the circle of acceleration within the horizon of systemic processes of modernity that are taking on a life of their own (*sich verselbständigenden*). It would require a mobilization of just those forces and motivations that take the *project of modernity* to consist above all in the promise of (individual and) political autonomy.

7

ACCELERATION AND GROWTH: EXTERNAL DRIVING FORCES OF SOCIAL ACCELERATION

WHOEVER WANTS TO UNDERSTAND THE acceleration dynamic of modern society cannot avoid grappling with its *growth dynamic*, as the definition of the concept of acceleration in chapter 2.1 already shows. It is not a conceptual coincidence that a generalized concept of acceleration that covers all three of its dimensions can only be defined as *quantitative growth per unit of time*. In particular, it has been shown that, due to the relation between free time resources and bound ones, an acceleration of the pace of life is compatible with a simultaneously appearing technical acceleration of goal-directed processes only if there is a logically independent increase of quantities (of items transported, communicated, or produced or of actions and experiences). Time resources can become scarcer despite time savings only if the *rates of growth* exceed the *rates of acceleration* in the corresponding processes.[1] For this reason, I have characterized modern society specifically as an "acceleration society" in the sense that technical acceleration and the acceleration of the pace of life simultaneously appear in it: in other words, a connection between processes of growth and acceleration exists that is not logical or analytical, but rather *culturally or structurally grounded*. And in fact it is not at all difficult to identify relevant growth rates, among which one can reckon, for instance, the proliferation of options and contingencies, as well as that of goods and services, and the corresponding increase in possibilities of action and experience and the episodes related to these. There are actually good reasons to assume that in many respects an *exponential* quantitative growth has occurred rather than a "merely" linear acceleration.[2]

The question that stands at the center of part 3 of this work—what propels the acceleration process or, better, process*es* we find in modern society—is thus inevitably a question about the structural and/or cultural ways in which the quantitative logic of escalation and the acceleration dynamic of modernity are interwoven. The self-reinforcing circle of acceleration is not a sufficient answer here, since it can explain *growth processes* only to a very limited extent,[3] and we would anyway still be owed an account of what sets *it* in motion.

Therefore, in what follows I will first identify three social motors that are, as it were, "external" in the sense that they are analytically independent both from each other and from the circle of acceleration. They each link together the moments of escalation and acceleration in their own specific way and can be respectively classified as the primary driving force of one of the three dimensions of acceleration (cf. figure 7.1). Then in the following chapter I will take up the role played by the national state and the military in the acceleration process of modernity recently highlighted by writers like Paul Virilio, Anthony Giddens, and William Scheuerman and attempt to give a more precise account of it in the context of the theory developed here.

1. TIME IS MONEY: THE ECONOMIC MOTOR

One does not in fact have to look very long to identify a constitutive element of modern society that unites within itself both principles—acceleration and quantitative escalation or *acceleration for the purpose of escalation*—and binds them together in a common logic of action. In the capitalist economic system acceleration becomes an inescapable compulsion embedded in the material structures of society. The dissolution of the traditional, natural, so to speak, connection between production and the satisfaction of needs or meeting of requirements in the wake of the conversion of the economy to the logic of capital valorization or the production of surplus value—i.e., the replacement of production for (traditionally defined) needs by "production for production"[4]—set in motion a dynamic that overcomes all the limits of an economic form oriented to the satisfaction of needs. It allows the escalation of production and productivity, and thus the striving for time advantages (*Vorsprünge*) and time efficiency, to become inescapable systemic imperatives of a production process that develops independently of other social values (*sich verselbständigenden*) and, as it were, coproduces matching needs.

As a striking series of studies in the sociology of time has worked out in painstaking detail,[5] the concept of time that is "operative" in modern society is decisively shaped and formed by the reification and *commodification* of time characteristic of the capitalist production process,[6] i.e., by its transformation into a scarce good to be managed from the standpoint of efficiency, which is responsible for the fact that time is experienced as a linear, abstract magnitude without any qualities.[7] It is now "time" itself that the capitalist entrepreneur buys from his employees and no longer the product of their labor.

In this vein, capitalist economic activity constitutively rests in at least three respects on the acquisition and exploitation of time advantages, such that Marx's dictum that "in the final analysis, all forms of economics can be reduced to an economics of time" holds true in a very specific way for this economic form,[8] which is summarized in Benjamin Franklin's well-known formula, "Time is Money": "when time is money, speed becomes an absolute and unassailable imperative for business."[9] If one follows the analysis suggested by Marx, then in the first place *labor time* directly constitutes a decisive, i.e., value-creating, factor of production, as time is transformed by work into value.[10] Insofar as the exchange value of a commodity is determined by the (socially necessary) labor time embodied in it, the economization of production time can be immediately translated into (relative) profit: whoever is able to produce a commodity in less time, that is, less than the average labor time required, generates potentially higher profits and thus increases the "surplus value" of work (i.e., the ratio of "necessary" (and hence paid) work to "surplus labor" within one work day shifts in favor of the latter). Therefore an increase in *productivity*, which can indeed be defined as a *quantitative increase of output per unit of time* (e.g., per hour worked) and thus as *acceleration*, produces competitive advantages—but only up to the time at which the competition follows suit and the socially necessary labor time is depressed to the new amount, which unleashes a potentially endless spiral of acceleration.[11] Thus the acceleration of production, for example, through the intensification or "compression" of work, becomes a basic element of capitalist economic activity as result of the principle of competition.

In the second place, this is connected to the fact that the acquisition and exploitation of time advantages through the introduction of new production technologies or new products is of fundamental importance for the generation of the "surplus profits" necessary for survival in the struggle of competition, i.e., for the possibility of selling products for a short period of time at clearly higher prices than the costs of production or producing them at less than market value before the competition catches up. Here we have the "systemically conditioned" causes of the acceleration of innovation cycles and of technical progress as well as the shortening of product life cycles.[12]

Finally, in the third place, in virtue of the principle of interest,[13] and the "moral wear" of machines and facilities (i.e., due to the probability, constantly increasing in the wake of the acceleration dynamic, that machines will become economically worthless in light of the development of more efficient production technologies before they become unusable as a result of material wear and tear),[14] the accelerated reproduction of invested capital becomes necessary from a business point of view. The longer it takes to reproduce invested capital, the smaller the profits are and the worse the competitive odds become. The result of this is the necessity for the longest possible, and preferably continual, machine operating time. As Marx already noted, the capitalist economics of time therefore provides *one* explanation for the paradoxical link between the introduction of time-saving technologies and the consequent increasing scarcity of time resources, i.e., the heightening of the pace of life: "hence too the economic paradox that the most powerful instrument for reducing labor-time suffers a dialectical inversion and becomes the most unfailing means for turning the whole lifetime of the worker and his family into labor time at capital's disposal for its own valorization."[15] What Marx observes here is in fact a production-technical "circle of acceleration" in which faster machines bring in train an intensification of work, something that at least in the long run requires a shortening of the work day and thus in turn motivates the development of faster machines or technologies.

However, the dynamizing element of capitalism extends beyond the sphere of production. For the acceleration of production due to the capitalist economics of time necessarily requires the simultaneous acceleration of *distribution* and (at least when the possibility of opening up new markets is exhausted) *consumption*. This is of decisive importance for the constitutive connection between the capitalist economic form and the acceleration dynamic of modernity. Indeed, the tempo of the capital valorization process depends decisively on the speed of circulation, i.e., above all the transportation, storage, distribution, and sale of goods as well as the procurement of raw materials. Since no value is created here (rather, the realization of created surplus value is delayed) circulation time appears to be a "time of devalorization" according to Marx.[16] Hence the compulsion to accelerate weighs quite heavily on it.

Of particular interest with respect to the *genesis* of the modern dynamic of acceleration is the fact that from a historical point of view acceleration driven by the logic of capital valorization began not in the sphere of production but precisely in the spheres of distribution and circulation: as we have already seen, transportation and communication noticeably accelerate from the seventeenth century onward, long before the great technological innovations that led to the acceleration of production processes. One essential reason for this is that in the sixteenth and seventeenth centuries capital first accumulated in the area of trade, that is, in the sphere of circulation. This created a pressure to increase the speed of shipping because subsistence economies and guild systems at first prevented a corresponding development in the realm of production.[17] Thus, the acceleration of trade and transport historically precedes the acceleration of production, which first achieved its dramatic highpoint later in the industrial revolution. As a cursory glance at the breathtaking change and massively increased transaction speeds in the financial markets quickly makes clear, the progressive development of the monetary system functioned as a cardinal accelerator here, a development that is not yet finished.[18]

The escalation in the turnover of capital and commodities per unit of time, as an escalation of the rate of production, has a necessary economic correlate in a resulting increase in consumption acts per unit of time, since surplus value is first realized in consumption. Therefore the capitalist economics of time "forces" an escalation of the intensity of consumption analogous to that in the production process. It can thus be used to decipher the multiplication of episodes of action and experience per unit of time, i.e., the heightening of the pace of life, as an economic necessity. From a national-economic point of view, it is significant that the basic economic problem of a capitalist economy is not a (static) problem of distribution but rather one of maintaining accelerated circulation. Of course this systemic necessity cannot explain the corresponding escalation of the pace of life on the *consumption side* in an action-theoretical way: no one is compelled to increase the "number of acts of need-satisfaction per unit of time," and hence to measure the value of free time using that increased rate, on economic grounds.[19] The fact that people in modern society are inclined to this kind of valuation is neither an anthropological given, as Linder seems to assume,[20] nor simply derivable as an economic necessity, as Scharf implies.[21] Rather, its explanation requires a reconstruction of the cultural foundations of the individual action orientations that are characteristic of modernity.[22] In the next chapter I work out a sketch of a corresponding "cultural logic" of acceleration that is indispensable for a synchronization of systemic and individual time horizons.

However, the formation of this kind of time orientation is in any event tightly linked to the internalization of the concept of linear, abstract time by subjects and the transfer of economic norms of time use in the world of work to other domains of social life. As I tried to show in the introduction, it is in the first place time structures that represent the site of mediation between systemic imperatives and subjective action orientations (by way of synchronization). Consequently, a transformation of time horizons in the economy is necessarily accompanied by a corresponding alteration in the temporal action orientations of individuals. In fact, the compulsion to manage time resources efficiently that results from the capitalist economics of time began to impact the form and substance of the predominant temporal practices, perceptions, and orientations of the working population in a massive and wide-ranging way in the wake of industrialization. This reorganization, which was accompanied by hard-fought social struggles and, as E. P. Thompson demonstrated in an oft-cited essay on "Time, Work-Discipline and Industrial Capitalism,"[23] often implemented with every available means of coercion, resulted in the adaptation of subjective dispositions to the acceleration imperatives of the economic system. It was reflected in a *threefold decoupling* of industrial work time from traditional time patterns of everyday life.

1. In the first place, the time of wage labor was bound to the standards of the mechanical clock and thus completely separated from the rhythms of nature that had structured social life, at least in the temperate latitudes, for centuries if not millennia. Times of day, seasons, and the weather in principle no longer play a role for the industrial production process. This decoupling is visible in a particularly drastic form in *shift work*, which is, as Marx underscores in *Capital*, an, as it were, natural consequence of the fact that time remains *without qualities* in the capitalist economy: it runs during the day and at night, in summers as in winters, at the same pace and in a linear fashion, and it is always true that an hour in which the machines stand still and nothing is worked on, transported, or sold is economically a lost hour. "Capitalist production therefore drives, by its inherent nature, towards an appropriation of labor throughout all 24 hours of the day," as Marx logically concluded.[24] This is the economic core of a continuing process in which collective social rhythms of production, circulation, and consumption are dissolved in favor of a "qualityless," perpetual time of simultaneity. While natural collective rhythms were its first victims, later on newly emergent social rhythms in all three domains also fell under pressure (e.g., work time and free time, weekends and work days, business hours and closing times, on-air times and off-air times, in short: times of availability and times of nonavailability).

2. At the same time, in the course of industrialization a strict and almost complete temporal and spatial separation of work and free time developed, which had wide-ranging consequences for the temporal experience and planning of individuals and for the time structures of modern society as a whole. It was only once this separation was carried out that the institutions of "leisure time" and "work time" that are characteristic of modernity could emerge. These institutions then restructured, to varying extents, the lifestyle and conduct of subjects and hence the forms in which they sought to bring everyday time, the time of life, and historical time into accord. In this way the spatial and temporal separation of work and private life also had wide-ranging political consequences, which are revealed for instance in the specific boundary lines drawn between the *public* and the *private* in modernity.[25]

3. Finally, work time was decoupled from the object of work, i.e., it was arranged according to abstract periods determined by the calendar and the clock that were no longer dependent on the relevant tasks or events (through which activities in traditional and particularly in agrarian societies were and are temporally structured). The beginning and ending of work time was from then on fixed by the factory sirens or the time stamp clock and not by the requirements of the task at hand. Traditional "event time," according to which the duration and tempo of activities and events is set by their naturally or historically determined character or by an "intrinsic temporality" (*Eigenzeit*) subject to all kinds of fluctuations, is replaced by an abstract, linear time grid by means of which the temporal framing of activities and events is fixed in advance. This substitution is a presupposition for planning and thereby temporally manipulating and hence accelerating social processes. It shifts the temporal focus of attention from a task or event orientation to an abstract time orientation.[26] The time of industrial capitalism thus presents itself as both an *abstract, linear* time and, at the same time, a *polarized* one, something made clear in, for example, the struggles concerning the workday. As Anthony Giddens repeatedly and correctly emphasizes, it is determined, on the one hand, by the temporal economy of capitalism and, on the other, by the specifically technical logic of industrial production.[27]

The implementation of fixed work times and temporal rhythms in the factories during the industrial revolution was at times met with heavy resistance: for instance, workers destroyed the factory clocks as the central symbol of this social development or stopped the assembly line by stubbornly going on strike and thereafter were made to feel the full sanctioning violence of the new regime of production.[28] Far more important and consequential for the internalization of the new concept of time than direct *coercion*, however, were and are all the institutions of modern society in which corresponding orientations and practices are inculcated as *habits*, for instance (along with the factories), hospitals, prisons, asylums, kindergartens, and, above all, schools.[29] On a closer look time proves to be the main instrument of the disciplinary society analyzed in particular by Michel Foucault. Adherence to strict time discipline plays an outstanding role in all the aforementioned institutions. Their patterns of activity are constantly determined according to a usually very rigid, abstract time schema (one thinks of the time intervals of class schedules, train schedules, prison sentences, etc.) and time discipline appears to be a central goal of their disciplinary work. Clocks represent the surveillance instrument par excellence here because they break up *intrinsic rhythms* (*Eigenrhythmen*) defined by human nature and custom; they are also in this sense a precondition for unleashing the acceleration and growth dynamic of modernity, which led Lewis Mumford to his well-known observation that the *clock*, and not, for instance, the *steam engine*, was the "key-machine" of the industrial age.[30] The time discipline to be inscribed into the very body consists in the first place in the ability to orient one's own action according to an abstract time schema, that is, to be *punctual* and to defer given needs (e.g., sleep, hunger, or the urge to go to the bathroom) and give priority to the instructions of a fixed time schema, hence to delay gratification, to supress impulses, to condition peak performance and phases of recuperation on abstract time intervals, etc.[31]

Now this is by no means to assert that these social institutions and the time orientations imparted by them are exclusively a consequence and side effect of the capitalist organization of the economy in the sense of, say, a base/superstructure relationship. As remains to be shown, they are to the same extent side effects and requirements of functional differentiation (which is unthinkable without an orientation to abstract time grids for the coordination and synchronization of actions), the political organization and rationality of the national state and the military, and also the specifically Western culture of rationalism. The characteristic nexus of modern institutions is only formed by the union of these elements following the pattern of "elective affinities" worked out by Weber.[32] Insofar as one must assume that ideas and institutions evolve and change in a coevolutionary process of reciprocal and interdependent adjustment, the postulation of a monocausal or unilinear priority of economic, social-structural, or cultural development is avoided here.[33] We can also disregard the identification of a primary driving factor by some kind of philosophy of history because the tendency toward social acceleration pertains to the structural and cultural configuration *as a whole* and is inscribed into all of its parts equally.

Nevertheless, the economics of time in the competitive logic of capitalist economic activity is indisputably a primary and direct driver of technical and technological acceleration: it is the most prominent cause of the undeviating acceleration of transportation, communication, and production. The pressure to accelerate that issues from it quite evidently does not limit itself to the realm of technological innovation but extends to developments in the organization of work and from there as it were "radiates" into other spheres of society, into modern administration, the development of society, the adjustment of law, etc. In the final analysis the tremendous technical revolutions of early modernity stand in service of the clock and not vice versa: they enable (time efficient) acceleration. So behind the *logic of technology* that dominates industrial society stands the *logic of the clock*, which certainly lends plausibility to Paul Virilio's thesis that the "dromocratic revolution" is more profound and more comprehensive (as well as earlier) than the industrial one and marks its actual birthplace.[34]

The assumption that the acceleration dynamic of modernity undergirds its institutional arrangement, as opposed to growing out of the latter, quickly becomes more credible when we look at the institutional transformations of contemporary postindustrial societies under the pressure of "globalization." It turns out that the classical modern work time regime, and with it at least two of the three temporal "decouplings" of industrialized modernity discussed, is on the point of regressing to (what appear to be at first glance) precapitalist patterns.

According to the findings of contemporary industrial and work sociology,[35] current trends toward *flexible production*, spatial and temporal *deregulation*, and "just in time" preparation and delivery tend to erode the rigid regime of normal working time, to unmistakably introduce elements of task or event orientation into the work sphere once again and to effect a gradual spatial and temporal *dedifferentiation* of work and "life" or free time. This is particularly but not only true of new occupations, for instance, the working world of the so-called New Economy, and for highly qualified employees. With ever greater frequency, "work" in the late modern society is no longer over when the clock strikes five or the calendar announces the weekend, but rather when the appointed task is complete: and as a rule that means when the deadline is met or the terms of the project contract are fulfilled.[36] As a matter of fact conventional manufacturers have also begun to transition toward doing away with their factory and time stamp clocks and even their procedures for monitoring presence. The workload is thus no longer prescribed by the clock, but rather by the object once again, i.e., it is defined and oriented by tasks and events, which, from the perspective of Marxist-inspired industrial sociology, is tantamount to an almost unthinkable revolution in capitalism.[37] As an apparent return to premodern relationships, this inversion of capitalist time practices is just as striking as the recent spatial and temporal dedifferentiation of the spheres of life. In late modernity the job tends to become once again a part of the lifeworld and vice versa: work is taken home or even generally done there and lifeworld desires and claims are channeled back into the sphere of work. A paradigmatic example for the first development is so-called telework, or telecommuting, although its level of diffusion, in contrast to the amount of scholarly attention it has received, is still not very great.[38] Representative of the latter development are the efforts of many firms to enable their employees to bring their kids to work or to satisfy cultural and athletic needs there and thus promote new forms of operational "community."[39] In this way (as well as through a certain social softening up of, for instance, holiday hours and closing times) the boundaries between work time and free time once again become permeable and novel mixtures of public and private or work-related and personal interests emerge.[40]

This development testifies to the enormous mutability of capitalism, the transformative capacity and polymorphism of which have led some in recent times to place in question the unity or unitary developmental logic of "the" capitalist economic form in general.[41] In my view, however, this doubt is just the consequence of a one-sided analytical perspective.[42] The attempt to determine the historical meaning of this mode of production and its relevance for modern society and the modern form of life can in principle be developed in two directions. In the variant that has mostly dominated the social-scientific and political debate about capitalism, the focus is on the social *breaks, divisions*, and *contradictions* that accompany this economic form, in particular those between classes and strata or between developed and "backward" nations.[43]

In contrast, the other rather neglected direction of analysis concentrates on the formative elements that determine the form of life and dynamic of modern society above and beyond class boundaries. With respect to the topic of this book, the necessity of a renewed social-scientific engagement with capitalism primarily from this latter perspective seems to me to be obvious. For a closer analysis reveals that, far more than class oppositions and the related societal contradictions, it is the *compulsions and promises of growth and acceleration* inherent in the capitalist economy that shape modern society and its form of life in an ever intensifying way. These two principles of escalation, which converge in the capitalist economics of time, have endured through every historical transformation of capitalism. In liberal capitalist societies they shape culture and are formative aspects of social structure even if class oppositions have become more fluid, owners of the means of production and proletarians can no longer be distinguished, and a "revolutionary subject" is nowhere to be found. They exert an enormous influence on which forms of life and which societal projects are conceivable and feasible.[44]

So what remains unchanged beneath late modern developments and runs through the various forms of capitalist production like a common thread is the validity of the temporal economic imperative, and particularly the logic of acceleration, which as much as ever does the trailblazing work through and behind all the much admired flexibility and variability of capitalism, even though this logic leads to different arrangements in different historical, geographical, and cultural contexts, i.e., produces "Rheinland," "Anglo-Saxon," and "Asian" versions of capitalism.[45] What connects all these versions is their subordination to the laws of the capitalist economics of time, although it stands to reason that their horizons of calculation vary greatly in temporal extension. Thus Anglo-Saxon capitalism counts as oriented toward short-term, the Rheinland model, in contrast, as oriented toward long-term increases in efficiency.[46] If, as is often postulated, the first model in fact triumphs worldwide in the wake of "globalization," then from a temporal perspective this would be in a certain way tantamount to a shortening of the horizon of acceleration.

From this angle an astonishing view of the developmental dynamic of the capitalist system opens up: in analogy to Marx's account of the historical relation of the forces and relations of production, the striking impression arises that the escalation of speed or growth in the forces of acceleration is the genuine driving element of (capitalist) history. For the pressure to accelerate continually produces new time practices and institutions that can further heighten the acceleration dynamic for a while before they themselves run up against their speed limits, i.e., become hindrances to acceleration, and are therefore "overcome" in the end by the forces of acceleration that they themselves unleashed.

From this perspective the institutionalization of formal, strictly linear, abstract time in the age of industrialization and the accompanying strict spatiotemporal separation of work and "life" appear to be a "lever" for setting in motion a process of unimaginable acceleration, first in production and circulation and then in the life of society as a whole. The unfolding of acceleration potentials here rests precisely on unburdening the differentiated sphere of work from lifeworld interests: the closing of the "pores of the work day" was first made possible by their strict exclusion. With this move an economic temporal rationality could be fully implemented without hindrance in the sphere of work. Fordism and Taylorism and the work of the REFA and "methods-time measurement" engineers optimized time efficiency in a way possible only under the conditions of a "system of paid indifference,"[47] i.e., in a working world "purified" of all lifeworld, private, and subjective reference points. On the other hand, for subjects this strict separation of functions and spheres had the advantage of disburdening the private sphere, or the "lifeworld" in Habermas's sense, of economic demands and requirements (of instrumental-strategic rationalization).[48] Consequently, the most important question in the economic struggle between capital and labor in the industrialized "classical" modernity shaped by this work time regime was how much weight should be placed on the respective spheres, that is, how long work time should be.[49]

Moreover, in the late twentieth century the accelerative possibilities of the Fordist-Taylorist regime proved to be exhausted. The institutional work regime bound up with it mutated, as it were, from a time-economic "accelerator" into a "brake."[50]

If the work regime of classical modernity achieved an intensification of work (and hence an increase of productivity or acceleration) by excluding potentially retardant subjective *questions of meaning* and decelerative lifeworld practices, a situation now looms in which the economic dynamic is only possible by inverting the former process, i.e., re-subjectifying work and "colonizing" lifeworld competences and resources by sublating the separation of the spheres. Today work can be intensified when the firm consciously promotes the channeling of subjective motivational energies and abilities into the workplace and thereby takes into account the "intrinsic temporalities" (*Eigenzeiten*), individual rhythms, and spatiotemporal needs of subjects. For instance, when a project deadline regulates the rendering of work services instead of the company clock, space, on the one hand, is opened up for subjects to have control, and, on the other, there are new opportunities for the employer to increase productivity and hence to accelerate. It is obvious that a work (time) regime that "is indifferent to the individual rhythms of work capacity during a day, a week, a year and the career," and does not ask "whether the person is currently afflicted or has a cold" and "in principle [demands] equal effort in every hour," and remains, moreover, completely indifferent to the noneconomic motivations of workers, wastes possibilities of intensification in comparison to a system that limits itself to "control of the framework" and permits the subjectification and "boundary-blurring" of work matters and thereby dynamizes the provision of services itself.[51]

Furthermore, time-economic advantages for the employer also arise from the possibility of eliminating economically inefficient idle times and absences and also of switching to more efficient forms of "just in time production" that are capable of responding to rapidly changing demand. This is accomplished by various methods of making work time more flexible ("flexibilization"), for instance, using individually designed work contracts of increasingly shorter durations, work contracts "as needed and on call," forms of temporary labor, etc.[52] One way of interpreting this is as follows. While at first the modern work world had to be protected from the traditions of the lifeworld in order to successfully establish its time regime and to enable social acceleration through rationalization within its boundaries, in the meantime the time orientation and time discipline thereby developed has penetrated so deeply into the everyday conduct of life and even the institutions of the lifeworld that an, as it were, "reverse colonization" has become possible: the ethos of the Protestant ethic and its logic of rationalization have struck such deep roots in the lifeworld and leisure culture that they can no longer be endangered by such a dedifferentiation. Thus Gert Günter Voß presents the results of an intensive study of changes in the way employees lead their lives:

> Generalizing, one can assert: the more pronounced the blurring of worklife boundaries and hence the compulsion to actively restructure one's own work becomes, the stronger is the necessity of consciously orienting the entirety of daily life to professional demands and efficiently reorganizing it. . . . Weber observed such a development in specific social groups and historically generalized it. . . . However, he could not have suspected . . . that the "bureaucratic" ideal of the rationalization of organizations and the conduct of life might at some point run up against historical limits and could be then transformed into a flexible form that rests on the systematic blurring of boundaries. Precisely that seems to be occurring at present.[53]

The blurring of the boundaries of work and life can also be seen in the fact that many activities can no longer be unambiguously categorized as belonging to work or free time, for example, in the realm of continuing education or in "networking" to secure structures of opportunity or in monitoring the labor market. Whoever meets up with colleagues to go bowling in the evening but thereby gains important information about who is doing volunteer work or privately pursuing further education to heighten her chances of employment or takes to reading about the latest developments in computer technology out of both personal and professional interest or attempts to heighten his work capacity and joie de vivre in psychophysical wellness spas is always involved in activities that are simultaneously professional and personal. In everything that concerns the conduct of her life the "entrepreneurial worker" (Voß) is *also* interested in questions of economic valorization and is *also* for economic reasons perched in all areas of life on the "slipping slopes" that according to Marx *and* Weber characterize the situation of the capitalist entrepreneur: *if you aren't climbing up, you're climbing down.*[54]

In view of the late modern intermingling of time and task orientations, abstract and event-based time, work time and free time, in the wake of current transformations, several sociologists of time have suggested that the time structures of contemporary societies be interpreted using a concept of "multitemporality" that connotes a situational, flexible oscillation between planable linear time and event-oriented "temporalized" time. It emphasizes the newly won maneuvering room and temporal sovereignty of subjects: "it is most fruitful when one flexibly leaps back and forth between the worlds of event time and clock time, as the situation requires."[55] However, it seems very questionable to me whether this concept of time accurately characterizes the "blurred boundaries" of the late modern arrangement of work. The time-economic imperatives of capitalist economic activity continue to refer exclusively to the linear time defined by calendars and clocks, and precisely the latter is determinative where interaction chains within and between functionally differentiated systems have to be synchronized. If enterprises (and also increasingly public institutions) no longer abstractly prescribe work time but instead set employees or (only apparently) independent contractors deadlines for delivery, production, or submission, then linear time and event time come together here in a very precarious way: in the end an economic time efficiency is supposed to be achieved that is still *greater* than the efficiency of the old regulated, inflexible, linear time regime, but without the stable framework of collective time institutions and economically unburdened "free times." Therefore, it seems more appropriate to me to speak of a "colonization of event time by linear time" (and of temporal autonomy by temporal heteronomy). As I will show in part 4, this form of colonization leads to "highly situational time practices" not only on the microsocial level of individual life conduct but also in the macrosocial realm of governance and political organization, indeed, even in the field of economic *strategy* itself.[56]

Against this background, it is hardly surprising that in the writings of industrial sociologists and sociologists of work who are critical of capitalism one now observes a kind of yearning for the classical modern "institutionalized-linear" time that was previously (and on the basis of the same critical attitude toward capitalism) condemned as "dead," abstract, alienated, and "ruined" (*zerstörte*) time.[57] This inversion makes the guiding hypothesis that supports the foregoing reflections intuitively clear, namely, that the time-economic dynamic of capitalist acceleration has a knack for generating and then destroying institutions and types of action in accordance with the specific requirements of its own further development, including the requisite time orientations (as will be shown in more detail, this is also true with respect to forms of subjectivity). However, on the systemic macro level too acceleration and growth are so directly interwoven in the capitalist logic of escalation that the "tempo of the economy" is usually measured by its rate of *growth* and recessions interpreted as economic *slowdown*.

The resulting high speed of development and change in the economic-technical sphere of society creates dramatic problems for all the other realms of society, for politics, child rearing and education, for cultural reproduction, and even for the legal system. These will be at the center of the analysis in chapter 11.

2. THE PROMISE OF ACCELERATION: THE CULTURAL MOTOR

There is certainly no shortage of social scientists who defend the view that in the end it is the economic motor alone that is responsible for the accelerative tendency of modernity: the acceleration of all other social spheres follows the capitalist pacemaker more or less necessarily as its epiphenomenon, including the production of the corresponding cultural "superstructural phenomena," the ideology of tempo, and the modern yearning for acceleration.[58] Accordingly, acceleration has transformed from an economic-technical factor into a cultural one because the acceleration and escalation of production inevitably demands the growth of consumption and circulation. The rather absurd, and not economically justifiable, fascination of modern culture for phenomena like fast food, *Blitzkrieg,* or luge athletes is accordingly interpreted as an epiphenomenal cultural reflex of the imperatives of the material base.

However, this kind of reductionistic interpretation seems inadequate on two grounds. In the first place, it is precisely *not* capable of clarifying the process that mediates between economic structural imperatives and subjective and cultural patterns of meaning. Why should subjects get involved with an acceleration of their consumption behavior and thus their pace of life when for them it is not only the case that they have no economic incentive to do so but also that it would actually land them in financial difficulty (and, in addition, leave them short of time)? The capitalist compulsion to accelerate by itself is not sufficient to explain how the process of speeding up goes on almost without resistance even in the other nontechnical dimensions of acceleration, that is, it fails to theoretically justify the absence of structurally powerful cultural forms of resistance to the self-driving dynamic or to the "penetration" of economic imperatives of acceleration. From the perspective of the cultural self-understanding of modernity, the ongoing dynamization is quite evidently not a matter of *adaptation* to external forces, but rather an essential moment of *self-determination.*

In the second place, the materialistic reduction remains blind to the ideational and cultural *presuppositions* of the unleashing of the forces of production and acceleration, as the representatives of a culturalist criticism of the economic primacy thesis would argue.[59] The unfolding of the economic dynamic is the result of a specific cultural "constellation of needs" (*Bedarfslage*) or historical mentality.[60] However, according to the view defended here, any unambiguous and, as it were, a prioristic attributions of causality regarding fundamental historical transformations rests on an error of philosophies of history, since the development of ideas and institutions must be understood as a coevolutionary process in which both sides remain interdependently related, although they can develop in partial autonomy from each other in different directions within certain limits of elasticity until a crisis of legitimation or of institutions arises and there is a consequent rebalancing either through a revolution of the institutional base or through a paradigm shift in historically leading ideas.[61] In particular, my claim is that the reciprocal mediation between the two sides is again and again brought about via the time structures of society and the time orientations of social actors. So while it is, of course, correct to conclude from the ongoing success of the capitalist economic system that the culture of modernity is likewise oriented toward acceleration or must at least be compatible with it, it would be fallacious to derive from this the claim that the compatibility arises simply *because the imperatives of the economic system require it.* The main question is how the acceleration dynamic is culturally rooted in modernity, or in what form the escalatory logics of growth and acceleration are intertwined and anchored in its cultural foundation.

If one accepts the common view that the prevalent time consciousness of developed modernity can be described as *linear with an open future,* in other words, that the idea of a future that develops linearly out of the past but is open to development and in many respects indeterminate dominates our experience of time,[62] then the time scarcity and yearning for acceleration of late modern culture at first glance seem downright puzzling. If, on the one hand, *no* apocalypse, *no* end of the world threatens that would allow the remaining worldly time to be experienced as scarce, and, on the other, the irruption of a categorically new, better future *within time* or *beyond (worldly) time* (whose arrival could be hastened by, e.g., political action in the sense of an acceleration of progress) is likewise not to be expected, then there seem to be no grounds for ideologies of tempo.[63] Hence Luhmann also remarks that the unquestioned character of modern "variable-goal" tempo ideologies, for which increasing speeds are more important than the ends to be realized, is "all the more peculiar since our concept of time runs to infinity and suggests no final date, no end of the world. Accordingly, we have time, an infinite amount of time." For just this reason, he continues, the idea of a wealth of time must be "forbidden, even morally forbidden," because it is not compatible with the structural requirements of modern societies.[64]

Now there can be little doubt that the culture of modernity is familiar with a powerful source for such a moral "prohibition against wasting time," namely, the ethos of the *Protestant ethic* worked out by Max Weber and the sociologists (of time) inspired by him.[65] As we have already seen, the imperative of time efficiency, of the intensive usage and valorization of every minute, is a core element of this ethic, an ethic that unfolds its rationalizing and disciplining effect in the temporal practices of those ruled by its ethos. Thus the innerworldly asceticism highlighted by Weber took the form of a strict, fastidious time discipline. The congeniality of capitalism and Puritanism proves to be also and especially a congeniality of their orientations toward time: the Protestant ethic provides a perfectly fitting cultural counterpart for the capitalist economics of time; it views the idea that there is plenty of time as indeed morally forbidden: wasting time is, in the words of Richard Baxter, the "first and gravest of all sins."[66] Betrand Russell's "In Praise of Idleness" illustrates just how obligatory this time orientation became for the modern work society

(*Arbeitsgesellschaft*) when it begins with the following confession: "Like most of my generation, I was brought up on the saying 'Satan finds some mischief still for idle hands to do.' Being a highly virtuous child, I believed all that I was told, and acquired a conscience which has kept me working hard down to the present moment."[67]

However, to use a moral prohibition of wasting time that stems from religious history as a cultural explanation of the modern will to accelerate is insufficient for two reasons. In the first place, prohibitions do not generate efficacious ideologies.[68] So in order to understand the existence of variable-goal tempo ideologies it is not enough to identify a prohibition of wasting time. Rather, an interpretive explanation requires an additional moral or, better, ethical *commandment* that makes time gains seem full of promise. In the second place, the original moral and cultural force of the Protestant ethic rested on a conception of linear time with a *closed* future. Concerns for salvation and an afterlife beyond the end of the world were what legitimated and motivated the prohibition. Thus the question still remains: on what cultural motivational energies does the urge to accelerate of a secularized modernity with an *open* future rest?

With respect to this first question, it is clear that the temporal imperatives of the Protestant ethic, the prohibition of wasting time and the command to increase efficiency, were equally motivated by *fear* (*Angst*) and *promise* (*Verheißung*) (as the most fundamental human drives of all).[69] If one follows Weber, the Protestant rage for work was not least a consequence of the gnawing fear that resulted from a fateful religious individualization in the face of the torturous question of whether one was chosen and in a state of grace. Ascetic, disciplined activism served (Calvinist) Protestants as a kind of catalyst for the fears that dammed up within due to the joint effect of the doctrine of predestination and the disappearance of ecclesiastical, sacramental forms of salvation, in particular that of confession. It became, as it were, the only reliable "means of getting rid of the fear of damnation."[70] The corresponding *promise*, however, was salvation, being chosen for everlasting life or the state of grace. Although Calvinist doctrine held that salvation could not be earned in any way since it was predetermined as one's destiny, according to an increasingly widespread view one could nevertheless "read off" chosenness from the achievement of a temporally efficient conduct of life (and the occupational and material success made possible by it). This naturally tended to smooth out the difference between works and predestination in daily religious practice.[71]

Now, as motives of action and cultural development, *fear* and *promise* are self-evidently not specific to the Protestant ethic and hence not to the accelerative culture of modernity. They are the correlates in structures of meaning to the most fundamental psychic motivational elements of *pain* and *pleasure* and thus undoubtedly universal. By contrast, what is specific is a time-economic turn: *the characteristic feature of modern culture is the connection of those motivations with the principles of time efficiency and the related expectations of acceleration.* My claim then is that the connection survives even in the course of the secular transformation of the meanings that lie at its foundation.

Accordingly, as the modernization process advances, the cultural form of fear and promise obviously changes in that, so to speak, the screens on which they are projected become relocated from the realm of an extrasocial transcendence (eternal salvation or damnation) into a system-immanent realm of social competition. However, their function as motivators of processes of (growth and) acceleration is preserved despite the accompanying transition from a closed future horizon to an open one.

The generalized unease laid out in chapter 4 (originally that of the capitalist entrepreneur), namely, that of standing in all realms of existence, as it were, on slipping slopes, i.e., of being irrevocably suspended in a world of growing contingencies, of missing decisive opportunities, or of falling hopelessly behind, operates as the *basic fear* in the dynamized, mobile society of modernity. Time thus remains existentially scarce even after specifically religious foundations of meaning "die off."

What serves as a *promise*, however, is the prospect of "perpetual prosperity" (Burkhard Lutz) or the promise of *absolute wealth* (Christoph Deutschmann).[72] In this promise we find once again the connection of growth and acceleration that is so characteristic for modernity: as Deutschmann in particular makes clear, *money* (as, so to speak, congealed time) serves secularized capitalist society as a replacement for religion by taking the place of God as a *master of contingency*. In view of the fundamental uncertainties of the future within the horizon of cultural modernity, there is no longer a promise of peace of mind in the turn to a powerful, reassuring God who is ready to intervene with respect to the contingencies of life (the encouraging thought behind many prayers is precisely that, *whatever* may happen, it is all in God's hands *and therefore good*). What now serves as a functional equivalent is the idea that having the largest possible amount of money, and hence options, will allow one to appropriately react to future contingencies, i.e., new needs and new threats. In the form of capital, money has taken on the task of transforming indeterminable into determinable complexity and therefore of functioning "as a means of meaning-oriented control of the indeterminable."[73] In this way, capital induces "the obsession of individual omnipotence" (i.e., the ability to hold all options open). And, just as with the earlier religious promise, here too many feel themselves *called to* this "absolute wealth," even though it is clear that in the end only a few can be *chosen*.[74] Since time and money are equivalent in the capitalist economy, and the contingency of life is not only per se inconquerable but also massively increased in a continually self-dynamizing late modernity, it is plain that the desire for further acceleration (and additional growth) is just as insatiable as it is ineradicably inscribed in modern culture.

In fact, as Marianne Gronemeyer has pointed out,[75] the modern *need for security* (i.e., the desire to protect oneself against contingencies and create calculable foundations for action) is caught in a conflict with the desire for acceleration. Interestingly, the fundamental underlying thesis of this investigation, namely, that the acceleration dynamic of modernity is able to win out in a dialectical process involving the other principles of development, appears to be confirmed here once again: after the dynamizing inception of early modernity produced large individual and social uncertainties, the gradually forming welfare state of "organized" modernity erected a new "framework of security" that created stable conditions for calculation and precisely thereby unleashed an enormous accelerating effect.[76] However, just like the earlier Taylorist work regime, this (nation-state based) social security system fell under the compulsion to accelerate in late modernity and hence under an erosive pressure. Almost all contemporary diagnoses of the times agree on this point: in contrast to "classical modernity," late modern society is characterized by an increase of uncertainties and contingencies that are caused by the late modern surge of acceleration already identified.[77] The conclusion that forces itself on us is that modernity's need for security is ultimately sacrificed to its need for acceleration.

Moreover, this indicates that the modern promise of acceleration must go beyond the economically grounded *promise of security* developed here in connection with Deutschmann. And, indeed, a further "promising" aspect of the notion of acceleration can be discovered that endures as a constitutive element of modern culture independent of the complex of ideas and norms we call the Protestant ethic. Following the "culturalistic" arguments of Hans Blumenberg, Marianne Gronemeyer, and others,[78] one can assume that the authentic, hidden, but culturally powerful "salvific promise" of social acceleration is that it seems to offer a secular functional equivalent for the idea of "eternal life" and can therefore be understood as *modernity's answer* to that great and unavoidable cultural problem of human finitude, *death*.

What is decisive in the basic structure of this symbolic idea seems to be the following: in modernity the idea that slowly loses its cultural potency is that of a "higher" or sacral time that will first provide a true fullness to time in its entirety as well as life after death or after the end of the world. In comparison to this, *earthly time*, whether as the time of life or the time of the world, appears as merely transitory and vain, an ultimately meaningless cycle of repeating events.[79] For Gronemeyer, who here follows the monumental work of the cultural historian Egon Friedell,[80] the trigger for this development and for the loss of metaphysical certainties was the collectively traumatic experience of the Black Plague in the fourteenth century. The culture of modernity is in her reconstruction of the history of European mentalities interpreted accordingly as a panicked flight response (such that the wish for acceleration takes on the character of the desire to run away).

Even if one does not share this narrative of its origins, the argument still stands that the farewell to thought of an afterlife unavoidably had to place the foundations of subjective and collective meaning in question, since this was an obligatory cultural idea, taken for a certainty, toward which and in light of which life *before* death received its meaning and orientation. In addition, in Blumenberg's terms the coming apart of the time of the world and the time of life (or of history and individual lifespans) became at that point a dramatic new problem that had to be dealt with culturally. If previously one was able to adopt a perspective from which the end of one's own life was united with the forthcoming end of the world (which also signaled the beginning of the "true time"), then with the waning of this idea both time horizons conspicuously separate from each other:

> If the duration of the world from its creation until its end in the Final Judgment was once the unity of time with which human beings reckoned, then at the beginning of modernity the duration of life from birth until death became the defining unity. What human beings now find to be of most concern is the length of their own stay *in time*. The medieval human was sure of her own participation in the remaining time of the aged world beyond her death. . . . The only question that worried her was whether in the end she would be damned or enter into eternal bliss. But this worry had

nothing to do with the length of her earthly life, but rather with the way she lived it. . . . Ever since the span of life was so ungently cut out of the time of the world and holy time, since the life of the individual has been viewed no longer from the perspective of the aging world, but rather the world from the central perspective of the fragile life of the individual, a chronic lack of time has arisen.[81]

Now in principle there are several cultural ways to react to this situation or to manage it in terms of structures of meaning, and most of these were, at least to some extent, tried out in the course of modernity.[82] For example, an escape from this ethical state of emergency could consist in the unfolding of a stoic equanimity or an offensive negation of life and the world: whoever holds the world and life within it to be ultimately worthless or even a "vale of tears" has nothing to lose; death takes nothing from him. Another way to react to the irrevocable shortness of individual life lies in the development of a deindividualizing "species-level patience" (*Gattungsgeduld*), as has been proposed in several streams of Marxism: individual life takes meaning and consolation from conceiving of itself as a link in a long chain that, even if it does not amount to a new form of sacral time, at least bridges the gap between a lifetime and the time of the world.[83] Furthermore, the coming apart of life time and the world's time can be overcome subjectively through the attempt to "immortalize" oneself in one's "works," whether these are artistic, scientific, or political, i.e., to leave behind a trace that extends the span of effects one's own life has far beyond its own duration and thus at least approaches the time of the world. It is not hard to identify this latter motif as a culturally powerful one in the modern period.

In fact, however, a different alternative achieved cultural hegemony as modernity advanced, one that seems to be without competition as an answer to the problem of death in late modernity, namely, the idea that an *accelerated enjoyment of worldly options*, a "faster life," will once again allow the chasm between the time of life and the time of the world to be reduced. In order to understand this thought one has to keep in mind that the question concerning the meaning of death is indissolubly tied to the question of the right or "good life." Thus the idea of the good life corresponding to this answer, which historically became the culturally dominant idea, is to conceive of life as *the last opportunity*, i.e., to use the earthly timespan allotted to humans as intensively and comprehensively as possible before death puts a definitive end to it. This is Gronemeyer's captivatingly simple thesis. The resulting modern ideal regarding life and time is that the good life is *the full life* (*erfüllte Leben*), and it consists in savoring as much of what the world has to offer as possible and in making use of as many of its possibilities and offerings as one can. Goethe has Faust formulate just this principle of life in the following, striking way, and in so doing seems to anticipate in his last sentence the potentially disastrous consequences of this endeavor, which are just beginning to loom in the late twentieth century:

> And what is portioned out to all mankind,
> I shall enjoy deep in my self, contain
> Within my spirit summit and abyss,
> Pile on my breast their agony and bliss;
> And thus let my own self grow into theirs, unfettered,
> Till as they are, at last I, too, am shattered.[84]

The enduring cultural power of this secularized conception of happiness and time and the *logic of escalation* that underlies it has been demonstrated in recent times above all by the work of Gerhard Schulze. According to his diagnosis, it is even more strongly directed at the multiplication and compression of episodes of experience per unit of time: "Two techniques for supposedly increasing our experiential wealth have continually altered our everyday life in the last two centuries: multiplication and compression of the objects of experience. According to the simple calculation, the more means of experience (TV programs, clothes, vacations, partners, etc.) we appropriate (*multiplication*), and the more we concentrate them in time (*compression*), the richer our interior life will be—an increase in being through an increase in having."[85]

Alongside the thought of an *exhaustion of options* appears a complementary *humanistic ideal of self-actualization* (*Bildung*) that points in the same direction and according to which the good life consists first and foremost in the most comprehensive possible development of the talents and potentials of a subject.[86] To the extent that, from this perspective, the divergence of the time of life and the time of the world is a disparity between the almost inexhaustible options available in the world and the limited number of possibilities realizable in an individual life, the principle of acceleration is rooted in the idea of exhausting as many subjective and worldly possibilities as one can. The heightening of the pace of life is as it were a natural consequence: *because the faster one runs through the particular waypoints, episodes, or events, the more possibilities one can realize, acceleration represents the most promising, indeed the only strategy that will tend to bring together again the time of the world and the time of (one's own) life.* She who lives twice as fast can realize twice as many worldly possibilities, achieve two times as many goals, have twice as many experiences, and accumulate twice as many lived events: she thus doubles the amount of worldly options that she exhausts.[87] This makes clear how technical acceleration and the heightening of the pace of life are tied together in a cultural logic of *quantitative escalation* and how growth and acceleration are indissolubly bound together *even from the cultural perspective.* He who lives faster can then in a certain way complete a variety of life projects in a single life span and make their experiential possibilities accessible to himself. It is not difficult to see how the horizon of an "eternal life" can be won back here by imagining an unlimited acceleration. *One who lives infinitely fast no longer needs to fear death as the annihilator of options.* Between such a person and the intrusion of death lie infinitely many "life projects."

It is this connection that turns the heightening of the pace of life into the modern answer to the problem of death and hence lends the idea of acceleration the eudaimonistic overtones that are expressed as much in Marinetti's futurism as in the fascination of formula one racing or the advertising slogans of late modernity ("all you need is speed!"). The observation of Friedrich Ancillon, cited at the beginning of chapter 1, to the effect that in modernity one seeks the "true life" *in movement,* "and only in it," thus gets to the heart of acceleration's promise of happiness. It can be understood alongside the capitalist organization of the economy as the second external "motor" of the modern dynamic of speed (external in that it drives the circle of acceleration, as it were, from the outside). Cultural patterns of meaning and subjective action orientations are its causal foothold, which means that it drives the acceleration process through the desire to heighten the pace of life in order to increase the number of episodes of action and experience per unit of time and hence to save time resources for this purpose. From this perspective the capitalist organization of the economy does not appear as a *cause* of the ideology of acceleration but rather as its *instrument.* Entirely in line with this, Peter Heintel and Thomas Macho remark: "Our economic system can be classified as a compensatory endeavor rooted in the will to master death, the absolute limit, through the quantitative saturation (*Erfüllung*) of time."[88]

Moreover, the linkage of this dimension of acceleration with technical acceleration and social change produces a highly unwelcome and paradoxical consequence that turns the implementation of the modern program of acceleration into a Sisyphean task and necessarily dooms the "promise of happiness" implicit in acceleration. The very same inventions, techniques, and methods that permit the accelerated realization of worldly possibilities and hence the increase of the total sum of options *realized* in a life also multiply the number and variety of *realizable* options of the *time of the world*—indeed, as we have already seen, often in an exponential way.[89] One only needs to call to mind the immense proliferation of options in the new media like cable television and especially the Internet,[90] which not only accelerated previous information and communication processes but also brought forth entirely new spaces of possibility regarding services, entertainment, and ways of communicating. These are only two examples of the way the "degree of missing out" is exponentially increasing in modern society.

The multidimensional developments of societal flexibilization, deregulation, and deconventionalization and the advances of the natural sciences also continually augment the number of viable worldly possibilities and options. In late modern society *whatever* decision an actor makes, she thereby decides *against* more and more alternatives, even though she can then hold open the possibility of realizing the latter according to the logic of the "temporalization of complexity," i.e., by deferring them to a later point in time, which will be the subject of the next section of this chapter: "if I don't have kids now, maybe later"; "if I do an apprenticeship after high school, maybe I can get my bachelor's degree just after that"; "if you can't get to see the film in the theater, you can just rent the DVD," etc. However, as a rule, the number of options available at each later moment (at least in relation to the average remaining time of life) has not diminished, but rather grown even larger. The temporalization of complexity does not overcome the compulsion to accelerate, but strengthens it even more: rejected options come back and continue to weigh down future decisions.

The result of this is evident: contrary to the promise of acceleration, the *degree of exhaustion*, the ratio of worldly possibilities *realized* in a life to those that are *realizable*, continually *decreases* no matter how much we hurry around heightening the tempo of our lives. The modern strategy for realigning life time and worldly time therefore backfires. The *rate of growth* (of options) undeniably exceeds the *rate of acceleration*. So the time resources that are already in short supply anyway become even scarcer. The *meaningless infinity of progress* of which Weber speaks in the context of scientific research is thus transferred to life in general: unlike Weber's premodern peasant,[91] who does not live in a linear, progressive time with an open future but in a cyclical time with reiterated rhythms of day and night, summer and winter, youth and age, and thus dies "old and sated with life," the (late) modern person never reaches this point, never manages to reconcile the time of life with the time of the world, because everything through which he has lived has long been overtaken by escalating possibilities with respect to life, events, and experience. Now we have described the *cultural* side of the paradoxical phenomenon of increasingly scarce time resources despite simultaneous technical acceleration.[92] It keeps the spiral of acceleration going, as it were, at a redoubled pace.

3. THE TEMPORALIZATION OF COMPLEXITY: THE SOCIO-STRUCTURAL MOTOR

The logic of the modern economy worked out in the first section of this chapter does not provide a sufficient grasp of the social-structural side of the transformation of time structures in and by modernity. At first glance, it may appear that my identification of three fundamental motors (or logics) of the modern acceleration dynamic contains a grievous category mistake: if one analyzes the structural and cultural developments separately and weighs them against each other, then isn't the economic motor a *component* of the structural motor, so that it is false to present it as a third driving principle that stands on its own? A closer look quickly makes clear, however, that both of these causal factors of acceleration, which result on the one hand from the leading form of social differentiation and on the other from the specifically economic "operational code," are in fact distinguishable from each other in an analytically clear and empirically adequate way.

The idea that the nature of social time, i.e., the perception and structuring of time, is determined by given forms of social structure is a fundamental postulate of the sociology of time.[93] The question that concerns us here is to what extent the principle of *functional differentiation*—a central developmental principle of modern societies in the account given in chapter 1.2b—*in and of itself*, i.e., according to its own unfolding logic, leads to or necessarily brings about an acceleration of social processes. The analytical independence of this potential motor of dynamization is demonstrated by the fact that one can easily imagine functionally differentiated societies whose economic (sub)systems are *not* oriented by the axiom of capital valorization, but rather, for instance, on (per se speed-neutral) principles of need satisfaction and hence are not organized in a market capitalist way. Conversely, a society could certainly engage in production according to principles of capital valorization even if it was not primarily differentiated functionally, but rather in a stratified way (or if the economic, religious, or political domain had primacy in it). Therefore, the economic motor of acceleration and the social-structural one can be neither reduced to nor derived from one another.

Functional differentiation can in the first place be understood as a mechanism for increasing the speed of productive and developmental processes of all types because in each case points of view and constraints that are alien to the function or system are "switched off" or disregarded: scientific discoveries, technical innovations, commercial products, etc., can progress at a much faster pace when they are disencumbered of "external" expectations (for instance, of a religious or political nature or from the standpoint of any other respective system). Because of this accelerating effect, the principle of differentiation thus represents from the very beginning a successful reaction to the demand for acceleration or the problem of time scarcity. For the individuals who are, at the same time, *partially* and *multiply included* in the various functional spheres, the consequence is that they have to settle how much time they want to spend when in which differentiated functional sphere (work, family, volunteer work, church, etc.) in a sequential time schedule. As we have already seen, the development of temporal rhythms and hourly schedules is a natural correlate of functional differentiation.

Conversely, however, this form of differentiation also leads to an *increasing scarcity* of time because it enormously heightens complexity (this is a basic postulate of systems theory) and because growth in complexity, as Werner Bergmann emphasizes in connection with Niklas Luhmann, can be understood as an essential source of time scarcity: "the sensation of time scarcity emerges from the difference between the complexity of the world, the horizon of the possible, and the processing capacity of the system."[94] The exponential increase of alternatives and options and thus of systematic surpluses of possibility can no longer be managed by the (linear) acceleration of systemic processing alone. This is just the systemic-structural side of the cultural problem, identified in the preceding section, of dealing with an incongruence of "the time of life" and "the time of the world" that increases despite acceleration. Hence it is also another side of the internal connection between quantitative escalation and acceleration that is so characteristic of modernity.[95] According to Luhmann, the multiplication of distinct possibilities and the need to select among them as well as the requirement of synchronization compel the *temporalization* of complexity: unrealized possibilities are "suspended but preserved" (*aufgehoben*) for the future and held open for a possible later actualization. Options for selection are thus ordered along a time axis projected into the future: "it is only in the future that orientation in the dimension of time can achieve a degree of complexity that corresponds to the structural complexity of the contemporary social system."[96]

The temporalization of complexity thus denotes the attempt "to actualize more relations in succession than were possible simultaneously" and "to delay choices and use the present future as a kind of reservoir for decisions to be made later" by means of the sequencing of decisions.[97] Yet the growth in complexity does not end with the respectively current present and each future present will then be additionally encumbered by the delayed choices and surplus options of the past.[98]

Therefore, as a result of the complexity-increasing and complexity-temporalizing effect of functional differentiation, social systems (regardless of whether they are interaction systems, organizations, or societal systems) fall simultaneously under two kinds of pressure to accelerate. A compulsion to accelerate emerges *endogenously* because temporalized systems are, as Luhmann emphasizes, "immanently restless" and only stabilized *dynamically*, i.e., through ceaseless processing that forces them to permit systemic operations to be continuously linked with new operations that bring about *something else.* "From this it follows that temporalized systems have to be fast ("hot"), that they have to obtain closure and the ability to discriminate (self-observation) . . . in ways that can in fact satisfy tempo requirements. . . . Thus for systems with temporalized complexity reproduction becomes a lasting problem. This theory [systems theory —H. R.] is not concerned, as in classical equilibrium theories, with a return to a stable stasis after absorbing disturbances, but rather with the securing of a ceaseless renewal of the elements of the system, or in a word: not static, but dynamic stability."[99]

In fact, the time problem of modernity that is echoed here in system-theoretical parlance can be easily translated into the time perspective that sets in whenever interaction contexts are differentiated with a certain measure of autopoietic closure: from the "internal perspective" of such a context it is clear that there are, at every moment, decisions to be made and future operations that must be planned and, furthermore, connectivity that must be continually organized. Such systemic action compulsions and the resulting scarcities of time are unavoidably transferred to actors. Luhman formulates this in the following way: "A system steered in this way reaches into its environment and there forms persons and objects in such a way that they are connected to the system and can function in accordance with its steering impulses. Thus the temporalization of complexity . . . is relocated from within to without and includes the way persons conduct their lives and the wear and tear of objects."[100]

This reaching out of systems can be easily illustrated with the example of an actor who is simultaneously the father of a family, a high school teacher, and a member of a citizen's group. If he participates actively in family life, then the university and the citizen's group unavoidably appear as a "disruptive environment" that curbs the family's "speed of operation." The family system is again and again forced to take "breaks," is hindered in realizing options and in its connectivity and almost "immobilized" when the actor operates in other functional contexts (the university, the citizen's group): the aunt doesn't get invited, the son's bicycle doesn't get repaired, the daughter's birthday party is delayed. Because "autopoietic" social systems aim at achieving and maintaining "a tempo of event sequences which is for them normal or in the limit case at least tolerable," so that "free times are eliminated . . . and the sequences are closed,"[101] almost every minute the actor spends in other interaction contexts appears to be irrevocably lost. For, under conditions of time scarcity, time that is not used to execute "system operations" is lost time. From the system perspective, actions that forge connections to the system's further actions or to other systems in its environment are always already needed and expected; they are delayed by systemic "idling times" in which actors are doing something else, i.e., spending time in the *system's environment*. Therefore, the temporalization of complexity produces, according to Luhmann, a fundamental compulsion to act: "the time problem spills over from the realm of experience into the realm of action, and time then presses human beings not only from without but also from within. It compels them to be active," he remarks, and cites Karl E. Weick in agreement, "'Chaotic action is preferable to orderly inaction'; non-action is lost time, the mere duration of a present without reality."[102]

The situation from the internal perspectives of the other two systems in our example is obviously just a mirror image of the first: if the citizen's group doesn't think up, plan, and realize new activities in a continual series, again and again, it stands in acute danger of dissolving as an interaction context. So there too breaks become a problem. In contrast, if our actor sits down again at his work desk, overwhelmed by all his tasks, then the time he spends with his family or the citizen's group appears to him to be "wasted." Now *they* represent a disruptive and constraining environment. In fact, he will have to realize that even his university work is in turn differentiated into subareas that tend toward a similar "closure of the event chain" and are characterized by time scarcity resulting from ceaseless growth in complexity: when he is in the seminar room, he can't understand why he isn't more prepared for the lesson, why he hasn't read the seminar text in a more detailed way, designed his pedagogical plan better, made the PowerPoint slides more polished and lean. The book he is supposed to write about, let's say, a theory of social acceleration, is now displaced into the disruptive (because time-draining) "seminar environment." If the seminar has ended, on the other hand, and the meeting about the research project on the motives of civic engagement that he is leading begins, the time perspectives are displaced once again: how come he didn't read the interviews from yesterday, write up the new guidelines, or call the sick project member? Finally, if he's perched once more over his book, maybe he manages at last to really forget those disturbing environments . . . [103]

However, alongside this endogenous, system-internally produced pressure to accelerate, there enters a further, system-*exogenous* accelerating factor that stems from the structural conditions of functionally differentiated societies. This factor turns acceleration into an, as it were, "rational form of temporal experience" in such systems.[104] As Luhmann never tires of emphasizing, the *future*, as a *horizon of expectation*, serves in the manner I have described as a way to deal with surplus possibilities and to delay the need to select among options. Yet, as we have seen, functionally differentiated societies ineradicably tend to make this horizon of expectation more and more unstable, and hence the future, so to speak, "ever shorter." This is an inevitable side effect of the endogenously induced heightening of the tempo with which each respective system processes the *other* systems in its own system environment. "In short, all functional social subsystems stimulate each other and communication [i.e., each systems' own operations — H. R.] tends to provoke more and more communication," as Jean-Sebastien Guy summarizes this self-escalating interaction.[105] He argues that functional differentiation multiplies the acceleration of social change because each system operation represents *another* event in the environment from the perspective of every other system. Due to the resulting increasingly rapid change in environmental conditions, social systems are compelled to revise their horizons of expectation at ever shorter intervals (and the same goes for the horizons of experience projected into the past) and also to continuously escalate and fine-tune their efforts at synchronization. In the course of doing so, the delay of decisions becomes more and more risky: "No present point in time can act as guarantor for any other point in time because the social structure starts to modalize itself. Stable social structures of earlier societies could anticipate the future without much danger of disappointment by binding the expectations of future presents, say, by counting on the continuation of tradition. . . . In contrast, societal self-description in modernity must be reset. Increasingly one has to expect that structure-constituting expectations cannot be expected."[106]

This simply describes once again the systemic-structural correlate of the experience of "slipping slopes" (explained "phenomenologically" in chapter 4) and the postulate of a contraction of the present, and thus of accelerated social change.[107] The rapid transformation of system environments (in each case observed from the standpoint of the respective system) implies the accelerated alteration of the grounds for selection and the horizons of expectation and so also "externally" imposes a heightening of operational tempo on the respective differentiated systems.

Put in terms of our example: the working times for research projects, the reaction times for citizen initiatives, and the deadlines for completing pending family tasks seem to constantly shorten; the corresponding activities take on the character of things one *can't put off*, since otherwise the opportunity for them will have already *gone by*. For instance, on the level of social subsystems, politics and legislation as well as the educational system fall under pressure to keep pace with the changes provoked by the economy and the development of technology, while, on the level of organizations, for instance, firms are compelled not only to react to but also to anticipate input from volatile financial markets.[108]

Since the time of social systems thus becomes scarce on both system-endogenous and system-exogenous grounds and operational acceleration becomes an imperative of reproduction, the fact that these systems, especially at the level of organizations and interaction contexts, tend more and more strongly to burst their socially defined "time windows" and press toward making all their processes constant represents a consequence of highly developed functional differentiation that is just as "natural" as it is consequential. The drive toward a "closure of the sequence" and an elimination of empty times, then, leads, on the one hand, to the disappearance of collective temporal patterns and rhythms in favor of a constantly operating "Nonstop Society" in which systemic processes tend to run around the clock.[109] On the Internet one can at any time further develop products, perform financial transactions, access offers of continuing education, etc., such that the World Wide Web creates the impression that *everything is happening everywhere at the same time*. But, even beyond the Net, one sees ubiquitous tendencies to make availability times, operating times, and access times of all kinds perpetual: i.e., for example, to extend production times and business hours, offer worship services at many different times, schedule work meetings even on the weekend, distribute sporting events, in contrast, all through the week, eliminate ad-free times on TV, and so on. The examples show the social potency of this process of temporal dedifferentiation.

On the other hand, the effect of this development toward the perpetuation of systemic processing for individual actors is that social systems or organizations and institutions become "greedy" (Coser).[110] They are no longer satisfied with the time windows allocated to them by society and tend to demand the undivided attention and total resources of subjects. Since, from the internal perspective of a given system or interaction context, all other activities represent only disruptive delays and eliminable empty times, highly temporalized systems tend to become totalitarian in their demands for access to actors. For this reason, the latter are always under the compulsion to fend off demands made on their time budget; they constantly move, in Luhmann's words, within a *magnetic field of social demands*.[111] Therefore, the third decisive reason (alongside the economic and cultural explanations) that human beings in functionally differentiated societies so frequently report the feeling of being "always rushed" and of never "having enough time" for any activity is that organizations and institutions become "greedy" in this way and make, as it were, "total" claims on their time. Even if an actor invested all twenty-four hours of her day in *one* of the functional spheres, her time resources would not be sufficient for coping with the systemically generated tasks: there are always still further significant, if not entirely necessary (and always nonpostponable) things to do, which undeniably creates the desire to give up the other spheres of activity that are not currently being actualized.[112]

But even when actors continue to try to balance the various interaction contexts in which they participate against each other, they are compelled by the temporal "dissolution of boundaries" in systemic operating times to also "dissolve the boundaries" of their own tempos and rhythms insofar as these are bound up with their participation: as I have tried to demonstrate in the first section of this chapter, work currently tends to *never* end. One takes it home and even does it over the weekend. While one works, family concerns get "fit in" somewhere. Something similar also holds true for the citizens' initiative. In agreement with the analyses of many time budget studies, Karl Hörning, Daniela Ahrens, and Anette Gerhard argue in their investigation of late modern time styles and lifestyles,[113] because engagement in individual functional spheres is no longer determinable according to fixed schedules as a result of the "slipping slopes" that appear from respective system standpoints, the temporal pattern of the future is that of the flexible "player" (*Spieler*) who decides *what* he will do *when* and for *how long* in accordance with each newly given situation. This is the sociostructural foundation of the late modern "dissolution of the boundaries" of work, free time, and "life," one that naturally requires and enables a large measure of individual *time sovereignty*. The obsolescence of the time stamp clock is thus not only caused by the requirements of late capitalist production. In the context of late modernity it has rather become quite generally inappropriate as a sequencing instrument. Again, it is important to keep in mind here that the argument thus far only demonstrates a *tendency* of future development; there is no question of any claim that this pattern already covers the temporal order of contemporary society across the board. The argument here is simply that the logic of functional differentiation inherently leads to a ceaseless increase in complexity that is linked to an acceleration of social processes and, in particular, an acceleration of social change. It therefore tends toward a reversal of temporal differentiation. The latter proves to be part of a dialectical movement of acceleration whose form is quite characteristic for modernity: in early and classical modernity the spatial and temporal differentiation of functional spheres sets an unprecedented acceleration of social processes in motion, but, in late modernity, it turns out to be more and more of a hindrance to further systemic acceleration (or increasingly constant operationality) and, in this way, falls under erosive pressure.[114]

The corresponding changes in patterns of identity and the relations subjects have to themselves will be a theme of chapter 10. We can note here, however, that from a *structural* point of view rigid hourly, daily, yearly, and lifetime plans belong to the past: they cannot be maintained in the face of the temporal boundary dissolution in highly differentiated functional systems, above all where the continuation of systemic processes depends on the engagement of individual actors, i.e., where subjects as role bearers cannot relieve each other in the seamless maintenance of systemic operations. Hörning, Ahrens, and Gerhard conclude that exact time management and precise planning prove to be unworkable and anachronistic as instruments of time allocation: they were (and are) adequate only where functional differentiation did not lead (has not yet led) to temporal (and spatial) dedifferentiation. In an ideal-typical sense they are being replaced by flexible time arrangements that (similar to the processing of digital computers) involve microtemporal oscillation between the demands of distinct functional spheres that are all running as "non-stop" enterprises. To set our chosen example to work one last time: the civically engaged high school teacher and father of late modernity constantly switches back and forth, in irregular sequences and intervals, between the interaction contexts of family, university, and citizens' group. He no longer allocates to any of them fixed blocks of time independent from given pending tasks (and hence unburdened by the respective demands of the other fields of activity). Instead he proceeds to do his sequencing *in time itself,* something Hörning, Ahrens, and Gerhard, agreeing here with, for instance, Armin Nassehi or Mike Sandbothe, designate as the *temporalization of time.* "The immense potential for change makes it problematic to tie oneself down. The differences between the past and the future become more and more drastic. In view of the 'time of permanent change (*Wechsel*),' every long-term orientation has be redecided and rejustified again and again. Any constancy, any continuity has to be arduously maintained. When all we can expect with certainty is that expectations may be disappointed, we must embrace the insight that *time is only available within time.*"[115]

The *fragmentation* of late modern time praxis and the tendency to "multi-task" thus turn out to be, as it were, *structural consequences* of an "aged," functionally differentiated society. They are a result of deep-rooted systemic pressure toward a "closure of sequences" or the perpetuation of process chains. Modern technologies like the e-mail system *enable* qualitatively new forms of perpetual systemic operation and microtemporal oscillation between functional domains, but they do not *cause* them.

Moreover, at the level of the social system a question arises concerning the maintenance of the ability to synchronize or the social consequences of possible desynchronization phenomena: if the assumption that functionally differentiated systems are already for endogenous reasons inclined to accelerate their process chains is correct, then an obvious suspicion would be that they are not all equally good at doing so. In other words, the "intrinsic temporalities" of the various systems permit different speeds, such that the slower subsystems run up against (their own) speed limits, and this has potentially dysfunctional consequences for the social system as a whole when they try to keep up with transformations in their respective environments. In chapter 11 I will attempt to interpret the noticeable *loss of political control (Selbststeuerungsverlust)* in late modern society as a result of just such a desynchronization between social subsystems—one that is caused, in particular, by a disparity between the economic-scientific-technological rate of innovation and the political capacity to process its effects.[116]

Summing up, we can observe here that the search for the *causes* of the modern acceleration dynamic has led beyond the logic of the self-propelling circle of acceleration that was worked out in chapter 6 to three further, as it were, "external" driving motors whose complex complementary interaction

Driving Forces of Acceleration II: External Motors

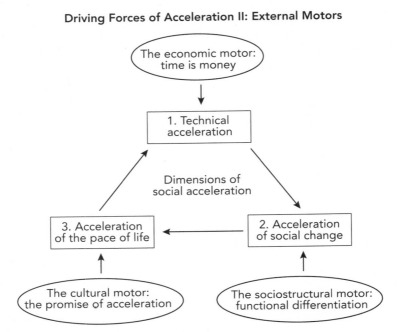

7.1. External Drivers of Acceleration

is capable of explaining the deep-seated relationship of mutual escalation between growth and acceleration that is so characteristic of modernity. This relation proves to be *structurally* a linkage of the increase and temporalization of complexity; *culturally* a consequence of a conception of the world in which acceleration, as a strategy for aligning the time of the world and the time of life, becomes a secular replacement for eternity; and *economically* a result of the logic of capital valorization (cf. figure 7.1). Each of these three driving principles can be primarily attributed to one of the three dimensions of acceleration, although, naturally, given the way the circle of speed functions, each "motor," in addition, always drives the spiral of acceleration as a whole: the economic logic serves as a primary accelerator for *technical acceleration*, the cultural logic of escalation drives forth the *acceleration of the pace of life*, and the structural principle of functional differentiation *accelerates social change* in a historically unprecedented way. In the last part of our causal analysis, we need to inquire about the institutional conditions that historically enabled and supported the unfolding of this interconnection of escalation and acceleration.

8

POWER, WAR, AND SPEED: THE STATE AND THE MILITARY AS KEY INSTITUTIONAL ACCELERATORS

ACCORDING TO THE CORE ARGUMENT worked out in the preceding chapters, the dynamic linkage and dialectical unfolding of growth and acceleration characterize the authentic nature of modernity and the logic of modernization. There is no doubt, however, that these occurred in the first instance in the shadows of the developing modern territorial state and the military apparatus that serves it. Many institutional boundary conditions of social acceleration and innumerable accelerative material innovations either would have been impossible without the modern institutions and initiatives of the national state and its military or must be in fact directly ascribed to them. Therefore, as more strongly political science–oriented engagements with the theme of social acceleration have convincingly shown,[1] the *state* and the *military* represent immensely powerful, historically central factors of acceleration that performed a decisive "maieutic" function for the birth of the modern dynamic of escalation and the development of corresponding *temporal practices*. However, as I argue in what follows, they seem to share the same fate, elaborated earlier in a different context, of all the other "classical modern" institutions: in late modernity they are threatened with erosion by the very forces of acceleration they set free because their functioning and their own intrinsic forms of stability have gone from being *accelerators* to being *brakes* or *hindrances to speed*.

It was nevertheless a long historical path that led to this point, in the course of which the modern territorial state replaced the static sociality of traditional states with dynamization in almost all social domains.[2] The acceleration of social processes and transactions was a special consequence of the *unification* of the conditions of action and development in the modern territorial state.

The implementation of unified national languages, currencies, time zones, educational systems, legal frameworks, administrative systems, tax liabilities, infrastructures, and centralized steering organs proved to be a massive accelerator of development and circulation, above all through the accompanying dismantling of intrastate transaction costs and obstacles to translation across domains. By systematically building up infrastructure, establishing legal certainty and security of trade, capturing the monopoly of violence and taxation inside its borders, and assuring a relatively reliable defense against external threats, the national state created the presuppositions of secure long-term planning and calculability that first made possible the systematic unfolding of scientific-technical and economic-industrial acceleration.[3]

Modern law also permitted—in contrast to traditional customary law or static conceptions of natural law—a similarly dynamic adaptation to changing needs since evolving political democracies turned out to be more adaptable and responsive than traditional monarchies.[4] At the same time, in its bureaucratic administrative system the modern state itself created a highly efficient apparatus for making and implementing decisions, one that was far superior in terms of speed and reliability than any previous system, particularly regarding information and the acquisition and utilization of resources (above all via tax revenues).[5] With its help the triumphant territorial states of modernity achieved an unprecedented acceleration of technical-economic and social development along the path of a state-centered, bureaucratic *regulation* and a political *steering* of social processes.

Furthermore, for a long time the competition among states, in particular that of European ones in their struggle for territorial expansion and for the conquest and opening up of ever more distant colonies, was one of the main causes of the technical acceleration of transportation and communication: in order not to fall behind in the battle for resources, markets, and territories, national states were compelled to invest massively in those technologies via military and civil programs.[6] *From this perspective modernization can be understood as an acceleration program of the central state that was driven by nothing other than the political quest to accumulate and preserve power in the system of competing states that formed after the Treaty of Westphalia.*

Of course, the tight link between domination and speed is not something that begins in modernity: political power is, as Virilio has argued, in the end a form of the *power to move* that allows the mastery of space through superior speed, so that domination always also means the *domination of the faster*—and of the *more flexible* who can shift at will between strategies of acceleration and deceleration.[7] This transhistorical principle gains a new meaning, however, as modernity unfolds because the form and the extent of political "time-space distanciation" (Giddens),[8] i.e., the ability to reach beyond the spatial and temporal limits of the immediately present, fundamentally change. Scheuerman therefore rightly states that "the modern nation state triumphed over an array of competing modes of political organization (empires, city-states, loose networks of city-states) in part because of its superior manipulation of speed. The competition for control over territory and population so pivotal to political success in a dangerous international environment has long constituted a major source of social acceleration. High-speed technologies and forms of social organization make up indispensable tools in the battle for territory and population."[9]

This is especially clear with respect to the military domain. The mastery of space no longer aimed at the occupation and control of strategically important sites, for example, castles and fortresses, but instead at the military and administrative mastery of closed territories over which the national state sought to obtain and defend a monopoly of violence. The preparation for war and the mode of warfare therefore fundamentally changed regarding both defense and attack: it became less a question of erecting impregnable fortresses or besieging and breaking them than of making spaces strategically attainable or defensible at any given point in a dynamic, flexible way. This presupposed a thick infrastructure and mobile military units. For Virilio this new form of military presence and power to move developed first at the end of the seventeenth century in England in its emerging "fleet in being": "The 'fleet in being' is logistics taking strategy to its absolute point, as the art of moving unseen bodies. It is the permanent presence at sea of an invisible fleet able to strike no matter where and no matter when, annihilating the enemy's will to power by creating a global zone of insecurity. . . . Thus it is a new idea of violence that no longer comes from direct confrontation and bloodshed, but from the unequal properties of bodies, evaluation of the number of movements allowed them in a chosen element, permanent verification of their dynamic efficiency."[10]

This military principle of rapid and quasi-total territorial presence across extended spaces is heightened in the twentieth century through the development of air force power with a potential "total surface coverage" and achieves a kind of logical and logistical end point in the production of intercontinental missiles that make every place on earth reachable from every other in mere minutes.[11]

The competitive and expansive logic of power accumulation among territorial states thus functions as a key factor in social acceleration not only because of the development of new military technologies and forms of organization in the narrower sense but also because of the complementary compulsion to enhance economic and "manpower" resources, scientific-technical progress, administrative control, and communications and transport infrastructure. The competitive political and military struggle therefore propels the acceleration of all domains of society in modernity until finally an almost "total mobilization" is achieved, as Matthias Eberling remarks, with clear echoes of Ernst Jünger, Peter Sloterdijk, and Paul Virilio: "The 'total mobilization' grips everything and everyone, the 'World War' and the 'world revolution' encompass the entire planet. Under the pressure of permanent military and ideological confrontation science, the economy, and other subsystems work faster and with less friction. The acceleration of all movement dissolves the remaining resistance. The complete exertion of all forces tolerates no doubts."[12]

So while *speed premiums* in politics and war are certainly nothing specifically modern, in the national context of an unfolding, dynamic dialectic of growth and acceleration they take on an unusually consequential quality, both culturally and structurally, in the form of the modern industrialization of war, the capitalization of the economy, and the bureaucratization of administration.[13]

Up to this point, I find myself entirely in agreement with the aforementioned scholarship from authors like William Scheuerman, Anthony Giddens, Charles Tilly, and Paul Virilio. The decisive question that must be posed now, however, concerns the role institutions of the national state and military play with respect to the transformation of the time structures of society in the early twenty-first century world of globalized relationships. Must they continue to be understood as the actual driving forces (or at least to a structurally relevant extent *codrivers*) of acceleration, such that from a causal point of view they are ultimately located on the same level as the three external motors of social acceleration, as Scheuerman implies in his critique of my conception?[14] Or are they to be counted among that ensemble of "classical modern" institutions that is threatened with erosion in late modernity by the very forces of acceleration it set in motion in accordance with the maieutic hypothesis developed here? On that view, this ensemble is the now dispensable midwife of a modern dynamization of growth and acceleration that rests solely on the three interlinked dimensions of the circle of acceleration. As already indicated, I defend the latter view. In what follows I would like to justify this claim first with respect to the military and then with regard to the state.

While the military apparatus that developed in modernity played a significant role in the acceleration of social change through its increased need for organizational power, i.e., above all for rapid acquisition of information, political-moral support, and supplies of material resources and personnel,[15] it occupied a much more direct and central place in the process of social acceleration in the other two dimensions, i.e., technical acceleration and the acceleration of the pace of life. On the one hand, military technology was undeniably the pacesetter of accelerative technical progress with respect to the development of land-, air- and sea-based weapon systems and the technical infrastructure for transportation and communication. Thus one can interpret, for instance, the outcome of the First World War with General Ludendorff as the victory of the more mobile French truck over the slower German railroad,[16] while contrariwise twenty-three years later the fast German Panzer formed the basis of the *Blitzkrieg* ("lightning war") and *Blitzsieg* ("lightning victory") against France. Inventions as consequential as the jet plane and rocket propulsion also represent military-technical results of the Second World War, and even the Internet, the cardinal accelerator of late modernity, owes its emergence to military-strategic considerations.

On the other hand, in the context of modern civilian-based mass armies and compulsory military service, the institution of the *barracks* is, next to the school, perhaps the most important educational establishment of the disciplinary society that Michel Foucault places at the center of the modernization process.[17] In it modern time discipline is more or less violently "inscribed" on the human body. There the new form of this discipline, which is immune to all natural rhythms and abstracts from all individual differences and subjective "intrinsic temporalities," is literally "beaten into" at least the male part of the population with the most extreme consistency, and soldiers are taught the ability to subordinate unreflecting and affective impulses to a formal, abstract regime of time and domination. At the same time, the "power to move" of the body is also increased by its physical acceleration in forced marches and assaults and unified in the temporal *Gleichschaltung* or mutual alignment of a large number of soldiers (for instance, in the lock step) in an exact "military machinery."

Thus the military apparatus is the paradigmatic site at which the abstract time regime of modernity developed long before it became generalized in the industrial revolution.[18] Moreover, it decisively drove the acceleration of action and interaction sequences through the strict ordering principle of hierarchical chains of command and the acceleration of information transmission through the consistent exclusion of noninformation-bearing elements of communication. Finally, it also represents an important moment in the process of the *temporalization of life* in that it projected, in the form of *military careers*, a possible temporal pattern of advancement in the life of a (professional) soldier that made the aspect of acceleration an almost quasi-natural component of his perspective on the future. Therefore, along with technological acceleration, the acceleration of the pace of life in modernity is also quite essentially a military achievement.

How does the situation look in the most modernized societies of the twenty-first century though? Let us turn first to the last aspect. There can be little doubt that military discipline in the form of soldierly drills does not contribute any longer, or at least not much, to the acceleration of the tempo of life. It is much more likely, rather, that many recruits experience their term of service as a phase of deceleration because of forced waiting periods and dull *monotasking*, in which the density of episodes of action and experience per unit of time drops in comparison to habitual everyday life rather than climbs. As the discussion of the transformation of the time regime in the late modern working world has already shown, today acceleration affects are far more likely to be achieved through *individualization*, i.e., by exploiting individual particularities, rhythms, and intrinsic temporalities, than through the *standardization* and harmonization (*Gleichschaltung*) of activities and movements. Furthermore, since hierarchical command chains have become inefficient or, in other words, *too slow* with respect to innovation, flexibility, productivity, and adaptation to rapidly changing demands, the military leadership principle is increasingly being replaced in almost all social domains, above all in business and administration, by flat hierarchies, teamwork, and an increase of individual responsibility. Finally, with respect to its linear career pattern too, the military proves unambiguously to be an institution of "classical modernity," the organizational principle of which is threatened with becoming anachronistic in the wake of the late modern temporalization of time. Professional careers designed for long-term development are losing their meaning and ability to provide orientation in the age of globalized capitalism; outside the military the only place they can still be found is in state bureaucracies that, as will soon be shown, can be similarly viewed as anachronistic.[19] A significant accelerative effect on the tempo of late modern life is thus not to be expected from the institutions of the military.

But what about the acceleration of transportation, communication, and production? As I have already indicated, the geostrategic logic of the defense and potential conquest of closed territories reached a decisive limit in the development of atomic long-distance rockets at the highpoint of the cold war. When weapons of mass destruction can reach any place on earth in minutes if not seconds, geostrategical military planning that rests on the basic distinctions between territories *to be protected* and (potentially) *to be conquered*, between *frontline* and *interior*, between *soldiers* and *civilians*, and between *near* and *far*, loses its meaning: "*the technological break-through*, the last form of the war of movement, ends up, with deterrence, at the dissolution of what *separated* but also *distinguished*, and this non-distinction corresponds for us to a political blindness."[20] As Virilio repeatedly emphasizes, the destruction threatened by such weapons is so fast and so total that it undermines the possibility of rational political decision because in the moment of existential danger *there is no more time* for a properly political mode of decision making, i.e., through common discussion and deliberation. The military possibilities of the second half of the twentieth century thus ultimately compel the permanent establishment of a "state of exception" (*Ausnahmestaat*) that has reached the limits of militarily controllable opportunities for acceleration:[21] "technology at the stage of perfection is so rational, so fast, and so successful . . . that its results are irrational and dysfunctional for the political system."[22]

If the "total war of acceleration" (*totale Beschleunigungskrieg*) toward the end of the twentieth century is thus so fast and destructive that it can only be waged at the price of one's own annihilation, then in the transition to the twenty-first century there suddenly develop forms of warfare that are at once old and new, that in many respects operate with the weapons and strategies and the speed of premodern or early modern times: in many regions of the world, wars are once again fought with conventional weapons, rifles, and even machetes and knives, and combatants more and more frequently follow terroristic or guerrilla strategies of momentary ambush (with the greatest possible radius of diffused fear) and rapid withdrawal instead of the modern military logic of comprehensive occupation of closed territories.[23]

Although the advantage enjoyed by the ability of selective acceleration and deceleration described earlier as transhistorical, and thus the "speed premium" in warfare, still holds good in these new wars, the classical modern institution of the military apparatus has nevertheless lost its pioneering role, especially from an acceleration-technical point of view: the military "machinery" of the national state, which for a long time was so successful precisely due to its superior speed, is almost powerless against this new-old mode of warfare; it is too slow, too rigid, and too cumbersome against an enemy operating with guerrilla tactics and in a world in which there are no longer any geostrategic limits. Because the mechanisms for setting the military in motion—for instance, conscription and political-diplomatic declarations of war, mobilization, and deployment—are too time consuming; today one must expect from the dynamization of warfare the forthright inversion of the relations of classical modernity, namely, the *demilitarization* of war, the decline of the monopoly of violence, and the "outbreak of civil wars" (*Enzsensberger*), as Herfried Münkler and also Martin van Creveld have shown.[24] The U.S. army's impressive display of muscle at the beginning of the twenty-first century cannot belie this: to react to the terrorist attacks of 9/11 in the manner of old interstate wars with field campaigns against Afghanistan and Iraq is as anachronistic and "old European" as it is inadequate as an answer to the new geopolitical dangers. The modern institution of the military has no chance against a terrorist network that operates with the possibilities of the information age. It proves to be quite simply "obsolete."[25] Aside from this fact, today genuine military innovations aim more at *slowing down* and *making more precise* the technology of destruction to such a degree that a *controlled* and hence *strategic deployment* of faster weapons is possible, rather than a direct acceleration of the weapons themselves. Smart bombs are not faster, but more exact and more selective in their destructiveness than their predecessors. The aim of technological development in the military today is not the faster destruction of the enemy, but the more precise neutralization of its infrastructure and its power of resistance.[26]

Interestingly, after a closer look even the apparent paradigm example of the military development of late modern accelerative technologies, the Internet, supports my thesis that the principle of acceleration has lost its former function in military logic. Even though the Internet is doubtless a principal accelerator not only of information-technical processes but also of social change, for its military-strategical "inventors" its networking logic served to *decelerate* rather than accelerate war: the original form of the Internet, the Arpanet, was something invented by the U.S. Department of Defense to prevent the neutralization of American information systems at a single blow in case of a (Soviet) nuclear attack by *scattering* and *decentering* American communicative arrangements. As Manuel Castells observes: "To some extent, it was the electronic equivalent of the Maoist tactics of dispersing guerrilla forces around a vast territory to counter an enemy's might with versatility and knowledge of terrain; the outcome was a network architecture that, as its inventors wanted, cannot be controlled from any center and is made up of thousands of autonomous computer networks that have innumerable ways to link up."

Meanwhile, Herfried Münkler, quite independently of these considerations, points out that such Maoist guerrilla tactics represent a form of the deceleration of warfare.[27]

So the Internet exemplifies the rare case of social acceleration as *an unintended side* effect of military-technical efforts to decelerate (hence a kind of complementary form of the third category of deceleration defined in chapter 2.3). Even if this example demonstrates that acceleration effects can still flow from military developments, it cannot be used as a counterexample for the thesis defended here, namely, that *in late modernity the institution of the military has by and large relinquished its function as the pacesetter of social acceleration.*

However, the same thing holds true for the institution of the state, as innumerable diagnoses of the transformation or loss of the national state's function in the age of globalization suggest.[28] As is well known, the claim that the national state is in the throes of decline and losing more and more of its power does not meet with universal agreement at all. The counterclaim asserts that states continue to be the main actors shaping the global rules of the game, that it is in fact ultimately treaties and conventions between governments, particularly those of the powerful industrial states, that have brought about and made possible the processes discussed under the catchphrase *globalization*. Furthermore, the national state is still the main addressee of the political demands of citizens, and these demands are (perhaps) even growing.[29] On the other hand, it can hardly be doubted that the power of national states is subject to novel forms of constraint with respect to both their sovereignty and their autonomy.[30] The *sovereignty* of national states is, on the one hand, limited by developments in international law, according to which certain situations, especially humanitarian catastrophes like genocide, but perhaps also the development of weapons of mass destruction, permit the intervention of the international community in the internal affairs of a country and, on the other, diminished by the voluntary transfer of rights to supranational institutions (like the EU). The latter represents above all a reaction to the progressive undermining of the *autonomy* of national states by the "globalization" of, first and foremost, economic and financial transactions, which enormously constricts the maneuvering room of governments in the areas of financial, economic, and social policy.[31] That the globalization—and this means, above all, *deregulation*—of the financial markets was a result of political projects pursued by the highly industrialized national states does nothing to change the fact of a loss of autonomy that cannot be offset by measures undertaken by individual states. In view of this there can be little doubt about the correctness of the argument, meticulously worked out by, for instance, David Held and colleagues, that the contemporary national state is not to be characterized as having suffered a simple and unqualified loss of power, but rather as having undergone a fundamental transformation of its *function*.[32]

This functional transformation can be seen particularly clearly from the standpoint of social acceleration. My diagnosis, to put a fine point on it, is that the national state has metamorphosed from a key accelerating agent into a key decelerating institution or an obstacle to acceleration. As I have argued, the centralization, standardization, and regulation of social developments and processes of exchange by national states in early and "classical" modernity unleashed an immensely dynamizing effect, the most important institutions of which were, on the one hand, the security organs of the military and, on the other, the highly efficient administrative machinery of the state bureaucracy. Regarding the military, tightly linked as it is to the national state, I have already laid out the postulated functional transformation from a modern accelerator to a late modern brake: the demilitarization of war is also its *denationalization* (*Entstaatlichung*), something shown for example by the increase of civil-war-type conflicts, which are, at the same time, an expression of a challenge to state sovereignty by substate movements *from within*.[33]

An analogous development can also be observed with respect to the second core element of the state, the bureaucracy. The structures and decision-making processes of bureaucratic administration have not only lost their status as the epitome of efficiency and temporal rationality. They are taken to be the paramount example of *inefficiency*, i.e., of *slowness* and *inflexibility*, and indeed precisely because of those principles that Weber once saw as grounding their rationality and speed, such as the basing of all processes on written documents (*Aktenmässigkeit*), the strict adherence to procedure ("always going through the proper channels"), the unilinear hierarchy of competencies and orders, the formation of fixed work routines, etc.[34] Because bureaucracies have become too slow, the *debureaucratization* of administrative processes today counts as the royal road to the acceleration of decisions. Therefore, the "crisis of statism" that Castells diagnoses during the last quarter of the twentieth century is above all a crisis of bureaucratic administration. The defeat of *state socialism* in the face of private-sector-oriented capitalism can be understood as a consequence of the fact that state-based steering reached the limits of its ability to accelerate. The centralized state is too slow and immobile an actor for the time structures of the "network society" created by the new information technologies; it no longer has any dynamizing force of its own to set against the last wave of acceleration in Western capitalist societies.[35] Social-scientific research on the systemic upheaval in Eastern Europe after the fall of the Soviet Union has consistently shown that time appeared to be for the most part "static" in socialist states and hence the system changeover was perceived as a massive acceleration process.[36]

The functional transformation that is expressed in the crisis of bureaucracy thus indicates much more than a mere administrative crisis: in a complete inversion of the circumstances of classical modernity, acceleration in late modernity is not achieved by state regulation of social, cultural, and economic processes and relations, but by their *deregulation*. As I will show in chapter 11, the accelerative effect of political control or steering has been exhausted because the economic, technological, and social or associational developments that were first propelled by it have become so fast and flexible that the political system can no longer keep up with them. This is particularly true for aspirations of *democratic* control: as will be shown, democratic will formation and decision-making processes are not only time consuming per se, but even develop an *increasing need for time* because of late modern transformations of associational structures and the public sphere. As a result of this temporal desynchronization, the relation between political steering and social acceleration in developed industrial states has almost completely reversed: while the dismantling of state regulation and the renunciation of steering promises further social acceleration, holding on to such aspirations of steering and regulation proves to be primarily an economic brake. This is revealed, for instance, in political initiatives like those launched by the German federal state of Bavaria in the winter of 2003: "Debureaucratization: the free state wants to eliminate one out of every three regulations—with a large Internet survey the government wants to find out which rules are slowing down the economy," as the *Süddeutsche Zeitung* reported on February 1 of that year. In the meantime, similar initiatives have been undertaken by other federal states.[37]

While states still definitely appear to be decisive agents of acceleration, the *mode* of governmental-political acceleration has fundamentally changed: instead of the dynamization of social development by regulation and national standardization in the sense of "progressive politics," there is a dynamization by *deregulation* and the successive *surrender* of specifically national standards (including even one's own currency). The accelerative competitive struggle between national states endures even into the present, though it has relocated to the field of economics in the fight to be the most capital-friendly place of

TABLE 8.1 The Dialectic of Acceleration and Inertia: Modern Accelerators and Late Modern "Brakes"

CENTRAL INSTITUTIONS OF SOCIETY	AS ACCELERATORS IN MODERNITY	AS "BRAKES" IN LATE MODERNITY
National state	Acceleration through unification (time, language, currency, law, etc.)	Hindrance of trans-and supranational exchange processes (i.e., of "global flows")
Bureaucracy	Acceleration of administration	Delay of social and economic development
Military	Acceleration through technical innovation and time discipline	Military apparatus/command structure too cumbersome and slow
Political steering	Dynamization through progressive politics	Aspiration to control as brake on dynamization
Democracy	Acceleration of succession of rulers; accelerated reaction to sociopolitical needs	As mode of political decision making too slow
Spatiotemporal division of "work" and "life"	Unhindered dynamization of the economic sphere	Slows down dynamization of the lifeworld
Stable personal identity (career, family, etc.)	Dynamization through individualization	Slows down dynamization of life through insufficient flexibility
Temporally extended individual life plans	Temporalization of life / acceleration of the pace of life	Delayed adaptation to social change; hindrance of acceleration in the sense of the *temporalization of time*
(Institutionalized form of the differentiation of functional spheres)	(Unhindered development of intrinsic functional logics of different spheres)	(Hindrance of transsphere dynamization)

For discussion, see chapters 9 and 10.3.

business, such that states paradoxically seek to gain the advantage primarily by eroding their own foundations, e.g., as when they contribute to the drying up of their own tax base.[38] If national unification and centralization functioned as an accelerator during the development of modernity, then in the second half of the twentieth century interstate differences regarding impediments to acceleration and faster transactions begin to become noticeable: the forces of acceleration have, as it were, outgrown the boundaries of national states. Thus, wherever the state appears as an agent of acceleration today, it does so primarily by intentionally enacting the erosion of its own (previously self-defining) institutional arrangements as well as its traditional aspirations for control. For this reason, it can hardly be surprising that the core of the recent globally successful ideology of "neoliberalism" is a policy of deregulation, debureaucratization, and downsizing of the state: in short, an *ideology whose policy is not to have any policy*.[39]

In part 4 of this book I will attempt to justify the claim that for temporal-structural reasons modernity in fact finds itself in a transition to a phase that is *posthistorical* and hence *postpolitical* in a specific sense. Nevertheless, summing up, it is important to hold on to the crucial point that the ensemble of social institutions defining "classical modernity" is now characterized by a comprehensive and consequential inversion of functions in the context of the dialectical development of forces of acceleration and institutional boundary conditions. Classical modern *accelerators* have become late modern *hindrances to acceleration* or *brakes* that are under transformative or erosive pressure from the unchained dynamizing forces that they themselves set in motion (cf. figure 8.1). Because of the interplay of cultural and structural "motors" articulated in the previous chapters, the dynamic of social acceleration has taken on a life of its own and is now turning against these institutions. This holds true for the institutions of the *military* and the *state bureaucracy*, but also in a certain way for the principles of *democratic control* and political regulation, as will be shown more clearly in chapter 11. Beyond this, the aforementioned dialectic can also be observed with respect to the institution of the industrial *labor time regime*, with its strict spatial and temporal separation of work and free time,[40] and possibly even regarding the specific spatiotemporal *institutionalization of functional differentiation*[41] and the *life course regime* of modernity that accompanies the idea of *stable personal identities* and orientating *normal biographies*.[42] Thus the previously stable societal framework of modernity has literally been set in motion, both semantically and institutionally. The task of the fourth and last part of this investigation is to reconstruct this movement as the consequence of the late modern stage of social acceleration in an empirically rich and theoretically substantial way and then to adequately determine its ethical and political effects.[43]

PART FOUR

CONSEQUENCES

9

ACCELERATION, GLOBALIZATION, POSTMODERNITY

IN MOST OF THE CURRENT diagnoses of the time the crisis of the ensemble of classical modern institutions exposed in the previous chapter appears to be the result of the developments that are commonly brought together under the catchphrase *globalization*. Thus Ulrich Beck, for example, interprets the globalization process not simply as a progressive *denationalization* (*Entstaatlichung*) but also explicitly as an "institution-softener" that has set in motion the rigid framework of the core elements of the welfare state, which were for a long time beyond the reach of the political process and, so to speak, "made them fluid":

> Institutions of the industrial society that appeared to be entirely closed off from political (re)organization, can be "cracked" and opened up to political intervention: the premises of the welfare state and the retirement pension system, of public benefits and community politics, of intrastructure policy, the organized power of the unions, the interfirm negotiation system of free collective bargaining as well as public expenditures, the tax system and "tax justice"—everything melts into political (expectations of) organizability under the new desert sun of globalization.[1]

In chapter 11 we will take a closer look at the fact that the breaking up of this institutional framework is not necessarily accompanied by the capacity to *politically* (or even *democratically*) reshape it, as Beck implies. On the contrary, it might rather be systematically linked to the progressive loss of the possibility that society can influence its own processes through political means. However, it is first necessary to grasp more precisely the common logic of the late modern processes by which social life becomes fluid and thereby to lay the ground for answering the notorious question concerning what is *genuinely new* in the contemporary phase of social development.[2]

Attempts at understanding this new element have not only been made under the heading of "globalized society" but also by means of various diagnoses of a "postmodernity" that is setting itself off from the previously developed or "classical" modernity.[3] They too perceive a "softening up" of classical modern institutions; they too postulate the end of stable personal and collective identities, the replacement of the meaning-embodying pattern of linear narratives by the principle of *fragmentary simultaneity*, the breaking up of national states and the overcoming of institutional boundaries between functional spheres, for instance, between art and the economy, the economy and politics, politics and science, etc.[4] More radical diagnoses of postmodernity announce at the same time the end of the project of modernity, of reason, of the subject, of politics and more or less everything else that functioned to generate meaning and legitimacy in modernity. Interestingly, the social-philosophical position of postmodernity here is also characterized by the idea that the world or "life" is no longer legible, comprehensible, and shapable from the perspective of subjects and politics—and also that it no longer needs to be, since aspirations to control and autonomy were only chimeras of modernity anyway. Philosophical postulates and sociological analyses are often juxtaposed in a disorderly way in this context, which appears particularly problematic where philosophical or normative projects are presented as empirical observations.[5]

The perception of a "break" in the development of modern society in the transition to the twenty-first century is shared, however, by an array of authors who follow the discourse of neither globalization nor postmodernity and for this reason use concepts like "second modernity," "late modernity," or "reflexive modernization" to characterize the new element. At the same time, these three concepts signal the assumption that what is new does not move *outside* the social-developmental framework of modernity but rather indicates simply a new phase or stage of development *within* the social paradigm of modernity.[6]

In the following three chapters I would like to demonstrate that both the *caesura* and the *continuity* of contemporary development can be grasped and situated in a theoretically precise and empirically fruitful manner only by way of a *temporal-analytic* definition of modernity. The claim to be justified in what follows is that developed societies of the Western type have experienced a further surge of acceleration in recent decades that once again transformed their foundational space-time regime and brought them to a critical tipping point for individual and collective forms of selfhood, identity, and agency.

The postulated surge of acceleration developed its economic, information-technological, and cultural driving forces at the latest in the 1970s,[7] though it gained its power to geographically expand and penetrate modern society as a whole (*raumgreifende Durchschlagskraft*) primarily from a confluence of three historical developments around 1989: the *political revolution* of those years, the collapse of East Germany and the Soviet regime and the political and economic opening up of East European states; the *digital revolution*, forced above all by the establishment of the Internet (and the buildup of satellite TV), which widened shortly thereafter into a *mobile revolution* that enabled microelectronic communicative availability unbound by location; and finally the *economic revolution* of flexible accumulation or post-Fordist just-in-time production in "turbo capitalism." They can all be understood as in essence *accelerative movements*.[8] Of course, the effects of these developments are interconnected and reinforce each other, as when the political upheavals after 1989 were favored by economic and information-technological networking and the latter in turn made possible new ways of accelerating production.

In particular, the achievement of *real time* information transmission has exerted a powerful accelerating undertow on almost all areas of economic and everyday life and thus created the impression that we are witnesses of a new, qualitative revolution of speed in whose wake speed is no longer symbolized by the breathless "running of the rattling, rotating machine wheel," but by the World Wide Web and catchwords like *instant gratification* and *instant delivery*.[9] The virtualization and digitization of once material processes (in model development, for example) and the embedding of digital information transmission in "analog," i.e., material processing chains, brings about the simultaneous acceleration of production, circulation, and consumption.[10]

As I already laid out in the analysis of the cultural self-observation of modernity in chapter 1, the cultural perception and processing of these events in many ways repeats the pattern seen in the reception and processing of the surge of acceleration around the previous turn of the century.[11] Beyond the strong discursive reaction to the postulated surge that is situated at the level of self-observation, sociological and economic analyses also deliver "material" evidence for the acceleration of production speed (and hence also of distribution and consumption), the tempo of life and social change.[12] However, the attempt to measure this acceleration encounters difficulties similar to those of the endeavor to determine the degree of globalization. So perhaps the degree of pressure under which the forces and niches of inertia discussed in chapter 2.3 fall might serve as an indicator for the postulated surge of acceleration: presumably it could be shown that natural speed limits are attacked with redoubled fury (for example, where an attempt is made to stimulate infant learning even *before* birth, where the acceleration of brain functions by computer-technological implantations is pondered, or where biological changes through genetic engineering are achieved in a fraction of the time that natural cultivation would require for a similar result); that social islands of deceleration are everywhere coming under increased erosive pressure (as when modern traditions practiced for decades, for instance, in university systems, but also in production processes and even in transportation systems, fall victim to rationalizing measures); and that at least in op-ed pages and academic journals there are increasing reports of dysfunctional side effects in the form of pathological individual "deceleration reactions" such as "hurry sickness" or the "national malaise," depression.[13] At the same time, it seems that in our cultural self-observation the impression is growing stronger that accelerated social change is only occurring at the "user interface" of society and actually hides a deep-seated cultural standstill.[14] Meanwhile, the "ideological" call for deceleration is swelling tremendously. Possibly the most interesting development, though, is occurring in the domain of *functional* or *accelerative deceleration.* As I worked out in the previous chapter, the pressure to accelerate has now become so great that the braking and steering institutional scheme of "classical modernity," which enabled long-term acceleration precisely through its short-term braking effect—the economic activity of the state is doubtless to be placed in this category[15]—can no longer withstand the "unlimited acceleration" of late modernity. The consequences are still unforeseeable.[16]

Moreover, for my thesis it is decisive that all three developments can also be understood as forms of globalization. Indeed, globalization discourse is defined by attention to the ramifications of just these late twentieth-century information-technological economic and political transformations of social relations. Yet an account of what is *qualitatively* new in these circumstances can only be successfully undertaken from a temporal-analytic angle: so long as diagnoses of globalization fail to recognize this, their attempts to justify claims about a "new age" remain unsatisfactory and confusing.[17] The exchange or movement of information, money, commodities, and people, or even of ideas and diseases, across large distances is not new: what is new is the *speed* and *lack of resistance* with which such processes transpire.[18]

Many long-distance transactions can be digitized and therefore performed in "real time," that is, practically without any time delay, without large costs or friction losses: capital investments, information transfers of all kinds, and the simultaneous processing of virtualizable products around the globe are the most well-known examples of this. The more directly place-bound infrastructural presuppositions of such transactions become dispensable in the wake of the further development of modern mobile technologies, especially the cell phone expanded into a personal computer with wireless Internet access. Alongside this, however, is the tremendous decline in the transfer times and costs for material movements of people and goods in the last few decades. Naturally, this reduction of the costs, resistances, and time needed to overcome distances has effected a quantitative increase of the corresponding *volume* of transactions. Therefore, David Held and his colleagues, in their meticulous empirical study, can characterize globalization as a state defined simultaneously by measures of extensity, intensity, velocity, and impact propensity.[19] Because *extensity*, i.e., the large spatial extension of transaction processes, is an analytically defining criterion of globality, an alteration in the degree of globalization can only be measured by the other three parameters. Thus the investigation of Held and colleagues quite consistently yields the result that the newness of contemporary globalization consists above all in an escalation of the global velocity and intensity of transactions in many spheres of society.[20] The heightening of the degree of *impact propensity* is then primarily a consequence of increases in those two dimensions. Both increases of velocity and of intensity, however, illustrate nothing other than processes of social acceleration: the first dimension comprises the acceleration of transportation and communication, the latter the escalation of the number of transactions per unit of time.

Yet this only registers a quantitative change. The thesis of a *qualitative* transformation in the social formations of modernity rests on the supposition that the accelerative processes summarized under the catchphrase of *globalization* lead, or have already led, to a recent transformation of the space-time regime of modernity. This is precisely what is postulated, either implicitly or explicitly, in most of the theoretically oriented diagnoses of globalization. The qualitative spatiotemporal change is revealed both in analyses of globalization as a *process* and in its definition as a new social *condition* or state of affairs and, interestingly, even when one conceives of globalization as a *political project*.[21]

As a *process*, globalization can be defined with David Harvey, as a new round or further escalation of time-space compression, or with Anthony Giddens, as the progressive achievement of a new level of time-space distanciation, i.e., the enlargement of the extent of temporal and spatial capacities of social coordination.[22] This process is characterized by the aforementioned technological and political reduction of the costs, resistances, and time needed for overcoming spatial distances. As a result *spatial distances become irrelevant* for many social processes and ever more events or actions are spatiotemporally "disembedded," i.e., have causes and effects that are largely or completely temporally and spatially separated from the event itself.[23] Because such disembedding processes release actions and events from their local contexts, they embody an essential cause for the *decontextualization* of lived events noted in chapter 5.2, which turns everyday experience into a series of mutually unconnected episodes.

Some facts that may serve as clear examples of spatial "disembedding" are, say, that politicians today can assert that the security of Germany is no longer defended at its borders, but in Iraq or Afghanistan, that a football game in Japan can set off riots in Moscow or a course of events in Argentina can produce a price slump in Wall Street, and all in *real time*. That such reciprocal effects seem to be extended not only spatially but also across social spheres may count as the escalatory aspect of this disembedding: economic events in Asia have implications for educational policy decisions in Europe and cultural preferences in the U.S., etc.[24] Naturally as a result of this development there are in turn *residual* gains in the relevance of space or locale and attempts at *reembedding* social events: precisely because space has become contingent for many decisions, regional or local differences and identities gain a new significance.[25] However, this is unambiguously a *consequence* of the prior disembedding.[26]

As I have already shown in part 1, the contraction or annihilation of space by time or, better, by acceleration is a constitutive feature of modernity per se and as such is certainly nothing new. But it occurs in historical waves that lead, in particular following the introduction of new transportation and communications technologies, to a step-by-step transformation of the social *space-time regime*, i.e., to altered relations to space, to things, and to fellow human beings as well as to changes in the relations subjects have to themselves, hence to a transformation of the objective, the subjective, and the social world.[27] Therefore, a new wave of time-space compression has wide-ranging social and cultural consequences, which are definitely capable of founding a qualitatively new society when the critical tipping points of an existing regime are passed. Moreover, the accounts of globalization as a new condition or state of affairs seek to prove that such a tipping point was reached by the late modern processes of globalization.

According to the most pregnant definition of globalization as a new *condition*, an altered space-time regime formed as a result of the most recent time-space compression. It is characterized *spatially* by the replacement of the stable and the fixed with perpetually moving "flows" and *temporally* by the dissolution of stable rhythms and sequences following the ubiquitous contemporization (*Vergleichzeitigung*) of even the noncontemporaneous.

An idea that is on the point of attaining cultural hegemony today is that the culturally and structurally significant spatial qualities are no longer defined by territorially or locally fixed, immobile institutions, by stationary sites and places, but, as it were, by *streams* or *flows* (of power, capital, goods, persons, ideas, diseases, risks, etc.) that continually alter their direction and shape as they flit here and there. At the very least, it dominates the discourses of globalization and postmodernity. It therefore seems to indicate a key aspect of the sensibility and mental state of contemporary society. Zygmunt Bauman concludes from this that the present epoch is most aptly characterized as "liquid modernity" and establishes the connection between the "institution-softening" aspect of globalization and the creeping irrelevance of space with respect to time in the following way:

> Liquids, unlike solids, cannot easily hold their shape. Fluids, so to speak, neither fix space nor bind time. While solids have clear spatial dimensions but neutralize the impact, and thus downgrade the significance of time (effectively resist its flow or render it irrelevant), fluids do not keep to any shape for long and are constantly ready (and prone) to change it; and so for them it is the flow of time that counts, more than the space they happen to occupy: that space, after all, they fill but "for a moment." In a sense, solids cancel time; for liquids, on the contrary, it is mostly time that matters. When describing solids, one may ignore time altogether; in describing fluids, to leave time out of account would be a grievous mistake. Descriptions of fluids are snapshots, and they need a date at the bottom of the picture. Fluids travel easily. . . . From the meeting with solids they emerge unscathed, while the solids they have met, if they stay solid, are changed—get moist or drenched. . . . *These are reasons to consider "fluidity" or "liquidity" as fitting metaphors when we wish to grasp the nature of the present, in many ways novel, phase in the history of modernity.*[28]

Manuel Castells also sees the new "Information Age" as defined by a change in the space-time regime. He tries to reconstruct the transition from a "space of places" to a "space of flows" in a more strongly empirically oriented analysis by means of, among other things, the investigation of changes in urban infrastructure and architectural principles. The *space of flows* is here characterized in particular by a network-like, nonhierarchically stabilized, centerless organization that operates only across temporary condensations and reversible inclusions.[29]

In connection with this, Castells then tries to work out the way a new structure of *social time* accompanies this changed morphology of space, one he calls "timeless time": "The space of flows . . . dissolves time by disordering the sequence of events and making them simultaneous, thus installing society in eternal ephemerality."[30] Underlying the concept of timeless time is the idea that time is formed by the duration, sequence, and rhythm of actions and events. Consequently, a social condition characterized by the elimination of duration, the purging of rhythm from social events, and the dissolution of fixed and stable sequential series (for instance, of the career or life course, the availability of foodstuffs in the course of the year, the types of action in the course of the day or week, etc.) can be described as "timeless" insofar as it is dominated by the modes of momentary *simultaneity* and, as its, so to speak, negative horizon, *eternity*.[31]

In agreement with David Harvey and Frederic Jameson, Castells points out that the predominance of these modes is, in the first place, tightly connected to the cultural perception of an *end of history* because the idea of a history "in the collective singular" (Koselleck) is bound up with a sequential temporality of development, progress, and order. Hence, in the second place, the former constitutes at the same time a fundamental principle of cultural "postmodernity," namely, the eclectic and arbitrary combination of historical set pieces at the price of the idea of sequential order and historical development.[32] Interestingly, the concept of a timeless time, and the fact that Harvey once quite unsystematically spoke of the annihilation of space *by* time and later of the annihilation of space *and* time,[33] gives rise to the suspicion that our sense of time is not unscathed by the complete separation of time from space and the "pulverization" of the latter: temporal orientation without a spatial foundation seems to be a difficult undertaking. Thus Bauman also surmises that the new irrelevance of space clothes itself in the form of an "annihilation of time" and then a bit later adds to an observation concerning the paradoxical structure of an extensionless, momentary time the ironic remark "Perhaps, having killed space as value, time has committed suicide? Was not space merely the first casualty in time's frenzied rush to self-annihilation?"[34]

Castells does not claim any more than the other aforementioned scholars that the space of flows and timeless time constitute the decisive space-time regime for *all* social groups in the globalized world. For most human beings, the *space of* (stable) *places* that prevails outside network streams and (linear) *clock time* are as dominant as ever, but the new modes of space and time determine the culturally and structurally decisive logics of development.[35] This is one manifestation of the dialectic of acceleration and the institutional regime of modernity worked out in chapter 8. As Bauman makes clear, in "classical modernity" the spatiotemporal unboundedness of nomadism (e.g., of the homeless, the gypsies, the *fahrendes Volk*, or travelling people, etc.) was a sign of backwardness in comparison to settledness in the sense of a "permanent address" (and the time discipline related to clocks) and thus led to social exclusion, while today it is precisely the reverse: being bound to a place and having insufficient time sovereignty (that is, being caught in the space of places and long-term commitments) are things that make the socially subordinate classes appear backward and "left behind" and signal a danger of exclusion. If again and again in globalization discourse there is talk of the growing supremacy of capital over labor, it is rooted precisely in this: capital can move, so to speak, "timelessly" across the entire earth, while the mobility of workers and their ability to accelerate and become more flexible remain very limited.[36] This idea of the *triumph of the nomadic* over that which is fixed in space and time also naturally connects the diagnoses of globalization with those of postmodernization. Indeed, the latter seem far more strongly oriented to the *temporal* than to the *spatial* reorganization of society. The dissolution of temporal orders and the dominance of *simultaneities* of all kinds, with associated connotations of liquefaction, dehistoricization, and "kaleidoscopic fragmentation," lie at the center of the discourse of postmodernity.[37]

Drawing on the work of John Urry, the following associative list of social phenomena that can be grouped together under the keyword of *contemporization*, or "instantaneous time," may clarify the ways in which diagnoses of globalization and postmodernization converge—and also how much they can be defined by the logic of social acceleration in its three forms of technical acceleration, the acceleration of social change, and the heightening of the pace of life.[38]

FORMS OF CONTEMPORIZATION

- Changes in information and communications technology that make possible a simultaneous worldwide exchange of and access to information and ideas

- (Organizational-)technological changes that make the distinctions between day and night, workdays and weekends, free time and work disappear
- The growing interchangeability of goods, places, and images in a "throw-away society"
- The increasing fluidity and ephemerality of fashions, goods, work processes, ideas, and images
- A sharpened "temporariness" of goods, jobs, careers, nature, values, and relationships
- The often boundary-crossing prevalence of new commodities, flexible forms of technology, and enormous trash heaps
- The growth of short-term labor contracts and a "just-in-time" workforce as well as the tendency to draw up long task lists
- The increase of worldwide nonstop trade in securities and currencies
- The growing "modularization" of free time, training and continuing education, and work
- The extreme increase in the availability of goods and customs from highly different societies in all parts of the world
- Growing divorce rates and other forms of the dissolution of households
- Disappearing intergenerational trust and decreasing intergenerational solidarity
- The (worldwide) feeling of an overly fast pace of life that is in contradiction with basic human experiences
- Growing volatility of political voting behavior

Urry speaks of "instantaneous time" and defines it as follows: "I . . . use the term . . . to characterise: first, new informational and communicational technologies based upon inconceivably brief instants which are wholly beyond human consciousness; second, the simultaneous character of social and technical relationships which replaces the linear logic of clock-time characterised by the temporal separation of cause and effect occurring over separate measurable instants; and third, a metaphor for the widespread significance of exceptionally short-term and fragmented time, even where it is not literally instantaneous and simultaneous" (2009:189).

Even authors that are rather skeptical of the diagnoses of globalization or postmodernization assert that contemporization is a fundamental trend of contemporary society.[39] Nevertheless, in many respects this idea of "timeless simultaneity" has in the end a merely metaphorical or even "illusionary" quality.[40] For this reason, the diagnoses discussed here still owe us a systematic explanation of why and in what ways the acceleration of numerous processes today leads to an inversion in our perception of time from sequential patterns to forms of simultaneity. I would therefore like to demonstrate in the remaining three chapters of this investigation that what is "new" about the contemporary age consists in the fact that the tempo of social change has surpassed a *critical threshold*—namely, that of the succession of generations—and therefore compels a pattern of time perception and time processing that can be described as the *temporalization of time itself* and hence as a *detemporalization* of life, history, and society. As I will show, the temporal-structural conditions of the predominance of ideas of a "timeless time," a static-dynamic simultaneity, and the end of history can be almost effortlessly reconstructed with the help of this concept of the acceleration-induced transformation of individual and cultural time perspectives.

In the course of doing so, I will analyze the process of the temporalization of time with regard to individual forms of identity, on the one hand, and the transformation of the conditions of political action, on the other, for this process first emerges at the interface or "translation point" between systemic-structural time patterns and cultural time perceptions and time horizons. Thus it is no coincidence that the change posited in the diagnoses of postmodernity is usually focused on just these two areas. Both the fragmentation, multiplication, and diffusion of social identities ("the end of the subject") and the apparent abandonment of a political shaping and normative steering of society ("the end of politics") are equally central themes of postmodern social theory.[41] In light of the reconstructed processes of liquefaction and contemporization, the diagnosis of postmodernity can then be reformulated as the attainment of a social state in which *the acceleration of social relations rooted in modernity surpasses a critical point or takes on a new quality such that the linearity and sequentiality of the perception and processing of problems and changes, at both individual and social levels, is broken up and the aspiration to integration is abandoned. The rapid pace compels a nonintegrated form of parallel processing that leads to fragmentation and a loss of steering, intelligibility, and malleability (Gestaltbarkeit) on the individual as well as the sociopolitical level.*

At first glance the diagnosis of an "end of politics" seems to stand in sharp contrast to the third of the possible perspectives on globalization,[42] which conceives globalization itself as a political project. This contradiction loses its sharpness, however, when one keeps in mind the character of the project, which is, namely, to eliminate the hindrances to the circulation of "global flows." Because it is in the nature of these streams, in particular streams of capital, to flow in another direction at the slightest political or economic re-sistance, it has become an urgent aim of (national state) politics to create the most favorable possible conditions of circulation in one's own area of influ-ence, because otherwise exclusion in the sense of avoidance or being passed by threatens — here one sees the novel *residual relevance* of territory postulated earlier. Moreover, this requires, above all, the removal of political claims to regulate and steer the "free flow" of global streams, though not an uncondi-tional abandonment of regulation per se. In fact, the *strengthened* regulation and sanctioning of place-bound and time-bound developments that *hinder* the free flow of streams of capital, commodities, experts, and information is definitely part of this political project, and this makes understandable the objections of "globalization-sceptics" who challenge the idea that national states have lost their claims to power. One should count here in particular the attempts to stop or at least contain *migration streams*. Insofar as it is not a question of members of the "global elite," the luring of whom into one's country is now on the agenda of most nation-states, migrants are not part of global networks, but rather are among the excluded whose presence can be reckoned among the conditions that hinder desired flows.

Unless it is acting to remove hindrances to circulation, national and demo-cratic political steering is, on the one hand, too time consuming and, on the other, incurs transaction costs and friction losses at the borders and thus functions as a brake on the hyperaccelerated circulation processes of global networks. These "fluid" networks are in turn certainly not free of relations of power and domination, although they embody a similarly fluid, depersonal-ized form of power.[43] Zygmunt Bauman conjectures that, in order to guaran-tee the free flow of these "global powers," the political project of globaliza-tion intentionally disintegrates all spatially and temporally bound communal social bonds, i.e., those located beyond the *space of streams* and *timeless time*: "For power to be free to flow, the world must be free of fences, barriers, forti-fied borders and checkpoints. Any dense and tight network of social bonds, and particularly a territorially rooted tight network, is an obstacle to be cleared out of the way. Global powers are bent on dismantling such networks for the sake of their continuous and growing fluidity, that principle source of their strength and the warrant of their invincibility."

Indeed, Bauman believes that the elimination of hindrances to circulation is the actual goal of the post-1989 "new wars," led above all by the U.S.: "Mili-tary force and its 'hit and run' war-plan prefigured, embodied and portended what was really at stake in the new type of war in the era of liquid modernity: not the conquest of a new territory, but crushing the walls which stopped the flow of new, fluid global powers; beating out of the enemy's head the desire to set up his own rules, and so opening up the so-far barricaded and walled-off, inaccessible space to the operations of the other, non-military, arms of power."[44]

The new world order identified in the diagnoses of globalization and post-modernity is therefore not free from relations of power and domination, but these are no longer democratically legitimated and no longer politically accountable: from the viewpoint of individual and collective actors they prove to be unchecked, unsteered, and unsteerable. In this sense acceleration is unmasked as a political strategy of immunizing the power of streams that underlies the political project of globalization, understood as a politics of eliminating the modern demand for democratic steering.[45] In the related, discourse-defining perception of globalization as a "brakeless train wreaking havoc,"[46] or as an unharnessed juggernaut driving at full throttle that grinds to a pulp and smashes to pieces everything that stands in its way (Giddens),[47] the tight connection between globalization as both *process, condition,* and *political project* and the achievement of a new level of acceleration is expressed once again, this time in a metaphorically condensed way. The goal of the following chapters is now to go beyond the level of the discursive self-observation of late modernity and arrive at a systematic understanding of this connection.

10

SITUATIONAL IDENTITY: OF DRIFTERS AND PLAYERS

1. THE DYNAMIZATION OF THE SELF IN MODERNITY

As I argued in the introduction to this work, time structures constitute the paradigmatic site for the linkage of culture and social structure. They are what primarily perform the necessary "translation" of systemic requirements into individual action orientations, because even in a posttraditional society they endow action with normatively binding force, largely stable expectations, and an orienting frame that is experienced as if it were a natural fact. This orienting frame is decisive for the time structure of identity patterns in which past, present, and future must necessarily be linked because the sense of who one is cannot be separated from the interpretation of who one was and will be or would like to be in the future.[1] Therefore the transformation of the *space-time regime* of a society has ramifications for the socially dominant forms of self-relation, i.e., the predominant *personality types* or *patterns of identity*. Forms of selfhood are set aflow because relations to things and other actors change along with the space-time regime as a result of the way the "relation to the self" and the "relation to the world" that subjects have are ineradicably interwoven.[2] As I have demonstrated in chapter 5.3, our sense of *who we are* (hence of our identity) is virtually a function of our relationship to space, time, fellow human beings, and the objects of our environment (or to our action and experience). Thus a fundamental question for the analysis of the postulated break within the development of modern societies is how the social change observed by the diagnoses of "globalization" and "postmodernization"—one that is constituted *spatially* as a process of the recent "contraction" or even irrelevance of space due to technical acceleration and *temporally* as a process of transformation in the direction of a "timeless" instantaneous time — impacts the forms of subjectivity in late modern society.

One has to keep in mind that the liquefactions or dynamizations dealt with under the keyword of *globalization* are per se nothing qualitatively new. Rather they are in the end simply the most recent stage of the three-dimensional process of acceleration that stands at the heart of this investigation. So we must again take up with particular care the question raised at the end of part 2, namely, whether and how the *quantitative* escalation of a constitutive principle of modernity can flip over into a *qualitative transformation* of forms of identity (or relations to oneself).

As we have seen, the perception of a shift in the balance between movement and inertia in favor of dynamization even with respect to one's very self is a basic experience of modernity. Indeed, one can read, for instance, Saint-Preux, the protagonist of Jean-Jacques Rousseau's epistolary novel *Julie, or the New Héloise*, describing his experience of arriving in Paris not just as a literary anticipation of Georg Simmel's theoretical attempts to define the influence of the metropolis on the individual but also as a foreshadowing of the calamities of the late modern, overwhelmingly relationally or situationally[3] defined self: "The good, the evil, the beautiful, the ugly, the true, the virtuous exist only in certain places and within certain limits. . . . One has to be more agile than Alcibiades, to change one's opinion at each meeting, revise one's understanding so to speak at every step and measure one's principles by the same standard." Soon afterward he states that he began "to feel the drunkenness this intoxicating, restless life gives to those who lead it; I fall into a daze that is like the condition of a man who sees a mass of objects rapidly pass by him one after the other. Nothing of what passes under my gaze penetrates to my heart; all together, though, it disquiets its movements and demands that they stop, *so that for several moments I forget who I am* and to whom I belong. . . . I move from one mood to the next and . . . *from one day to the next I cannot be sure . . . what I will love.*"[4]

One already sees here all the elements that characterize the diagnosis of *postmodern* identities: the liquefaction of previously stable structures of the self in favor of more open, experimental, fragmentary, and, above all else, consistently transitory forms of selfhood that reflect the dynamic of restless "global flows." As Douglas Kellner puts it: "Identity today . . . becomes a freely chosen game, a theatrical presentation of the self, in which one is able to present oneself in a variety of roles, images, and activities, relatively unconcerned about shifts, transformations, and dramatic changes."[5] And Iain Chambers describes late modern identity management in the following way: "you constantly shift where you stand, you subdivide your life into separate areas and into differences, you construct your lifestyle in a mobile way. You consciously make decisions about how you will appear in this moment, how you will present yourself."[6] But even much more cautious social-scientific observers who are rather skeptical of the thesis of an epochal break detect a shift from stable identities to dynamic relations to self that are characterized by a "permanent revision" of biographies or at the very least by the way formerly *fixed* building blocks of identity become contingent.[7]

Moreover, if modernity is characterized by the "love of movement for its own sake" and seeks "the true life in it and in it alone" (Friedrich Ancillon) and if as a consequence even "identity is caught up in movement,"[8] then the real question concerning an identity-theoretical definition of what is new in late modernity runs: *what is the difference between the classical modern and late modern forms of the liquefaction and dynamization of identity?* My thesis, which remains to be explicated, is that the difference lies in the fact that the predominance of *individualization* in the transformation of relationships to self and world in classical modernity leads to a *temporalization of life*, i.e., to a perspective on one's own life as a project to be given shape in time, while the same process of dynamization in the late modern phase of its development effects a "detemporalized," *situational* definition of identity. Thus the "acceleration of being" in modernity mentioned at the end of part 2 manifests itself as, so to speak, a double break in the socially dominant form of selfhood, one I will now sketch with the help of the guiding concepts of individualization and acceleration and ideal-typically reconstructed transitions from premodernity to "classical modernity" and from the latter to late modernity.

2. FROM SUBSTANTIAL A PRIORI IDENTITY TO STABLE A POSTERIORI IDENTITY: THE TEMPORALIZATION OF LIFE

With respect to the predominant form of selfhood or *personality type*, modernization has been viewed since the time of the sociological "classics" as a process of *individualization*.[9] This is inherently linked to the dynamization of social relations insofar as it designates the detachment of individual actions and lives from rigid, pregiven social roles and positions and from obligatory traditions and conventions and also clearly heightens the scope of individual freedom and responsibility regarding the shaping of one's own life. Even though it is historically problematic to speak of "the" premodern identity in general since there certainly is no such thing as premodernity in the sense of a unified social formation, one can nevertheless justify the claim that in traditional societies (and well into early modernity) the substantial social identity of subjects was, as it were, fixed and predefined *externally*. The question of identity (insofar as it was even posed at all as a practical life problem in such societies) was answered by looking outward: tradition and religion show the premodern subject its place in the world and in society, and predefine who it is, where it stands in society, and what it has to do. Things like religion, place of residence, "political orientation," occupation, form of life, etc., are *given*, not *chosen*, which already makes clear that questions about political orientation, religion, form of life, or occupation are meaningless within the horizon of the traditional society. In fact, these "identity parameters" are only recognizable as such at all when traditions and conventions have *become questionable*.

As Charles Taylor has argued, relations of social recognition are already secured "a priori" in societies that start out from a meaning horizon that includes a divine or at any rate pregiven "great chain of being": the measure of social esteem that is due someone can be almost entirely read off from his place in the social order.[10] The correlative concepts of identity and recognition, which become more and more important for culture and politics as modernity advances, play practically no role in the vocabulary and self-understanding of premodern societies (with the exception of sharpened crises involving conflicts of loyalty, as one sees in exemplary fashion in *Antigone*, for instance). They denote nothing that could be influenced by an individual and hence might become questionable. For this reason, self-relations or identities are scarcely a theme of reflexive contestation in strictly traditional societies. This occurs only in the wake of the reflexive *inward turn* that becomes, especially after the Reformation, the dominant practice of self-determination in modernity.[11] Thus subjects in traditional societies have, as it were, a *substantial a priori identity*.

Individualization thus designates a process beginning with modernity in which substantial *alternatives* for life and action open up and a gradually increasing amount of responsibility for shaping their own lives is transferred to individuals. One presupposition of this is social change in the form of a liquifying of traditional standards and role patterns. Who one is can no longer be determined externally, but rather depends increasingly on one's own collaboration. So individualization means primarily the possibility as well as the task of discovering and choosing identity-constituting roles and relationships for oneself (e.g., profession, spouse, religious community, political convictions)—and then bearing the consequences. Hence the self becomes much more strongly a "reflexive project" than before.[12]

Now it is of decisive importance that individualization in this sense is necessarily correlated with a *temporalization of life*. The development or "realization" of identity becomes a temporal project that unfolds in a day-to-day conduct of life: this is the classical modern form of the "setting-in-motion" of identity. If responsibility for what one's life becomes, for the *leading* of that life, and for the pursuit of one's own identity-constituting project lies with the individual herself, then she is forced to provide for her future and sound out alternative (future) possibilities. This is why Norbert Elias in *The Civilizing Process* also notes a growing "compulsion of foresight" (which complements the spread of self-constraint).[13] In contrast, an orientation to the past loses some of its importance.[14]

However, the objective susceptibility of the future to planning (*Planbarkeit*) is an essential condition for such a rearrangement of identity-constituting time horizons. Identity as the directed movement of life along alternative developmental paths could only become a socially binding project when the liquefaction of forms of life and community, which reached epoch-making levels during the industrial revolution, was steered onto relatively fixed, institutionalized rails in the increasingly "organized modernity"[15] of the welfare state and thereby dynamically stabilized. Martin Kohli has worked out this process in particular detail by showing the significance of the institutionalized "life course regime" for the identity patterns of classical modernity. "The modernization process is a transition from a pattern of relatively contingent life events to one of a foreseeable life course,"[16] he states and further points out that a life course divided into temporal sequences has a double function: on the one hand, it undergirds the institutional order of the welfare state (the educational system, the social insurance system, the pension system, etc.) and conversely becomes a socially obligatory standard through this system of institutions; but, on the other hand, it establishes an identity-guiding, orienting schema in the conception of the "normal biography," which allows for respective three-stage "schedules" in professional life (education, gainful employment, retirement) and the familial structuring of life (childhood in the ancestral family, own family with kids, older phase after the kids move out). Kohli summarizes the *classical-modern conception* of an individually shaped life as follows: "The development leading to modernity is a process of the *temporalization of life*. . . .

The change has led from a form of life in which old age was only relevant as a categorial status to a form of life in which the course of a lifetime is a central structural principle: a form of life mainly ordered biographically, i.e., by lifelong 'schedules,' has taken the place of a mainly static or situational one ordered by stable belonging."[17]

An identity that is temporalized in this sense is thus closely tied to a conduct of life that sets out from the premise of temporal sequences with reliably foreseeable contents, for instance, in educational and career patterns, family planning, and retirement provision. It thereby replaces premodern society's form of life, correctly described by Kohli as being at once static (in the substantial definition of identity and social order) *and* situational (in the conduct of life as a reactive adaptation to unforeseeable, exogenously determined contingencies and vicissitudes of the world).

In this context the reliability of social institutions corresponds to the idea of the stability of one's own identity unfolding in the progress of life. For this reason, the "classical modern" identity appears to be, so to speak, a *stable a posteriori identity*. The identity-constituting task given to the modern individual is: *find your own place in the world*, i.e., choose a career, start a family, decide on a religious community, and find a political orientation. Yet finding one's identity in this way is inherently a *one-time* process. As a rule, it follows the standards of sturdily interlocking social milieus and thus often results in typical "identity clusters" in which specific educational paths, professional activities, forms of life, political orientations, etc., are tightly correlated, which limits the free combination of the "building blocks" of identity. However, to me this fact seems less relevant than the empirical fact that once one's identity has been "found," along with the role patterns that define it, it is only rarely substantially revised. Thus in classical modernity divorce and career change as well as conversion to another religion or another political camp are always possible, but remain exceptions and so constitute indexes of a failed or at least endangered identity project: they represent, as it were, emergency revisions of identity.

All the same, of course, *revision* and *conversion* were already real possibilities of biographical development within the horizon of "classical modernity," but where they do occur they are as a rule narratively reconstructed as a *story of progress*, i.e., as important stages on the way to a more authentic life or as an emancipation from bondage and a liberation from error.[18] So a revised identity always reproduces a comprehensive perspective on the continuous development and unfolding of a total life project. The narrative representation

of the linkage of past, present, and future bears the form of a story of progress and development that contains a reconstructible, meaning-constituting
goal horizon.[19] One can say that its most prominent cultural model is the
bourgeois *Bildungsroman*, the coming-of-age novel or developmental narrative, in which it is almost invariably a question of finding a self-determined
identity and asserting and unfolding it in a potentially hostile or indifferent
environment.[20]

It seems to me that a biographical development of a life plan or a project
of identity like this is inextricably, as it were, "structurally" coupled to a "generational" tempo of social change in the sense defined in chapter 4. For it
presupposes, on the one hand, that the space of experience and the horizon
of expectations are sufficiently different to allow one to conceive of one's life
(as well as the development of society) as a *directed motion* and not to have to
carry on traditions in a unreflective way and, on the other, that the horizon of
expectations remains stable enough to allow long-run, time-resistant life perspectives to develop, the gratification of needs to be systematically postponed,
and the completion of the biographical pattern to be patiently awaited.

In contrast, in *premodern* society time necessarily appeared as *motionless*
and static, as a foil against whose traditionally defined background the undirected contingencies and vicissitudes of life transpired. The reason for this is
that fundamental social structures changed *more* slowly than the complete
turnover of the three generations that can be alive together at any given time.
If the pace of social change is instead *higher* than that of the replacement
of generations, then, as I will soon argue, the idea of *stable* personal identities can no longer be sustained. It is only in classical modernity, which lies
between these two dynamic limiting cases, that each respective new generation can become the bearer of structural and cultural innovation, as Ansgar
Weyman has shown.[21] Thus a kind of intergenerational work of renewal, or
generational project, is contained in the identity-finding task as previously
defined, but this also comes with a promise of generational stability.

This stability is quite evident in the kind of employment relations that
were undoubtedly central for the modern identity. It is no coincidence that
Zygmunt Bauman, drawing on Daniel Cohen, describes the contract of employment between a "Fordist factory" and its workers using the vocabulary of
bourgeois marriage: it was inherently oriented toward stability ("until death
do us part") and calculable career patterns and routines ("divorce was out of
the question"), but in each case it had to be individually accepted.[22] Naturally,
such secure forms of employment were quite exceptional, even in classical

modernity, but they defined the paradigmatic form of a successful identity in one's professional biography and counted for a long time as the epitome of modernness. This kind of generational stability not only covered central areas of life (marriage, occupation, political orientation, etc.) but also to a large extent peripheral dimensions like membership in associations, voluntarily acquired social obligations, insurance providers, banking institutions, and even automobile brands. The meaning of this kind of constancy for the possibility of stable identities only becomes visible when one contrasts it to the instability of late modern social relations.

3. FROM TEMPORALLY STABLE TO SITUATIONAL IDENTITY: THE TEMPORALIZATION OF TIME

Because individual self-relations require a constant balancing of *continuity* and *coherence* against *change* and *flexibilization*, the socially determined relationship of movement and inertia is immediately relevant to them.[23] It should be clear from the preceding arguments that this balance is produced more dynamically in modern societies than in traditional societies; and it is just as evident that the classical modern identity was nevertheless constructed in a relatively time-resistant fashion and hence rooted in biographical coherence and continuity even when it had to preserve itself in the face of change and upheaval. As opposed to this, observations of a *second wave of individualization* and hence *pluralization* have been mounting in the cultural and social sciences since the 1970s (thus in roughly the same time period that diagnoses of a transformation of the space-time regime of modernity emerged).[24] The finding they suggest is that the aforementioned balance shifted once again, this time enduringly in favor of a dynamization of identity or the self.

So it is not surprising that the diagnoses of a "postmodern" identity, which are otherwise quite heterogeneous, converge in the thesis of a liquefaction of stable personal identity in favor of more open, experimental, and often also fragmentary self-projects. Even in its late modern form, *individualization* means the increase of possible choices and contingencies with respect to the shaping of one's biography, where this increase primarily involves freer *combinability* and easier *revisability* of the building blocks of identity. Thus in late modernity there is, on the one hand, a considerable increase in available choices and ways of differentiating oneself not only regarding *central* dimensions of life and identity like profession, family, religion, residence, and, tendentially, nationality, sexuality and gender as well, but also relatively *peripheral* areas of life that, nevertheless, contribute to the shaping of everyday existence, such as one's telephone, insurance or energy provider, unions and associations, favored forms of investment, etc.

On the other hand, however, the identity building blocks in both central and peripheral areas are now, as I said, almost freely combinable and revisable at will: families, professions, religious membership, political preferences, insurance companies, and friendship networks are no longer fixed points in the conduct of life that endure for a lifetime after a (one-time) choice. They can all be revised at any time by one's own choices or by the decisions of others. Therefore the *consciousness of contingency* is unavoidably heightened even where old patterns are handed down and almost no use is made of the new options and possibilities of change.[25] At the same time, a choice made in *one* dimension is losing its power to determine which possibilities remain open in *other* dimensions. In the wake of the looming progressive dissolution of rigid, identity-shaping milieus, on the one hand, and fixed sequential and career patterns, on the other, a given education no longer necessarily leads to a given profession, and a given profession is no longer accompanied with a high probability by a given preference of political party. Nor do either of these coincide any longer with particular religious orientations or free time activities. *Chronological phases of life* are similarly losing their tight correlation with specific activities and orientations: for instance, periods of education that are traditionally associated with youth are increasingly common at older ages and after periods of extended gainful employment; the same holds true for biographical phases of falling in love, getting married, and having children, while conversely lasting involuntary exclusion from employment can even be experienced in youth.[26] Even involvement with so-called youth cultures no longer seems to be regimented in age-group-specific ways.

So what is new in this situation is, on the one hand, the progressive dissolution of "clusters" of identity features found together with a high probability, i.e., an increasing differentiation of individual life situations, and, on the other hand, a loss of *predictability* in biographical development, such that one can no longer infer its probable course from an individual's decision in particular areas of life. And revisability here means nothing other than the *temporalization of personal identity*: one can no longer read off who someone is from a traditionally defined cultural and social model of order that lasts for many generations (as in premodernity), nor can one determine it for an entire individual lifespan (as in classical modernity). Instead, it depends on the particular *point in time* within an individual's life. Identity thus becomes *transitory*;[27] it alters at an *intragenerational* rate of change. As I have shown in chapter 5.3, identity-specifying predicates must be given a time index in late modernity: it is no longer the case that one is a baker, conservative, or Catholic per se. Instead one is such "for the moment" and for tendentially shrinking periods of a nonpredictable length. One was something different and (possibly) will be something else. Therefore the transformation of patterns of identity in the course of modernity can likewise be described as an acceleration from multi-generational identity sequences to infragenerational ones. This is strikingly clear in the "serial monogamy" within intimate relationships and professional life that has taken the place of lifelong monogamy in both areas.[28]

Thus what Luhman conceived as an unavoidable effect of functional differentiation and the temporalization of complexity, namely, the consistent rearrangement of the semantics of the "schema of being" into that of the "schema of time," seems to have occurred with respect to the practice of identity. As a result, all (identity-constituting) positions and decisions become, so to speak, *time relative* instead of being, as previously, *ontologically relative*.

> [In this way] time is not only thematically but also operationally much more profoundly built into the self-description of society and its world. In fact, one can no longer hold fast to the idea that identities, whether of objects or subjects, are pre-defined for time. Rather they are constructed and reproduced within time and in each respective present moment in order to generate for a while temporal connections that mediate between the extremely different time horizons of the past (memory) and the future (oscillation of all distinctions relevant to observation).[29]

The concept of the temporalization of time is by now well-established as a label for this understanding of time in both philosophy and the social sciences. "Temporalization of time" means that the duration, sequence, rhythm, and tempo of actions, events, and relationships are first decided in the course of their execution, that is, *within time itself*. They no longer follow a predefined time schedule. Thus "temporalization of time" paradoxically signifies exactly what Castells describes as "timeless" time.[30]

Two facts are primarily decisive for the transformation of patterns of identity that is postulated here as a consequence of social acceleration: first, the *temporalization of time* is diametrically opposed to the *temporalization of life* discussed, which provided the classical modern form of identity with an authoritative life course regime and normal biography. The first surge of dynamization in modernity led to a view of life as directed motion along presequenced alternative paths of development that were defined by the formal stability of expectations and planning regarding the future and that therefore issued in the devising of "lifeplans." The second surge supersedes (*aufhebt*) precisely this presequencing and calculability. *The temporalization of time therefore means the revocation of the temporalization of life in the sense of a temporally extended project.* Second, the temporalization of time that has thus far been a rather theoretically derived idea is by now well confirmed empirically as a tendency shaping the development of contemporary Western societies. For instance, Kohli claims that there is an unmistakable tendency toward the deinstitutionalization of the life course regime and a diminishing ability of the normal biography to provide orientation.[31] On the one hand, conventional professional and familial sequences (education, gainful employment, retirement or falling in love, getting married, having kids) are less and less linked to one another and to biological age, and, on the other hand, they are run through multiple times and their sequential ordering is broken up. Yet the temporalization of time can also be empirically verified in rather semiperipheral and peripheral areas of life. So, for instance, in the area of civic engagement for a long time now a change in the form of volunteer work (*Ehrenamtes*) has been diagnosed (from the "old" to the "new" volunteerism) that can be described precisely with the conceptual framework of temporalized time: younger volunteers are less and less prepared to commit themselves to "volunteer roles" in a *long-term* way and within a *predefined* scope.[32] Instead, they prefer flexible forms of engagement, the duration of which they determine on a case by case basis and to which they devote a portion of their weekly or monthly time budget that they can decide *flexibly*—which means that the concept of the volunteer "role" is obviously misleading for this kind of activity. In the wake of the temporalization of time, civic engagement and professional activity, as well as tendentially the activities and commitments of private life take on the form of "projects": one flexibly decides their length, sequence, and often tempo too; but projects can always be ended within the short term and their duration is limited.[33]

Moreover, the late modern temporalization of time, which follows the logic of timeless time, is not only revealed by the temporal destructuring of the life course but also by the flexibilization of *daily life*. As I have already shown, time use patterns in the classical modern, functionally differentiated society are by and large determined by the standards of a linear time that is external to events, i.e., the activity patterns of individuals are adjusted by means of exactly sequenced hourly, daily, weekly, and monthly plans within the "time windows" of various functional spheres of society. Good time management then distinguishes itself by ensuring that the respective action sequences follow one another with as little "loss" as possible, i.e., without undesired pauses, idle times, and overlaps, and that the pending tasks and obligations can actually be performed in the time provided. So the length and sequence of activities within a segment of time are here fixed and planned *ahead of time* in order to guarantee a social synchronization and coordination of actions.[34]

Yet today a "paradigm shift" is looming in the area of everyday time strategies and practices in the wake of 1. the perpetuation and contemporization of systemic processing, 2. the dissolution of the boundaries of "systemic time windows" by a tendentially limitless extension of availability, operating, and access times that erodes the collective rhythms of social life, and finally, 3. the accompanying flexibilization of the time individuals spend engaged in specific areas.[35] When there is no longer any predefined time window for the activities of everyday life like working, shopping, meeting friends, taking care of correspondence, looking after one's family, etc., because, in the first place, it is possible to do these things at any time and in the second place, unforeseeable events may make an unplanned or more intensive engagement necessary, it becomes rational to organize daily life in a flexible way whereby particularly new mobile technologies can be used for the coordination and synchronization of action chains. The "classical modern" everyday routine was characterized by a predefined time schedule (and a time routine developing within it) of roughly the following shape: 7 A.M. wake up, 8 A.M. start work, 12 P.M. lunch break, 5 P.M. end work/go shopping, 6 P.M. pick up the kids, 7 P.M. dinner, 8 P.M. meet up with friends. In contrast, the temporalized everyday time of late modernity stays, to a great extent, flexible regarding the occurrence, length, and sequence of events. It might already begin when one gets up and run all the way until one goes to bed. When work time has become flexible and is only coordinated by *deadlines*, and, at the same time, many activities are possible around the clock, each decision to do a particular possible activity requires its own *motive*.[36] Private and professional appointments can both be flexibly arranged with the help of mobile coordination techniques: "When and where I'm meeting with X depends on how far I get with my work and how long her meeting runs. She's going to call me as soon as it's over. If I'm at home by then, we'll meet near my place. If I'm still in the city, we'll meet at café Y. I'll decide whether to go shopping or not based on the situation." Time orderings are thus individually and flexibly created within time itself.

In turn, the number of options and contingencies—hence also surprises, imponderables, and sudden changes of situation—rises rapidly as an unavoidable consequence of this kind of *temporalization of complexity*, which makes classical time management in the style of disciplined control using time schedules increasingly impossible. This is the reason why Karl Hörning, Daniela Ahrens, and Anette Gerhard believe that their empirical study of emerging late modern time practices, which is based on individual interviews and group conversations, can demonstrate that the classical modern form of linear time management and sequential time planning has become untenable and that the figure of the "time manager" is gradually being supplanted by a new lifestyle: that of the "time-juggling player."[37] The "player" overcomes the linear, calculating, and planning time orientation of modernity and replaces it with a situationally open, "event-oriented time praxis" (that has a certain premodern sound, but is fully reflexive).[38]

Hörning, Ahrens, and Gerhard also conceptualize this newly established time praxis using the notion of a temporalization of time because the "player" does not decide the tempo and length of events and connected actions within the frame of an overall plan or an abstract, linear conception of time, but in a flexible and situation-dependent way, as it were, on the basis of the intrinsic temporality and the time horizon of each respective event.[39] "The 'player' does not want to have what, when, how fast, why and how prescribed to him anymore, nor does he want to prescribe such things for himself. He no longer wants to lay down which form of temporalization is appropriate when. Rather, he wants to know that he always has time to make his own arrangements."[40] According to the authors, he thereby succeeds in "constantly placing given situations in varying perspectives and thus appropriately handling the 'vicissitudes' of late modern everyday life. By 'having' to begin, interrupt, prolong, and end 'games,' he develops the particular quality of an *event-oriented time praxis* that seeks to keep its own parts as flexible as possible in the 'game of games.'"[41] In this way the "player" learns what Richard Sennett sees as the late modern corrosion of character by delinearizing and temporalizing time, that is, by treating "disturbances like temporal uncertainties, nonsimultaneities, disadjustments, collision of different time cultures, the occurrence of breaks," etc., precisely *not* "as anomalies . . . but [as things] to be included in the current, highly situationally oriented time practice as normality."[42]

In this new form of "highly situational" time practice, then, the late modern perspectives on everyday time and the time of life combine into a *new form of identity* that is itself situational. It no longer reacts to the openness and unforeseeability of the future with the need for control and security of "classical modernity." The hyperacceleration of late modernity that is unmanageable for the lifestyle models and identity types of classical modernity no longer appears as a threat to the "player." Rather he is excited by it and affirms it as a generator of possibility through which "an ever faster 'temporalization of time' becomes possible." He "sheds time compulsions, time obligations and time imperatives that are externally given. He moderates and modulates his own highly situational intrinsic temporalities (*Eigenzeiten*). Thus the 'player' reflects within his own orientation the growing dynamism and complexity of a society that increasingly can only recapture its identity from the flood of events in momentary descriptions of situations."[43]

Gert Günter Voß also demarcates this *situational conduct of life* from tendentially obsolete patterns: namely, from the *traditional conduct of life*, on the one hand, and the *strategic conduct of life*, on the other. The inner logic of the former lies in "stability and self-evidentness: persons who conduct their lives in this way shape their daily life by means of a strong orientation to predefined ideas of an 'orderly' life and try to 'adjust' themselves. Here the central values are security and regularity."[44] One recognizes the correspondence between this mode of life conduct and the previously discussed diachronic logic of the stable a posteriori identity, which is characterized by the temporally stable maintenance of an arrangement of identity building blocks that is chosen once at the outset of adult life: "whoever has found her 'life' in this sense has also, so to speak, already ended it—from here on out it should change as little as possible."[45] In contrast, the strategic conduct of life is held by Voß to be a more modern variant and an appropriate way of organizing daily life even in many late modern circumstances of life, but his characterization of it leaves little doubt that it stems more from Fordist industrialized modernity than from flexibilized late modernity and hence that it is likewise tendentially anachronistic. "A 'strategic' conduct of life rests . . . on systematic planning, calculation and active mastery of the conditions and resources of life for the purpose of realizing life plans: the ongoing optimization and condensation of the course of the day is an important aspect of this."[46] He then summarizes the opposition between the situational and strategic conduct of life as follows:

> A *strategic* conduct of life relies on strict planning and rigid, thorough organization that reminds one in many respects of the bureaucratization or centralization (if not outright Taylorization) of firms. In contrast, the *situational* form follows a logic of flexibilization or even decentralization and

thus resembles recent business strategies in an astonishing way. The strategic logic correlates with work circumstances that involve complex, but still comparatively calculable, relatively long-term and stable conditions (*Vorgaben*). On the other hand, when circumstances become increasingly dynamic and de-structured, a situational logic becomes more and more functional.[47]

My thesis is that a situational logic for the daily and biographical conduct of life directly shapes identity because it forces one to maintain, both synchronically and diachronically, flexible and variable time horizons and perspectives. Where past, present, and future are continually reconnected and reinterpreted situationally, the conception of who one was, is, and will be likewise continually changes. The character and weighting of the parameters of identity alter from situation to situation: who one is depends on which social sphere one is currently engaged in and with whom one is currently dealing (which is why Kenneth Gergen thinks he can discern an imminent replacement of personal identity by a purely "relational" self).[48] It becomes unclear which dimensions of identity (profession, religion, family, sexual and political orientation, style of consumption, free time activities, etc.) are central and which are peripheral. Hence the coherence and continuity of the self become context-dependent and flexibly constructed; its stability no longer rests on substantial identifications.

For this reason, Gergen (among others) sees empirically discernible indications that the perspectives and horizons of the self can no longer be integrated in a unified or even temporally stable identity project.[49] This is true not only diachronically regarding the various phases of life but also synchronically with respect to the various social contexts in which an individual is involved. This is a reflection of the structural logic of the spatiotemporal "disembedding" of episodes of action and experience discussed in the previous chapter from the viewpoint of persons, who thereby lose any sense of intercontextual relations between episodes. Hence the fragmentation, pluralization, or multiplication of the self in highly developed Western societies that is repeatedly postulated in "postmodern" theories of identity seems to me to be nothing other than a logical consequence of the synchronic and diachronic *temporalization of time* in the conduct of life, which is in turn to be conceived as an effect of the acceleration of the social rate of change beyond a critical threshold marking the limits of the capacity for integration.

It is thus the idea of an identity project oriented toward duration or the long-term that is surrendered under the compulsions of the acceleration society. It also follows that the notion of autonomy in the sense of a context-transcending and temporally stable personal pursuit of self-defined values and goals must be surrended as well.[50] The figure of the situational, "shapeshifting" self (Robert Jay Lipton), or the "pastiche personality," steps in to take the place of the classical modern personality type characterized by a relatively time-resistant identity.[51] Gergen defines the new character as follows: "The pastiche personality is a social chameleon, constantly borrowing bits and pieces of identity from whatever sources are available and constructing them as useful or desirable in a given situation."[52] Of course this just sketches out the radical logical vanishing point of this development, at which one could no longer speak of *identity* any more at all, because the balance between continuity and coherence, on the one hand, and flexibility and change, on the other, would have shifted so far in favor of the latter that the former would have simply dissolved. In the debates surrounding identity research there have been legitimate objections raised to such an idea. The empirical accuracy of the corresponding observations has been questioned as well as the bare existential possibility of such a relation to self.[53] As opposed to this, I hold that the previously discussed empirical findings converge on the diagnosis of a tendency toward a late modern form of *situational identity* that is capable of uniting the paradoxical characteristics of situationality and identity.[54]

If one defines identity as that which lends a subject coherence and continuity across varying contexts, then the concept of situational identity seems to become a sort of *contradictio in adjecto*. Yet if one understands identity as a *sense of who one is* that provides an ability to orient oneself and to act, then situational identities are quite conceivable as, so to speak, logical vanishing points of heightened individualization and acceleration: the sense changes in its substance from context to context and from situation to situation, but the feeling of identity that guides choice and action in all circumstances remains. After all, the idea of such an identity does not imply that *all* the characteristics of an identity are altered from situation to situation. On the contrary, one would assume that in fact several remain synchronically and diachronically constant across a plurality of situations and contexts, such that situational identities, while no longer susceptible to, so to speak, definitive definition, can certainly be connected by "family resemblances" in the Wittgensteinian sense. Nevertheless radical swings and reversals are also quite possible. Ultimately the concept simply indicates that there are no longer any definitions of identity that are per se temporally stable and that the weighting, relating, and interpreting of aspects of identity changes from situation to situation. In my view, the following four factors secure a rudimentary *trans-situational* unity and continuity of the self that justifies the use of the identity concept in the first place:

1. In the first place, even a situational identity allows at least a minimal narrative connection of past, present, and future and the various provinces of life with their meanings and functions. However, in each case this connection follows narrative patterns that stem from the respective situational context.[55]

2. One should assume that subjects are shaped by an as it were *habitualized* continuity of a relatively temporally fixed nature. For, apart from our own reflexive self-definition, our feeling of identity also emerges and is preserved, to a great extent, by what we may call, following Pierre Bourdieu, our *habitus*: our embodied likings and aversions, our gestures and expressive idiosyncrasies, peculiarities of taste, etc. The habitus is certainly neither immune to change nor context-invariant (our likings and aversions are also partly determined by situations), but its basic patterns presumably change only gradually and rarely in an intentional way. Thus the feeling of the self that is embodied in our practices and our relationship to our bodies can establish continuity even where it seems lost behind a situational change of reflexive identity and lifestyle. Furthermore, a natural thought here is that in the course of modernity continuity and coherence have increasingly changed from being a question of *substance* to being one of *style*: who one is gets characterized less and less by the roles one takes on, the convictions to which one subscribes, and the positions one holds and more and more by the way one handles the contingencies and vicissitudes of life. Nevertheless, even this form of coherence belongs more to the romantic, expressivist side of "classical modernity" than to a radicalized "postmodernity":[56] a genuinely postmodern self is characterized precisely by the fact that it feels no inner compulsion to have a unified style, neither synchronically nor diachronically. So a radically situational identity is marked out by the fact that a subject can be, say, faithful and introverted in church, "soft and feminine" in intimate relationships, chauvinistic and full of vitality at work, pacifist and counterculture at a peace demonstration, militantly aggressive and atheistic at the party convention, all without feeling the related inconsistencies as problematic. In contrast, the attraction of the postmodern credo "I am many" rests precisely on flexibly trying out possibilities and accepting *pastiche* and *collage* even in such questions of style. This internal pluralization does become problematic, though, when a person is forced to define relevancies and priorities and when conflicting demands for action result from such plurality.

3. Tilmann Habermas draws our attention to a further, surprising way in which continuity is created in times of accelerated change in his study on the connection between *beloved objects* and identity formation. According to him, objects to which individuals have developed a personal and emotional attachment can take on the function of, as it were, "transitional objects" that represent and symbolize continuity at just those times when identities and relationships change. In this sense, personal objects (and also pets) become possible "placeholders" for temporally stable substantial identities when they are by conscious decision at least temporarily withdrawn from the predominating contingency of the "disposable goods" that surround us. They establish momentary continuities while one's own personality is being reorganized and thus contribute to a seamless transition between divergent contexts and situations.[57]

4. Against the assumptions of, for instance, symbolic interactionism, recent social-psychological research suggests that subjects possibly have at their disposal, beyond any such stabilizing elements, an, as it were, "innate," predicateless "core self" that allows them to preserve a *feeling* of identity, in certain circumstances even when there is complete situational discontinuity.[58]

So it seems clear that the idea of a situational identity is both philosophically and psychologically coherent and within the realm of the empirically possible in late modernity. It constitutes the personality-related correlate of the space of flows and timeless time, though it certainly does not define the social reality of all or even the majority of human beings in the globalized world. Rather, it describes the pattern of a form of selfhood that corresponds to the developmental logic that is structurally and culturally dominant in contemporary society.

At the same time, it is clear that the relationships that people have to space, time, and objects, and thus to themselves and to the world, are undergoing a sustained transformation. With respect to *space*, if in modernity there was a deeply rooted movement toward a detachment of personal identity from a fixed place from which the world disclosed itself, then this movement has been radicalized anew. The more strongly selfhood is defined and stabilized in the space of flows, the more identity literally loses its geographical "location": there lies a gaping chasm in terms of identity between the "classical modern" form of mobility, which allowed an immensely maneuverable form of life centered around a fixed "place of residence" and, at the same time, enabled sequential change in that place of residence, and the late modern *return of nomadism* (Zygmunt Bauman) or *polygamy of place* (Ulrich Beck).[59] Whoever understands himself as residing in Hamburg, but living in Spain and Egypt for five months a year, is "situated in space" in a different way than someone who actually no longer wants to or even can say where he really lives.

Beyond this, the process of distancing between the self and its local environment that was already noted by Simmel is also being heightened once again on account of the high rate of change in the structures of our material surroundings:

> The process of objectification of culture that, based on specialization, brings about a growing estrangement between the subject and its products ultimately invades even the more intimate aspects of our daily life. During the first decades of the nineteenth century, furniture and the objects that surrounded us for use and pleasure were of relative simplicity and durability and were in accord with the needs of the lower as well as of the upper strata. This resulted in people's attachment as they grew up to the objects of their surroundings, an attachment that already appears to the younger generation today as an eccentricity on the part of their grandparents.[60]

One can conclude from this that in the process of modernization identities withdraw more and more from their spatial surroundings and the material structures of the environment: they no longer extend into the latter and, conversely, are no longer defined by the former. Nothing of the (temporalized) place where the late modern person lives adheres to her "essentially," and, conversely, she no longer enters into "her" place.[61] This is, as it were, the *literal* side of what Taylor posits as a "shrinkage" of the self into a point from which all relationships (spatial, thematic, and social) become contingent and malleable such that it can *choose* almost without constraint. However, in so doing it remains, as it were, predicateless, because there is nothing it simply *is*.[62]

Yet note that this is exactly what becomes a functional requirement in a radicalized "acceleration society" in which reference groups, communication partners, objects, ideas, jobs, etc., switch so quickly that their *contents* become increasingly indifferent and interchangeable; put the other way around, this means that the more indifferent persons become with respect to the *contents* of their social identity, the better they can adapt to the requirements of acceleration and flexibility. This tendency was also anticipated by Simmel, whose great popularity in the discourse of postmodernity stems in no small part from such observations.[63] Thus Stefan Breuer postulates, drawing on Paul Virilio, that subject and object only "occasionally" (or punctually) come into contact with each other, such that the world "ceaselessly" breaks in on us "with the violence of an accident," whereas Virilio himself believes that *substance* and *accident* have switched roles since the time of Aristotle: the ephemeral is now necessary, substance is a side issue.[64] Correspondingly, the permanent revolutionizing and hence devaluation of fashions, styles, contents, and objects in capitalist society must lead to a necessary shift of emphasis: the assumption that the content or object of an experience or relationship has a (lasting, "deep," identity-constituting) value per se is permanently frustrated, and one may presume that ultimately it will no longer be formed at all or only rarely.[65]

Therefore, in late modernity self-projects that are oriented toward stability appear to be anachronistic and condemned to failure in a highly dynamic environment, while forms of identity based on flexibility and readiness to change are systematically favored. Of course, self projects that have an affirmative and constitutive relation to the idea of continual change themselves become driving forces of the acceleration of the pace of life and social change.[66]

As I will now show in what follows, however, the temporalization of time in life and daily practice also transforms *temporal experience*, i.e., the way in which people find themselves *placed in time* (and hence in history and in society), with far-reaching ethical, cultural, and political consequences. For the interweaving of the time horizons of daily life, one's own lifetime and history at large that is the everyday work of identity becomes extraordinarily precarious if the aspiration to autonomy is supposed to be maintained in these changed circumstances. What is striking about the many investigations of the identity-constituting time experience of individuals in contemporary society, not only those of social psychology but in particular those of sociology, is the flagrant contradiction between an evident gain in practical, everyday *time sovereignty* and the simultaneous feeling of a loss of *autonomy* and *control* over one's own life. This contradiction is the consequence of a paradoxical situation. On the one hand, since the orientation to predefined normal biographies and standardized life course schedules is eroding and the content and temporal structure of life is left more open, life must be planned out in the short-, middle-, and long-term much more than before and also led actively if the aspiration to autonomy is to be preserved. However, on the other hand, as a result of the further heightening of social dynamization, such long-term organization becomes more difficult or even simply impossible. Thus it becomes "more and more necessary to plan for and make decisions about the unplannable, the unforeseeable and the undecidable. In other words: things past and things to come can be formulated less and less, but more and more one has to formulate them, *now*."[67] Since this kind of demand is on a par with a demand to square the circle, the most obvious expedient is to give up the aspiration to autonomy and escape into a new or "second" fatalism, a strategy that Manfred Garhammer, on the basis of his empirical studies, and Peter Sloterdijk, from a philosophical perspective, believe they can already observe (to name just two examples).[68]

The perception of an unsteered and unsteerable "drifting" amid a sea of options and contingencies thus appears to be an inevitable consequence of the growing impossibility of making long-term life plans and developing reliable outlooks on the future. This is not just a reflection of the abandonment of the *aspiration* to an active shaping of one's own life but also of the fact that, even when greater contingency enters into the picture, an increase in autonomy does not necessarily result—quite the contrary.[69] That people are increasingly doing without the making and pursuit of long-term "life" plans is by now an empirically well-confirmed finding, one on which, though by different paths, the perspectives of writers like Manfred Garhammer, Richard Sennett, Karlheinz Geißler, or Hörning, Ahrens, and Gerhard all converge.[70]

Another informative empirical indicator for this claim is the decreasing willingness to postpone the satisfaction of wants in favor of long-term goals, since this willingness "is most likely to occur when future rewards are both reasonably certain, and to some degree under a person's control."[71] Both qualitative and standardized investigations in recent years indicate that these conditions can no longer be taken for granted and that, as a result, the *present-orientedness* of younger people is clearly on the rise.[72]

On the basis of narrative interviews, and taking up Walter Lippman's metaphor of *drift*, Sennett conceives the late modern experience of how the self changes over the course of time in a clearly pessimistic way as an "erratic experience" of "aimless inner drift" that stands in sharp contrast to the feeling and aspiration of "mastering events" through one's own action.[73] We encounter here, in an "experience which drifts in time, from place to place, from job to job,"[74] the pattern of behavior and choice that Hörning, Ahrens, and Gerhard identify as the lifestyle of the "time-juggling player." He too relinquishes the aspiration of reflexively controlling and actively *leading* a life that was still central for classical modernity; he too does without a quest for authenticity or genuineness. Although the *evaluation* of this fact varies greatly in social-scientific studies, they nevertheless agree on the diagnosis that the new *situationality* and *temporalization* of decisions and actions is incompatible with the modern notion of autonomy, which refers to the temporally stable and trans-situational pursuit of individual lifeplans and hence to stable future (and past) horizons.

Robert Lauer also holds that dispensing with rational planning for the future results in "societal drift, or worse, societal chaos," and he conjectures that a systematically situational present-centered orientation will undeniably generate social pathologies.[75] Sennett's judgment is not much more favorable. He believes he has found empirical indications that the drift of the "player" leads to a fragmentation of personality or character, the erosion of social relationships, and the undermining of social trust. "The conditions of time in the new capitalism have created a conflict between character and experience, the experience of disjointed time threatening the ability of people to form their characters into sustained narratives. . . . Perhaps the corroding of character is an inevitable consequence. 'No long term' disorients action over the long term, loosens bonds of trust and commitment, and divorces will from behavior."[76]

In contrast, Kenneth Gergen arrives at a directly opposite and highly optimistic evaluation of the new situationalism, according to which everything that Sennett believes to be undermined is in fact fulfilled: "The rewards can be substantial—the devotion of one's intimates, happy children, professional success, the achievement of community goals, personal popularity, and so on. All are possible if one avoids looking back to locate a true and enduring self, and simply acts to full potential in the moment at hand." However, even he makes clear that the price of *drifting* consists in the *loss of autonomy* and of the claim to be the (co-) author of one's own life. In the introduction to the new edition of his book, he describes his own experience of being on the path to "multiphrenia" in a section titled, "Out of Control": "I am also struggling against my modernist training for constant improvement, advancement, development, and accumulation. Slowly I am learning the pleasures of relinquishing the desire to gain control of all that surrounds me. *It is the difference between swimming with deliberation to a point in the ocean*—mastering the waves to reach a goal—and floating harmoniously with the unpredictable movements of the waves."[77]

Without a doubt, this way of "letting oneself drift" ought not to be misunderstood as a lifestyle of passivity: the situational self can make tremendous context-dependent efforts to achieve its goals and/or fulfill social demands, but it does so without setting long-term, authoritative, context-transcending "life goals."

Nevertheless, that means—and this is the point I am driving at—that the biographical course of life as a whole loses *its direction*. It can no longer be understood as *directed motion* and narratively reconstructed in the sense of a history of progress or development. *Life doesn't head anywhere; in the end, it goes nowhere (very fast)*. This is the sense in which the temporalization of time implies the *detemporalization of life* and hence displays a tendential return to the static, situational form of life of premodernity,[78] even though the contingencies and vicissitudes of life today are of a different, namely, societally *endogenous*, reflexive kind. The "events" that determined the course of the day and the unfolding of life in premodernity were embedded in a broadly stable, static natural and social-institutional fabric. While they were often not concretely expected, they were understood to be continuously present possibilities (as is still true of, for instance, droughts, wars, and famines). Their relevancies were laid down in routines and/or by tradition. In contrast, possible events in late modernity are often unpredictable and are themselves subject to rapid change within a horizon of possibility that is no longer determined by routine and tradition, but instead has been escalated into unforeseeability. Within this horizon relevancies are no longer there to be recognized but must rather be set by actors for themselves.

The setting of priorities and relevancies is an indispensable presupposition of temporal planning and organization. However, it is only possible where *several* parameters and basic orientations are withdrawn from the play of contingencies and hence can serve as ordering factors. For this reason, as many authors have independently observed, the inability (or unwillingness) to set temporally stable relevancies and to develop corresponding priorities of action in the sense of a "task" that is built into the character of situational identity[79] leads to a paradoxical inversion in which the experience of *detemporalization*, of temporal *standstill*, suddenly emerges out of the experience of "temporalized" and so accelerated or "racing" time. As the philosopher Klaus-Michael Kodalle writes:

> If you devote yourself to a task in a "reasonable" way, you do not experience time as an independent dimension at all. You only experience it as compulsion and pressure if you overburden yourself. And at the other extreme, if you don't know how to leave yourself aside for something, some idea, or other people, in other words, if you keep entirely "to yourself," then however

many superficial activities you may be caught up in, you experience a kind of temporal standstill, a viscosity that makes time appear like the repetition of the same even when things are definitely happening.[80]

This is a significant reason why the perception of a deep-seated structural and cultural rigidity that constantly accompanies the modern history of acceleration like a shadow was able to gain the upper hand in the cultural self-perception of late modernity: it is the paradoxical but complementary *flip side* of social acceleration. In any case, the metaphor of a *racing standstill* seems to be doubly appropriate for describing the time experience tied to the late modern form of situational identity. Firstly, time *races* because in the space of flows the rate of social change rises and because the decontextualization and increasingly episodic character of lived events and actions tendentially shrinks the traces they leave in memory and thus favors the experience of an accelerated passing of time, as the discussion of subjective time experience in chapter 5.2 showed. Secondly, it *stands still* because within timeless time no development can be discerned behind changes. There are no stable perspectives that organize time. So life seems like an aimless drift through changing situations, as if the *same things happen again and again.* "In 1996, the proportion of those who affirmed, 'There is nothing genuinely new to be expected in my life. Things happen but I have no control over them,' rose from 14% to 32%," runs the finding of a study of Michael Häder's cited by Garhammer.[81] Hörning, Ahrens and Gerhard also observe this tendency: "One increasingly has to assume that the struggle with time has reached a threshold that indicates the limits of the dominant understanding of time's linearity: the 'cult of speed' is being carried to its extreme and the dynamic it has unleashed threatens to congeal into a 'frenetic standstill' (Virilio)."[82] As I have already laid out, this temporal standstill corresponds to an experience that pervades the culture of late modernity and is reflected in the titles of records that sell millions (*Everything Stays Different* [Herbert Grönemeyer] or *Nowhere—Fast!* [Fury in the Slaughterhouse]), in newspaper headlines ("Everything stays the same, but goes faster and faster"), or also in best sellers like Douglas Coupland's *Tales for an Accelerated Culture* from Texlahoma, a city in which time is frozen in 1974 (!) forever.

Lothar Baier also examines this self-perception in detail and points to what may be its most significant pathological manifestation:[83] according to many findings, there has been a dramatic increase in *depressive illness* in modern societies, and according to the statistics of the W.H.O. it has already become the world's second most common kind of sickness after cardiovascular disease.[84] Depression can doubtless be conceived as a *pathology of time* in a threefold sense.

In the first place, it is well-established today that it *can be* a consequence of increased stress, i.e., undesired time pressure, including hectic rates of change and great uncertainty or insecurity.[85] In the second place, it represents a psychic reaction that is characterized by the experience of a *viscous, stagnant time* and *futurelessness*. Baier summarizes the testimony of depressed persons as follows:

> The damage to the experience of time wrought by depression is what seems to be so hard to measure, a way of living time which, even when it has not come to a standstill, resists being put into words. . . . Those who are depressed perceive . . . a kind of knotting up of time that provokes something like an attack of temporal asphyxiation: they can't pull themselves through the past and the future. This strengthens the sensation of falling out of a world in which the ceaseless transformation of future into present and present into past is something self-evident.[86]

In connection with this Baier then cites the psychiatrist Eugène Minkowski: "Our life is essentially geared to the future. Wherever a pathological slow-down occurs, this orientation is deeply altered; corresponding to the extent of the slow-down it will be either the present or the past that will exert an enormous influence."[87] Robert Levine also postulates such a connection in light of psychiatric findings. He cites a depressive patient who makes the observation (reminiscent of Coupland's Texlahoma) that "the future looks cold and dry and I seem to be frozen in time."[88]

Thus, in the third place, depression becomes the *pathology of late modernity*, not only because it is on the rise and increasingly afflicts young persons, which is a historical novelty, but even more because it seems to embody the temporal experience of a *frenetic standstill* in a pathologically pure form. It thus confirms the theoretical derivation of this experience from the previously outlined temporal perspective of situational identity. "Depression is the handrail of the rudderless person and not just his suffering," writes Alain Ehrenberg, "it is *the reverse side of the expression of his energy*."[89] According to Ehrenberg's diagnosis, this energy has insurmountable difficulties in unfolding productively when every possible relationship into which it can be invested will be transitory, passing, and hence not constitutive of identity. And, for the reasons already mentioned, we can assume that condition to be increasingly met in late modern society. Interestingly, the history of social dynamization in modernity is constantly accompanied by this problem, which expresses itself in shifting cultural diagnoses and discourses, first as *acedia*,[90] then secularized as *melancholia*,[91] as *ennui*, later as *neurasthenia*,[92] and today as *depression*. In every case it is a matter of a psychic condition that is characterized by an as it were artificial lethargy, tedium, and emptiness (accompanied by inner restlessness), by "spiritual paralysis" *in the face of the inability of the soul to direct its energy towards a fixed, constant, subjectively worthwhile goal and to express it in action.*

Because there was a strong cultural counterweight in the "classical-modern" ideal of a (authentically determined and authentically unfolded) lifeplan, these experiences were at first picked up and interpreted as individual (though historically typical) pathologies or peculiar dispositions of the "sensitive," of poets, artists, or philosophers. In late modernity they may be condensing into a structurally inescapable universal experience.

If melancholia belonged to extraordinary people, then depression bears witness to the democratization of the exception. We live with the truth and in the belief that each person must have the possibility to shape her own life instead of enduring it as a fate. Through individual initiative and the opening up of possibilities, humankind has set itself in motion, even in its most intimate realms. This dynamic heightens the lack of fixed character in the human being, accelerates the dissolution of constancy, multiplies the guiding principles on offer and at the same time makes them confusing. Musil's "Man without Qualities" is open to the indeterminate and gradually sheds every externally predefined identity that gives him a structure. "Human beings are like the blades of tall grass; they were probably blown back and forth by God, hail, firestorm, pestilence and war more fiercely than they are now, but then it was as a whole, as a city, a land." The new traumas are individual. They come from within. . . . . *Depression is melancholia in a society in which all are free and equal; it is the sickness par excellence of democracy and the market society. In this respect, it is the unavoidable reverse side of the sovereignty of the person, not the one who acts in the wrong way, but the one who cannot act at all. In depression, one does not think in the concepts of rightness or law, but in those of an inability to act.*[93]

The inability to act here ultimately refers to the effect of an inability to form relationships and bonds with others (in the sense described by Kodalle). Its cause lies in the fact that no component of the self appears to be absolutely given anymore such that it could or must be *discovered* and authentically *expressed* in a process of *acting upon the world* in which (again in the sense of a *Bildungsroman* or self-development narrative) self and world reciprocally reshape and develop each other. Instead, as Gerhard Schulze observes, in late modernity the action-type of opportunity-dependent *choice* drives out that of *affecting* or acting upon the world. This endangers the ability to indicate *in the name of what* one desires or chooses.[94]

Beyond these paradigmatic pathologies, however, it also seems to be characteristic of late modern identity that there is *a loss of the perception of the directed movement through time of the self or of life, and hence of a developmental perspective.* "If, as Benjamin wrote, 'the sick have a very special knowledge of the condition of society,' then today depressives . . . are probably the most sensitive seismographs of existing and approaching faultlines. Their stupor proclaims the desolate standstill that gapes beneath the colorfully animated *user interfaces* that have been broken up by a new obscurity."[95]

However, the full import of this individual experience of time and the accompanying switchover from a semantics of progress to a rhetoric of objective necessity can only be grasped in light of an analysis of the *collective* side of the acceleration-induced temporalization of time, i.e., in light of an analysis of *situational politics* and the underlying late modern *experience of history.* That is the theme of the next chapter.

11

SITUATIONAL POLITICS: PARADOXICAL TIME HORIZONS BETWEEN DESYNCHRONIZATION AND DISINTEGRATION

1. TIME IN POLITICS—POLITICS IN TIME

The political project of modernity and the underlying idea of a democratic organization of the lifeworld and our collective form of life rests on two fundamental assumptions about societal time structures that have rarely been the subject of explicit reflection. In the first place, there is the conviction that society is a project *to be politically organized in time*. The territorial, representative, and mass democracies of modernity developed against the background of a dynamic understanding of history according to which legislation in particular was not an act to be completed once and for all, not, as it were, an everlasting inscription, but rather a continuous task of progressively steering the path of societal development in the historical process. Therefore, in agreement with Uwe Schimank and against Niklas Luhmann, I defend the view that functional differentiation and political steering must be thought together in order to understand modernity. Schimank writes that modern societies are, first, *functionally differentiated*, second, *growth societies*, and, third, *steered societies*:

> This is not to say that societal steering is always or even in the majority of cases successful, i.e., that the goals set are reached. Everyone knows that is not the case. Nevertheless, social actors make a demand of themselves that is just as counterfactual as it is binding, namely, to be the conscious shapers of societal structures and not merely entities that de facto produce them: that is, to have a steering influence on the construction, preservation or transformation of specific structures. This modern aspiration to control was

first formulated by the Enlightenment. Its range and radicality are entirely alien to premodern societies. It is especially, though not exclusively, manifest in measures of political steering.[1]

Linked with this is a series of presuppositions whose fulfillment could be taken for granted on temporal-structural grounds during the age of "classical" modernity, but that, as I argue in what follows, necessarily become problematic in late modernity: namely, the expectations that the future will be different from the past, that societal development in this future is subject to our *understanding* and is supposed to be *steered* or *shaped* in a democratic political fashion, and that the *normative criteria* or *objectives* that will guide this shaping activity are either already available or at least can be established by means of collective political agreement, even if this is open to revision. Therefore democratic politics as understood in modernity has a direct correlate in a "temporalized" view of history, as in particular Koselleck and the school of historians working on the *Geschichtliche Grundbegriffe* project have worked out. According to this view, politics is held responsible for a very specific task *within historical time*. The most unambiguous indicator of this is that fact the two great political camps in classical modernity could be distinguished along a temporal directional index, namely, as *progressive* and *conservative*. I will come back to this point shortly.

The second fundamental assumption is that the diverse, institutionalized temporal structures of political will-formation, decision-making and decision-implementation in representative-democratic systems are compatible with the rhythm, tempo, duration and sequence of social developments: in other words, that they are essentially synchronized with the path of societal development such that the political system has time to make fundamental decisions and to organize the deliberative, democratic process for this purpose.

However, the possibility of controlling or guiding the development of framing conditions in a democratic way depends on the success of a series of highly time-sensitive processes of transmission and translation. As I have already made clear, up to now the superiority of modern, democratic models of politics with respect to their predecessors and competitors rested above all on their ability to react to emerging needs in the various spheres of society in a sensitive, fast, and flexible way.[2] Thus its adeptness for this function decisively depends on whether collective interests can be aggregated and articulated, translated into political programs, channeled through political parties into decision-making or legislative processes, and implemented by the executive branch, all in a quick and timely fashion. At the same time, a steering framework has to emerge that, on the one hand, exhibits enough institutional and institutionalized stability to be able to guarantee the security of expectations that is socially indispensable and, on the other, remains sufficiently flexible and changeable to be able to react to shifting constellations of needs and new developments.

The dynamic element in these systems is rooted not least in the clearly demarcated length of legislative terms, usually either four or five years. When contrasted to the time monarchical princes spent controlling the government, which was as a rule much longer, this explains why democracy was experienced as an element of political acceleration deep into the era of classical modernity. Dynamic, democratic regulation assumes that this period of time is long enough to give a new government the chance to test and implement its political program, but short enough to prevent political rigidity or the creation of irreversible arrangements (*Verhältnisse*). The presupposed temporal interlocking of political and societal changes becomes particularly conspicuous at this point. Furthermore, as the controversies in political science about the limits of majoritarian democracy in the 1980s made clear, the *temporal scope* of the *consequences* of political decisions plays a central role for the functional capacity and legitimation of democratic systems of the Western type: if political decisions have serious, long-term, *irreversible* consequences, then, to the extent that the legitimacy of decisions in the eyes of a minority disappears, the general basis for democratic decisions seems to become questionable.[3] At the same time, the acceptance of majority rule also presupposes that the representatives of the minority opinion see social and political relations as being dynamic enough to sustain the hope that they might themselves become the majority after the next election.

On the basis of this sensitive temporal interdependency between political structures of decision and implementation and the "intrinsic temporalities" of other social spheres, it is clear that processes of social acceleration have consequences for the functioning and efficiency of the political system and substantially influence society's possibilities of political self-control. Both John Locke and Charles de Montesquieu[4] pointed in prominent passages to the temporal difference between the deliberative mode of the legislative and the flexible and fast action of the executive and thus adumbrated the acceleration-induced displacement of political decision-making competences from the legislative to the executive[5] that was later observed by John Stuart Mill, John Dewey, and Carl Schmitt.[6] The latter situation is accompanied by a tendency to replace formal laws with (executive) orders and to "evacuate" them of material content in favor of more content-variable procedural determinations, frameworks, or guidelines (*Rahmenordnungen*).[7] Hence the central specifically temporal difficulty of democratic politics proves to be the fact that a participatory and deliberative will formation that includes a broad democratic public is capable of being accelerated only to a very limited extent and under specific social conditions. The aggregation and articulation of collective interests and their implementation in democratic decision making has been and remains time intensive.[8] For this reason democratic politics is very much exposed to the danger of desynchronization in the face of more acceleratable social and economic developments.

From the standpoint of their institutional orders, the political systems of the developed national states have turned out to be astonishingly indifferent, if not frankly *blind* to this danger: to take one example, Gisela Riescher's study of the institutionalized time structures of parliamentary and presidential systems of government reveals that the "intrinsic temporalities" of the political system (e.g., speaking times, consultation cycles, question hours, voting modes, etc.) are to the greatest extent possible "self-referentially" oriented to the logic of the interaction between government and opposition (in parliamentary systems) or between executive and legislative (in presidential ones) and as such amazingly stable. Acceleration and deceleration (most strikingly in the form of the "filibuster" in the American Senate) overwhelmingly appear in this context as tactical instruments of "politics," i.e., the power struggle between the antagonists of a political confrontation.[9]

The difficulty of even conceiving of an institutional solution for the time dilemma sketched here thus awakens a suspicion that the political project of modernity might ultimately prove to be incompatible with the social conditions indicated by the concepts of a "space of flows," a "timeless time" of ubiquitous simultaneity, and a situational form of identity.[10] On the other hand, a certain minimum tempo of social change is among the conditions of possibility for the dynamic organizational idea of political modernity. Thus it turns out that the political system underlying that project as well as the stable personal identity that corresponds to it can only exist within certain speed limits of social change: above and below the tempo of transformation characteristic of classical modernity, the aspiration of determining the basic parameters of the shared form of life in a deliberative-democratic way loses its credibility. This is the thesis that will be explicated in what follows.

2. THE TEMPORALIZATION OF HISTORY IN THE MODERN AGE

The first of the specifically temporal difficulties I have identified, namely, that society is a *political project to be shaped within historical time*, constitutes one of the cultural roots of modernity in general. Indeed, this is actually one of its conceptual underpinnings: following the Enlightenment and the French Revolution, a qualitatively different "new time" (*Neue Zeit*) is no longer conceived as and expected to be the irruption of a transcendent sacred time at the end of earthly, historical time (in Christian belief, after the second coming of Christ and the end of the world). Instead, it is secularized and thus, so to speak, hauled down into history itself: it becomes the mission of political organization.[11] As Reinhart Koselleck and, following him, Niklas Luhmann have meticulously worked out, a far-reaching reorganization of the societal semantics of time was linked with this temporalization of new or modern time (*Neuzeit*) that reached its high point during the "epochal threshold" between 1770 and 1830.[12]

Koselleck's central thesis is that a fundamental change in the perception and experience of *history* underlies this development. A new individual and collective perception of *how we are placed in time* (*In-die-Zeit-Gestelltseins*) is expressed and made conscious in this change, one that had been looming with increasing strength since the beginning of modernity (which in this context is held to date back some three hundred years to roughly 1500). Before this, historical time was experienced as a static temporal space in which diverse histories took place, often repeating themselves, so that history could serve the purpose of learning from the mistakes of past generations, in the sense of the old commonplace according to which history is a teacher of life (*historia magistrae vitae*).[13] Koselleck summarizes this premodern and early modern form of historical time experience in the following way:

> Time as the formal and generalized condition for possible events remained quite neutral with respect to epochal episodes and historiographic periods. "*Historia omnis Chronica est, quoniam in tempore fit*" (history is a chronicle of everything that happens in the course of time), as Alsted said. Even

Bacon, who distinguished ancient from modern history, dealt with *Historia temporum* according to method, type, domain, but not according to temporal criteria of modernity or of archaism, which would have been close to his new science and his dictum of "veritas filia temporis." It was Bodin who came up with perhaps the most pithy formulation for the constant projection of historical events into time: while empires age, history remains eternally young. *The additive mode of historical writing corresponds to a uniform and static experience of time, registering ever-present novelty from event to event.* . . . "The world remains the world; therefore all action remains the same in the world, though people die," as Melanchthon, invoking Thucydides, stated in his best Lutheran tones. . . . Such a view presupposes, however, that all histories resemble each other or are structurally similar: only on this condition is it possible to learn from them in the future.[14]

In contrast to this, during the "epochal threshold" a new time experience forges ahead with seemingly unstoppable force, one in which history turns into a "collective singular" in that it is no longer experienced as static, but as *in motion*. Koselleck locates the core of this new perception of history in the divergence of the space of experience and the horizon of expectation.[15] In the new creed, which is undoubtedly grounded in a fundamental transformation of the quality of the present, the future becomes something structurally different from the past: as I have tried to show, the divergence of time horizons is a predictable and indeed unavoidable consequence of the escalation of the pace of social change beyond the critical perceptual threshold of three (or at most four) historically coexisting generations. The experience of historical motion is thus as it were an epiphenomenon (*Begleiterscheinung*) of the gradual transition from an *intergenerational* to a *generational* pace of change.[16] Quite consistently with this, Koselleck also states that the experience of historical acceleration and the surpassing of an epochal threshold underlies the temporalization of history in the epochal threshold and hence the divergence of the time horizons of experience and expectation, yet he remains ambivalent regarding the interpretation of the causal explanation of this perception.[17] After examining a multitude of historical testimonies about the altered experience of time, he states that

two specific temporal determinants characterize the new experience of transition: the expected otherness of the future and, associated with it, the alteration in the rhythm of temporal experience: acceleration, by means of which one's own time is distinguished from what went before. In his analysis of the eighteenth century, Humboldt had expressly emphasized this, and in this he was not alone: "Our epoch appears to lead out of one period, which is passing, into another, which is no less different." The criterion of this shift was based upon a historical time which generated ever-shorter intervals of time. For whoever compares even superficially the present state of affairs with those of fifteen to twenty years ago will not deny that there prevails within this period greater dissimilarity from that which ruled within a period twice as long at the beginning of this century. The abbreviation of the periods which allow for a homogeneity of experience — stated differently, the acceleration of a change which consumes experience — has since then belonged to the topoi characteristic of the prevailing *neueste Geschichte*.[18]

On the basis of this historical finding, which culminates in the "Law of Acceleration" formulated by Henry Adams at the beginning of the twentieth century,[19] Koselleck then interprets acceleration as the decisive and categorially new foundational experience of history, and the rapid establishment of the concept of modernity (*die Neuzeit*) as "an indicator of an acceleration in the rate of change of historical experience and the enhancement of a conscious processing of the nature of time."[20] Thus history is no longer a static space or a neutral foil against which varying *histories* transpire, but is rather itself *temporalized*. "Time is no longer simply the medium in which all histories take place; it gains a historical quality. Consequently, history no longer occurs in, but through, time. Time becomes a dynamic and historical force in its own right. Presupposed by this formulation of experience is a concept of history which is likewise new: the collective singular form of *Geschichte*, which since around 1780 can be conceived as history in and for itself in the absence of an associated subject or object."[21]

This transformation of the experience of history lies at the root of the reconceptualization of the role and status of the political in modernity. This occurs in part through the formulation of modern *philosophies of history* that attempt to define the direction and goal of the perceived movement of history and thereby become constitutively tied to the idea of *political movement*: society becomes a task of political organization within time in accordance with the principles of social development. The category of social and political *progress*, as the "first genuinely historical category of time,"[22] constitutes the key concept for this expectation of goal-directed historical development. It acquires its cultural impetus not least from the modern *temporalization of utopias*: political conceptions of an alternative, better society are no longer projected into an imaginary u-topian space, but into the future, and hence pulled into the space of history and politics. As Jürgen Habermas aptly remarks: "In fact, modern time consciousness has opened up a horizon in which the utopian merges with historical thinking. This migration of utopian energies into historical consciousness characterizes the spirit of the times that has shaped the political public sphere of modern peoples since the days of the French revolution. Political thinking which draws on the current spirit of the times is charged with utopian energies—but at the same time this surplus of expectation should be controlled by the conservative counterweight of historical experiences."[23]

However, Koselleck states that as a consequence of this development more or less *all* political and social theories and programs are temporalized and become ordered along temporal lines of movement such that the *pressure to move* produces a *compulsory time grid*. Things can no longer be recognized or argued about, let alone politically legitimated, without temporal coefficients of movement and change.[24] Almost all the political groupings and streams of modernity conceive of themselves as *movements*, right down to the new social movements that emerge following the revolts of 1968.

As I have already remarked, the great political camps of modernity are ordered along the directional time index of the dividing line designated by the terms *progressive* and *conservative*, whereby the specific forms of respective movement can be read in the various *ism* concepts, newly coined as the high point of classical modernity approached: *republicanism, liberalism, conservatism, socialism,* etc.[25] However, these movements become structurally asymmetrical because of the assumed irreversibility of historical development: even a conservative politics cannot stop history; it can only ensure gentle, cautious transitions and the preservation of that which is worth preserving. Thus progressive and conservative often designate different *speeds* rather than genuinely different directions: according to its own self-understanding, progressive politics strives toward an *acceleration* of the expected development of history, conservative politics toward its *deceleration* or temporary suspension.[26] *But in each case politics becomes the pacesetter for societal development in the context of the (classical) modern experience of history; it is given a peremptory formative task.* This constitutes an indispensable correlate to political modernity's *promise of autonomy*, according to which the organization of the societal project lies in the hands of human beings themselves in their role as citizens.

In what follows, I will argue that the "end of history" diagnosed by the advocates of *posthistoire* is only plausible if understood as the end *of this specific form of temporalized history* and that this fundamentally alters not only the experience of historical time but also the conception and form of politics and the political. At the same time, it will turn out that this epochal transition can ultimately only be understood and precisely defined from an acceleration-theoretical perspective.

3. PARADOXICAL TIME HORIZONS: THE DETEMPORALIZATION OF HISTORY IN LATE MODERNITY

The time structures of late modernity cause the basic temporal assumptions of the political project of modernity worked out in the first section of this chapter to become problematic, if not plainly to fail: as a consequence of the most recent wave of social acceleration both our received understanding of the role of *politics in (historical) time* and the classical modern conception of the *pattern of time in politics* or of the interface between politics and society seem to become untenable.

This *temporal crisis of the political* comes to light most clearly in something we have already thematized on several occasions, the *desynchronization* between the "intrinsic temporality" of politics and the time structures of other social spheres, in particular the economy and technological development, but increasingly also between political organization and sociocultural development. The American political scientist Sheldon Wolin summarizes this shift as follows:

> Starkly put, political time is out of synch with the temporalities, rhythms, and pace governing economy and culture. Political time . . . requires an element of leisure. . . . This is owing to the needs of political action to be preceded by deliberation and deliberation, as its "deliberate" part suggests, takes time because, typically, it occurs in a setting of competing or conflicting but legitimate considerations. Political time is conditioned by the presence of differences and the attempt to negotiate them. The results of negotiations, whether successful or not, preserve time. . . . Thus time is "taken" in deliberation yet "saved."[27]

Wolin's last sentence makes clear that up to now politics was assigned the task of preserving the cultural *unity of time* in the face of all the disintegrative tendencies of society. This preservation of the integrity of the political past, present, and future is achieved through the deliberative process of political contestation, not the decision as such.

Moreover, at least with respect to *democratic* forms of politics, the fact of desynchronization is by now a commonplace not only in social and political theory,[28] but in practical politics itself. As evidence of the latter, I will simply remind the reader of the aforementioned initiative of the Bavarian government to eliminate political regulations that slow down the economy, of the North Rhine-Westphalian political campaign of 2000, in which the Free Democratic Party received a sensational 10 percent of the vote with the ever-present slogan *NRW needs Tempo*, while the Green party, labeled as a "modernization retardant" by Governor Clement and perceived as such by the public, lost almost a third of its votes, or of the Swiss "Acceleration Initiative," a legislative program likewise launched in 2000 that aimed at getting rid of democratic rights of participation with the argument that the directly democratic Swiss referenda, which can take up to three years, are too slow for developments in the economy and in research and are therefore damaging to them.[29]

What is common to all three examples is the politically highly influential idea that *less politics* in the sense of democratic regulation means *higher speed* and thus the abolition of societal desynchronization. It is grounded in the observation that the differentiated social subsystems have become quite independent of each other even in their time horizons and time patterns, that is, they have each formed their own *new* intrinsic temporalities and can therefore be accelerated to different degrees (contrary to the widespread opinion that modernity replaced the variety of quasi-natural intrinsic temporalities and rhythms with a *single* linear, abstract, and, as it were, "empty" worldly time to which everything was ruthlessly related).[30] This fact is what first makes possible systemic social desychronization and the appearance of the *nonsimultaneity of the simultaneous*, which only becomes a manifest problem in view of the temporal-structural coupling of systems.[31]

This development is not at all limited to the relation between politics and the economy. It appears within and between all possible social subsystems, for instance, between education and science, law and the economy and beyond this along the boundary between the economy and the ecological realm. As David Harvey remarks: "The time-horizon set by Wall Street simply cannot accommodate to the temporalities of social and ecological reproduction systems in a responsive way. And it goes without saying that the rapid turnover time set in financial markets is even more stressful for workers (their job security, their skills etc.) and for the lifeworld of socio-ecological reproduction."[32]

Relatedly, Thomas Assheuer finds that it is "self-deception to believe that one can accelerate a society at will and despite that hold together its lifeworlds."[33] The intergenerational disintegration of cultural lifeworlds in late modernity has already been dealt with in detail in chapter 4.

Yet even within the economy itself the pressure to accelerate generates massive synchronization problems whose costs are as a rule externalized. In the context of booms and the crisis of the "New Economy" this is particularly visible in the divergence between the high speed world of financial markets and the sphere of real investment or even in the development of business and production itself. In the latter, for instance, test phases for new products or materials are shortened and the products themselves are introduced to the market *before* the test phase ends, thus drawing the consumer into the preparation of a new product as a test person. Innovation cycles (the time between a scientific or technological invention and its introduction to the market) and product cycles (the lifetime of a given model) have been accelerated so much in certain sectors (for instance, in entertainment electronics and, to some extent, even in the automobile industry) that often even the dealer is unable to identify the most up-to-date product, let alone the consumer. The number and succession of new medicines has been heightened so much that when doctors go to write prescriptions they now have to trust the information given to them by the pharmaceutical industry instead of their own experience.[34]

Furthermore, it seems that even the traditional paths of adjudication have become too slow to resolve conflicts in economic relations, especially in the context of transnational operations, which have therefore increasingly deployed alternative forms of conciliation (like mediation or arbitration procedures) and thereby produced novel configurations of "project law" or even "neo-spontaneous law."[35] Thus the growing compulsion to accelerate also has effects on the forms of international law. As Klaus Dicke shows, here too traditional procedures can no longer satisfy the demands for speed, so pressure grows to turn the General Assembly or even the Security Council of the United Nations into a "legislator."[36] This is also illustrated by the tendency to transfer (quasi-)legislative competences to executive organs for reasons of time scarcity: the International Criminal Tribunal for the former Yugoslavia in May 1993 was successfully established *by the Security Council*, which appealed to chapter 7 of the UN Charter and drew legal support from a report by the secretary-general declaring that the "normal" procedure of a multilateral treaty was *too slow*. The chosen procedure was simply faster and more immediately effective.[37]

My thesis is thus that toward the end of the twentieth century the role of politics as a social *pacesetter* that was undisputed in classical modernity has been lost because the intrinsic temporality of the political is largely resistant to or incapable of acceleration (the pacesetter role now seems to be occupied by the economy). Political time horizons increasingly exhibit a highly paradoxical structure. As I hope to show, *time within politics* is becoming thoroughly disorganized and confused (*durcheinander*), and this is also bringing the classical modern conception of the role of *politics in time* to the brink of collapse.

The paradoxical nature of political time in late modernity consists in the development of a twofold divergence of its constitutive time horizons and in the relationship of time resources to time needs (cf. figure 11.1).

The accelerative pressure on the political system to deliver collectively binding decisions rapidly is in the first place a direct consequence of the acceleration of the tempo of development and change in other social systems, in particular in the areas of economic circulation and scientific-technical

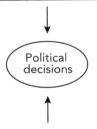

Shortening of time horizon/ scarcity of time resources:
- Time period for decisions shrinks
  (Speed of technical and social innovations rises)
- Number of necessary decisions grows – growing scarcity of time
  resources per decision
- Horizon of predictability shrinks (contraction of the present)

Political decisions

Consequence:
Relocation of decisions into faster systems:
- Juridification
- Deregulation
- Privatization
- Preponderance of executive
  over the legislative

Widening of time horizon/ increase in the need for time:
- Scope of the effects of decision grows
  (e.g., genetic engineering)
- Need for planning per decision rises due to growing contingencies
- Erosion of cultural and sociostructural bases of decision
  (*disintegration*) leads to heightened need for time

11.1. Paradoxes of Political Time

innovation. It brings about a situation in which the time resources available for a political decision on taxes or regulation continually diminish. This occurs for three reasons:

First, if and so long as politics wants to maintain its claim to regulate the parameters of economic and technological development, it must *either* adapt itself to the accelerated rate of innovation in the relevant social spheres and become, as it were, a "motorized legislator" (Carl Schmitt) *or* decisively intervene in their developmental autonomy and thereby repeal the principle of functional differentiation in favor of a renewed political dominance.[38] It could thus impose the (slower) change tempo of the political system on the other functional systems and bring about a kind of "forced resynchronization." The latter option is the solution that acceleration-skeptical authors like Fritz Reheis or Matthias Eberling have in mind when they call for a *politics of time* intent on social deceleration: "the politics of time must stop the artificial acceleration of evolutionarily emergent processes through phased interventions or introduce deceleration," as Reheis succinctly puts it.[39] Eberling provides an even more pregnant formulation: "the core thesis runs: if acceleration is the problem, the solution lies in slowdown. . . . Here democracy is the key to the slowdown," because it consciously makes the exercise of power slow.[40] However, due to the economic and social costs that a politically imposed resynchronization would cause, and above all due to the crisis of the modern conception of the role of politics in time, to which I will shortly return, this idea is very unrealistic, particularly because it remains unclear who could be the political *bearer* of such a politics of deceleration. In any case, present levels of desynchronization put politics ever more frequently at risk of making anachronistic decisions that have already been made obsolete by social reality at the time of their implementation: one thinks for instance of questions concerning stem cell research or cloning or of legal questions relating to information transfer on the Internet.

Second, due to the already discussed "contraction of the present," i.e., the growing instability of horizons of expectation and conditions of action in the postconventional age, there is an increase not only in the rate of innovation but also in the number and scope of social areas requiring political regulation. This fact lies behind the observation made by Beck, for instance, that in a certain sense the extent and significance of the political constantly increases: as is well known, there is no longer any area of human life, from waste disposal to vacation time to gender relations, that might *not* be the object of political contestation. Yet this expansion of the area to be regulated implies that the amount of time *per decision* available to the legislator or the politically responsible official sinks in inverse proportion to the rise in the number of decisions to be made.[41]

Third, and finally, as a result of the rapidly altering background conditions of social action, the very same contraction of the present causes a progressive shortening of the temporal range of what can be rationally assessed in the course of political planning. As I have shown, the *need* for planning in late modernity increases to the same extent that the range of what *can* be planned decreases. As a result, fewer and fewer things can be provided with regulations once and for all or at least for the period of one or more generations; the limit of the foreseeable moves steadily closer to the present, and politics has to shift over to a mode of muddling through where the urgency of the fixed-term reigns and temporary and provisional solutions take the place of larger political designs.[42] For this reason the same problems (for instance, pension or health insurance reforms) repeatedly return to the political agenda at short intervals. Thus politics loses its role as an influential actor that shapes the playing field itself and takes on the status of a predominantly *reactive* fellow player of the game.[43]

However, the dilemma of time in politics is not only caused by the external pressure to accelerate. It is further sharpened by a growing internal *inability to accelerate* and even a manifest *tendency of slowdown* in the way democratic politics operates. It is this that first makes the time horizons of the political in late modernity truly paradoxical. It looks as if once again there are three reasons for this involuntary deceleration of political decision making, corresponding to the three causes of the pressure to accelerate.

In the first place, the temporal range of the *effects* of political decisions increases. Many of their consequences reach further and further into the future. Matthias Eberling illustrates this using the example of the development of technology:

> Traditional technology offers each new generation in principle the possibility of a critical assessment and possible rejection. . . . This already becomes more difficult with the introduction of atomic technology, because the radioactive by-products would remain a danger to the next hundred generations even if all atom-splitting immediately ceased. However, genetic engineering [itself a technique for the immense acceleration of traditional breeding procedures —H. R.] will produce consequences endlessly, since its mistakes can reproduce themselves. It can shape not only present-day society, but every other society that comes after us.[44]

Yet irreversible decisions require significantly more careful planning and information gathering and are therefore unavoidably more time intensive than reversible ones. In fact, other things equal, the following holds: the longer the temporal range of a decision is, the longer the period of time required to make it on the basis of a given substantive standard of rationality. This illustrates the paradox of contemporary temporal development: the temporal range of our decisions seems to increase to the same extent that the time resources we need to make them disappear.

In the second place, however, the time expenditure needed to make political decisions that meet a given substantive (time-insensitive) standard of rationality rises even where the range of its effects is *not* larger: the more uncertainty that prevails about the stability of the parameters in light of which a decision is made, the greater the amount of information required to take account of contingencies and alternative possibilities and consequently the amount of time expended for making a rational decision.[45] For instance, it might already seem a difficult enterprise to design a secure pension system when the demographic variables (especially the ratio of gainfully employed persons to the unemployed) are stable or at least calculable. However, it becomes almost impossible when it is unknown (a) how long future generations will live, (b) how long they will work, (c) what percentage of the population at what point in time will be gainfully employed, (d) which forms of private pension scheme will develop, and (e) which trans- and international agreements will come into conflict with a given design. The escalating political and legal uncertainty regarding national and supranational competences and available leeway for making decisions thus sharpens the problem.

In the third place, finally (and this seems to me to be the most serious finding), the genuinely political processes of interest articulation and aggregation and (democratic) deliberation, i.e., will formation and decision making, become ever more difficult and hence time consuming on account of the cultural and social-structural development of late modern society. For the smaller the taken-for-granted value consensus of a society is, and the less traditional or conventional the principles of justification and legitimation in political contestation are, the more difficult it becomes to find agreement or to form a political will capable of meeting with consensus. And, according to all existing diagnoses, late modern society tends to become at once more pluralistic and more postconventional. The accompanying level of social *disintegration* can itself be interpreted to a great extent as a consequence of social *desynchronization*: as I have already laid out, the late modern simultaneity of the nonsimultaneous also encompasses the various cultural, ethnic, and religious subgroups, which develop in a, so to speak, "desynchronized" fashion in accordance with their own respective rules,[46] such that a "mosaic of time ghettoes" emerges (as one can observe above all in the United States, although the development of, for instance, Germans and Turks in Germany points in a similar direction). These "ghettoes" may be partially withdrawn from the compulsion to accelerate (and hence from the time structures and horizons of modernity in general) and in this way their continued existence becomes more secure (e.g., the Amish in the U.S.). However, where the pressure to accelerate drives social spheres and social groups, one may presume that it will ultimately force them to make their boundaries more diffuse since such boundaries form evident barriers to speed (the creeping irrelevance of national boundaries is just one example of this).[47] Despite attempts at creating functionally equivalent but temporary forms of association, however, the resulting postmodern *dedifferentiation* will hardly lead to a *reintegration*. Rather it will end up in further atomizing *disintegration*. What could emerge from the mosaic of ghettoes is a structureless or kaleidoscopic (i.e., rapidly altering) social formation of fluctuating associations and temporary milieus.

Yet, even leaving aside such speculative scenarios, it seems clear that the progressive dissolution of stable social milieus, the instability of forms of social belonging, and the volatility of political preferences, all discussed under the heading of the "individualization of life situations," make it increasingly difficult to articulate and organize collective interests, not least because it is more and more unclear which social groups, associations, and partners are even relevant for which negotiation processes. Interestingly, John Dewey already saw the related, specifically temporal problem of organizing a stable political public sphere as a core presupposition of a functioning democracy. "How can a public be organized, we may ask, when literally it does not stay in place? Without abiding attachments, associations are too shifting and shaken to permit a public readily to locate and identify itself," he observed already in 1927. The problem he sketched out is no less pressing in the age of digital media and global flows.[48]

Nevertheless, in this context hopes for a *resynchronization* and the establishment of new forms of a public sphere rest above all on the democratic potential of new interactive media, that is, on procedures like Internet debates and Internet voting.[49] However, I fear that while this could clearly accelerate the process of *voting*, the same is not the case for the formulation and bundling of interests and *deliberation*.[50] Under the aforementioned conditions of a diffusion of political publics, translation of aggegrated "private opinions" that can be surveyed via the new media into a genuinely public and political (i.e., reasoned) opinion may in fact be more time consuming than ever.[51] Given the enormous time required for such translations, they may increasingly not even be attempted: in place of a contestation with justified and justifiable *arguments* there is then the political struggle of images and symbols. The latter are more quickly communicated than words. Therefore, in the struggle for the ever scarcer resource of *attention*, politics is in danger of ultimately being reduced to a question of the better *marketing strategy*.[52] In any case, in view of the difficulties of democratic will formation in pluralized societies, it is not surprising that the pressure to decide can be and also is used to unburden the political system of expectations of protracted or even impossible processes of deliberation and consensus making, i.e., in Luhmann's sense, to bring the time dimension into play for the purpose of unburdening the social dimension.[53]

The dilemma of late modern politics that these six points comprehensively describe leads quite evidently to a *displacement of the decision-making process* from the realm of democratic politics into other faster realms of society (cf. figure 11.1): Alongside the long-noticed shift of emphasis from the democratic form of legislative lawmaking to the flexible institution of executive decisions,[54] there is the transfer of politically controversial questions to the jurisdiction of constitutional courts (juridification), the self-regulating ability of the economy (economic deregulation), or the realm of each individual's own personal responsibility (ethical privatization). Beyond this, at the international level authoritative decisions are often negotiated by experts and interest groups that are either not democratically legitimated at all or only insufficiently. From this perspective, the notorious democratic deficit of the European Union seems to be no coincidence.

Nevertheless, in this context the most weighty consequence of the time crisis of politics is the retraction of its claim to shape society (*Gestaltungsanspruch*) and the connected fundamental change in the conception of the status and function of politics in history. As I have already suggested, this transformation indicates a deep-seated faultline in modernity's understanding of history.

In fact, all the previously discussed political developments seem to point to the conclusion that the time of modern politics has run out. Because the time horizon and working speed of politics in late modernity lags behind changes in the economy and in society, it can no longer perform the function of *setting the pace* for social development and being a *shaper of history* (which the culture at large still imputes to it). Where it does still hold to its steering aspiration, it no longer appears as progressive, as driving historical development forward, but rather as a "modernization brake" (this is the reason why it appears in the list of classical modern accelerators that have become late modern brakes, cf. figure 8.1). Insofar as the distinction between left- and right-wing politics still has any meaning at all, today "progressives" find themselves mostly on the side of *deceleration* (a direct inversion of classical modern relations) because they advocate political control of the economy, processes of democratic negotiation and protection of the environment, and local cultural particularities, while "conservatives" seem to pursue a strategy of acceleration at the cost of the genuinely political insofar as they, for instance, campaign for the rapid introduction of new technologies, the dismantling of political hurdles for the circulation of global flows, the predominance of the market and accelerated forms of decision making.

The resulting loss of a temporal-political directional index provides a tangible sign of an altered form of historical perception and a related change in the role of politics. Both strategies, namely, the attempt to hold on to the ideas of control by means of delaying tactics and the effort to resynchronize by revoking the claim to regulate, ultimately lead to a politics that no longer acts, but *reacts* in accordance with the requirements of the given situation: such a politics is forced to conform to the standards of faster systems. Consequently, the relinquishment of political control is explicitly defended in political argument with the claim that a single state's hindrance of the intrinsic developmental dynamics of, for instance, genetic research would undeniably lead to a genuine inability to influence or steer *future* conditions. For instance, during debates about the therapeutic cloning of embryoes, the German chancellor Schröder argued in January 2001 that Germany could not, in the end, do with a "No," since it would then be left far behind in international development and would no longer be able to play a role in decisions about *future* "applications and consequences" of genetic technology. This is a signal of nothing other than a renunciation of political control today in order to preserve potential future opportunities of control. It is thus a form of, as it were, "idling" synchronization.[55]

In other words, strategies of muddling through that orient themselves to the urgency of the fixed term take the place of political conceptions aimed at shaping society.[56] If political exhaustion and increasing voter volatility are political characteristics of late modern democracies, their causes lie not least in the conceptions offered by political parties insofar as they do not limit themselves to the mere withdrawal of political aspirations of control (which is nevertheless a genuinely political program). The things that sail under the banner of a political vision for society (platforms, ideas for reform, strategic plans) turn out to be unable to redeem this claim, and on a closer look reveal themselves to be simply a desperate effort of adaptation.[57] Perhaps the advancing decline in voter participation in almost all developed democracies does not simply reflect a decline in the consciousness of civic duties, but rather a deeper rationality of voters who thereby express their sense of the increasing insignificance of politics for the course of history by withdrawing from it.

There are also precipitates of this loss of significance in the transformation of political vocabulary, a transformation that seems to eliminate almost all of the characteristics of (classical) modern political vocabulary. Thus the resynchronization efforts of politics are clearly correlated with a rhetoric of *objective forces* (*Sachzwangs*) that hides behind concepts like "globalization," "locational competition," or "the pressure to modernize." At the beginning of the twenty-first century, the semantics of progress that accompanied all earlier phases of modernization almost completely disappears behind the rhetoric of objective forces: technological and social changes are no longer pushed through in the name of progress; they are justified by a threatened loss of competitiveness.[58] In this context *growth* and *acceleration* go completely unquestioned as the prescribed goals of societal development, though the basis of their legitimacy correspondingly shifts from promise to necessity or even threat. This is yet another signal of the growing predominance of the *compulsion* to accelerate that results when the contraction of the present and the slipping slope phenomenon occur together with the horizon of the utopian *promise* of acceleration.[59] Processes of acceleration that were once politically set in motion inspired by utopian hopes have in the meantime become so autonomized (*verselbständigt*) that they compel their own continuation *at the cost* of this political hope for progress.

In the course of this, the system as a whole becomes, as Elmar Altvater remarks, "myopic": in place of philosophical-historical conceptions or long-term political strategies one finds short-term operation according to the requirements of the respective situation.[60] Therefore, *situational politics* is a collective correlate to the late modern form of *situational identity*: the situationality is in both cases a consequence of heightened social acceleration and here as there it brings about a transformation of the dominant experience of time that can be most clearly grasped using the concept of the temporalization of time. "Since the modern risk society is permanently aware of the riskiness of binding time commitments, it experiences the paradox that it can only make use of time within time, i.e., that it is always bound to present moments whose succession makes time continually appear different. . . . The world changes with each new present, and one can tell from this that the future exists only as the future of a present. The future itself is inevitably unknown."[61]

In this description of the temporalization of time in politics formulated by Armin Nassehi, one cannot fail to recognize parallels with the figure of the player as characterized by Karl Hörning, Daniela Ahrens, and Anette Gerhard: politics too is increasingly caught in the logic of drifting and (noncommittal) playing.[62] At any rate, Luhmann also catches sight of one of the "most important problems of the present" at precisely this juncture.[63]

Just as the temporalization of time causes a *detemporalization of life* with respect to individual selfhood, so it brings about a *detemporalization of history* in the context of late modern politics. Instead of being experienced as a directed, dynamic process that can be politically accelerated (or decelerated), history once again takes on the form of an almost "static" space of juxtaposed and successively unfolding histories. Insofar as Lübbe is correct in claiming that the projection of a utopia conceived as something *realizable in time* presupposes the perception of one's own historical condition as in the midst of *directed change*,[64] the exhaustion of utopian energies diagnosed by Habermas is not only a crisis of the developmental perspective of a welfare state tied to a work society but a crisis of history-making political steering energies in general: their conditions of emergence as laid out by Koselleck and Lübbe no longer exist.[65] In this way, Frederic Jameson's astonishment at the fact that late modern society can more easily imagine *the end of the world* than an end of the liberal capitalist political system can be explained by a theory of acceleration.[66]

The temporalization of political-historical time can also be seen in the fact that the movement concepts that formed during the epochal threshold no longer indicate movement in late modernity, but simply set up a static space of alternative forms of politics: the political isms (republicanism, socialism, liberalism, conservatism, etc.) have forfeited their dynamic force and no longer assume any irreversible developments. They indicate only *reversible alternatives* that are experienced as being at once timeless and simultaneous in the "timeless time" of late modernity. Thus one may predict that the so-called new social movements are the last offshoots of classical modernity and have also exhausted the typical *movement-involving character* of modern politics. One can no longer foretell what the respective next stage or movement will be in the manner of theories of progress or philosophies of history. From now on this will be decided once again *within time*, i.e., in political action itself.

The new dominant experience of time in the form of "timelessness" is undoubtedly *not* a return to the cyclical time of premodernity.[67] The various states of the world do not repeat again and again in an, as it were, "natural" rhythm (as in Polybius's cyclical view of constitutional forms, for instance), but exist alongside one another simultaneously. Which forms are actualized in which place, when, in what sequence, and for how long is decided within time itself according to unpredictable developments that are *endogenous* to society.

At this point, though, it should be clear how it is possible that in the hyperaccelerated society of the present perceptions of the total contingency and complete openness of historical development and the experience of standstill, of the *end* of any development, become dominant simultaneously. In Jean Baudrillard's essay "The Pataphysics of the Year 2000," the internal affinity of both these historical and societal tendencies—dynamization and rigidification—is reflected in the fact that they are two opposed modes of the *dissolution of history* that ultimately lead to the same result, namely, the disappearance of history and a historical sense. The first mode is the unstoppable *acceleration* of all facts and events up to a point ("escape velocity," *vitesse de liberation*) at which they can no longer have any duration and hence also no effects, such that a situation emerges that Thomas Jung, in connection with Baudrillard, characterizes as follows: "History loses . . . its validity when events implode into 'current events,' when the facts become messages whose function lies only in the circulation of media information. History becomes meaningless because 'no history can bear the centrifugation of facts for their own sake.'"[68]

In contrast, the second mode consists in a *slowing down* and gradual crystallization of history (inertness, *Trägheit*) until it finally congeals and is extinguished under the weight of its own "mass":

That is where *the* crucially significant event of [our modern] societies is to be found: the advent of their revolutionary process along the lines of their mobility (they are all revolutionary with respect to the centuries gone by), of their equivalent force of inertia, of an immense indifference, and of the silent power of this indifference: the so-called "masses." . . . It is the cold star of the social, a mass at the peripheries of which history cools out. Successive events attain their annihilation in indifference. . . . History can no longer play itself out . . . it blows itself out in its immediate effect, it exhausts itself in special effects, it implodes in current events. Essentially one can no longer speak of the end of history since it has no time to rejoin its own end. As its effects accelerate, its meaning inexorably decelerates. It will end up stopping and extinguishing itself like light and time at the peripheries of an infinitely dense mass.[69]

As I have already shown, such rapid change is experienced as a *frenetic standstill* in the absence of a goal or a direction. If this experience potentially leads to individual depression insofar as it touches one's own life, then as a collective form of historical perception it winds up in the paralytic experience of *posthistoire*.[70] Thus the experience of *history* in the sense of the "collective singular" and the interpretation of politics as a democratic project of shaping society are only possible when social change remains within a definite "speed window." In the epochal threshold its lower limit was obviously crossed. It could be that its upper bound has now been reached in late modernity. The diagnosis of Baudrillard agrees precisely with the argument developed here: he remarks that "a certain slowness (i.e., a certain speed, but not too fast) . . . is necessary for this condensation to take place, for the signifying crystallization of events that we call history."[71]

Beyond this speed limit, political events again take on the situational character of episodes and are comparable to the compressed episodes of individual experience discussed earlier. However, because they lose their status as elements of a meaningful historical chain of development and can no longer be transformed into genuine historical *experience* (*Erfahrung*) in Benjamin's sense, they also lose any ("deeper") significance in general, as countless cultural (and pop-cultural) observers of the present attest. Quite in the spirit of Marx's dictum that history only repeats itself *as farce*, the documents of contemporary culture observe (occasionally even very turbulent) historical events in terms of the peculiar waning of their personal and collective significance. "From the turn of the twentieth century up to the present, the semantics of time has developed from a field upon which there are still victories to be won to an area in which all battles have already been fought and *nothing more can happen*," as Nassehi summarizes this feeling of an end of history; his summary is confirmed by Imre Kertész, the Hungarian winner of the Nobel prize for literature in 2002, who writes: "everything keeps on going, but somehow flatter, if also more bluntly."[72] Similar to Hans Magnus Enzensberger or Martin van Creveld, Kertész also remarks that while the ideologies that motivated violence and excess of course still exist, they no longer claim to affect the course of history, but assume the appearance of sheer contingency. Nationalism, war, anti-Semitism, economic crises, secularization and new fundamental-isms, struggles over wages, foundings of new states and state failure, recently even manifestations of (neo-) colonialism: all the historical forms, elements and conflicts of modernity return in unordered sequences in a space of, so to speak, neostatic simultaneity and situational politics.

The heroes of Douglas Coupland's *Generation X* suffer from a *history poison-ing* that illuminatingly and pregnantly encapsulates the dialectical, paradoxi-cal simultaneity of frenetic change and historical lack of development.[73] Ironi-cally, Coupland's list of key cultural concepts, itself a diagnosis of the times, reads like a caricature of Koselleck's list of temporalized motion concepts from the epoch of temporalized history written in light of the now temporalized time: "historical slumming," "vaccinated time travel," "decade blending," "leg-islated nostalgia," "ultra short term nostalgia," "now denial," etc., designate the temporalization strategies in the glossary appended to Coupland's novel. The first-person narrator there explicitly remarks that the Vietnam War and the revolts caused by it are the last offshoots of *genuine history*.[74]

Quite in line with this, the social scientist and music theorist Bill Martin observes that the revolts and movements of 1968 now appear to us as "the last gasp of something we used to call 'history,'" and it is no coincidence that they were characterized by the musical trend of "progressive rock," which was nourished by the idea of a better future that remained to be (musically and politically) given shape, while the music of the 1980s and '90s was character-ized by "retro waves" and the negation of hopes for progress: "Yesterday's alter-native rock included the idea of going somewhere, whereas the predominant ethos in today's 'alternative' music is that there is nowhere to go." Hence it has become difficult to get a deeper meaning from things in general: "We live in a time when it is very hard for anything to be significant or important, a time of an immense cultural machinery of pure distraction."[75] Roger Waters, the former creative leader of the rock group Pink Floyd, interprets this process as "the peeling away of feeling" and dedicated to it an elaborate album he entitled *Amused to Death*.[76]

The cultural experience of crisis connected to this perception of history is rooted in the simultaneous loss of a past providing a reference point and a meaning-constituting future. Without these a workable definition of the pres-ent is also impossible, a point on which Lutz Niethammer and Armin Nassehi concur when they declare that the problem the *posthistoire* diagnoses pose to us is "not the end of the world, but the end of meaning," while Jean Chesneaux shows that a central task of political democracy lies in mediating between "the inheritance of the past," the "priorities of the present," and the "challenges of the future."[77] The simultaneity of the crisis of democracy and the increasingly problematic character of that mediation is thus no coincidence.

Thus what is experienced in this way as a *time of crisis* from within the cultural horizon of modernity is certainly *not* a time of great upheavals or decisions that can be faced, as it were, "chronopolitically" by means of a reorientation of political action.[78] The crisis consists rather in the fact that *there is no longer anything left to decide*: social processes of action and systemic developments have become independent with respect to political steering, and the cultural foundations of the latter's meaning have been stripped away. Ultimately this too can be interpreted as a form of *desynchronization*: systemic processing in the structures of late modern society has become *too fast* to carry along the cultural resources of meaning that upheld the unifying political project of modernity and its understanding of history. In the longing for a plausible construal of an end of history, Nassehi believes that "a certain non-simultaneity is expressed that obviously seeks to rescue semantically that which seems to have become impossible socio-structurally."[79]

Accordingly, the desynchronization of politics and economics would be only a *symptom* of a deeper-seated desynchronization of structure and culture in late modernity. The end of the world proves to be the single remaining history that can still be coherently recounted from the horizon of (classical) modernity: "if the end of history were itself a historical event, history would be continued, because there would still be differences between events, and, as is well-known, time functions as their unity."[80] For this reason, the protagonists of *Generation* X see the fact that we can produce a nuclear (or, varying the motif, an ecological or [genetic]-technological) *catastrophe* as not only less frightening than an *endless time without history* but also something that definitely bears the marks of a hope for salvation, for it still promises the chance of "finding an end . . . for the history of the world," as one of the main characters of the novel declares.[81]

Thus it should not be surprising that a frivolous playing around with the apocalypse (so understood) is not only omnipresent in Coupland's books but also belongs to the phenotype of postmodernism in general, as Klaus Scherpe has observed.[82] The destruction of the world becomes a kind of exciting antipode to the creeping apocalypse of an everyday existence that, as I have shown, appears rigid in virtue of its contingent openness and ubiquitous simultaneity, like the world of Texlahoma, a central setting of the stories told in *Generation X*, which is *frozen for all eternity in the year 1974*, "the year after the oil shock and the year starting from which real wages in the U.S never grew ever again."[83]

However, in the systems-theoretical approach represented by, for instance, Nassehi, the desynchronization of "semantics" and "social structure" that underlies the drying up of historical and political visions bemoaned by Jameson and Habermas is unequivocally attributed to modernity as such. This approach sees it as a direct consequence of functional differentiation. Because Nassehi and Luhmann can only identify *one* process of temporalization, they are unable to specify precisely the *break* between classical modernity and late modernity.[84] Indeed, the temporalized concept of history that develops in the epochal threshold appears to them as anachronistic from the start, as a mere *simulation* of unity or as a semantic fiction. "This semantics of social unity," as Nassehi writes in connection with Peter Fuchs, "has [from the start —H. R.] the function of compensating for the loss of meaning in the social dimension that arises due to functional differentiation and all the functional crises of early modernity that accompany it. *It serves to establish unity where from a social-structural point of view it has ultimately already been lost.*"[85] According to this view, what I have described as the "temporalization of time" is nothing other than a delayed adaptation of our cultural consciousness to the structural conditions of modernity as such.

In my view, however, this interpretation suffers from two grave defects: By reducing the temporalization of life and of history to mere "simulations" of unity and anachronistic attempts at compensation, it misjudges the extent to which the related conceptions of politics, history, and identity shaped and defined the project of modernity. Luhmannian systems-theory can only manage this without losing its plausibility because it almost programmatically ignores or downplays the promises of autonomy and control in modernity. In the second place, though, it can convincingly reconstruct neither the emergence of the earlier form of temporalization nor the transition to the "temporalization of time" and hence the break *within* modernity. If systems theory reduces this understanding to an anachronistic fiction or simulation, then ultimately it still owes us an explanation for the emergence of such a historically influential conception of history and it can provide no convincing reason why this fiction is given up in the late twentieth century with such obviously serious consequences for individuals and societies.

In contrast to this, the two specifically temporal breaks in the transitions first to modernity and then to late modernity can not only be more precisely *defined* and *explained* by the interaction of structure and culture from the acceleration-theoretical perspective proposed here, but they can further be reconstructed as consequences of a unified escalatory relationship between growth and acceleration that characterizes modernity as a whole. Therefore in the next chapter I will try to summarize the findings presented in part 4 of this work and flesh them out into a sketch of a theoretical redefinition of modernity in light of the dialectical relationship between acceleration and inertia.[86]

12

ACCELERATION AND RIGIDITY:
AN ATTEMPT TO REDEFINE MODERNITY

IN A WRITTEN SURVEY IN North Thuringia, in 2002, a seventeen-year-old student answered the question "In your view, what are the main problems of youth today?" by checking off two bullet points: "no hope for the future" and "a rigid and at the same time hectic society in which everyone only thinks about themselves and it is difficult to find a place for oneself without help."[1] In this succinct, everyday diagnosis of the problem, one sees the basic temporal-structural difficulties of late modernity worked out in the previous chapters bundled together with astonishing precision: on the one hand, the action-orienting capacity of future horizons and the meaning-constituting unity of past, present, and future become problematic (under pressure from autono-mized systemic necessities), and, on the other, there is a simultaneous percep-tion of higher rates of change and rigidity beneath the surface.

Now one may with good reason wonder just how much these represent time problems that are really specific to our epoch. Doesn't the two-sided fear of both change *and* stasis reflect the ineradicable duality of Herclitus's παντα ρει (everything is in flux) and Parmenides' εν χαι παν (permanent, unchanging being), which presents itself as an invariant given in the world? For instance, Georg Simmel finds that "if we consider the substance of the world, then we easily end up in the idea of . . . an unchangeable being, that suggests, through the exclusion of any increase or decrease in things, the char-acter of absolute constancy. If, on the other hand, we concentrate upon the formation of this substance, then constancy is completely transcended; one form is incessantly transformed into another and the world takes on the aspect of a *perpetuum mobile*. This is the cosmologically, and often metaphysically interpreted, dual aspect of being."[2]

If one views the world from these two extreme perspectives, however, the horizon of the future almost inevitably becomes cloudy: as Pausanias had already complained in the second century before Christ, the future—set in motion by "demonic powers"—appears either as highly transitory and uncertain or as the result of an inalterable, eternal fate.[3] But *whether* such a perspective is taken depends not least on the chances that an individual (or collectivity) has of shaping its own existence, and these are themselves conditioned by education and material well-being. This argument can be strengthened in light of the findings of current research.[4]

In contrast to such ontologizing or at least anthropologizing interpretations of the experience of time and the future, I have tried to consistently adopt a perspective oriented toward cultural and social history. This has delivered conclusive evidence that a given epoch's image of history and the temporal life perspectives of its participants are highly dependent on the social and cultural *speed of change* endogenous to society and that this speed of change continually increases as modernity unfolds. The time perspectives attributed to Heraclitus and Parmenides gain their plausibility from a philosophically distanced view wherein history and the world appear to be a static space of changes or, in other words, a stable space in which various histories transpire. Yet in the Christian worldview this space of histories was already overlaid by the dimension of "salvation history," the linear time of which spans from the creation through the birth of Christ to its ending with his return.[5] This does not at first alter the experience of worldly time much; it remains a space for exogenously produced, uncontrollable vicissitudes of life, although movement and inertia now appear in the paradigmatic form of an opposition between the worldly/temporal and the transcendent/eternal.[6]

Then in the wake of an increasingly dynamic modernity a direction of movement and a developmental perspective enter into the worldly or secular space of history. This leads to a different experience of historicity and the time of life, one in which movement and inertia no longer form the supratemporal, ahistorical frame of life and history, but where *dynamization* becomes a basic element of society and history in such a way that the relationship between the two principles appears from then on as historically *asymmetrical* and the continual displacement of the balance between them can become the characteristic experience of modernity. Quite surprisingly, though, at this point a countertendency to the historical tendency of acceleration or dynamization makes its appearance, namely, an inclination toward structural and cultural *rigidity* that manifests itself ever more strongly during the advance of modernity. As I have shown, this principle must be understood as a paradoxical complement of modern acceleration.

In the concepts of acceleration and rigidification, which characterize the modern experience of time, the timeless principles of movement and inertia thus themselves appear to be dynamized once again. Thus the "hectic" and "rigid" qualities spoken of in the quotation at the beginning of this chapter cannot be simply reduced to those supratemporal basic principles. They are rather expressions of a dynamized experience of time that belongs to a specific epoch. That these two tendencies are beginning to be radicalized in recent times at the cost of the future horizon that characterized classical modernity (something also apparent in the quotation) points to a new transformation of an epoch-specific experience of time and the world. As we have already seen, this change can only be coherently conceived from an acceleration-theoretical perspective as both a break *and* a continuation of modernity. For the history of modernity can not only be plausibly reconstructed as a history of acceleration; this is in fact the only way in which the unity of its driving forces, its contradictions, and its historical phases can be revealed. Therefore, it is now time to return to the question raised in chapter 1 regarding the status of the principle of acceleration in the context of the driving forces of modernity as they have been traditionally identified by sociology. In doing so, we will provide sharper contours for the epoch-specific breaks and continuities discussed here in part 4 and thereby deepen them into a diagnosis of the times.

In chapter 1.2.b, I argued in connection with the work of Hans van der Loo and Willem van Reijen that analyses of social formations and their transformations usually begin from a perspective that is focused on either *structure*, *culture*, the dominant *personality type*, or, lastly, on the *relationship to nature*. Analyses of modernity are thus developed that tend to be, in accordance with the perspective chosen, structuralist, culturalist, subject-centered, or materialist. It turned out, however, that the corresponding definitions of modernization as a process of *differentiation, rationalization, individualization,* or *domestication* each leave out the specifically temporal dimension of the development of modernity that so undeniably constitutes a basic experience of the modern era. One of the main aims of this book has been to fill in this lacuna. The course of its argument has entirely confirmed the thesis formulated in chapter 1, namely, that *acceleration* is of constitutive significance for each of the four dimensions of development (cf. figure 12.1). While it is, of course, true that not all regions and segments of the population of the modern world are caught up in the transformative dynamic of social acceleration to the same degree, it is nevertheless the *logic of acceleration* that determines the structural and cultural evolution of modern society.

If one attempts to transfer the results of this investigation into the schema of modernization developed in chapter 1.2.b, the following picture emerges. To begin with, it is undoubtedly the case that *technical acceleration* is of fundamental importance with respect to the relationship of society to nature and that it is closely interwoven with the process of the domestication and domination of nature. The acceleration of transportation, communication, and production implies the enhancement of natural processes themselves (consider, for instance, the agricultural revolution) and the overcoming of natural limits, and hence at the same time an acceleration of processes of exchange with nature.

Moreover, the progressive *acceleration of the pace of life* has weighty consequences for developments in the dominant forms of identity and personality. As has been shown, the concepts of individualization and the dynamization of perspectives on life correlate to each other in many domains.

Finally, the *acceleration of social change* is intrinsically linked just as much with the structural as with the cultural transformation of society. In fact, structural and cultural changes (as one can see in the concept of rationalization, for instance) are not only empirically but also analytically so tightly bound up with each other that from the very start they could both be subjected together to a specifically temporal analysis under the wider concept of the acceleration of social change. With respect to the social-structural side of modernization, two analytically separable but interconnected aspects appeared. If one sees functional differentiation as the decisive structural feature of modern societies, then, as the inquiry in chapter 7.3 revealed, there can hardly be any doubt that while it may be interpreted as an adaptive *reaction* to the pressure to accelerate, it also generates in turn an immense heightening and accelerating *effect* as a result of the temporalization of complexity. Therefore, the acceleration of systemic processing in differentiated subregions (i.e., the acceleration of financial transactions, artistic and economic production, scientific discoveries, technical developments, etc.) through the externalization of all points of view irrelevant to the given system is an ineradicable tendency of the process of functional differentiation. In contrast, if one starts from the assumption that the basic structure of society is defined now as ever by the fabric of social associations, groups, and role patterns that ensures the production and reproduction of society, then it is undeniable that modernization implies an acceleration of structural change insofar as it increases the speed of change in familial and employment structures and causes associations and milieus to tend to become short-lived and volatile.[7] This makes it increasingly difficult to identify associational structures that are socially and politically significant. Both structural developments are accompanied by potentially problematic side effects: in the course of the argument, we have seen that the process just mentioned produces the danger of social *disintegration*, while functional differentiation, due to the fact that the respective subsystems can be accelerated to different extents, leads to the problem of *desynchronization*.

From a cultural perspective the most wide-ranging consequence of social acceleration proves to be what I have described, following Hermann Lübbe, as the contraction of the present, i.e., the progressive shortening of the periods of time for which one can count on stable stocks of knowledge, action orientations, and forms of practice. It leads in the first place to a divergence of the space of experience and the horizon of expectation and thus to a temporalization of history (and life) that is then taken back again in late modernity in favor of a highly dynamic *contemporization*. This was the thesis developed in the previous chapters. The acceleration of cultural change in the form of comparatively faster and easier changes in lifestyles, fashions, leisure time practices, stocks of knowledge, familial, spatial, political, and religious bonds and orientations thus constitutes one of the main traits of cultural modernization.[8] It also harbors far-reaching consequences for the political self-understanding of modernity and for the culturally dominant forms of individual self-understanding; thus acceleration represents not only a formal parameter of the cultural modernization process but also to a great extent determines its direction *substantively* or in the dimension of *content* (*Sachdimension*). Therefore, modernization can in fact be seamlessly reconstructed as a process of social acceleration (figure 12.1, cf. chapter 1.2.b, figure 1.1).

This reconceptualization of the modernization process seems to be fruitful for the formation of social-scientific theories for two reasons: first, it makes possible a new view of the paradoxes and ambivalences of modernity and, second, it allows a precise definition of both rupture and continuity at the threshold between modernity and late modernity. I begin with the first.

Contrary to the diagnosis of an accelerated structural transformation, one can observe a complementary process of structural rigidification in the course of modernity. It is noticeable primarily in the autonomization and immunization of the operational logic of social systems. In particular, the mutual escalation of growth and acceleration standing at the center of this investigation appears to be an unavoidable structural compulsion that mercilessly propels the development of society and turns the "zero-growth option" into an unreachable utopia. "A seemingly paradoxical status quo bias and immobility of

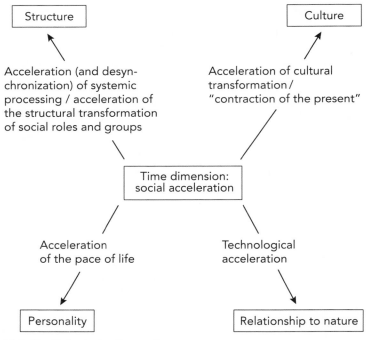

12.1. The Modernization Process IIa

society as a whole appears to be to the flipside of the modernization process. There is nothing in common between this and the basic motif of modernity, the heightening of the capacity to dispose over and select among options," finds Claus Offe, and indicates that the multiplication of options only occurs within the bounds set by the selection filters that govern systemic operations and *grow increasingly narrow* precisely as a result of the heightening of complexity that systems are compelled to achieve: "Regardless of how self-evident and commonplace they may sound, all these claims about growing choices over social contexts give not just a crude but a downright misleading and one-sided picture of the realities of a modern social structure. They serve me here merely as a foil against the backdrop of which I would like to consider the exactly opposite claim: namely, that it is precisely modern societies which are characterized by a high degree of *rigidity and inflexibility*."[9]

He comes to the conclusion that this structural rigidity is the result of the specific mode in which contingency is processed in modernity. Through specialization and functional differentiation, this mode simultaneously brings about 1. a tremendous heightening of complexity and thus contingency *and*, as a result, 2. a sharpening of the systemic processing filters with which political, economic, scientific, and legal problems are identified and "solved." The more options multiply and change, the more "the institutional and structural premises according to which contingency operates . . . transcend being at our political, or even intellectual, disposition."

Offe then tentatively derives from these considerations a *principle of constant sums*: "the more options that we make available to ourselves, the less optional is the institutional framework with whose help we make them available."[10] Transferred to the dialectic of movement and inertia, this constancy principle can illuminate social acceleration in a very instructive way with the help of the "motors" represented above in figure 7.1: the greater the dynamization of the three spheres of acceleration (techniques/technology, social change, the pace of life), the more fixed and unshakable the three external principles linking growth and acceleration and the (internal) circle of acceleration appear. Put otherwise, to the extent that the material structures of the lifeworld, the networks of relationships and associational structures, and the concrete value orientations, practices, and action orientations change, the abstract structural logics that drive substantial societal transformations harden into the "iron cage" bemoaned by Max Weber. Frenetic standstill therefore means that *nothing remains the way it is* while at the same time *nothing essential changes*. Furthermore, this paradoxical dualism of late modernity may help explain a peculiar phenomenon in the debate about globalization. The defenders of the cultural *homogenization* or convergence diagnosis seem to have arguments that are just as plausible as those of the partisans of the *pluralization* thesis: whether globalized societies are experienced as converging or diverging depends on whether one adopts a structure- or a content-oriented perspective.

"Structural crystallization" also obviously has massive consequences for the *cultural* development and self-perception of society. Thus it is tightly connected to the phenomenon of cultural rigidity in modernity. The counter-diagnosis here is that the rapid cultural change actually hides a lack of development. For reasons specifically arising from acceleration that I have worked out in previous chapters, the perception of an "end of history" and a "return of the ever same" even comes to overshadow the perception of profound transformation.[11] Society thereby loses its character as a project, as something to be shaped through political action; it has exhausted, so it seems, its utopian energies and resources of meaning. Correspondingly, one can observe an astonishing stability and solidification on the cultural side of the modernization process, a fact that is quite susceptible to interpretation as ongoing "pattern maintenance," to use Talcott Parsons's term. From a cultural perspective, the value orientations of activism, universalism, rationalism, and individualism prove to be the necessary complementary principles of the mutually escalating interconnection of growth and acceleration.[12]

Therefore, from both cultural and structural points of view, the history of acceleration and modernity can also be told without contradiction as the story of a progressive rigidification whose traces are also visible from a psychological perspective, i.e., in relation to the development of personality and individual relations to self. As I have shown, the acceleration or compression of episodes of action and experience constantly threatens to flip over from a stimulating "heightening of sensory life" (*Steigerung des Nervenlebens*, Simmel) into its opposite, namely, the experience of an eventless, existential tedium (*l'ennui*) and, in extreme cases, even the pathological experience of the "frozen" time of depression. Our finding, then, is that in both the individual and the collective case the impression of a *standstill* (in spite of or precisely because of a very dynamic field of events) is created by the transition from a form of movement that is experienced as directed to a *directionless dynamization*.

Interestingly, Paul Virilio, who holds that the modern history of acceleration ceaselessy strives toward the frenetic standstill of a "polar inertia,"[13] essentially bases his claim on *technical acceleration* and thus, in the end, on a perspective centered on society's relation to *nature*. According to him, the progressive speed revolutions of transportation, transmission, and finally transplantation lead paradoxically to a growing physical immobility of, in the first place, the human body, but potentially of the whole material universe. The switch from forward motion with the help of one's own bodily power to motion using the *metabolic* speed of external entities (e.g., riding horses or carriages) already slowed down the speed and movement of one's own body. However, it was only in the wake of the "dromocratic revolution," in which the discovery of *technical* speed replaced the metabolic, body-bound production of tempos, that human beings became a passively borne, more or less tied up, "parcel": for instance, in automobiles, planes, and, above all, in rockets. In other words, they became by and large unmoving moved objects that sit tight in a "projectile" and are thereby also increasingly sealed off from the sensory experience of movement.[14]

Self-driven human and animal movement thus noticeably loses its social function.[15] It is relegated to sport arenas and in this way, so to speak, turned into a "museum piece." The fact that we have to move our bodies from time to time while we are, as it were, "idling," i.e., not really going anywhere at all (for instance, running on treadmills), simply in order to keep them functional, just confirms their acceleration-historical *obsolescence* from this point of view. As I have argued in chapter 3, with the transition from transportation to transmission as the leading medium of acceleration, the movement of one's own body across the surface of the earth is increasingly replaced by the "channeling and downloading" of the world through the TV and the computer: to the extent that physical mobility is replaced by much faster digital and virtual transmission, Virilio's apocalyptic vision of polar inertia gains in plausibility.

Beyond this, the technologically accelerated mastery and processing of nature is accompanied by a growing risk of systematically incalculable breakdowns and accidents, as Charles Perrow showed in a much discussed study.[16] These suddenly and unexpectedly bring the rapid processing of nature enabled by modern industrial technology to a standstill. So here again accelerated movement flips over into paralyzed inertia: a server crash in a computer network can illustrate this just as well as a necessary shutdown of a nuclear reactor. Thus *rigidification* (*Erstarrung*) indeed proves to be an inherently complementary principle of social acceleration in all four aspects of societal development (figure 12.2).

This also makes clear both how much the four paradoxical complementary principles of differentiation, rationalization, domestication, and individualization, which were introduced in chapter 1.2.b as descriptions of the modernization process, can be understood as *consequences* of social acceleration and how they are linked with the designated tendencies of rigidification (cf. figure 1.1). As I have shown, the processes of *losing control* (*Steuerung*) and *disintegration* that accompany the functional differentiation of society can be interpreted as an effect of desynchronization under conditions of acceleration. Moreover, the *erosion of resources of meaning*, as the "flip side" of rationalization that seemingly culminates in the extinguishing of meaning once and for all in *posthistoire*, is caused not least by the accelerated devaluation or invalidation of traditions, bodies of knowledge, and action routines as well as the continual alteration of associational structures. Further, the inversion of the mastery of nature into the *destruction of nature* (and the potential destruction of ourselves *by* nature) seems to be primarily a result of a lack of respect for the "intrinsic temporalities" of nature. Last, the widespread alarm in cultural criticism concerning a *loss of autonomy* (in "mass culture") that paradoxically accompanies and complements the process of individualization is grounded in the acceleration-induced experience of "uprootedness" and/or

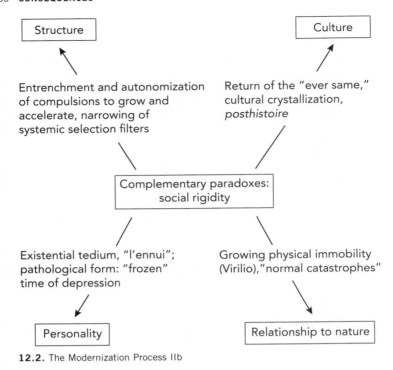

12.2. The Modernization Process IIb

"alienation." Such an experience is expressed, for instance, in the growing feeling of not having any time (for that which is "genuinely" important) even though more and more time resources are being saved by means of technological acceleration.[17]

Thus the thesis that the basic processes of modernization identified in classical sociology can be interpreted from a specifically temporal perspective as mechanisms and manifestations of social acceleration has been confirmed. *Individualization* is a cause as well as an effect of social acceleration insofar as individuals are more mobile and flexible in adapting to social change and faster in making decisions than collectivities. *Functional differentiation* causes acceleration and at the same time represents a promising strategy in the face of the pressure to accelerate because it makes possible the externalization of costs and the acceleration of systemic processing, hence also the (mutually reinforcing) escalation and temporalization of complexity. The same holds true for processes of *rationalization* in the sense of efficiency increases in means-ends relationships and for processes of *domestication* in the sense of an escalation of exchange processes with nature. However, this still does not answer the question whether social acceleration constitutes an independent basic principle of modernization or rather merely opens up an illuminating perspective on modernity as defined by the other four processes and so, as it were, simply describes the temporal dimension of modernization.

I do indeed defend the thesis that social acceleration should be understood as an irreducible and tendentially *dominant basic principle* of both modernity and modernization for three interconnected reasons. In the first place, social acceleration and its underlying logic of escalation have proved in the course of the present work to be the unified principle that links together not only the four dimensions of modernization but also the various *phases* of the modernization process. We will come back to this point shortly. In the second place, however, the principle of acceleration has even turned out to be *primary* with regard to the other tendencies of modernization insofar as it can provide the key to explaining the historical changes in their manifestations. So, for instance, it was shown in chapter 7.1 that the various phases and manifestations of capitalism can be conceived as expressions of a unified logic of acceleration. Connected to this is the partial retraction or modification of "classical modern" forms of differentiation: as I have made clear, in late modernity many of the temporally and spatially differentiated social processes or spheres (e.g., the separation of realms of work and leisure, of commercial, cultural, and athletic institutions, etc.) are once again dedifferentiated. In the domain of social institutions a similar hybridization of economic, civil society, and state elements can be observed.[18] Thus the developmental transition to postmodernity is frequently described in social diagnoses as a process of dedifferentiation and hybridization, one that even makes the boundaries between science and religion, culture and commerce, art and technology, economics and politics, etc., porous once again.[19] I have interpreted this development by postulating that after the acceleration of the respective system processes, rigid system boundaries function as brakes on intersystemic exchange processes. From this point of view, the principle of differentiation itself could even prove to be a further element of the dialectic of acceleration and deceleration summarized in figure 8.1: it accelerated social processes in classical modernity, but increasingly becomes an impediment to acceleration in late modernity. Yet even if one can interpret the observable changes more as modifications of differentiation than as actual *de*differentiation (the other possibility of hybridizations on the level of the system *codes* is almost entirely ruled out from the start on conceptual grounds),[20] it still appears to be the case that the process of differentiation formally follows the logic of acceleration.

This is even truer of the process of individualization. If one conceives of the unfolding of a self-determined, stable identity and the autonomous pursuit of a "life plan" in accordance with freely chosen but relatively time-resistant principles as the correlate or core of modern individualization,[21] then the tendential development of late modern situational forms of identity can actually be understood as an acceleration-induced *decline* of individualization; in any case, however, it represents a serious change in the manifestations of this process.

Finally, indications of a modification or tendential retrogression of rationalization may be found wherever the substantial rationality of decisions or determinations sinks in favor of shorter processing and execution times, for example, in the legislature, the stock market, or in certain production decisions, or where the "situational" exploitation of contingent opportunity structures replaces the principles of a systematic conduct of life or even in phenomena such as the abandonment of the theoretical and deductive derivation and calculation of new combinations of active ingredients in chemistry in favor of the accidentally innovative products of excessive amounts of practical experimentation. From a perspective that is indifferent to the demands of time rationality, such phenomena can indeed be interpreted as forms of *de*rationalization; but from a time-sensitive angle, in contrast, they seem to be rather modifications of the rationalization process under conditions of acceleration.[22]

In the third place, however, the weightiest and most consequential argument for the independence and potential dominance of social acceleration as a basic process of modernization lies in the fact that the results of my inquiry impressively confirm the assumption that the nature of individual and collective human existence has an essentially temporal and processual character, such that what an individual or society ultimately *is* is quite fundamentally determined by the time structures and time horizons of this existence. Transformations of the latter are therefore immediately transformations of the former and vice versa.[23]

Yet this holds true a fortiori for the analysis of modernity: when considered on its own, the structural and cultural nexus characterized by differentiation, rationalization, individualization, domestication and their paradoxical countertendencies seems to be an "ultrastable arrangement" and hence to guarantee the continuity of societal development as well as that of personal identity.[24] Now with respect to this nexus, indeed, *nothing* has changed about the character of modernity. In my view, however, it is this constriction of perspective, this "forgetfulness of time," that leads the critics of diagnoses of rupture to categorically reject any questioning of the continuity of modernity. Yet the fact that remains hidden from this involuntarily "static" view of modernity, and that first comes into view in a temporalized, acceleration-theoretical perspective, is that *even though the basic framework of the principles of modernization (including the tendencies of growth and acceleration) persists unaltered and uncontested* individuals and societies can be (and are) exposed to radical and fundamental transformation *because of* an alteration of their temporal structures. As I have argued here in part 4, it is an acceleration-induced transformation in the dimension of time that first allows the epochal breaks in the process of modernization to come to light and to be explained. It is what is responsible for the fact that individuals and societies from early modernity through "classical modernity" to late modernity were exposed to a wide-ranging, double transformation.

Table 12.1 summarizes this twofold transformation process and its characteristic dialectic of temporalization and detemporalization in an ideal-typically sharpened fashion. The guiding hypothesis here is that the dynamization of society and the acceleration of endogenous social change lead to a progressive alteration of the individual and collective experience of time and history. This also brings about a transformation of individual and collective sociopolitical self-relations as a consequence. I assume here that the effects of the modern process of dynamization do not operate in a linear way but rather reach critical points of inflection that are linked to the tempo of the succession of generations.[25]

If the tempo of social change that is systematically self-produced (and in this sense expected) becomes *higher* than the turnover rate of the three or at most four generations that coexist within a society at any given historical moment, then the space of experience and the horizon of expectation come apart: one expects something different from the future than one knows from the past. It seems that this threshold was crossed at the latest during the "epochal threshold" of the late eighteenth century in such an enduring way that the experience of history and the life perspectives of individuals have been correspondingly temporalized. History and life are temporalized, in the sense characteristic for "classical modernity," insofar as they are projected into the future as malleable and susceptible to planning and thus bear the promise of individual and collective autonomy. Social acceleration thus sets history and

TABLE 12.1 From "Temporalized" History to "Frenetic Standstill": The Acceleration-Induced Dialectic of Temporalization and Detemporalization in Modernity

	PREMODERNITY AND EARLY MODERNITY	CLASSICAL MODERNITY	LATE MODERNITY
Pace of endogenous social change	Structural and cultural transformation below the tempo of generational turnover (intergenerational)	Structural and cultural transformation approximate a "generational" rate of change	Rate of structural and cultural transformation higher than the speed of generational turnover (intragenerational)
Indicator: occupational and family structures	"Occupational" and family structures (family in the sense of an economic unit) intergenerationally stable	Family structures and occupations change at a generational tempo: "starting a family" and "choosing a career" as individual, identity-constituting acts; generations as bearers of innovation	Family structures and occupations change at a faster pace than turnover of a generation: the career becomes a series of activities (jobs); the life partner is replaced by a series of "life period partners"
Time perspective	Congruence of space of experience and horizon of expectations (cyclical time)	Divergence of time horizons of past and future (linear time)	"Timeless time" and "temporalization of time": rhythm, duration, sequence, and point in time decided in the course of performance
Historical perspective	Static historical perspective; historical time as "space of histories"	Temporalization of history: history as intelligible and malleable; directed process (idea of progress); temporal index of direction (progressive versus conservative); politics as historical "pacemaker"	The "end of history" in the sense of the idea of progress and the philosophy of history; loss of the political index of direction (situational politics): "detemporalization of history"
Life perspective	"Situational" life perspective: mastery of (exogenously determined) daily problems on the basis of "substantial a priori identities"; vicissitudes of life on the one hand exogenous, on the other hand metaphysically and culturally embedded	Temporalization of life: perspective of planable life course whose history is a narrative of development on the basis of stable, self-determined a posteriori identity and institutional safeguards (life course regime)	Deinstitutionalization of the life course; abandonment of stable identity in the sense of a "life project"; "situational" identity and conduct of life: "detemporalization of life"

identity in motion in a very specific way. The fundamental transformation of individual and political forms of selfhood that goes along with this is, from a historical point of view, unquestionable. Therefore, it cannot be weakened by a doubtlessly justified reference to the fact that premodern societies were not nearly so stable and static as the schema presented here suggests at first glance. In order to prevent misunderstandings, let me just point out once again that the model of historical development proposed here is not at all forced to deny or ignore any of the sometimes dramatic historical upheavals and phases of accelerated societal transformation in premodernity, for instance, subsequent to the Crusades or during the urban development that began in the high Middle Ages. The claim defended here is rather that *unexpected* or *exogenous* upheavals, however fast and violent they may be, do *not* lead by themselves to a temporalization of the horizon of expectation: they appear as more or less surprising "histories" within a per se static historical space, where they can possibly be *repeated*.[26] Innovations that are, so to speak, erratic cannot be systematically located within a stable horizon of expectation. Thus even after a phase of upheavals sociocultural realignment occurs within the horizon of a situational, static experience of time and an orientation toward inherently enduring structures. Under such conditions, historical shocks do not bring about temporalization. Rather they cause a one-time transformation of the space of experience and the horizon of expectation, which quickly adjust and become restabilized in a more or less static form, though they naturally do have to systematically take into account the unpredictable vicissitudes of ordinary life.

In contrast to this, "classical modern" society presents itself as a social order that, after its consolidation, changes continually, controllably, and above all in a directed and thus politically malleable process within a growing framework of institutional safeguards against those vicissitudes and hence precisely *without* dramatic structural upheavals.[27]

The temporalization of individual life in "classical modernity" first takes root on a broad scale sometime after the temporalization of history does, lagging behind the latter until around the end of the nineteenth century. Two factors may be responsible for this: on the one hand, the biographical and identity-constituting orientation toward a planned-out, *temporally extended life course* needed an institutional safeguard in the structures of the nascent welfare state, which was for its own part a product of the historical conceptualization of society as a project to be shaped politically. On the other hand, however, this time lag may reflect the fact that the temporalization of one's own individual life seems to be more strongly bound to a genuinely *genera-tional* rate of change, whereas the temporalization of the horizon of history could already set in as a consequence of the acceleration of the historical rate of change beyond the critical threshold of three (or four) coexisting genera-tions. A possible reinforcement of this argument lies in the fact that at the second threshold, namely, that of an *intragenerational* rate of change and hence a late modern temporalization of time, no corresponding shift to a new phase can be observed.[28]

Interestingly, alongside the temporalization of (social) history observed by Koselleck there is also a temporalization of the perceptual patterns of the natu-ral sciences. According to Wolf Lepenies, it is precisely during this period that the view of a categorial juxtaposition of natural things is increasingly replaced by the analysis of their *succession* in developmental histories.[29]

However, what is of decisive importance is that the temporalization of life and of history in the sense of their progressive motion along preestablished pathways was accompanied and supported by the formation of a stable institu-tional arrangement that was centered, on the one hand, around the national state institutions of law, democracy, and security apparatuses and, on the other hand, around those of the welfare state, marriage, and the classical modern labor regime that constituted the material foundation of the institutionaliza-tion of the "life course regime."

But the dynamization of society and self-relations did not stop there. To-ward the end of the twentieth century it reached the critical threshold of an intragenerational rate of change, which once again brought in train severe mutations in the individual and collective experience of time and hence also in the dominant forms of individual and sociopolitical identity. At the same time, it led to a steadily advancing erosion of the classical modern institutional arrangement, which likewise fell under pressure to become more dynamic (cf. figure 8.1).[30] Now *time itself* is temporalized, that is, the various qualities that define temporality such as the point in time, the sequence, the duration, the rhythm, and the tempo of events and actions are no longer determined in accordance with a "metatemporal," preinstitutionalized plan, but are rather decided *within time itself*. This has serious consequences in the form of a "detemporalization" of history and life, which thereby lose the character of directed, planned temporal processes. The ubiquitous simultaneity of late modernity that rests on this constellation is thus, strictly speaking, no longer a simultaneity of the nonsimultaneous, since that presupposes the idea of a temporalized, directed, and moving (though asynchronous) history. Instead, it is, as it were, a static, situational, "timeless," and orderless *simultaneity of historical fragments.*[31]

As the replies of Barbara Adam and Carmen Leccardi to an earlier version of my temporalization thesis have made clear,[32] the concepts I have chosen easily give rise to a confusion, the cause of which lies once again in the very inconsistent conceptual repertoire of the contemporary debate concerning the philosophy and sociology of time. Just as the phenomenon of the future becoming contingent or uncertain can be apprehended under the concept of the contraction of the present (Lübbe) as well as the "extension of the present" (Nowotny), so too the late modern development of a ubiquitous simultaneity that determines the temporal qualities of events and processes in daily life, life as a whole, and in historical time during the course of their performance gets described using the catchword of "timeless" time (Castells) as well as the concept of "temporalized" time (Luhman and Hörning, Ahrens, and Gerhard). In both the latter cases the same thing is meant: since nothing can be said beforehand about the sequences, speeds, rhythms, and durations of events, time appears to some as detemporalized (it lacks the corresponding basic qualities), but to others it seems only now to be truly temporalized (the specific form those qualities take is decided within time).

Consequently, I suggest that from a conceptual point of view this development can be most clearly described as a temporalization of time and a detemporalization of history, life, and also partly of everyday practice. What has been lost are the, so to speak, "metatemporal" plans of history, life, and daily activities that determined the temporal qualities of events and actions beforehand and made the time of everyday practice, of life, and of history susceptible to planning and allowed them to appear *directed.*

Thus, regardless of the terminological confusion, it seems to me that the arguments are in both cases unmistakable and clear. Nevertheless, one must keep in mind that I am using the concept of temporalized time in the social-phenomenological or systems-theoretical sense described earlier and not (as Adam erroneously assumes) in the philosophical meaning proposed, with varying accents, by Bergson, Mead, and particularly Heidegger, one that was above all directed against the notion of clock time. So "temporalization of time" does not mean anything like the return to the "originary temporality of Dasein" that constitutes itself out of the certainty of death and hence out of an authentic future that first brings forth and connects the present and the past.[33] From a Heideggerean perspective, the late modern form I have in mind would appear to be rather a radicalized "flight in the face of what passes" (*Flucht vor dem Vorbei*)[34] and hence from the authentic core of the temporality of Dasein in the "anyone's time" (*Man-Zeit*) that is caught up in the present, or in other words, as a radicalized detemporalization.[35]

In any case, as a diagnosis of the times the core thesis of part 4 runs as follows. It is above all the transformation of the socially dominant experience of time, grounded in the acceleration-induced dialectic of temporalization and detemporalization, that has led to two key conditions: the rigidifying side of the relationship of complementarity between movement and inertia has gained the upper hand in the cultural self-perception of late modernity and the related autonomization of systemic processes appears to be irreversible. Thus the observations of an "end of history" diagnose nothing more than the end of the temporalized history of modernity, i.e., the end of an experience of time in which historical development and the unfolding of one's life history appeared to be both directed and controllable, hence in which changes bore, as it were, visible indexes of movement. In late modernity this is replaced by the experience of unforeseeable and undirected, and hence, as it were, unmoving, un-(trans-situationally)controllable, and continuous change. The "law of acceleration" postulated by Henry Adams can no longer be understood as a "law of progress." Insofar as the modern promise of progress was the promise of individual and political autonomy, the transition to this experience of time is diametrically opposed to the idea of progress. For I follow Jürgen Habermas in holding that the project of modernity is centered on the idea that persons can and should themselves take responsibility for the progressive shaping of their own individual lives (ethical autonomy) and their collective form of life (political autonomy).[36] Yet the new experience of time is constitutively related to the feeling of a loss of autonomy that is manifested in the disappearance of any possibility of control and the erosion of opportunities to shape one's own affairs. It leads *individually* to the experience of drift, or, put positively, of situationally open play, and *politically* to the fatalism of a rhetoric of objective forces and inevitable structural adjustment.

Thus Claus Offe comes to the conclusion that "precisely as a result of rapid modernization and rationalization processes, societies can regress into a condition of mute condemnation to fate and inflexibility, the overcoming of which was the original motive of processes of modernization," and Peter Sloterdijk complains that "modernity left all to itself" evidently no longer has any strength "to fend off its fatal drift; before our very eyes enlightened secularism, with its double commitment to self-determination and large-scale technology, seems to be saying goodbye in the midst of a global state of ne-

glect—things now run as they please, human intentions are no longer necessary."[37] Sloterdijk also diagnoses the emergence of a "second fatalism."

In this way the *core* of modernization, the acceleration process, has turned
against the very *project* of modernity that originally motivated, grounded, and
helped set it in motion. Indeed, the acceleration process appeared to be what
was promising in the possibility of modernity: growth and acceleration served
as the societal precondition on which the *promise of autonomy*, in the sense
of a liberation from material and social compulsions of all forms, was based.
As I have shown, it was not least visions of progress and utopian energies that
drove social acceleration in early and classical modernity before it became so
independently entrenched (*verselbtständigte*) in the structures of modernity
that it no longer needed a pronounced orientation toward the future to maintain itself. However, it is now precisely the relationship of mutual escalation
between growth and acceleration and its impact on temporal structures that is
beginning to undermine the promise of autonomy in an ever sharper fashion.
It has become an inescapable compulsion. The conclusion my arguments
yield is thus that the project of modernity itself can be placed among the classical modern accelerators that now fall under a growing pressure of erosion
as late modern "brakes." What was once an alluring possibility now appears
to be a threat. The original promise of happiness presented by growth and
acceleration is noticeably waning and being transformed into the curse of an
ever increasing endangerment of individual and collective autonomy.

The compulsion to accelerate that is rooted in the social structure of "slipping slopes" forces people, organizations, and governments into a *reactive
situational attitude* instead of a self-determining conduct of individual and
collective life. According to Virilio, they thus begin to look like a racing car
driver who, in the face of the highly automated processes he is trying to control, "is no more than a worried lookout for the catastrophic possibilities of
his own movement."[38] However, taken by itself, this image is misleading because it suggests a direct reduction of options. Social acceleration does not
simply erode potentials for autonomy in a unilinear way. Instead it makes their
use problematic precisely by multiplying them. Despite all the uncertainties
and dangers, for individuals the temporalization of time in everyday practice
and the life course always means in the first place an immense growth in
the number of possible decisions and the temporal horizons of availability,
precisely because actions and events become more freely sequenceable, combinable, and revisable. Further, in politics the setting aflow of the solidified
institutional arrangements of "classical modernity" opens up maneuvering

room and new organizational possibilities. Nevertheless, these developments become *autonomy-endangering* precisely through the transformation of the late modern time structures with which they are linked. The self-determined organization of individual and/or collective life presupposes 1. that the space of options remains stable for a certain period of time (since well-grounded decisions become impossible when their utility, opportunity costs, and consequences cannot be foreseen with a certain minimal temporal stability), 2. that conditions of action are enduring enough for processes of change to be comprehensible and at least partly controllable, and finally 3. that there is sufficient time available to actually shape the spaces of action that constitute life and society through planned intervention.

Therefore, the possibility of genuine ethical and political self-determination also depends on the formation of time-resistant or *trans-situational* preferences and goals according to which organization, progress, and movement can be defined and measured. Autonomy in this sense is equivalent to the temporally stable pursuit of self-determined plans even *against the resistance of changing situational conditions*. Naturally this does not exclude the revision of these plans within time itself, but these changes should not exclusively be induced by external forces or be entirely situation dependent, that is, the urgency of the fixed term and the pragmatic necessity of holding options open must not hinder the formation and pursuit of a self-determined preference ordering.

Thus, to the extent that the institutions safeguarding this stability dissolve under the pressure to dynamize and identities and political programs do indeed become situational, the horizons of choice become politically and ethically unfruitful. This is due not least to the fact that the holding open of options and opportunities becomes a categorical imperative in view of uncertainty regarding the future conditions of action and decision. But this imperative cuts ever more strongly against substantial bonds, and this in turn produces a state in which experiences have little power to bind expectations and hence in which the connection between past, present, and future, both individually and politically, is sundered in such a way that the supposedly autonomous spaces for organization turn into a static space of fatalistic standstill. Here the return of the ever same, the "timeless time" of what is at once eternal and ephemeral, of what is, in the words of the schoolgirl cited at the beginning of the chapter, simultaneously hectic and rigid, is hidden behind the rapid turnover of episodes. In such a context the very idea of organizing or shaping (*Gestaltung*) becomes literally meaningless.[39] The full significance of this dilemma is first revealed in a truly paradoxical historical situation in which the *technical* and *social presuppositions* for a political shaping of society (particularly in light of burgeoning genetic technology and the extinguishing of the binding force of tradition) are more favorable than ever, while the *actual* organizational possibilities (*Gestaltungsmöglichkeiten*) seem to be even scarcer than in premodernity *for temporal-structural reasons*.

The break between classical and late modernity can therefore be quite exactly determined as the moment in the "history of acceleration" at which the forces of acceleration so greatly surpass the organizational and integrative capacity of individuals and societies that the temporalization of life and of history is supplanted by the temporalization of time itself and thus replaced by the latter as the dominant experience of time. It is also, therefore, the moment at which *the cultural project* and the *structural process* of modernization come into insurmountable contradiction.[40] Furthermore, this moment is closely tied to the fact that the speed of social change crosses the generational threshold and heads toward an *intra*generational pace that erodes the conditions of continuity and coherence for stable personal identities, thus creating massive difficulties for the formation of time-resistant preferences.

The resulting state of affairs only appears problematic or even worthy of lament as long as one believes that the normative project of modernity must be sustained. An abandonment of the ideal of autonomy and the connected claim to shape and control circumstances thus opens up the possibility of a positive relationship to the autonomization of the modernization process and the new modes of time experience, something that is expressed in the affirmative stance toward acceleration in philosophies of *postmodernity*. From their perspective, the claim to be able to theoretically understand and adequately describe societal development,[41] and to shape it practically through political action, is delusory and always already latently totalitarian. This claim, which is now untenable for temporal-structural reasons, must be given up. The resulting loss of control is celebrated as a liberation from a compulsion to control that, even in classical modernity, could only be maintained by formidable social demands of continuity, integration, and coherence (the "terrorism of identity"). Therefore, so the argument goes, social acceleration does not simply undermine the possibility of subjectivity per se; it also liberates it from restrictive demands of stability.[42] Social fragmentation and desynchronization and the absence of an integration of experiences into an identity-constituting whole can be affirmed as pleasurable and satisfying *just insofar as* it is possible to develop an ironic, playful relation to the uncontrollable vicissitudes of life and to do without a representation of the world as a meaningful whole and enduring bonds to places, people, practices and values.[43]

Our confrontation in this work with the self-autonomizing acceleration dynamic of modernity has at several places brought to light arguments *against* such an uncritical affirmation of hyperacceleration. They relate, for instance, to the fundamental conditions of cultural reproduction, the presuppositions of a minimally sufficient amount of social synchronization, or the quasi-anthropological givens of time experience. I will not repeat any of the details of these arguments here. Beyond the ethical and political critique from within the horizon of classical modernity, the doubts are, above all, addressed to the question of the consequences that unchecked further dynamization would have for the earth's ecosystem, for the various modes of the (temporal) "structural coupling" of desynchronized social subsystems, for the maintenance of the sociomoral conditions of the existence of society and intergenerational cultural transfer, and finally, for the possibility of experiencing the world as meaningful. They make clear that the determination of the temporal-structural or speed limits of subjectivity and sociality require, so to speak, a *critical theory of acceleration* that is capable of identifying acceleration-induced social pathologies without relying on the normative criteria of a now questionable philosophical anthropology or philosophy of history.[44] Peter Sloterdijk suggested this path more than a decade ago in his attempt to develop a "critique of political kinetics" and of "mobilization" that he wanted to understand as a third version of critical theory. Marx and the Frankfurt School had supposedly failed by misunderstanding or even uncritically supporting the immense kinetic forces of modernity.[45] However, Sloterdijk's own conception remains highly speculative, rather unsystematic, and lacking an empirical grounding. Therefore, in the conclusion I would like to sketch out, drawing on a summary of the argument of the book, an outline of a critical theory of acceleration. At the same time, I will sound out the various scenarios that remain open with regard to the continuation of the modern history of acceleration.

CONCLUSION: FRENETIC STANDSTILL? THE END OF HISTORY

The command bridge isn't answering any more. What should we do?
—From a documentary on the effects of globalization in Haiti, aired on the channel Arte

IF ONE TAKES SERIOUSLY THE idea that the constitution of society and social processes is radically temporal in nature, then talk of the acceleration *of* society does indeed appear to be justified. The time structures of modernity change according to a unified pattern as it develops. The upshot of this investigation is, in brief, that this pattern can be grasped in an analytically informative and empirically fruitful way using the concept of social acceleration.

From the beginning of modernity onward—one could say since Hamlet's complaint that his time was "out of joint"—the perception of the progressive dynamization and shortening of the periods of time associated with events, processes, and changes is constitutive of the basic experience of modernization, as I argued in chapter 1. Consideration of the findings of cultural history led to the conclusion that the experience of modernization is practically equivalent to the experience of acceleration: "modernity is about the acceleration of time," ran Peter Conrad's influential formula. This is confirmed by the testimonies from the "epochal threshold" investigated by Koselleck as well as by the theoretical frameworks of "classical" sociology. From Simmel's observation of the continuous "heightening of nervous life" in the modern metropolis to Weber's analysis of the time discipline of the Protestant ethic, for which wasting time is the "the deadliest of all sins," and from Durkheim's fear of anomie as a result of overly rapid social change to Marx and Engel's dictum that capitalism's inherent tendency is to make all that is solid "melt into air," classical sociological analyses of modernity can always be reconstructed as *diagnoses of acceleration*.

However, this aspect of societal development was very much forgotten in the social scientific analysis that followed them. The reason for this is above all the "forgetfulness of time" in twentieth-century social-scientific theory, which notoriously preferred "static" models of society and modeled the modernization process (almost entirely according to the analytical pattern of a "comparative statics") along the dimensions of structural *differentiation*, cultural *rationalization*, the *individualization* of personality, and the *domestication* of nature. The aim of this book was to close up the holes in the analysis of modernity that thereby arose with the help of an outline of a systematic theory of social acceleration.

It is doubtless the first and foremost task of such a theory to clear up what underlies such an experience of acceleration *materialiter*, i.e., in the structures of social processes. Thus the first step should be to ask about the substantial content of the experience. Here the wavelike ebb and flow of acceleration discourse and cultural-critical calls for *deceleration* already indicate that social acceleration, just like other basic tendencies of modernization such as individualization or differentiation, unfolds in phases, encounters forms of resistance as well as countertendencies, and occasionally produces qualitative shifts in social arrangements by reaching certain thresholds: in this case, speed levels. The years between 1880 and 1920, when a multitude of significant technical innovations had a widespread social impact, and the period following the digital and political revolution circa 1989, the consequences of which are mostly discussed under the heading of *globalization*, can be considered two such phases in which massive surges of acceleration occur and are immediately followed by debates about the inevitability of adaptive increases of tempo or the harmfulness of an overly high social tempo. One may assert more generally that in the history of modernity each wave of technological, organizational, or cultural acceleration at first encounters massive resistance and widespread skepticism but eventually triumphs, gradually silencing its critics.

Nevertheless the simple claim that in modernity "everything goes faster and faster," which is pervasive not just in the features pages and the popular press but also in academic works, is both undifferentiated and transparently false. This is why in chapter 2 I developed a categorial framework for the systematic discernment of empirically demonstrable acceleration phenomena that is supplemented by a survey of corresponding tendencies of slowdown and forces of inertia. It thereby avoids proceeding according to a logic of subsumption.

My proposal is that the three fundamental dimensions of social acceleration, which are mostly not differentiated from one another in contemporary discourse about acceleration, can be distinguished in a way that is both analytically and empirically illuminating. In the first place, we have the phenomena of *technical acceleration*, that is, the intentional acceleration of goal-directed processes. From this perspective, the acceleration history of modernity essentially represents a history of the progressive acceleration of transportation, communication, and production. The second dimension concerns the *acceleration of social change*, that is, the escalation of the rate of social change with respect to associational structures, knowledge (theoretical, practical, and moral), social practices, and action orientations. Here "acceleration" means primarily the accelerated change of fashions, lifestyles, work, family structures, political and religious ties, etc. For the definition and empirical operationalization of this form of acceleration I drew on the concept of the contraction of the present introduced by Hermann Lübbe, but also justifiable on systems-theoretical grounds. Accordingly, "the acceleration of social change" means the following: the intervals of time for which one can assume stability in the sense of a general congruence of the space of experience and the horizon of expectation (and hence a secure set of expectations) progressively shrink in the various domains of society, whether these are understood in terms of values, functions, or types of action, although this shrinkage neither occurs in a unilinear way nor at the same tempo across the board. Thus the acceleration of social change can be defined as the increase of the rate of decay of action-orienting experiences and expectations and as the shortening of the periods of time that are defined as "the present" in the respective spheres of society.

Finally, the third form of social acceleration, the *acceleration of the pace of life*, represents a reaction to the scarcity of (uncommitted) time resources. This is why, on the one hand, it is expressed in the experience of stress and a lack of time, and, on the other, it can be defined as an increase in the number of episodes of action and/or experience per unit of time.

Futhermore, as I have shown, technical acceleration and the acceleration of the pace of life stand in a peculiar paradoxical relationship to each other: the former frees up time resources by shortening the duration of processes and thus by itself leads to a *decrease* of the pace of life; prima facie, it makes more free time available. Therefore, the fact that modern society is characterized by the simultaneous appearance of both forms of acceleration requires an additional explanation. I have located this in a specific connection between growth and acceleration: a scarcity of time resources in the face of simultaneous technical acceleration can only occur when the *quantitative rates of increase* (of the production of goods and services, of the number of communications performed, of the distances covered, of the completed activities, etc.) surpass the *rates of acceleration* of the corresponding processes. The more the rates of acceleration lag behind the rates of growth, the greater the time scarcity will be. On the other hand, the more the former outpace the latter, the more time resources will be freed up.

Therefore, one can speak of an acceleration of the pace of life as a society-wide phenomenon if and only if the average rate of growth is higher than the average rate of technical acceleration. This raises the question of what drives this typically modern linkage of growth and acceleration and what forms it takes, a question to which part 3 of this work was devoted. However, prior to this, it was necessary to more precisely determine the relation of the forces of acceleration and inertia in modernity by means of a categorization of the latter.

As I have shown, five categories of phenomena that elude or even run counter to the process of dynamization can be distinguished.

1. First, there are still, and probably always will be, *natural* geophysical, biological, and anthropological speed limits, that is, processes that either absolutely cannot be manipulated or only at the price of a massive qualitative transformation of the process to be accelerated.

2. Next there are territorial, cultural, and structural "islands of deceleration," i.e., areas that are in principle susceptible to modernization and hence to processes of acceleration but that have, up till now, not been caught up in them or have managed (at least for the time being) to remain idle. They thus appear to be places where "time stands still."

3. Furthermore, in many fields of action blockages and slowdowns occur again and again as *unintended side effects* of acceleration that can lead to dysfunctional and, to some extent, pathological consequences. The most well-known example of this is the traffic jam, though economic recessions and forms of depressive illness can also be placed under this heading. Yet beyond this, acceleration-induced unintended slowdown also occurs at the interface points of functional systems or processing cycles when these prove to be capable of acceleration to different extents, which causes desynchronization

problems that are expressed in unwanted waiting times: for instance, when the new long-distance express train arrives at the station twenty minutes earlier than the old long-distance train did, but the local commuter train comes at the same time it did before.

4. To be distinguished from these are phenomena of *intentional deceleration*, which appear in two different forms: either as "functional" or "accelerative" deceleration in the sense of individual and collective moratoria or phases of recuperation (as in the four-week retreat of a CEO to the tranquillity of a monastery) that ultimately serve the goal of further increases of speed (for example, in the form of an increased capacity for innovation) or as "ideological" deceleration movements that often have a fundamentalist or antimodernist character and aim at genuine social slowdown or a stalling of the acceleration process in the name of a better society and a better form of life. This idea of deceleration may even be on the verge of becoming the dominant counterideology of the twenty-first century.

The existential guarantees and "institutional pausing" of the fundamental social framework of "classical modernity" should be counted here among the manifestations of functional deceleration. In many areas acceleration was made possible by the fact that leading institutions and the action orientations connected with them were for a long time secured against change: for instance, law, political steering mechanisms, the stable industrial work (time) regime, or the "life course" regime. For this reason they created secure expectations and stable conditions for planning and calculation that could serve as a basis for economic, technical, scientific, and political-organizational acceleration along stable "developmental pathways." This raises the question whether the erosion of those institutions through the, as it were, "unbounded" social acceleration of the late modern era will in the long run undermine its own preconditions.

5. Finally, as the fifth category of decelerating forces, I identified the cultural and structural phenomena that embody a tendency toward rigidity. This tendency does not appear to be a self-standing principle, but rather the paradoxical flip side of social acceleration. These phenomena constitute the basis for the experience of an uneventfulness and standstill that underlies the rapidly changing surface of social conditions and events, one that accompanies the modern perception of dynamization from the very beginning as a second fundamental experience of modernization. It is often precisely in phases of an intense surge of acceleration that this phenomenon is reflected individually in manifestations of "ennui" or "existential boredom" and collectively in the

diagnosis of cultural crystallization, or the "end of history," but in both cases as the perception of a *return of the ever same*.

This last form of slowdown is not directed against the modern process of acceleration, but rather is, so to speak, constitutively inherent in it. Furthermore, the other four categories (where they do not appear to be in fact functional for acceleration) can be understood as either *residual* or *reactive*: they are either processes that have not (yet) been accelerated or reactions to prior social acceleration. Therefore, to the extent that no corresponding tendency of slowdown stands against it, the guiding hypothesis of this investigation, namely, that social acceleration represents one, if not *the*, fundamental tendency of modernity, appears to be justified. The process of modernization indeed proves to be a ceaseless displacement of the balance between the forces of movement and those of inertia in favor of the former. This fact is responsible for the considerable plausibility of the erroneous claim that in modernity "everything" goes faster and faster.

The categorial groundwork for my theory of acceleration ended with this observation. Part 2 of the investigation was then dedicated to an inquiry into the concrete mechanisms and empirical manifestations of social acceleration by means of a phenomenology of its three leading dimensions. Here I argued that the primary effect in the domain of *technical acceleration* is a phased transformation of the social space-time regime. The acceleration of transportation, communication, and production does not only bring about an alteration of the spatiotemporal patterns of usage, movement, and settlement and the very experience of space (space seems literally to shrink and lose significance in comparison to time). It also changes the quality and quantity of social relationships, practices, and action orientations. In short, technical acceleration always harbors a tendency to transform the objective, the social, and (mediated through these) the subjective world, because it implicitly transforms our relations to things (i.e., to the material structures of our environment), to our fellow human beings, and to space and time. For this reason, it also alters the form of our relation to ourselves and hence the mode and manner of our being-in-the-world.[1] The linkage of growth and acceleration thus implies a tendential loosening of concrete ties to particular persons, places, or things as a result of increased speeds of change and exchange.

A central result of the analysis of the consequences of *accelerated social change* was that the quantitative increase of speed can cause qualitative shifts in the experience of time. The temporal relationship between the succession of generations and the fundamental structural and cultural processes of change proved to be decisive here. If the latter transpire at a speed that is slower than the span of time required for the complete turnover of three or at most four generations, then the space of experience and the horizon of expectation remain essentially congruent in the human experience of history and life. One expects from the future what one knows from the past. However, if the tempo of social change surpasses this critical threshold and approaches an approximately "generational" speed of change, then these time horizons separate from one another: both history and life history become *temporalized*, that is, they are (under conditions of stability like those that emerged in modernity) experienced as directed motion. As has been shown, the conception of stable personal identities and a form of constructive politics accompanied by indexes of direction from "conservative" to "progressive" corresponds to this pace of change.

Then the next critical threshold is crossed when the tempo of social change reaches an *intragenerational* level. As indicators that this is in fact occurring, I pointed to familial and employment relations that in late modernity no longer tend to be stable over an entire adult life but rather lead to a form of life in which the life partner is inconspicuously replaced by the "life period partner" and a serial sequence of jobs takes the place of an identity-constituting profession. This further dynamization can also be demonstrated in less central or even peripheral areas of life: political orientation, car brand, insurance provider, financial institution, telephone number, and newspaper of choice no longer remain unquestionably the same for the duration of a working life. Even where they remain, in fact, unchanged, they fall under the suspicion of being merely contingent. As I argued in part 4, this leads to an altered form of time experience and hence to new forms of personal identity and political self-understanding that have come to be defined by the metaphors of *flows* and *fluids*. As a result of the erosion of the institutions of the welfare state, the experience of a progressive development along preestablished tracks is gradually transitioning into a perception of undefined situations with high, unforeseeable rates of change. An intragenerational tempo of change thus undeniably raises the question of the temporally specific, so to speak, load-bearing capacity of cultural reproduction and social integration. The consequences of the growing intergenerational divide in lifeworld orientations and everyday practices as well as the ongoing devaluation of experience for the exchange between generations, for the passing on of cultural knowledge, and for the maintenance of intergenerational solidarity have hardly been studied at all. In this context the progressive contraction of the present implies that not only one but increasingly two or more age fault lines are developing to separate the lifeworlds of different generations. Currently coexisting generations are themselves becoming, as it were, a manifestation of the nonsimultaneity of the simultaneous.

However, the most important finding of the discussion on the ramifications of accelerated social change is that high rates of change produce a growing pressure to adapt for both individuals and organizations. This leads to the widespread feeling that one is standing not just on a slippery slope but on terrain that is itself slipping away (at varying speeds), as if one were on "slipping slopes" or a down escalator: in order to maintain one's position, to avoid lost opportunities, and to meet the requirements of synchronization, one has to constantly monitor and keep pace with changes in the social environment. One has to compensate for phases of standstill or temporary withdrawal with an increased catchup tempo. Yet since the conditions of action and choice are themselves multidimensional and constantly changing, there is no longer any resting place from which options and opportunities can be sounded out "at leisure." The high "kinetic energy" or notorious unrest that pervades modern societies in the diagnoses of its observers is rooted in this basic experiential condition of slipping slopes. For this reason, it is perhaps no coincidence that Adorno in his *Minima Moralia* defines the "true society" as that which "will grow tired of development and, out of freedom, leave possibilities unused, instead of storming distant stars under a confused compulsion."[2]

The *acceleration of the pace of life*, on the other hand, can be measured objectively as the increase of the number of action episodes per unit of time. This can be achieved, first, by the direct acceleration of actions, as symbolized in fast food, speed dating, or drive-through funerals; second, by shortening pauses or empty times between actions; and, third, by the compression of action episodes in the form of multitasking, i.e., the simultaneous performance of several actions. Such acceleration leads directly to a progressive *fragmentation* of the strands of action. The spans of time in which actors are exclusively concentrated on one thing become shorter and shorter. The technical and social presuppositions of being permanently reachable and available play a significant role here.

While these changes can in principle be grasped empirically by means of time use studies, the evaluation of previously available data has been extremely disappointing in this respect because the relevant national and international surveys, in particular the longitudinal studies, are almost monomaniacally fixated on shifts in the comparative time resources devoted to various kinds of activity (e.g., changes in the distribution of free time and work time). Nevertheless, the results we have at present seem to clearly confirm the hypothesis of acceleration, although one can naturally discern significant class-specific differences here. The evidence for the subjective experience of a progressively increasing scarcity of time resources, however, is much more convincing. This experience constitutes a natural correlate of the acceleration of the pace of life: in all industrial states (despite certain decreases for Japan) citizens complain of large, and in the last few decades increasing, amounts of stress and shortage of time as well as a fear of "not keeping up." In this context the *fear of missing things* and the *compulsion to adapt* are two alternative causes of this experience of stress that appear to be equally at work, although I believe I have found evidence that the latter is beginning to outweigh the former because of the sharpening "slipping slope syndrome."

I justified the further claim that the increase in episodes of experience per unit of time has the potential to dramatically alter the pattern of cultural perception and processing of time by drawing on social-psychological studies of the subjective experience of time as well as social-philosophical considerations developed by, among others, Walter Benjamin. The findings brought together in relation to the idea of the "TV paradox" back up the suspicion that the rapid succession of decontextualized, mutually unconnected but highly stimulating sequences of events characteristic of late modernity hinders the transformation of lived events (*Erlebnisse*) into genuine experience (*Erfahrung*). According to this research, contemporary forms of activity like television and computer games produce a novel "short-short" pattern of time perception that stands the subjective time paradox on its head (i.e., displays both rapidly elapsing experiential time and rapidly erased memory traces). The lived events *remain* episodic. They are no longer linked to each other, to history, and to one's own individual identity. On account of this, time begins in a certain way to race "at both ends": *during* activities, which are felt to be short (and often stressful), it elapses very rapidly, but, at the same, *in retrospect* it seems to "contract" or shrink because they hardly leave any memory traces behind (as Benjamin argued, we remember with the help of photos and souvenirs). Thus, on the one hand, the days and years seem to "fly" by, while, on the other hand, looking back, we have the feeling that time literally slipped through our fingers. To sum up, the society characterized by the short-short pattern could prove to be one that is just as *rich in lived events* as it is *poor in experience*.

In part 3 I considered the question of the motors that drive the escalatory logic characteristic of modernity and the specific ways in which each of them links growth and acceleration. The underlying conjecture of the book is that social acceleration constitutes a basic tendency of modernity that is sui generis and shapes both the social structure and the culture of modern societies. This implies in the first place that it cannot be reduced to other fundamental processes of modernization like rationalization, differentiation, or even economization. Indeed, the analysis showed that it is in fact a self-re-inforcing process that is no longer immediately dependent on external drivers at all. Processes of acceleration in the three identified dimensions interact in such a way that an almost unstoppable "feedback loop" arises. Because the process of technical acceleration unremittingly tends to transform the estab-lished space-time regime, and with it the relationships that individuals have to society, things, and themselves, it also spurs on the logically and analytically independent process of social change. Thus the spread of the automobile or the creation of the Internet, for example, had momentous consequences for movement in space and the social forms of interaction, for communicative structures, for occupational, everyday, and free time practices, and even for as-sociational structures and patterns of identity. *Therefore, technical innovations represent a powerful instigator of social change.*

Moreover, new possibilities and opportunities are thereby opened up for individuals, though, on the other hand, compulsions to adapt and the pressure of having to keep up with the pace of transformations arise as well. In short, the "slipping slope syndrome" that subjects people to stress and time shortage is made more acute. The threat of not being able to keep up with change and thus losing out on opportunities produces an immediate pressure to heighten the pace of life or, in other words, to "stay current." *Accelerated social change thus represents a forceful driver of increases in the pace of life.* It is only by way of this "detour" that one can construct a nonparadoxical connection between technical and individual acceleration: the widespread prejudice that techni-cal, and especially technological, acceleration is "guilty" for our scarcity of time, a view that seems absurd in light of the previously discussed relation-ship between technical acceleration and the saving of time resources, is thus indirectly confirmed.

The circle of acceleration presented in chapter 6 then comes to a complete close when we note how individuals and organizations react to the scarcity of time resources resulting from an increased pace of life by calling for techni-cal acceleration. *Because their time becomes scarce, they demand faster con-nections in transportation and computer technology, shorter waiting times and service times, etc.* As I have demonstrated, the search for technical possibilities of acceleration is a rational strategic reaction to the problem of scarce time resources. Nevertheless, within the dynamic of the circle of acceleration it leads to an unintended *sharpening* of just this very problem and thereby ceaselessly spurs on the acceleration process. Therefore, social acceleration has become a self-reinforcing process in modernity. It places the three domains of acceleration into a reciprocal relationship of mutual escalation that takes on a circular form and is almost entirely impervious to social or political interventions.

The constitutive link between the logics of acceleration and escalation continuously sharpens the scarcity of time through the juxtaposition in many domains of a quasi-exponential quantitative growth (of options, products, and changes) and a "merely" linear acceleration of the ability to process it. Furthermore, the roots of this linkage also lie in three other fundamental principles of modernity that propel the circle of acceleration as, so to speak, "external," i.e., logically independent, "motors." These include the *economic motor* of capitalist enterprise, the operational principle of which inherently rests on the acquisition and exploitation of time leads that function as competitive advantages; the *structural motor* of functional differentiation, which leads to a heightening of production and processing speeds in each differentiated subsystem through the externalization and temporalization of complexity; and the *cultural motor* of a modern ethos in which acceleration has become, as it were, a substitute for eternity and a strategy for aligning the time of life and the time of the world. In the case of each respective motor, growth and acceleration mutually drive each other on in a specific way.

In the first place, the scaling up and acceleration of production, which together compose the principle of heightening productivity, represent the fundamental constants of capitalist enterprise. They are preserved in all the developmental forms and manifestations of this economic system. This fact justifies speaking of *capitalism* in the singular (as against the plurality of capitalisms). As a result of the logic of capital valorization, social acceleration becomes an, as it were, objective compulsion (*Sachzwang*) that is embedded in the material structures of modern society and determines the development and transformation of the capitalist regime of production, for instance, from early capitalism to Fordism and finally to flexible accumulation. Thus, in capitalism, *time becomes money*, and acceleration profit. Because growth and acceleration in the realm of production inevitably express themselves in the speed of circulation and consumption, the dynamizing force of this motor radiates out into almost all fields of society. Yet above all else the economic motor can be understood as the primary impetus of technical acceleration.

Niklas Luhmann and other representatives of systems theory have defended the idea that the principle of functional differentiation is generally accompanied by the heightening and temporalization of complexity: decisions are not all made simultaneously, but rather a growing number are displaced into the future, thus constantly increasing the amount of open and realizable options. This leads to social acceleration because, first, complexity and contingency continue to increase more and more and, second, temporalized systems can only be stabilized in a dynamic fashion (i.e., there is great pressure toward a closure of their operational sequences). If one accepts this line of thought, then at first glance it may appear as though the economic motor is not an independent source of acceleration, but rather just the concrete economic form of a general principle of escalation. A closer look, though, reveals that, on the one hand, capitalist enterprise is analytically independent from functional differentiation and can arise without it (and vice versa). On the other hand, time in the form of the duration of production processes in the modern economy plays a different role than in, for example, science or art. An artwork or a scientific truth never loses its value simply through the passage of time or through the duration of production (naturally both can become worthless through a shift in the dominant aesthetic or scientific paradigm, but this requires the introduction of an extratemporal dimension). But a commodity progressively loses its economic value for the producer as the duration of production increases. Therefore, capitalism and functional differentiation prove to be two logically and analytically independent motors of acceleration, although ones that are empirically and historically closely linked. The identified structural motor can thus be viewed as the main impetus for the acceleration of social change in the sense of the "contraction of the present." Its accelerating effect is expressed in particular through the synchronization requirements of differentiated subsystems and their unavoidable temporal-structural coupling.

Then the paradox that emerged in the wake of functional differentiation, namely, that the problem of processing the consequences of such heightening of complexity is continually worsened by the way the means deployed for coping with it cause further, even exponential, heightening, was reduplicated in the analysis of the *cultural motor*. It was shown that acceleration represents an intuitive solution to the problem of a limited lifetime or the divergence of the time of the world and the time of life in a secular culture. In this context the maximal enjoyment of worldly opportunities and the optimal actualization of one's own abilities, and hence the ideal of the *fulfilled life*, has become the paradigm of a successful life. Whoever lives twice as fast can realize twice as many worldly possibilities and thus, as it were, live two lives in the span of one. Whoever becomes infinitely fast approaches the potentially unlimited horizon of the time of the world (and of worldly possibilities) within one life-time to the extent that she can realize a plurality of life possibilities in a single earthly lifespan. She therefore no longer needs to fear death, the annihilator of options. In this way acceleration as a strategy of aligning world time and life time becomes a secular substitute for eternity, a functional equivalent for religious ideas of an eternal life and thus a modern response to death. This promise in contemporary culture turns out to be a primary external impetus for the heightening of the pace of life. For this very reason it cannot be merely understood as a result of systemic or structural compulsions.

However, this strategy for raising one's "degree of exhaustion" of worldly possibilities is in the end doomed to fail by the functional mechanisms of the circle of acceleration. For the very same inventions and methods that permit the accelerated enjoyment of worldly possibilities, and thus the increase of the total sum of *realized* options in a single life, also multiply the number and diversity of *realizable* options, in fact exponentially, so that the *degree* of exhaustion—the ratio of realized to realizable worldly possibilities—continu-ally decreases while the spiral of acceleration is relentlessly driven onward. This is the cultural side of the paradoxical phenomenon of ever scarcer time resources in the face of simultaneous technical acceleration, and it demon-strates with an almost mathematical clarity that acceleration is, at least in the long run, *no* solution at all to the problem of "missing things." Indeed, it cannot even *soften* the problem.

Yet the analysis of the way the modern process of acceleration was set in motion remains incomplete as long as it leaves out of consideration the devel-opmental and functional logics of the modern national state and its military apparatus. As the course of the inquiry in chapter 8 made clear, the unfolding of that process can only be adequately grasped in light of the military and state-centered competition for the conquest, control, and defense of national territories. From this perspective, modernization is an accelerative project of national states that was driven by nothing more than the political striving to preserve and accumulate power within a system of competing national states that took shape after the Treaty of Westphalia.

The national state and the military can thus be seen as institutional "key accelerators" that performed an indispensable "maieutic" function for the development and stabilization of the acceleration dynamic. However, as we have also seen, the ensemble of societal institutions centered around the national state and the military are now marked by a comprehensive and consequential *functional inversion* in the wake of the characteristically dialectical development of the forces of acceleration and their institutional parameters. Classical modern *accelerators*—most strikingly bureaucracy and the Fordist work (time) regime—have turned into late modern *hindrances to acceleration* or *brakes* that are now placed under pressure to transform or else erode by the very dynamizing forces they themselves helped to unleash.[3] In the interplay of the cultural, structural, and internal motors, the dynamic of social acceleration has become autonomous from these institutions and is now turning against them.

This fact by itself already supports the conjecture that the often postulated but endlessly contentious break between classical modernity and late modernity can only be reconstructed in an analytically precise and empirically substantial way from the perspective of a theory of social acceleration. Accordingly, a reversal occurs within modernity when critical speed limits are reached beyond which society takes on a new quality even though nothing in the ensemble of modernization principles has fundamentally changed (acceleration, differentiation, rationalization, individualization, domestication).

As I have tried to show in this work, the time patterns of society link together and assimilate structural developments and requirements, on the one hand, and cultural action orientations, on the other. In the final analysis they ensure the compatibility of systemic imperatives and perspectives on life and action at both individual and collective levels. The acceleration-induced alteration of time structures in late modernity therefore has massive consequences for the culturally dominant forms of individual and collective identity. This was the guiding hypothesis of part 4.

The late modern surge of acceleration that began in the 1970s but culminated in the digital and political revolution circa 1989, for which there are clear indicators in all three fields of social acceleration, had two notable effects: first, it eroded the basic institutional arrangement of "classical" modernity and once again transformed the predominant space-time regime and, second, it brought about a fundamental change in the individual and collective experience of time, a shift occurring simultaneously in the structure of personal identities and the political self-understanding of society. In the diagnostic lexicon of the present, the first set of changes is mostly discussed under the catchphrase *globalization*. What is *new* in them, as I have argued, is not the global expansion of processes and transactions of various kinds, but the *speed* with which they transpire. This tendentially transforms the "classical modern" space of stable localities into a late modern space of *dynamic streams* and replaces the linear and sequential temporal order with a new form of "timeless" and, at the same time, "temporalized" time defined by ubiquitous simultaneity.

If the acceleration of social change and the concomitant contraction of the present in early and classical modernity caused the upheaval in the experience of time that received cultural expression during the "epochal threshold" between 1770 and 1830, and that I described, following Reinhart Koselleck and Martin Kohli, in the political dimension as the temporalization of history and in the personal dimension of an analysis of identity as the temporalization of life, then the transition to late modernity can be identified as a converse process of the *detemporalization* of history and life. While history took on the character of a directed and politically shapable movement in classical modernity, in late modernity the perception of a directionless historical transformation that can no longer be politically steered or controlled becomes more and more prevalent. Politics forfeits its directional index, and the concepts "progressive" and "conservative" lose or switch their meanings: progressive politics no longer has any accelerating function and its insistence on the political possibility of controlling social development makes it rather a late modern *decelerator*. As I concluded from an analysis of its temporal structures, the political project of modernity has perhaps come to its end as a result of the desynchronization of socioeconomic development and political action. Under the pressure of an ongoing contraction of the present, late modern politics becomes *situational*. It reacts to emerging problems without being able to maintain its claim to shape history and society.

The resulting perception of an "end of history" only reflects the end of the history of classical modernity that was centered on, directed toward, and temporalized by the idea of progress. It marks the transition to a condition in which the historical forms previously thought of as noncontemporaneous once again become timelessly contemporaneous alternatives (monarchy, democracy, state formation, state disintegration, colonization, decolonization, constitutional state, welfare state, etc., no longer designate specific historical stages of development). There is a parallel to this in individual life in the experience of a "temporalized" time of everyday practice whose sequential temporal order likewise appears contingent: what occurs when, for how long, in what rhythm, and in which order is increasingly decided in the course of acting itself (that holds true for everyday tasks like shopping, work, relaxation as well as for "life events" like starting to pursue a degree, entering the workforce, having kids, getting married, etc.). Therefore, the perception of an end of history corresponds to the perception of a transition from a life based on a stable identity and the institutional safeguards of the life course regime and organized according to a "lifeplan" to one that is playful, open, and unpredictable, that is experienced as a *game* or as *aimless drifting*, depending on individual or cultural temperament.

In this way the situational politics of late modernity is reflected in a new form of *situational identity*. In concrete contexts, both prove to be very capable of acting, making choices, and finding some kind of orientation, but in virtue of a contraction of the present defined by an intragenerational pace of social change, they are also trans-situationally directionless. Decisions no longer unfold a morally binding effect or radiate into the future or the past. The events they bring about remain *episodic* in both individual and collective experience and no longer solidify into (life-)historically "embedded" and narratively connectable experiences.

The same dynamization process that first made possible the experience of directed, progressive movement and individual and collective development when a generational rate of change was achieved in "classical modernity" also gave rise to the perception of a *directionless movement* and hence a "frenetic standstill." The latter eludes intentional control in both its two dimensions of rigidity and change and thus conflicts with the modern promise of autonomy. The dialectical inversion of acceleration and movement into rigidity and standstill, which is, so to speak, the leitmotif of my analysis of the modern acceleration process, culminates in a "postmodern" political culture that dispenses with the claims to autonomy and identity that have always characterized the project and ethos of modernity. Imposed by late modern time structures, this situation is constituted by the peculiar concurrence of a similarly designated "postmodern" antinomy: a condition where *nothing remains the same but nothing essentially changes*.[4]

Part 4 ended with this finding, but left open two questions that I would now like to discuss in closing, even though here I will only be able to provide, so to speak, an outlook on them. The first question concerns the possible or probable continuation of history (as it were, without quotation marks), that is, the ways the history of acceleration might end, a history that, insofar as the analysis presented here is correct, is still going on as the constant *behind* all the openness and directionless indeterminacy of late modernity. The second question pertains to the *critical* potential of a theory of acceleration like the one attempted here. Does it offer normative criteria for the *desirability* of any particular further development of the modern dynamization process, that is, does it go beyond the observation that the autonomization of the acceleration process is incompatible with an ethos and project of modernity that rests on the promise of individual and collective autonomy? If it does not do this, then it remains, as I indicated at the end of chapter 12, "toothless" in the face of a competing systems-theoretical or "poststructuralist" diagnosis of time and society that celebrates an abandonment of the claims of identity and autonomy as a liberation from "old European" illusions and/or as an emancipation from limiting expectations of control, continuity, and coherence, to give just one example. I will start with the second question.

As a matter of fact, I hope that the outlines of a critical theory of society are already visible in this work, one that is not aimed at the *relations of production* (the approach of the older critical theory), the *relations of understanding* (Habermas), or the *relations of recognition* (Honneth), all of which involve normative criteria and empirical anchorings that seem to be increasingly problematic, but rather one that emphasizes a critical diagnosis of *temporal structures* or *relations of time*.[5] For these designate the site at which systemic imperatives are transformed into cultural orientations for living and acting, as it were, "behind the backs of actors."

As the course of the argument has made clear, sociostructural modernization processes are inevitably reflected in the construction of individual and collective identities or self-relations. However, the mechanism by which this translation of functional necessities (roughly, the requirements of growth and acceleration) into cultural orientations is accomplished in the individualized and ethically rather unrestrictive liberal societies of modernity is largely mysterious.[6] My thesis is that the path to understanding it leads directly to the investigation of societal time structures.

The sociology of time has left little doubt about the fact that both methods of measuring time and ways in which it is perceived (i.e, the formation of time horizons and temporal perspectives) are subject to historical change dependent on the structure of society. Nevertheless, time always appears to have a solid, objective facticity. From the standpoint of actors it is undeniably a natural, unquestionable given whose compulsions and patterns of order are deeply and unreflectively engraved in the habitual and dispositional structures of individuals as a "second nature." In this capacity they steer the orientations of actors in the context of everyday time and the time of life. Therefore time is always both private and intimate—"How do I want to spend my time?" is the temporal version of the ethical question, "How do I want to live?"—and also thoroughly socially determined. The rhythms, sequences, durations, and speeds of social time as well as the correlative time horizons and perspectives are almost completely beyond the control of individuals. Yet, at the same time, they undoubtedly exert a great normative, i.e., action-coordinating and action-regulating, effect. Particularly in modern society, transgressions against norms of time have weighty sanctions attached to them. Today more than ever ignoring deadlines and speed imperatives leads to *social exclusion*. This is the reason why time appears to be the actual way that structural imperatives and cultural orientations are linked. It explains the way in which the conditions of individual ethical autonomy and maximal social action coordination can be simultaneously fulfilled. Enlightenment concerning the "mute normative violence" of temporal structures is therefore a primary and pressing aim of a critical theory of acceleration.

Moreover, time structures also appear to be a privileged site for the genesis, and hence the analysis, of social maldevelopments or *suffering-inducing social pathologies*, because an illusion of almost unlimited individual freedom is produced by the minimally restrictive ethical code that predominates in late modern society, while, at the same time, an ever greater need for coordination emerges in view of the ever more complex, unsteered, and self-autonomizing interaction chains and the need to fulfill the resulting structural imperatives (roughly, the compulsions of growth and acceleration). So the ethically and politically uncontrollable trend of acceleration does not just exert an increasing normalizing force; it also harbors a growing potential to produce "pathologies of acceleration."

On this point, the critique of temporal relations at which I aim can in fact be linked up with the critique of relations of recognition proposed by Honneth: if social exclusion as the experience of disrespect leads to subjective suffering, then in modern society one can clearly discern a progressive *dynamization* of exclusion-induced suffering. There is no doubt that this produces fear and anxiety in those who are not (or not yet) excluded. It therefore decisively shapes the action orientations of individuals, because the premodern experience of *being* excluded on categorical grounds (for instance, in the denial of specific rights and forms of esteem to certain classes or "estates") is replaced in modernity by the constantly present, fear-inducing possibility of *becoming* excluded in the sense of "getting left behind." Almost every form of social recognition (with the exception perhaps of the legal dimension) increasingly stands under temporal qualification: love and friendship come to be viewed as contingent and conditional arrangements and personal achievement must be ceaselessly renewed and improved if it is not to lose its function of securing social esteem. This may be one of the essentially subject-related causes of the oft-observed *restlessness* of modern societies and the dominance of a rhetoric of "must" that contradicts their ideology of freedom.

But hiding behind this rhetoric there may be a creeping and unnoticed *restructuring of the order of values as a result of problems with time.*[7] On the one hand, this occurs because subjects as well as organizations are constantly involved in "putting out fires," that is, managing pressing problems while also trying to hold future options and opportunities open, so that, in the long term, the connection between the sequencing of their actions and their preference orderings becomes impaired. On the other hand, it is a consequence of the social advantages of *short-termism* under conditions of structural uncertainty. As I argued, there are serious empirical indications that individual cost-benefit calculations are increasingly oriented to short-term expectations because of high rates of subjective and objective instability and change. Moreover, in an environment in which, for example, the entertainment industry creates innumerable, literally "attractive" possible experiences that promise immediate gratification with minimal investments of time and energy, actions that only bear fruit under conditions of long-run stability and with significant investments of time and energy are no longer performed even when they provide subjects with far higher levels of (empirically measurable) satisfaction and are thus not only cognitively judged to be "more valuable" by the subjects themselves but are also felt and experienced as such.

Together these two factors produce the widespread feeling that one no longer has any time for the "genuinely important things" in life. As confirmed by qualitative time use studies, this feeling occurs independently of the quantity of free time resources and thus can only be interpreted as an experience of alienation in the sense of Ödön von Horváth's bon mot: "I'm actually a quite different person, I just never get around to being him." I concluded from this that *the time structures of the acceleration society get people "to will what they do not will,"* that is, to pursue, of their own volition, *courses of action that they do not prefer from a temporally stable perspective*. Therefore, the normative criteria of the kind of *critique of time* aimed at here are delivered by individuals themselves.

It has thus become clear at many points in this investigation that the mechanisms of social acceleration offer a series of possibilities for a new, as it were, acceleration-theoretical *critique of alienation*. Multidimensional and high rates of change and instability transform the relationships of human beings to the places in which they live, the material structures that surround them (including the clothes that they wear and the instruments with which they work), the people with whom they are in contact, the institutions in which they move, and, finally, their own feelings and convictions. The faster these things change or are replaced, the less it is worth the effort of becoming intimately familiar with them and, as it were, "assimilating oneself" to them. As I have shown, the more indifferent individuals become with respect to the *content* of such relationships, the better they can adapt to the demands for acceleration and flexibility in late modernity. However, where the process of becoming at home and familiar with feelings and lifestyles or acquaintances and friends, with tradition- and work-related objects or the physical environment of a home or workplace, fails to occur, then, at the very least, a feeling of alienation sets in if one still adheres to the idea of "depth" in relationships, sentiments, and convictions (which can in principle be sounded out narratively). Therefore, it is no coincidence that the apologists of a postmodern culture celebrate precisely the abandonment of all ideas of "depth" and "authenticity."

Against the abandonment of this claim to lend a depth, direction, and meaning to experiences there speaks the potentially anthropologically justifiable finding that it leads to an experience of life and time in which episodic lived events can no longer be transformed into experiences because they lack a connection to stable future horizons and reliable images of the past. This leads to a verifiable impairment of subjective capacities of orientation and action and possibly to a significant increase in the incidence of depression and depressive moods. The latter also appears to be facilitated, above all, by the way the perspectives of everyday time, the time of life, and historical time fragment or become mutually incompatible. I discussed the empirical findings supporting such an interpretation at length in chapters 5 and 10. The experience of alienation accordingly results in particular from living in the condition of "frenetic standstill" already discussed.

Yet, as the history of modern acceleration shows, one must be very cautious with respect to the postulation of anthropological speed limits. It certainly cannot be ruled out that such "pathologies of acceleration," insofar as they can be empirically confirmed at all, are *transitional phenomena* that are not due to the late modern level of speed per se, but rather to its incompatibility with the value orientations of "classical modernity" and hence will likely disappear in the long term. Nevertheless, as long as and to the extent that they produce real experiences of suffering they must be taken seriously by a critical theory of society. In any case, the diagnosis of such experiences would have to carefully weigh the speed-induced experiences of loss against the gains in freedom, mobility, and nimbleness.

If even a critique of alienation remains in the end reliant on the normative basis of individual and collective claims to autonomy (it is difficult, though by no means impossible, to diagnose experiences of alienation that are *not* linked with the feeling of a loss of self-determination), this is no longer true of a critical diagnosis of the previously identified phenomena of *desynchronization*. As I have made clear, the different capacities of social subsystems to rapidly accelerate leads to their potential desynchronization and endangers the modes of their temporal-structural coupling (and hence their coupling in general). Synchronization problems appear in sharpened form both within and also between the functional spheres of society, though primarily between scientific-technological and economic developments, on the one hand, and politics and the educational system, on the other. The rapid tempo of socioeconomic and technological change systematically overtaxes the temporal structures and horizons of democratic, deliberative politics, which actually tends to *slow down* its processes of will formation and decision making in response to the highly dynamic nature of the acceleration society. Moreover, it is easy to show that social acceleration places great pressure on the capacities of both social integration and cultural reproduction, in particular where an overly rapid tempo endangers the continual interchange of generations. Furthermore, wherever the time pattern of society overstrains the reproductive and regenerative capacities of the natural environment, what is potentially the most devastating form of desynchronization shows up: in other words, social acceleration threatens to lead to ecological catastrophe.

Nevertheless, the strongest foundation for a critical theory of acceleration remains modernity's *broken promise of autonomy*. If this promise once inspired and spurred on the project and ethos of modernity, it can no longer be redeemed in either its individual or its political form on account of the altered time structures of late modernity. The normative foundations of this idea continue to provide the most convincing criteria for a critical diagnosis of the times, because the moral convictions bound up with it are employed by the members or the political actors of late modern societies themselves in order to evaluate their own action. The apologists of a farewell to this project, despite their full-throated avowals, still owe us proof that genuinely postmodern forms of subjectivity and politics that get by without any claim to autonomy whatsoever can even be coherently thought. Instead, their affirmation of acceleration seems to be grounded again and again on an assumption, mostly left implicit, that autonomy is heightened by speed.

With this I come to back to the first question: how will the history of acceleration unfold, or how will it end? Does it have, so to speak, a center of gravity toward which it continually strives or are alternative forms of new equilibria between movement and inertia conceivable? Within the horizon of the theory developed here, four alternatives are conceivable, although they are certainly not all equally probable.

The first possibility consists in the formation of a new form of institutional facilitation and stabilization of the acceleration process and thus the attainment of a new equilibrium at a higher level of speed. This would repeat the organizational and orientational achievement of "classical modernity" by replacing the social, political, and juridical institutions of the national welfare state that have become too slow by more dynamic arrangements that reconcile the project of modernity with the speeds of late modernity at both individual and collective levels. Hopes for reform by those who press for adaptive political measures while maintaining the claim to autonomy aim at this goal. Their optimistic stance is based on the idea that the enlarged scope of action resulting from increased dynamism can be translated into improved opportunities for individuals and polities to shape their existence and hence make redemption of the modern promise of autonomy truly possible for the first time. Individual, cultural, and political action would gradually adapt to late modern speeds of change through the development of new forms of perception and control, perhaps even with the help of new genetic and implanted computer technologies.

However, I think these hopes are unrealistic because it is difficult to see how such reforms could come to grips with the problem of the desynchronization of deliberative-democratic politics and economic-technological development and how they could be politically achieved at all when political steering with existing means is becoming more and more improbable. Yet, even if such a revision of modern institutional arrangements and related individual and collective identities were successful, the novel emerging forms would likely not long be able to withstand the newly fostered forces of acceleration in view of the institution-disintegrating character of the primacy of dynamization: in accordance with the previously discussed dialectical logic of the development of the forces of acceleration and their institutional enabling conditions, one should expect that the lifetime of a "second modernity" created in this way would be even shorter than that of the first.

Therefore, a second possibility would be the definitive abandonment of the project of modernity, which could lead to the emergence of genuinely "post-modern" forms of subjectivity and a new kind of (sub-)politics (for instance, in the sense of the spontaneous self-organization of the "multitude" hoped for by Hardt and Negri) that would dispense with the claims of autonomy and control and for just this reason be able to affirm late modern manifestations of social acceleration. New modes of perception, new ways to process speed, and new forms of individual and collective self-relations would have to develop, and, by definition, nothing can yet be said about them. Of course, synchronization problems would persist. The end of the history of acceleration would remain unforeseeable.

If the second possibility represents, as it were, the triumph of the modernization process over the cultural and political project that originally consolidated it, then a third possibility consists in the converse attempt to assert the modern *aspiration to shape human affairs* against the self-autonomizing forces of acceleration. As I have shown in chapter 11, this requires that we, as it were, "reach for the emergency brake" to prevent the social tempo from surpassing the threshold beneath which it can still be politically and individually controlled. Such a solution would demand both a decisive political intervention in the developmental autonomy of the faster functional systems so as to "forcibly resynchronize" them as well as a deceleration of the movement of dynamization to a level that is, in accordance with the ideas of "classical modernity," compatible with humanity (*humanverträgliches*).

However, this idea is highly unrealistic because it remains unclear *who* the political and institutional *bearers* of such a politics of deceleration could be, and also because of the unpredictable economic and social costs that such a forced resynchronization would engender, but above all in virtue of the crisis of the modern conception of the role of politics in time. For it would mean in principle not only the reversal of functional differentiation but also an exit from the modernization process in general. Its aim of holding onto the classical modern idea of progress and conserving the experiential space of temporalized history by stalling the spiral of growth and acceleration is inherently self-contradictory: as I have tried to show, the idea of progress and hence the project of modernity already irrevocably entail the modern process of dynamization, and they are indeed themselves a *reaction* to the historical experience of social acceleration. Progress and acceleration were indissolubly linked together from the very beginning. They were both thought to be unstoppable. Therefore, the idea of reaching for the emergency brake can only be consistently conceived with Walter Benjamin as a radical and revolutionary exit from history,[8] as a *revolution against progress*,[9] and hence in the end as a "saving leap" out of modernity itself, i.e., equally out of the project and the process.[10]

The triumph of the project over the process would thus be limited to the brief moment of autonomy exercised in the very act of exit, and this is all that ultimately distinguishes the third endgame scenario for the history of acceleration from the fourth and, according to the logic laid out in this work, *most likely* possibility: namely, the unbridled onward rush into an abyss. From a logical point of view, this abyss is characterized by the final collapse of the antinomies of movement and inertia and the realization of the vision, which has accompanied modernity from the very start, of a *frenetic standstill* as the flip side of a *total mobilization*. From an empirical point of view, however, presumably long before that point is reached the abyss will be embodied in either the collapse of the ecosystem or in the ultimate breakdown of the modern social order and its values under the pressure of growing acceleration pathologies and the power of the enemies these foster. It stands to reason that modern society will have to pay for the loss of the ability to balance movement and inertia with nuclear or climatic catastrophes, with the diffusion at a furious pace of new diseases, or with new forms of political collapse and the eruption of uncontrolled violence, which can be particularly expected where the masses excluded from the processes of acceleration and growth take a stand against the acceleration society.

The alternative of a final catastrophe or a radical revolution hardly represents the kind of ending for which one begins to read or write a book. In both cases one is dealing with an extremely disconcerting finale. Yet perhaps it is in precisely this kind of disquiet that a creative contemporary social theory can find the impulse to discover a fifth ending for the history of acceleration. "When it is profound and consistent, sociology is not satisfied with a kind of mere observation that could be deemed deterministic, pessimistic or demoralizing," as Pierre Bourdieu maintains in his contribution to defining the task of a contemporary sociology. He goes on to say that it does not rest until it can offer means "to work against the immanent tendencies of the societal order. And whoever calls that deterministic should recall that the law of gravity must first be known by those who build the flying machines that effectively overcome it."[11] Today, however, the challenge lies in overcoming the laws that made the invention of flying machines possible: a no less difficult task.

NOTES

Translator's Introduction

1. Meghnad Desai, *Marx's Revenge: The Resurgence of Capitalism and the Death of Statist Socialism* (New York: Verso, 2002), 47.

2. All parenthetical chapter and page references in this introduction are to the present work. For relevant excerpts from Adams's famous autobiography, *The Education of Henry Adams*, see Adams 2009.

3. Cf. chapter 1, this volume.

4. For some examples of this feature of sociological inquiry, see Randall Collins, *Sociological Insight: An Introduction to Non-Obvious Sociology* (New York: Oxford University Press, 1992). As Luhmann often puts it, sociological understanding involves the conscious theoretical endeavor to succeed in making clear the improbability of socially normal states of affairs. See, for instance, Niklas Luhmann, *Social Systems*, trans. John Bednarz Jr., with Dirk Baecker (Stanford: Stanford University Press, 1995), 114–15.

5. Charles Duhigg, "Stock Traders Find Speed Pays, in Milliseconds," *New York Times*, July 24, 2009, A1.

6. Graham Bowley, "After the Flash Crash, Still Reason for Anxiety," *New York Times*, November 9, 2010, B1.

7. The circuit breakers were first put in place in 1988 in response to the 1987 crash, one in which high-frequency computer trading already played a major role.

8. Paul A. David, "May 6th—Signals from a Very Brief But Real Catastrophe on Wall Street," *real world economics review*, no. 50 (June 26, 2010): 2–27, http://www.paecon.net/PAEReview/issue53/David53.pdf, 12.

9. See particularly chapter 11.

10. "The State of Emergency," in Rosa and Scheuerman 2009:201–15, here p 205.

11. Saskia Sassen, *A Sociology of Globalization* (New York: Norton, 2007), 25–28. Sassen even speaks of the "incipient formation of transnational urban systems" (28).

12. Hauke Brunkhorst, "The Analysis of Contemporary Mass Society," *The Cambridge Companion to Critical Theory* (Cambridge: Cambridge University Press, 2004), 248–80, here p. 255.

13. Sheldon Wolin, *Politics and Vision: Continuity and Innovation in Western Political Thought*, expanded ed. (Princeton: Princeton University Press, 2004), 46–47.

14. Plato, *Statesman*, 269a. The idea of the "golden age" stems from Hesiod, *Works and Days*, ll.111–222.

15. J. G. A. Pocock, *The Machiavellian Moment: Florentine Political Thought and the Atlantic Tradition* (Princeton: Princeton University Press, 1975).

16. For a seminal analysis of the social-political implications of this semantic transformation, see Hannah Arendt, *On Revolution* (New York: Viking, 1965).

17. See Johan Heilbron, Lars Magnusson, and Bjorn Wittrock, eds., *The Rise of the Social Sciences and the Formation of Modernity: Conceptual Change in Context, 1750–1850, Sociology of the Sciences Yearbook, 1996* (Dordrecht: Kluwer, 1998). In particular, Peter Wagner, "Certainty and Order, Liberty and Contingency: The Birth of Social Science as Empirical Political Philosophy," ibid., 241–63. Consider Theodore M. Porter's claim that "social science . . . developed during the middle third of the nineteenth century above all as a liberal, reformist answer to the upheavals of the era." Theodore M. Porter, "Genres and Objects of Social Inquiry, the Enlightenment to 1890," in *The Cambridge History of Science*, vol. 7: *The Modern Social Sciences* (Cambridge: Cambridge University Press, 2008), 13–39, here p. 28.

18. A figure from a different intellectual tradition altogether who is also a master of such historical and social "differential diagnoses" is Michel Foucault. For an articulation and application of this form of "historical epistemology," see Arnold Davidson, *The Emergence of Sexuality: Historical Epistemology and the Formation of Concepts* (Cambridge: Harvard University Press, 2004).

19. For a seminal account of the normative aspects of a key pair of clinical categories that inspired some of Foucault's own work, see Georges Canguilhem, *The Normal and the Pathological* (New York: Zone, 1991). On the centrality of the concept of pathology for critical forms of social philosophy, see Axel Honneth, "Pathologies of the Social: The Past and Present of Social Philosophy," in David Rasmussen, ed., *The Handbook of Critical Theory* (London: Blackwell), 369–99, and "A Social Pathology of Reason: On the Legacy of the Frankfurt School," in *Cambridge Companion to Critical Theory* (Cambridge: Cambridge University Press, 2004), 336–61.

20. In a recent work, Rosa has singled out experiences of suffering, insofar as they systematically result from existing social relations, as the normative anchor of critical social theory. See his "Kapitalismus als Dynamisierungsspirale—Soziologie als Gesellschaftskritik," in Klaus Dörre, Stephan Lessenich, and Hartmut Rosa, *Soziologie, Kapitalismus, Kritik: Eine Debatte* (Frankfurt: Suhrkamp, 2009), 90–93. On the various "generations" of the Frankfurt School tradition, see Joel Anderson, "The 'Third Generation' of the Frankfurt School," *Intellectual History Newsletter* 22 (2000), also at http://www.phil.uu.nl/~joel/research/publications/3rdGeneration.htm).

21. See Seyla Benhabib, *Critique, Norm, and Utopia: A Study of the Foundations of Critical Theory* (New York: Columbia University Press, 1986).

22. Adorno's treatment of modernist art in his *Aesthetic Theory* (Minneapolis: University of Minnesota Press) is an example of the latter, expressive mode of immanent critique. However, for Adorno, this expressive or articulate endeavor is also in the service of a wider immanent critique of society as a whole, and that wider critique can certainly be said to subject society to a rather negative judgment.

23. Talcott Parsons, *The Structure of Social Action*, 2d ed. (New York: Free Press, 1967); Jürgen Habermas, *The Theory of Communicative Action*, 2 vols. (Boston: Beacon, 1984, 1987).

24. See chapter 1.2.

25. While Friedrich Nietzsche, Søren Kierkegaard, and Alexis de Toqueville, each in his own way, helped set the tone for a new form of individualist social and cultural criticism, a classic and eloquent expression of a widespread reaction among modern intellectuals to the phenomena of massification is José Ortega y Gasset's *The Revolt of the Masses* (New York: Norton, 1994), first published in 1930. In the English-speaking world this book, which is quite brilliant, if overly elitist, has unfortunately overshadowed Ortega's other much more important and philosophically interesting works. See, e.g., the works cited in note 57.

26. For evidence that this is not solely a problem faced by modern societies, see Jared Diamond, *Collapse: How Societies Choose to Succeed or Fail* (New York: Viking 2005).

27. See the introduction.

28. See chapters 2–5.

29. See chapter 6.

30. See chapter 7.

31. Anthony Giddens, *Runaway World*, rev. ed. (London: Routledge, 2002).

32. Page 000.

33. "Angelina on Brad, Her Religious Beliefs and Life Before Fame," July 12, 2010, www.msn.com, At http://movies.msn.com/movies/article.aspx?news=510226&gt1=28101.

34. On this and what follows, see chapter 10.

35. See chapter 2.2.b.

36. On globalization and temporal-structural transformations of politics, see chapters 9 and 11.

37. See chapter 7.3.

38. Luhmann, *Social Systems*.

39. In the conclusion, this volume, p. 000.

40. For a now standard historical overview of critical theory and the Frankfurt School, see Rolf Wiggershaus, *The Frankfurt School* (Cambridge: MIT Press, 1994).

41. Benhabib, *Critique, Norm, and Utopia*, 1–19. For classic statements, see Max Horkheimer, "Traditional and Critical Theory," *Critical Theory* (New York: Continuum, 2002), 188–244; Herbert Marcuse, "Philosophy and Critical Theory," in David Ingram and Julia Simon-Ingram, eds., *Critical Theory: The Essential Readings* (Paragon House, 1991), 5ff.; and Jürgen Habermas, "The Classical Doctrine of Politics in Relation to Social Philosophy," in *Theory and Practice* (Boston: Beacon, 1973), 41–82.

42. The term *old European* comes from Niklas Luhmann. For the debate between Luhmann and Habermas, see *Theorie der Gesellschaft oder Sozialtechnologie? Was leistet die Systemforschung* (Frankfurt: Suhrkamp, 1971); and also Jürgen Habermas, *Legitimation Crisis* (London: Heinemann, 1976), 130–44.

43. John Rawls, A *Theory of Justice* (Cambridge: Belknap, 1999), § 5, 21–22.

44. See Jürgen Habermas, "Morality and Ethical Life: Does Hegel's Critique of Kant Apply to Discourse Ethics?" in *Moral Consciousness and Communicative Action* (Cambridge: MIT Press, 1990) , as well as the first three essays of *Justification and Application* (Cambridge: MIT Press, 1993).

45. See Thomas McCarthy, "Practical Discourse: On the Relation of Morality to Politics," *Ideals and Illusions: On Deconstruction and Reconstruction in Contemporary Critical Theory* (Cambridge: MIT Press, 1993), 181–200, and "Legitimacy and Diversity: Dialectical Reflections on Analytical Distinctions," *Cardozo Law Review* 17 (1995–96): 1083–1125; Richard Bernstein, "The Retrieval of the Democratic Ethos," *Cardozo Law Review* 17 (1995–96): 1127–46; and Benhabib, *Critique, Norm, and Utopia*, chapter 8. Martin Seel has subtly worked out an argument for the interdependence of the two concepts in his *Versuch über die Form des Glücks: Studien zur Ethik* (Frankfurt: Suhrkamp, 1999).

46. This is broadly the response of contemporary neo-Aristotelians such as Charles Taylor, *The Sources of the Self: The Making of the Modern Identity* (Cambridge: Harvard University Press, 1989); Alasdair MacIntyre, *After Virtue* (South Bend: University of Notre Dame Press, 1981); Michael Sandel, *Liberalism and the*

Limits of Justice (Cambridge: Cambridge University Press, 1998); and Martha Nussbaum, *Frontiers of Justice: Disability, Nationality, Species Membership* (Cambridge: Harvard University Press, 2006).

47. Axel Honneth, *Struggle for Recognition: The Moral Grammar of Social Conflict* (Cambridge: MIT Press, 1995). On the notion that this work is a touchstone for an "ethical turn" in critical theory, see Nikolas Kompridis, "From Reason to Self-Realisation? Axel Honneth and the 'Ethical Turn' in Critical Theory," *Critical Horizons* 5, no. 1 (2004): 323–60. For another important example of this trend, see Maeve Cooke, *Re-presenting the Good Society* (Cambridge: MIT Press, 2006).

48. Hartmut Rosa, *Identität und kulturelle Praxis*. Politische Philosophie nach Charles Taylor, with a foreword by Axel Honneth (Frankfurt: Campus, 1998).

49. See his "What Is Human Agency?" and "The Concept of a Person," in Charles Taylor, *Human Agency and Language: Philosophical Papers*, vol. 1 (Cambridge: Cambridge University Press, 1985), pp. 15–45 and 97–115, respectively.

50. For a good overview of these debates, see Stephen Mulhall and Adam Swift, *Liberals and Communitarians*, 2d ed. (Oxford: Wiley-Blackwell, 1996).

51. The distinction between established and engendered (dis)advantages comes from Thomas Pogge, *Realizing Rawls* (Ithaca: Cornell University Press, 1989), p. 35ff.

52. Hartmut Rosa, "On Defining the Good Life: Liberal Freedom and Capitalist Necessity," *Constellations* 5, no. 2 (1998): 201–14.

53. Jürgen Habermas, "Consciousness-Raising or Redemptive Criticism: The Contemporaneity of Walter Benjamin," *New German Critique*, no. 17 (Spring 1979): 20–59, p. 57.

54. See chapters 5 and 8.

55. For cultural factors, see chapter 7.2; For social-structural factors, see chapter 7.3.

56. Page 00.

57. "Kapitalismus als Dynamisierungsspirale — Soziologie als Gesellschaftskritik," in Klaus Dörre, Stephen Lessenich, and Hartmut Rosa, *Soziologie Kapitalismus Kritik: Eine Debatte* (Frankfurt: Suhrkamp, 2009), 87–126, 87.

58. Rosa thus continues a critical and selective appropriation of the Heideggerian themes by other critical theorists such as Marcuse, Habermas, and Honneth. The insight into the correlation between time structures, agent identity, and social-systemic structures also allows Rosa to provide a reinterpretation of the Hegelian notion of the "substance" of the ethical life of a community such as the ancient Greek polis in terms of the "substantial a priori identity" of subjects in premodern societies in which the pace of social change was much slower than the pace of generational turnover (chapter 10.2). The central role

of the generation as an explanatory factor in historiography and social theory was again explored and anticipated by José Ortega y Gasset in various works, including, in addition to *The Revolt of the Masses* (see note 26), *The Modern Theme* (New York: Harper and Row, 1961), and *Man and Crisis* (New York: Norton, 1962).

59. Page oo, this volume.

60. Dörre, Lessenich, and Rosa, *Soziologie, Kapitalismus, Kritik.*

61. For another recent interesting contribution to this endeavor, see Rahel Jaeggi, *Entfremdung: Zur Aktualität eines sozialphilosophischen Programms* (Frankfurt: Campus, 2005).

62. This is another way in which Rosa's project can be read as a means of retrieving Hegelian themes that is different enough to be an interesting alternative, within contemporary critical theory, to Honneth's recognition-theoretical way of doing the same. In particular, one could see Honneth as focusing on Hegelian freedom in the institutional and social domain of objective spirit, roughly, the family or intimate personal life, civil society and the economy, and the polity and its laws, while Rosa focuses on Hegelian freedom in the "higher" domain of absolute spirit (though Rosa substitutes the Romantic emphasis on nature for the place of philosophy in the Hegelian schema). See Axel Honneth, *The Pathologies of Individual Freedom: Hegel's Social Theory*, trans. Ladislaus Löb (Princeton: Princeton University Press, 2010) and *Das Recht der Freiheit: Grundriß einer demokratischen Sittlichkeit* (Frankfurt: Suhrkamp, 2011).

63. Hartmut Rosa, *Weltbeziehungen im Zeitalter der Beschleunigung. Umrisse einer neuen Gesellschaftskritik* (Frankfurt: Suhrkamp, forthcoming).

In Place of a Preface

1. Cf. Erhard 1997.

2. Linder 1970:1.

3. Russell 1985.

4. Cited in Putnam 1997:xiii.

5. The best known may be Heinrich Böll's (1963) version in the "Anekdote zur Senkung der Arbeitsmoral."

6. The terms *horizon of expectation* and *space of experience* come from the work of the German historian Reinhart Koselleck. Wherever they appear in the text they are translations of the respective German terms that are in parentheses in the sentence preceding this note. The horizon of expectation is essentially the set of possibilities, and associated judgments on the relative probability of the possibilities' realization that one holds regarding the future. The space of experience, on the other hand, is the set of things, events, and situations that

one has experienced in the past and has stored up in memory. There are individual and collective applications of both these closely interrelated concepts. See Koselleck's essay "'Space of Experience' and 'Horizon of Expectation': Two Historical Categories," in Koselleck 2004:255–77. —TRANS.

7. I will generally translate *Zeitstrukturen* as "temporal structures," but often I use the variant "time structures" for reasons of style and euphony, i.e., to avoid repetitiveness. *Time structure* is a term found in economics and management literature, so in some ways it is an already established English expression that can be used for this purpose. However, *temporal structure* follows the precedent of related, more widespread, and established terms in sociology and political science like *material structure* and *social structure* (e.g., one doesn't say *society structure*). On the other hand, *time horizon* is definitely part of established English usage, and *temporal horizon* would sound needlessly stilted. —TRANS.

Introduction

1. On techniques of domination, see Levine 2006:101ff.; Lauer 1981; Virilio 2006; and Bourdieu 1977. Overviews concerning class distinctions are offered by Lauer 1981 and Bergmann 1983:466ff. On time and multiculturalism, see Levine 2006 and Marschall 1997; Lauer (1981:135ff.) discusses the connection of temporal structures and development. For gender relations, cf. Hufton and Kravaritou 1996; Shaw 1997; or Tronto 2003. Garhammer 1999 analyzes the relationship between temporal patterns and welfare regimes. For the last three themes, cf. Zerubavel 1979; Brown 1998; and Flaherty 1999:63ff., 152ff.

2. For an example representative of many, see Zerubavel 1981:ixff.

3. Lauer 1981; Bergmann 1983; cf. further Adam 1990:13; and Nowotny 1993:8.

4. Bergmann 1983:462. Cf. Adam 1990:5f.

5. Cf., for example, Lauer 1981; Garhammer 1999; Nassehi 1993; Adam 1990; Giddens 1987a; Nowotny 1993; or also Elias 1988. See further Maurer 1992 for a more recent survey of work in the area.

6. Examples of this kind are the aforementioned works of Bergmann 1983; Maurer 1992; and Lauer 1981.

7. See Geißler 1999; Levine 2006; Reheis 1998; Gronemeyer 1996; Eberling 1996; Backhaus/Bonus 1998; Sennett 1998; Zoll 1988a; Klein, Kiem, and Ette 2000.

8. Nassehi 1993; Luhmann 1990a; Rammstedt 1975; Sandbothe 1998.

9. Adam 1990:14f. Unfortunately Adam's own attempt to create a unified grand theory using theories of time drawn from social science, natural science, and philosophy and to make this the basis of a new social theory does not change this lamentable situation very much. Her book leaves the reader puzzled as to how the accumulated theses from varied disciplines and schools can be

put together into anything other than a vague, rather esoteric holism à la David Bohm, Rupert Sheldrake, or Fritjof Capra. In the meantime, the social-scientific relevance of, say, reflections on quantum physics remains (as so often happens in popularizing literature) much more of an assumption than a demonstrated fact.

10. Anthony Giddens declares that this state of affairs is a fundamental misfortune of the social sciences, i.e., that they have split up into diachronic, historical disciplines on the one hand and synchronic, structure-analyzing ones that are forgetful of time on the other (1987a, 1995:17ff.). In this way they became blind to the fact that societies constantly extend over portions of space-time in order to reproduce themselves (*Time-Space-Distanciation*). Despite the distinction, drawn from Henri-Louis Bergson, Alfred Schütz, Martin Heidegger, and Fernand Braudel, between three simultaneous temporal forms of social life (time as *durée*, *Dasein*, and *Longue-Durée*, cf. Giddens 1987a:144ff.), time ultimately remains a simple physical given or *one* dimension of society in Giddens's theory of structuration. In this way his concept of society ultimately becomes static again. See Berman (1988:495); and Hans Joas's critique of Giddens's concept of time (1992:214ff.).

Time is also constitutive for social systems according to Niklas Luhmann. The most elaborate social-scientific engagements with time have undoubtedly emerged in the context of his systems theory (Rammstedt 1975; Bergmann 1981; and above all Nassehi 1993). The third category of investigations in the sociology of time captures Nassehi's book perfectly: it begins with a journey through the philosophy of time (inspired by Luhmann) and ends with an abstract, esoteric systems-theoretical concept of time that can only be fruitfully applied to the kinds of questions I am asking in marginal respects. In chapters 1.2a and 7.3, I will discuss the systems-theoretical perspective in detail.

11. Compare the debate concerning McTaggart's (1908) influential thesis of the unreality of time. For a literature review, see Zimmerli and Sandbothe (1993:304f.) and, further, Browning and Myers 1998.

12. Tabboni 2001:6.

13. Augustine, book 11, chapter 14, 239.

14. Bourdieu 1977:9.

15. Compare, for instance, Willems and Hahn 1999 or Keupp et al. 1999; see also Rosa 2002a:267f.

16. For instance, growth-oriented capitalist societies require the majority of the actors operating within them to understand themselves as producers and consumers who are always willing and able to step up their production and consumption (and not as, say, self-sufficient, world-renouncing ascetics or artists or as political citizens or warriors), even though the political-legal possibility

of orienting themselves differently in the conduct of their lives is naturally left open. On this point, in greater detail, see Rosa 1999a).

17. Cf. Habermas 2003:1ff. The classical formulation of the quintessential ethical question, "How do I want to live?" can be reformulated without any loss of meaning as "How do I want to spend my time?" and even here one sees that this cannot be a purely individualistic ethical question: "my time" is always social time — its beat, rhythms, perspective, and horizons are not at my disposal. The question concerning time is therefore always also a political question. Temporal structures determine how we live together and have an ineradicably normative character (cf. Lauer 1981:86ff.).

18. Rammstedt 1975.

19. "Always already" is the standard translation for the adverbial phrase *immer schon*, which in recent German philosophy typically denotes a structure of cognition, action, and experience that is "transcendental" in the Kantian sense of being a condition of possibility for a given cognitive-practical activity or experiential capacity. This usage of the phrase stems from certain formulations of Heidegger in his influential work *Being and Time* (2008). In the text the idea is that even if in a very abstract sense the representations of past and future have a transcendental status in human experience, i.e., all human beings mark some such distinction, the specific content and interrelationships of the two sides of the distinction vary quite considerably, such that a purely "a priori" or transcendental philosophical approach to them is ruled out. One must instead investigate historically the actual and quite different ways people in various places and times have fleshed out the abstract categories of past and future. —TRANS.

20. On the concepts of the space of experience and the horizon of expectation and their gradual separation in the early modern period, cf. Koselleck 2004:255ff.

21. The telos of history can then be either fulfilled in the irruption of a radically different temporality at the "end of time" (as in the Kingdom of God or, more weakly, in the time of the classless society) or realized in historical time itself; cf. chapter 11.2.

22. Cf., for instance, Zerubavel (1981:112f.); Adam (1990:133ff.). An "occasional" time consciousness can also predominate in high-modern cultures, for instance, under the influence of drugs or in extreme exceptional situations. It is accompanied by a feeling that the flow of time is standing still or has come to a stop. A survivor of the terrorist attack on the World Trade Center on 9/11 reported the following of his experience immediately after the plane had flown into the building and caused the tower to wobble, "The building must not have moved like that for very long, maybe fifteen or twenty seconds, but it felt like forever," and then of his perception of time on the way down from

the seventieth floor through the (repeatedly jammed) stairwell: "I couldn't tell how long we'd been in there. Time had vanished. There was no time. There was only descent. There was only counting [the floors — H.R.] and waiting and counting, circling around again and again" (Charles 2002:31f.).

23. Durkheim had already formulated the thesis in the second part of his introduction to *The Elementary Forms of Religious Life* (1995 [1912]); as did Sorokin and Merton 1937; Gurvitch 1963; Bergmann 1983:471ff.; Elias 1988; and today, for instance, Giddens 1987a; Luhmann 1980:260f.; or Nassehi 1993:249ff. For instructive empirical examples of different forms of time consciousness, see, e.g., Evans-Pritchard 1969:94ff.; Dux 1989; or Bourdieu 1977.

24. Elias 1988:122. Cf. Nowotny: "like a test fluid flows through the body to demonstrate the presence and pathways of particular substances, so runs . . . social time through a life, however individually distinct and directed it may be. For time, which is a deeply collective, symbolic product of human coordination and meaning ascription, retains its reference to other persons even in moments of markedly individual feeling" (1993:9). In a similar way, Durkheim saw in socially constructed, structure-dependent concepts of time central and indispensable categories of the understanding, or *necessary ideas*, that individuals cannot do without. Somewhat like Kant's a priori forms of intuition, though sociohistorically variable, these categories serve more to shape the dispositional structure of consciousness than its cognitive content.

25. Elias 2000:379.

26. Cf. Foucault 1995. For this reason, Tabboni views norms of time as collective norms "par excellence" (2001:18); and Lauer conjectures that implicit temporal norms are of such great consequence that they can lead to traumatic psychological disturbances and even complete spatiotemporal disorientation in nonconforming individuals (1981:72f.).

27. Thus the institution of the prison is almost defined by the dispossesion of time; there the only relevant question consists in a monotonous, "How much (longer)?" (Brown 1998). On the strict time regime in hospitals, cf. the informative study by Zerubavel 1979. Countless studies of schools demonstrate that temporal discipline plays an outstanding role in almost all educational matters: the child is compelled to wake up early in accordance with the clock, to show up regularly, to sit still for timed periods, to regulate and delay need gratification, to learn in a planned fashion, and to master time pressures in test situations. On this and temporal disciplining in the industrial revolution, see chapter 7.1.

28. Cf. Ahlheit 1988; Giddens 1987a:144ff.

29. Following Bergson and Schütz, Giddens describes this time as "durée" and interprets it as reversible time. Adam rightly criticizes this, pointing out that ac-

tually the activities are recursive and not time itself. Repetitiveness (of events) and reversibility (of time) should not be confused (Adam 1990:24ff.).

30. While the "being-in-time" of actors is repeatedly spoken of here, this should in no way be taken as implying an as it were ontological time independent of subjects. As may be already sufficiently clear, I share the view that time is to a great extent historically and culturally variable. It is first constituted as determinately and qualitatively capable of being experienced in social contexts. Nevertheless, as I have tried to show, it confronts acting subjects as a solid facticity and, so to speak, a fact of nature. From the (individual or collective) actor perspective, then, human beings are always "placed in time."

31. Robert Lauer has suggested that five variables should be distinguished in the analysis of temporal structures of social phenomena (1981:28ff.): 1. the *periodicity* or the rhythm of events; 2. the *speed* of processes and changes; 3. their *synchronization* (internal and "external," i.e., with respect to other events/actions); 4. the *duration* of actions, events, or conditions; and last, 5. their *sequence*. From the *actor* perspective, there are also temporal *orientations* or *perspectives* to consider, i.e., the weighting and specific quality of past, present, and future. Weighting and specific quality are definitely not identical in their effects: two actors or groups may agree in orienting their actions to the future, but this future might be dominated for one group by an approaching Second Coming, and for the other by developments in computer technology, which amounts to a significant difference in temporal perspective. I hold this categorization to be heuristically useful and thus in what follows I will occasionally rely on it. Similar distinctions can be found in Adam (1990:106); Zerubavel (1981:1f.); and Gurvitch (1963:174f.).

32. For a more detailed treatment, see Garhammer 1999:28ff.

33. "The fact that there is a time for each of many different activities . . . keeps the claims of each from interfering with those of the others. In fact, a society so complex as ours probably could not function without relatively rigid time scheduling," writes Parsons (1951:302); cf. Zerubavel 1981, especially 31ff.

34. Cf. MacIntyre (2007:208ff.), Taylor (1994:615), also, in further detail, Rosa (1998:166ff.). This connection between life history and "History" becomes very clear, for instance, when older interviewees from the former East Germany recount their life history against the background of two regime changes. One sees immediately in that context that after the upheaval of 1989 the linkage of past, present, and future occurred, and had to occur, in a different way than it had before.

35. Cf. Blumenberg 1986; Gronemeyer 1996; and also chapter 7.2.

36. The significance and socially constitutive role of sacred time has been worked out particularly well by Durkheim and successors like Hubert and Mauss

(Watts Miller 2000); see, further, Achtner, Kunz, and Walter 1998; as well as Zerubavel 1981.

37. Zerubavel 1981:101ff.; Eliade 1991 [1954].

38. Zerubavel describes the Jewish Sabbath, for example, in accordance with Durkheim and Eliade, as a "cultural recess" from, or standing still of, the continuous flow of profane time (1981:112ff.). He impressively lays out the diverse ways the holiday becomes a period and institution of striking "deceleration" that is consciously set off from the hectic time of the work week: through the kind of clothing and walk, through forbidden and prescribed activities, through the lengthening of mealtimes, etc. (ibid., 121f.).

39. Virilio 2006; cf. Wallis 1970; and Rifkin 1987, who describes the *war for time* as the most fundamental conflict in human history.

40. See the striking arsenal of temporal strategies laid out by Bourdieu (1977:7).

41. See, for instance, the contributions in Zoll 1988a or Rinderspacher 2000.

42. See in greater detail Zerubavel 1981, 1985.

43. Zerubavel 1981:70ff., 1985:130ff.

44. Thompson 1967; compare also on this point, in greater detail, chapter 7.1.

45. Cf. for instance the impressive literature, with no fewer than twenty-two suggested definitions of contemporary society, in Beniger 1986:4f. A good overview of current diagnoses of the time can be found in the anthology edited by Schimank and Volkmann 2000.

46. Hamlet already complained that "the time is out of joint" (Shakespeare 1991: 188, act 1, scene 5) and thereby anticipated the experience of time of coming generations, the looming alterations in the structure of time being registered by the highly sensitive poetry of Shakespeare (cf. Harvey 1990:247).

47. See Koselleck 1989:321, 336f., further 2000; and Achtner, Kunz, and Walter 1998:5.

48. Brunner, Conze, and Koselleck 1972–1997.

    From here on out, I will translate *Sattelzeit* as "epochal threshold," though the literal meaning is that which is indicated in the text. I am following the precedent of other translators of Reinhart Koselleck, the most prominent member of the *Geschichtliche Grundbegriffe* project. —TRANS.

49. For evidence, see chapter 2.1.

50. Conrad (1999:9). An even more pointed formulation is given by Thomas H. Eriksen: "Modernity *is* speed" (2001:159).

51. Freyermuth (2000:75). In the same vein, the American James Gleick, in his best seller *Faster: The Acceleration of Just About Everything* (1999), observes the comprehensive acceleration of our everyday life in work, free time, and even love life, while matching this is the German government's view that *acceleration* is at the top of the list of trends leading the way into the society of the future

(cf. the advertisement 'Den Wandel gestalten,' signed by Joschka Fischer and Gerhard Schröder, in *Der Spiegel*, January 17, 2000, 47–49).

52. Breuer 1988:309.

53. Jameson 1998:50.

54. Cf. Fukuyama 1992 or Gehlen 1994.

55. On this see, in further detail, Rosa 1999c, d.

56. Rosa is referring to a German translation of Virilio (1999) that translated Virilio's French term *inertie polar* with *rasender Stillstand*. Rosa makes the latter term a name for a central theorem of his theory of acceleration, and I have translated it consistently as "frenetic standstill." —TRANS.

57. As Joachim Radkau (1998) shows, in his brilliant study on the age of nervousness, the diagnosis of "neurasthenia" as a consequence of an overstimulating pace of life was widely made at the beginning of the twentieth century (of interest here as well is Simmel 1995 [1903]), while in our own times a very similar form of "hurry sickness" was discovered in the U.S., with the same supposed causes (Levine 2006:21–22; on the "yuppie flu" as a diseaselike reaction to stress, cf. Harvey 1990:287).

58. Conrad 1999:16f. Cf. in more detail Lepenies 1981. The main problem of the protagonists in Douglas Coupland's novel, *Generation X*, whose descriptive subtitle is "Tales for an Accelerated Culture" is also this uneventful boredom *after the end of history*, as it is explicitly called in the text.

59. Cf. chapter 10.3.

60. Ende 1973. The elegant book title, *In Search of Gained Time* (*Auf der Suche nach der gewonnenen Zeit*), trenchantly expresses this paradox (Auer, Geißler, and Schauer 1990). The close connection between the heightened perception of "rushing" time and a condition of debilitating standstill, even on the level of everyday experience, may perhaps be made clear by the following lines of Michel Quoist, which Staffan B. Linder (1970) uses to introduce his book (cf. the following note): "Good-bye, Sir, excuse me, I haven't time / I'll come back, I can't wait, I haven't time / I must end this letter—I haven't time / I'd love to help you, but I haven't time / I can't accept, having no time / I can't think, I can't read, I'm swamped, I haven't time / I'd like to pray, but I haven't time."

    The original title of the German-language work by Auer, Geißler, and Schauer, appearing in parentheses here, alludes to Proust's great work, *A la recherche du temps perdu*, the title of which is standardly translated in German as *Auf der Suche nach der verlorenen Zeit*. So I have given a similarly allusive title that references the standard English translation of Proust's title. —TRANS.

61. Linder (1970) postulates an "axiom," according to which, for reasons of rational time allocation, there is a virtually necessary inverse proportional relationship between temporal well-being (*Zeitwohlstand*) and material well-being (*Güter-*

wohlstand), such that the modernization process inevitably becomes a process in which societies of surplus time are transformed into societies of time deficit.

62. Robinson and Godbey 1999:33.

63. The acceleration-induced problem of translation or synchronization can be made clear with very simple examples: as a rule almost every citizen wants, on the one hand, to be served as quickly as possible as a customer or client (in the train station, at a café, at the doctor's, on the telephone information hotline, etc.) and on the other hand, however, to have more time and less stress at work (i.e., as the provider of services). One cannot fail to see that this idea—*everything should go as fast as possible, so I can have more time*—is self-contradictory at the collective level.

64. Simmel 1992a [1897]: 228; also Lauer 1981:70ff.

65. Such bifurcating developments are clearly what Gurvitch has in mind when he distinguishes between social temporal forms like "time remaining behind itself," "time alternating between advance and backwardness" or "time in advance of itself," without, however, sufficiently clarifying their structural basis (1963:176ff.). The division in social structures of time and temporal perspectives that becomes clear in these "temporal forms" does not infrequently result in a revolutionary upheaval whose "explosive time" makes possible a realignment of temporal structures (ibid., 178).

66. Richard Sennett is a prominent proponent of this thesis (1998); see also Fritz Reheis (1998) as well as numerous authors in Backhaus and Bonus (1998). Robinson and Godbey also conjecture that "internal," i.e., actor-related, and "external," i.e., systemically observable, time perspectives have come apart (1999:304).

67. Ahlheit (1988); cf. Sennett (1998) as well as Achtner, Kunz, and Walter 1998; Lübbe 2009; Rosa 1999c.

68. Beyond this, desyncronization phenomena also occur where actors from different social strata or cultural milieus, whose temporal practices and orientations are palpably different, encounter each other. The *noncontemporaneity of the contemporaneous* is without a doubt one of the gravest problems of "multiculturalism" (cf. Marschall 1997).

69. See, for instance, Eberling 1996; Scheuerman 2001a; also, in detail, chapter 11.3. A further variant of these diagnoses of systemic desynchronization can be identified in investigations in the context of the ecological movement that defend the thesis that the "system of society," or the *economic* system, has become too fast for the *ecological* system of nature: the desynchronization postulate here rests on the supposition that society is not leaving nature enough time, on the one hand, to reproduce raw materials and, on the other, to recycle pollutants and waste (cf. Reheis 1998:34ff.).

70. On structural coupling, a central concept of Luhmannian systems theory, see Luhmann 1991. Two systems, A and B, that are structurally coupled will exhibit various interconnected properties: in general, no change in the state of A will lack a corresponding change in the state of B and vice versa; this mutual influence, reiterated over time, will powerfully determine the structure and process, and hence the evolution, of both A and B; and the coupling of A and B will tend to last as long as the mutual interaction of the two systems, since the decoupling of one system from other systems in its environment will in the long run imperil its own survival. To give an example: a nation's health care system and its economic system form various interconnections via prices, on the one hand, and diagnostic decisions to render treatment, on the other. This constitutes a form of structural coupling. If the health care system's operation, or other disturbing causes in its environment, e.g., the operation of the political system or the energy system, impair its coupling with the economic system, pathological and even system-endangering side effects can develop, e.g., skyrocketing costs that make treatments impossible to afford. —TRANS.

71. On this concept, cf. Beck 1997:25, note 8.

72. Beck, Giddens, and Lash 1994.

73. Wagner 1994.

74. E.g., Hörning, Ahrens, and Gerhard 1997.

75. Lyotard 1984; cf. Jameson 1998; Harvey 1990; Welsch 1994.

76. Cf. here Berger 1986.

77. Since, as I will soon explain, I assume that there is in fact a significant break in the structure and culture of modernity that can only be adequately defined in terms of a theory of acceleration, in what follows I will use the concepts of *classical modernity* and *late modernity* to identify the formations before and after the critical turning point that will be more precisely defined in the course of this work (cf. also note 79).

78. In order to overcome the usual completely arbitrary usage of terms on this point, I propose discussing *late modernity* from a structural perspective and *postmodernity* from a cultural one. To me this seems justified on two grounds: first, the debate concerning postmodernity is overwhelmingly shaped by cultural studies and philosophy and sets out from aspects of aesthetic style, intelligibility, and the malleability of the world, while the concept of *late modernity* is used more often in the context of analyses of structural alterations in modern society. Second, however, *postmodernity* naturally indicates a much stronger break in or *after* modernity than *late modernity*: the first concept implies the appearance of something qualitatively new, while the second indicates, rather, a new form of the old (i.e., modernity itself). As I would like to show in the course of the book, this corresponds exactly with my own diagnosis of a qualita-

tive cultural shift, i.e., in individual and collective self-understandings, on the basis of unchanged structural principles.

79. Cf. for instance, Jameson 1998, especially 51ff.; Jameson 1994; Welsch 1994:1ff.

80. Brose 2000:130; cf. Nowotny 1993.

81. As Jean Chesneaux therefore rightly laments, "the notion of acceleration, which originally described the condition of material bodies in motion, has gradually and unwarrantedly migrated into the sphere of social relations, and now claims to control history itself" (2000:417).

82. Breuer 1998:309. One must however reject Breuer's proposal of a disciplinary division of labor: the economic, sociological and political domains of wealth, meaning and domination are self-evidently linked together with both the roots and the effects of acceleration as tightly as can be.

83. Cf. on this Koselleck 2004 and 2000, who cites innumerable documents that diagnose a historical acceleration (his quotations also make clear just how much the aforementioned categories are treated interchangeably) and at the same time undertakes one of the very few attempts to grasp the idea of a historical acceleration in an analytically sharp way.

84. E.g., Coupland 1991.

85. Thus, for instance, Simmel 1992a [1897] or, more recently, Levine 2006.

86. Gurvitch 1963 or Schmied 1985:86ff.

87. Representative of this view are Altvater 2002:285, § 22, cf. 281; Heylighen 2001; Garhammer 1999:114; Gross 1994:155; Gleick 1999 (see his title); and Eriksen 2001:50.

88. Weber 1988. For a critical discussion of recent empirically oriented investigations of this theme, cf. my literature review, Rosa 2001a.

89. I have made use of, in particular, Garhammer 1999; Robinson and Godbey 1999; Benthaus-Apel 1995; Gershuny 1990 and 2003; as well as Holz 2000.

90. Cf., on this especially, Hörning, Ahrens, and Gerhard 1997; as well as Sennett 1998.

91. In particular, Castells 1996; Harvey 1990; and Held et al. 1999.

92. Just this "empirical saturation" of the acceleration diagnosis by means of its reformulation into verifiable hypotheses is what the circle of researchers around Reinhart Koselleck have, in his own estimation, so far failed to achieve despite intense efforts (so Koselleck in a personal letter to the author, dated November 26, 2001; cf. also Koselleck 2000).

93. Cf. on this Castells 1996:476f. Zygmunt Bauman (1998:324, 326) and, following him, Ulrich Beck (1997:102f.) speak in the same sense of a "numerically ceaselessly growing" group of "structurally superfluous persons."

94. Cf. for instance, Elchardus and Glorieux 1992; Hufton and Kravaritou 1996; Leccardi 1996; Shaw 1997.

95. Giddens 1987a:148ff., 1990.

96. Harvey 1990.

97. Cf. along with Harvey, also Schivelbusch 2000 [1977]; Waters 1995; and Robertson 1992.

98. Appadurai 1990; Castells 1996:376ff.; similarly, Bauman 2000, especially 1ff.

99. Cf. Kant 1998 as well as the second part of the introduction to Durkheim 1995 [1912].

100. Cf. for example, Schaltenbrand 1988:46ff.

101. Cf. Piaget 1980.

102. Cf. for instance, Elias 1988; Dux 1989; Evans-Pritchard 1969; Giddens 1990:17ff. At the same time, our temporal ordering concepts normally follow a spatial semantics (*before* and *after*, etc.; cf. Schaltenbrand 1988:47).

    The semantic connection of the temporal concepts to spatial vocabulary is clearer in the German prepositions *vor* and *nach*, translated here as *before* and *after*. However, *after* bears obvious etymological relations to *aft* which is a spatial designation, as in seafaring vocabulary ("The captain is currently aft" or "What's the situation aft?") and *before* of course is (or was) used in obviously spatial locutions such as "He stood before me and wept," not to mention a similar etymological connection to *fore* which is evidently spatial (cf. *forwards, to the fore*). —TRANS.

103. On the observation that in modernity the idea of movement gains priority in rank over inertia and hence time comes to dominate in its relation to space, cf. Harvey 1990:205. At the same time, the need for explanation and justification is thereby displaced in favor of movement: since Thomas Hobbes, it is *inertia* that requires justification, as, for instance, Otthein Rammstedt remarks (1975:47ff.).

104. Bauman gives a similar formulation: "In the modern struggle between time and space, space was the solid and stolid, unwieldy and inert side, capable of waging only a defensive, trench war—being an obstacle to the resilient advances of time. Time was the active and dynamic side in the battle, the side always on the offensive: the invading, conquering and colonizing force" (2000:9).

105. Harvey 1990:240, cf. 270ff. and 293.

106. For a systematic justification of this thesis providing strong empirical plausibility for it, see Linder 1970; cf. also Lauer 1981.

107. Cf., representative of many here, Adam 1990:89f. or Nowotny 1993:157ff.

108. Adam 1990:154; Geißler 1999:152f.; cf. on this in more detail Rosa 2001a:341ff.

109. On the extraordinarily complex way in which our theoretical interpretations of the world and our social institutions and practices mutually influence one another, cf. Rosa 2004b.

110. The most profound philosophical justification for this connection was without a doubt made by Heidegger (1992 [1924], 2008).

111. Thus, even in the title of the empirical analysis of United States time use data by Robinson and Godbey (1999), *Time for Life*, suggests the quite Aristotelian idea that alongside time for (re)production and consumption there also can and must be time for "real life" (*das wirkliche Leben*). Cf. further Gershuny 2003:242ff.; Sennett 1998; Gronemeyer 1996; Reheis 1998; or Nowotny 1993, especially 135ff. In fact, it is more difficult to find studies in which the ethical dimension plays *no* role than the reverse.

112. In "Four Levels of Self-Interpretation" (Rosa 2004b), I have attempted to explore the conditions under which a "successful life" is possible on the basis of a systematic model of coherent ethical agency that accords with criteria used by subjects themselves. Such conceptions of successful life are generally explicitly formulated and brought into a system of reflective convictions only to a very small extent. To a much greater degree, they underlie our feelings, values, and decisions in an *implicit* fashion and are reflected in our individual and collective narratives, symbols, and doctrines.

1. From Love of Movement to Law of Acceleration

1. Conrad 1999; Berman 1988; Borscheid 2004; Gronemeyer 1996; Kern 1983; Harvey 1990.
2. Conrad 1999:9.
3. Berman 1988:15.
4. In Faust's restlessness and disquietude, Marianne Gronemeyer also sees the paradigmatic expressions of the modern ideal of life (1996:121ff.).
5. Cited Koselleck 2004:241 (translation emended).
6. Berman 1988:294f.
7. On the latter, cf. especially Osten 2003, 2004. In a letter of 1825, Goethe describes the new age with the neologism *velociferian* and remarks: "I hold the fact that nothing is allowed to ripen, that one eats up what came before in the next moment, squanders the day in the day, and thus always lives from hand to mouth without bringing anything to fruition, to be the greatest malady of our time" (Goethe 1825:37; cf. in detail Osten 2004).

   The quotation comes from a letter written to Goethe's great-nephew Georg Heinrich Ludwig Nicolovius in 1825, for which I have not been able to find a published English translation. —TRANS.
8. Nietzsche 1996:132 (§ 282), 133 (§ 285). See also Osten 2003 and 2004.
9. Nietzsche 1997:108 ("On the Use and Abuse of History for Life," § 9). Cf. Frisby 1988:28ff.
10. Nietzsche 1997:148 ("Schopenhauer as Educator," § 4).
11. Baudelaire 1975:37 (translation altered). David Frisby (1988) also sees the fundamental characteristic of modernity in this Baudelairean definition of

modernity as the *transitory, fleeting and contingent*, taken up by Benjamin (1980).

12. Cf. Baudelaire 1964:82–84. On this see also Berman 1988:138f. and 142; Frisby 1988:14–20.

13. For Stephen Kern, modern culture is shaped by a multidimensional alteration of the experience of time and space as such. However, it is no coincidence that in the center of his cultural-historical study, at the interface between his investigations of the transformed experience of time and the analyses of the perception of space, stands a chapter on (increasing) *speed*, with regard to which Kern explicitly observes that it represents a decisive link and point of intersection between spatial and temporal structures (1983:3, 189ff.).

14. Above all in his famous picture of 1844, *Rain, Steam and Speed*—The Great Western Railway; cf. Braun 2001:87ff.

15. Cf. Conrad 1999:82f.

16. "Ford . . . fragmented tasks and distributed them in space. . . . In effect, he used a certain form of spatial organization to accelerate turnover time of capital in production. Time could then be accelerated (speed-up) by virtue of the control established through organizing and fragmenting the spatial order of production" (Harvey 1990:266f.). Cf. here, for instance, the dictum of Jean Metzinger's that "the Cubists . . . have allowed themselves to move round the object, in order to give, under the control of intelligence, a concrete representation of it, made up of several successive aspects. Formerly a picture took possession of space, now it reigns also in time" (cited in Kern 1983:145).

17. The same appears to be true of the speed of dialogue in the theater. Eriksen reports that the length of a performance of Ibsen's *Rosmersholm* dropped from four to two hours in less than a century (2001:49).

18. This is not without a certain irony, since Beethoven's metronome indications for tempo are notoriously fast, which led to speculations that his metronome might have been defective, i.e., too slow, or that he might have taken two beats to be one (cf. Hagmann 2003); on the almost revolutionary, dynamic temporality of, for instance, the *Eroica* and the new experience of a "time that races away" made possible by it, see also Brinkmann 2000.

19. Cf. Lübbe 2009.

20. Cf. Kern 1983:124.

21. Volkwein 2000.

22. Gaines 1998:203 and Volkwein 2000:403ff., esp. 407.

23. Cf. Kemper 1995; Schneider and Geißler 1999; Gleick 1999; Großklaus 1997:11ff.

24. Cited in Koselleck 2009:113f.

25. "What changes must occur in our experience and in our thoughts! Even the basic concepts of time and space have become unstable. Space has been killed

by the railroad, and only time remains," writes Heine in 1843 (Heine 1974:449), and, in another passage, "A new period of world history is beginning. . . . We merely note that our entire existence is being carried away, hurled forth, that new relations, joys and tribulations await us, and the unknown works a frightful charm, alluring and at the same time frightening" (ibid., 448f.)

26. On Proust's confrontation with the heightened tempo of social change and the "shrinkage of space" through the new technologies of movement, cf. also Conrad 1999:91ff.

27. Also noteworthy in this connection is Robert Musil's *Man Without Qualities*, whose protagonist is characteristically introduced with a (stop)watch in his hand as he counts pedestrians and cars: "he was gauging their speeds, their angles, all the living forces of mass hurtling past that drew the eye to follow them like lightning, holding on, letting go. . . . If all those leaps of attention, flexings of eye muscles, fluctuations of the psyche, if all the effort it takes for a man just to hold himself upright within the flow of traffic on a busy street could be measured. . . . The grand total would surely dwarf the energy needed by Atlas to hold up the world, and one could then estimate the enormous undertaking it is nowadays merely to be a person who does nothing at all" (1995:6–7). Interestingly, the compulsion to count is among the symptoms of *hurry sickness* (Levine 2006:21f.), which gains a certain intuitive plausibility in our time when some meticulously follow even the smallest change in the numbers on their blood pressure device, while others do the same with hundredths and sometimes thousandths of a second between athletes, and still others follow the most minimal trend changes in the stock markets with the help of the Internet, television, and newspapers.

28. Harvey 1990:240ff., 267, 284ff., 305ff.

29. Breuer 1988:323; on the meaning of "accident" in Virilio, cf. Crogan 2000; and Virilio 1998c:183ff.

30. Cf. also Kern 1983:109ff.; Conrad 1999:91ff. On shock and trauma, cf. the interesting reflections of Schivelbusch 2000 [1977]:142ff.

31. Cited in Levine 2006:206.

32. On "bicycle face," cf. Kern 1983:111; on the social struggles surrounding the railroad, see, inter alia, Schivelbusch 2000 [1977]:35ff. and 106ff.; cf. further Levine 2006:65ff.

33. With respect to television, this type of thought has continued even into the present. Thus Robert Putnam (1995) traces the loss of social capital in the U.S. and other developed countries back to the damaging influence of TV.

34. So, for example, the neurologist Willy Hellpach records at the beginning of the twentieth century not only an "overwhelming increase in the speed of mental processes" but also, at the same time, an entire series of phenomena

of slow-down running parallel to this: "it essentially takes a longer time for us to be raised. . . . Nearly all civilized peoples (*Kulturvölker*) eat slower, more politely than most 'primitive' peoples ('*Natur*'-*Völker*); during the nineteenth century with its furious acceleration of transportation almost all careers have slowed down, advance in one's profession has become more of a trudge" (cited in Radkau 1998:25; cf. Kern 1983:136).

35. It is important to note that the heightened perception of processes of dynamization, i.e., the appearance of "discourses of acceleration" can by all means be out of phase with materially observable processes of acceleration; indeed, such a displacement and partial independence is frankly to be expected. However, it appears indubitable that there is a strong relationship of interdependence between discourse and "material" reality; the assumption that acceleration might be a purely discursive phenomenon without a material experiential basis is groundless and can also be refuted with empirical evidence.

36. "For every speed lover like Marinetti there were thousands who preferred the way rivers wandered and the way barges drifted on them. The Danube never seemed so deliciously slow until he [Marinetti —H. R.] suggested speeding it up" (Kern 1983:129f.; for Marinetti see 1966 [1909]:26 and 2009 [1916]).

37. Benjamin 1982:532; Heintel 1999:231ff.

38. Stephen Kern therefore concentrates his analysis on the years 1880–1918, and Harvey follows him insofar as he postulates a new round of time-space-compression for this period; for Marshall Berman as well the modernization processes enters a new, heightened phase around 1900 (Berman 1988:17).

39. Cited in Koselleck 2000:178.

40. Adams 1999 [1904]:411f.

41. Radkau 1998; cf. Kern 1983:124ff.

42. The diagnosis of a new wave of acceleration is also made on all sides in the social sciences, although there is just as much unclarity over its beginning as there is over its predecessor: Castells (1996:5), for instance, discerns an information technology revolution that he categorically places on a level with the industrial revolution and dates from the 1970s, while, for example, Thomas H. Eriksen (2001:2), who interprets the same revolution still more precisely as an *revolution of acceleration*, places its beginning at the second half of the 1990s. Harvey is very precise about the matter when he dates the beginning of a new round of time-space-compression to the year 1972 (1990:vii). Cf. on this as well, chapter 9.

43. Harvey 1990:287; Levine 2006:21f.; Ulmer and Schwarzburd 1996; Ehrenberg 2000.

44. Cf. for instance Lothar J. Seiwert's (2000) best seller "If You're In A Hurry, Go Slow: New Time Management in an Accelerated World" (*Wenn Du es eilig*

hast, gehe langsam: Das neue Zeitmanagement in einer beschleunigten Welt), already in its fifth edition.

45. Reheis 1998; Nadolny 1987; Heintel 1999; Glotz 1998.

46. Compare Kay Kirchmann's comprehensive study on the interrelationship of media development and acceleration in the modernization process in which she juxtaposes the apologists of medial acceleration around Peter Weibel, whose tone is reminiscent of the futurists, to the apocalyptic soothsayers about the new tempo around Paul Virilio (Kirchmann 1998:16ff.).

47. Koselleck 2000:152f.

48. When David Harvey expressly warns of the "geopolitical dangers" he sees issuing from the increased speed of time-space-compression, while he defines this compression itself as acceleration, as we have seen, he is thereby postulating nothing other than an *acceleration of acceleration* (Harvey 1990:305).

49. Blumenberg 1986; Nowotny 1993:47ff.; Gronemeyer 1996. Cf. Koselleck (2000:157): "One of the findings of our epochal threshold is that before the invention of the steam engine, the mechanical loom, the telegraph, which accelerated transportation, textile production (then the leading economic sector), and the transmission of news, *an increasing velocity of life as a whole was already being registered*" (my emphasis —H. R.).

50. Berman 1988:17; Harvey 1990:242f.

51. Cf., for instance, Schings 1977; also chapter 10.3.

I have here translated *Steigerung* with "escalation," although in many other contexts "increase" or "heightening" are appropriate and have been used. For instance, when translating the terms *Komplexitätssteigerung* or *Steigerung der Komplexität* from sociological systems theory, "heightening of complexity" has often been used. I have chosen to use "escalation" for contexts in which Rosa is referring to a central concept of his theory or making a theoretically central claim related to that concept. I have done this for at least four reasons: first, it preserves semantic connections with English words that refer to related social phenomena such as "to scale up" and "scaling up," while also bearing the meaning of a quantitative increase; second, it has a nice semantic connection to the down-escalator effect of the "slipping slopes" phenomenon Rosa discusses in chapter 4; third, it draws on the use of the term to refer to arms races in international relations and, more generally, to "arms-race" type processes that are classic examples of collectively irrational outcomes resulting from individually rational action in specific scenarios of strategic interaction, and the functioning of the escalatory principles of acceleration and growth in the modern spiral of acceleration is a species of this genus; last, insofar as it has a slightly unexpected ring in the given passage of the text it serves to highlight and mark out a specifically theoretical idea, as opposed to the anodyne and unremarkable connotations of "increase," which in nontheoretical contexts might otherwise serve equally well, while it avoids the overly unexpected ring that "heightening" would have. I will include the original term *Steigerung* in parentheses for the first few occasions of this specifically theoretical context. Thereafter, I assume the reader will have become accustomed to the intended meaning. Since Rosa is drawing on Simmel to point out one of the key phenomena that he aims to explain in his theory of acceleration, it seemed appropriate to reflect this by translating Simmel's use of the word to indicate its connection to central aspects of Rosa's own theory. —TRANS.

52. Conrad 1999:17. On the social-discursive and historical location of melancholia, see also Lepenies 1981.

53. Cf. on this side of the dialectical reversal from frenzied change to pregnant standstill, also Frisby 1988:11–37.

54. Cf. Conrad 1999:17; also Radkau 1998.

55. Cf. in more detail Rosa 1999c and, in addition, Rushkoff 1994.

56. Coupland 1991:17.

57. Cf. for example Frisby 1988:2.

58. *The Communist Manifesto*, in Marx and Engels 1978:476 (translation altered).

59. Ibid., 477.

60. Cf. Marx 1976:chapters 1.1, 10, 15.3, 17, and 19–21; on this see also Postone 1996; and Giddens 1987a:149ff, 1995a:129ff.

61. On "escalatory" and "escalation" as translations of *Steigerung*, see my discussion at note 51. —TRANS.

62. Weber 2001:xxxi.

63. Weber thus attempts to show how this form of ascetic orientation toward time could unfold in the context of Puritanism by, for example, citing the doctrines of the Presbyterian Richard Baxter, for whom "waste of time is thus the first and in principal the deadliest of sins" (ibid., 104f.). The span of life is "infinitely short and precious to make sure of one's own election. Loss of time through sociability, idle talk, luxury, even more sleep than is necessary for health, six to at most eight hours, is worthy of absolute moral condemnation" (ibid.).

64. Weber 1978; cf. Schluchter 1998.

65. Cf. Weber 1978:223ff., 956ff.; also on this Segre 2000:154.

66. Cf. for instance, chapter 2 of the second book of *On the Division of Labor in Society* (Durkheim 1997 [1893]), where Durkheim makes the "growing movements of exchange among the parts of the social mass" and the "resulting active intercourse" between them, which he describes as the heightening of the "dynamic or moral density" of society, the main cause of the advancing division of labor and thus declares it to be the driving principle of development in modern society.

67. Ibid., 421–25.
68. Luhmann 1990a:119ff., 139.
69. Ibid., 122f. (my emphasis). Cf. on the other hand, p. 137, where Luhmann interprets alterations in temporal structures as a *consequence* of social change.
70. Luhmann 1990a: 143.
71. Luhmann 1990a:137f.; cf. Luhmann 1980.
72. In the remark concerning the title of Nassehi's book, Rosa is alluding to a series of works by Niklas Luhmann whose titles in German all follow the pattern *The ___ of Society*: for instance, translated literally some of them would be *The Art of Society, The Law of Society, The Economy of Society*. The series culminates in his last two-volume magnum opus, *The Society of Society* (*Die Gesellschaft der Gesellschaft*). Given Luhmann's stated view of the centrality of time to social theory, it is surprising that not he but a follower of his wrote *The Time of Society*. —TRANS.
73. In the connected belief that instead of events appearing *in* time (considered abstractly or "absolutely"), they themselves rather produce time (and thereby in each case their own horizons of past, present and future), the most various scientific disciplines (physics, biology, psychology, sociology) appear to converge (cf. Adam 1990; Nowotny 1986:135ff.; Bergmann 1983:496f.). The meaning of this claim for the social sciences is so far completely unclear. It appears that no systematic theoretical gains can be drawn from it for an analysis of the *diachronic transformation* of temporal patterns and perspectives in modern society. Its owes its current popularity, in my view, rather to the late modern phenomena of a "temporalization of time" at the expense of a *detemporalization* of individual life and history, something which should be understood as a result of *social hyperacceleration*, as I argue in part 3.
74. Luhmann 1994 [1968].
75. Simmel 1950:409–27; cf. also Frisby 1988:77ff.
76. Simmel 1950:410f.
77. Simmel 1992a [1897]:215 as well as Simmel 2004:504.
78. Cf. Simmel 2004:407, 490.
79. Ibid., 512.
80. Ibid., 2004:511f.
81. Cf. Frisby 1988:38ff.
82. Simmel 1919:185.
83. Simmel 1992a [1897]:230ff. and 2004:515ff.
84. Simmel 2004:517 (translation emended).
85. "The lack of something definite at the centre of the soul impels us to search for momentary satisfaction in ever new stimulations, sensations and external activities. Thus it is that we become entangled in the instability and helpless-

ness that manifests itself as the tumult of the metropolis, as the mania for travelling, as the wild pursuit of competition and as the typically modern disloyalty with regard to taste, style, opinions and personal relationships" (Simmel 2004:490).

86. Cf. Frisby 1988:75f.; Radkau 1998; Simmel 1995 [1903].
87. Schneider and Geißler 1999; Weibel 1987.
88. Sennett 1998; Garhammer 2001.
89. Myerson 2001; Eriksen 2001.
90. Cf. for instance the contributions in Backhaus and Bonus 1998.
91. Exemplary here are, for instance, Gleick 1999 or Gronemeyer 1996.
92. For a critical literature review, see Rosa 2001a.
93. Above all, Virilio 2006, cf. also 1998b.
94. Virilio 2006:27f.
95. See Virilio 1993:7ff., 17f.; cf. also Breuer 1988.
96. Virilio 1999 as well as his reflections on "escape velocity" in Virilio 1997:119ff.
97. Reheis 1998:35ff.
98. Ibid., 62, 83.
99. Cf. for a critique of Reheis in greater detail, Rosa 2001a:350ff.
100. Kirchmann 1998.
101. Van der Loo and van Reijen 1997:30ff.
102. Cf. for instance Parsons 1971:4–28, as well as an attempt to make the view clearer in von Adriaansens 1980.
103. An alternative analytic grid of *institutional* dimensions of modernization has been proposed by Anthony Giddens (1990:59ff., cf. 1996). According to his grid, industrialization, capitalization, the formation of the surveillance apparatus of the national state, and the development of a military with a monopoly of violence are the main characteristics of modernity. Indicative here is the fact that contrary to his assertion that temporal structures are fundamental for his theory of structuration (1995a:90), and contrary to his observation of a growing time-space distanciation that results in a "disembedding" of time and space in modernity, temporal structures are not taken into account in Giddens's categorial framework of modernity. The dimensions of capitalism and industrialism distinguished by him both appear in my schema as elements of the process of domestication (together they determine the form of the social process of exchange with nature), and while the national state and the military, as I would like to show in chapter 8, of course played an important "maieutic" role in unleashing the modern dynamic of cumulation (*Steigerung*), nevertheless they cannot be viewed as part of its indispensable structural elements.
104. Cf., inter alia, Habermas 1984, 1987a, or 1987b.
105. Horkheimer and Adorno 2002.

106. Van der Loo and van Reijen also point out this inherently paradoxical nature of the fundamental processes of modernization (1997:36ff.). However, they identify no countertendencies to the four main developments, but rather see these as *in themselves* contradictory: differentiation thus displays at once elements of both enlargement of standards and shrinking of standards (130ff.), rationalization is characterized by the contradictory principles of pluralization and generalization (176ff.), individualization processes lead as much to greater individual independence as they do to stronger dependency (216f.), and domestication finally means at the same time (physical) deconditioning and (social and psychological) reconditioning (260ff.).

107. Simmel 1992b [1908]:791ff. For a similar diagnosis of more recent data, cf. for instance Riesman, Denney, and Glazer 2001 [1950].

108. Cf. on this Lübbe 2009. Interestingly, Weber already characterizes the ethical foundation of modern capitalism, the Protestant ethos, as a highly irrational attitude toward the world, insofar as it aims (on the basis of the world-denying, active character of Protestant Christendom) at the maximal accumulation of wealth under a simultaneous renunciation of the enjoyment of its fruits. The "most fateful power" of our modern life thus rests, as it were, on irrational ethical foundations.

109. Cf. for example, Luhmann 1996:256ff.

110. Cf. on this in greater detail, Rosa 1998:305ff., 417ff.

111. I owe this insight not least to the critical objections Andrew Arato and Hanns-Georg Brose directed against my first attempt at a conceptualization of this constellation.

112. Differentiation, rationalization, individualization, and domestication can all be interpreted equally well as strategies of acceleration. In my opinion, among the other processes, only rationalization can claim a similar transcategorial pervasiveness.

2. What Is Social Acceleration?

1. The desolate condition of research into this context is also reflected in Lothar Baier's confession, presented with an honesty as striking as it is disarming, in his philosophical and belle-lettristic "18 Essays on Acceleration" (2000:12): "How one can discern the acceleration values of a society has not become clear to me. Even if it is correct that our societies are in ceaseless inner movement, something hardly ever intelligibly described, let alone defined, in anything more than catchphrases, that is still a long way from saying that they are moving forward, however fast or accelerated they may be."

2. The existence of the latter trends is definitely controversial; I will come back to the question of the cogency of the corresponding empirical findings.

3. Nowotny 1993:97 (my emphasis).

4. Ibid., 98 (my emphasis).

5. When, for instance, Matthias Eberling (1996:41), in his investigation of the effects of acceleration on politics, defines acceleration as "increase in developmental speed, that is, of socially relevant changes in politics, economics, culture, science and technologically per unit of time," he has this dimension of acceleration exclusively in mind. The basic problem with this definition naturally lies in the concept of relevance, i.e., in the notorious problem of distinguishing fundamental innovations and secondary alterations, which we can safely ignore here since we are only concerned with making the acceleration concept more precise.

6. "The rise of world population from around a half a billion persons in the seventeenth century to around six billion around the year 2000 can be interpreted as acceleration: it is an exponential time curve in which humanity doubles itself at ever shorter intervals," finds Reinhart Koselleck, who at the same time conjectures that the gradual differentiation and biological "development of the human being" since the solidification of the earth's crust, and after that the history of culture, and within that, moreover, the development of great civilizations, can be similarly interpreted as histories of acceleration and thus as growth curves (2000:199).

7. Cf. for an entire series of such growth curves, see Eriksen 2001:78ff.

The "kairotic" society imagined at the beginning of this work [i.e., in "In Place of a Preface" —TRANS.] can now be defined as a "uchronia" in which freed-up time resources are directly transformed into "free time," that is, in which corresponding processes of growth remain absent.

8. Anyone to whom these reflections are too abstract can easily help themselves make it more concrete with a contemporary example: without a doubt, the establishment of e-mail essentially accelerated communication. Writing and sending an e-mail message may take only half as much time as a conventional letter. However, when the quantity of e-mails written daily exceeds the number of letters one wrote daily by a factor of four, the amount of time dedicated to correspondence climbs by 100 percent! That this corresponding growth relates to the speed of communication transmission, moreover, is incontestable. If the answer to the morning message has already been received by nightfall while previously one required at least fourteen days, then it seems that an inherent impulse toward the accelerated continuation of chains of communication and action results. Nevertheless, this impulse can be neither logically nor causally

reduced to technical acceleration: *the heightening of the quantity of communication is made possible by technology, but not compelled by it.* The perceptible compulsion to heighten therefore results not from technics itself, but rather from the contraction of the present enabled by it, i.e., from the *accelerated transformation of the context of communication and action.* Thus this example illustrates in a paradigmatic way the mechanism (*Wirkungsweise*) of the circle of acceleration that is presented in chapter 6.

9. I assume along with Luhmann 1994 [1968]; Bergmann 1983:484; and Linder 1970; and against Moore 1963; and Balla 1978, that despite the limits of a natural lifetime, time scarcity is *not* an invariant phenomenon of human life, but rather is influenced, at least in the degree of its severity, by structural factors (which the first three cited authors emphasize), and cultural forces (which I will work out in chapter 7.2 in connection with Blumenberg and Gronemeyer).

10. Robinson and Godbey 1999:258.

11. Ibid., 259.

12. Robinson and Godbey assume that the "Parkinson law" (originally formulated for the allocation of time in organizations) is at work here, according to which a (work) task takes as much time as there is available regardless of how large the quantity of work is. "Put in Parkinson's terms, there is some norm or 'mental image' of the amount of time that should be devoted to certain activities. Whatever can be accomplished within that time is what determines the time spent on the activity" (ibid., 260).

13. Robinson and Godbey use the concept of the tempo of life very inconsistently, however; their presentation shows just how important it is to distinguish between technical acceleration and the acceleration of the pace of life and exactly define their relation. On the one hand, the authors are inclined (on the grounds given), to hold the acceleration of the tempo of life for a paradoxical problem of perception ("The problem of lack of time is, in most senses, a perceptual problem" [1999:25, cf. 229ff.]), yet, on the other, they see in it a constitutive element of modernization, but only by identifying it with technical acceleration: "from the Middle Ages through the Industrial Revolution, the pace of life began an unprecedented process of speeding up" (ibid., 29).

14. Cf. in more detail and with greater precision, chapters 2.2.c and 6.1.

15. This will be described in terms of industrial sociology and in connection with Marx as the intensification of work through the closing of the pores of the work day; cf. chapter 7.1.

16. Cf. on this in greater detail, chapter 7.3.

17. Cf. Geißler 1999:89. Heylighen (2001) starts from the assumption of a heightening of "several quantitative orders" in two-hundred years of the history of

technology. Cf. further Beniger 1986: inter alia, 208–14, as well as, on the history of technical acceleration as a whole, Virilio 1980, 1993, 1998.

18. Heylighen (2001:2) and Beniger (1986) leave no doubt that the sum of these values increases, although they forego corresponding estimations, let alone calculations.

19. Harvey 1990:240ff.; cf. also chapter 3.

20. For Beniger (1986), the acceleration of communications and information technology represents the attempt to win back control over the accelerating processes of transport and production. On the acceleration of communication in general, see Virilio 1993; Kirchmann 1998; Großklaus 1997; Myerson 2001; and Eriksen 2001.

21. Geißler 1999:89; Heylighen 2001:2f.

22. While some services can be accelerated through specialization and the use of technology, there are many realms (for instance, the education of children and care for the elderly or even shoe cleaning) in which no significant increases in tempo can be achieved, for which reason they become relatively more expensive and therefore, as Staffan Linder remarks (1970:38ff.), promote the tendency toward a "disposable society" in which, for example, cleaning, repair, and maintenance services are minimized by continually replacing used products with new ones.

23. Beniger 1986:vii, cf. 169ff., 427.

24. Recounted by, for instance, David S. Landes in "The Unbound Prometheus" (1969).

25. Freyermuth 2000:75.

26. Cf. Geißler 1999:89.

27. Ibid., 155; for a criticism of Geißler, cf. Rosa 2001a:341ff.

28. In this wider sense, the various types of "human-technical" rationalization of the work process can also naturally be counted as technical acceleration, for instance, Frederick W. Taylor's methods of "Scientific Management" or also current forms of flexible "just in time" production, of "lean management," etc. Furthermore, time-saving improvements in, say, running and swimming techniques in sports or reading techniques in studying also fall into this category.

29. Eriksen 2001:97; cf. further Beniger 1986:324ff., 362ff.

30. Heylighen 2001:3.

31. As just one example among many, cf. Robinson and Godbey 1999:46.

32. Cf. Sztompka 1993; Müller and Schmidt 1995; and Eder 1995.

33. Jahoda 1988:169.

34. Laslett 1988:31ff. Interestingly, Laslett postulates that political change, in contrast to most of the other types of change, cannot be accelerated, which suggests the possibility of desynchronization phenomena as discussed in part 3 of

this work. Nevertheless Laslett defends what is in my view a highly implausible equation of the personal tempo of life with the speed of political change, whereas in what follows I would like to show that the increase of the pace of life must itself be considered one of the three basic forms of social acceleration.

35. Cf. on the following, the keywords *Vergangenheit, Gegenwart,* and *Future* in the lexicon *Gedächtnis und Erinnerung* (Rosa 2001b).

36. Luhmann (1997: 1073) also suggests the same definition.

37. Cf. Koselleck 1989:323ff.

38. Cf. Lübbe: "['Contraction of the present'] means that in a dynamic civilization, in proportion to increases in the number of innovations per unit of time, the number of years decreases over which we can look back without seeing a world alien to our trusted present-day lifeworld as well as outdated in signifcant experiental respects. . . . Moreover, the innovation-dependent contraction of the present implies that in accordance with the shortening of the chronological distance to a past that has become alien, the number of future years for which we can infer the likely conditions of life decreases. Beyond these years, the future can no longer be compared in its essential respects to our present living conditions. In short, the contraction of the present entails a process whereby the space of time for which we can calculate our living conditions with a degree of constancy is shortened" (2009:159f.). In contrast to Lübbe, it seems to me inappropriate here to tie the concept of a contraction of the present to that of innovation: the form of contraction described by Lübbe can be the consequence of any kind of accelerated sociocultural transformation (thus, for instance, also of a partial return to old relations); it does not require any genuine innovations (unless one wants to, for example, describe the dismantling of the welfare state or the return to a militaristic, nationalist politics as innovations).

39. Cf. Koselleck 1989:328ff., 367 or 2000:150ff. David Harvey, who interprets modernity as an advancing process of "time-space compression," also sees in the progressive shortening of time horizons and stability horizons a constitutive sign of this process and a core characteristic of modern societies, although in his terminology he deviates diametrically from Lübbe: "As space appears to shrink to a 'global village' . . . and *as time horizons shorten to the point where the present is all there is* . . . so we have to learn how to cope with an overwhelming sense of compression of our spatial and temporal worlds" (1990:240; my emphasis).

40. Nassehi 1993:342.

41. "First in modernity and only *through a shortening of the temporal extension of the present* is the problem of inertia or conservatio a living one. . . . By restructuring time in the last two hundred years, the present has specialized itself in

the function of temporal integration; it does not, however, have enough time available to manage this" (Luhmann 1990a:135f. (my emphasis); cf. Nassehi 1993:342 and 375f.).

42. Cf. Guy 2002:2 and Nassehi 1993:342, 375f.

43. Cf. Guy 2002:7.

44. This viewpoint is also suggested by Nassehi (1993:370ff.) when he interprets the loss of binding expectations that follows the shortening of time horizons as an acceleration of social change in the shape of a "modalization of social structure."

45. Another entirely conceivable reaction to the shortening of time horizons and the resulting instability of expectations is a passive, fatalistic, and action-reducing stance, while conversely stable horizons of expectation and experience can also go along with an increase in the speed of action and (the feeling of) a dearth of time resources, as Ernst Benz (1977) and Reinhart Koselleck (2000:177ff.) have shown, using the example of Christian eschatological conceptions of time. On the historical-empirical interaction of the three forms of modern social acceleration in a self-reinforcing circle of acceleration, cf. chapter 6.

46. Garhammer 1999:470ff.; Robinson and Godbey speak of "time-deepening" (1999:24ff.).

47. Whoever eats, irons, calls people on the phone, and watches television at the same time will presumably be relatively time-inefficient regarding each particular task, but nevertheless complete them all faster than in the case of a sequential performance of the four actions.

48. I will return to factual empirical evidence for such a development in chapter 5.1; it is in fact postulated everywhere, but only seldom verified.

49. Geißler 1999:92; Garhammer 1999:448ff.; Levine 2006:146f.; and above all Robinson and Godbey 1999:229ff.; for a critical discussion of the evidence, cf. chapter 5.2.

50. On the concept of deceleration, popularized by Fritz Reheis (1998), see the corresponding entry in the dictionary *Umweltbildung* (Reheis 1999): "Deceleration means negative acceleration, that is, decreasing speed, slowing down, hesitation or even stretching out time" (53). In distinction from my use of the concept, however, Reheis wants it to be understood as a *prescriptive* concept for the characterization of an "alternative plan" in contrast to the "high-speed and non-stop society." "In transportation, deceleration means the reduction of speed. . . . In the economy, deceleration means a decrease in the technical rate of innovation, a rise in the shelf life of products and an orientation of production and consumption towards the goal of sustainability. . . . In politics, the deceleration concept is opposed to attempts to curtail the working of political

processes under pressure from the economy. . . . In the context of the human psyche, deceleration opposes the attempt of many people to heighten the enjoyment of life by heaping up and compressing external events" (ibid.).

51. See here, for instance, Pöppel 1997.

52. This is one of the central arguments of Fritz Reheis (1998).

53. Schivelbusch 2000 [1977]:16, 35ff.

54. Ibid., 51ff; cf. also Treptow 1992:4f. and Eriksen 2001:54f.

55. "The railroad produced (*inszeniert*) a new landscape. The speed that volatilizes objects in the perception of a Ruskin [a paradigmatic representative of the "old" mode of perception] and strips them of their contemplative existence, becomes an elixir of life for the new perception. It is through speed that the objects of the visible world obtain an allure" (Schivelbusch 2000 [1977]:58, cf. 143).

56. Eriksen 2001:54f.

57. Cf. the CD publications of the *Jazz Heritage Society*. For this reference I thank Bethany Ryker, who investigated the connection between social and musical experiences of time in an excellent term paper at the New School for Social Research (Ryker 2002). Cf. also Ogren 1989.

58. Schivelbusch 2000:142ff.

59. Cf. Armitage 2000:49ff.

60. In the meantime such acceleration-resistant forms of practice have been idealized in advertisements, for instance, in the well-known Jack Daniel's ad from Tennessee (which has since been caricatured in a cigarette ad coming down on the side of acceleration) or in the advertising images for Werther's Original that suggest that precisely through this acceleration-immune practice a transgenerational solidarity is established that, outside this protected world, is becoming increasingly fragile because of the acceleration of social change to an *intragenerational* pace of change (see chapter 4).

61. Nowotny 1993:127, 133; Lübbe 2009.

62. See chapter 10.3.

63. Cf. Sennett 1998:159ff. On the transformation of the structure and perception of time as an effect of unemployment, see Jahoda 1988:169ff. and, also still instructive, Jahoda, Lazarsfeld, and Zeisal 1933.

64. Cf. for instance Hall 1988.

65. This can be directly observed, for instance, when the harried manager is held up in his attempt to ask directions by the kiosk salesperson who has an endless amount of time or the hurrying professor's schedule is ruined by the (slow) library circulation desk or even where a highly accelerated industrial production process is knocked off its stride by the obsolete, slow repair service.

66. Cf. for instance Lauer 1981:30. On the three second window, see Pöppel 1997:64ff., 84ff.
67. Cf. also Levine 2006:72ff.
68. This can also be seen, for example, in popular best sellers like the books of Reheis (1998) and Gronemeyer (1996).
69. Glotz 1998:75; cf. Eriksen 2001:29f.
70. Cf. on this, for instance, the numerous publications of the Tutzinger Project "Ecology of Time" (for an overview, see Adam 2002).
71. So says the subtitle of Reheis 1998.
72. Cf. Glotz 1998:76.
73. Cf. Lafargue's *Right to Be Idle* (*Recht auf Faulheit*) of 1883 (Lafargue 1998 [1883]) and Russell's *In Praise of Idleness* (Russell 1985).
74. From a historical perspective, violent protests against accelerative technologies, e.g., the destruction of factories or railroad lines, naturally lead to temporary delays, but never to a reversal of the direction of development.
75. The first movement mentioned sets itself the goal of enjoying organically grown nutrition in a stylish and unhurried way, while the second movement, which emerged in the more well-off strata of the U.S. several years ago, purposefully tries to break through the "vicious circle of acceleration" of more work, higher income, and increased consumption by abstaining from consumption. The latter, at least, seems to have passed its zenith without achieving any noteworthy effects.
76. Cf. the instructive essay of Dieter Ronte (1998) on experiences of time in art and in museums.
77. Radkau 1998:220ff.
78. This is not to deny that monasteries and yoga techniques cannot be utilized in other ways, namely, in the sense of a genuinely alternative and decelerated form of life. In this case they fall under category (d.1).
79. On such strategies, see Seiwert 2000. The title itself, "if you're in a hurry, slow down," denotes one.
80. For Chesneaux (2000:411) such moratoria belong essentially to democracy, and hence to modernity, because, against all the acceleration-induced tendencies toward closure, they hold open the horizon of the future and thus enable future development. Cf. further Eberling (1996), who suggests that decelerating moratoria be made into a central instrument of politics in the struggle for control of processes in science, technology, and the economy that are taking on a life of their own (*sich verselbständigenden*); similarly also Reheis (1998:217ff.).
81. On the latter as stable fundamental values of Western, modern societies in the sense of an almost Parsonian "pattern maintenance," cf. Voß 1990.

82. I will go into this argument in greater detail in chapter 2.4; cf. also Bonus 1998.
83. As in the title of an essay by Claus Offe (1992).
84. In fact, Schumpeter defended the preservation of several braking, static, inefficient constraints on the rapid and free economic unfolding of markets in the form of state interventions, price fixing, and cartels with the functionalist argument that in the end they are accelerating factors of a "long-run process of expansion which they protect rather than impede." This observation is "no more paradoxical than saying that motorcars are travelling faster than they otherwise would *because* they are provided with brakes" (Schumpeter 1994:88–89). As Offe remarks, for Schumpeter the massive growth dynamics of capitalism thus "do not rest on free price competition and on the unfettered development of market conditions, but on their [temporary — H. R.] shackling by monopolistic practices" (1992:73).
85. Lübbe 2009:175f.; cf. Brose 2002:126f. Also informative on the question of cultural reproduction is Bonus 1998.
86. Fukuyama 1992; Habermas 1989; Gehlen 1978 and 1994; Offe 1987, respectively.
87. Cf. Baier 2000.
88. Cf. Rosa 1999b.
89. Cf. Hörning, Ahrens, and Gerhard 1997:176ff.; Baier 2000:12ff.
90. Wagner (1994) identifies in the history of modernity a similar three-stage process of liquefaction, reorganization, and late modern destabilization of institutions and orienting patterns.
91. So runs the title of an essay by Holger Bonus (1998).
92. Nietzsche 2005:214–15 (*Twilight of the Idols*, "Skirmishes of an Untimely Man," § 39).
93. On this see Rosa 1999b:393f.; as well as figure 8.1.
94. Schulze 1997b:79.

3. Technical Acceleration and Revolutionizing Space-Time

1. Cf. Rosa 1998 and 2004b for a justification of the claim that the altering forms of self-interpretation and world interpretation are, in the final analysis, constitutive for both subjects and social reality. I follow there, on essential points, the philosophical approach of Charles Taylor.
2. Of course, Koselleck here commits the fallacy identified in chapter 2.1 of interpreting quantitative growth as an inherent consequence of acceleration. To be correct, it would have to read: "the cargo loads, that . . . could be hauled." The acceleration of transport *makes possible* a corresponding increase in quantity.

3. Koselleck 2009:119–20.

4. Cf. above all, Harvey 1990:201ff.

5. In 1870 alone, there were supposedly over two hundred different local times used on the track from Washington to San Francisco (Kern 1983:12; the U.S. first introduced a national standard time in 1883); cf. Levine 2006:63ff.; Schivelbush 2000 [1977]:43ff.

6. It had already been invented at the end of the thirteenth century in late medieval cloisters and then quickly acquired a function regulating work and trade in city life (cf. LeGoff 1977; Dohrn-van Rossum 1988; Thrift 1988).

7. Cf. Kern 1983:12ff.

8. Cited in Koselleck 2000:160.

9. Virilio 2006; Gronemeyer 1996:107ff.

10. In her prize-winning contribution to the Fourth German Student Prize, Tempo! The Accelerated World, Johanna Marxer (2003) has so to speak "verified," in a brilliant, artistic-poetic way, the transformation in the human being's relationship to self and world through the dominant form of movement and the measure of its mobility that is ever postulated, but never demonstrated in the sociology of time literature. With the wonderful double entendre of her title, "Way from Würzburg" (Weg aus Würzburg), she documents in text and image specific modes of perceiving self, world, and time while underway using eight different technologies or media. Her verification succeeds through the original and consistent self-experiment she undertook, which enabled her to make an unusually sharp and detailed observation of her own perception of space, of interaction partners, and the specific kinds of time (Eigenzeiten) in persons, forms of movement, flows of traffic, and the conflicts that emerge from these, as well as through the artistic concordance of this transformation into writing, image, layout, etc. She thereby achieves impressive insights about the effects of the selected forms of movement and media on our objective, subjective, and social relationships to the world.

11. Harvey 1990:271ff.; cf. Castells 1996:376ff.

12. Virilio 1999, cf. 1993:7ff., 17, and further 2006, passim, and 1997:9ff.

13. Cf. Baur 1989; Fölling-Albers 1992.

14. Perhaps the most interesting example of the cultural processing and artistic presentation of the loss of sequential ordering in the experience of the world is Christopher Nolan's film Memento, whose protagonist has lost the ability to record experiences and information in long-term memory, for which reason the world appears to him as an incomprehensible series of sequences of experiences through which the film gropes its way "backward" chronologically.

15. On the systematic interpretation of this perception, see the considerations on the detemporalization of history developed in chapter 11.3.

16. Giddens 1990:21ff.

17. Castells 1996:464. Interestingly, this time appears to be just as motionless and "frozen" as Virilio's space-centered *inertie polaire*. Both conceptions, however, very clearly refer to the social rigidity identified in this work as the inherent and paradoxical flip side of social acceleration, whose logic will be deciphered in part 4 of this investigation.

18. Cf. on this Zygmunt Bauman's diagnosis of "liquid modernity" (2000).

19. Cf., Myerson 2001:12ff.

20. "In the face-to-face community the cast of others remained relatively stable. There were changes by virtue of births and deaths, but moving from one town—much less state or country—to another was difficult. The number of relationships commonly maintained in today's world stands in stark contrast. Counting one's family, the morning television news, the car radio, colleagues on the train, and the local newspaper, the typical commuter may confront as many different persons (in terms of views or images) in the first two hours of a day as the community-based predecessor did in a month," observes Kenneth Gergen (2000:62) and thus ascribes to technological acceleration a key role in the heightening of the number and intensity of social relationships in modernity that leads in postmodernity to the condition of a self "saturated" by the social world: "Through the technologies of the century, the number and variety of relationships in which we are engaged, potential frequency of contact, expressed intensity of relationship, and endurance through time all are steadily increasing. As this increase becomes extreme we reach a state of social saturation" (ibid., 61, cf. 49ff.). On the alteration of social relationships as a result of the technological acceleration of communication, see further, Eriksen 2001; Myerson 2001; Kirchmann 1998; as well as Hörning, Ahrens, and Gerhard 1997; cf. see also chapter 4 und 10.3.

21. If essential parts of the fittings of a home that are today called "furniture" (*Möbel*) were, well into the modern period, literally unalterable components of a house, "immovables" (*Immobilien*)—something Simmel already noted (2004:464f.)—then today, at least in the U.S., houses are themselves becoming mobile.

    The point of the note makes use of an etymological connection between *Möbel* (furniture) and *Immobilien* (real estate) that is lost in English. The latter term literally connotes immobility and hence is appropriate for denoting real estate, and the former, by contrast, denotes things which can be "moved in" to pieces of real estate, such as a house, office, condo, etc. —TRANS.

22. As Linder (1970:38ff.) has shown, the trend towards a "throw away society" has its rational basis in the fact that production processes have been more strongly

accelerated than the hardly acceleratable processes of repair, which is why the latter have become ever more expensive in comparison to the former.

23. Cf. on this chapter 10.3. See also Frisby's reflections in connection to Walter Benjamin (Frisby 1988:230ff.) as well as Simmel (2004:465) and Rosa (2002a).

24. Cf. Augé 1994; Bauman 2000:98ff.; Lübbe 2009:162ff.; in addition, Rosa 1998: 205ff. and 2002a.

4. Slipping Slopes

1. Goethe 1988:113 (*Elective Affinities*, part 1, chapter 4); cf. Koselleck 2009:125.

2. For the suggestion of explaining social change by reference to the "kinetic energy" of a society, see Radkau 1998:13f.

3. Appadurai 1990, 1996. Cf. also Urry 2000, 2002; and Castells 1996:376ff. on the question of empirical evidence.

4. Assmann 1992; Koselleck 1989:328ff., 366ff.; cf. Bering 2001.

5. Mannheim 1964. Cf. further Ahmadi 2001:194 and Lauer 1980:144. On the last argument, see, for example, Lübbe 2009 and Lauer 1981:113, 140.

6. Cf. Lübbe 2009:173ff..

7. At first glance, this seems to contradict the Goethe citation from the beginning of the chapter in which a cultural speed of obsolescence that demanded *re-learning every five years* was already diagnosed for the early nineteenth century. This "speed indicator," however, as I would like to show, does not refer to the tempo with which the existential foundations of social life alter, but rather to peripheral realms of knowledge. Nevertheless the cogency of the diagnosis of an acceleration of social change does not rest on the correctness of this specific generational argument.

8. Cf. for instance, Castells 1996:228. Representatives of Luhmannian systems theory take up an anomalous position according to which the primary type of social differentiation (usually segmentary, stratificational, or functional) determines the basic form of society. An acceleration of the transformation of this foundational differentiation is scarcely conceivable. From this perspective, however, one cannot get an angle on the phenomena that interest us in this context, namely, the contraction of the present or the continual shortening of the duration of stable time horizons diagnosed by Luhmann himself. As I will later show, the apparently unshakable stability, indeed rigidity, of systemic processing in modern societies is not a contradiction of the diagnosis of an acceleration of social change, but rather its complementary flip side: the imperturbability of (sub)systemic operational logics is a necessary correlate of the

continual revolutionizing of material, social, and cultural relations in modern society (cf. Jameson 1998:57f.).

9. Cf. Nassehi 1993:346, n. 104.

10. Imhof 1984:188. Luhmann also notes the transition from the "institutional indissolubility" of the family structure of the Middle Ages to the discontinuous new foundings of such structures in the tempo of generational succession in modernity (1980:299).

11. On the alteration of family structures, cf. Laslett 1988:33; Brose 2002:137; Castells 1997:chapter 4; Hildenbrand 2001; Beck and Beck-Gernsheim 1994; and Bauman 2000:16off..

12. Cf. for instance, Fuchs-Heinritz 2000.

13. Burkart, Fietze, and Kohli also identify "romantic partners for a time" as the most modern form of pair bonding (1989:244ff.), although other forms like the traditional marriage or the modern love marriage are still dominant in certain milieus. They thereby indirectly confirm the conjecture that even in this respect acceleration is equivalent to modernization.

14. "Serial monogamy is one of the best extant examples of life's tendency to stand still at great speed around the turn of the millenium" (Eriksen 2001:131).

15. Neckel 2000:40.

16. This stability covered in an ideal-typical way not only one's occupational identity, but even concrete relations of employment. As Zygmunt Bauman remarks: "The 'Fordist factory,' that most coveted and avidly pursued model of engineered rationality in times of heavy modernity, was the site of . . . a 'till death do us part' type of marriage vow between capital and labour. . . . It was meant to last 'for ever' (whatever that might have meant in terms of individual life), and more often than not it did. The marriage was, essentially, monogamic—and for both partners. Divorce was out of the question" (2000:116).

17. Sennett 1998:25. "Whoever begins a career at Microsoft has not the slightest idea where it will end. Whoever started it at Ford or Renault could be well-nigh certain that it will finish in the same place," as Daniel Cohen summarizes this change (cited in Bauman 2000:116).

18. Cf. for instance Bertholt 2002; Donges 1992.

19. Grotheer and Struck 2003:35.

20. The average duration of employment or membership at a firm declined from 1991–92 to 1998–99 from 11.6 to 10.1 years (not including public officials), while at the same time the proportion of short-term labor rose in the course of the nineties from barely 20 percent to barely 27 percent (ibid., 14f., data for West Germany). With respect to the development of labor *contracts*, one sees a decline of 7 percent in regular forms of labor (*Normalarbeitsverhältnisse*) during the last 15 years; "Beyond the so-called 'normal forms of labor,' there have been

rises in West Germany above all in the proportion of fixed-term contracts (from 3.2% to 5.7%), temporary work (from 0.2% to 1%), part-time labor (from 9% to 11.7%) and marginal employment (2.4% to 7.3%)" (ibid., 11). Concerning the job mobility rates, it turns out that of the positions begun after 1976 that are subject to social insurance contributions, around 60 percent ended after two years, and a further 20 percent ended after five (ibid., 5).

21. Ibid., 30f.

22. Cf. ibid., 3, 17.

23. Cf. for instance, Beck and Beck-Gernsheim 1994.

24. On the empirical findings, see, alongside Grotheer and Struck 2003, Garhammer 2001, 2002; Kohli 1994; Kommission für Zukunftsfragen 1996, 1997; Sennett 1998; Hoffmann and Walwei 1998; Beck 1999; Dörre 1997. Erlinghagen 2002 along with Bertholt 2002 and Donges 1992 are critical of the erosion thesis.

25. Weymann 2000:44.

26. Cf. Walzer (1990:11ff.), who does not, however, mention religious mobility, though it is covered by social status, which he treats as an independent category.

27. An increase in political volatility or "swing voters" is a well-documented phenomenon in electoral research.

28. "Which religion is the right one for me?" runs the recent cover page headline of a modern lifestyle magazine, provocatively getting to the heart of the idea of a frictionless religious mobility ("Testing Religions," in *XXLiving. Der Navigator für das moderne Leben* 6 [1998]: 44–52).

29. Cf. Backhaus and Gruner 1998.

30. Lübbe 2009:175.

31. Cf., for instance, Francis-Smythe and Robertson 1999:286. These authors suggest, contrary to the *cohort effect* postulated here, an *age effect* as the root of the difficulties the older generation has with multitasking, without, however, providing any evidence for this claim.

32. De Haan 1996:123.

33. Incidentally, Clemens Theodor Perthes had already remarked, in view of the political acceleration resulting from the French Revolution, "our time has . . . united in three contemporary, existing generations, the completely incommensurable. The monstrous contrasts of the years 1750, 1789, and 1815 dispense with all interim and appear in men now living not as a sequence but as coexistence, according to whether they are grandfather, father, or grandson," and in another place he states that "the more directly that history presses together the sequence of events, the more severe and universal the conflict will be" (cited in Koselleck 2004:269).

34. Cf. Gaines 1998:256, 257; Eriksen 2001:133f.; de Haan 1996:122ff. More than thirty years ago, Margaret Mead had already pointed to this fact in her analysis of generational rifts: "In the past there were always some elders who knew more than any children in terms of their experience of having grown up within a cultural system. Today there are none. It is not only that parents are no longer guides, but that there are no guides, whether one seeks them in one's own country or abroad. There are no elders who know what those who have been reared within the last twenty years know about the world into which they were born" (1970:61).

35. Cf. Sennett 1998. Recently, there are traces of a (probably transitory) counter-trend: not least because of the dramatic downfall of the "New Economy," many enterprises have once again emphasized *experience* at the management level.

36. Cf. Krappmann 1997. Using the example of Stefan Zweig's autobiography, Ahmadi shows that in the prewar generation of the early twentieth century *experience* and *age* were still preferred to *flexibility* and *youth*, as a result of which the young tried in all sorts of ways to appear *old*, exactly as today the old pay a fortune in order to be able to present themselves as *young*. This transformation is an impressive indicator of the acceleration of social change to a tempo beyond the succession of generations.

37. Cf. Rosa 1999b, d and 2002a.

38. An interesting illustration of what happens when one rejects this pressure to accelerate and adapt can be found in Levine (2006:44). He cites a North American colleague who evaded the fast pace of life of U.S. culture through long stays in South America. About his experiences on occasional returns to the U.S., the colleague reports: "Every time I visit I am surprised by how foreign I feel. It's as if the people have completely abandoned and replaced the fashions of yesterday—not only in clothing, but also in music and art and everything else. Even the language seems to change. I don't know how I should dress, what I should talk about or which words will sound completely silly. Sometimes, especially with young people, I can't even follow the conversation." The experience of being completely unable to understand what people are talking about has occurred to many older people with respect to what appears to them as the "techno-bubble" of the youth.

39. Luhmann 1980. On this see chapter 7.3.

40. The first American newspaper appeared in 1784 in Pennsylvania; cf. Beniger 1986:183.

41. Cf. on this also Eriksen 2001:66ff.

42. The news reports of the radio program MDR-Info (in 2003), broadcast every fifteen minutes, begin with the slogan: "The world: state of the art." Its ads

use the sayings "The world doesn't take breaks" and "News, new every fifteen minutes!"

43. Lübbe 2009:164 (translation emended). A side effect of the acceleration of social change is the chaotic quantitative growth of *relics* that have become functionless and, if need be, are preserved from decay through *musealization* (*Musealisierung*), i.e., by being turned into museum pieces.

44. Conrad 1999:6; Robinson and Godbey 1999:33. It is perhaps no coincidence that the most monumental symbol of this *getting nowhere fast*, the treadmills in gyms and fitness studios, enjoy such great popularity that since the turn of the century one cannot even imagine urban centers, particularly those of "global cities," without them. The phenomena investigated in this work seem to be bundled together in them as if in a magnifying glass. They illustrate above all the efficient commodification of so simple an activity as running: while the jogger needs as good as no technological apparatus, the *gym* is almost unlimitedly commodifiable—the TV above the treadmill, the CD in the ear, the pulse rate and blood pressure measuring devices buckled on (as if in confirmation of the number obsession of late modernity that is linked to hurry sickness), and the clock solidly in view provide an almost ritualized staging of *mobility-without-advance* (*Mobilität-ohne-Fortbewegung*). Time becomes endlessly long for the destinationless runner (which perhaps explains the fascination of the treadmill: finally for once an otherwise steadily contracting time is extended), and every additional laborious minute on the treadmill is experienced as a personal triumph, celebrated as gained time, and perhaps even felt to be revenge against time. The immensely popular activity of training in the gym is quite aptly characterized as a "workout": insofar as the longing for acceleration that leads into the paradoxical situation of a *speeding standstill* has its roots in the Protestant work ethic, one could hardly have found a more appropriate concept.

5. The Acceleration of the "Pace of Life"

1. Simmel 1992a [1897]:215.
2. In a representative survey performed by Nadine Schöneck, 80.4 percent of the respondents agreed that *in essential respects their life has accelerated in the last few years* (2004:32).
3. Ibid. Cf. Simmel 2004:504; see also chapter 1.2.
4. Cf. Simmel 2004:511. Simmel derived from this the dramatically heightened pace of life in modern societies as compared to agrarian societies: "If one compares the velocity of circulation of landed property with that of money, then this

immediately illustrates the difference in the pace of life between periods when the one or the other was the focal point of economic activity" (ibid., 513).

5. Levine 2006:8–9; cf. in more detail on this, Rosa 2001a:343ff.

6. Levine's studies overwhelmingly confirm presumptions one always had: economically more developed regions are faster than backward, poorer ones (ibid., 9ff.); thirty years ago, the Swedish economist Staffan B. Linder [1970] had already given a brilliant economic justification for treating time as a scarce [life] resource whose allocation followed rational considerations of utility, which leads to an analytically grounded inverse proportional relation between material and temporal well-being); localities with hot climates are slower than those in moderate latitudes (Linder 1970:47ff.) and—confirming Simmel's essay "The Metropolis and Mental Life"—larger cities have a faster pace of life than smaller ones (Simmel 1995 [1903]:46f.; Levine refers here for the most part to other studies). It is striking that western Europe appears to be by far the fastest cultural space (in the first three places are Switzerland, Ireland [!], and Germany), while Canada and the U.S. land toward the back of the middle range.

7. Correspondingly, the U.S. ranks twenty-three out of thirty-one in Levine's list for the speed of postal service (2006:132).

8. I thank Manfred Garhammer for this suggestion.

9. This is in my view correct, but it does not prove, as Geißler thinks, that clock time in general has become insignificant. The phenomenon can be explained rather by means of the universal diffusion of individual timekeeping devices. That clock time in airports and train stations has lost significance is, in my opinion, an absurd claim—it is even more important for coordination and synchronization now than it is was before. However, the disappearance and neglect of public clocks does seem to be a remarkable symptom for the loss of significance of *collective* temporal rhythms: the work clock displaying 12 o'clock no longer always means lunch break, 5 o'clock no longer necessarily means evening, 6:30 doesn't mean closing time everywhere, neither does midnight mean channels go off the air nor Friday night necessarily signify the beginning of collective leisure time (cf. Rosa 2001a:342f.).

10. Maybe this explains why Switzerland and Italy come in at first and second place on this indicator, while the U.S. has to be satisfied with being twentieth (Levine 2006:132).

11. Which can be in turn explained as an "objective" effect of a ratio of the rate of increase in the quantity of actions and the speed of completion where the former is greater than the latter. Cf. chapter 2.1, figure 2.3.

12. Robinson and Godbey 1999:39. Cf. Schmahl's list, as extensive as it is impressive, of 18 everyday strategies for saving and manipulating time (1988:362ff.).

13. At the same time, this entails the conjecture that the tempo of life in modern societies is higher than in all (or almost all) premodern cultures. An empirical testing of this thesis fails, however, due to the difficulty of generating the corresponding comparative data. Linder (1970:chapter 2) derives the existence of three different types of culture from his axiom of the inverse proportional relation of temporal and material well-being: societies with an excess of time and a scarcity of goods, societies with an equilibrium of economic well-being and time resources, and surplus societies with a marked scarcity of time. In his analysis these societal types broadly correspond to premodern, modernizing, and high modern societies. Some empirical evidence from ethnographical research does speak in favor of this theory. For instance, Allen Johnson (1978) reports that the Peruvian Machiguenga Indians have *more than four hours more* of activity-free time (which they spend, e.g., sleeping, dozing, or talking) than their French contemporaries who spend three to five times more time on the consumption of goods. For further evidence, see Sahlins 1972; Cherfas and Lewin 1980; and the discussion of these in Robinson and Godbey 1999:26f.; as well as Levine 2006:5–19. and Dux 1989.

14. Cf. Marx 1976:chapters 1, 10, 15, 17, 19–21, inter alia.

15. See note 13.

16. Cf. chapter 1.1.

17. Thus for instance Gleick reports that the average speaking time without interruptions attributed an American presidential candidate has shortened from around forty seconds in 1968 to "soundbites" 8.2 seconds long. Cf. also Weibel 1987 and Kirchmann 1998.

18. Cf. Eriksen 2001:71.

19. Schulze 1994, 1997a and 1997b.

20. I follow the usage of the concept recommended by Schulze (1997a:735, 738), not Luhmann's distinction between experience and action (1996:161f.).

21. Schulze 1997b:90f.

22. Cf. Eriksen 2001:84. In this context, a further astonishing phenomenon is the by now routine practice in Hollywood films of accelerating action and battles scenes so much that the effects flash thick and fast across the screen, making it, however, completely impossible for the viewer to follow the action: what exactly happened is either only apparent afterward — or remains entirely unclear. For an informative presentation of the history of the acceleration of film, see Peter Wollen (2002:109ff.). Wollen arrives at cinematic vision of "paralysis by hyperacceleration," or frenetic standstill, that is clearly reminiscent of Virilio and Baudrillard (ibid., 114).

23. Levine 2006:45.

24. Robinson and Godbey (1999:136ff., 229ff., 319ff) and also 1996.

25. Cf. Schulze 1997a:43ff., 735.

26. Eriksen 2001:148, cf. 141. See further Bauman 1995.

27. One can use this to illustrate in a trivializing way the connection that systems theory posits between the temporalization of complexity (as a response to its increase) and acceleration: naturally, when we buy books or CDs, we "console" ourselves with the thought that we don't after all have to consume them all in a month, since we have years to do that; this calculation works out only if we lower the quantity of new acquisitions in the future, and we are highly unlikely to do this, which means that compulsions to accelerate are unavoidable: the situation will look even worse next month or next year.

28. Everyday examples of this are, for instance: which kind of computer is right for me in view of the cost, versatility, connectivity? Which cell phone? Which health insurance is the best short-, mid-, and long-term deal for me (keeping in mind the fact that my professional and familial life path are uncertain)? Which investment fund is the most promising? The growing need for information accompanied by shrinking time resources is the reason for the proliferation of professional consulting and advisory services of all kinds.

29. "One actually *wants* to be influenced by advertising to get an instant feeling that one has a perfectly good reason to buy this or that commodity, the true properties of which one knows dismally little about. Only unintelligent buyers acquire complete information" (Linder 1970:74).

30. For an empirical confirmation of such time/decision dilemmas, see Hörning, Ahrens, and Gerhard 1997.

31. See Linder 1970:chapter 6, "The Rationality of Growing Irrationality."

32. For instance, work times, holiday dates, business hours, times of religious services, weekend regulations, news broadcasts, etc. For a more detailed treatment, see Garhammer 1999:30ff., 347ff., 474ff..

33. Eriksen provides an illustrative example: "A major preoccupation for many parents is the industrial organisation of family time. It goes like this: if you take X to her violin lesson today, I will go and collect Y at kindergarten. If you take both of them to the country on the weekend so that I can get down to doing something, I'll take them to my parents next weekend. Can you stay at home today, so that I can go to that meeting? If I can leave early for work tomorrow, you can do it on Thursday. Deal!" (2001:132).

34. Geißler 1999:142. The phenomenon of interest here is that relevancies and priorities can shift literally overnight: what was yesterday a sufficient motive for setting the alarm clock, may today be an incitement to fail to get up.

35. Gehlen 1986.

36. Garhammer 1999:412f.

37. Luhmann 1994 [1968].

38. It is an astonishing phenomenon that a large number of scholars who work on the analysis of temporal structures see themselves driven to append to their investigations a kind of practical how-to guide on deceleration. See, for instance, Reheis 1998; Levine 1999; Geißler 1999; Eriksen 2001; and even Luhmann 1994 [1968].

39. Luhmann also comes to this conclusion in the end: "Only institutionalized excuses can protect one against demands for cooperation" (ibid., 158).

40. Eriksen infers from this that in modern societies *fast time kills slow time.* Wherever fast and slow processes encounter each other, there is an asymmetry such that the slow process falls under pressure to accelerate (and not the other way around).

41. Cf. for instance, Robinson and Godbey (1999), who assert a slight decline of work time in the U.S. even in the 1980s, and Schor (1992), who postulates a clear rise. The varying results here should be traced back to diverging interpretations of the question concerning what counts as work time (contentious here, for example, are work breaks, travel time, and continuing education or training arrangements). In this context, Garhammer's conjecture that the still observable shortenings of work time (insofar as they are not traceable to growing unemployment) are offset or surpassed by work-related but unpaid activities (of information gathering, networking, retraining, etc.) does not seem implausible (1999:293ff.). See here, further, Hochschild 2000. In recent years, however, a trend reversal in the direction of *longer* working times has become unquestionable.

42. Particularly interesting here is the observation of a "more-more" pattern systematically demonstrated by Robinson and Godbey: the more active a person is in a given social realm, the higher the probability is that she is active in other sectors (1999:41 and passim). The people who are most ready to take on an honorary office or an additional task are not those who work little and hardly have any hobbies, but rather just the opposite: such readiness increases with the number of offices and tasks already performed, which is of great interest, for instance, for the question of how motivational resources for civic engagement can be promoted and utilized (cf. Giegel and Rosa 2000 and Giegel, Rosa, and Heinz 2001).

    See, further, Robinson and Godbey 1999 for the U.S.; Garhammer 1999 and Gershuny 2003 for Europe; Holz 2000 for Germany; and, further, Schor 1992; Gershuny 1990; Benthaus-Apel 1995; Statistisches Bundesamt Wiesbaden 1994.

43. Cf. on this point, for instance, Robinson and Godbey's declaration of the "zero sum property" of time, which displays an amazing insensitivity toward their own formulation of the possibility of temporal condensation: "Simply put, if

one increases time spent on some new activity . . . time on some other activity must show a decrease" (1999:15).

44. Data from Robinson and Godbey 1999:336ff.

45. Garhammer 1999:378.

46. Ibid., 379.

47. Curiously in particular by Robinson and Godbey (1999), whose data make the development of male sleep behavior between 1985 and 1995 appear to be rather an anomaly or outlier; even for the other two forms of activity this study yields a rather uneven picture in comparison to other periods. Gershuny asserts, on the basis of the longitudinal international comparative data since 1960 he evaluated, that the average "condensation of sleep" of the better employed or more educated was around 20 minutes (2003:219).

48. Zulley and Knab 2000:118f. The latter argument is not valid, however, for the similarly asserted decline of the duration of sleep for the gainfully employed in general; see here also Holz 2000:14 and Gershuny 2003:218.

49. On fragmentation, cf. for example Robinson and Godbey 1999:56 or Holz 2000:19f.; see also Eriksen 2001. On multitasking, cf. Gleick 1999:171ff.; Garhammer 1999:472f.; Benthaus-Apel 1995.

50. Cf. on this, Verkaaik 2001 as well as Michelson and Crouse 2002.

51. Garhammer 1999:466ff.

52. Robinson and Godbey 1999:29, cf. 33, 35, 46.

53. "[Our] results seem to be seriously at odds with the time patterns that many social observers have reported and that many of our own respondents report are affecting their lives—*such as the faster pace of American life*" (Robinson and Godbey 1999:8 [my emphasis]). For the authors, the contradictions arise above all from the fact that available free time and (stressless) time spent in front of the TV seem to be increasing. I have tried to set out why this in no way contradicts the diagnosis of an escalating pace of life.

54. Cited in Koselleck 2000:161, n. 17.

55. Cf. the preface, note 4. On this "problem of free time," cf. also Gershuny 2003:58ff. The argument consistently rests on the claim (whose consequences are misinterpreted) that work time decreases and free time increases. Curiously, Gershuny himself seems to hold the possibility of excessive available time, as against leisure time stress, to be the greater of the two "dangers of free time." He correctly points, however, to the still considerable *gender differences* with respect to work burdens and the experience of time scarcity, which stem primarily from the double burdening of women by work and home or child-raising responsibilities. Because men still manage to avoid most of the latter, women have both objectively fewer time resources and subjectively higher

stress rates (cf. here also Schor 1992; Hochschild 2000; Robinson and God-bey 1999:197, 349, whose data, however, indicate a gradual lessening of the differences).

56. Insofar as the feeling for elasped time is gained from the action that is now being accelerated, this is not surprising.

57. Cf. for instance, Geißler 1999:92; Garhammer 1999:448ff.; Levine 2006:145f.; Robinson and Godbey 1999:229ff., 319ff. as well as numerous research papers on this theme on the Web page of the International Time Use Conference, "Time Pressure, Work-Family Interface, and Parent-Child Relationships" of 2002 (www.lifestress.uwaterloo.ca).

58. Robinson and Godbey 1999:232. The international comparative data of Gar-hammer point in the same direction (1999:450ff.). According to them, in 1991–92 roughly 78 percent of the German labor force complained about lack of time. Holz, in contrast, presents astonishing numbers according to which 71 percent of German citizens as reported in the representative time budget survey of 1991–92 were not subject to any notable time stress (2000:10ff.). This divergence arises in my view from the fact that the stress indicator in the ques-tionnaire (*desire for more time for specific areas of activity*) was very vague. The respondents might have interpreted the desire for more time for a specific activity in the sense, typical of time budget thinking, of a zero-sum game, i.e., as a desire for "time redistribution." As a matter of principle when dealing with stress data, of course, one must consider that not all groups in the population are equally affected; for example, the retired or the unemployed suffer mark-edly less from it (Holz 2000:13). The central argument of this work is that acceleration is a fundamental tendency or basic property of modernization. Thus, where population groups are culturally or structurally excluded from modernization processes, one ought not to except any significant experience of acceleration.

59. Robinson and Godbey 1999:239ff., 314ff.; cf. 1996. According to the numbers presented by John Robinson in his lecture, "Is There an Acceleration of the Pace of Life? Some Empirical Evidence" (RC 35), at the Fifteenth World Con-gress of Sociology in Brisbane on July 10, 2002, this trend also continues in the most current U.S. time use data.

60. Robinson and Godbey 1999:279ff.

61. In this respect, the results of the new representative time budget survey of the Statistical Office of Germany (2001–2) are eagerly awaited.

62. Data from Robinson and Godbey 1999:339. The differences between men and women are considerable in terms of composition, but not, however, in the overall result: for women housework time declined tremendously, while

work time rose, whereas for men family and household time climbed but work time dropped. Nevertheless, both sexes registered a significant rise in free time (ibid., inter alia, 346). This rise in free time is also confirmed by Garhammer's international comparative data (E.U. and U.S.) between 1960 and 1995; yet, according to this data, this can be traced back to an acceleration of self-care rather than a reduction of housework or overall work time: "The development of *paid* labor and the time bound up by it . . . significantly sinks from 7.6 to 6.5 hours per day. . . . Otherwise than expected, *unpaid labor* from the 1960s into the 1990s *rose* (significantly) from 1.7 to 2.8 hours by the same amount, *so that overall work at 9.29 hours remained the same almost to a hundredth.* Accordingly, the expansion of daily free time since the sixties by 38 minutes to 4.9 hours (sic.) did *not* result from the employed working less. The source of the 'gain in time' is rather a compression of their personal needs by an hour [!], from ten and a half to nine and a half hours (sig.). . . . This trend is unmistakeable in spite of any doubts about the sources of data" (Garhammer 1999:427f.).

63. Robinson and Godbey 1999:135, cf. table 30 on p. 279.

64. From a macrosociological and economic perspective it is evident that these resources are primarily bound to acts of consumption, whose rise is a necessary correlate of the capitalistic growth of production (Linder 1970).

65. Cf. Luhmann 1994 [1968]:149.

66. Cf. Michelson and Crouse 2002; Garhammer 1999:32ff.; Benthaus-Apel 1995; Robinson and Godbey 1999:290ff.

67. Cf. the striking list of such quasi obligations that produce "free time stress" in Opaschowski 1995:85f.

68. Gergen 2000:75; Opaschowski 1995:85f..; Robinson and Godbey 1999:305.

69. Rosa 2002b; cf. chapters 10.3 and 11.3.

70. Cf. Gamm 1992:80. See also Rosa 1999a and 2002b.

71. "'Work before play' is an ordering of activity that reflects a value hierarchy" (Lauer 1981:35).

72. Luhmann 1994 [1968]:143.

73. Robinson and Godbey 1999:292.

74. Luhmann 1994 [1968]:148. Cf. also, ibid., 154, where Luhmann's description of the workplace context of administrative officials seems to characterize late modern life as a whole: "Occupied with numerous cooperative obligations, the individual finds his time so scarce and so fragmented that he can, to be sure, still function in cooperative relationships, and above all still transfer current information from one work context to another, but he no longer finds any time for longer deliberation. In his work he remains dependent on quickly graspable and utilizable data and symbols: temporally, thematically, or socially distant

information will not be called upon, circuitous ways of thinking no longer used, unless of course cooperative routines are set up for that."

75. Something expressed in the fact that respondents indicate that this is the activity that they would be most ready to give up (Robinson and Godbey 1999:242).

76. Data from ibid., 241ff.

77. Things that received very high satisfaction values (between 9.0 and 9.3) were, in particular, sex, ball sports (to which increasingly less time is devoted in comparison to jogging and the "workout" in the fitness club), fishing, as well as engagement with art and music (ibid., appendix O, 374). Visits to friends and relatives also receive as a rule high values on the satisfaction scale, but, at least in the U.S., continually dwindling time resources (ibid., 297).

78. Ibid., 126, 292.

79. Ibid., 311.

80. Cf. here the comprehensive studies on the level of attention, etc., of Kubey and Csikszentmihalyi 1990.

81. As Kubey and Csikszentmihalyi show (1990), TV consumption indeed relaxes one during viewing. However, it leaves behind rather stressed and unrecuperated actors. With sports, in contrast, it is just the opposite: they are strenuous in the performance, but develop into a relaxing effect afterward.

82. Cf. for instance Achtner, Kunz, and Walter 1998:1ff.

83. Nietzsche 1974:259 (*The Gay Science*, book 4, § 329).

84. Cf. the data in Kubey and Csikszentmihalyi 1990:122ff.

85. It is instructive to view this argument in light of Linder's initial hypothesis that a rational allocation of time always aims at optimizing the relation of input to output, i.e., to draw the greatest possible utility from the least possible expenditure of time (Linder 1970:2ff.). In my opinion, this argument itself still needs to be "temporalized": whether the utility calculation is oriented toward short-, mid- or long-term time horizons seems variable. In a society with high rates of instability in which expectations and the conditions of their future fulfillment are uncertain, it stands to reason that the rationality criteria will shift in favor of short-term utility calculations: it becomes irrational to count on long-term fulfillment.

86. Luhmann 1994 [1968]:148. On these arguments, compare Eriksen 2001:63f.

87. Cf. in more detail, Rosa 1999a:753ff.

88. The term *oasis of deceleration* should be understood in the sense laid out in chapter 2.3. Instead, we are on the verge of shortening the time spent in secondary education and thereby placing the potential oasis of deceleration offered by the school under a pressure to accelerate.

89. Robinson and Godbey 1999:152, 255f.

90. Cf. Kubey and Csikszentmihalyi 1990:140ff.

91. James 1890:624. To illustrate, one might for instance imagine a day's journey in which one starts out in the morning in Stuttgart, eats lunch at the Vierwaldstättersee Lake, sees the cathedral in Milan after coffee and cake there, and in the evening goes for a walk on the Riviera. Going to bed, one would undoubtedly ask whether the trip really just began this morning—it seems like so much longer, even though throughout the day time went by fast. On the contrary, on the evening of a day that was overwhelmingly spent waiting in line at government offices and at the dentist's (assuming one has no phobia about dentists that would make the visit unforgettable), one would have the impression that one had just woken up. Flaherty's observation that time also occasionally flows slowly precisely when we are exposed to a very high input of information with great affective concern, i.e., in particular in extreme situations like accidents, crimes, or natural catastrophes (cf. the introduction, note 21). This does not contradict the general correctness of the claims of James and Mann.

92. In his study of the experience of time, Michael Flaherty explains this with reference to varying erosion times in episodic memory: "Episodic Memory is oriented towards the recollection of activity. Situtions in which there is an abnormally low level of overt activity generate the experience of protracted duration. But while these situations may seem to last forever as one endures them, little or nothing 'happens,' and they leave only a faint and waning residue in one's episodic memory" (1999:112). Cf. the neurophysiological research of Ernst Pöppel 1997 or Frederic Vester 1998.

93. Cf. Barth 1989:208f.

94. Who hasn't had the experience of just wanting to check out what's on TV "for a moment" and then, after turning it off, being astonished that two hours have passed by?

95. Kubey and Csikszentmihalyi 1990:145 (my emphasis).

96. The reflections presented here, however, gain empirical plausibility from, on the one hand, the widespread qualitative reports of the experience of television viewers and, on the other, the fact that I have tested them countless times on sometimes extraordinarily critical and contrary teachers, high school students, undergraduates, colleagues, and other members of an interested public, which almost always led to an "aha effect" in the interlocutors, namely, the identification of the short-short pattern. (My particular thanks go here to the equally persevering and creative participants of the *Deutschen Schüler Akademie* in Braunschweig from 1998–2003.)

97. Cf. the detailed reports in Flaherty 1999:40ff. and 69ff.; see also Levine 2006:33ff.

98. Kubey and Csikszentmihalyi reported a comparatively low level of cortical stimulation and the phenomenon of "attentional inertia": the longer the gaze is directed at the screen, the stronger an external stimulus needs to be in order to disengage it again (1990:135ff.).

99. Cf. Rosa 2004d. If the thesis that experiences of time in late modern society increasingly follow the television pattern is correct, this could also prove to be a side effect of the commercialization or colonization of the lifeworld: it is activities like the visit to the amusement park or the dance club or the recreational pool that most strongly exhibit the discussed features of "decontextualization."

100. The study was undertaken in March 1990, so "last year" referred to 1989.

101. Flaherty 1999:115ff. The value was higher than 4 in all age groups. Contrary to the assumption that time flows faster in old age, it was astonishingly not the oldest group (with an average age of over seventy years), but the (professionally active) middle age group (average of 38.4 years) that reported the highest value (4.328). Diverging from my interpretation, Flaherty construes this result as a "normal" memory effect that arises from the erosion of episodic memory over time: after a year the subjects can hardly remember their experiences and activities. I hold this interpretation to be implausible insofar as, taken by itself, the effect Flaherty has in mind should have led to the answer "fast as normal" (3): a year goes by as fast as a year goes by, and the erosion of memory is equally great every year, so from every year "just as much" (or little) remains. Therefore, the significantly higher numbers point, in my view, to an *acceleration effect*: time elapsed too *fast* for the respondents (in retrospect); *less* remained than they expected or hoped (on the basis of experience).

102. The decontextualization of lived experiences could contribute in this way to a diminishment of the intensity of experience. Georg Simmel already anticipated that individuals would react to it with a decline in their psychological "reactivity" (1950:415ff.). That the *longing* for intense experience in the late modern ("experience") society is at the same time great may in turn cause the contents of the envisaged experiences to become ever more "extreme," which might help explain the quest for ultimate "kicks" and possibly even a heightened disposition to violence (on the latter cf. Enzensberger 1994:33; Nassehi 2000; Assheuer 2000).

103. Cf. Benjamin 1974c, especially 609ff., and further 1974a, 1974b.

104. Cf. Honneth 1999:especially 101ff.

105. Cf. on this Giorgio Agamben's diagnosis of the destruction of experience: "Modern man's average day contains virtually nothing that can still be translated into experience. . . . It is this non-translatability into experience that now makes everyday existence intolerable" (1993:13f.). Cf. also Ahmadi 2001:191ff.

106. Cf. Benjamin 1974c:612ff.

107. Benjamin 1974a; cf. also Frisby 1988:262.

108. I have tried to define this dynamic relationship in my book, *Identität und kulturelle Praxis* (1998).

109. Cf. for example, Willems and Hahn 1999, Keupp et al. 1999, and also Rorty 1989; cf. here Rosa 2002a.

110. Cf. on this point, Straub 1993 and 1998a.

111. See Lauer 1981:35ff., 63ff. and 112ff.

112. Cf. Straus and Höfer 1997 and Ahlheit 1988. See also the introduction, section 1.

113. "The temporary contract is in practice supplanting permanent institutions in the professional, emotional, sexual, cultural, family and international domains, as well as in political affairs" (Lyotard 1984:66).

114. Amir Ahmadi, in connection with Paul Valéry and Walter Benjamin, diagnoses just this disassociation between the self and its roles as an unavoidable consequence of social acceleration: "While individuals take up and fulfill various roles in their day-to-day life, their engagement remains just that, playing roles, which they feel does not address the core of their existence. Thus everyone becomes a Sartrean for-itself. Perched above and beyond the everyday affairs, the self anxiously looks on in a perpetual expectation as its worldly shadow exhausts itself in its daily battles with time" (2001:192).

115. Taylor 1989:159ff., 196; Sandel 1984; also here Rosa 1998:342ff., 403ff. and 2002a.

116. Cf. on this point, Straub 1998b and 2001 or Wenzel 1995.

117. Gergen 2000; Willems and Hahn 1999:19 (introduction); Willems 1999; Harvey 1990:286ff.

118. Cf. Rosa 2002a:§ 2.1.

6. Speeding Up of Society as Self-Propelling Process

1. As I tried to show using the example of improved running techniques and the shortening of track and field competitions, technical acceleration leads to a heightening of the tempo of life only if it is used to shorten episodes of action or experience. The "saved" time can be used equally well for a lengthening of breaks, a slowing down of preparatory and follow-up activities, or a sequenced performance of previously simultaneous activities (i.e., mono- instead of multitasking). While increasingly scarce time resources thus lead, as it were, "naturally" to a desire for technical acceleration, the paradox lies in the fact that the converse does not hold: technical acceleration *does not lead* to a scarcity of time resources.

2. Heinrich Heine already anticipated the way the railroad would alter our *form of life* when (although with an ironic undertone) he conjectured that with it a new section of world history was beginning: "I just want to remark

that our entire existence is being carried away, hurled forth along new tracks, that new relations, joys and hardships await us" (Heine 1974:448f.). Cf. chapter 2.3a.

3. Cf. chapter 4, note 31.

4. Cf. for example, Birkefeld and Jung 1994.

5. Cf. for instance, Thompson 1967 or the contributions in Zoll 1988a, and further Virilio 2006; also chapter 7.1.

6. In particular, there came to be an almost complete separation of the financial and stock markets, on the one hand, and the real economy, on the other, which the collapse of the so-called new markets in the summer of 2000, leading in the end to a worldwide crisis even in the standard stock markets, made completely clear to everyone.

7. Very informative on this point are Held et al. 1999:189ff.; cf. chapter 9.

8. Thus the title of a three-volume work by Manuel Castells (1996, 1997, 1998); cf. Eriksen 2001 and Lestienne 2000.

9. On the development of novel forms of social identity through the Internet, see, for example, Turkle 1995 or Buchstein 1997.

10. Naturally that does not mean that technical acceleration is the *sole cause* of an accelerated social change. Indeed, it could be objected to the argument formulated here that technical acceleration certainly causes social change in the way described, but not necessarily its *acceleration*. This objection can in turn be parried by two counterarguments: in the first place, all societies are in the end already subject to processes of social change due to altering environmental conditions even if they produce no technological innovations (cf. Laslett 1988). These, so to speak, "natural" rates of change (which are dependent on social structure) are also without a doubt increased by the emergence of technical acceleration. The latter is therefore a motor of social change. In the second place, technological innovations seem to have as it were *exponentially escalating* side effects on the social world: particular inventions, for example, the acceleration of transport by the railroad, have *multidimensional* effects on society (it simultaneously changes social practices, communicative relations, patterns of perception, housing developments, etc.) and accelerate social change in that their effects are multiplied through mutual reinforcement. Beyond this one can also argue, naturally, that the innovation process itself accelerates (though as we have seen this is difficult to demonstrate given that it is often unclear what counts as a fundamental innovation versus a mere further development). Insofar as this is correct, this too is then a matter of accelerating social change: the escalation of the rate of innovation is not a technical achievement (although there may be social techniques aimed at achieving it).

11. "One can naturally expect any arbitrary number of objective events, but of one's own experience and action there is only as much as can fit within

one's own time" (Luhmann 1994 [1968]:159). Lübbe speaks in this context of how "the compression of innovation through the narrow temporal boundaries of the individual life course," has the effect of making time scarce (2009:165).

12. Hermann Lübbe puts this in a somewhat stilted form as follows: "The compression of cultural innovation specific to this period increased time pressure in the form of an experience of a time shortage: the growing structural incongruity of the rising wealth of possible acquisitions on offer, on the one hand, and the relatively decreasing opportunities to make use of them, on the other, constrained as the latter were by the duration of a life course that remained fundamentally constant" (2009:165).

13. The citation stems from an interview with André Kemper, the manager of the Hamburg advertising agency, Springer and Jacoby, with the magazine *Stern* on July 2, 1998. On the latter point, cf. for instance Myerson, who speculates that meaning as a medium has become too slow for the interaction speed required in contemporary society (2001:46).

14. Anders 1987:338.

15. Lübbe illustrates the heightening of the tempo of life using the example of the heightening of *reading speed* as the culturally "standard reaction of the reading public" to the "journalistic compression of innovation" in the late eighteenth century (2009:164f.).

16. The title of a book by Anthony Giddens (1999).

17. Eriksen 2001:70.

18. In the context of these reflections I thank Nancy Fraser for valuable suggestions.

19. But the awareness that one *could* meanwhile take care of the pressing phone call, watch the interesting program, send the attachment, and make the visit (which all fall into the category of what can be felt to be necessary) inconspicuously changes the context, character, and quality of those "simple" activities: even in an oasis of deceleration we can't escape the (late) modern space-time consciousness (cf. the reflections on the difference between the angler and the entrepreneur developed in "In Place of a Preface").

20. Reheis 1998:217ff.; Eberling 1996; Rifkin 1987:189ff.; Eriksen 2001:147ff.

21. Cf., for instance, Rosa 2003:20ff.; Scheuerman 2001a and 2003.

7. Acceleration and Growth

1. See chapter 2.1, figure 2.4.

2. Eriksen 2001:78ff; cf. chapter 2.1.

3. As we have seen, technical acceleration grounds the possibility, but not the actual appearance of quantitative increases. The acceleration of social change

as such does not correspond to any "real growth"; it results in growth only when the change is culturally processed and is supposed to be "translated" into "knowledge" or action orientations. This form of growth then functions as *one* causal factor in the heightening of the tempo of life, which is itself of course defined as a growth process, viz., an increase in the number of episodes of action or experience per unit of time.

4. Reheis 1998:66ff. Compare Schlote: "The conversion of the goal of the economy from the satisfaction of needs to the production of surplus value [i.e., replacement of the circulation cycle of commodity-money-commodity by that of money-commodity-*more money* —H. R.] is the basis on which the specifically capitalist 'economy of time' needs to be understood" (1996:63).

5. Representative for many here are, for instance, Thompson 1967; Zoll 1988b; Scharf 1988a; Adam 1990; Giddens 1995; Sennett 1998; Reheis 1998; Rinderspacher 2000; Schlote 1996; Richter 1991; and in particular Postone 1996. For a review of the literature, cf. further Bergmann 1983:483ff.

6. Here I completely agree with Barbara Adam, who singled out the aspect of *commodified* time as a consequence of capitalist economic activity in her reply to an earlier version of my arguments (Adam 2003).

7. Time's "lack of quality," i.e., the fact that in the capitalist process of production and accounting time displays no "coloring" by circumstances (by festivals and ordinary days, day or night, youth or age, etc.), is mainly responsible for the ever repeated experience and description of it as "dead."

8. Marx 1971:75–6.

9. Adam 2003:50. Cf. Postone 1996:378ff.; Giddens 1987a:150ff.; Garhammer 1999:73ff., 88ff. The commodification of time in capitalist modernity and its equivalence with money reveal themselves today as facts of experience in many aspects of daily life and language: just like money, time is always scarce, regardless of how much one has, and exactly like money one can *lose it, invest it, waste it, save it, allocate it,* etc. And one can convert time and money into each other like two currencies: whoever lacks money must *invest* time in order to *earn* money (as babysitter, lawn mower, wage laborer, etc.), or he must *spend* time and, for example, walk or wash clothes by hand or darn socks, in order to *save* money. In contrast, whoever lacks time can *invest* money in order to gain time: he travels by cab in order to get home faster, hires the gardener, cleaning service, pizza takeout, in order to *save* work time on cooking, cleaning, and gardening. However, as is well known, this free convertibility finds its limits where time is no longer in demand (unemployment) and in the impossibility of saving up time (building interest) for the future.

10. Cf. Schlote 1996:66 and Richter 1991:57.

11. Cf. Schlote 1996:67. The acceleration of production through growth in productivity thus compels in turn a quantitative increase in production, hence

economic growth, as long as the goal of full employment is maintained (since more can be produced with the same quantity of social work): acceleration spirals and growth spirals mutually drive each other on.

12. Cf. Garhammer 1999:79.

13. Marx already attributed to the credit system the function of "acceleration . . . of the particular phases of circulation or the transformation of commodities, further of the transformation of capital, and thus acceleration of the reproduction process in general" (1957:685). On the connection between the interest principle and acceleration, see as well Reheis (1998:181ff.), who draws here on the (controversial) theses of Silvio Gesell.

14. Marx 1976:528ff.

     I have altered the translation from "moral depreciation" to "moral wear" to keep it in line with the parenthetical remark of Rosa. The meaning should be clear. —TRANS.

15. Ibid., 532. For Marx, however, the contradiction is explained by the shift in the ratio of constant (machines) and variable, surplus-value producing capital (labor) in favor of the former and from the resulting tendency of decline in the rate of profit (cf. also ibid., 772ff.).

16. Marx 1957:458:ff.; cf. Schlote 1996:72.

17. Cf. for instance Richter 1991:27ff. or Dohrn-van Rossum 1988.

18. Cf. Marx (1951:§ 5, especially chapter 27, 436ff.), who noticed this early on, as well as Simmel 1992b [1908].

19. Scharf 1988a:157.

20. Linder 1970:77ff.

21. Scharf 1988a.

22. Cf. also, in more detail, Rosa 1999a.

23. Thompson 1967; cf. further, for instance, the contributions in Zoll 1988a or Richter 1991:61ff. It has been objected against Thompson that the formation of a linear concept of time and maintenance of temporal discipline does not first begin in the industrial revolution, but rather has a series of important historical forerunners, for instance, in monasteries, and that social time orientations are always "plural," complex, and multileveled, so that there could never be a simple and complete separation between "the" time orientations of one epoch and those of another (Thrift 1988; Glennie and Thrift 1996; Garhammer 1999:73ff.; cf. also Dohrn-van Rossum 1988). Neither point is in dispute here, but they do not change the fact that it is only in the wake of the industrial revolution and the institutional regime of the industrial age that a rigorous and extensive, socially obligatory establishment of the aforementioned temporal patterns and structures occurred and that these from then on dominated the temporal order of modern societies in spite of the continued existence of alternative time orientations.

24. Marx 1976:367 (trans. altered). Cf. Garhammer 1999:79.

25. Cf. for example Giddens 1987a:151.

26. The central focus of Thompson (1967) is on this transformation.

27. Giddens 1990:59ff. and 1987a:149ff.

28. Cf. for instance, Scharf 1988b; Negt 1988; or Thompson 1967.

29. But even the timetables and maps of public transportation systems or the schedules of the theater or the cinema contribute to orienting everyday consciousness and social practices in accordance with the concept of linear and abstract clock time.

30. Mumford 1934:14. On the complex connection between the development of modern time consciousness and the history of the introduction and diffusion of the mechanical clock, the chime clock, and finally the precision clock in the context of monastery routines, city government, and (later) industrialization, cf. also Dohrn-van Rossum 1988; LeGoff 1977; Thrift 1988.

31. In this respect, the time regime of schools, through which children are accustomed to the corresponding temporal practices, is quite instructive. "The school day consists in a permanent confrontation with linear time. Early in the morning the alarm clock, during breakfast presumably regular announcements of the time on the radio, then on the way to school the departure times (to be followed as exactly as possible) of buses and trains, once one finally arrives the minute hand admonishes students in the hallway and the classroom, at the end of the hour the bell announces the break. The school serves as an 'apparatus for the intensification of time use'" (Richter 1991:40; cf. further Treptow 1992:9ff. and Garhammer 1999:73ff.).

32. Cf. Giddens 1990:59ff.

33. Cf. Rosa 2004b; see also Garhammer 1999:75ff.

34. Cf. Virilio 1980:61f.; in addition, Breuer 1988:314ff.

35. Piore and Sable 1984; Behr 1999; Voß 1998 and 2001; Sennett 1998; Garhammer 1999 and 2002.

36. The widely observable transition from long-term, routinized work to "project work" or work projects (often accomplished by teams) is here just *one* symptom of the replacement of abstract rigid work oriented to externally prescribed time patterns by short- to mid-term but relatively autonomous and flexible activities.

37. The (at this point quite comprehensive) research on this topic rightly warns against overgeneralizing this finding: in many firms, above all in those that are highly mechanized and whose personnel have few qualifications, the "classical modern" work time regime still dominates and has even appeared to retrench for the moment in the wake of the fall of the "New Economy" and the generation of young managers that rose with it, thus making clear the much discussed "limits of the dissolution of the limits of work." However, it seems to me that

the demonstrated development is indisputable in its *tendency* to point in a certain direction (cf. also Döhl et al. 2001; Moldaschl and Sauer 2000; further, see Schneider, Limmer, and Ruckdeschel 2002).

38. Naturally teleworkers aren't the only ones for whom the new-old task orientation is applicable: due to the new technical possibilities of continuous, need-oriented availability and spatial independence through portable computers and phones, it is no longer only (social) scientists but also, in the meantime, for example, real estate brokers, programmers, and insurance agents who distinguish less and less between work time and free time or who switch back and forth in short and irregular rhythms and in relative disregard of space between free time and work. On telework cf., for example, Garhammer and Mundorf 1997.

39. Cf. Behr 1999:145ff. or Deutschmann 1989.

40. The current discussion in the sociology of work regarding late capitalist "dissolution of the boundaries" and "subjectivation" of work stands in this context. Cf. Voß 1998 and 2001; Behr 1999; Schneider, Limmer, and Ruckdeschel 2002; Döhl et al. 2002; and Moldaschl and Sauer 2000.

41. Cf. Elmar Altvater's essay for the journal, *Erwägen, Wissen, Ethik* (Altvater 2002) and the other discussion pieces printed there.

42. On the following, cf. Rosa 2002b.

43. The much-noticed recent work of Michael Hardt and Antonio Negri (2001) falls in this category. The distinction or "fundamental contradiction" between "empire" and "multitude" forms its analytical (or "ontological") basis. However, Hardt and Negri's adherence to the definition of a proletariat as a potentially revolutionary, oppositional class makes the inadequacy of their approach for the interpretation of late modern social reality clear. "All of [the] diverse forms of labor are in some way subject to capitalist discipline and capitalist relations of production. This fact of being within capital and sustaining capital is what defines the proletariat as a class," write Hardt and Negri (53) and involuntarily demonstrate that this "proletariat" does *not* form a class, but rather describes the life circumstances of *all* actors in developed societies. For to whom is this definition *not* applicable? Insofar as more or less *all* actors in modern societies are subject to the compulsions of capital, which reach deep into the forms of subjectivity and the relations we have to our own bodies, potential resistance is certainly not in the first place to be found along lines of class conflict or in the "working class," as Hardt and Negri imply, but rather in the traditions aiming at *individual and political self-determination* that are found in these societies.

44. Precisely this second variant also seems to be gaining the upper hand in recent neo-Marxian research in the Anglo-Saxon realm, for instance, in the works of David Harvey, Fredric Jameson, or Moishe Postone.

45. William Scheuerman's criticism of my identification of "the" social form of capitalism as one of the main motors of social acceleration, namely, that it leaves unclear *which manifestation of capitalism I had in mind*, therefore misses its target (Scheuerman 2003:42): the argument is precisely that the dynamization effect is the characteristic that connects all the manifestations of this mode of economic activity.

46. See, for instance, Sennett 1998; in addition, see Garhammer comparative study (1999) as well as Streeck and Höpner 2003.

47. Thus Behr (1999:44), drawing on Luhmann. Cf. also Richter 1991:65f.

   REFA (Verband für Arbeitsgestaltung, Betriebsorganisation und Unternehmensentwicklung) is a German organization that studies industrial organization and offers consulting services for businesses that want to optimize their productivity by making relations between management, labor, and the means of production as smooth and efficient as possible. According to its Wikipedia page, it was "founded in the tradition of 'Scientific Management' and represents the perspective of 'industrial engineering' in German-speaking lands." —TRANS.

48. Habermas 1987a:318ff.

49. Cf. Behr 1999:34f. The intensification of work already represents, then, the second stage of the unfolding of the capitalist logic of acceleration: as Marx had already worked out in a historically meticulous way, capitalism accelerated capital accumulation in the eighteenth and early nineteenth centuries first by the *extensification* of work, i.e., by *lengthening the work day* to up to fourteen, sixteen, and extreme cases even more hours. The way of accelerating production quickly ran up against its limits, however – it lead to the loss of the ability to reproduce itself and made the actual, paid labor process become inefficient. The economic system reacted to this with its first transformation, which generated at one and the same time a shortening of work time (and hence also sufficient time for consumption and training) and economic acceleration through the *intensification* of work.

50. Gert Günter Voß, for instance, postulates a "far-reaching structural transformation" of the world of work in all its dimensions along the lines of development indicated here (1998:1, cf. 2001).

51. The citations are from Garhammer 1999:74. Michael Behr also defends this claim (1999:cf. especially 171).

52. Cf. in more detail Garhammer 1999 and Grotheer and Struck 2003.

53. Voß 1998:25ff. Cf. also Voß 1990 and Sennett 1998.

54. In fact, Weber characterizes this principle as an unavoidable consequence of (economic) processes of rationalization (2001:30). Richard Sennet in turn, in his essay on the culture of the new "Turbo Capitalism," judges that precisely

this feeling that all *standing still* unavoidably means *going backwards*, leads in the end to a hyper-activism that is irrational even from an economic point of view (1998:99ff.). Interestingly, Robinson and Godbey identify just this stance as a dominant trend in the conduct of life: "From such a perspective, the line between free time and work is largely irrelevant—to do nothing is to be nothing, and both work and free-time activity are important in defining who we are. It is little wonder that the preparation of résumés has become a science and that such résumés now often include information about people's free-time activities as well as their work activities" (1999:45).

55. Levine 2006:97, cf. 283; also Geißler 1999:168ff.

56. Thus Piore and Sable, for instance, describe the contemporary economic strategy of *flexible specialization* as "a strategy of permanent innovation: an adaptation to lasting transformation instead of the desire to try and master it" (cited here from Sennett 1998:64; cf. also Backhaus and Gruner 1998).

57. For instance, Sennett 1998 and Garhammer 1999. Cf. also Rinderspacher 2000.

58. This approach is taken above all by Reheis 1998, cf. especially 64; Jameson 1994 and 1998; and, in a highly elaborated way, Harvey 1990; cf. also Scheuerman 2001a:2ff. and Postone 1996:224f.

59. Cf. Rosa 1999b:395ff.

60. A classic formulation of this point of view was provided by Max Weber in his study on the Protestant ethic (2001). Cf. further Gronemeyer 1996; Blumenberg 1986; or Heintel and Macho 1985.

61. Cf. in detail Rosa 2004b as well as 1998:271ff.

62. Cf. on this the introduction, especially section 1.

63. The Christian origin of the idea that the course of history has a fixed direction and aim and can be accelerated has been pointed out in particular by Ernst Benz (1977) and then Reinhart Koselleck (2000:168ff., 177ff.). In an altered form it became a driving force of the Enlightenment project (*aufklärerischen Handelns*), which wanted to accelerate, with all its power, a human progress that had been delayed for too long and whose aim was now conceived as *historically immanent* (cf. ibid.; and Blumenberg 1986:218ff.). On the basis of deterministic philosophies of history, the idea of a revolutionary political-historical task of acceleration was derived that inspired revolutionary social movements well into the twentieth century (Lübbe 2009:168ff.).

So the element of an *expectation of salvation*, at first Christian and later secularized, should not be underestimated in the genesis of the modern urge to accelerate. Yet Hans Blumenberg also points out in this context that while "acceleration ideologies" lie close at hand in the case of closed, deterministic conceptions of history, they are actually very improbable in conceptions of time with an open future. He emphasizes that "insight into the necessity of the course of history [is] by itself . . . the sufficient motivation for the readiness to support with all one's accelerating power something known in advance," in contrast, "something unknown [must do without] any inclination to influence or cooperate with it," i.e., an acceleration through our own actions. What needs to be explained here, then, are the ways in which the impulse to accelerate has been preserved and even further entrenched across the transformation of historical conceptions of time.

64. Luhmann 1994 [1968]:156.

65. Weber 2001; cf. chapter 1.2.a above, and further Neumann 1988 or Sparn 1999.

66. Cf. chapter 1.2a, note 62. We find the same moral rigorism in a secularized variant in Benjamin Franklin, who reminds one that each person who fails to acquire a five-shilling piece out of laziness "murders" this and all its potential capital gains "to the thousandth generation" (cited in Weber 2001:15). The heinousness of wasting time is thereby placed on a level with the worst capital crimes.

67. Russell 1985. Voß (1990) has attempted to show the ways in which this Protestant ethos has remained decisive as a paradigm for the conduct of life in a transformed and even expanded form.

68. This is why, for instance, the strict moral prohibitions of *murder* or *stealing* do not produce any corresponding positive motivational energies.

69. While *Angst* in other contexts would likely be best translated by "anxiety," "angst," or "dread," none of these could plausibly represent one of the two most fundamental human drives, while fear would immediately be recognized as a viable candidate. Similarly, while *Verheißung* does not have the same range of connotations as "promise," it is captured perfectly in expressions like "a promising situation" or "the promised land" (indeed the German for the latter is *das Land der Verheißung*). It also incorporates the idea of hope or something hoped for. However, "hope" would not be a good translation of *Verheissung*, despite the intuitive quality that a pairing of fear and hope has as well as the support of philosophical tradition for their identification as two basic human drives (as in the work of thinkers like Hobbes and Spinoza). —TRANS.

70. Weber 2001:69. The "means of periodically 'working off' the affect-laden consciousness of guilt" were removed by the abolition of confession (ibid., 124). Restless professional work and a methodical conduct of life that was self-conscious about time were then a sharpened psychological "antidote."

71. Taken strictly, both interpretations contradict Calvin's own teaching according to which predestination cannot be discerned by any external signs.

72. Lutz 1984; Deutschmann 1999.

73. Deutschmann 1999:100. Deutschmann's thesis draws on the work of Luhmann.
74. Ibid., 177, 179.
75. Gronemeyer 1996.
76. Cf. chapter 2.4.
77. On the "wave of acceleration" at the end of the twentieth century, see also chapter 9.
78. Blumenberg 1986; Gronemeyer 1996; and, in addition, de Haan 1996; Geißler 1999; and Achtner, Kunz, and Walter 1998:76ff.
79. The question of the relationship between acceleration and secularization in modernity is in fact as interesting as it is complex. Somewhat in tension with foregoing reflections (cf. note 63, this chapter), according to which the thought of acceleration is above all a consequence of the Judeo-Christian expectation of salvation, one can actually argue with equal plausibility that (traditional) religiosity constitutes a massive cultural obstacle to acceleration. For religious ideas almost always include a reference to a "transcendent dimension of time" (sacral time) that contains an element of stability or even a static condition (cf. Achtner, Kunz, and Walter 1998; Sparn 1999:19ff.). Perhaps, then, the comprehensive secularization of society was a *presupposition* for its revolutionary acceleration, even though it may also be in part its *consequence*. "The causal arrow runs," as Taylor once formulated the point, "in both directions . . . the skein of causes is inextricable" (Taylor 1989:206). If one nevertheless wanted to undertake an "extrication," one obvious way would be to see here as well the dialectical dynamic of acceleration already noted in various contexts at work: the Christian expectation of salvation set in motion a dynamic of acceleration which in the end became so strong that it was incompatible with religious ideas and thus began to erode them.
80. Friedell 1976.
81. Gronemeyer 1996:91f.; cf. further Blumenberg 1986:86ff.
82. On the following, cf. Gronemeyer 1996:92ff.
83. Rosa is punning on the Marxian idea of the "species being" or "species essence" (*Gattungswesen*) of humanity, the idea that what is essential to being human cannot be found in individuals considered apart from their relations to wider human groupings, and that ultimately the "essence" of humanity, such as it is, can only be found in the history of the human species as a whole. —TRANS.
84. Goethe 1961:189 (*Faust*, part 1, second scene in Faust's study, lines 1770–75). On Goethe's clear-eyed interpretation of the "velociferian" essence of modernity, cf. in greater detail Osten 2003 and 2004.
85. Schulze 1997b:90, cf. 87. Cf. also his 1997a and 2003.

86. To stick with Goethe for the moment, this idea finds its classic literary expression in *Wilhelm Meister's Apprenticeship* (though it is pessimistically retracted at the end).

87. That this abstract idea has definitely struck roots in contemporary conceptions of how to lead a (good) life is shown in my view by the time practices and time problems of, above all, many women (which are well documented in time budget studies): because they desire to lead the life of a "good mother" as well as a successful career woman, but both life projects make potentially total claims on their time, they try to live as it were two complete lives in the span of one by doubling their pace of life—either by trying to take care of all the justified demands made on a mother and all the legitimate claims on a professional *in parallel* (which despite increases in tempo leave them continually short of time) or by *first* pursuing a professional career and *afterward* the life of a housewife and mother (or the reverse; as a successful female British colleague recently explained to me with respect to her own high work tempo, one has to *work at a fanatic pace when one starts an academic career only after raising two children*). The same holds true in a certain way for all those who plan to live the life of an artist after being a business consultant or be a manager in professional life but a teacher and parent in free time.

88. Heintel and Macho 1985:66. Castells likewise diagnoses, in the culture of the "Information Age," the attempt to overcome death and achieve eternity within our life span through a hyperacceleration that appears to be simultaneity (which leads to a cultural repression of death). However, he explicitly emphasizes that there is no connection between this idea and the capitalist economy. He thus overlooks, in my view, the constitutive bond between this culture and that economy that results from the principle of acceleration (Castells 1996:452ff.).

89. Cf. also Nowotny 1993:139ff.

90. Even into the 1970s, whoever turned on a TV channel missed at the same two other programs. Today, one potentially misses hundreds—which has produced the accelerated consumption habit of "channel surfing."

91. "Abraham, or some peasant of the past, died 'old and sated with life' because he stood in the organic cycle of life; because his life, in terms of its meaning and on the eve of his days, had given to him what life had to offer; because for him there remained no puzzles he might wish to solve; and therefore he could have 'enough' of life. Whereas civilized man, placed in the midst of the continuous enrichment of culture by ideas, knowledge, and problems, may become 'tired of life,' but not sated with life. He catches only the most minute part of what the life of the spirit brings forth ever anew, and therefore death for him is a meaningless occurrence. And because death is meaningless, civilized life as such is meaningless; by its very 'progressiveness' it gives death the imprint

of meaninglessness" (Weber, from "Science as a Vocation," cited in 1946:140). With this observation on the "meaninglessness" of scientific progress, Weber unknowingly formulates at the same time the failure of the program of acceleration as an answer to death.

92. When Bálint Balla claims that time scarcity is a universal phenomenon that is not dependent on culture, because there is always a "deficit between the time required to satisfy needs, to realize desired objectives, on the one hand, and the de facto amount of available time, on the other" (1978:26), he overlooks the fact that an acceleration-theoretical interpretation of his argument reveals precisely the way that time scarcity is rooted in the cultural pattern he describes. The problem of time scarcity can indeed be in principle overcome by the acceleration of goal-directed processes: the time needed for the satisfaction of existing needs and desires can be successively harmonized with the amount of time available—unless the former multiply at the same or at a higher rate. Then, of course, a sharpening of the problem of time scarcity occurs despite the accelerated satisfaction of needs.

93. I use the concept of social structure here in the sense proposed by Luhmann or Durkheim, which refers to the foundational lines of social differentiation; hence not in the sense of social-structural research that pertains to the analysis of inequality, social milieus, and status positions.

    Cf. section 1 of the introduction and, further, Bergmann 1983:476ff.

94. Bergmann 1983:483; cf. Luhman 1990a:131f.

95. On this relationship of reciprocal escalation, cf. also Luhmann 1980:251f.

96. Luhmann 1991:124.

97. Luhmann 1980:238; 1990:141; cf. 1996:76ff.; cf. also Nassehi 1993:199ff.

98. This problem can be illustrated with the example of choice-delaying technical achievements like the video recorder: if you can't decide between two shows in light of the diversity of options on television and you therefore decide to watch the one and record the other, you'll realize the next time you sit down to watch TV that you now have not only the agony of deciding between whichever programs are currently on but also of deciding for or against the recorded shows. Temporalizing complexity in this sense leads to a floodlike growth of complexity.

99. Luhmann 1996:79.

100. Luhmann 1980:255, cf. 1990b:114f.

101. Luhmann 1990b:117, 126.

102. Luhmann 1980:279f.

103. The transfer of the scarcity of time from the internal systemic perspective to that of actors requires strong assumptions from the point of view of systems theory because conscious or "psychic" systems, which, according to this ap-

proach, first become persons through self/other attributions, are not operationally coupled to the communicative process (*Geschehen*) in social systems. That time becomes scarce in social systems only implies in a very mediated way that it also does so for individual actors. Then how is the transfer mechanism to be reconstructed in a systems-theoretical way? The path has been illustrated by Armin Nassehi. In *Time of Society* (*Zeit der Gesellschaft*), he demonstrates, in the first place, that the structural coupling of psychic systems and social systems is in the end a temporal coupling that is, however, of a merely temporary nature, i.e., a psychic system and a social system operate in the mode of simultaneity when and just so long as the former adjusts itself to the social context, in other words, is in a certain way "latched on" (1993:175). ("Structurally coupled systems ultimately converge only through a reciprocal simultaneity of system and environment, but they give the simultaneous events differing selectivities and connections.") However, because at each moment psychic systems have the option of once again "unlatching" themselves or pursuing other selectivities and connections, this form of temporal coupling is not yet sufficient to ground the accelerating effect of functional differentiation on persons. The latter only becomes unavoidable on the basis of the mutual functional necessity of the historical coordination and synchronization of individuals and social systems. According to Nassehi, this occurs by means of process structures that make action routines and event chains predictable (*erwartbar*) and thus temporally couple psychic and social systems to one another. "Process structures are capable of achieving the synchronization of society and consciousness in such a way that they treat individuals as addressees of communication. . . . Not only in the social, but also in the temporal dimension, consciousnesses find themselves to be persons who, through the experience of communication, not only know what is expected from them, but also when" (ibid., 353f., note 111). In particular, where the continuation of systemic operations decisively depends on the activity of individual persons in this way, the latter fall under temporal pressure as a result of the scarcity of time systemically induced through the temporalization of complexity.

104. Rammstedt 1975:50, 55ff.; cf. also Nassehi 1993:194f., 376f.
105. Guy 2002:4.
106. Nassehi 1993:376f., cf. 332ff. See also Luhman 1980:296ff.
107. Luhmann himself again and again refers to this effect of a shortening of the present as a result of the increased temporalization of complexity. Cf. for instance 1980:242ff., 261, 296; or 1990:119ff. Cf. also Nassehi 1993:342f.
108. Luhmann himself leaves little doubt about this (doubled) acceleration effect of functional differentiation (cf. 1980:239, 288, 296, or also 1990a), however he holds that the related perception of "tempo increases, shortenings of the

present . . . mutability even of what is constant and the like" are the consequence of an obsolete semantics that ultimately rests on an anachronistic concept of motion that is no longer appropriate for contemporary structural complexity. Nevertheless, he then proves unable to indicate how an appropriate description of this phenomenon using other concepts is supposed to look (Luhman 1980:296). But his conjecture that "much stress and hurry" could thus be just "the consequence of a disparity between structure and semantics" (ibid.) is highly implausible against the background of his own theory of the temporalization of complexity, because the latter appears to present the increasing scarcity of time as a necessary result of the way functionally differentiated systems operate.

109. Cf. for instance Adam, Geißler, and Held 1998.

110. Cf. here Coser's (1974) instructive analysis of "greedy institutions." Coser still starts out from the assumption that a clear functional differentiation works against the principle of the "greedy organization," which aims at "total commitment." Simultaneous inclusion in several overlapping organizations offers protection against the threatened loss of autonomy due to "greedy" monopolization (ibid., 21). Coser argues that this multiple commitment prevents the claims of the organizations on the resources of individuals from becoming total because it rests on collectively binding normative and legal regulations and delimitations of the conflicting claims and thus allows a relatively conflict-free "sequential inclusion." "Thus . . . the amount of time that an individual legitimately owes to his employer is normatively and even legally established; this makes it possible for him to have time for his family or other non-occupational associations. Similarly, democratic societies limit the areas in which the claims of the state upon the citizen are considered legitimate. . . . Modern non-totalitarian societies typically come to terms with . . . competing demands on individuals through a structural arrangement by which these individuals, far from being fully immersed into a particular sub-system, are in fact segmentally engaged in a variety of social circles, none of which should demand exclusive loyalty. . . . Their multifaceted involvements with a plurality of role-partners . . . are not likely to present insolvable dilemmas . . . as long . . . as all of them are content with controlling only a segment . . . of the personality. To put the matter a little differently, the segmental structure of a society is viable to the extent that concommitant patterns of normative priorities assign the claims for loyalty in such a way that little choice has to be made by the individuals concerned" (ibid., 2f [my emphasis]). Yet according the thesis developed here, at the beginning of the twenty-first century the "segmentally" differentiated organizations themselves become "greedy" and overstep the (time-, space-, and resource-specific) limits placed on their control in the wake of spatial and temporal

processes of boundary dissolution and subjectivation. The obligatory normative and legal limitations are caught in a process of erosion—with possibly
grave consequences for the individual (and collective) capacity for autonomy,
as still remains to be shown in a more detailed way. Now individuals no longer
see themselves confronted by just one, but rather by several "greedy" organizations (cf. on this tendency, Bennis and Slater 1968).

111. Connected to our example, this means that the (legitimate) claims of the family must take a backseat to those of professional life and the citizens' group, the
(legitimate) demands of career must be held back by those of the family and
civic engagement, the possibility of being overly taxed by family and work life
must be taken into account if the citizen initiative is to continue to exist, etc.

112. Cf. Bennis and Slater 1968:93.

113. Hörning, Ahrens, and Gerhard 1997; cf. for instance, Garhammer 1999:157ff.,
411ff., 463ff.; Robinson and Godbey 1999:286ff.; or Benthaus-Apel 1995; as well
as Sennett 1998; Eriksen 2001.

114. On the pattern of dialectical formation and erosion that the characteristic institutional patterns of modernity display as its forces of acceleration unfold, cf.
chapter 8, especially figure 81.

115. Hörning, Ahrens, and Gerhard 1997:168 (my emphasis), cf. 179; as well as
Nassehi 1993; Sandbothe 1997, 1998. See also Luhmann's concept of "temporalization" (1997:2:997ff.).

116. In this I follow Schimank (2000:cf. especially 274f.) rather than Luhmann
in assuming that functional differentiation and the claim of political control
(Steuerung; at least regarding the social framework) are equally fundamental
for the structural and cultural arrangement of modernity.

8. Power, War, and Speed

1. Cf. in particular, Virilio 2006; Scheuerman 2003 and 2004; Tilly 1990; or Eberling 1996, as well as Giddens 1987b, 1990, 1995a:182ff.; and Münkler 2009.

2. Cf. Giddens 1990:59ff.

3. Cf. chapter 2.4.

4. I agree on this point with Scheuerman's (2003:43) remarks on my reflections.

5. Thus Max Weber already praised modern bureaucracy as the fastest and most
efficient—and just for this reason inescapable—form of administration. "In
the classical model, administrative activity is . . . an efficient time-saving instrument since it minimizes the need for time-consuming deliberation during the
implementation of policy. Administrative officials need not engage in ambitious debate, or worry about reaching an agreement about the aims of policy,
since others have already done so for them. They ideally do nothing more than

apply standing general rules, and like 'automatons' should properly 'spill forth the verdict' on any particular issue at hand 'with the reasons read mechanically from codified paragraphs,'" summarizes Scheuerman in connection with the time efficiency of the bureaucratic decision-making process (2003:45f).

6. Cf. in greater detail, Held et al. 1999:39ff. 58ff.; Münkler 2009:§ 4, 21f.; and Virilio 1998b:22f.

7. "Speed has always been the advantage and the privilege of the hunter and the warrior. Racing and pursuit are the heart of all combat. There is thus a hierarchy of speeds to be found in the history of societies, for to possess the earth, to hold terrain, is also to possess the best means to scan it in order to protect and defend it. Real-estate property is linked, directly or indirectly, to the faculty of its penetration" (Virilio 1998b:24). On the power to move, cf. Virilio and Lothringer 1984:57; Breuer 1988:316ff.; further Eberling 1996:59ff. On the "dialectic" of acceleration and deceleration in war, cf. Münkler 2009.

8. Cf. for instance Giddens 1990:14ff., 66f.

9. Scheuerman 2003:43.

10. Virilio 2006:62.

11. Cf. Virilio 2006:159ff.

12. Eberling 1996:62. Cf. Virilio 2006 and Sloterdijk 1989:21ff. On the partly accelerating, partly delaying effect of war itself on social and political development, cf. in more detail, Münkler 2009:§ 2.

13. On the reciprocal links between the military, the administrative surveillance state, industrialism, and capitalism, cf. Giddens 1990:59ff. On the irreducibility of the nation-state principle to the needs of developing capitalism (and vice versa), cf. ibid., 66f., and also in greater detail Giddens 1995a:182ff.

14. Scheuerman 2003.

15. Cf. Münkler 2009:257ff.

16. Cf. Eberling 1996:61.

17. Cf., inter alia, Foucault 1995.

18. In fact, the meticulous analysis of military actions into their component parts in Holland in the late sixteenth century seems to anticipate the accelerative idea of Taylorism. According to Giddens, for instance, Moritz von Oranien analyzed the operation of a musket into a series of forty-three particular steps and that of a pike into twenty-three individual movements (1986:148). McNeill also emphasizes that the new forms of military drill in the seventeenth century brought *to each individual movement a new measure of exactness and speed* (1982:130; cf. on this also Scheuerman 2003:44f.).

19. "'Career' brings to mind a set trajectory . . . with a sequence of stages marked in advance and accompanied by moderately clear conditions of entry and rules of admission. . . . Whatever happens to the employees of Microsoft or its count-

less watchers and imitators, where all concern of the managers is with looser organizational forms which are more able to go with the flow, and where business organization is increasingly seen as a never conclusive, ongoing attempt to form an island of superior adaptability in a world perceived as multiple, complex and fast moving . . . militates against durable structures, and notably against structures with a built-in life-expectation commensurable with the customary length of a work-life. Under such conditions the idea of a 'career' seems nebulous and utterly out of place," observes Zygmunt Bauman (2000:116f.) drawing on Nigel Thrift. Cf. Sennett 1998 as well as the literature discussed in chapter 7.1.

20. Virilio 2006:157.

21. Ibid., 147ff.

22. Eberling 1996:63f.

23. Münkler 2002:13ff., 175ff.; and van Creveld 1998; further Enzensberger 1994.

24. Münkler 2002 and 2009, van Creveld 1998, Enzensberger 1994.

25. Cf. in addition Castells 1997:chapter 4.

26. "Of course, here the latest developments, like the so-called stealth bomber, show that new military developments need not be toward further increases of speed, but instead can be devoted to reducing detectability, which may involve sacrifces of speed," as Münkler thus also finds (2009:251). Scheuerman's examples for the recent acceleration effects of military technology are therefore unconvincing: the bombing of English cities by the German Luftwaffe is not "recent," the transmission of the bombing of Baghdad on TV screens is not an achievement of military technology, and the success of "smart bombs" does not rest on acceleration effects (2003:46).

27. Castells 1996:6f. Münkler 2002:25f., 55. The *acceleration* and *deceleration* of warfare are here naturally complementary principles of military strategy: *defenders* always react to the increased power to move of potential attackers by developing new methods of *hindering, braking, and delaying*—the clearest historical examples of which are castles and fortresses as well as city walls and moats. As Virilio tries to show, however, up to now the technological and organizational impetus has come as a rule from the increase of attack speed and hence from progress in accelerative technologies—thus here again acceleration and deceleration prove to be *asymmetrical*. So, from this point of view, the Arpanet only represents a compensatory or *catch-up deceleration* (*nachholende Entschleunigung*).

Interestingly, one can see the same "dialectic" of acceleration and deceleration in the history of soccer: new strategies and techniques of acceleration in the offensive game meet with reactions of improved defensive "versions of deceleration," while the game as a whole has become faster and faster in the last few decades. Of course, even here one should expect that football is in a way asymptotically approximating its biophysically conditioned absolute speed limits.

28. For example, Beck 1997:34.

29. Cf. for instance Gilpin 1987. On this skeptical position regarding globalization, see also Held et al. 1999:5ff.

30. *Sovereignty* here designates the legal guarantee of a nation's freedom to act, while *autonomy* refers to the de facto existence of such maneuvering room, i.e., the actual power to act; cf. Held et al. 1999:441ff.

31. Cf. Beck 1997:chapter 1; Harvey 2000b:65; Castells 1997; Held et al. 1999.

32. Held et al. 1999:especially 436ff., cf. 82ff. Similarly, although with a clearer emphasis on the loss of power, Castells 1997:chapter 4.

33. Cf. von Creveld 1998 and 1999, who likewise suggests the parallel between the functional transformation of the national state and the military.

34. Cf. Weber 1978:956ff. See further Beniger 1986:13ff., 184f. on the connection of bureaucratization and rationalization in the age of industrialization. Surprisingly, Scheuerman appears to hold just these rigid characteristics of bureaucracy to be, even today, extraordinarily accelerative.

35. Cf. Castells 1998:chapter 1.

36. One finds in Chesneaux the following quotation from the former Czechoslovakian president, Vaclav Havel, in 1990: "When I began to work in my presidential office in the Prague Castle, I found no clocks at all, and this was for me a strong symbol; for long, endless years there had been no need to look at the time, because time did not exist. History had stopped, and not only in the Castle of Prague, but in the whole country. Today, history is rushing ahead . . . and seems to be making up for lost time. All of us . . . have to re-enter the course of time" (2000:419). Priller points to the meager dynamism of the time use patterns of the East German Republic from the 1970s to the reunification of Germany, which he interprets as a sign of the absence of innovation and modernization (1992:610f.). See further Borneman (1993:105) and Keane (1991:189) as well as Urry (2005:20). This experience of time is also given an eloquent expression in Wolfgang Becker's successful film about reunification, "Good-Bye Lenin," in which the young protagonist observes that life afterward has gotten faster and faster and gives one the feeling of being in a particle accelerator. On the differing paces of life in East and West Germany and the experience of reunification as one of acceleration, cf. also Hofmann 2004.

37. *Süddeutsche Zeitung*, February 1–2, 2003, 48.

38. Cf. for instance, Beck 1997:13ff.; Castells 1997:chapter 5. Thus one may agree with Scheuerman's (2003) criticism of an earlier formulation of my thesis of the loss of function of the national state insofar as important accelerating impulses

still come from this actor, but he overlooks their paradoxical structure, and this is what underlies my own interpretation of the state as a late modern obstacle to acceleration.

39. Cf. Beck 1997:203ff.
40. Cf. chapter 7.1.
41. Cf. chapter 11.3 and 13.
42. In greater detail here, see chapter 10.2 and 10.3.
43. For discussion of figure 8.1, see chapters 9 and 10.3.

9. Acceleration, Globalization, Postmodernity

1. Beck 1997:16, 13f.; cf. Harvey 2000b:62f.
2. I would like to recall here once again that this *new* element cannot consist in the liquefying of institutions and social relations per se, because modernity is characterized from the very beginning by a tendency toward the dynamization of "all that is solid." The institutional ensemble of "classical modernity" that formed after a first wave of dynamization of static traditional institutions in the wake of the industrial revolution achieved, however, an astonishing high level of time resistance because it took account of the dynamizing character of modernity and proved itself to be capable of guiding the social world's processes of acceleration and change onto stable paths and in just this way driving them onward. Cf., in greater detail, chapter 2.4 as well as Wagner 1994 and Bauman 2000:2f.
3. On the conceptual distinction between late and postmodernity, cf. the introduction, note 76.
4. Cf., representative here for many, Harvey 1990:113ff.; Jameson 1998; Giddens 1990:150, 163; Welsch 1994:introduction; or Urry 2009.
5. Cf. here Peter Wagner's (1994) illuminating attempt to clarify the empirical foundations of the postmodernity diagnoses.
6. On the sociological debate surrounding the question of rupture and continuity in modernity, cf. Berger 1986.
7. Castells discerns three main driving forces in the information age: the *cultural revolution* since 1968 and the new social movements that arose from it, the *technological breakthrough* in microelectronics, and the political-economic *crisis of statism* (1996:5ff. and 1998:355ff.). Datings of developmental tendencies of society as a whole are, however, always to be undertaken with extreme caution: on this point a broad consensus reigns in the social sciences after the debates concerning the beginning of modernity or capitalism.
8. On the "digital revolution," cf. for example Freyermuth 2000 and Eriksen 2001. The latter mentions the collapse of the Soviet Union, the disintegration of Yugo-

slavia, and the second Gulf War as the political events that developed a cardinal surge of acceleration around 1991 (ibid., 8ff.). On the dynamizing effect of the "political revolution," see, further, Urry 2009:193f. On the "mobile revolution," see Myerson 2001. On the "economic revolution of speed" of "turbo capitalism," driven above all by multinational firms with new strategies of centralization and decentralization, altered employment circumstances, and a new spatial distribution of production, see chapter 7.1; further Sennet 1998; Harvey 1990:141ff.; Jameson 1998:67f. The thesis that these developments together introduce a new epoch—i.e., a transformation of the modes of production, politics and cultural experience—is at the root of Castells's three-volume work on the information age (1996, 1997, 1998). A similar point of view is represented by Hardt and Negri in their controversial diagnosis of the times, *Empire* (2001).

9. Freyermuth 2000:75.

10. Cf. chapter 2.2a.

11. Cf. the introduction, section 2, and chapter 1.1.

12. Cf. here especially the findings discussed in part 2.

13. Cf. chapter 2.3 and also chapter 10.3.

   "National malaise" is my attempt to capture the meaning of the German term *Volkskrankheit*, which literally means "sickness of the people." —Trans.

14. Baier 2000; Jameson 1998:50ff.

15. Compare Harvey: "Capitalism is always under the impulsion to accelerate turnover time, to speed up the circulation of capital and consequently to revolutionize the time horizon of development. But it can do so only through long-term investments (in, e.g., the built environment as well as in elaborate and stable infrastructures for production, consumption, exchange, communication, and the like). Moreover, a major stratagem of crisis avoidance lies in absorbing overaccumulated capital in long-term projects (e.g., the famous 'public works' launched by the state in times of depression) and this slows down the turnover time of capital" (2000b:58). Cf., in greater detail, chapter 2.3d.

16. That, in contrast, *individual* forms of functional deceleration are experiencing an economic boom may count as a further index of a continuing surge of acceleration: courses, spa treatments, techniques, and vacations that suggest "pausing" represent one of the few boom sectors of the free time economy, and trendsetting "wellness oases" are doubtless the paradigmatic example of intentionally created islands of deceleration.

17. This is shown even in the attemped definitions of the new by Harvey (2000b:67f.) and Held et al. (1999:424), which otherwise possess a sharp consciousness of temporal-structural changes, as well as in Castells's almost helpless-seeming list of new aspects of society (1998:356).

18. Cf. also Jessop 2009.

19. Held et al. 1999:14ff.

20. Ibid., 433. At the same time, the analytical framework developed by Held et al. makes it clear that globalization as a process displays thoroughly uneven and occasionally contrary developmental tendencies: for example, dimensions regarding migration streams or in some regions even regarding the proportion of external trade, the degree of globalization may have even been markedly higher in earlier historical epochs.

21. On these three possible interpretations of globalization, cf. Harvey 2000b:53f. Beck suggests an analogous conceptual differentiation when he describes the process dimension as *globalization* and the project dimension as *globalism* (1997:26ff.).

22. On the first, cf. Harvey 1990; see also the introduction, section 3, and chapter 1.1. On the latter, see Giddens 1995a:90ff. Interestingly, Giddens himself (in contrast to other authors who have taken up his conception) fails to consistently apply this perspective to the globalization process. Thus it is left out of his conception of the dimensions of globalization (1990:71ff.). For the definition of globalization as a corresponding alteration of the spatiotemporal dispositive, cf. Jessop 2009 or Waters 1995.

23. "By disembedding I mean the 'lifting out' of social relations from local contexts of interaction and their restructuring across indefinite spans of time-space" (Giddens 1990:21). This is accompanied by processes of "dis-placement" (ibid., 140f.). *Familiarity* and *foreignness* no longer correspond with *near* and *far*, because what is far can be very familiar, and what is near, in contrast, completely "alien(ated)" on account of rapid change.

24. Cf. Jessop 2009:135f.

25. Giddens 1990:79f., 88f.

26. Cf., in greater detail, chapter 3.

27. See chapter 3; cf. further Virilio (1998b:24): "The arrival of a new infrastructural-vehicular system always revolutionizes a society in overthrowing both its sense of material and its sense of social relationships—thus the sense of the entire social space."

28. Bauman 2000:2 (my italics); cf. also Urry 2009. Arjun Appadurai conceptualizes the geography of this new space-time regime consistently, no longer on the model of "static" maps that represent fixed territorial "aggregate conditions" or (relatively) time-resistant ties of territories, ethnies, religions, political forms of domination, modes of economic activity, and technological levels of development, but "cultural flows" that disjunctively separate from and displace each other as *ethno-, techno-, finance-, media-,* and *ideoscapes* that can only be pictured in the dynamic visualization of flickering screens (1990 and 1996:33ff.).

29. Castells 1996:276ff., 469ff.

30. Ibid., 467.
31. Ibid., 464ff.
32. Castells 1996:4, 462f.; cf. Harvey 1990:240, 304f. and Jameson 1998:58f.
33. Cf. for instance, the index and chapter headings in Harvey 1999.
34. Bauman 2000:116, 118f.
35. Castells 1996:476f.
36. "We are witnessing the revenge of nomadism over the principle of territoriality and settlement. In the fluid stage of modernity, the settled majority is ruled by the nomadic and exterritorial elite," writes Bauman (2000:13) and reflects on the temporal consequences: "Being stuck with things for a long time, beyond their 'use up and abandon' date and beyond the moment when their 'new and improved' replacements and 'upgrades' are on offer, is . . . the symptom of deprivation. . . . Durability loses its attraction and turns from an asset into a liability" (ibid., 126).
37. David Harvey has worked this out in great detail (1990:285ff.). For an overview, cf. the anthology edited by Bertens and Natoli (2002).
38. On the constitutive connection of contemporization, acceleration, and globalization, cf. further the contributions of the "Time and Globalization" symposium in *Time and* Society (Lestienne 2000).
39. Hanns-Georg Brose, for instance, interprets them as signs of a transformed time consciousness: after a linear, sequential time perspective directed toward the difference between past and future predominated, we find ourselves "presently in a phase of social development . . . in which the perception of the temporal dimension of the world grounded in discontinuity and non-simultaneity . . . is supplemented by a semantics of the simultaneity (of the non-simultaneous)" (2002:30). Cf. further Nowotny (1993:17ff.), who, like Castells, glimpses in this simultaneity a form of "extended present," or Geißler 1999:111ff.
40. Nowotny 1993:17ff.
41. Cf. here Eriksen: "The fragmentation of work, consumption, family life and the public sphere brings us to a world beyond ready-made "identity packages". Each must create their own coherent totality out of the disjointed fragments. A far from irrelevant question is whether such a task is at all manageable, or whether life is inevitably becoming more collage-like and filled with singular events and impressions, arbitrariness and spontaneity, short-term choices rather than some over-arching direction—that is, *of a hegemonic fast mode* rather than a mix between fast and slow modes. Many hold the view that this is exactly what happens in a lot of areas, from work to ethics, *and commonly, the suggested shift is described as a transition from modernity to postmodernity*" (2001:140f. [my emphasis —H. R.]).

42. Cf. for instance, Welsch 1994:21 or the contributions in Georg-Lauer 1992.
43. Thus Hardt and Negri (2001), following Foucault, speak of "governance without government," while Castells remarks that the "power of streams" itself guides the "streams of power" (1998:366ff.; also 1997:chapter 5).
44. Bauman 2000:14, 12.
45. Thus, insofar as this strategy can be conceived as following an "ideology of having no politics" (Beck 1997:203ff.), it can be understood as an element of the end of politics and a political project at the same time.
46. Thomas Friedman, cited in Harvey 2000b:61, 68.
47. Giddens 1990:139f., 151–54.

10. Situational Identity

1. On this see, in greater detail, chapter 5.3.
2. Cf. Giddens 1990:92f.; Wenzel 1995:124; and in detail, Rosa 1998:84ff.
3. For the relationally defined self, cf. Gergen 2000:139ff.; for the situationally defined self, cf. Rosa 2002a. For further analyses of the transitory character of late modern identity, see Wenzel 1995 or Straub and Renn 2002.
4. Rousseau 1997:part 2, Fourteenth Letter, part 2, Seventeenth Letter (my emphasis); cf. the beginning of the Seventeenth Letter. See here also Berman 1988:18f.
5. Kellner 1992:157f.
6. Cited in Kemper 1995:24. An overview of sociological and social-psychological theories of postmodern forms of selfhood can be found in Wenzel 1995. Cf. further, Gergen 2000 for a comprehensive analysis of late modern identity that systematically includes a perspective of (spatio-)temporal dynamization and instability.
7. Wenzel 1995:114; Straub and Renn 2002:7; Schneider, Limmer, and Ruckdeschel 2002:13ff.
8. Straub and Renn 2002:13.
9. Cf. chapter 1.2b. The concept of "personality" has fallen out of fashion in social-scientific discourse and been almost entirely replaced by that of (personal) identity. Presumably this conceptual shift has to do with the subject matter itself: it signals the aversion to substantialistic or even essentialist ideas of the self in favor of dynamic, flexible, strongly reflexive, mutable or even selectable forms of *self-representation*.
10. Taylor 1994.
11. Taylor 1989:185ff. On this, see Rosa 1998:181ff., 351ff.
12. Cf. in connection with Giddens, Wenzel 1995:127.

13. Elias 2000:379ff.

    Elias's translator uses "pressure for foresight" to translate *Zwang zur Lang-sicht* in the original, but this notably weakens the force of *Zwang*, which in other contexts is translated as "force" or "compulsion." —Trans.

14. Robert Lauer distinguishes modern from traditional societies precisely on this point (1981:117). The latter take their criteria of value and legitimation from the past, but turn out to be oriented to the present in the everyday conduct of life, insofar as it remains in essence limited to a reactive adaptation to unforesee-able events and a concern for daily survival.

15. Wagner 1994; cf. Wagner 2002.

16. Kohli 1986:185. Cf. Wenzel, in connection with Giddens: "The [modern] individual thinks autobiographically, produces a coherent, continuing identity *by shaping his own life history, anticipating his future in a strategic, calculating attitude, having a lifeplan calendar*" (1995:127 [my emphasis]).

17. Kohli 1986:184 (my emphasis).

18. Cf., in detail, Rosa 1998:166ff.

19. One finds an interesting distinction between modern and postmodern forms of narrative identity that makes use of these features in Kraus 2002.

20. Cf. on this, for instance, Petersen 1991.

21. "Each generation functions as a collective actor that shapes and creates in-novations in the social structure in modern society, in each case under the respective historical circumstances of the generation" (Weyman 2000:44).

22. Cf. chapter 4, note 16.

23. Cf. Rosa 2002a:268ff. Further Krappmann 1997 and Straub 1998b.

24. A classical formulation is Beck 1992.

25. *This is how it is: it could also be different* is the striking title of a book by Helga Nowotny (1999).

26. Martin Kohli (1990, 1994) therefore diagnoses a gradual *de*institutionalization and *de*standardization of the life course, similar to Castells (1996:445ff.).

27. Straub and Renn 2002.

28. On this see chapter 4.

29. Luhmann 1997:1014ff.

30. Cf. here chapters 3 and 9 and, in particular, chapter 12. On the establishment of such an understanding of time in philosophy and natural science, see Sand-bothe 1998.

31. Kohli 1986, 1990, 1994; and also Castells 1996:439ff., 445ff. The erosion of pre-defined career sequences in the professional world is interpreted in the same way by Bauman (2000:116f.) and Sennett (1998).

32. Cf. for instance Heinze and Olk 1999; but see also Giegel and Rosa 2000 and Corsten et al. 2005.

33. On this, see also Garhammer 1999:157ff., 411ff., 463ff.
34. Cf. the introduction, section 1, and chapter 7.3.
35. On the causes of this paradigm shift, see chapter 7.3. On its empirical cogency, cf. for instance Seiwert 2000:15ff.; Levine 2006:139ff.; Geißler 1999:111ff.; Hörning, Ahrens, and Gerhard 1997.
36. Geißler 1999:142f.
37. However, the authors somewhat misleadingly describe the type of the classical modern *time manager* as a "technology-obsessed surfer" on account of his attempt to maintain control over daily life and win back the ability to make secure plans by applying the most modern technology (cf. Hörning, Ahrens, and Gerhard 1997 and 1999).
38. In the words of an interviewed, "newly converted" player: "My priority is, if one likes, to be able to approach my day as spontaneously and unstructured as possible. Naturally I too make appointments and set up meetings, but always in such a way that I can also occasionally shake things up a bit. An insistence on the good old days just gets in the way of this. Everything was different before. Back then my weekly schedule and everything else was divided up all nice and neat into a half-hour tempo, and then I put blocks in, but that's history. Now I can approach things more spontaneously. That's a good way to 'handle' things" (Hörning, Ahrens, and Gerhard 1997:142).
39. Ibid., 145ff.
40. Ibid., 178. Of course, one should not forget here that even the player—in particular in the sphere of gainful employment—is tied to deadlines and appointments over which he has no influence. These, as it were, "colonize" his play with the temporalities of events (*Ereigniszeiten*). Cf. here, in greater detail, chapter 7.1.
41. Hörning, Ahrens, and Gerhard 1997:16.
42. Ibid., 178. In their investigation of late modern forms or types of life conduct using the example of temporary workers, Brose, Wohlrab-Sahr, and Corsten find that in our changed circumstances the most well-adapted and hence "most modern" pattern of biographical organization or the conduct of life is that of the "decentered type," which is very similar to the "player": "What other types experience as problematic is given an offensive turn in the decentered type. . . . The time perspective of this type is shaped by the 'present future.' And this future appears to be open. . . . The future is open in the sense of the possibility of different developments. . . . If there is no longer any central perspective, no fixed, unique life goal; if it is rather a matter of realizing oneself in diverse ways within the change of perspectives, then the contingency of the future is no cause for vexation" (Brose, Wohlrab-Sahr, and Corsten 1993:322).
43. Hörning, Ahrens, and Gerhard 1997:179, 174.

44. Voß 1998:20f.

45. Ibid., 21.

46. Ibid. Voß's strategic conduct of life is strongly reminiscent of the lifestyle figure of the technology-obsessed surfer (or time manager) identified by Hörning, Ahrens, and Gerhard.

47. Ibid., 25.

48. Gergen 2000:156ff.

49. Bilden 1997; Helsper 1997; cf. also Wenzel 1995.

50. In what follows I do not use the concept of autonomy in a narrow Kantian sense of moral self-legislation, but in an ethical and identity-based understanding of living an autonomous life of one's own.

51. Lifton 1993; cf. here Wenzel 1995:121f.

52. Gergen 2000:150.

53. Straub 2001; Joas 1994. Lifton himself emphasizes that the shapeshifting, protean self must continually produce coherence and continuity, even if in a nonlinear and episodic way.

54. Cf. also Rosa 2002a.

55. Cf. here Anderson 1997; Kraus 2000, 2002.

56. On the romantic, expressivist side of the modern identity worked out by Charles Taylor, cf. in greater detail, Rosa 1998:351ff. See also Gergen (2000:18ff), who holds, however, that the romantic idea of the self precedes the modern version, though it remains culturally influential.

57. For example, Habermas quotes a medical student who says of his beloved bike that it stands "for the only worldview I have left" (Habermas 1999:431, cf. 506). As if in confirmation, the chief executive of MontBlanc International, Ltd., Norbert A. Platt, traces the attractiveness of luxury brands to the fact that they embody "recurring values like tradition and constancy, thoughtfulness and slowness" in a "time of furious change" (Platt 1998:179). That the beloved objects of the respondents interviewed by Habermas were on average less than five years old certainly might say something about the tempo of change even in this area (Habermas 1999:457).

58. Cf., for example, Glass 1993.

59. Bauman 2000:13; Beck 1997:127ff.

60. Simmel 2004:464. Cf. Harvey's interpretation of late modernity as the escalation of the pattern described by Simmel: "The bombardment of stimuli, simply on the commodity front, creates problems of sensory overload that makes Simmel's dissection of the problems of modernist urban living at the turn of the century seem to pale into insignificance by comparison" (1990:286).

61. Cf. in greater detail, Rosa 2002a:286ff.

62. Taylor 1989:159ff.; cf. chapter 5.3. Werner Helsper also observes just this kind of distancing from one's own predicatively determined self in his reflections on the possible form of a postmodern self: "The modern self is . . . *especially reflective*, or better, self-referential, because the plurality of forms of life, interpretations of the world, cultural style, and possibilities for the conduct of life and the continually renewed need to make decisions in view of increasing options places the self into a distanced relationship to the social and subjective world. . . . A reflexive relation to self and world distances the self from itself and the world" (1997:177).

63. "People who know only one uniform style which permeates their whole life will perceive this style as being identical with its *contents*. Since everything they create or contemplate is naturally expressed in this style, there are no psychological grounds for distinguishing it from the material of the formative and contemplative process or for contrasting the style as a form independent of the self. Only where a variety of given styles exists will one detach itself from its content so that its independence and specific significance gives us the freedom to choose between the one or the other. . . . The fact that the entire visible environment of our cultural life has disintegrated into a plurality of styles dissolves that original relationship to style where subject and object are not yet separated. Instead, we are confronted with a world of expressive possibilities each developed according to their own norms, with a host of forms within which to express life as a whole. Thus these forms on the one side, and our subjectivity on the other, are like two parties between whom a purely fortuitous relationship of contacts, harmonies and disharmonies prevails" (Simmel 2004:467f.). On the reception of Simmel as a predecessor of postmodern thought, cf., for instance Kaern, Philips, and Cohen 1990; Dörr-Backes and Nieder 1995; or Moebius 2002.

64. Breuer 1988:323; Virilio 1998a:184f.; cf. Crogan 2000:17f.

65. As Harvey remarks in connection with Toffler's best seller, *Future Shock*, the concept of the Throw Away Society implies "more than just throwing away produced goods . . . but also being able to throw away values, life-styles, stable relationships, and attachments to things, buildings, places, people, and received ways of doing and being" (1990:286). Thus when Bill Martin complains that we live in a time in which it is almost impossible for something to achieve genuine significance, this difficulty seems to be an unavoidable consequence of the late modern tempo of change.

66. This thought is also already present in Simmel, which should hardly be surprising by now: "The lack of something definite at the centre of the soul impels us to search for momentary satisfaction in ever new stimulations, sensations and

external activities. Thus it is that we become entangled in the instability and helplessness that manifests itself as the tumult of the metropolis, as the mania for travelling, as the wild pursuit of competition and as the typically modern disloyalty with regard to taste, style, opinions and personal relationships." (2004:490).

67. Hörning, Ahrens, and Gerhard 1997:180.

68. "The second fatalism that is awakening all around us belongs to a consciousness which notices that even today what happens is very different than what one thinks or expects" (Sloterdijk 1989:112, cf. 126; Garhammer 1999:482).

69. Cf. Garhammer 1999:482.

70. Cf. further, also Gergen 2000:xx ff.

71. Adam 1990:124.

72. On the former, see for instance Urry, who also reports a corresponding reorganization of the spaces of free time, work, and experience in cities (2006:17f.). On the latter, cf. Garhammer 1999:482; Robinson and Godbey 1999:137; Brose 2002:131f.; and Fuchs-Heinritz 2000. However, the data of the Shell Study are contradictory, insofar as they also suggest that the scope of ideas about one's life in the future has slightly climbed from 1991 to 1999 (Fuchs-Heinritz 2000:30). In contrast, a large survey of students from the graduating classes of all types of secondary institution in Thüringen (N = 407) in 2002 found that over 40 percent of the students answered a question about the period of time they believed they could envision and plan with "today one can no longer plan for the future" (40.3 percent). Only 4.2 percent believed that they could envision their entire future life course (Behr, Kottman, and Seiwert 2002:14). At the same time, 78.7 percent of the respondents indicated that they had only vague ideas about their life course, and, of the rest, more students (10.8 percent) held that they had absolutely no ideas about the life course than that they had already planned the rest of their lives step by step (9.3 percent) (ibid., 16).

73. Sennett 1998:119, 133.

74. Ibid., 26–27.

75. Lauer 1981:37, 114. One should not exclude the possibility that the "highly situational time practices" of late modernity dam up undirected psychic energies that can be discharged in apparently unmotivated violence. This may occur on account of their lack of narrative perspective and the short half-life of their future and past horizons as well as their so to speak *structural indifference*. "The attraction of physical violence consists in the way it shortens time, produces immediate results and—literally causes short breaths and demands no long ones." Nassehi 2000:36; cf. Reheis 2000:1; and, further, Enzensberger 1994:33; Assheuer 2000.

76. Sennett 1998:31.

77. Gergen 2000:150, xviii (my emphasis).
78. Garhammer also diagnoses a "reversion to a situational form of life" in this sense (1999:476). And Brose, Wohlrab-Sahr, and Corsten end their book with the observation that "a break with teleological ideas of life-historical development" is characteristic of the genuinely "late modern" form of life conduct that they investigate: "it is not only a departure from the 'external' form of an ordering teleology, something observed in a certain way in the stepwise progression through sequences of positions, but also from its 'internalized' version, which no longer reads off the attainment of life goals from status markers, but interprets it as a maturation process oriented by ideas of perfectibility. The continuity and linearity of life-historical development—whether external or internal—no longer counts as a self-evident basis of orientation. In the pattern of biographical development reconstructed by us, life goals become contingent—in a sense different from that implied by the utilitarian theory of action" (1993:323).
79. "The highly dynamic form of communication of the 'player,' which aims at opening up ever new worlds of meaning, can lead one to lose oneself in the fascinating play of communicated messages. One follows up the ceaselessly offered, endless references and has enormous difficulties—since after all almost everything is possible—in still managing to recognize relevancies and keep significances in view. The problems of the 'player' are: to self-referentially set boundaries, to let go of things once again, to develop one's own 'stop' rules, to designate something as ended" (Hörning, Ahrens, and Gerhard 1997:165).
80. Kodalle 1999:12; cf. also Robinson and Godbey 1999:47f.; further Garhammer 1999:482; Sennett 1998:121; and, in greater detail, Rosa 1999d.
81. Garhammer 1999:482.
82. Hörning, Ahrens and Gerhard 1997:60.
83. Baier 2000:147ff.
84. Schulte-Strathaus 1999:29. From the empirical finding that seven out of ten mentally ill patients in France exhibit symptoms of pathological time experience, Baier concludes that "a considerable part of the population of developed countries at the end of the twentieth century must experience feelings of being overstrained that do not simply arise from a tempo-related hustle and bustle" (2000:160). For other forms of contemporary "time sickness" like "hurry sickness" or the experience of a schizophrenic that time for him had "stopped; there is no time, . . . The past and the future have collapsed into the present and I can't hold them apart," see Levine 2006:28ff. (the quotation is found at ibid., 37).
85. Cf. for instance, Nuber 1999; Levine 2006:28ff., Ulmer and Schwartzburd 1996.

86. Baier 2000:157f.
87. Ibid., 158.
88. Levine 2006:36–37.
89. Ehrenberg 1999:250, in the translation of Baier 2000:159 (my emphasis).
90. Cf. Kessel 2001:20f.; Schings 1977.
91. Schings 1977.
92. Cf., in great detail and very instructive, Radkau 1998.
93. Ehrenberg 2000:124f. (my emphasis). Axel Honneth reaches a similar conclusion in his discussion of (late) modern paradoxes of individualization (2002).
94. Schulze 1997b. Werner Helsper also sees here a problematic feature of the postmodern self that can potentially lead to a depressive inability to act: "In the face of the pluralization of the world, social organizations tend to become 'strange' or 'alien' and the subject seeks stability in its own self. But here too in view of the plurality of possible options imposes on the self by the social frame within which it deliberates, this stability is precarious. . . . Thus the dilemma of the self-referentiality of the modern self consists in the fact that it needs this self-referentiality to remain capable of action in the face of such open choice-horizons. If the self falls below the required level of self-referentiality, it becomes the plaything of distant social compulsions. If self-referentiality is heightened as a response to the interminable array of possible decisions, then this leads to a practical inability to choose and act whereby the self is likewise determined from without. The reflexive self expands at the price of practical, sensory experience, and feelings of emptiness and tedium result" (1997:177f).
95. Baier 2000:161.

11. Situational Politics

1. Schimank 2000:274f.
2. On this in greater detail, see Chesneaux 2000.
3. Guggenberger and Offe 1984.
4. Locke 1980:§ 156ff., § 159ff. Montesquieu 1989:159ff. (*The Spirit of the Laws*, book 11, chapter 6).
5. In fact, one can make out a *threefold division* in the democratic political order of modernity from the perspective of speed or the relation between inertia and motion: the *constitution* is slower, or more static, than ordinary legislation because of higher legal hurdles for change and hence exhibits a strong element of inertia and, as a rule, allows only for incremental change, if one leaves aside the possibility of revolutionary upheaval. Therefore constitutions are in danger of becoming anachronistic under the pressure of increased social acceleration. The political system can react to this by either interpreting the

constitutional norms in an increasingly abstract way as minimal *procedural norms* or enabling an accelerated adaptation of it to the changing social realities (cf. Howard 1990:17f.). Scheuerman appears inclined toward the latter solution when he writes, in view of the problem of, as it were, constitutions being "frozen" in time, that "we need to consider the possibility that contemporary instantiations of constitutionalism fail to provide adequate possibilities for modifying the original compact for the sake of adapting to fast-paced social and economic change. . . . Once we recognize that time and space compression constantly forces constitutional courts to adapt constitutional norms to the restless pace of social and economic life, we can at least begin to consider institutional reforms that honestly acknowledge the impressive powers of constitutional lawmaking now possessed by most constitutional courts" (2001a:64). The institution of the *constitutional court* can also be used, moreover, to short-circuit deliberative democratic decision-making processes, as when difficult decisions—for instance, about abortion, immigration law, or participation in war—are withdrawn from political discussion and transferred to the courts (cf. Howard 1990:17f.). I will come back to this.

6. Mill 1977:428ff.; Dewey 1954; Schmitt 1950.

7. Scheuerman 2001a:62f. and 2001b:118. On the realm of international treaty law, see Dicke 2001:22. See further the contributions in the third part of Rosa and Scheuerman 2009.

8. As Scheuerman shows, in the tradition of liberal political thought—in Locke and Montesquieu as well as in Hamilton, Madison, or even John Dewey—it was precisely this slowness that counted as a specific virtue, and not a defect, of the legislative process in contrast to the faster decisions of the executive: the presumption was that it ensured the high quality of legislative decisions (2001a:49ff., cf. 2004:39ff.).

9. Riescher 1994.

10. In a number of publications, William Scheuerman pursues the aim of finding paths to an institutional reform of liberal democracy, "for the sake of transforming time and space compression into an *ally*, rather than an *enemy*, of liberal democracy" (2001a:67; cf. 2004). In my view, however, he has so far not gotten much farther than the well-grounded postulate of this necessity. The same goes for his German colleagues Eberling (1996) or Reheis (1998).

11. Cf. also Habermas 1989.

    In German, one refers to modernity (or the modern age, or the modern period) using, among others, the words *Moderne* and *Neuzeit*. The latter literally means "new time." Hence this sentence is setting up the emergence of the genuinely modern understanding of history by contrasting it to a premodern way of understanding what a break between a currently existing time and a "new" time would look like, namely, the Christian understanding. This aspect of the discussion is difficult to capture in English translation, but it is important to the reflections that follow. —TRANS.

12. Koselleck 2004:247; cf. here also Brunner, Conze, and Koselleck 1972–1997; and Luhmann 1997:866ff., especially 997ff., as well as his four-volume study on *Gesellschaftsstruktur und Semantik* (1980–1999).

13. Cf. Koselleck 2004:26ff.

14. Ibid., 230f. (my emphasis).

15. Ibid., 255ff., Koselleck 2000:331ff.

16. On this see chapter 2.2b and chapter 4.

17. In Koselleck's two more recent essays on the question, "Is There an Acceleration of History?" (2009) and "The Shortening of Time and Acceleration: A Study of Secularization" (2000:177–202), he seems more strongly inclined than in his earlier works to interpret historical acceleration as, in the first instance, a secularized category of a now politically oriented expectation that only became genuinely empirically fulfilled in the wake of the industrial revolution. His claim is that "acceleration as a historical category of expectation is old, that new expectations accrue to it after the sixteenth century, and that, however, it could first become a saturated concept of experience in the wake of the industrial revolution" (ibid., 153). The eighteenth-century experience of acceleration was at best empirically grounded in the rapid series of political shocks. This result remains unsatisfying since it is ultimately circular: the reorganization of the time horizon of politics becomes at once the explanans and the explanandum. In my view, the inadadequacy of Koselleck's explanation lies in the fact that he seeks empirical grounds for his unambiguous finding of a perception of historical acceleration in the epochal threshold only in the form of technological acceleration (ibid., 167) and thus overlooks the separate possibilities of an acceleration of the pace of life and of social change.

18. Koselleck 2004:241–42.

19. Adams 1999 [1904]:406ff., also 2009.

20. Koselleck 2004:235, cf. 243ff.

21. Ibid., 236.

22. Koselleck 2000:163, cf. 172ff. and 2004:140f., 268ff. On the centrality of the idea of progress for the temporalization of history, cf. further Nowotny 1993:17.

23. Habermas 1989:49. Compare Lübbe's statement: "The temporalization of utopia, by transposing the perfection realized in literature from distant places to distant times, also presupposed that the social condition in which we now find ourselves is at the same time part of a directed process of transformation" (2009:167).

24. Koselleck 2004:247, 248ff.

25. Ibid., 248ff.

26. Compare Koselleck: "The Revolution was transformed for everyone into a historico philosophical concept, based on a perspective which displayed a constant and steady direction. There might be arguments over "earlier" versus "later," or "retardation" versus "acceleration," but the actual direction appeared to have been established once and for all" (ibid., 51). With this the concept of revolution was itself temporalized: it no longer indicated the "rotation" or return of the social order to an earlier or cyclically repeating state, but rather a historically irreversible and directed social change to be brought about (or accelerated) through politics (and in the form of revolutionization potentially become permanent). Cf. further, Nowotny (1993:152) for the equation of "Progress" and acceleration (*Fortschritt durch Beschleunigung*).

27. Wolin 1997:2. Cf. on this in detail, Chesneaux 2000.

28. Representative here are Eberling 1996, Chesneaux 2000 and Scheuerman 2001a; one finds in these authors numerous further confirmations of this. See also Hennis 2000:175ff.

29. "Dictate instead of debate," headline from the *Weltwoche* of February 24, 2000. The representatives of the (Denner) initiative argued that, for instance, plans in genetic research are simply obsolete after three years of discussion time, so that decisions, when they are finally made, are already anachronistic by the time they are passed. Nevertheless, the initiative was rejected by Swiss voters on April 14, 2000.

30. On this in greater detail, Nassehi 1993:323ff.

31. In this way acceleration in late modernity could lead to a condition of marked *structural decoupling*—contrary to Schwinn's (1999) thesis on the formation of a new kind of interplay between formal rationalities in new structures (cf. here also chapter 7.3). If one tries to make the effect of acceleration more intuitively accessible in the sense of a thought experiment, say, by analogy to physics, one can speculate as follows: the principle of the differentiation of functional spheres enabled a significant acceleration of the processing of emerging, quasi-autopoietic systems. However, the "centrifugal forces" that accompany the increasing speed will produce a progressive erosion of system boundaries and therefore a postmodern *de*differentiation, which must not be confused with a *re*integration, for it signals rather the atomization and fragmentation of particular system connections: thus today there is already presumably no longer a unitary scientific system, nor any ordered formation of corresponding (roughly disciplinary) subsystems, but rather a "kaleidoscope" of schools, approaches, research projects, journals, conferences, etc. Therefore, wherever art, commerce, politics, and science intermingle in new (by all means creative) symbioses and syntheses, the resulting processes can be planned, controlled, or

steered *neither* politically *nor* economically nor in any other way—not at any rate over the long term. In addition, it may seem problematic to identify which *code* they follow.

In systems theory every system, in particular every subsystem, follows its own specific "code." The code consists in a binary sorting of all possible "messages" or operations into one of two possibilities given by the system's code. For instance, the legal system "perceives" or "understands" everything in terms of the code legal/illegal, the political system in terms of the code government/opposition, etc. If it is becoming deeply problematic to identify which code certain social processes are following, this may constitute a rather dramatic challenge to the basic presuppositions of systems theory as formulated by Niklas Luhmann and his followers. —TRANS.

32. Harvey 2000b:59. Reheis's (1998) central thesis is similar, namely, that the "systems" individual, society, and nature have become desynchronized with pathological consequences. Bergmann also diagnoses a desynchronization of social time and the times of the psyche, physiology and the biological-physical environment (1981:166ff.).

33. Assheuer 2000:38.

34. On these desynchronization phenomena, see in particular the contributions in Backhaus and Bonus 1998.

35. Cf. Scheuerman 2001b:115ff. and Günther 2001. On the concept of "neo-spontaneous law", cf. Teubner 2000. This is accompanied by a potential dissolution of *legal monism* in the globalized world: which courts and which legislatures are responsible and competent for which conflicts and decisions is once again becoming increasingly unclear and hence a question of power—the undermining of the UN by the foreign policy of the U.S. in the early twenty-first century and the associated suspension of the validity of international law and its scope of application are perhaps the most visible symptoms of this.

36. Dicke 1988:217ff. In contrast, Dicke proposes the expansion of regulation in the form of treaties and international or cooperative law (cf. Dicke 2001:13ff.).

37. Cf. Dicke 2001:15f.

38. Schmitt 1950. Cf. also Scheuerman 2000:especially 189ff. On the dynamization and "motorization" of international law, cf. Dicke 1988:200, 202ff.

39. Reheis 1998:215.

40. Eberling 1996:14.

41. On this in detail, Scheuerman 2001a:57ff.

42. Cf. in greater detail, Denninger 1988.

43. Cf. also Kielmansegg (2003a, b), who attributes the "denial of future" by German political parties, i.e., their manifest inability to develop and implement

workable designs for the future, to the logic of party competition and of course to the parties themselves.

44. Eberling 1996:68.

45. As I have already shown, one must also naturally consider the climbing opportunity costs incurred by increasing temporal expenditures on decisions when judging the rationality of a decision. But in the present context the only thing that follows from this is that it becomes politically rational to lower the substantial criteria of rationality for reasons of time. Incidentally, the growing indeterminacy of decision parameters is a necessary effect of the compression of innovation.

46. *Multiculturalism* here represents an interesting phenomena of "time pluralism": time horizons, patterns, and practices of various cultures are without doubt significantly distinct, but they inevitably collide in the public sphere, which is governed by the time structures of the dominant culture. Cf. here Marschall 1997.

47. For the argument that social disintegration in late modernity is becoming a requirement of acceleration or a presupposition for the free flow of global streams, see Baumann 2000:14f., 168ff. See also chapter 9.

48. Dewey 1954:140f. "The increasing fragmentation and heterogeneity of political space . . . leads to cooperation problems. Parties realize that they are no longer dealing with stable milieux for which an overall interest could be defined. Instead, they have be attuned to highly distinct social situations that are differentiated in many ways and the individually combined bundles of interests tied to them which can hardly be reduced to a common denominator given their internally contradictory nature. Under these conditions an articulated program must appear to be strategically counterproductive. But the diffuse mixture of single points of a (possible) program accentuated for publicity purposes that replaces genuine platforms can only strengthen the fragmentation of voters and the problem of integration" (Giegel 1999:108f.; cf. Scheuerman 2001a:60f.).

49. See here, for example, Connolly 2000; Barber 1998/99; and Buchstein 1997.

50. On the fundamental difference between "poll government" and the idea of political democracy, cf. Chesneaux 2000:409. He sees an (ominous) attempt at political acceleration in the growing dependence of democratic governments on opinion surveys.

51. For a brilliant attempt to distinguish between (aggregated) private opinions and genuinely political or public opinion, cf. Hennis 2000:37ff.

52. Here see also Weibel 1987.

53. Thus already Luhmann 1994 [1968]; cf. Bergmann 1983:483.

54. Cf. Scheuerman (2001a:57): "Not surprisingly, legislatures tend to throw their hands up in the air in frustration when faced with these contradictory demands. Too often, contemporary parliaments abandon their lawmaking duties—to an executive envisioned as better equipped to grapple with the imperatives of speed."

55. On Schröder's argumentation, see Rulff 2001:8.

56. "The more clearly this style of pragmatic 'muddling through' takes shape, the more a form of politics is suppressed that could be an important motivational resource for political organization," remarks Hans-Joachim Giegel (1999:109) and draws our attention to a "vicious circle" in the context of the late modern problem of control (*Gestaltung*).

57. This is clear, for instance, in the debate surrounding the 'Reform Agenda 2010' initiated by the former German chancellor Schröder. Its defenders almost exclusively appealed to the argument of an unavoidable (structural) adaptation, while many of its critics faulted it for not going far enough.

58. On the progressive erosion of the idea of progress, cf. Nowotny 1993:17f., 52ff., 151ff.

59. Cf. here also Rosa 2002b.

60. Altvater 2002:290, § 44.

61. Nassehi 1993:377.

62. This may partially explain the appearance of a novel, "playful" type of politician like Arnold Schwarzenegger in California, Berlusconi in Italy, or Pim Fortuyn in Holland.

63. "Perspectives on the future become more obscure and thus at the same time the pressure on decisions in the present grows, for one can only make decisions and act in the present, in the context of a simultaneously given world. One of the most important problems of the present is how much the decision-making organizations, above all those of the political system, can absorb this pressure and the growing mistrust connected with it" (Luhmann 1997:1074).

64. See note 26, this chapter.

65. Habermas 1989.

66. Jameson 1998:50.

67. For a basically opposed view, Nowotny 1993:56.

68. Jung 1989:178f.; cf. Baudrillard 1992.

"Escape velocity" is used here to translate *Befreiungsgeschwindigkeit*. The connected ideas of Baudrillard and Virilio exploit a double meaning or perhaps an ironic pun in the French term for the aeronautical or ballistics concept of escape velocity, *vitesse de liberation*, literally "speed of liberation." The irony is that once historical events reach this "speed," the experience of history is not at all that of a liberation, but rather a vertiginously oscillating experience reminiscent of Weber's famous "iron cage." —TRANS.

69. Baudrillard 1992 (translation altered).

70. See the introduction, section 2. For an overview of the posthistoire diagnoses, cf. Niethammer 1989.

71. Baudrillard 1992 (translation altered).

72. Nassehi 1993:364f. (my emphasis). Kertész 2002:70. Cf. also Baudrillard 1992: "Already, political events no longer conduct sufficient autonomous energy to rouse us and can only run their course as a silent movie in front of which we all sit collectively irresponsible. That is where history reaches its end, not because of the lack of actors or participants, not due to a lack of violence (with respect to violence, there is always an increasing amount), not due to a lack of events (as for events, there will always be more of them thanks to the role of the media and information!)—but because of a slowing down or deceleration, because of indifference and stupefaction."

73. Cf. chapter 1.1, note 56.

74. "Okay, yeah, of course, I thought silently to myself, they *were* ugly times. But they were also the only times that I had ever had; genuine moments in *history*, before history only existed for a wild press, for marketing strategies and as the tool of cynical campaigns" (Coupland 1991:131).

75. Martin 1998:58f., 5.

76. Columbia Records, 1992. On this feeling of time, characteristic of *posthistoire*, see in greater detail Rosa 1999c.

77. Niethammer 1989:9; cf. Nassehi 1993:359ff.; Chesneaux 2000:415ff. For Coupland's protagonists, history tellingly becomes a "debris heap" on which they lose their maps and suffer an "option paralysis" in view of a surfeit of options ("the tendency, when given unlimited options, to choose none," 1991:121).

78. Cf. Wallis 1970.

79. Nassehi 1993:367; similarly, see Harvey 1990:305f.

80. Nassehi 1993:366.

81. Coupland 1991:90.

82. Scherpe 1986:275.

83. Coupland 1991:34. Perhaps studio films like *Armageddon*, *Titanic*, or *Godzilla* have just this motif to thank for their enormous and unbroken popularity. They not only always present the destruction of the everyday world in aesthetically pleasing and exciting ways. They also represent variations of the idea that there is still a possibility of finding a history for the end of the world (Rosa 1999c:260ff.).

84. Cf. in particular Luhmann 1997:1143ff. and 997ff.

85. Nassehi 1993:320 (my emphasis).
86. In a certain way I am thus also attempting to incorporate into a theory of acceleration the dynamization of our understanding of modern society called for by Luhmann (1997:1144).

12. Acceleration and Rigidity

1. From the data set of the study by Behr, Kottman, and Seiwert (2002), which the authors kindly made available to me.
2. Simmel 2004:515.
3. "Because I know that the daemonic powers love to turn things continually upside down, and I know that fortune alters everything, strong and weak, things at their beginning and things at their ending, and drives everything with a strong necessity *and* [!] according to her whim" (Pausanias, *Travels in Greece*, as cited in Frisby 1988:11 [my emphasis]).
4. On the future perspectives of youth in the German Federal Republic, cf. Fuchs-Heinritz 2000:41ff.
5. Naturally, one also finds similar ideas in non-European cosmologies, for instance, in conceptions of a determinate series of ages of the world.
6. Andreas Gryphius's lyric poem "Es ist alles eitel," written under the impact of the turmoil of the Thirty Years' War, is thoroughly shaped by this opposition: "Du siehst, wohin Du siehst, nur Eitelkeit auf Erden. / Was dieser heute baut, reißt jener morgen ein; / Wo jetzund Städte stehen, wird eine Wiese sein, / Auf der ein Schäferskind wird spielen mit den Herden // Was jetzund prächtig blüht, soll bald zertreten werden; / Was jetzt so pocht und trotzt, ist morgen Asch und Bein; / Nichts ist, das ewig sei, kein Erz, kein Marmorstein. / Jetzt lacht das Glück uns an, bald donnern die Beschwerden. // Der hohen Taten Ruhm muß wie ein Traum vergehn. / Soll denn das Spiel der Zeit, der leichte Mensch, bestehn? / Ach, was ist alles dies, was wir für köstlich achten, // Als schlechte Nichtigkeit, als Schatten, Staub und Wind, / Als eine Wiesenblume, die man nicht wiederfind't! / Noch will, was ewig ist, kein einzig Mensch betrachten."

   Gryphius (1616–1664) is one of the most important German poets of the seventeenth century and several of his poems are among the German language's greatest lyric poetry. Many of these poems are in addition remarkable poetic expressions of a deep religious mysticism. What follows is a translation, "All Is Vanity," by Scott Horton, from *Harper's Magazine* (August 2007), available at http://harpers.org/archive/2007/08/hbc-90000849: "You will see wherever you look only vanity on this earth. / What one man builds today, another tears down tomorrow; / where now cities stand, a meadow will be, / upon which a shepherd's child will play with the herds. // What now blooms in magnificence, will soon be tread asunder; / what today pounds with defiance, tomorrow is ash and bone; / there is nothing which is eternal, neither ore nor marble. / Now fortune smiles upon us, but soon troubles will thunder. / The fame of great deeds must pass like a dream. / Why should the game of time, the simple human, persist? / Oh, what is all of this that we hold to be exquisite, / but wicked vanities, as shadow, dust and wind, / but a meadow flower which one can find no more! / Yet not a single man wants to contemplate what is eternal." —Trans.

7. Cf. in further detail chapter 4.

8. Cf. here also Offe 1987:3f.

9. Ibid., 4.

10. Ibid., 9.

   Offe translation slightly modified. —Trans.

11. This point was postulated not only by Nietzsche, Baudelaire, and Benjamin but also, for example, by Horkheimer and Adorno (2002:106).

12. Cf. for instance, Voß 1990; as well as Schulze 1997b:79.

13. Virilio 1999; cf. introduction, section 2.

14. Cf. Virilio 1993. As Schivelbusch (2000 [1977]:53ff., 116ff.) further demonstrates, this form of travel very quickly produces of itself a growing sense of monotony, boredom, and a feeling of inactivity that has to be combated with activities of "motionless engagement" like reading or, later, listening to the radio or watching television; cf. the instructive contribution of Thomas Bourry (2004) on the use of media in airplanes and also, in general, Gronemeyer (1996).

15. In this sense it is only consistent that in modern mass production factory farming animals are almost entirely "immobilized."

16. Perrow 1999.

17. On the psychological explanation of this perception, cf. chapter 5.2.

18. Cf. Evers, Rauch, and Stitz 2002.

19. Cf. quite early on, Adorno 1993:75f.; further, Lash 1996; Harvey 1990:291; Jameson 1998; Lash and Urry 1987:285ff.; or Welsch 1994; and from a skeptical point of view, Schwinn 1999.

20. On this debate, cf. Luhmann 1997:1145ff. as well as Schwinn's 1999 critique of Beck.

21. Honneth (1994:20–29) suggests that we conceive of becoming autonomous (*Autonomisierung*) (alongside the privatization of the conduct of life and the individual differentiation of life circumstances) as the decisive component of individualization. Insofar as "becoming autonomous" means that the unmistakable increase in the variety of options and the amount of contingency faced by individuals can be used by them in a way that enables them to have greater, more reflective, and more "rational" self-determination in light of their respective life histories and identities, the findings discussed in chapter 10.3

undoubtedly point to a diminishment of the potential for autonomy; cf. also Rosa 2002a:271f.

22. Linder (1970) therefore speaks of the rationality of growing irrationality; cf. chapter 5.1.

23. Precisely this is emphasized by Robert Lauer when he writes, in a passage reminiscent of Heidegger, that "the self is process; the temporal dimension is fundamental. To neglect the temporal dimension is to neglect the essence. We shall never understand the human by simply analysing the individual as a stable configuration of traits, qualities, or attitudes" (1981:56). Cf. Heidegger's basic definition of *Dasein* as *Zeitlichkeit* (1992 [1924]:20 cf. also 2008:chapter 3).

24. Domestication here includes the principles of *industrialization, economization*, and *commodification* that are derivable from the social arrangement of modernity as a whole.

25. Cf. chapters 1.2.b and 4.

26. The idea of historically repeating constellations or successions of events (one thinks, for example, of the ancient doctrine of the series of constitutional forms) naturally allows such things to be *expected*, however, it definitely does *not* lead to a temporalization and singularization of "history" itself, but rather just strengthens the impression of an underlying stasis because these repetitions are always ultimately a return of the ever same; cf. in greater detail, Koselleck 2004.

27. Nevertheless, let us note that I do not connect this hypothesis with any universal-historical or ethnological claims. For me it is only a question of understanding developments and transformations in modernity and not of describing the experiences of time and history of decidedly "extramodern" societies. The characterization "of premodern society" should thus be understood more in the sense of an ideal-typical model-like abstraction for comparative purposes than as a strictly historical description of facts. On this procedure, see Kirchmann 1998:30f.

28. Admittedly, Kohli expressly places the beginning of the modern temporalization of life back in the "epochal threshold" (1985:12); however, it was adumbrated at first only in the milieu of high culture—for instance, in the change from an "annalistic" to a "developmental-historically" temporalized form of autobiography based on a life perspective, first visible in *Anton Reiser* by Karl Philipp Moritz (1988). Only with the emergence of the welfare state was it diffused among the wider populace.

29. Lepenies 1976.

30. In Bauman's view, the dissolution of traditional institutions in early and classical modernity had the aim of replacing them with self-determined, more stable, and more reliable institutions, while the liquefaction of the "classical"

modern institutions in late modernity (Bauman prefers the concepts of "heavy" and "light modernity") is bent on the rejection of institutional consolidation as such (2000:3ff.); cf. chapter 2.4.

31. Here, as well, one sees how much the philosophical idea of an (eclectic) "postmodernity" that first developed in architecture is an expression of an altered experience of time.

32. Adam 2003:51f.; Leccardi 2003:39ff.

33. Heidegger 1992 [1924]:12ff. In fact, from Heidegger's point of view the phenomena of acceleration (of racing around [*Gerennes*] and not-having-any-time [*Keine-Zeit-Habens*]), and also the corresponding experiences of emptiness and tedium, are consequences of the (modern) fixation on the "inauthentic time" of the present as a flight before the temporally uncertain certainty of the future (namely, of one's own death): "Time suddenly becomes long for Dasein as being-present, for this Dasein that never has time. Time becomes empty because Dasein, in asking about the 'how much,' has in advance made time long, whereas its constantly coming back in running ahead towards the past never becomes boring" (ibid., 16 [my emphasis]). On a concept of temporalization oriented toward Heidegger that is, however, in my view not incompatible with my own usage, cf. Sandbothe 1997 and 1998.

34. Heidegger 1992 [1924]: 20.

35. The complete confusion of time concepts in the contemporary theoretical debates about time that has come to light here no doubt itself represents a sociologically significant phenomenon of late modernity to which one could devote an entire work and which is presumably to be interpreted as a symptom of the "time crisis" of our epoch (Achtner, Kunz, and Walter 1998:5).

36. Cf. for instance, Habermas 1996:83ff.

37. Offe 1996:29; Sloterdijk 1989:87f. Cf. Nassehi: "After early modernity took up the task of making the world and time malleable and initiating future progress by means of historical legitimation, in more developed modernity time itself does not admit steering potentials or the possibility of shaping or influencing development, neither materially (*sachlich*) nor socially" (1993:375).

38. Virilio 2006:158; cf also Chesneaux 2000:413f.

39. Something Nassehi also notes: "Possibly the *most modern* version of . . . the semantics of time is Nietzsche's: what appears to be at first glance a restoration of the mythical form of cycles is rather the diagnosis of the *eternal return of the same*, that is, of present times that are confronted with the irresolvable dilemma of not being able to use their past as a resource and not knowing their future" (1993:378).

40. This contradiction is also revealed in the antagonism of "Cosmopolis vs. Empire" (the theme of the International Philosophy and the Social Sciences Conference at the Czech Academy of the Sciences in Prague, 2003) that is in-

herent within the globalization process. The *project of modernity*, which aims at a cosmopolis, is being undermined by empire, that is, the self-steering and autonomizing escalatory dynamic (*Steigerungszusammenhang*) of the *process of modernization*. Interestingly, the "postmodern" overcoming of imperial heteronomy postulated by Hardt and Negri is supposed to be achieved not by a reestablishment of the intentional, rational, political, and institutionalized claim (*Geltungsanspruch*) of classical modernity, but rather by the *vitalistic, spontaneous* activity of a "multitude" that is as diffuse as it is dubious. The kind of politics manifest in the multitude is, however, as difficult to conceive as the possible form of a postmodern subjectivity. Further, it would be interesting to interpret the rift between "old Europe" and the U.S., deepening since the most recent Iraq war, in terms of this dividing line. Whereas Europe experiences more and more the inevitability of an involuntary but functionally required *structural adaptation* to the modernization process and falls into a fatalistic pessimism about the gap between project and process, the U.S. ideologically holds onto the modern project's idea of being able to make and shape circumstances, of course at the price of eliminating any aspirations of control that might hinder the escalatory process of modernization.

41.   Wolin answers his own question—why is political theory so difficult today?—by pointing to the desynchronization of political theory, whose time patterns are tied up with (slow-moving) deliberative politics, but whose effects "preserve" historical time within themselves, and economic and cultural change in society: "Political theory might . . . be said to be governed by political time. It has its preservative function which is partly reflected in the amount of labor, perhaps even affection, that accompanies its perpetuation of a canon, but partly, too, in the deliberations about political life that figure in each and every theory and make their construction such a slow and drawn out process" (1997). On the way the intelligibility and describability of the world is placed in question by postmodernity, see Wagner (1994:175ff.) and Turner (1990:1ff.).

42.   Within the discourse surrounding acceleration, such an affirmative position is represented by Peter Weibel (1987), for instance. Of course, also of interest here is the question of how one is supposed to conceive of a genuinely *postmodern* form of subjectivity. Dieter Henrich, who has vehemently opposed the postulation of an *end* of art and subjectivity, defends the thesis that the growing dynamism of subjectivity does not necessarily destroy it because the incommensurable experiences of different life stages can be bound together into a whole by memory, on the one hand, and in the work of art, on the other. "Memory is the epistemic mode by which any synthesis is performed that bridges over the incommensurability of the stages of life," writes Henrich (2001:260). Later one reads that the formal process of the work of art discloses to every subject

"the movement of life in its whole dynamic in such a way that life is actually consummated through an experiential process to which the subject can attribute its own experiences and in which the sequence of stages, the conflicts between them and the prospect of a continuation come together in a closure" (ibid., 263). Yet this form of subjectivity remains unmistakably bound to the time experience of classical modernity. The idea of *life as a whole*, one that can be understood as a development through various life stages by way of a course of experience whose recollection is mediated by art, is constitutively dependent on a concept of *temporalized life*, i.e., one in which lived episodes can be transformed into experience in such a way that, at least in artistic reenactment, the life as a whole appears as *directed*. However, in view of the difficulties of even conceiving of a "postmodern" form of subjectivity, it may very well turn out that it is ultimately an "existential impossibility" (Löw-Beer 1991).

43. See for example, Rorty 1989.

44. An analysis of social pathologies oriented toward the investigation of time structures could thereby help to overcome the dilemma of contemporary social philosophy identified by Honneth (2007b), namely, that it cannot demonstrate the validity of its critical standards.

45. Sloterdijk 1989:12f., 27f., 52f. Sloterdijk makes the assertion that "firstly, both of the versions of critical theory previously known to us (those of Marxism and the Frankfurt School) have remained objectless (*gegenstandslos*) because they have either not grasped their object, the kinetic reality of modernity as mobilization, or could not critically differentiate themselves from it since on their own understanding they function as mobilizers; . . . secondly, a kinetic and kinaesthetic dimension must be introduced into the diagnostics of the present because without this all the talk about modernity simply misses what is most important" (ibid., 27f.; cf. the introduction of Rosa and Scheuerman 2009).

Conclusion: Frenetic Standstill?

1. Cf. figure 3.2.

2. Adorno 2005:156 (§ 100).

3. Cf. figure 8.1.

4. Jameson 1998:51ff.

5. Cf. for instance, Honneth (2007a:63ff.) on the empirical and theoretical presuppositions of a continuation of the project of critical theory. Among these are the interdisciplinarity of the approach and the diagnostic identification of social pathologies (*Fehlentwicklungen*), something that should rest on the real moral experiences of social subjects as well as an empirically discernible "interest in emancipation." It seems to me that these conditions can definitely

be fulfilled by a critique of temporal relations. Furthermore, if both Honneth (ibid., 88) and Helmut Dubiel (2001) believe that an analysis of the fundamental "objective laws of motion" of society—something still demanded by, for instance, Adorno (1993:42)—is no longer possible *on account of the rapid pace of social change*, then this seems to me to speak in favor of nothing so much as a critical analysis of precisely the laws and consequences of the *dynamization* that hinders both theory formation and political party formation.

6. For an attempt to decipher it, see Rosa 1999a.

7. See chapter 5.2.

8. "Marx says that revolutions are the locomotives of history. But perhaps it is quite otherwise. Perhaps revolutions are an attempt by the passengers on this train—namely, the human race—to activate the emergency brake" (Benjamin 2003:402; cf. ibid., 396, on the idea of a "messianic arrest of happening" (*messianische Stillstellung des Geschehens*).

9. "The concept of progress must be grounded in the idea of catastrophe. That things are 'status quo' *is* the catastrophe. . . . Redemption depends on the tiny fissure in the continuous catastrophe" (ibid., 184–85; on the critique of progress, see further ibid., 392ff.).

10. I draw here on the interpretation of Claus Offe, who remarks: "This vision obviously does not focus on purifying and defusing the rationalization process [or the acceleration process —H. R.] of modernity, on overcoming its contradictions and continuing to develop in accordance with its better possibilities; it focuses instead on a revolutionary act *in which the entire dynamics of modernity is brought to a standstill*" (Offe 1992:75).

11. Bourdieu 1996:70.

BIBLIOGRAPHY

Achtner, Wolfgang, Stefan Kunz, and Thomas Walter. 1998. *Dimensionen der Zeit. Die Zeitstrukturen Gottes, der Welt und des Menschen.* Darmstadt: Wissenschaftliche Buchgesellschaft.

Adam, Barbara. 1990. *Time and Social Theory.* Cambridge: Polity.

———, ed. 2002. "The Multiplicity of Times: Contributions from the Tutzing Time Ecology Project." *Time and* Society 11:87–146.

———. 2003. "Comment on 'Social Acceleration' by Hartmut Rosa." *Constellations: An International Journal of Critical and Democratic Theory* 10, no. 1: 49–52.

Adam, Barbara, Karlheinz A. Geißler, and Martin Held, eds. 1998. *Die Nonstop-Gesellschaft und ihr Preis.* Stuttgart: Hirzel.

Adams, Henry. 1999 [1904]. *The Education of Henry Adams.* Ed. Ira B. Nadel. Oxford: Oxford University Press.

———. 2009. "A Law of Acceleration." in Rosa and Scheuerman 2009:33–41.

Adorno, Theodor W. 1993. *Einleitung in die Soziologie,* vol. 15: *Nachgelassene Schriften.* Frankfurt: Suhrkamp.

———. 2005. *Minima Moralia: Reflections from Damaged Life.* New York: Verso.

Adriaansens, Hans P. M. 1980. *Talcott Parsons and the Conceptual Dilemma.* London: Routledge.

Agamben, Georgio. 1993. *Infancy and History: The Destruction of Experience.* London: Verso.

Ahlheit, Peter. 1988. "Alltagszeit und Lebenszeit." In Zoll 1988a:371–86.

Ahmadi, Amir. 2001. "On the Indispensability of Youth for Experience: Time and Experience in Paul Valery and Walter Benjamin." *Time and* Society 10:191–212.

Altvater, Elmar. 2002. "Kapitalismus—Zur Bestimmung, Abgrenzung und Dynamik einer geschichtlichen Formation." *Erwägen, Wissen, Ethik* 3:281–92.

Anders, Günther. 1987. *Die Antiquiertheit des Menschen.* Vol. 2. Munich: Beck.

Anderson, Walter Truett. 1997. *The Future of the Self: Inventing the Postmodern Person*. New York: Tarcher.

Appadurai, Arjun. 1990. "Disjuncture and Difference in the Global Cultural Economy." In *Global Culture. Nationalism, Globalization and Modernity*, 295–310. Ed. Mike Featherstone. London: Sage.

——. 1996. *Modernity at Large: Cultural Dimensions of Globalization*. Minneapolis: University of Minnesota Press.

Armitage, John. 2000. "From Mondernism to Hypermodernism and Beyond: An Interview with Paul Virilio." In *Paul Virilio*, 25–56. Ed. John Armitage. London: Sage.

Assheuer, Thomas. 2000. "Rechte Gewalt und Neue Mitte. Die Sehnsucht des Bürgers nach symbolischer Autorität und seine Gedankenflucht vor dem Rechtsradikalismus." *Die Zeit* 36 (August 31, 2000): 38.

Assmann, Jan. 1992. *Das kulturelle Gedächtnis. Schrift, Erinnerung und politische Identität in frühen Hochkulturen*. Munich: Beck.

Auer, Frank von, Karlheinz Geißler, and Helmut Schauer, eds. 1990. *Auf der Suche nach der gewonnenen Zeit. Beiträge für eine neue gesellschaftliche Zeitgestaltung*. Mössingen-Talheim: Talheimer.

Augé, Marc. 1994. *Orte und Nicht-Orte. Vorüberlegungen zu einer Ethnologie der Einsamkeit*. Frankfurt: Fischer.

Augustinus, Aurelius. 1912. *Confessions*. Trans. William Watts. Loeb Classical Library. 2 vols. New York: MacMillan.

Backhaus, Klaus, and Holger Bonus, eds. 1998. *Die Beschleunigungsfalle oder der Triumph der Schildkröte*. 3d ed. Stuttgart: Schäffer/Pöschel.

Backhaus, Klaus, and Kai Gruner. 1998. "Epidemie des Zeitwettbewerbs." In Backhaus and Bonus 1998:107–32.

Baier, Lothar. 2000. *Keine Zeit! 18 Versuche über die Beschleunigung*. Munich: Kunstmann.

Balla, Bálint. 1978. *Soziologie der Knappheit*. Stuttgart: Ferdinand Enke.

Barber, Benjamin. 1998/99. "Three Scenarios for the Future of Technology and Strong Democracy." *Political Science Quarterly* 113:572–87.

Barth, Ariane. 1989. "Im Reißwolf der Geschwindigkeit." *Spiegel*, no. 20: 200–20.

Baudelaire, Charles. 1964. "Exposition Universelle (1855)." In *Baudelaire as a Literary Critic*, 78–85. Ed. and trans. Lois Boe Hyslop and Francis E. Hyslop Jr. University Park: Pennsylvania State University Press.

——. 1975. *My Heart Laid Bare, and Other Prose Writings*. Ed. Peter Quennell. Trans. Norman Cameron. New York: Haskell.

Baudrillard, Jean. 1992. "The Pataphysics of the Year 2000." http://www.egs.edu/faculty/jean-baudrillard/articles/pataphysics-of-year-2000/.

Bauman, Zygmunt. 1995. *Life in Fragments*. Oxford: Blackwell.

———. 1998. "Schwache Staaten. Globalisierung und die Spaltung der Weltgesell-schaft." In Ulrich Beck, ed., *Kinder der Freiheit*, 15–332. Frankfurt: Suhrkamp.

———. 2000. *Liquid Modernity*. Cambridge: Polity.

Baur, Jürgen. 1989. *Körper- und Bewegungskarrieren. Dialektische Analysen zur Entwicklung von Körper und Bewegung im Kindes- und Jugendalter*. Schorndorf: Hofmann.

Beck, Ulrich. 1992. *Risk Society: Towards a New Modernity*. London: Sage.

———. 1997. *Was ist Globalisierung? Irrtümer des Globalismus, Antworten auf Globalisierung*. Frankfurt: Suhrkamp.

———. 1999. *Schöne neue Arbeitswelt. Vision: Weltbürgergesellschaft*. Frankfurt: Campus.

Beck, Ulrich, and Elisabeth Beck-Gernsheim, eds. 1994. *Riskante Freiheiten. Individualisierung in modernen Gesellschaften*. Frankfurt: Suhrkamp.

Beck, Ulrich, Anthony Giddens, and Scott Lash. 1994. *Reflexive Modernization: Politics, Tradition and Aesthetics in the Modern Social Order*. Stanford: Stanford University Press.

Behr, Michael. 1999. *Perspektiven eines neuen Arbeitstyps. Wandlungstendenzen im Verhältnis Person-Organisation*. Jenaer Beiträge zur Soziologie Heft 9. Jena: Institut für Soziologie.

Behr, Michael, Andrea Kottmann, and Tina Seiwert. 2002. "Schülerbefragung Nordthüringen Sommer 2002. Zukunftsaussichten, Berufsorientierungen und Abwanderungsmotivationen." Jena: Unpublished MS.

Beniger, James R. 1986. *The Control Revolution. Technological and Economic Origins of the Information Society*. Cambridge: Harvard University Press.

Benjamin, Walter. 1974a. "Zentralpark." In *Gesammelte Schriften*, 1.2:655–90. Ed. Rolf Tiedemann und Hermann Schweppenhäuser. Frankfurt: Suhrkamp.

———. 1974b. "Über den Begriff der Geschichte." In *Gesammelte Schriften*, 1.2:691–706. Ed. Rolf Tiedemann and Hermann Schweppenhäuser. Frankfurt: Suhrkamp.

———. 1974c. "Charles Baudelaire. Ein Lyriker im Zeitalter des Hochkapitalismus." In *Gesammelte Schriften*, 1.2:509–690. Ed. Rolf Tiedemann und Hermann Schweppenhäuser. Frankfurt: Suhrkamp.

———. 1980. "Das Paris des Second Empire bei Baudelaire." In *Gesammelte Schriften*, 1.2:509–604. Ed. Rolf Tiedemann und Hermann Schweppenhäuser. Frankfurt: Suhrkamp.

———. 1982. "Der Flaneur." In *Das Passagen-Werk, Gesammelte Schriften*, 5.1:524–69. Ed. Rolf Tiedemann und Hermann Schweppenhäuser. Frankfurt: Suhrkamp.

———. 2003. *Selected Writings*, vol. 4: 1938–40. Ed. Howard Eiland and Michael Jennings. Cambridge: Harvard University Press.

Bennis, Warren G., and Philip E. Slater. 1968. *The Temporary Society*. New York: Harper and Row.

Benthaus-Apel, Friederike. 1995. *Zwischen Zeitbindung und Zeitautonomie. Eine empirische Analyse der Zeitverwendung und Zeitstruktur der Werktags- und Wochenendfreizeit*. Wiesbaden: Deutscher Universitäts-Verlag.

Benz, Ernst. 1977. *Akzeleration der Zeit als geschichtliches und heilsgeschichtliches Problem*. Abh. der geistes- und sozialwissenschaftl. Klasse der Mainzer Akademie der Wissenschaften und der Literatur, Jg. 1977:2. Mainz.

Berger, Johannes, ed. 1986. *Die Moderne—Kontinuität und Zäsuren*. Soziale Welt, Sonderband 4. Göttingen: Schwartz.

Bergmann, Werner. 1981. *Die Zeitstrukturen sozialer Systeme. Eine systemtheoretische Analyse*. Berlin: Duncker and Humblot.

——. 1983. "Das Problem der Zeit in der Soziologie. Ein Literaturüberblick zum Stand der 'zeitsoziologischen' Theorie und Forschung." *Kölner Zeitschrift für Soziologie und Sozialpsychologie* 35:462–504.

Bering, Dietz. 2001. "Kulturelles Gedächtnis." In Nicolas Perthes and Jens Ruchatz, eds., *Gedächtnis und Erinnerung. Ein interdisziplinäres Lexikon*, 329–32. Reinbek: Rowohlt.

Berman, Marshall. 1988. *All That Is Solid Melts Into Air: The Experience of Modernity*. New York: Penguin.

Bertens, Hans, and Joseph Natoli, eds. 2002. *Postmodernism: The Key Figures*. Oxford: Blackwell.

Bertholt, Norbert. 2002. *Deregulierung und Flexibilisierung des Arbeitsmarktes in Zeiten der Globalisierung. Gutachten für den deutschen Bundestag*. Enquête-Kommission "Globalisierung der Weltwirtschaft"—AU Stud 14/23. Würzburg.

Bilden, Helga. 1997. "Das Individuum—ein dynamisches System vielfältiger Teil-Selbste. Zur Pluralität in Individuum und Gesellschaft." In Keupp and Höfer 1997:227–50.

Birkefeld, Richard, and Martina Jung. 1994. *Die Stadt, der Lärm und das Licht. Die Veränderung des öffentlichen Raumes durch Motorisierung und Elektrifizierung*. Seelze: Kallmeyer.

Blumenberg, Hans. 1986. *Lebenszeit und Weltzeit*. Frankfurt: Suhrkamp.

Böll, Heinrich. 1963. "Anekdote zur Senkung der Arbeitsmoral." In *Romane und Erzählungen*, 4:267–69. Cologne: Kiepenheuer and Witsch.

Bonus, Holger. 1998. "Die Langsamkeit der Spielregeln." In Backhaus and Bonus 1998:41–56.

Borneman, J. 1993. "Time-Space Compression and the Continental Divide in German Subjectivity." *New Formations* 21:102–18.

Borscheid, Peter. 2004. *Das Tempo-Virus. Eine Kulturgeschichte der Beschleunigung*. Frankfurt: Campus.

Bourdieu, Pierre. 1977. *Outline of a Theory of Practice*. Cambridge: Cambridge University Press.

———. 1996. "Störenfried Soziologie. Zur Demokratie gehört eine Forschung, die Ungerechtigkeiten aufdeckt." In Joachim Fritz-Vannahme, ed., *Wozu heute noch Soziologie?* 65–70. Opladen: Leske and Budrich.

Bourry, Thomas. 2004. "Wie die Zeit im Flug vergeht. Stillstand und Beschleunigung beim Reisen in Jetgeschwindigkeit." In Rosa 2004a:101–14.

Braun, Andreas. 2001. *Tempo, Tempo! Eine Kunst- und Kulturgeschichte der Geschwindigkeit im 19. Jahrhundert*. Werkbund-Archiv 28. Frankfurt: Anabas.

Breuer, Stefan. 1988. "Der Nihilismus der Geschwindigkeit. Zum Werk Paul Virilios." *Leviathan* 16:309–30.

Brilling, Oskar, and Eduard W. Kleber, eds. 1999. *Handwörterbuch Umweltbildung*. Hohengehren: Schneider.

Brinkmann, Reinhold. 2000. "Die Zeit der Eroica." In Klein, Kiem, and Ette 2000: 183–211.

Brose, Hanns-Georg. 2002. "Zeit-Kulturen im Umbruch." In Günter Altner et al., eds., *Jahrbuch Ökologie 2002*, 123–36. Munich: Beck.

Brose, Hanns-Georg, Monika Wohlrab-Sahr, and Michael Corsten. 1993. *Soziale Zeit und Biographie. Über die Gestaltung von Alltagszeit und Lebenszeit*. Opladen: Westdeutscher Verlag.

Brown, Alyson. 1998. "'Doing Time': The Extended Present of the Long-Term Prisoner." *Time and* Society 7:93–103.

Browning, Douglas, and William T. Myers, eds. 1998. *Philosophers of Process*. New York: Fordham University Press.

Brunner, Otto, Werner Conze, and Reinhart Koselleck, eds. 1972–1997. *Geschichtliche Grundbegriffe: Historisches Lexikon zur politisch-sozialen Sprache in Deutschland*. 8 vols. Stuttgart: Klett-Cotta.

Brüsemeister, Thomas. 2000. "Das überflüssige Selbst. Zur Dequalifizierung des Charakters im neuen Kapitalismus nach Richard Sennett." In Uwe Schimank and Ute Volkmann, eds., *Soziologische Gegenwartsdiagnosen*, 307–22. Opladen: Leske and Budrich.

Buchstein, Hubertus. 1997. "Bytes That Bite: The Internet and Deliberative Democracy." *Constellations* 4:248–63.

Burkart, Günter, Beate Fietze, and Martin Kohli. 1989. *Liebe, Ehe, Elternschaft. Eine qualitative Untersuchung über den Bedeutungswandel von Paarbeziehungen und seine demographischen Konsequenzen*. Wiesbaden: Bundesinstitut für Bevölkerungsforschung.

Castells, Manuel. 1996. *The Information Age: Economy, Society and Culture*, vol. 1: *The Rise of the Network Society*. Oxford: Blackwell.

———. 1997. *The Information Age: Economy, Society and Culture*, vol. 2: The Power of Identity. Oxford: Blackwell.

———. 1998. *The Information Age: Economy, Society and Culture*, vol. 3: *End of Millennium*. Oxford: Blackwell.

Charles, Bryan. 2002. "The Numbers. The World Trade Center." In Thomas Bellers, ed., *Before and After: Stories from New York*, 25–36. New York: Mr. Beller's Neighborhood.

Cherfas, Jeremy, and Roger Lewin, eds. 1980. *Not Work Alone: A Cross Cultural View of Activities Superfluous to Survival*. Beverly Hills: Sage.

Chesneaux, Jean. 2000. "Speed and Democracy: An Uneasy Dialogue." *Social Science Information* 39:407–20.

Connolly, William. 2000. "Speed, Concentric Cultures, and Cosmopolitanism." *Political Theory* 28:596–618. Repr. in Rosa and Scheuerman 2009.

Conrad, Peter. 1999. *Modern Times and Modern Places: How Life and Art Were Transformed in a Century of Revolution, Innovation, and Radical Change*. New York: Knopf.

Corsten, Michael, Hans-Joachim Giegel, Niki Gudulas, Michael Kauppert, and Hartmut Rosa. 2005. *Politische Kultur und Bürgerschaftliches Engagement*. Jenaer Beiträge zur Soziologie Heft 15, Institut für Soziologie, Jena.

Coser, Lewis A. 1974. *Greedy Institutions: Patterns of Undivided Commitment*. New York: Free Press.

Coupland, Douglas. 1991. *Generation X. Tales for an Accelerated Culture*. New York: St. Martin's.

van Creveld, Martin. 1998. *Die Zukunft des Krieges*. Munich: Gerling Akademie.

———. 1999. *The Rise and Decline of the State*. Cambridge: Cambridge University Press.

Crogan, Patrick. 2000. "The Tendency, the Accident and the Untimely. Paul Virilio's Engagement with the Future." In John Armitage, ed., *Paul Virilio: From Modernism to Hypermodernism and Beyond*, 161–76. London: Sage.

Cwerner, Saulo B. 2000. "The Chronopolitan Ideal: Time, Belonging, and Globalization." *Time and Society* 9:331–346.

De Haan, Gerhard. 1996. *Die Zeit in der Pädagogik. Vermittlungen zwischen der Fülle der Welt und der Kürze des Lebens*. Weinheim: Beltz.

Denninger, Erhard. 1988. "Der Präventionsstaat." *Kritische Justiz* 21:1–15.

Deutschmann, Christoph. 1989. "Der Clan als Unternehmensmodell der Zukunft?" *Leviathan* 17:85–107.

———. 1999. *Die Verheißung des absoluten Reichtums. Zur religiösen Natur des Kapitalismus*. Frankfurt: Campus.

Dewey, John. 1954. "The Eclipse of the Public." In *The Public and Its Problems*, 138–42. Athens: Ohio University Press. Repr. Rosa and Scheuerman 2009.

Dicke, Klaus. 1988. "Völkerrechtspolitik und internationale Rechtssetzung. Grundlagen—Verfahren—Entwicklungstendenzen." *Zeitschrift für Gesetzgebung* 3, no. 3: 193–224.

———. 2001. "Globales Recht ohne Weltherrschaft. Der Sicherheitsrat der Vereinten Nationen als Welt-Gesetzgeber?" *Forum Politicum Jenense*, no. 11, Jena.

Döhl, Volker, Nick Kratzer, Manfred Moldaschl, and Dieter Sauer. 2001. "Die Auflösung des Unternehmens?—Zur Entgrenzung von Kapital und Arbeit." In Ulrich Beck and Wolfgang Bonß, eds., *Die Modernisierung der Moderne*, 219–32. Frankfurt: Suhrkamp.

Dohrn-van Rossum, Gerhard. 1988. "Zeit der Kirche—Zeit der Händler—Zeit der Städte." In Zoll 1988a:72–88.

Donges, Juergen B. 1992. *Deregulierung am Arbeitsmarkt und Beschäftigung*. Tübingen: Mohr and Siebeck.

Dörr-Backes, Felicitas, and Ludwig Nieder, eds. 1995. *Georg Simmel zwischen Moderne und Postmoderne*. Würzburg: Königshausen and Neumann.

Dörre, Klaus. 1997. "Unternehmerische Globalstrategien, neue Managementkonzepte und die Zukunft der industriellen Beziehungen." In Ulf Kadritzke, ed., *Unternehmenskulturen unter Druck: Neue Managementkonzepte zwischen Anspruch und Wirklichkeit*, 15–44. Berlin: Sigma.

Dubiel, Helmut. 2001. *Kritische Theorie der Gesellschaft. Eine einführende Rekonstruktion von den Anfängen im Horkheimer-Kreis bis Habermas*. 3d ed. Weinheim: Juventa.

Durkheim, Emile. 1995 [1912]. *The Elementary Forms of Religious Life*. New York: Free Press.

———. 1997 [1893]. *The Division of Labor in Society*. Ed. Lewis Coser. New York: Free Press.

Dux, Günter. 1989. *Die Zeit in der Geschichte: ihre Entwicklungslogik vom Mythos zur Weltzeit*. Frankfurt: Suhrkamp.

Eberling, Matthias. 1996. *Beschleunigung und Politik*. Frankfurt: Peter Lang.

Eder, Klaus. 1995. "Die Institutionalisierung sozialer Bewegungen. Zur Beschleunigung von Wandlungsprozessen in fortgeschrittenen Industriegesellschaften." In H.-P. Müller and M. Schmied, eds., *Sozialer Wandel. Modellbildung und theoretische Ansätze*, 267–90. Frankfurt: Suhrkamp.

Ehrenberg, Alain. 1999. *La fatigue d'être soi: Dépression et société*. Paris: Odile Jacob.

———. 2000. "Die Müdigkeit, man selbst zu sein." In Carl Hegemann, ed., *Endstation. Sehnsucht. Kapitalismus und Depression*, 103–39. Berlin: Alexander.

Elchardus, Mark, and Ignace Glorieux. 1992. "The Search for the Invisible Eight Hours: The Gendered Use of Time in a Society with a High Labor Force Participation of Women." *Time and Society* 3:5–28.

Eliade, Mircea. 1991 [1954]. *The Myth of the Eternal Return; or, Cosmos and History*. Princeton: Princeton University Press.

Elias, Norbert. 1988. *Über die Zeit. Arbeiten zur Wissenssoziologie*. Vol. 2. Frankfurt: Suhrkamp.

———. 2000. *The Civilizing Process*. Ed. Eric Dunning, Johan Goudsblom, and Stephen Mennell. Trans. E. Jephcott. London: Blackwell.

Ende, Michael. 1973. *Momo oder die seltsame Geschichte von den Zeit-Dieben und von dem Kind, das den Menschen die gestohlene Zeit zurückbrachte (Ein Märchen-Roman)*. Stuttgart: Thienemann.

Enzensberger, Hans-Magnus. 1994. *Aussichten auf den Bürgerkrieg*. Frankfurt: Suhrkamp.

Erhard, Ludwig. 1997. *Wohlstand für Alle*. Munich: Econ.

Eriksen, Thomas Hylland. 2001. *Tyranny of the Moment: Fast and Slow Time in the Information Age*. London: Pluto.

Erlinghagen, Marcel. 2002. "Entwicklung der Arbeitsmarktmobilität und Beschäftigungsstabilität im Übergang von der Industrie zu Dienstleistungsgesellschaft." *Mitteilungen der Arbeitsmarkt und Berufsforschung* 35:74–89.

Evans-Pritchard, Edward E. 1969. *The Nuer: A Description of the Modes and Livelihood and Political Institutions of a Nilotic People*. Oxford: Oxford University Press.

Evers, Adalbert, Ulrich Rauch, and Uta Stitz. 2002. *Von öffentlichen Einrichtungen zu sozialen Unternehmen*—hybride Organisationsformen im Bereich sozialer Dienstleistungen. Berlin: Sigma.

Flaherty, Michael G. 1999. *A Watched Pot: How We Experience Time*. New York: University Press.

Flaherty, Michael G., and Gary Alan Fine. 2001. "Present, Past, and Future. Conjugating George Herbert Mead's Perspective on Time." *Time and Society* 10:147–61.

Fölling-Albers, Maria. 1992. *Schulkinder heute*———*Auswirkungen veränderter Kindheit auf Unterricht und Schulleben*. Weinheim: Beltz.

Foucault, Michel. 1978. "Recht der Souveränität/Mechanismus der Disziplin." In *Dispositive der Macht. Über Sexualität, Wissen und Wahrheit*, 75–95. Berlin: Merve.

———. 1983. "The Subject and Power." In Hubert L. Dreyfus and Paul Rabinow, eds., *Michel Foucault: Beyond Structuralism and Hermeneutics*, 208–29. 2d ed. Chicago: University of Chicago Press.

———. 1992. *The History of Sexuality*, vol. 2: *The Use of Pleasure*. London: Penguin.

———. 1995. *Discipline and Punish: The Birth of the Prison*. New York: Vintage.

Foucault, Michel et al. 1993. *Technologien des Selbst*. Ed. Luther H. Martin et al. Frankfurt: Fischer.

Francis-Smythe, Jan, and Ivan Robertson. 1999. "Time-Related Individual Differences." *Time and* Society 8:273–92.

Freyermuth, Gundolf S. 2000. "Digitales Tempo. Computer und Internet revolutionieren das Zeitempfinden." *c't, magazin für computer technik* 14:74–81.

Friedell, Egon. 1976. *Kulturgeschichte der Neuzeit. Die Krisis der europäischen Seele von der schwarzen Pest bis zum Ersten Weltkrieg*. Munich: Beck.

Frisby, David. 1988. *Fragments of Modernity: Theories of Modernity in the Work of Simmel, Kracauer und Benjamin.* Cambridge: MIT Press.

Fuchs-Heinritz, Werner. 2000. "Zukunftsorientierungen und Verhältnis zu den Eltern." In Deutsche Shell, ed., *Jugend 2000,* 23–92. Opladen: Leske and Budrich.

Fukuyama, Francis. 1992. *The End of History and the Last Man.* New York: Free Press.

Gaines, Donna. 1998. *Teenage Wasteland: Suburbia's Dead End Kids.* Chicago: University of Chicago Press.

Gamm, Gehrhard. 1992. "Das metaphorische Selbst. Über Subjektivität in der modernen Gesellschaft." In Jutta Georg-Lauer, ed., *Postmoderne und Politik,* 79–96. Tübingen: diskord.

Garhammer, Manfred. 1999. *Wie Europäer ihre Zeit nutzen. Zeitstrukturen und Zeitkulturen im Zeichen der Globalisierung.* Berlin: Sigma.

——. 2001. "Von Jobhoppern und Jobnomaden—Zeitinstitutionen und Unsicherheit in der spätmodernen Arbeitswelt." Jena: Unpublished MS.

——. 2002. "Changing Job Careers and Work Environments in the EU and Their Effects on Time-Pressure and the Work-Family Interface." Lecture presented at the Conference on Time Pressure, Work-Family Interface, and Parent-Child Relationships, March 23, Toronto.

Garhammer, Manfred, and Norbert Mundorf. 1997. "Teleheimarbeit und Telecommuting. Ein deutsch-amerikanischer Vergleich über kulturelle Bedingungen und soziale Auswirkungen einer neuen Arbeitsform." *Zeitschrift für Arbeitswissenschaft* 51, no. 4: 232–39.

Gehlen, Arnold. 1978. *Einblicke.* Frankfurt: Klostermann.

——. 1986. *Der Mensch. Seine Natur und seine Stellung in der Welt.* 13th ed. Wiesbaden: Aula.

——. 1994. "Über kulturelle Kristallisation." In *Wege aus der Moderne. Schlüsseltexte der Postmoderne-Diskussion,* 133–43. Ed. Wolfgang Welsch. Berlin: Akademie.

Geißler, Karlheinz. 1999. *Vom Tempo der Welt. Am Ende der Uhrzeit.* Freiburg: Herder.

Georg-Lauer, Jutta, ed. 1992. *Postmoderne und Politik.* Tübingen: diskord.

Gergen, Kenneth. 2000. *The Saturated Self: Dilemmas of Identity in Contemporary Life.* New York: Basic Books.

Gershuny, Jonathan. 1990. *The Multinational Longitudinal Time Budget Data Archive.* European Foundation for the Improvement of Living and Working Conditions. Dublin: Foundation.

——. 2003. *Changing Times: Work and Leisure in Postindustrial Society.* Oxford: Oxford University Press.

Giddens, Anthony. 1986. *The Constitution of Society: Outline of the Theory of Structuration.* Berkeley: University of California Press.

————. 1987a. "Time and Social Organization." In *Social Theory and Modern Sociology*, 140–65. Stanford: Stanford University Press.

————. 1987b. *The Nation-State and Violence*. Berkeley: University of California Press.

————. 1990. *Consequences* of Modernity. London: Polity.

————. 1995. *A Contemporary Critique of Historical Materialism*. 2d ed. Stanford: University Press.

————. 1996. *Kritische Theorie der Spätmoderne*. Passagen Heft 5. Wien: Passagen.

————. 1999. *A Runaway World*. London: Profile.

Giegel, Hans-Joachim. 1999. "Strukturveränderungen und Problementwicklungen in der Demokratie." In Dirk Berg-Schlosser and Hans-Joachim Giegel, eds., *Perspektiven der Demokratie. Probleme und Chancen im Zeitalter der Globalisierung*, 100–33. Frankfurt: Suhrkamp.

Giegel, Hans-Joachim, and Hartmut Rosa. 2000. "Politische Kultur und Bürgerschaftliches Engagement." In *Gesellschaftliche Entwicklungen nach dem Systemumbruch. Diskontinuität, Tradition und Strukturbildung*, 485–521. Projektantrag zum Sonderforschungsbereich 1811/580 der DFG in Jena/Halle.

Giegel, Hans-Joachim, Hartmut Rosa, and Jana Heinz. 2001. *Zivilgesellschaft und Lehrstellenkrise in Ostdeutschland. Eine Untersuchung über die Bedingungen bürgerschaftlichen Engagements angesichts funktionaler Defizite*. Jenaer Beiträge zur Soziologie Heft 8. Jena: Institut für Soziologie.

Gilpin, Robert. 1987. *The Political Economy of International Relations*. Princeton: Princeton University Press.

Glass, James M. 1993. *Shattered Selves: Multiple Personality in a Postmodern World*. Ithaca: Cornell University Press.

Gleick, James. 1999. *Faster: The Acceleration of Just About Everything*. New York: Pantheon.

Glennie, Paul, and Nigel Thrift. 1996. "Reworking E. P. Thomspon's 'Time, Work-Discipline and Industrial Capitalism.'" *Time and* Society 5, no. 3: 275–300.

Glotz, Peter. 1998. "Kritik der Entschleunigung." In Backhaus and Bonus 1998a: 75–89.

Goethe, Johann Wolfgang. 1825. *Briefe*, Ende November 1825. Frankfurter Ausgabe II, vol. 10. Frankfurt: Deutscher Klassiker Verlag.

————. 1961. *Faust: A Tragedy, Part One*. Trans. Walter Kaufmann. New York: Anchor.

————. 1988. *The Sorrows of Young Werther; Elective Affinities; Novella. Collected Works of Goethe*. Vol. 12. Ed. David E. Wellbury. Trans. Victor Lange and Judith Ryan. New York: Suhrkamp.

Gronemeyer, Marianne. 1996. *Das Leben als letzte Gelegenheit. Sicherheitsbedürfnisse und Zeitknappheit*. 2d ed. Darmstadt: Wissenschaftliche Buchgesellschaft.

Großklaus, Götz. 1997. *Medien-Zeit, Medien-Raum. Zum Wandel der raumzeitlichen Wahrnehmung in der Moderne.* 2d ed. Frankfurt: Suhrkamp.

Gross, Peter. 1994. *Die Multioptionsgesellschaft.* Frankfurt: Suhrkamp.

Grotheer, Michael, and Olaf Struck. 2003. *Beschäftigungsstabilität: Entwicklung und Arbeitszufriedenheit. Ergebnisse aus der IAB-Beschäftigtenstichprobe 1975–97 und der BIBB/IAB-Erhebung.* Institut für Soziologie, Universität Jena (forthcoming).

Guggenberger, Bernd, and Claus Offe. 1984. *An den Grenzen der Mehrheitsdemokratie.* Opladen: Westdeutscher Verlag.

Günther, Klaus. 2001. "Rechtspluralismus und universaler Code der Legalität: Globalisierung als rechtstheoretisches Problem." In Lutz Wingert and Klaus Günther, eds., *Die Öffentlichkeit der Vernunft und die Vernunft der Öffentlichkeit,* 539–67. Frankfurt: Suhrkamp.

Gurvitch, Georges. 1963. "Social Structure and the Multiplicity of Time." In E. A. Tiryakian, ed., *Sociological Theory, Values, and Sociocultural Change,* 171–85. London: Free Press of Glencoe.

Guy, Jean-Sebastien. 2002. "The Acceleration of Time from Luhmann's Theoretical Perspective." Montreal. Manuscript read at Session 3, "Temporal Structures and the Concept of Acceleration," of Research Group 35 at the Fifteenth World Congress of Sociology in Brisbane, July 7–13, 2002.

Habermas, Jürgen. 1984. *The Theory of Communicative Action,* vol. 1: *Reason and the Rationalization of Society.* Boston: Beacon.

———. 1987a. *The Theory of Communicative Action,* vol. 2: *Lifeworld and System: A Critique of Functionalist Reason.* Boston: Beacon.

———. 1987b. *The Philosophical Discourse of Modernity: Twelve Lectures.* Cambridge: MIT Press.

———. 1989. "The New Obscurity: The Crisis of the Welfare State and the Exhaustion of Utopian Energies." In *The New Conservatism: Cultural Criticism and the Historian's Debate,* 48–71. Cambridge: MIT Press.

———. 1996. *Between Facts and Norms: Contributions to a Discourse Theory of Law and Democracy.* Cambridge: MIT Press.

———. 2003. *The Future of Human Nature.* Malden, MA: Polity.

Habermas, Tilmann. 1999. *Geliebte Objekte. Symbole und Instrumente der Identitätsbildung.* Frankfurt: Suhrkamp.

Hagmann, Peter. 2003. "Beethoven—von heute? Eine neue Gesamtaufnahme der Symphonien." *Neue Zürcher Zeitung,* March 19, 2003, 3:10.

Hall, Peter. 1988. "The Intellectual History of Long Waves." In Young and Schuller 1988:37–52.

Hardt, Michael, and Antonio Negri. 2001. *Empire.* Cambridge: Harvard University Press.

Harvey, David. 1990. *The Condition of Postmodernity: An Enquiry Into the Origins of Cultural Change*. Oxford: Blackwell.

———. 1999. *The Limits to Capital*. New York: Verso.

———. 2000a. *Spaces of Hope*. Edinburgh: Edinburgh University Press.

———. 2000b. "Contemporary Globalization." In *Spaces of Hope*, 53–72. Edinburgh: Edinburgh University Press.

Heidegger, Martin. 1992 [1924]. *The Concept of Time*. Trans. Will McNeill. Malden, MA: Wiley-Blackwell.

———. 2008. *Being and Time*. Trans. John MacQuarrie and Edward Robinson. New York: Harper Perennial Classics.

Heine, Heinrich. 1974. *Lutetia*. In *Sämtliche Schriften*, 5:217–48. Ed. Klaus Briegleb und Karl-Heinz Stahl. Munich: Hanser.

Heintel, Peter. 1999. *Innehalten. Gegen die Beschleunigung—für eine andere Zeitkultur*. Freiburg: Herder.

Heintel, Peter, and Thomas Macho. 1985. *Zeit und Arbeit. Hundert Jahre nach Marx*. Vienna: Verlag des Verbandes der wissenschaftlichen Gesellschaften Österreichs.

Heinze, Rolf G., and Thomas Olk. 1999. "Vom Ehrenamt zum bürgerschaftlichen Engagement. Trends des begrifflichen und gesellschaftlichen Strukturwandels." In Ernst Kistler, Heinz-Herbert Noll, and Eckhard Priller, eds., *Perspektiven gesellschaftlichen Zusammenhalts*, 77–100. Berlin: Sigma.

Held, David, Anthony McGrew, David Goldblatt, and Jonathan Perraton. 1999. *Global Transformations: Politics, Economics and Culture*. Cambridge: Polity.

Helsper, Werner. 1997. "Das 'postmoderne Selbst'—ein neuer Subjekt- und Jugend-Mythos?" In Keupp and Höfer 1997:174–216.

Hennis, Wilhelm. 2000. *Regieren im modernen Staat*. Politikwissenschaftliche Abhandlungen, vol. 1. Tübingen: Mohr.

Henrich, Dieter. 2001. *Versuch über Kunst und Leben. Subjektivität—Weltverstehen—Kunst*. Munich: Hanser.

Heylighen, Francis. 2001. "Technological Acceleration." http://pespmc1.vub.ac.be/TECACCEL.html.

Hildenbrand, Bruno. 2001. "Zum Verhältnis von Tradition und Wandel in Paarbeziehungen." Lecture delivered to the 6th Symposium of the Working Group "Zweite Moderne" on May 20. Weimar: Unpublished MS.

Hochschild, Arlie Russel. 2000. *Time Bind: When Work Becomes Home and Home Becomes Work*. New York: Holt.

Hoffmann, Edeltraut, and Ulrich Walwei. 1998. "Normalarbeitsverhältnis: ein Auslaufmodell? Überlegungen zu einem Erklärungsmodell für den Wandel der Beschäftigungsformen." *Mitteilungen der Arbeitsmarkt- und Berufsforschung* 31, no. 3: 409–25.

Hofmann, Wilhelm. 2004. "Zusammenprall der Zeitkulturen. Lebenstempo und Zeitempfinden in Ostdeutschland vor und nach der Wiedervereinigung." In Rosa 2004a:57–72.

Holz, Erlend. 2000. *Zeitverwendung in Deutschland: Beruf, Famile, Freizeit*. Schriftenreihe, Spektrum Bundesstatistik, vol. 13. Wiesbaden: Statistisches Bundesamt.

Honneth, Axel. 1999. "Kommunikative Erschließung der Vergangenheit. Zum Zusammenhang von Anthropologie und Geschichtsphilosophie bei Walter Benjamin." In *Die zerrissene Welt des Sozialen. Sozialphilosophische Aufsätze*, 93–113. 2d ed. Frankfurt: Suhrkamp.

——. 2002. "Organisierte Selbstverwirklichung. Paradoxien der Individualisierung." In Axel Honneth, ed., *Befreiung aus der Mündigkeit: Paradoxien des gegenwärtigen Kapitalismus*, 141–59. Frankfurt.

——. 2007a. *Disrespect: The Normative Foundations of Critical Theory*. Malden, MA: Polity.

——. 2007b. "Pathologies of the Social. Past and Present of Social Philosophy." In Honneth 2007a:3–49.

——. 2007c. "The Social Dynamics of Disrespect: On the Location of a Critical Social Theory." In Honneth 2007a:63–79.

Horkheimer, Max, and Theodor W. Adorno. 2002. *Dialectic of Enlightenment*. Ed. Gunzelin Schmid Noerr. Trans. E. Jephcott. Stanford: Stanford University Press.

Hörning, Karl H., Daniela Ahrens, and Anette Gerhard. 1997. *Zeitpraktiken. Experimentierfelder der Spätmoderne*. Frankfurt: Suhrkamp.

——. 1999. "Do Technologies Have Time? New Practices of Time and the Transformation of Communication Technologies." *Time and Society* 8:293–308.

Howard, A. E. Dick. 1990. *The Road to Constitutionalism*. Budapest: Sonderdruck der Konferenz Democracy and Constitution-Making in Central Europe.

Hufton, Olwen, and Yota Kravaritou. 1996. "Gender and the Use of Time." *Time and Society* 5:339–98.

Imhof, Arthur E. 1984. "Von der sicheren zur unsicheren Lebenszeit. Ein folgenschwerer Wandel im Verlaufe der Neuzeit." *Vierteljahresschrift für Sozial- und Wirtschaftsgeschichte* 71:175–98.

Jahoda, Marie. 1988. "Time: A Social Psychological Perspective." In Young and Schuller 1988:154–72.

Jahoda, Marie, P. F. Lazarsfeld, and H. Zeisel. 1933. *Die Arbeitslosen von Marienthal*. Leipzig: Hirzel.

James, William. 1890. *Principles of Psychology*. Vol. 1. New York: Holt.

Jameson, Fredric. 1994. *The Seeds of Time*. New York: Columbia University Press.

——. 1998. *The Cultural Turn. Selected Writings on the Postmodern, 1983/1998*. London: Verso.

Jessop, Bob. 2009. "The Spatiotemporal Dynamics of Capital and Globalization—How They Challenge State Power and Democracy." In Rosa and Scheuerman 2009:135–59.

Joas, Hans. 1992. *Pragmatismus und Gesellschaftstheorie*. Frankfurt: Suhrkamp.

——. 1994. "Kreativität und Autonomie. Die soziologische Identitätskonzeption und ihre postmoderne Herausforderung." In Christoph Görg, ed., *Gesellschaft im Übergang. Perspektiven kritischer Soziologie*, 109–19. Darmstadt: Wissenschaftliche Buchgesellschaft.

Johnson, Allen. 1978. "In Search of the Affluent Society." *Human Nature* (September): 50–59.

Jung, Thomas. 1989. *Vom Ende der Geschichte. Rekonstruktionen zum Posthistoire in kritischer Absicht*. Münster.

Kaern, Michael, Bernhard S. Philips, and Robert S. Cohen, eds. 1990. *Georg Simmel and Contemporary Sociology*. Dordrecht: Kluwer.

Kamper, Dietmar, and Christoph Wulf, eds. 1987. *Die sterbende Zeit. Zwanzig Diagnosen*. Darmstadt and Neuwied.

Kant, Immanuel. 1998. *Critique of Pure Reason*. Ed. and trans. Paul Guyer and Allen Wood. Cambridge: Cambridge University Press.

Keane, John. 1991. *The Media and Democracy*. Cambridge: Polity.

Kellner, Douglas. 1992. "Popular Culture and the Construction of Postmodern Identities." In Scott Lash and Jonathan Friedman, eds., *Modernity and Identity*, 141–77. Cambridge: Blackwell.

Kemper, Peter. 1995. "Weltfernsehen MTV: Ein Clip zielt ins Herz, nicht ins Hirn." *Frankfurter Allgemeine Magazin* 823, no. 49 (December 8, 1995): 18–24.

Kern, Stephen. 1983. *The Culture of Time and Space, 1880–1918*. Cambridge: Harvard University Press.

Kertész, Imre. 2002. *Ich—ein anderer*. 2d ed. Reinbek: Rohwohlt.

Kessel, Martina. 2001. *Langeweile. Zum Umgang mit Zeit und Gefühlen in Deutschland vom späten 18. bis zum frühen 20. Jahrhundert*. Göttingen: Wallstein.

Keupp, Heiner et al. 1999. *Identitätskonstruktionen. Das Patchwork der Identitäten in der Spätmoderne*. Reinbek: Rowohlt.

Keupp, Heiner, and Renate Höfer, eds. 1997. *Identitätsarbeit heute. Klassische und aktuelle Perspektiven der Identitätsforschung*. Frankfurt: Suhrkamp.

Kielmansegg, Peter Graf. 2003a. "Zukunftsverweigerung." *Frankfurter Allgemeine Zeitung*, May 23, 2003, 11.

——. 2003b. "Können Demokratien zukunftsverantwortlich handeln?" *Merkur* 651:584–94.

Kirchmann, Kay. 1998. *Verdichtung, Weltverlust und Zeitdruck. Grundzüge einer Theorie der Interdependenzen von Medien, Zeit und Geschwindigkeit im neuzeitlichen Zivilisationsprozess*. Opladen: Leske und Budrich.

Klein, Richard, Eckehard Kiem, and Wolfram Ette, eds. 2000. *Musik in der Zeit. Zeit in der Musik*. Weilerswist: Velbrück.

Kodalle, Klaus-Michael, ed. 1999. *Zeit-Verschwendung. Ein Symposion*. Würzburg: Königshausen and Neumann.

Kohli, Martin. 1985. "Die Institutionalisierung des Lebenslaufs. Historische Befunde und theoretische Argumente." *Kölner Zeitschrift für Soziologie und Sozialpsychologie* 37:1–29.

——. 1986. "Gesellschaftszeit und Lebenszeit. Der Lebenslauf im Strukturwandel der Moderne." In Johannes Berger, ed., *Die Moderne—Kontinuitäten und Zäsuren*, 183–207. Göttingen: Schwartz.

——. 1990. "Lebenslauf und Lebensalter als gesellschaftliche Konstruktionen: Elemente zu einem interkulturellen Vergleich." In G. Elwert, M. Kohli, and H. K. Müller, eds., *Im Lauf der Zeit. Ethnographische Studien zur gesellschaftlichen Konstruktion von Lebensaltern*, 11–32. Saarbrücken: Breitenbach.

——. 1994. "Institutionalisierung und Individualisierung der Erwerbsbiographie." In Ulrich Beck and Elisabeth Beck-Gernsheim, eds., *Riskante Freiheiten*, 219–44. Frankfurt: Suhrkamp.

Kommission für Zukunftsfragen der Freistaaten Bayern und Sachsen. 1996. *Erwerbstätigkeit und Arbeitslosigkeit in Deutschland—Teil 1. Entwicklung von Erwerbstätigkeit und Arbeitslosigkeit in Deutschland und anderen frühindustrialisierten Ländern*. Bonn.

——. 1997. *Erwerbstätigkeit und Arbeitslosigkeit in Deutschland—Teil 3. Maßnahmen zur Verbesserung der Beschäftigungslage*. Bonn.

Koselleck, Reinhart. 1989. *Vergangene Zukunft. Zur Semantik geschichtlicher Zeiten*. Frankfurt: Suhrkamp.

——. 2000. *Zeitschichten. Studien zur Historik* (with a contribution by Hans-Georg Gadamer). Frankfurt: Suhrkamp.

——. 2004. *Futures Past: On the Semantics of Historical Time*. New York: Columbia University Press.

——. 2009. "Is There an Acceleration of History?" In Rosa and Scheuerman 2009:113–35.

Krappmann, Lothar. 1997. "Die Identitätsproblematik nach Erikson aus einer interaktionistischen Sicht." In Keupp and Höfer 1997:66–92.

Kraus, Wolfgang. 2000. *Das erzählte Selbst. Die narrative Konstruktion von Identität in der Spätmoderne*. Herbolzheim: Centaurus.

——. 2002. "Falsche Freunde." In Straub and Renn 2002:159–86.

Krugman, H. E. 1977. "Memory with Recall, Exposure Without Perception." *Journal of Advertising Research* 17:7–12.

Kubey, Robert, and Mihaly Csikszentmihalyi. 1990. *Television and the Quality of Life: How Viewing Shapes Everyday Experience*. Hillsdale, NJ: Lawrence Erlbaum.

Lafargue, Paul. 1998 [1883]. *Das Recht auf Faulheit. Widerlegung des, Rechts auf Arbeit' von 1848.* Grafenau: Trotzdem.

Landes, David S. 1969. *The Unbound Prometheus. Technological Change and Industrial Development in Western Europe from 1750 to the Present.* Cambridge: Cambridge University Press.

Lash, Scott. 1996. "Tradition and the Limits of Difference." In Paul Heelas, Scott Lash, and Paul Morris, eds., *Detraditionalization: Critical Reflections on Authority and Identity,* 250–74. Cambridge: Blackwell.

Lash, Scott, and John Urry. 1987. *The End of Organized Capitalism.* Madison: University of Wisconsin Press.

Laslett, Peter. 1988. "Social Structural Time: An Attempt at Classifying Types of Social Change by Their Characteristic Paces." In Michael Young and Tom Schuller, eds., *The Rhythms of Society,* 17–36. New York: Routledge.

Lauer, Robert. 1981. *Temporal Man: The Meaning and Uses of Social Time.* New York: Praeger.

Leccardi, Carmen. 1996. "Rethinking Social Time: Feminist Perspectives." *Time and Society* 5:169–86.

——. 2003. "Resisting 'Acceleration Society.'" *Constellations: An International Journal of Critical and Democratic Theory* 10, no. 1: 34–41.

LeGoff, Jacques. 1977. "Zeit der Kirche und Zeit des Händlers im Mittelalter." In *Schrift und Materie der Geschichte,* 393–414. Ed. Claudia Honegger. Frankfurt: Suhrkamp.

Lepenies, Wolf. 1976. *Das Ende der Naturgeschichte. Wandel kultureller Selbstverständlichkeiten in den Wissenschaften des 18. und 19. Jahrhunderts.* Munich: Hanser.

——. 1981. *Melancholie und Gesellschaft.* 2d ed. Frankfurt: Suhrkamp.

Lestienne, Remy, ed. 2000. "Time and Globalization." *Time and Society* 9:289–346.

Levine, Robert. 2006. *A Geography of Time: The Misadventures of a Social Psychologist, or How Cultures Keep Time a Little Differently.* Oxford: Oneworld.

Lifton, Robert Jay. 1993. *The Protean Self: Human Resilience in an Age of Fragmentation.* New York: Basic Books.

Linder, Staffan B. 1970. *The Harried Leisure Class.* New York: Columbia University Press.

Löw-Beer, Martin. 1991. "Living a Life and the Problem of Existential Impossibility." *Inquiry* 34:217–36.

van der Loo, Hans, and Willem van Reijen. 1997. *Modernisierung. Projekt und Paradox.* 2d ed. Munich: dtv.

van Loon, Joost. 2000. "Imminent Immanence: The Time-Politics of Speed and the Management of Decline." *Time and Society* 9:347–54.

Lübbe, Hermann. 2009. "The Contraction of the Present." In Rosa and Scheuer-man 2009:159–79.

Luhmann, Niklas. 1980. "Temporalisierung von Komplexität. Zur Semantik neuzeitlicher Zeitbegriffe." In *Gesellschaftsstruktur und Semantik. Studien zur Wissenssoziologie der modernen Gesellschaft,* 1:235–313. Frankfurt: Suhrkamp.

——. 1980–1999. *Gesellschaftsstruktur und Semantik. Studien zur Wissenssoziologie der modernen Gesellschaft.* 4 vols. Frankfurt: Suhrkamp.

——. 1990a. "Die Zukunft kann nicht beginnen. Temporalstrukturen der modernen Gesellschaft." In *Vor der Jahrtausendwende: Berichte zur Lage der Zukunft,* 1:119–50. Ed. Peter Sloterdijk. Frankfurt: Suhrkamp.

——. 1990b. "Gleichzeitigkeit und Synchronisation." In *Soziologische Aufklärung,* vol. 5: *Konstruktivistische Perspektiven,* 95–130. Opladen: Westdeutscher Verlag.

——. 1991. "Weltzeit und Systemgeschichte." In *Soziologische Aufklärung,* vol. 2: *Aufsätze zur Theorie der Gesellschaft,* 103–33. 4th ed. Opladen: Westdeutscher Verlag.

——. 1992. "Operational Closure and Structural Coupling: The Differentiation of the Legal System." *Cardozo Law Review* 13:1419–42.

——. 1994 [1968]. "Die Knappheit der Zeit und die Vordringlichkeit des Befriste-ten." In *Politische Planung. Aufsätze zur Soziologie von Politik und Verwaltung,* 143–64. 4th ed. Opladen: Westdeutscher Verlag.

——. 1996. *Soziale Systeme. Grundriss einer allgemeinen Theorie.* 6th ed. Frankfurt: Suhrkamp.

——. 1997. *Die Gesellschaft der Gesellschaft.* Frankfurt: Suhrkamp.

Lutz, Burkhard. 1984. *Der kurze Traum immerwährender Prosperität.* Frankfurt: Campus.

Lyotard, Jean-Francois. 1984. *The Postmodern Condition: A Report on Knowledge.* Minneapolis: University of Minnesota Press.

MacIntyre, Alasdair. 2007. *After Virtue: A Study in Moral Theory.* 3d ed. Notre Dame: University of Notre Dame Press.

McLuhan, Marshall. 1966. *Understanding Media—The Extensions of Man.* New York: McGraw-Hill.

McNeill, William H. 1982. *The Pursuit of Power: Technology, Armed Force and Society Since AD 1000.* Chicago: University of Chicago Press.

McTaggart, John Ellis. 1908. "The Unreality of Time." *Mind* 17:456–73.

Mannheim, Karl. 1964. "Das Problem der Generationen." In Kurt H. Wolff, ed., *Wissenssoziologie,* 509–65. Berlin: Luchterhand.

Marinetti, Filippo Tomaso. 1966 [1909]. "Gründung und Manifest des Futurismus." In Christa Baumgarth, ed., *Die Geschichte des Futurismus,* 23–29. Reinbek: Rohwolt.

——.2009 [1916]. "The New Religion-Morality of Speed." In Rosa and Scheuerman 2009:57–61.

Marschall, Wolfgang. 1997. "Zeitkonflikte in multikultureller Konfrontation." In Peter Rusterholz and Rupert Moser, eds., *Zeit. Zeitverständnis in Wissenschaft und Lebenswelt*, 161–76. Bern: Peter Lang.

Martin, Bill. 1998. *Listening to the Future: The Time of Progressive Rock, 1968–1978*. Chicago: Open Court.

Marx, Karl. 1951. *Das Kapital. Kritik der politischen Ökonomie*. Vol. 3. Berlin: Dietz.

——. 1957. *Das Kapital. Kritik der politischen Ökonomie*. Ed. Benedikt Kautsky. Stuttgart: Kröner.

——. 1971. *The Grundrisse*. Ed. and trans. David McLellan. Harper: New York.

——. 1976. *Capital: A Critique of Political Economy*. Vol. 1. Trans. Ben Fowkes. London: Penguin.

——. 1983 [1857]. *Grundrisse der Kritik der Politischen Ökonomie*. In *Marx-Engels-Werke*, 42:15–770. Berlin: Dietz.

Marx, Karl, and Friedrich Engels. 1978. *The Marx-Engels Reader*. Ed. Robert Tucker. New York: Norton.

——. 1986. "Manifest der Kommunistischen Partei." In *Ausgewählte Werke*, 34–63. Moskau: Progress.

Marxer, Johanna. 2003. "Weg aus Würzburg." First-prize contribution to the Fourth Deutschen Studienpreis der Körberstiftung. Hamburg: Unpublished MS.

Maurer, Andrea. 1992. "Stand und Perspektiven zeitsoziologischer Forschung." In Hansgünter Meyer, ed., *Soziologie in Deutschland und die Transformation großer gesellschaftlicher Systeme*, 590–607. Berlin: Akademie.

Mead, Margaret. 1970. *Culture and Committment: A Study of the Generation-Gap*. Garden City NY: Doubleday.

Michelson, William, and David Crouse. 2002. "Changing Demands on the Time-Use Analysis of Family, Work, and Personal Outcomes: Implications for Trend Analysis of Time Pressure." www.lifestress.uwaterloo.ca/papers/michelson.pdf.

Mill, John Stuart. 1977. *Essays on Politics and Society: Collected Works of John Stuart Mill*. Ed. J. M. Robson. Vol. 19. Toronto: University of Toronto Press.

Moebius, Stephan. 2002. *Simmel lesen. Moderne, dekonstruktive und postmoderne Lektüren der Soziologie Georg Simmels*. Stuttgart: Ibidem.

Moldaschl, Manfred, and Dieter Sauer. 2000. "Internalisierung des Marktes—Zur neuen Dialektik von Kooperation und Herrschaft." In Heiner Minssen, ed., *Begrenzte Entgrenzungen—Wandlungen von Organisation und Arbeit*, 205–24. Berlin: Sigma.

Montesquieu, Charles de. 1989. *The Spirit of the Laws*. Ed. Anne Cohler, Basia Miller, and Harold Stone. Cambridge: Cambridge University Press.

Moore, Wilbert E. 1963. *Man, Time, and Society*. New York: Wiley.

Moritz, Karl Philipp. 1988. *Anton Reiser. Ein psychologischer Roman.* 7th ed. Frankfurt: Insel.

Müller, Hans-Peter, and Michael Schmid, ed. 1995. *Sozialer Wandel. Modellbildung und theoretische Ansätze.* Frankfurt: Suhrkamp.

Mumford, Lewis. 1934. *Technics and Civilization.* New York: Harcourt Brace.

Münkler, Herfried. 2002. *Die neuen Kriege.* Reinbek: Rowohlt.

——. 2009. "Temporal Rhythms and Military Force: Acceleration, Deceleration and War." In Rosa and Scheuerman 2009:243–61.

Musil, Robert. 1995. *The Man Without Qualities.* Trans. Sophie Wilkins and Burton Pike. Vol. 1. New York: Vintage International.

Myerson, George. 2001. *Heidegger, Habermas and the Mobile Phone.* Cambridge: Icon.

Nadolny, Sten. 1987. *Die Entdeckung der Langsamkeit.* Munich: Piper.

Nassehi, Armin. 1993. *Die Zeit der Gesellschaft. Auf dem Weg zu einer soziologischen Theorie der Zeit.* Opladen: Westdeutscher Verlag.

——. 2000. "Schläger schaffen ohne Waffen. Die offene Gesellschaft produziert ihre Feinde: Vermutungen über den 'Kampf gegen Nazis.'" *Die Zeit* 35 (August 24, 2000): 36.

Neckel, Sighard. 2000. "Identität als Ware. Die Marktwirtschaft im Sozialen." In *Die Macht der Unterscheidung. Essays zur Kultursoziologie der modernen Gesellschaft,* 37–47. Frankfurt: Campus.

Negt, Oskar. 1988. "Der Kampf um die Arbeitszeit ist ein Kampf um die Lebenszeit." In Zoll 1988a:531–43.

Neumann, Enno. 1988. "Das Zeitmuster der protestantischen Ethik." In Zoll 1988a:160–71.

Niethammer, Lutz. 1989. *Posthistoire. Ist die Geschichte zu Ende?* Reinbek: Rowohlt.

Nietzsche, Friedrich. 1974. *The Gay Science.* Trans. Walter Kaufmann. New York: Vintage.

——. 1996. *Human, All-Too-Human.* Ed. Richard Schacht. Trans. R. J. Hollingdale. Cambridge: Cambridge University Press.

——. 1997. *Untimely Meditations.* Ed. Danieal Breazeale. Trans. R. J. Hollingdale. Cambridge: Cambridge University Press.

——. 2005. *The Anti-Christ, Ecce Homo, Twilight of the Idols and Other Writings.* Ed. Judith Norman and Aaron Ridley. Trans. Judith Norman. Cambridge: Cambridge University Press.

Nowotny, Helga. 1993. *Eigenzeit. Entstehung und Strukturierung eines Zeitgefühls.* Frankfurt: Suhrkamp.

——. 1994. *Time: The Modern and Postmodern Experience.* Cambridge: Polity.

——. 1999. *Es ist so. Es könnte auch anders sein. Über das veränderte Verhältnis von Wissenschaft und Gesellschaft.* Frankfurt: Suhrkamp.

Nuber, Ursula. 1999. "Stresskrankheit Depression." *Psychologie Heute* 26, no. 3: 20–25.

Offe, Claus. 1987. "The Utopia of the Zero-Option: Modernity and Modernization as Normative Political Criteria." *Praxis International* 7, no. 1: 1–24.

———. 1992. "Bindings, Shackles, Brakes: On Self-Limitation Strategies." In Axel Honneth, Thomas McCarthy, Claus Offe, and Albrecht Wellmer, eds., *Cultural-Political Interventions Into the Unfinished Project of Enlightenment*, 63–95. Cambridge: MIT Press.

———. 1996. *Modernity and the State*. Cambridge: MIT Press.

Ogren, Kathy J. 1989. *The Jazz Revolution: Twenties America and the Meaning of Jazz*. New York: Oxford University Press.

Opaschowski, Horst W. 1995. *Freizeitökonomie: Marketing von Erlebniswelten*. 2d ed. Opladen: Leske and Budrich.

Osten, Manfred. 2003. *"Alles veloziferisch" oder Goethes Entdeckug der Langsamkeit*. Frankfurt: Insel.

———. 2004. "Accelerated Time. A Few Remarks on the Modernity of Goethe." In Helmut Heinze and Christiane Weller, eds., *Die Lektüre der Welt: zur Theorie, Geschichte und Soziologie kultureller Praxis*, 373–80. Frankfurt: Peter Lang.

Parsons, Talcott. 1951. *The Social System*. New York: Free Press.

———. 1971. *The System of Modern Societies*. Englewood Cliffs, NJ: Prentice Hall.

Perrow, Charles. 1999. *Normal Accidents: Living with High-Risk Technologies*. Princeton: Princeton University Press.

Petersen, Jürgen. 1991. *Der deutsche Roman der Moderne. Grundlegung—Typologie—Entwicklung*. Stuttgart: Metzler.

Piaget, Jean. 1980. *Die Bildung des Zeitbegriffs beim Kinde*. Stuttgart: Klett-Cotta.

Piore, Michael J., and Charles F. Sable. 1984. *The Second Industrial Divide: Possibilities for Prosperity*. New York: Basic Books.

Platt, Norbert A. 1998. "Faszination Beständigkeit." In Backhaus and Bonus 1998:179–94.

van der Poel, Hugo. 1997. "Leisure and the Modularization of Daily Life." *Time and Society* 6:171–94.

Pöppel, Ernst. 1997. *Grenzen des Bewusstseins*. Frankfurt: Insel.

Postone, Moishe. 1996. *Time, Labor, and Social Domination: A Reinterpretation of Marx's Critical Theory*. Cambridge: Cambridge University Press.

Priller, Eckhard. 1992. "Zeitverwendung in der ehemaligen DDR—Ergebnisse von Zeitbudgetuntersuchungen." In Hansgünter Meyer, ed., *Soziologie in Deutschland und die Transformation großer gesellschaftlicher Systeme*, 608–15. Berlin: Akademie.

Putnam, Robert D. 1995. "Bowling Alone: America's Declining Social Capital." *Journal of Democracy* 6:65–78.

——. 1997. "Foreword." In John Robinson and Geoffrey Godbey, *Time for Life: The Surprising Ways Americans Use Their Time*, xiii–xvi. University Park: Pennsylvaina State University Press.

Radkau, Joachim. 1998. *Das Zeitalter der Nervosität. Deutschland zwischen Bismarck und Hitler.* Munich: Propyläen.

Rammstedt, Otthein. 1975. "Alltagsbewußtsein von Zeit." *Kölner Zeitschrift für Soziologie und Sozialpsychologie* 27:47–63.

Reheis, Fritz. 1998. *Die Kreativität der Langsamkeit. Neuer Wohlstand durch Entschleunigung.* 2d ed. Darmstadt: Primus.

——. 1999. "Entschleunigung." In Oskar Brilling and Eduard W. Kleber, eds., *Handwörterbuch Umweltbildung*, 53–54. Hohengehren: Schneider.

——. 2000. "Zeit lassen als Qualität. Zeitökologische Überlegungen zur, guten Gesellschaft.'" Lecture at the Thirtieth Congress of the DGS in Cologne ("Gute Gesellschaft? Zur Konstruktion sozialer Ordnungen") on September 26–29, 2000.

Richter, Götz. 1991. *Die lineare Zeit. Eine Untersuchung zum Zusammenhang von Zeitform und Entfremdung.* Edition Philosophie und Sozialwissenschaften 21. Hamburg: Argument.

Riescher, Gisela. 1994. *Zeit und Politik. Zur institutionellen Bedeutung von Zeitstrukturen in parlamentarischen und präsidentiellen Regierungssystemen.* Baden-Baden: Nomos.

Riesman, David, Reuel Denney, and Nathan Glazer. 2001 [1950]. *The Lonely Crowd: A Study of the Changing American Character.* New Haven: Yale University Press.

Rifkin, Jeremy. 1987. *Time Wars: The Primary Conflict in Human History.* New York: Holt.

Rinderspacher, Jürgen. 2000. *"Ohne Sonntag gibt es nur noch Werktage." Die soziale und kulturelle Bedeutung des Wochenendes.* Bonn: Dietz.

Robertson, Roland. 1992. *Globalization: Social Theory and Global Culture.* London: Sage.

Robinson, John. 2002. "Is There an Acceleration of the Pace of Life? Some Empirical Evidence." Lecture of Research Committee 35 at the Fifteenth World Congress of Sociology in Brisbane, October 7, 2002.

Robinson, John, and Geoffrey Godbey. 1996. "The Great American Slowdown." *American Demographics* (June 1996): 42–48.

——. 1999. *Time for Life: The Surprising Ways Americans Use Their Time.* 2d rev. ed. University Park: Pennsylvaina State University Press.

Ronte, Dieter. 1998. "Die Langsamkeit der Ewigkeit." In Backhaus and Bonus 1998:239–62.

Rorty, Richard. 1989. *Contingency, Irony and Solidarity.* Cambridge: Cambridge University Press.

Rosa, Hartmut. 1998. *Identität und kulturelle Praxis. Politische Philosophie nach Charles Taylor*. With a foreword by Axel Honneth. Frankfurt: Campus.

———. 1999a. "Kapitalismus und Lebensführung. Perspektiven einer ethischen Kritik der liberalen Marktwirtschaft." *Deutsche Zeitschrift für Philosophie* 47, no. 5: 735–58.

———. 1999b. "Bewegung und Beharrung. Überlegungen zu einer sozialen Theorie der Beschleunigung." *Leviathan. Zeitschrift für Sozialwissenschaft* 27:386–414.

———. 1999c. "Am Ende der Geschichte: Die, Generation X' zwischen Globalisierung und Desintegration." In Karsten Fischer, ed., *Neustart des Weltlaufs? Fiktion und Faszination der Zeitwende*, 246–63. Frankfurt: Suhrkamp.

———. 1999d. "Rasender Stillstand? Individuum und Gesellschaft im Zeitalter der Beschleunigung." In Jürgen Manemann, ed., *Befristete Zeit*, 3:151–76. Jahrbuch Politische Theologie. Münster: LIT.

———. 2001a. "Temporalstrukturen in der Spätmoderne: Vom Wunsch nach Beschleunigung und der Sehnsucht nach Langsamkeit. Ein Literaturüberblick in gesellschaftstheoretischer Absicht." *Handlung, Kultur, Interpretation* 10:335–81.

———. 2001b. Entries on "Vergangenheit," "Gegenwart," and "Zukunft." In Nicolas Pethes and Jens Ruchatz, eds., *Gedächtnis und Erinnerung. Ein interdisziplinäres Lexikon*, 210–12, 617–20, and 677–78. Reinbek: Rowohlt.

———. 2002a. "Zwischen Selbstthematisierungszwang und Artikulationsnot? Situative Identität als Fluchtpunkt von Individualisierung und Beschleunigung." In Straub and Renn 2002:267–302.

———. 2002b. "Wachstum und Beschleunigung—Angst und Verheißung der kapitalistischen Gesellschaft." *Erwägen Wissen Ethik* 13, no. 3: 330–33.

———. 2003. "Social Acceleration. Ethical and Political Consequences of a Desynchronized High-Speed Society." *Constellations: An International Journal of Critical and Democratic Theory* 10, no. 1: 3–52.

———, ed. 2004a. *Fast Forward. Essays zu Zeit und Beschleunigung*. Hamburg: Körber-Stiftung.

———. 2004b. "Four Levels of Self-Interpretation. A Paradigm for Social Philosophy and Political Criticism." *Philosophy & Social Criticism* 30:691–720.

———. 2004c. "Wider die Unsichtbarmachung einer Schicksalsmacht. Plädoyer für die Erneuerung der Kapitalismuskritik." *Berliner Debatte/Initial* 15 (1): 81–90.

———. 2004d. "Zeitraffer und Fernsehparadoxon oder: Von der Schwierigkeit, Zeitgewinne zu realisieren." In Rosa 2004a:19–28.

Rosa, Hartmut, and William Scheuerman, eds. 2009. *High-Speed Society: Social Acceleration, Power, and Modernity*. University Park: Pennsylvania State University Press.

Rousseau, Jean-Jacques. 1997. *Julie, or the New Heloise: Letters of Two Lovers Who Live in a Small Town at the Foot of the Alps. Works of Jean-Jacques Rousseau,* vol. 6. Ed. Philip Stewart and Jean Vache. Hanover: Dartmouth University Press.

Rulff, Dieter. 2001. "Schröders Totipotenz." *Die Woche*, January 26, 2001, 8.

Rushkoff, Douglas, ed. 1994. *The Gen-X Reader*. New York. Ballantine.

Russell, Bertrand. 1985. *In Praise of Idleness*. London: Routledge.

Ryker, Bethany. 2002. "Keepin' Time: Breaking the Past and Sounding the Future." Term paper at the New School for Social Research, New York, June 2002.

Sahlins, M. 1972. *Stone Age Economics*. New York: Aldine Atherton.

Sandbothe, Mike. 1997. "Die Verzeitlichung der Zeit in der modernen Philosophie." In Antje Gimmler, Mike Sandbothe, and Walther Ch. Zimmerli, eds., *Die Wiederentdeckung der Zeit. Reflexionen, Analysen, Konzepte*, 41–62. Darmstadt: Wissenschaftliche Buchgesellschaft.

——. 1998. *Die Verzeitlichung der Zeit. Grundtendenzen in der modernen Zeitdebatte in Philosophie und Wissenschaft*. Darmstadt: Wissenschaftliche Buchgesellschaft.

Sandel, Michael. 1984. "The Procedural Republic and the Unencumbered Self." *Political Theory* 12, no. 1: 81–96.

Schaltenbrand, Georges. 1988. "Zeit und Bewusstsein." In Zoll 1988a:37–58.

Scharf, Günter. 1988a. "Zeit und Kapitalismus." In Zoll 1988a:143–59.

——. 1988b. "Wiederaneignung von Arbeitszeit als Lebenszeit." In Zoll 1988a: 509–30.

Scherpe, Klaus R. 1986. "Dramatisierung und Entdramatisierung des Untergangs—zum ästhetischen Bewusstsein von Moderne und Postmoderne." In Klaus R. Scherpe and Andreas Huyssen, eds., *Postmoderne. Zeichen eines kulturellen Wandels*, 270–301. Reinbek: Rowohlt.

Scheuerman, William E. 2000. "The Economic State of Emergency." *Cardozo Law Review* 21:1869–94.

——. 2001a. "Liberal Democracy and the Empire of Speed." Polity 34, no. 1: 41–67.

——. 2001b. "Global Law in Our High Speed Economy." In Richard Appelbaum, Volkmar Gessner, and William Felstiner, eds., *Rules and Networks. The Legal Culture of Global Business Transactions*, 108–24. Oxford: Hart.

——. 2003. "Speed, States, and Social Theory: A Response to Hartmut Rosa." *Constellations: An International Journal of Critical and Democratic Theory* 10, no. 1: 42–48.

——. 2004. *Liberal Democracy and the Social Acceleration of Time*. Baltimore: Johns Hopkins University Press.

Schimank, Uwe. 2000. *Theorien gesellschaftlicher Differenzierung*. 2d ed. Opladen: Leske and Budrich.

Schimank, Uwe, and Ute Volkmann, eds. 2000. *Soziologische* Gegenwartsdiagnosen I. Opladen: Leske and Budrich.

Schings, Hans-Jürgen. 1977. *Melancholie und Aufklärung. Melancholiker und ihre Kritiker in Erfahrungsseelenkunde und Literatur des 18. Jahrhunderts*. Stuttgart: Metzler.

Schivelbusch, Wolfgang. 2000 [1977]. *Geschichte der Eisenbahnreise. Zur Industrialisierung von Raum und Zeit im 19. Jahrhundert*. Rev. ed. Frankfurt: Fischer.

Schlote, Axel. 1996. *Widersprüche sozialer Zeit. Zeitorganisation im Alltag zwischen Herrschaft und Freiheit*. Opladen: Leske and Budrich.

Schluchter, Wolfgang. 1998. *Die Entwicklung des okzidentalen Rationalismus. Eine Analyse von Max Webers Entwicklungsgeschichte des Okzidents*. Frankfurt: Suhrkamp.

Schmahl, Kurt. 1988. "Industrielle Zeitstruktur und technisierte Lebensweise." In Zoll 1988a:344–370.

Schmied, Gerhard. 1985. *Soziale Zeit. Umfang, "Geschwindigkeit," Evolution*. Berlin: Duncker and Humblot.

Schmitt, Carl. 1950. "Der motorisierte Gesetzgeber." In *Die europäische Rechtswissenschaft*, 18–21, 29–31. Tübingen: Universitätsverlag. English translation in Rosa and Scheuerman 2009.

Schneider, Manuel, and Karlheinz Geißler, ed. 1999. *Flimmernde Zeiten. Vom Tempo der Medien*. Stuttgart: Hirzel.

Schneider, Norbert F., Ruth Limmer, and Kerstin Ruckdeschel. 2002. *Mobil, flexibel, gebunden. Familie und Beruf in der mobilen Gesellschaft*. Frankfurt: Campus.

Schöneck, Nadine M. 2004. "'Stets ein bisschen getrieben.' Die Zeitwahrnehmung meiner Mitmenschen im Fokus." In Rosa 2004a:29–46.

Schor, Juliet B. 1992. *The Overworked American: The Unexpected Decline of Leisure*. New York: Basic Books.

Schulte-Strathaus, Regine. 1999. "Bei Anruf Rat." *Psychologie Heute* 26, no. 3: 29.

Schulze, Gerhard. 1994. "Das Projekt des schönen Lebens. Zur soziologischen Diagnose der modernen Gesellschaften." In A. Bellebaum and K. Barheier, eds., *Lebensqualität. Ein Konzept für Praxis und Forschung*, 13–39. Opladen: Westdeutscher Verlag.

——. 1997a. *Die Erlebnisgesellschaft. Kultursoziologie der Gegenwart*. 7th ed. Frankfurt: Campus.

——. 1997b. "Steigerungslogik und Erlebnisgesellschaft." *Politische Bildung* 30, no. 2: 77–94.

——. 2003. *Die Beste aller Welten. Wohin bewegt sich die Gesellschaft im 21. Jahrhundert?* Munich: Hanser.

Schumpeter, Joseph A. 1994. *Capitalism, Socialism, and Democracy*. London: Routledge.

Schwinn, Thomas. 1999. "Gibt es eine 'Zweite Moderne'?" *Soziale Welt* 50:423–32.

Segre, Sandro. 2000. "A Weberian Theory of Time." *Time and Society* 9:147–70.

Seiwert, Lothar J. 2000. *Wenn Du es eilig hast, gehe langsam. Das neue Zeitmanagement in einer beschleunigten Welt.* 5th ed. Frankfurt: Campus.

Sennett, Richard. 1998. *The Corrosion of Character: The Personal Consequences of Work in the New Capitalism.* New York: Norton.

Shakespeare, William. 1991. *Hamlet, Prince of Denmark.* In *Complete Works*, 870–907. Ed. W. J. Craig. Leicester: Bookmart.

Shaw, Jenny. 1997. "'Feeling a List Coming On': Gender and the Pace of Life." *Time and Society* 6:383–96.

Simmel, Georg. 1919. "Rodin." In *Philosophische Kultur*, 168–86. Leipzig: Kröner.

——. 1950. *The Sociology of Georg Simmel.* Ed. Kurt Wolff. New York: Free Press.

——. 1992a [1897]. "Die Bedeutung des Geldes für das Tempo des Lebens." In Simmel 1992b:215–34.

——.1992b [1908]. *Soziologie. Untersuchungen über die Formen der Vergesellschaftung.* Ed. Otthein Rammstedt. Gesamtausgabe, vol. 11. Frankfurt: Suhrkamp.

——.1995 [1903]. "Die Großstädte und das Geistesleben." In *Aufsätze und Abhandlungen 1901–1908*, 1:116–31. Ed. R. Kramme et al. Gesamtausgabe, vol. 7. Frankfurt: Suhrkamp.

——. 2004. *The Philosophy of Money.* Ed. and trans. Tom Bottomore and David Frisby. London: Routledge.

Sloterdijk, Peter. 1989. *Eurotaoismus. Zur Kritik der politischen Kinetik.* Frankfurt: Suhrkamp.

Smentek, Martin. 1991. *Arbeitszeitflexibilisierung. Zwischen kapitalistischer Zeitökonomie und sozialer Zeitstruktur.* Hamburg: VSA.

Sorokin, Pitirim A., and Robert Merton. 1937. "Social Time. A Methodological and Functional Analysis." *American Journal of Sociology* 42:615–29.

Sparn, Walter. 1999. "' . . . Solange es heute heißt.' Zeitverknappung und Zeitverschwendung in neuesten Zeiten." In Klaus-M. Kodalle, ed., *Zeit-Verschwendung: Ein Symposion*, 17–27. Würzburg: Königshausen and Neumann.

Statistisches Bundesamt Wiesbaden, ed. 1994. *Datenreport 1994. Zahlen und Fakten über die Bundesrepublik Deutschland.* Bonn: Bundeszentrale für politische Bildung.

Straub, Jürgen. 1993. "Zeit, Erzählung, Interpretation. Zur Konstruktion und Analyse von Erzähltexten in der narrativen Biographieforschung." In H. Röcklein, ed., *Möglichkeiten und Grenzen der psychohistorischen Biographieforschung*, 143–83. Tübingen: diskord.

——, ed. 1998a. *Erzählung, Identität und historisches Bewusstsein. Zur psychologischen Konstruktion von Zeit und Geschichte*, Frankfurt: Suhrkamp.

———. 1998b. "Personale und kollektive Identität. Zur Analyse eines theoretischen Begriffs." In Aleida Assmann and Heidrun Friese, eds., *Identitäten. Erinnerung, Geschichte, Identität*, 73–104. Frankfurt: Suhrkamp.

———. 2001. "Zur Psychologie des flexiblen Menschen'. Ein Leitbild für jüngere Generationen?" In Franz Lehner, ed., *Erbfall Zukunft. Vordenken für und mit Nachkommen*, 357–68. Munich: Rainer Hampp.

Straub, Jürgen, and Joachim Renn, eds. 2002. *Transitorische Identität. Der Prozesscharakter des modernen Selbst*. Frankfurt: Campus.

Straus, Florian, and Renate Höfer. 1997. "Entwicklungslinien alltäglicher Identitätsarbeit." In Keupp and Höfer 1997:270–307.

Streeck, Wolfgang, and Martin Höpner, ed. 2003. *Alle Macht dem Markt? Fallstudien zur Abwicklung der Deutschland AG*. Frankfurt: Campus.

Sztompka, Pjotr. 1993. *The Sociology of Social Change*. Oxford: Blackwell.

Tabboni, Simonetta. 2001. "The Idea of Social Time in Norbert Elias." *Time and Society* 10:5–27.

Taylor, Charles. 1989. *Sources of the Self: The Making of the Modern Identity*. Cambridge: Harvard University Press.

———. 1994. *Multiculturalism and "the Politics of Recognition."* Ed. Amy Gutmann. Princeton: Princeton University Press.

———. 2004. *Modern Social Imaginaries*. Durham: Duke University Press.

Teubner, Günther. 2000. "Privatregimes: Neo-Spontanes Recht und duale Sozialverfassung in der Weltgesellschaft?" In Dieter Simon und Manfred Weiss, eds., *Zur Autonomie des Individuums*—Liber amicorum für Spiros Simitis, 437–53. Baden-Baden: Nomos.

Thompson, Edward P. 1967. "Time, Work-Discipline and Industrial Capitalism." *Past and Present* 38:56–97.

Thrift, Nigel. 1988. "Vivos Voco: Ringing the Changes in the Historical Geography of Time Consciousness." In Young and Schuller 1988:53–94.

Tilly, Charles. 1990. *Coercion, Capital, and European States, AD 990–1992*. Oxford: Blackwell.

Treptow, Rainer. 1992. "Schneller und langsamer leben." In Hans-Uwe Otto, Paul Hirschauer, and Hans Thiersch, eds., *Zeit-Zeichen sozialer Arbeit. Entwürfe einer neuen Praxis*, 7–15. Neuwied: Luchterhand.

Tronto, Joan. 2003. "." *Feminist Theory* 4, no. 2: 119–38.

Turkle, Sherry. 1995. *Life on the Screen: Identity in the Age of the Internet*. New York: Simon and Schuster.

Turner, Bryan S. 1990. "Periodization and Politics in the Postmodern." In *Theories of Modernity and Postmodernity*, 1–13. London: Routledge.

Ulmer, Diane K., and Leonard Schwartzburd. 1996. "Treatment of Time-Pathologies." In R. Allen und S. Scheidt, eds., *Heart and Mind: The Practice of Cardiac Psychology*, 329–62. Washington, DC: American Psychological Association.

Urry, John. 2000. *Sociology Beyond Societies. Mobilities for the Twenty-First Century*. London: Routledge.

———. 2002. "Time, Complexity, and the Global." In G. Crow and S. Heath, *Social Conceptions of Time: Structure and Process in Everyday Life*, 11–24. Basingstoke: Palgrave.

———. 2009. "Speeding Up and Slowing Down." In Rosa and Scheuerman 2009: 179–201.

Verkaaik, Oskar. 2001. "Rezension von Pascale Peters: The Vulnerable Hours of Leisure (Amsterdam 2000)." *Time and* Society 10:407–10.

Vester, Frederic. 1998. *Denken, Lernen, Vergessen*. 25th ed. Munich: dtv.

Virilio, Paul. 1993. *Revolutionen der Geschwindigkeit*. Berlin: Merve.

———. 1997. *Open Sky*. New York: Verso.

———. 1998a. "Continental Drift." In *The Virilio Reader*, 183–95. Ed. James Der Derian. Oxford: Blackwell.

———. 1998b. "Military Space." In *The Virilio Reader*, 22–28. Ed. James Der Derian. Oxford: Blackwell.

———. 1999. *Polar Inertia*. London: Sage.

———. 2006. *Speed and Politics*. Trans. Marc Polizzoti. Los Angeles: Semiotext(e).

Virilio, Paul, and Sylvère Lotringer. 1984. *Der reine Krieg*. Berlin: Merve.

Volkwein, Barbara. 2000. "130 Beats Per Minute: Techno." In Klein, Kiem, and Ette 2000:399–409.

Voß, Gert Günter. 1990. "Wertewandel. Eine Modernisierung der protestantischen Ethik?" *Zeitschrift für Personalforschung* 3:263–75.

———. 1998. "Die Entgrenzung von Arbeit und Arbeitskraft. Eine subjektorientierte Interpretation des Wandels der Arbeit." *Mitteilungen aus der Arbeitsmarkt- und Berufsforschung* 3:473–87.

———. 2001. "Neue Verhältnisse?—Zur wachsenden Bedeutung der Lebensführung von Arbeitskräften für die Betriebe." In Burkart Lutz, ed., *Entwicklungsperspektiven von Arbeit. Ergebnisse aus dem Sonderforschungsbereich 333 der Universität München/DFG*, 31–45. Berlin: Akademie.

Wagner, Peter. 1994. *Liberty and Discipline: A Sociology of Modernity*. London: Routledge.

———. 2002. "Die Problematik der 'Identität' und die Soziologie der Moderne." In Straub and Renn 2002:303–17.

Wallis, George W. 1970. "Chronopolitics: The Impact of Time Perspectives on the Dynamics of Change." *Social Forces* 49:102–8.

Walzer, Michael. 1990. "The Communitarian Critique of Liberalism." *Political Theory* 18, no. 1: 6–23.

Waters, Malcolm. 1995. *Globalization.* New York: Routledge.

Watts Miller, William. 2000. "Durkheimian Time." *Time and* Society 9, no. 1: 5–20.

Weber, Max. 1946. *From Max Weber: Essays in Sociology.* Oxford: Oxford University Press.

——. 1978. *Economy and Society: An Outline of Interpretive Sociology.* Ed. Guenther Roth and Claus Wittich. Berkeley: University of California Press.

——. 2001. *The Protestant Ethic and the Spirit of Capitalism.* Trans. Talcott Parsons. New York: Routledge.

Weibel, Peter. 1987. *Die Beschleunigung der Bilder. In der Chronokratie.* Bern: Benteli.

Welsch, Wolfgang, ed. 1994. *Wege aus der Moderne. Schlüsseltexte der Postmoderne-Diskussion.* 2d ed. Berlin: Akademie.

Wenzel, Harald. 1995. "Gibt es ein postmodernes Selbst? Neuere Theorien und Diagnosen der Identität in fortgeschrittenen Gesellschaften." *Berliner Journal für Soziologie* 1:113–31.

Weyman, Ansgar. 2000. "Sozialer Wandel, Generationsverhältnisse und Technikgenerationen." In Martin Kohli and Marc Szydlik, eds., *Generationen in Familie und Gesellschaft,* 36–58. Opladen: Leske and Budrich.

Willems, Herbert. 1999. "Institutionelle Selbstthematisierungen und Identitätsbildungen im Modernisierungsprozess." In Herbert Willems and Alois Hahn, eds., *Identität und Moderne,* 62–101. Frankfurt: Suhrkamp.

Willems, Herbert, and Alois Hahn, ed. 1999. *Identität und Moderne.* Frankfurt: Suhrkamp.

Wolin, Sheldon. 1997. "What Time Is It?" *Theory and Event* 1:1–4. http://muse.jhu .edu/journals/theory_&_event/v001/1.1wolin.html.

Wollen, Peter. 2002. "Speed and the Cinema." *New Left Review* 16 (July/August 2002): 105–14.

Young, Michael, and Tom Schuller, eds. 1988. *The Rhythms of Society.* London: Routledge.

Zeiher, Hartmut J., and Helga Zeiher. 1994. *Orte und Zeiten der Kinder. Soziales Leben im Alltag von Großstadtkindern.* Weinheim: Juventa.

Zerubavel, Eviatar. 1979. *Patterns of Time in Hospital Life.* Chicago: University of Chicago Press.

——. 1981. *Hidden Rhythms: Schedules and Calendars in Social Life.* Berkeley: University of California Press.

——. 1985. *The Seven Day Circle. The History and Meaning of the Week.* New York: Free Press.

Zimmerli, Walther Ch., and Mike Sandbothe, eds. 1993. *Klassiker der modernen Zeitphilosophie.* Darmstadt: Wissenschaftliche Buchgesellschaft.

Zoll, Rainer, ed. 1988a. *Zerstörung und Wiederaneignung von Zeit*. Frankfurt: Suhrkamp.

———. 1988b. "Zeiterfahrung und Gesellschaftsform." In Zoll 1988a:72–88.

Zulley, Jürgen, and Barbara Knab. 2000. *Unsere Innere Uhr. Natürliche Rhythmen nutzen und der Non-Stop-Belastung entgehen*. Freiburg: Herder.

INDEX